Thy Honored Name

Anthony J. Kuzniewski, S.J.

Thy Honored Name

A History of The College of the Holy Cross, 1843–1994

The Catholic University of America Press
Washington, D.C.

Copyright © 1999
The Catholic University of America Press
All rights reserved
Printed in the United States of America

The paper used in this publication meets the minimum requirements of American
National Standards for Information Science—Permanence of Paper for Printed
Library materials, ANSI Z39.48-1984.
∞

LIBRARY OF CONGRESS CATALOGING-IN-PUBLICATION DATA

Kuzniewski, Anthony J.
    Thy honored name : a history of the College of the Holy Cross,
  1843–1994 / Anthony J. Kuzniewski.
      p.   cm.
  Includes bibliographical references and index.
    1. College of the Holy Cross (Worcester, Mass.)—History.
  I. Title.
LD2281.H32K89   1999
378.744'3—dc21
98-17977
   ISBN 0-8132-0911-0 (alk. paper)

For the students at Holy Cross,
with thanks for the inspiration

CONTENTS

ILLUSTRATIONS

CHARTS

"WILL NOT THIS be a bold undertaking? Nevertheless I will try it." With these words, Benedict J. Fenwick, the second Roman Catholic Bishop of Boston, committed the resources of Catholic New England to a new boarding college in Worcester in 1843. It was named Holy Cross after Fenwick's cathedral church in Boston. In an era when four out of five new colleges failed, chances that this institution would survive were slight: nine years after the burning of the convent school in Charlestown, nativist violence was still a concern; the Catholic population of the region, mostly Irish immigrants, lacked the resources and ambition for lengthy formal study; and the Maryland Province of the Society of Jesus (Jesuits), who reluctantly agreed to staff the new school, were already overextended in their institutional commitments, and more eager to sponsor day schools in large cities than remotely situated boarding colleges like Holy Cross. Yet the corporate strength of the Jesuits, and the lack of Catholic alternatives in New England during the first twenty years, were advantages that helped the College survive. The oldest school of its type in New England, Holy Cross became the first point of contact between the educational system sponsored internationally by the Society of Jesus since the 1550s and the academic tradition carried by the sturdy group of Yankee colleges whose New England antecedents were only eighty years younger.

The corporate sponsors of Holy Cross, the Jesuits, were a religious order founded in the mid-sixteenth century by Ignatius of Loyola. The Society of Jesus gained notoriety among Protestant reformers for its forcefulness in asserting the Catholic point of view during the Reformation; but by 1600 Jesuits were known primarily for sponsoring schools that followed the classical humanism of the Renaissance, and for work in the missions. Jesuit sponsorship, and the fact that many of the early administrators and faculty were from outside the region, made Holy Cross an outsider in the institutional and cultural life of Yankee New England. The school gained support only slowly: it barely survived a disastrous fire in 1852 and did not gain a charter from the General

Court until 1865, when the new concept of private, state-chartered colleges was also being applied to Harvard, Williams, and Amherst.

Late in the nineteenth and early in the twentieth centuries, Holy Cross graduates played a major role in the development of Catholic life in the Northeast. At the same time, David I. Walsh (Class of 1893) became the first Irish Catholic to serve as Massachusetts governor and U.S. senator. At the turn of the century, controversy with Harvard's Charles W. Eliot about the prescriptive curriculum ended in a compromise: Holy Cross did not abandon its humanities requirements, but re-cast them to conform to American patterns of organization and amplified the curriculum in social and natural sciences. For the first half of the twentieth century, Holy Cross was distinguished within the Jesuit network of colleges and universities as a defender of the humanistic tradition. But the declining attractiveness of classical languages to young Americans forced administrators to de-emphasize the tradition and a period of drift ensued after the Second World War. After 1960, Raymond Swords and his successor, John Brooks, rebuilt the school to a level of academic excellence that was associated both with traditional institutional affiliations and with contemporary standards.

The broadest theme that emerges is the idea that the school's excellence and reputation are the result of creative tension between the persistent strength of its Jesuit and Catholic identity, and the enduring influence, by virtue of geographic proximity, of the strongest network of undergraduate schools in the nation. In the nineteenth century, College administrators took it as a challenge to protect the first influence from the second; in the twentieth century, increasingly, the challenge was to integrate the two, enhancing the school's profile within the institutional network of the Northeast by accepting the standards and approaches of academically outstanding neighbors while upholding a specific institutional heritage. The assertion of traditional affiliation *and* academic excellence made Holy Cross the country's most highly rated Catholic-sponsored undergraduate liberal arts college at the time of its sesquicentennial.

In a further sense, this study discloses the diversification of the educational landscape in New England as Holy Cross was led away from institutional isolation, through the intervention of outsiders like Harvard's Charles Eliot and the choice of presidents like Joseph Hanselman, Raymond Swords, and John Brooks. Within this pattern, the story describes the sporadic conflict between the traditional Jesuit spirit of adaptation to persons and cultures, and a defensive tendency to be merely reactive to challenges from the outside. The secularization that has tended to characterize church-sponsored colleges and universities is a subsidiary theme, particularly after 1960, when Jesuits increasingly delegated responsibility for the mission and goals of the College to lay individuals. Within these broader parameters, the history of the College falls into three distinct stages, designated in this study as the first, second, and third Holy Cross.

The first Holy Cross was an institution completely determined by the traditional Jesuit *Ratio Studiorum* (Plan of Studies); its seven-year course made the College more like a European *lycée* or *gymnasium*. At the insistence of Boston's bishops, administrators were forbidden to admit non-Catholic students—a restriction that differentiated Holy Cross from every other Jesuit college in the nation. The bishops reasoned (correctly, it turned out) that a boarding school limited to Catholic students would foster religious vocations: about one student in six opted for the priesthood in the nineteenth century. For all students, life on the hill was isolated and rather strictly regimented, but the arrival of intercollegiate sports after the Civil War helped open contact with other schools.

The second Holy Cross developed at the turn of the century, when in response to direct pressure from President Eliot of Harvard, College authorities altered the academic program by separating the preparatory and collegiate divisions, adding a year of studies at the top end of the academic ladder, and eventually dropping the prep school. By the time of the First World War, the school was well established in its middle stage: an American college with an academic program that was heavily laden with required courses reflective of the old Jesuit plan, an athletic program that achieved a certain amount of notoriety in intercollegiate competition, a building program that afforded facilities to a student population that gradually rose to 1900, a faculty dominated by Jesuits, and a growing group of alumni successful in ecclesiastical, public, and professional life.

After 1960, the third Holy Cross emerged as a result of deliberate efforts to upgrade the academic quality of the faculty, to introduce lay persons into all facets of the operation, and to make the curriculum more consonant with professional standards that developed in the postwar era while, at the same time, asserting the importance of a liberal education. The first East Coast Jesuit school to undertake institutional separation of the College from the Jesuit community, Holy Cross introduced laymen as trustees in 1969 and then adopted co-education in 1972. In 1986, the College was the only Catholic school among the founding members of the Patriot League, an athletic conference that was dedicated to the ideal of the scholar-athlete and associated primarily with the Ivy League for non-conference games. By 1994, the student body numbered 2700; the curriculum included distribution and language requirements but no core courses, and a broadly supported mission statement that integrated the specific institutional traditions with the quest for academic excellence in the contemporary world.

Research on the book has proceeded along two lines: traditional archival work, and data analysis. Archival holdings dealing with the history of Holy Cross are especially rich. The College Archives contain materials dating back to the opening of the school, including the original *Matricula* book and a College diary kept by the Jesuit minister (the second-in-authority in the Jesuit community). The latter source contains a daily account (Latin in the early years) of the College from 1845 until about 1970. I have had access to College materials through the administration of Raymond Swords (president from 1960 to 1970), and access upon request to many papers of John Brooks (1970–1994). Other rich sources include the archives of the Maryland Jesuit Province, deposited at Georgetown University, and of the New England Jesuit Province, now at Holy Cross. The Roman Archives of the Society of Jesus, available at Georgetown and Holy Cross in microfilm and Xerox copy, are available for about the first eighty years of the College's history.

Data-based analysis has been facilitated through the assistance of Emmett Curran, Georgetown University's historian, whose program was adapted to devise a 75-line questionnaire covering the students of the past. All students who studied at the College in the nineteenth century were profiled, plus every class in the twentieth century for years ending in zero and five. In all, over 11,000 profiles have been gathered by a group of undergraduate research assistants. The search for information proved both enlightening and disappointing. Although tens of thousands of details have been gathered into the data base, the irregularity of sources and the impossibility of tracking down every item have left considerable gaps. The available information has been incorporated into the text by providing summaries of the findings, and also by utilizing charts and graphs to show geographic origins, vocational choices, and other variables. Charts and graphs also illustrate material gathered from traditional sources—annual budgets and indebtedness, number of graduates and type of degree, rising tuition and financial aid, the growth of the endowment since 1970, and characteristics of the faculty.

This is not the first attempt at a history of Holy Cross. The College Archives contain about a dozen such efforts, starting with a short chronology of the founding and early years written by the first president, Thomas F. Mulledy. The best of the early histories, "College of the Holy Cross, 1843–1914," was published by Jesuit Edward I. Devitt in *The Woodstock Letters* (vol. 64, 1935). Another Jesuit, Walter J. Meagher, wrote a more substantial history as his doctoral dissertation at Fordham University in 1943; but efforts to polish and publish this work proved difficult. When he offered the manuscript to publishers in 1951 under the title *The Crusaders' First Century*, Meagher was urged to make the text "more readable." Holy Cross President John O'Brien then searched for someone to revise the book. He eventually settled on Professor Frank Drumm of the English Department. Drumm started on the project in 1954, completed revision of the first three chapters over the next several years, and received $2000 for his services. In 1957, the remainder of the text was entrusted by College President William A. Donaghy to Professor William J. Grattan of the History Department. Grattan was given a stipend during the summers he worked on the project, which he completed in 1963. Two years later, an agreement was reached with Vantage Press in New York City to publish the book for $6000 under a new title, *The Spires of Fenwick*, which had been suggested by Professor Grattan. The history appeared under the co-authorship of Meagher and Grattan, a gesture characterized by College President Raymond Swords as "an act of pure charity" on Grattan's part. (For further details, see the Grattan Papers, ACHC, 14.8-1.)

Because it was published through a vanity press, *The Spires of Fenwick* failed to receive a thorough editorial critique. The result was a flawed book that did not, ultimately, surmount the difficulties associated with its origins. Moreover, it lacked critical perspective, as even charitable reviewers pointed out; and its questions were shaped within an era that soon yielded to the Catholicism of Vatican II and the Holy Cross of separate incorporation and diminished Jesuit presence. But if it was flawed, *Spires* was also useful. Its factuality, and particularly its presentation of the early years of the College's life, have served for several decades to illuminate important aspects of the institutional past.

Now, with the passing of the sesquicentennial, the time seems ripe for a new history of the College. Among the highly rated undergraduate liberal arts colleges in the Northeast, Holy Cross is distinct because of its Catholic and Jesuit connections. This history is an effort to explain, in a critical manner, the origins and development of that distinctiveness and academic excellence. Appreciating Holy Cross, what it can contribute to the academic enterprise, and what goals are appropriate for a school of its quality, very much depends on historical understanding.

This book is an abridgment of a longer manuscript, deposited in the Holy Cross Archives; persons desiring a more detailed account of the College history should consult that source. The Mission Statement of 1992 and lists of Holy Cross presidents and Jesuit leaders before separate incorporation are included in the appendices of the present volume.

ACKNOWLEDGMENTS

S O MANY PEOPLE have contributed time, talent, advice, and encouragement to this project that formal acknowledgments fall far short of addressing the debt of gratitude I owe to so many. To all the unnamed individuals who have helped—the Holy Cross faculty, administrators and staff, professional colleagues, fellow Jesuits, alumni of the College, family, friends—I offer deep thanks.

At the beginning, when I was uncertain about shifting fields from my earlier work in immigration history, Oscar Handlin, Gerry McKevitt, and Emmett Curran '58 nudged me in this direction. Emmett also shared his experience from work on the history of Georgetown University, setting me on the path of data gathering, answering questions, giving me the benefit of his knowledge in researching Jesuit sources. Philip Gleason, the dean of the history of Catholic higher education in the United States, introduced me to the field during my sabbatical stay at Notre Dame in 1986, and afterwards critiqued the manuscript for the Catholic University of America Press with suggestions that only a historian of his competence could offer.

John E. Brooks, the College president until 1994, kept his promise to support the project. He provided research assistants, granted access to archival materials covering the third Holy Cross, and reviewed the latter chapters for accuracy and confidentiality, but without interfering with the presentation. Gerard Reedy, his successor, also offered strong support. Their encouragement lightened the burden and confirmed a long personal commitment. I am also grateful to Deans Frank Vellaccio and James Kee and to my colleagues in the History Department for approving sabbatical leaves, and to the former Committee on Professional Standards for two Faculty Fellowships to work on the book.

The staff of the Holy Cross College Archives extended themselves beyond the call of duty, responding patiently to my many impatient requests. The late Father Gene Harrington, Arlene Long, and Suzanne Sylvester were there at the start. For most of the period, I relied on the help of Father Paul Nelligan,

Mark Savolis '77, and Jo-Anne Carr. At Georgetown, Jon Reynolds was very helpful; in Worcester, Bishop George Rueger (EX '53) readily supplied access to the Diocesan Archives; and two Jesuit provincials, Robert E. Manning and William A. Barry, authorized use of the New England Province Archives.

All of the illustrations in the book are from the Holy Cross College Archives and are used with permission of the College. A number of individuals read sections of the manuscript and were frank enough with their critiques to improve the quality of the book immeasurably. Two Jesuit associates, Bill Rieser and Michael Boughton, offered helpful comments at the beginning. Later, Lorraine Attreed, David O'Brien, and Father Paul Harman supplied pointed comments at times where I needed their perspective and advice. Two Holy Cross Jesuits read the entire manuscript—Paul Nelligan, who corrected dozens of factual errors and later offered invaluable help with the illustrations; and Phil Rule, whose knowledge of grammar and style helped to clarify the text. Michael Perko, a Jesuit at Loyola University of Chicago, offered a sage critique for the CUA Press.

Several Jesuit associates provided assistance with translations from Latin and (in the case of Anthony Ciampi) Italian: Alfred Desautels, David Gill, Lionel Honoré, Vincent Lapomarda, Edward Vodoklys '72, and the late Robert Healy. A lay colleague, Maurizio Vannicelli, now deceased, helped with Ciampi's papers and explained the elegance of his Italian. Father Michael Ford of the Chaplains' Office adapted an 1843 engraving of Fenwick Hall for the dust jacket.

From 1987 to 1994, summer research assistants provided assistance, enthusiasm, and good humor in equal measure: Edward T. O'Donnell '87, James T. Phalen '88, Timothy S. Delahaunty '90, Allan M. Harper '91, Robert B. Roche '91, Andrew W. Sullivan '93, James P. Heidbreder '94, and William J. Phoenix '95. During the academic year, work-study researchers patiently collected data on former students and tracked down details when I was writing: James J. Nolan '91, Matthew A. Smith '91, Patrick J. Murphy '92, Mark T. Gunn '93, Matthew W. Hughes, '93, Julia F. Gentile '94, Matthew M. Marakovitz '94, and Joshua M. Whittaker '95. Special thanks go to Richard Wareing '90, who modified Georgetown's data gathering instrument for Holy Cross, and Christine C. Gowen '92, who captained the data-gathering crew for several years.

Brendan Collins '78 was one of my first students at Holy Cross and one of the best. He died suddenly and unexpectedly in 1996 as this book was nearing completion. In his memory, his parents, Don '49 and Louise, provided support to make this history available to a wider audience. Early in 1998, while the book was being edited, Don also died. His enthusiasm for this project was a wonderful gift. Father and son, may they rest in peace.

Finally, my thanks go to the students of Holy Cross. For these many years, they have communicated interest and enthusiasm. "How's the book coming?"—a question asked a thousand times, everywhere on campus—was an expression of support I came to value. Their eagerness to hear the stories, their sense of wonder that the people of the past were so much like themselves in having to make choices without knowing the future, their conviction that the project was important, have inspired and blessed me. To them, with affection, I dedicate this book.

Anthony J. Kuzniewski, S.J.
April 1998

ABBREVIATIONS

In footnotes, the following abbreviations are used:

ACHC   Archives of the College of the Holy Cross
ARSI   Roman Archives of the Society of Jesus
         [*Archivum Romanum Societatis Iesu*]
GUA   Georgetown University Archives
MPA   Maryland Province Archives
NEPA   New England Province Archives
UNDA   University of Notre Dame Archives
WDA   Worcester Diocesan Archives
WL   *The Woodstock Letters*

Thy Honored Name

The Origins of a New England College

HOLY CROSS is New England's first Catholic and first Jesuit college. That historical fact suggests what was at stake when Benedict J. Fenwick and Thomas F. Mulledy set the College cornerstone in place in June of 1843. Their hopes and plans were influenced by a long-established Jesuit educational tradition and by the particular historical circumstances of ante-bellum New England. Holy Cross was built in the heart of Yankee America by men from Maryland and Virginia at a time when regional traditions were distinctive and strong. The College's Catholic sponsorship and Jesuit affiliation made it resistant to outside influences and vulnerable to misunderstanding by local observers schooled in the heritage of Calvinism. But the founders were determined to begin, to establish a college in Worcester as an act of faith in God and in human potential. What they had of human wisdom and physical resources, they gave to Holy Cross, gambling that those assets would enable the school to flourish. It was an attempt to alter the educational landscape of New England—a departure, they were convinced, whose time had come.

The primary influence on the new college was the enduring spirit of Ignatius of Loyola (1491–1556), founder of the Society of Jesus.[1] Born into a

---

1. Ignatius of Loyola's autobiography has been published under the title *St. Ignatius' Own Story As Told to Luis Gonzales de Camara*, trans. William J. Young (Chicago: Loyola University Press, 1956). Recent biographies include Mary Purcell, *The First Jesuit: St. Ignatius Loyola (1491–1556)* (Chicago: Loyola University Press, 1981); and Candido de Dalmases, *Ignatius of Loyola, Founder of the Jesuits*, trans. Jerome Aixala (St. Louis: The Institute of Jesuit Sources, 1985). See also George Ganss' introduction to *The Constitutions of the Society of Jesus* (St. Louis: The Institute of Jesuit Sources, 1970), 3–33. Summaries of the Loyola's life prior to the founding of the Society of Jesus may be found in William J. Bangert, *A History of the Society of Jesus* (2d ed.; St. Louis: The Institute of Jesuit Sources, 1986), 3–22; and John O'Malley, *The First Jesuits* (Cambridge: Harvard University Press, 1993), 23–36.

noble Basque family at the castle of Loyola near the town of Azpeitia, Ignatius was educated in the household of the chief treasurer of Ferdinand of Aragon and entered young adulthood longing for a chivalrous life. All changed, however, after his right leg was shattered by a French shell at Pamplona in 1521. During a long convalescence, he developed a deeply religious orientation toward life. After his recovery, he slowly worked out the implications of his conversion. He spent a year of prayer and reflection that ran the gamut from near-despair to intense experiences of divine love, then another year as a pilgrim to the Holy Land. When he returned to Spain in 1524, Ignatius was 33 years old. His openness to opportunities and his personal magnanimity now prompted him along a path that eventually extended his influence through time and space. Utilizing his religious experiences, he composed a book of spiritual direction that he continuously revised until its publication in 1548 under the title *Spiritual Exercises.*[2] The book was a practical guide to prayer and decision-making. It incorporated exercises in the methods of prayer, and specific considerations designed to lead an individual to understand, and respond to, inner promptings inspired by God. The *Exercises* incorporated considerations on the meaning of creation, human freedom and sin, reflections on the life of Christ, and a concluding contemplation on divine love. The goal was personal freedom, a capacity for responding as fully as possible to a loving God. The principle that animated the *Exercises* came to be called the *magis* (the "more"), the understanding that the most authentically human life involves the free choice, among available possibilities, of the alternative that renders greater service to God.

As he searched his mind and heart, Ignatius found himself drawn to the idea that the way to incorporate the *magis* into his life was "to help souls," an understanding that at least implicitly committed him to prepare for the priesthood.[3] To do so, he had to amplify his rudimentary education. After studying Latin in Barcelona, he enrolled in the universities in Alcala and Salamanca. These efforts proved unsatisfactory—partly because he lacked focus, and partly because his work in offering catechetical instruction and spiritual advice twice led to encounters with the Inquisition. Although he was exonerated, he decided to continue his studies in the less suspicious atmosphere at the University of Paris, where he arrived in 1528 and remained until 1535. That interlude proved to be a second turning point in his life.

---

2. Modern English-language translations include: Louis J. Puhl, *The Spiritual Exercises of St. Ignatius, Based on Studies in the Language of the Autograph* (Chicago: Loyola University Press, 1951); and David L. Fleming, *A Contemporary Reading of the Spiritual Exercises: A Companion to St. Ignatius' Text* (2d ed.; St. Louis, The Institute of Jesuit Sources: 1980).

3. Dalmases, *Ignatius,* 85.

The University of Paris was at that time a center of the new learning that was supplanting the old scholastic tradition with the classical humanism of the Renaissance. Students encountered a graduated program of studies, and could progress to the next level as soon as they mastered the material in a given class. Between 1529 and 1534 the university was the locus of intense controversy between the Catholic theological faculty and a group of critics who included Erasmus, Luther, Melanchthon, Calvin, and their supporters. In its more dramatic moments, the conflict included public protests, and imprisonment, exile, even execution, for some of the participants. A mature adult, Ignatius was critically appreciative of the goals and methods of the academic program and keenly aware of the stakes involved in the ideological and religious conflicts. He progressed quickly, studying Latin at the College of Montaigu for eighteen months, then enrolling at the College de Sainte-Barbe, where he received a Licentiate and a Master's Degree in Philosophy. In 1533, he turned to the study of theology.[4]

As a student, Ignatius held to his desire to help souls, in part by directing fellow students in the Spiritual Exercises. Over the years, six companions associated themselves with Ignatius, constituting what historian William Bangert has called "a loose and informal brotherhood" known for their "striking harmony of learning and devotion."[5] Following the lead of Ignatius, the group decided to dedicate their lives to working among the Muslims in the Holy Land. In August 1534, as a token of their earnestness and to associate themselves with each other more formally, they vowed poverty, chastity, and a journey to Jerusalem. The following spring, under a doctor's advice, Ignatius traveled south, eventually stopping in Venice, where he continued to study theology while waiting for his companions to join him for the journey to the Holy Land.

The companions were reunited in January 1537 and ordained to the priesthood in June; but growing tensions between Venice and the Ottoman Empire delayed their journey eastward. While they waited, they undertook works of

4. Georg Schurhammer provides a thorough description of the University of Paris at this time. *Francis Xavier: His Life, His Times*, trans. M. Joseph Costelloe, 3 vols. (Rome: The Jesuit Historical Institute, 1973–80), 1:79–269 passim. See also William Bangert, *Claude Jay and Alfonso Salmeron: Two Early Jesuits* (Chicago: Loyola University Press, 1985), 11–13; François de Dainville, "Saint Ignatius and Humanism," in *Jesuit Educational Quarterly* 21 (March 1959), 191–96; Allen P. Farrell, *The Jesuit Code of Liberal Education: Development and Scope of the Ratio Studiorum* (Milwaukee: Bruce Publishing Co., 1938), 29–36; and Dalmases, *Ignatius*, 106–25.

5. William Bangert, *Jerome Nadal, S.J., 1507–1580, Tracking the First Generation of Jesuits*, edited and completed by Thomas M. McCoog (Chicago: Loyola University Press, 1992), 6; Bangert, *Jay and Salmeron*, 358. On the first companions, see also Schurhammer, *Xavier*, 1:189–224, 247–310, and Dalmases, *Ignatius*, 117–22, 138–56.

ministry and decided to name themselves the Society of Jesus. By late 1538, it was clear that adverse international circumstances would indefinitely postpone their dream of serving in Jerusalem. The companions then agreed to make their way to Rome and offer their services to Pope Paul III. The pontiff accepted their offer; but his desire to send them to various places raised the necessity of organizing themselves so that they could maintain their unity after the group had been dispersed. In the spring of 1539, they met daily, drawing up the basic outline of a new religious order, which the companions submitted to the pope for approval. It included a statement describing the spirit they intended to sustain.

Whoever desires to serve as a soldier of God beneath the banner of the cross in our Society . . . , should, after a solemn vow of perpetual chastity, poverty, and obedience, keep what follows in mind. He is a member of a Society founded chiefly for this purpose: to strive especially for the defense and propagation of the faith and for the progress of souls in Christian life and doctrine, by means of public preaching, lectures, and any other ministration whatsoever of the word of God, and further by means of the Spiritual Exercises, the education of children and unlettered persons in Christianity, and the spiritual consolation of Christ's faithful.[6]

In September of 1540, Paul III formally established the Society of Jesus as a canonical order. The following year, Ignatius was elected to the office of father general. The fundamental principle of the new order was the *magis*, expressed by Ignatius in the motto *Ad Majorem Dei Gloriam* (For the Greater Glory of God), a phrase he used 376 times in drawing up the Constitutions of the Society of Jesus.[7]

The Society grew quickly, to about a thousand members at the time of Ignatius' death in 1556.[8] The first members worked as university professors and college chaplains, assistants at the Council of Trent, and missionaries; but in the mid-1540s, education unexpectedly emerged as a major commitment. One reason was the rapid increase in numbers, with the necessity of educating the younger Jesuits. In 1545, Ignatius found that the theology program the Society was utilizing at the University of Padua was inadequate; so he directed Jesuit professors to supplement the curriculum with courses at their residence. In the same year, he accepted Francis Borgia's offer to found a college for Jesuit

6. The statement is taken from "The Formula of the Institute" (1540). *The Constitutions of the Society of Jesus*, trans. George E. Ganss (St. Louis: The Institute of Jesuit Sources, 1970), 66–67.

7. Schurhammer, *Xavier*, 1:341–671 *passim*; Dalmases, *Ignatius*, 157–72; Xavier de Franciosi, *The Spirit of St. Ignatius* (New York: Benziger Brothers, 1892), 14.

8. Bangert, *History*, 25.

scholastics at Gandia; soon lay students were also being admitted. These decisions were part of a general movement for Jesuits and other Catholic religious communities to begin sponsoring and staffing schools that were supported by wealthy benefactors, and to take over communal schools supported by public funds.[9]

The matter of schools reached a definitive turning point in 1548 when Ignatius decided to accept an offer to open a college for lay students at Messina "to reform the island" by educating Christian gentlemen. Ignatius sent ten of his best-trained men to initiate the venture; their unexpected success helped convince him that extending Jesuit sponsorship to schools was an authentic application of the *magis*.[10] In organizing the studies at Messina, he was particularly concerned that the methods used at Paris be employed in specific ways: subjects were to be studied in progressive order; books and authors were to be carefully chosen and specified, with an emphasis on Cicero and Vergil; there was to be written work, speaking in Latin, and competitive disputation; classroom work was to be active; and there was to be a moderate workload that allowed for regular recreation.[11]

The curriculum rather freely adopted the literary classics that lay at the heart of the Renaissance humanities schools that had flourished in Italy since the first half of the fifteenth century. After learning Latin grammar as a tool for reading texts, students concentrated on classical authors, especially Cicero, who modeled the ideal prose style and introduced the topic of ethical conduct, and Vergil, whose skill in poetry extended the students' virtuosity in Latin. Other poets and historians rounded out the field. Some schools also offered Greek, particularly focusing on the writing of Aristotle. The goal of the system, historian Paul Grendler has demonstrated, was both practical and moral: "The Latin school taught schoolboys sufficient Latin to enable them to attend university or to pursue professional careers as civil servants and clergymen. It also expected to train wise and morally upright future leaders of society."[12] These Latin schools differed from vernacular schools, some also sponsored by religious communities, that taught reading, writing, and practical commercial skills in Italian.

9. Paul Grendler, *Schooling in Renaissance Italy* (Baltimore: The Johns Hopkins University Press, 1989), 367–68, 398–99.

10. Dainville, "Humanism," 200; Ganss, *St. Ignatius' Idea of a Jesuit University* (2d ed.; Milwaukee: The Marquette University Press, 1956), 166.

11. Dainville, "Humanism," 202–5; Grendler, *Schooling*, 377. The Jesuit course of studies is outlined in Part IV of the Jesuit *Constitutions*, Ganss ed., 171–229; Dalmases, *Ignatius*, 275.

12. Grendler, *Schooling*, 201–2, 219, 270–71, 398–99.

Ignatius asked his assistant Jerome Nadal to codify the Messina program, which was written up in 1551 under the title *De Ratione Studiorum Colegii Messanensis* (The Plan of Studies of the College at Messina). The plan described the piety and good conduct required of students, and contained a 26-point academic program that guided students from Latin grammar to rhetoric, philosophy, and theology. Texts were specified, including Aristotle's *Ethics*, Paul's epistles, Euclid, and contemporary texts on astronomy and mathematics. The document stipulated pedagogical method, the length and content of classes, the kinds of exercises to be used, and the manner of keeping discipline.[13] The Messina plan of studies incorporated Ignatius' ideal of the *magis* into a practical plan that combined Renaissance humanism with Ignatian religious ideals.

Ignatius directed that the Messina plan be adopted at the Roman College he established in February 1551, intending it as a model for all Jesuit schools, a showplace of pedagogical and educational excellence. Here, Ignatius substituted the *Summa Theologiae* of Thomas Aquinas as the principal theological text in place of Peter Lombard's *Book of Sentences*, then in use throughout Italy. By the end of the year, over 250 students were enrolled at the Roman College, and soon its system was being applied at colleges in Germany, France, Portugal, Spain, the Netherlands, Austria, Bohemia, and Poland. Gradually, sponsorship of schools became a defining feature of the order, as Ignatius explained to Philip II in 1556: ". . . Christ our Lord has inspired the Society with a zeal to undertake this very humble, but nonetheless valuable, task of educating youth. Consequently, the administration of colleges for extern students must be accounted as one of the Society's most important apostolates [ministries]."[14] Ignatius devoted about two hundred paragraphs of the Jesuit Constitutions to the colleges and universities conducted by the Society. By the 1770s, the number of schools surpassed 800.[15]

It fell to the fifth Jesuit general, Claudio Acquaviva, to refine the *Ratio Studiorum* and give it a more permanent form after he took office in 1581. Under his guidance, the period of testing and adaptation gave way to sorting and codification. The *Ratio Atque Institutio Studiorum Societatis Iesu* (or *Ratio Studiorum*, the Plan of Studies) was circulated among Jesuit educators for private review in 1586, revised in 1591, and given final form and sanction in 1599.[16] The 1599 version of the *Ratio*, running to 208 pages, featured progressively more difficult classes (or "schools," as they were called), individual progress through the

13. Bangert, *Nadal*, 68–70; Dainville, "Humanism," 202.
14. Cited in Dainville, "Humanism," 200–201. See also Ganss, *St. Ignatius*, 158–59.
15. Bangert, *Nadal*, 69; Farrell, *Jesuit Code*, 219; O'Malley, *First Jesuits*, 16.
16. Farrell, *Jesuit Code*, xi, 224–35, 314–16.

course, competition as a stimulus to learning, frequent holidays and opportunities for sports, and personal mentoring relationships between teachers and students.[17] As a systematic expression of the humanists' approach to education, it was, in John O'Malley's words, "a species within the genus," a system that employed the same texts and exercises as other humanistic schools within a more rigid syllabus. The *Ratio* also elevated Greek to a more prominent position by working it in through the program of five units of material, designated (in ascending order) First, Second, and Third Grammar, Humanities, and Rhetoric.

The Humanities class ordinarily took two years to master; each of the other classes required about a year. Students in the Grammar classes used standard language manuals and progressed through a series of classical authors and orators.[18] Beyond the educational goals lay formation of the intellect, emotions, and spirit of each student as a human being involved in a personal relationship with God. The program stressed compatibility between classical humanities, Aristotelian philosophy, and Thomistic thought. The Jesuit alumnus was to strive for both knowledge and charity, to position himself for useful insertion into his society as an active Christian.[19] The *Ratio* of 1599 accorded humanities teachers equal status with the philosophy and theology faculties. The complete educational scheme required fourteen years, starting at age ten: five years of humanities; three of philosophy and natural sciences; six of Scripture and theology; plus concurrent classes in mathematics and science. Many schools, designated as colleges, offered only the humanities portion of the program to students typically aged ten to sixteen. Schools with the full complement of philosophy and theology studies were considered universities.[20]

The *Ratio* specified the use of prelection, disputation, and competition in

17. Ibid., 317–18. In the mind of Ignatius, student discipline had to be subordinate to the development of student-teacher bonds. Jesuit masters were told to administer discipline "gently, sparingly, by word rather than deed." Ignatius was adamant in prohibiting Jesuit teachers from administering physical punishment, even when it was required to maintain good order. O'Malley, *First Jesuits*, 230.

18. O'Malley, *First Jesuits*, 210, 253–56; Grendler, *Schooling*, 377–81.

19. Farrell, *Jesuit Code*, 352–53; William Henry Dixon, "An Historical Survey of Jesuit Higher Education in the United States with Particular Reference to the Objectives of Education" (Ph.D. Dissertation, Arizona State University, 1974), iii–iv, 30; see also Ganss, *St. Ignatius*, 153–87, 191–201. O'Malley, *First Jesuits*, 218–27, gives a systematic explanation of the characteristics of early Jesuit schools.

20. Farrell, *Jesuit Code*, 342–48, 365, 371–73, 378, 384; Ganss, *St. Ignatius*, 32–34; O'Malley, *First Jesuits*, 215–16; Grendler, *Schooling*, 375.

the classroom. Prelection, used in place of the lecture method, was essentially a process of emulation. The master read, translated, and explained the text; students were then invited to emulate his performance, using their own examples and applying his method. Disputation encouraged students to argue points with their masters and with each other to foster quickness of mind. Students were regularly ranked in their class according to academic achievement, and could raise their ranking by challenging and besting a higher student in an academic topic. There were rules for promoting rivalry and awarding prizes—sometimes in the form of titles like *imperator* or *praetor*, which frequently changed hands. Masters were given rules to ensure that their classroom manner would prepare students in vocabulary, idiom, and style, and that their comments would be "of an elevating and religious character."[21]

The Jesuit Constitutions specified that teachers had a key role in the religious formation of students. Ignatius encouraged masters to "inspire the students to the love and service of God our Lord, and to a love of the virtues by which they will please Him. They should urge the students to direct all their studies to this end."[22] Thus, beyond the humanists' expectation that the classics would inspire virtue, Jesuit schools became an expression of the desire "to help souls." Since the upper levels of the *Ratio Studiorum* (intensive philosophy and theology studies) were omitted at most Jesuit schools, religious instruction and motivation were communicated through personal example, devotional exercises, religious dramas, weekly instruction in Christian doctrine, and the formation of Sodalities. The latter were student confraternities whose members pledged themselves to daily Mass, weekly confession, monthly Communion, daily meditation, and other pious practices and works of charity. Despite the emphasis on religious practice, Jesuit authorities were careful to specify that students be invited rather than coerced into participation. Exemptions for Protestant students varied according to circumstance.[23]

The *Ratio Studiorum* of 1599 designated the governance structure of each institution. Each college or university was headed by a rector, who was both the local superior of the Jesuit community and the chief executive officer of the school. Under the rector was a vice-rector, commonly called the minister, who managed the house and attended to the physical needs of faculty and stu-

---

21. Farrell, *Jesuit Code*, 291–301; Ruth Bradbury LaMonte, "Early Maryland Education: The Colonials, the Catholics, and the Carrolls" (Ph.D. Dissertation, Ohio State University, 1976), 125–28. For a discussion of the pedagogical techniques employed in Jesuit and other humanistic schools, see Grendler, *Schooling*, 162–271.

22. Constitutions, 486.

23. O'Malley, *First Jesuits*, 197–99, 207, 219–27.

dents. The prefect of studies, analogous to a modern secondary school principal or a college dean, was responsible for the daily academic operation of the schools. Institutions also had a prefect of discipline, the prototype of a modern dean of students, who worked with the prefect of studies for the orderly management of common life according to the rules. A spiritual prefect served as chaplain and counselor.[24]

George Ganss has argued that the Jesuit concept of education was particularly successful because it was adaptive—that is, the *Ratio* was designed for "transmitting, discarding, and adding in such a way" that Jesuit colleges were responsive to "the emerging needs and interests of the men of their own day." Jesuit schools, said Ignatius, "ought to be adapted to places, times, and persons."[25] Thanks to the *Ratio*, the character of Jesuit education was well defined by the end of the sixteenth century. Each school had to have a broadly representative humanities curriculum that prized academic excellence; it had to be oriented toward values, particularly religious values, that propelled alumni into society as intelligent and generous contributors to the common good; and it had to be adapted to the developmental level of the students and appropriately lodged within the culture of the region or country. Nevertheless, the effort to fix the content proved to be a mixed blessing: while the revision of 1599 saved and codified the educational experience of the first half-century, it also tended to thwart further development. A plan that started as an innovative response to a historically conditioned set of circumstances would, in time, acquire an intrinsic authority that was hostile to the spirit of adaptation.

Although the *Ratio* was sacrosanct in aims, methods, and organization, the approach took on coloration from the host culture. In the United States, the initial identity of Jesuit colleges was associated with the specific cultural backgrounds of their founders. Before the Civil War, that often connected a school with the specific European Jesuit province that missioned its members to educational work in the United States.[26] Belgian Jesuits, for example, initiated

24. Farrell, *Jesuit Code*, 286–87, 317–62; Constitutions, 419–39.

25. Constitutions, 455; Ganss, *St. Ignatius*, 115. Under 16 headings, Ganss summarizes Ignatius' thoughts on education as he incorporated them into the *Constitutions* of the Society. Pp. 191–201. The points include the training of human faculties for a devout and useful life in imitation of Christ; the intellectual primacy of theology as supported by philosophy; active, participatory learning on the part of students; the mentoring relationship between master and student; adaptability; openness to educational innovations; and the importance of liberal education.

26. These ideas were expressed by historian Philip Gleason in several conversations held in March 1986. See also Christa Ressmeyer Klein, "The Jesuits and Catholic Boyhood in

their work through St. Louis University; Italian Jesuits started from a staging area at Santa Clara University. Holy Cross was founded by Jesuits from Georgetown College, which, in turn, reflected the tradition and experience of the English recusant college operated by Jesuits in the town of Saint-Omer in Flanders, not far from Calais and Dunkirk. There the specific institutional lineage of Holy Cross began.

Saint-Omer had been the home of a Jesuit college for Walloon boys since 1567;[27] the English school was established there in 1593, at a time when Catholic schoolmasters were being persecuted, sometimes executed, in Britain. The college, anglicized as St. Omers, was expected to furnish vocations for the Society of Jesus and for the English seminary at Douay, but students were not required to be candidates for the priesthood. Primarily, it was envisioned as a place for Catholic youth "to escape heretical education in England."[28] By 1614, it had acquired sufficient stability for the Jesuit general to allow it to function independently of the Walloon college. The curriculum offered the first five classes of the Jesuit plan, designated, in ascending order: Figures, Grammar, Syntax, Poetry, and Rhetoric. About 1632 a sixth class was added, without an agreed-upon name. In their free time, the boys (especially the older ones) were encouraged to read and write English prose and poetry, and to study modern history and other subjects. Throughout the seventeenth century, the college was the largest English Catholic school and became a symbol of Roman Catholic persistence through the English Reformation. Enrollment averaged above one hundred students, with the peak coming in 1635, when 200 boys and 25 Jesuits were engaged. During the English Civil War, a number of students were withdrawn to fight for the king; later in the century, St. Omers boys spread the school's reputation when several of them testified at the Popish Plot trials in 1679.[29] Not long afterwards, the rector reported that "religion and learning, and in that order, were unobtrusively combined, with the aid of grace, to produce cultivated, solid, devout Catholic gentlemen."[30]

In fact, St. Omers held a unique position within the international Jesuit system as the one Jesuit boarding college that adapted the customs of the hu-

---

Nineteenth-Century New York City: A Study of St. John's College and the College of St. Francis Xavier, 1846–1912" (Ph.D. Dissertation, University of Pennsylvania, 1976), 3.

27. Bangert, *Nadal*, 332–33, 335.

28. A. C. F. Beales, *Education under Penalty: English Catholic Education from the Reformation to the Fall of James II (1547–1689)* (London: The Athlone Press, 1963), 39–42, 45–48, 64–73.

29. Hubert Chadwick, *St. Omers to Stonyhurst: A History of two Centuries* (London: Burns and Oates, 1962), 69–79; Beales, *Education*, 158, 166–71.

30. Cited in Chadwick, *St. Omers*, 214–15.

manistic English boarding schools. As late as the 1730s, the Jesuit general was disturbed that the students were allowed to go horseback riding and duck shooting: these were English gentlemen's customs and deemed inappropriate student behavior in the host country.[31] Students kept a rigorous 16-hour daily schedule. Two weekday afternoons were free, and there was a monthly holiday. The diet was simple, and weak beer was served at every meal. The prescribed uniforms resembled Jesuit cassocks. To foster the use of classical languages, students were ordinarily forbidden to speak English. Classroom procedures followed the rules for prelection and disputation; in the Grammar and Syntax classes, disputations were held in Greek and Latin. Monthly examinations (called "compositions") determined class standing, with the top six in each class receiving a special holiday. At the end of the academic year, students displayed linguistic and dramatic accomplishments in a public "academy."[32]

The House of Commons declaration, in 1689, that the ousted James II had subverted the English constitution "by the advice of Jesuits and other wicked persons" signaled that the Glorious Revolution would not be propitious for English Jesuits. Indeed, the persistence of penal laws kept the English college on the continent until the French Revolution. Still, the school's reputation attracted the sons of Catholic gentry in the colony of Maryland; more Americans enrolled there in the eighteenth century than at Oxford and Cambridge combined.[33] Charles Carroll of Annapolis, a second-generation Marylander, attended St. Omers in the 1720s. His son, Charles Carroll of Carrollton, destined one day to sign the Declaration of Independence, and his nephew John Carroll, who was to become the first Roman Catholic bishop in the United States, also studied there and assimilated the essentials of the *Ratio*. After St. Omers, John joined the Jesuits and later taught at his alma mater; Charles pursued a legal education in London.[34]

---

31. Ibid., 220–21, 266. Lawrence Stone, *The Crisis of the Aristocracy* (London: Oxford University Press, 1965), 676–83, 686–87. About 1570, Sir Humphrey Gilbert drew up plans for the education of noble English youth that included, in addition to humanistic studies, instruction in such "gentlemanly accomplishments" as horsemanship, shooting, dancing, and fencing. Stone, *Crisis*, 679.

32. Good descriptions of life at the English Jesuit college may be found in Beales, *Education*, 162–65; and Chadwick, *St. Omers*, 75, 80–89, 125–40, 223–36, 365–66.

33. Robert Emmett Curran, *The Bicentennial History of Georgetown University*, vol. 1, *From Academy to University, 1789–1889* (Washington, D.C.: Georgetown University Press, 1993), 5.

34. LaMonte, "Early Maryland Education," 164; Kate M. Rowland, *The Life of Charles Carroll of Carrollton, With His Correspondence and Letters* (2 vols.; New York, G. P. Putnam's, 1898), 1:14–19. See also the correspondence of Charles Carroll of Carrollton during his 5½ year stay at St. Omers, in *Maryland History Magazine*, Vol. X.

Bowing to concerted pressure from Europe's Bourbon monarchs, Pope Clement XIV suppressed the Society of Jesus in 1773.[35] The twenty Jesuits assigned to Maryland, Pennsylvania, New Jersey, and New York comprised the entire Catholic clergy for approximately 30,000 Roman Catholics in the thirteen colonies. The papal directive deprived them of their formal organization, while pre-revolutionary tensions deterred them from submitting to the authority of the Catholic vicar apostolic in London, who headed England's Roman Catholics. In 1774, John Carroll returned from Europe and found a way to bring advantage from the circumstances by rallying his fellow priests behind three key ideas: an organization of ex-Jesuits to hold formerly Jesuit properties as a legal corporation, pending a hoped-for restoration of the Society; a distinct American Catholic church, connected directly with Rome; and a college to train educated laity and American priests. All three objectives were speedily accomplished after the conclusion of the War for Independence. In 1783, the priests organized themselves legally under the title of "The Select Body of the Clergy" and petitioned Roman authorities to appoint an American as their religious head. Partly through the intervention of Benjamin Franklin, who was then in Paris, Carroll was named prefect apostolic of the United States in 1784. Five years later, he was named bishop of Baltimore. In the same year, 1789, Bishop Carroll founded Georgetown College, averring that "on this Academy is built all my hope of permanency and success to our H. Religion in the United States." The college was entrusted to ex-Jesuits to be conducted according to the method of the *Ratio Studiorum*.[36]

When Georgetown opened in 1791, Bishop Carroll intended that the learning environment and academic program should resemble St. Omers. For several generations, his blueprint was followed. Students had to be at least eight years old and literate in English; they encountered the humanities segment of the *Ratio*, with the addition of English grammar, arithmetic, and geography. Before the Civil War, the "lower schools" ordinarily required three years of work, designated as Rudiments (English syntax and grammar, mathematics); Third Humanities (beginning Latin and French, mathematics, English); and Second Humanities (Latin syntax and grammar, Julius Caesar, French, mathematics, geography). The "higher schools," or college division, incorporated four years, designated First Humanities (beginning Greek, Latin

---

35. Bangert, *History*, 363–406.

36. Bangert, *History*, 407; Jay P. Dolan, *The American Catholic Experience* (Garden City: Image Books, 1985), 103–7; Joseph T. Durkin, "The Mission and the New Nation, 1773–1800," in *The Maryland Jesuits*, 35–38, 43–44. The Carroll quote is taken from his letter to Charles Plowden, March 1, 1788, MPA, 202 B 17, in Daley, *Georgetown*, 47.

authors, French); Poetry (Latin and Greek poets, including Vergil and Homer, and French works of LaFontaine); Rhetoric (Cicero, Demosthenes, other Latin and Greek works, and English literature); and Philosophy, which was divided into moral philosophy (logic, metaphysics, natural theology, psychology, and ethics) and natural philosophy (mechanics, physics, calculus, chemistry, astronomy). All courses except natural sciences were taught in Latin. The Georgetown program included daily prelections and weekly class repetitions; competition was fostered by announcing student rankings at a monthly assembly; semi-annual examinations, lasting about a month, were capped by an assembly at which students were praised or scolded.[37] The daily schedule lasted 15 hours, beginning at 5:30 A.M., and included 5½ hours of classes, about 3½ hours of individual study, nearly 2 hours of recreation, in addition to religious exercises and meals. A school uniform was also prescribed. Non-Catholic students, who numbered between 21 and 35 percent of the student body before 1850, were subject to all rules except those touching upon religious practice. Separate religious instructions for the upper and lower schools were given on Saturdays; Catholic students received additional instruction in Christian doctrine on Sundays. A Sodality was established in 1810; but debating was the most favored student activity by mid-century, when non-Catholic Southern students became more dominant.[38]

After the opening of Georgetown, a new turn of events again altered the status of the ex-Jesuits in the world. In 1801, Pope Pius VII extended recognition to the remnant of Jesuits who had maintained their existence in the Russian Empire under the protection of Catherine the Great and Paul I, by allowing them to accept members from outside the Russian borders. For the ten American ex-Jesuits who were still alive, the papal decision afforded an opportunity to re-affiliate with the Society; in 1805, five of them chose to renew their Jesuit vows. The following year, they opened a novitiate at Georgetown to accept new members. The first group of novices included Benedict J. Fenwick.[39] The partial restoration of the Jesuits meant that Georgetown could now be formally entrusted to the Society of Jesus. This change was effected in 1805 when the trusteeship of the school passed from the Select Body of the Clergy to the Society of Jesus, which subsequently operated the school through its network of provincial and local officers of the Maryland Mission, which

37. Daley, *Georgetown*, 54–71; R. Emmett Curran, "From Mission to Province: 1805–1833," in *Maryland Jesuits*, 64–65; Curran, *Georgetown*, 1:190–94, 197–200; Edward J. Power, *A History of Catholic Higher Education in the United States* (Milwaukee: Bruce Publishing Co., 1958), 114–15.

38. Curran, *Georgetown*, 1:170–74, 193–94, 200–202, 408–12.

39. Bangert, *History*, 423–26.

became the autonomous Maryland Province in 1833. Meanwhile, an influx of European Jesuits made it possible to expand the humanities offerings; in 1815, Georgetown received a Congressional charter.[40] The American application of the *Ratio* at Georgetown influenced the thinking of the Jesuits who eventually shaped Holy Cross. Benedict Fenwick was rector at Georgetown twice between 1817 and 1825. Thomas Mulledy, the first Holy Cross president, had also held that office. Many of the other Jesuit administrators and teachers who were to introduce Ignatian educational concepts into New England gained experience at Georgetown.

The full restoration of the Jesuits took place in 1814, when Pius VII allowed the Society to organize along the lines that existed before the suppression. His successor, Pope Leo XII, noted that the chief motive for restoring the Society had been "that it might undertake the intellectual and moral instruction of youth."[41] By then, Jesuits were already at work on a revision of the *Ratio* that was issued in 1832. This version added vernacular languages, physics, chemistry, mathematics, geography and history to the humanities curriculum, but otherwise took a cautious approach to innovation. Jan Roothaan, who was elected Jesuit general in 1829, advised Jesuits to hold the line of tradition as much as possible. New methods and innovative curricula, he warned, tended to be "self-contradictory and mutually repugnant—how could all this be taken as a norm for our studies?"[42] Roothaan's approach reflected the post-Napoleonic restorationist spirit of many European Catholics and Jesuits, who lost the feel for what William Bangert called "the pulse of the times and the sense of change in history."[43] Roothaan maintained these views until his death in 1853, setting in place a pattern that influenced Jesuit education well into the twentieth century.

Benedict J. Fenwick, who was destined to found Holy Cross, was well suited for the challenge. He was a fifth-generation Marylander who finished the course at Georgetown in 1801 at the age of 19. By then, Benedict wanted to become a Jesuit and was awaiting the order's restoration. He stayed at the college as a private student and teacher, and then studied theology at a Baltimore seminary until the Jesuit novitiate opened in 1806. After his ordination in 1808, he headed a successful but short-lived school in New York City, the New York Literary Institute, until it was closed in 1814. Afterwards, he was administra-

---

40. Curran, *Georgetown*, 1:58–59, 64–66, 75, 115.
41. Farrell, *Jesuit Code*, 383–95.
42. Roothaan's letter was dated July 25, 1832. Cited in Farrell, *Jesuit Code*, 388–89.
43. Bangert, *History*, 497.

Benedict J. Fenwick (1782–1846), Second Bishop of Boston, Founder of the College of the Holy Cross.

tor of the New York diocese for two years, then rector of Georgetown in 1817–18. From 1818 to 1822, he served under Bishop John England as vicar-general of the Charleston diocese. He was at Georgetown in his second term as rector when he received word of his appointment as second bishop of Boston.[44]

Fenwick had reservations about accepting the Boston see. Always dedicated to the Society of Jesus, he had shown his sentiments at the time of its restoration: "What a triumph! How glorious to the Society! How confounding to her enemies!"[45] Fenwick would think again about confounding enemies as bishop of Boston, but at first he tried to avoid the position altogether. In early 1823, when rumors about his episcopal candidacy were circulating, he denied any desire for the office. Yet Baltimore's Archbishop Ambrose Maréchal, as head of the Catholic Church in the United States, was promoting Fenwick for Boston, whose first bishop, Jean Cheverus, wanted to return to France.[46] Eventually, Maréchal overcame Fenwick's reluctance by appealing to his sense of responsibility. Accepting the appointment was a personal sacrifice: Fenwick had to give up companionate life in a Jesuit community, for his new position superseded his Jesuit commitments to religious obedience and poverty. As his thoughts turned toward New England, he promised, "I shall never cease to be a sincere friend & well wisher to the Society."[47] Because of his personal background and his family connection to the Society through his Jesuit brothers Enoch and George, and given the potential that Jesuits might eventually help in meeting the needs of New England's Catholic population, his promise of friendship was willingly kept.

Benedict Fenwick was consecrated by Archbishop Maréchal on November 1, 1825. Then he headed north. A Marylander accustomed to neither the social nor the meteorological climate of New England, he faced a hard assignment: his diocese encompassed the six New England states, but he had only one

44. For biographical summaries of Benedict Fenwick's early years, see Robert H. Lord, John E. Sexton, and Edward T. Harrington, *A History of the Archdiocese of Boston*, 3 vols. (New York: Sheed and Ward, 1944), 2:3–23; Fenwick's autobiographical account in *Memoirs to Serve for the Future*, ed. Joseph H. McCarthy (Yonkers: U.S. Catholic Historical Society, 1978), 180–82; and Daley, *Georgetown*, 156–58, 174–81.

45. The letter was dated December 23, 1814, MPA, 204 M 20, cited in Daley, *Georgetown*, 188–89.

46. Lord et al., *History*, 23, 25; and Benedict Fenwick to George Fenwick, Georgetown, January 14, 1823, MPA, 206 S 2a.

47. Letters to Francis Dzierozynski, Port Tobacco, August 5, 1825, MPA, 207 P 11; and Baltimore, September 4, 1825, MPA, 207 P 19. On Jesuits who become bishops, see Ganss, *Jesuit Constitutions*, pp. 334–45.

priest in Boston and twenty others in an area that had nine Catholic churches. Fortunately, he was blessed with strong faith, buoyant energy, and practical imagination as he summoned his resources for the new challenge. His enthusiasm for life extended to the dinner table and he gradually developed a portly figure; one estimate has him weighing 300 pounds in his latter years. Calm and deliberate, Fenwick got along well with the Whig aristocracy of the Bay State; and his sympathy toward the Irish immigrants who were pouring into New England earned the respect of the radical Yankee publicist Orestes Brownson, who approached him about embracing Catholicism. When the bishop died, Brownson described Fenwick as "a great and good man, a man of various and solid learning, a tender heart, unaffected piety, and untiring zeal in the ministry."[48]

Fenwick needed all of his gifts to confront the problems that surfaced during the two decades he headed the diocese. His predecessor, Jean Cheverus, was a cultivated French aristocrat whose erudition and willingness to build bridges of understanding with Protestants after the diocese was established in 1808 helped assuage old antipathies. In 1821, the commonwealth's constitutional prohibition against Catholic office-holders was rescinded; three years later, religious taxation was informally ended; and in 1833 the Congregational Church was formally disestablished. But anti-Catholicism, fostered through popular textbooks like the *New England Primer*, remained a fact of public life for the time being. The number of Catholics was relatively low during the Cheverus era; only at the very end of his Boston years did poverty-ridden Irish immigrants begin to seek work in Lowell, Boston, and elsewhere. Boston, whose population was about 50,000 when Fenwick arrived, reached 137,000 in 1850, when over 35,000 Bostonians had been born in Ireland. In the same period of time, the city's Catholic population rose to about 60,000. The physical and cultural poverty of the Irish, no less than the rapid increase in their numbers and the social impact of their presence, brought opportunities for exploitation and reawakened nativist and anti-Catholic fears.[49]

48. Brownson, *The Convert* (1857), in *The Works of Orestes Brownson*, collected and arranged by Henry F. Brownson, 20 vols. (Detroit, Thorndike Nourse, 1884), 5:164; Thomas H. O'Connor, *Fitzpatrick's Boston, 1846–1866* (Boston: Northeastern University Press, 1984), 44–45, 91, 95, 171, 181–83; Fenwick, *Memoirs*, 181–83; Joseph M. McCarthy, "Introduction" to *Memoirs to Serve for the Future*, vii.

49. A classic account of the impact of Irish immigrants on the city of Boston is Oscar Handlin, *Boston's Immigrants* (rev. ed.; New York: Atheneum, 1972). The statistics are taken from Handlin, 239, 243, and from Vincent A. Lapomarda, *The Jesuit Heritage in New England* (Worcester: The Jesuits of Holy Cross, Inc., 1977), 79. See also Cecelia Meighan, "Nativism and Catholic Higher Education, 1849–1860," (Ed.D. dissertation, Columbia University, 1972),

At first the social displacement and cultural qualities associated with the Catholic immigrants produced a war of words. In January 1829, Bishop Fenwick noted that "Yankee Calvinist Preachers" had begun to issue an anti-Catholic paper called *The Anti-Jesuit*.[50] By September, the bishop had readied his response, a weekly entitled *The Jesuit, or Catholic Sentinel*. Polemical in tone, the paper was more reflective of Fenwick's combative spirit than of his charity. When his cousin, Bishop Edward Fenwick of Cincinnati, urged him to be more moderate, Benedict replied that he was only responding to "the outrageous provocation of some of our Boston Calvinistic Papers":

> There is no lie, no calumny, no misrepresentation that they will stop at, or which they do not insert in their scandalous papers against Catholics & their tenets. So bold had they become of late that it was deemed necessary to twitch them in their own style by way of shewing them the absurdity of it.[51]

During the winter of 1830–31, the hostility was aired in the lecture circuit, when Fenwick arranged a series of public lectures at the cathedral in response to the series being given by Lyman Beecher at the Park Street Church. Soon, verbal skirmishing gave way to legal discrimination and physical attack. In 1832, the selectmen of Charlestown passed an ordinance forbidding Boston's deceased Catholics burial in the Catholic cemetery Fenwick had established on Bunker Hill. Two years later, the convent school run by Ursuline Sisters in Charlestown fell victim to the overheated circumstances when it was torched by a mob and burned down on August 11, 1834. The local Brahmins, some of whom had sent their daughters to the academy, recommended that the injured parties be reimbursed by the state. But the episode generated little remorse among Boston's militant nativists. The courtroom audience applauded when the ringleaders were acquitted after a trial laced with anti-Catholic sentiment and biased procedures.[52]

87–92; and Ronald P. Formisano, *The Transformation of Political Culture: Massachusetts Parties, 1790s–1840s* (New York: Oxford University Press, 1983), 170. On the background of anti-Catholic and anti-Jesuit sentiment in New England, see Ray Allen Billington, *The Protestant Crusade, 1800–1860*, (Chicago: Quadrangle Paperbacks, 1964), 14–16; and Lord et al., *History*, 2:205–65; Lapomarda, *Jesuit*, 70–77.

50. Fenwick to Francis Dzierozynski, Boston, January 5, 1829, MPA, 209 Z 3.

51. Fenwick to Edward Fenwick, Boston, July 19, 1830, UNDA, Cincinnati Collection, 11-4-d; Victor F. O'Daniel, *The Right Rev. Edward Dominic Fenwick* (Washington: The Dominicana, 1920), 379; Lord et al., *History*, 2:191–201.

52. Benedict Fenwick to George Fenwick, Boston, May 21, 1832, MPA, 210 R 9; Billington, *Protestant Crusade*, 70–90.

The winter of 1834–35 was a low point for Bishop Fenwick. On the last day of the trial, he sadly predicted acquittal for the rioters on account of a regional spirit he found difficult to accept: "A Yankee jury, where religion is concerned, will seldom be brought to convict . . . Yankee criminals." He was also concerned that new violence would ensue if new outrages were added to the public insult which had been dealt to "our good Irish men."[53] A few weeks later, the bishop was reporting anonymous threats of violence. And, although many people were having second thoughts about the destruction of the school, he was furious that anti-Catholic polemicists were endeavoring to keep the antipathy alive—"They are certainly incarnate Devils."[54] The wound inflicted by the convent fire and its aftermath never completely healed; rather, it seems to have sustained Fenwick's militant determination to assert Catholic presence.

A major reason for Benedict Fenwick's lingering outrage about the convent fire must have been that the attack had been mounted against a school. As bishop, his first major project had been the relocation of the academy to the Charlestown site, "Mount Benedict," where its success eventually rendered it so intolerable to some. At the same time he was dreaming of a college for male students, partly as a seedbed for priests in his critically understaffed diocese. Less than four months after his arrival in Boston, he wistfully invited the Jesuit superior of the Maryland Mission to sell some property and "purchase a lot on one of the beautiful hills around Boston & build a College on it. [I can] insure you as many scholars as you please, where you will make five jesuits for every one you will make where you are."[55] From afar, he monitored the progress of Georgetown College and corresponded with Edward Fenwick about the opening of a college in Cincinnati.[56]

Fenwick's concern with Catholic education had several sources. Obviously, his experience as an educator, his need for priests, his desire to improve the lot of the Catholic immigrants, and his wish that Catholic youth be educated in atmosphere free from hostility to their faith all came into play. During Fenwick's Boston years, Catholic colleges were beginning to come into their own in the United States. In 1829, the Maryland Jesuits opened St. John's Literary

53. Letter to George Fenwick, Boston, December 29, 1834, MPA, 211 S 11.

54. Letter to George Fenwick, Boston, February 4, 1835, MPA, 211 R 7.

55. Fenwick, *Memoirs*, 183–85; Fenwick to Francis Dzierozynski, Boston, April 11, 1826. MPA, 207 K 12[?].

56. Fenwick to Edward Fenwick, Boston, July 19, 1830, UNDA, Cincinnati Collection, 11-4-d; Fenwick to Dzierozynski, Boston, January 5, 1829, MPA, 209 Z 3.

Institute in Frederick, Maryland, and assumed responsibility for St. Louis University. And in the 1840s, in addition to Holy Cross, Jesuits from several provinces and missions assumed responsibility for Xavier University in Cincinnati, Fordham University in New York, Gonzaga College in Washington, and Spring Hill College in Mobile. Other bishops and religious congregations were also establishing schools: forty-two Catholic colleges were founded in the United States between 1789 and 1850, and an equal number was added during the 1850s. They offered preparatory and collegiate training, and religious instruction; and, despite the fact that Protestant students were an important part of the clientele, the schools were a source of new members for the congregations and dioceses which sponsored them.[57]

By 1830, Bishop Fenwick was calling a college and seminary "the thing I want most."[58] Late in 1831, he told George Fenwick that he was "about to erect a College" that would cost $20,000. The following April, he reported that he had bought property adjacent to the Boston cathedral for "a College *in miniature*," but the enterprise dragged along. In 1833, he told George that "next May, I, too, mean to open a College." But 1834 brought no developments; and in 1835, the Jesuits declined to staff such a school.[59] Up to this point, the order had resisted his invitations; but, given his predilection for the Jesuit approach to education and the general shortage of priests, he had no alternative but to repeat his request for "respectable" Jesuit educators for a region where "our holy Religion is so continually assailed."[60]

After 1835, the bishop made plans for a college in Maine, where he had bought 11,000 acres in Aroostook County, seventy miles north of Bangor. Named Benedicta, the settlement was a social experiment intended as an agricultural refuge for needy Irish immigrants. By 1838 lumber and grist mills were

57. Philip Gleason estimates that a third to a half of the enrollment in Catholic colleges between 1825 and 1850 may have been Protestant students. "Changing and Remaining the Same: A Look at the Record," *Current Issues in Catholic Higher Education* 10 (Summer 1989), 4–5, cited in Curran, *Georgetown*, 1:128. Meighan, "Nativism," 3, 26–31, 35–41; Helen Lefkowitz Horowitz, *Campus Life: Undergraduate Cultures from the End of the Eighteenth Century to the Present* (Chicago and London: The University of Chicago Press, 1987), 59. For a listing and brief history of men's ante-bellum Catholic colleges, see Powers, *History*, 255–88.

58. Benedict to Edward Fenwick, Boston, July 19, 1830, UNDA, Cincinnati Collection 11-4-d.

59. Letters of Benedict Fenwick to George Fenwick, all from Boston, December 21, 1831, MPA, 210 S 4; April 25, 1832, MPA, 210 R 7; August 1, 1833, MPA, 210 F 10; Benedict Fenwick to William McSherry, Boston, August 18, 1835, MPA, 211 N 9; McSherry to Francis Dzierozynski, Georgetown, August 27, 1835, MPA, 211 N 11; Lord et al., *History*, 2:320–21.

60. Quoted by William McSherry to Dzierozynski, Georgetown, August 27, 1835, MPA, 211 N 11.

under construction; the bishop intended their revenues for the college he constructed there between 1839 and 1841—a two-story wooden structure with dimensions of 84 × 42 feet.[61] The following year, after failing to attract Canadian Jesuits to the project, Bishop Fenwick informed Francis Dzierozynski, acting provincial of the Maryland Province, of his "earnest desire to have the Society permanently established in this Diocese" and formally requested him to draw the matter to the attention of Jan Roothaan. The offer included the school at Benedicta, pastoral opportunities in Maine, the sawmill revenues, and 2000 acres of land. In transmitting the offer to Rome, Dzierozynski added his personal view that Fenwick was well disposed toward the Society.[62]

By this time, Bishop Fenwick was clear on two points about the college he intended to found: it was to be run by Jesuits according to the *Ratio Studiorum*; and it was to be exclusively Catholic. His preference for the Jesuit educational program was an understandable by-product of his experience and connections, but his desire for Catholic exclusivity was a surprising innovation. After all, his principal collegiate experiences, as student and administrator, had occurred at Georgetown, which was open to students of all faiths and whose progress Fenwick extolled after he came to Boston. Nevertheless, as early as 1835, he told the Jesuit provincial that he was planning his school in Boston along exclusionary lines: "Aware long since of the great disadvantage of mixing Catholic with Protestant students I have concluded to admit none of the latter . . . under any pretence whatsoever; and furthermore none shall be admitted in to it who do not affirm themselves, or who are not offered by their Parents, as candidates for the Church." This line suggests that, so soon after the Charlestown episode, he was wary of the potential for violence in Boston if Protestant zealots learned that Protestant children were again being educated by Catholics.[63] But later in the same letter, when Fenwick returned to the issue of exclusivity, he placed it in a different context: "Parents will prefer & select it . . . on account of it, being *strictly & purely* Catholic, *to the exclusion of all protestants*—and consequently will have a just hope that their children, when sent hither, will not be biassed by the conversation of such, & will more surely follow the vocation upon which they set out." The rationale thus combined several justifications: his sense that exclusivity would be a drawing card for

61. Walter J. Meagher and William J. Grattan, *The Spires of Fenwick* (New York: Vantage Press, 1966), 37; Lord et al., *History*, 2:322—23.

62. Fenwick to Dzierozynski, Boston, August 27, 1842; MPA, 213 H 9; Dzierozynski to Roothaan, Georgetown, September 6, 1842, ARSI, MD 7-VIII, 7.

63. Fenwick to William McSherry, Boston, August 18, 1835, MPA, 211 N 9; Meighan, "Nativism," 100.

Catholics; his frustration with anti-Catholic nativism; his need for priests; and his conviction that isolation would best nurture the vocational aspirations of students who were candidates for the priesthood.[64]

In 1838, when his hopes for a college had shifted to Benedicta, Fenwick maintained his ideas about exclusivity. Since, presumably, there would be no immediate threat from contact with anti-Catholics at Benedicta, the vocational issue was uppermost. To his brother George, he wrote:

I shall erect a College into which no Protestant shall ever set foot; for I cannot persuade myself that it is much to the advantage of Catholicity to have that mixture of boys of different creeds which prevails in all our Catholic establishments throughout the country. What is gained by removing the prejudices of Protestants is lost by impairing the devotion, & in some cases, the religion of the Catholics. It cannot but strike everyone that fewer boys take to religion, or to the ecclesiastical state in a College where this mixture prevails than in one in which it does not.[65]

Five years later, when he was negotiating with Father Dzierozynski about staffing a college, he made an identical point: "I venture to say there will be more vocations to the ecclesiastical state manifested in this *purely Catholic Institution* than in any other . . . as they now are with Protestants and Catholics mixed up."[66] The same motives prompted Fenwick to insist upon a boarding rather than a day school; for in a boarding school, contact with the predominant Protestant culture could be limited. Thus, his antipathy toward anti-Catholic Yankees and his desire to stimulate vocations to the priesthood became mutually reinforcing arguments.[67]

But still there was no school. After more than a decade of careful thought, of planning and cajolery and begging, there was no formal sponsor, no administrator to assume responsibility, no situation attractive enough to lure Jesuits (or others) to stretch their slender resources for the Diocese of Boston. Then, early in 1843, everything changed. In remarkably short order, Bishop Fenwick secured tentative sponsorship, an administrator, and an acceptable location.

The location came first. Worcester, in the middle years of the nineteenth century, was becoming an industrial city. Between 1840 and 1860, its popula-

64. William McSherry to Francis Dzierozynski, August 27, 1835, MPA, 211 N 11.
65. Boston, November 27, 1838, MPA, 212 M 7.
66. Fenwick to Dzierozynski, Boston, February 4, 1843, MPA, 214 Z 5.
67. In Philadelphia, the Augustinians founded a college (Villanova) in 1842, soliciting only Catholic patronage. Nativist violence and threats of violence forced the closing of the school for nineteen months in 1845–46. Meighan, "Nativism," 7–8, 29.

tion rose from 7500 to 25,000, spurred by the opening of the Blackstone Canal to Providence in 1828, and by its location at the intersection of railroad lines from Boston, Springfield, and New York City (through a boat connection at Norwich)—a network constructed between 1835 and 1847.[68] In 1836, Bishop Fenwick assigned Father James Fitton[69] to Worcester as its first resident Catholic pastor, though his "parish" extended to Worcester, Hamden, and Middlesex counties of Massachusetts and part of eastern Connecticut. Confronting the challenge, Fitton opened a small church in the city in 1836 and also, for $2000, bought 52 acres of farm land two miles south of Worcester "on the northerly side of Bogachoag[70] hill" to establish a Catholic academy. The farm occupied the lower level of the slope, approximately from the river to the present site of Fenwick Hall, and included a house near the river and a barn. Fitton turned the farm over to his brother's management. For the academy, named Mount Saint James Academy after his patron saint, he erected a two-story frame building, 70 feet long, near the present location of Fenwick Hall,[71] to receive the thirty students who enrolled during the first year. The contractor also built a small cottage for Fitton's private residence. The location enchanted Bishop Fenwick from the beginning. On his first visit, he described it as being "on the declivity of an extensive hill which is watered at the base by a little stream of pure water." The place, he thought, was "well adapted to an institution of that nature. . . . I . . . could not but entertain the hope that sooner or later something would grow out of it useful to the Church."[72]

The academy accepted boys who were at least eight years old. Terms ran September to March and March to mid-August. Tuition was $80 per semester. Conducted with the help of a layman, Joseph Brigden, the academy offered a

68. John L. Brooke, *The Heart of the Commonwealth: Society and Political Culture in Worcester County, Massachusetts, 1713–1861* (New York: Cambridge University Press, 1989), 332, 389; Roy Rosenzweig, *Eight Hours For What We Will: Workers and Leisure in an Industrial City, 1870–1920* (New York: Cambridge University Press, 1983), 11.

69. Fitton was descended from an old English Catholic family that came to Boston about 1800. He was ordained by Bishop Fenwick in 1827. As a young priest, Fitton wanted to be a Jesuit, but Fenwick told him he was too much needed where he was. L. P. McCarthy, *Sketch of the Life and Missionary Labors of Rev. James Fitton*, Publications of the New England Catholic Historical Society, No. 8 (Boston: George F. Crosby Co., 1908), 1–18.

70. From Pakachoag, "Hill of Pleasant Springs," once the site of a settlement of native Americans attracted there by the source of water. Meagher and Grattan, *Spires*, 24–25.

71. William Lucey, in a note dated April 25, 1965, states that the altered academy building was moved twice—first to the edge of the present Jesuit cemetery, and later to a site to the east of the cemetery where the Millard Art Center is currently located. ACHC, Fact File.

72. Fenwick Diary, August 8, 1836, copy, GUA, "Holy Cross, 1843–47."

diversified practical curriculum that included Latin, English grammar and composition, history, geography, and bookkeeping. Presumably, the students availed themselves of the Blackstone's "pure water" for fishing, swimming, and ice-skating, but they were also encouraged to "exercise" at the task of leveling the upper and lower terraces. The enterprise was successful enough to attract students from New Orleans and Texas, but there were chronic financial difficulties and Fitton was heavily overextended.[73]

In the fall of 1842, Bishop Fenwick, still waiting for an answer from the Jesuits about Benedicta, settled on the Fitton academy and farm as the best location for a seminary to be staffed by diocesan priests. At that point, apparently, he envisioned a Jesuit college in Maine and a diocesan seminary at Fitton's site. Fitton agreed to part with the property on condition that it be used for educational purposes and that the bishop assume the $1500 mortgage. In October, Fenwick purchased 22 acres of land adjacent to the academy property and visited Worcester again to examine the site. In the same month, he disclosed to his brother George the magnitude of his dream:

Next May I shall lay the foundation of a splendid College in Worcester. I have bought 50 acres of land for that purpose. It is to be modelled after your new college [building] in Geo-Town, but *prodigeously* improved. . . . Will not this be a bold undertaking? Nevertheless I will try it.

He supplied the dimensions of the building and a freehand sketch, noting that the building "will stand on a beautiful eminence & will command the view of the whole town of Worcester." He anticipated an enrollment of 100 and tuition of $125.[74] Fenwick closed his agreement with Fitton on February 2, 1843.[75] He now owned 74 acres of the Pakachoag hillside, with its farm, barn, farmhouse, cottage, and academy. And he had plans for an imposing college building.

By the time Fenwick and Fitton signed their agreement, a major development had altered the bishop's thinking about the use of the academy property. Early in 1843, Father Dzierozynski had received Father General Roothaan's response to Fenwick's offer of the college in Benedicta. The general understood

73. Meager and Grattan offer a good summary of the history of Fitton's academy, 22–30. See also James Fitton, *Sketches of the Establishment of the Church in New England* (Boston: Patrick Donohoe, 1872), 289; Edward I. Devitt, "College of the Holy Cross, 1843–1914," in *WL*, 64:204–7; and Lord et al., *History*, 2:42–43, 323–24.

74. Benedict Fenwick to George Fenwick, Boston, October 3, 1842, MPA, 213 G 4; Fenwick Diary, September 22 and October 18, 1842, copy, GUA, "Holy Cross, 1843–1847"; Lord et al., *History*, 2:323.

75. Lord et al., *History*, 2:323–24; Meagher and Grattan, *Spires*, 29–30.

that the situation was delicate: Fenwick's requests could no longer be honorably refused, but his specific offer presented objections because of the shortage of qualified personnel.[76] Roothaan chided the Maryland superior gently for making no specific recommendation and asked him to refer the matter to the Province Consultors (the advisory council in each Jesuit province). He also suggested that Dzierozynski press the bishop to commit diocesan priests to assist the Jesuits in staffing the school in Maine. On January 9 Dzierozynski informed Fenwick of Roothaan's "very sincere wish to comply with yr pious intentions." There were, however, prior questions: How many teachers could Fenwick free for the work? When and where would the school begin? The latter question is curious, since only Benedicta had been proposed; and it is quite likely, given the correspondence that followed, that Dzierozynski was hinting at a preference for a site in Boston. He pledged to Fenwick his "hearty cooperation. . . . I will do my utmost."[77] This was the most positive signal the bishop had yet received from the Jesuits. It was all he needed to stimulate his enthusiasm.

On the very day he received Dzierozynski's letter, Fenwick added the site at Pakachoag to the negotiations and then drew upon his persuasive powers to induce the Jesuits to accept. He expressed "infinite delight" at Roothaan's response: "I now see clearly that it is the will of God that a new career should be opened to the zeal of these Fathers." He continued his offer of $10,000 worth of property at Benedicta and promised also the farm in Worcester and the new building, whose contract estimate was $14,000 and had a estimated completion date of October 1. And he praised the Worcester location: "There is not one to surpass it in the United States."[78] Although the Benedicta offer remained on the table, it became essentially a dead letter since subsequent negotiations focused on Worcester. As the dialogue proceeded, the bishop had to carry two points to convince the Jesuits to accept his plan: first, that the boarding school he had in mind was as legitimate an application of Jesuit manpower as a day college would be; and second, that Worcester—not

76. There were only about three dozen priests in the Maryland Province in 1842, a number of whom were unavailable for regular work by reason of infirmity or personal qualities. R. Emmett Curran, "Troubled Nation, Troubled Province, 1833–1880," (unpublished MS), 17–18.

77. Roothaan to Dzierozynski, Rome, October 29, 1842, ARSI, MD I:204; Dzierozynski to Fenwick [early January, 1843], MPA, 214 Z. Dzierozynski's reference to alternatives may be an indication that he was aware that Father John McElroy, then at the Jesuit school in Frederick, Maryland, and unaware of the Worcester project, had just proposed to Bishop Fenwick a Jesuit day school in Boston near the cathedral. Letter of January 7, 1843, Boston Archdiocesan Archives, cited in Lord et al., *History*, 2:325.

78. Fenwick to Dzierozynski, Boston, January 11, 1843, MPA, 214 Z 3.

Boston—would be the starting point for Jesuit educational work in New England.

Dzierozynski raised these objections in his response to the bishop's amplified offer. He reported his consultors' sense that the Maryland Province lacked the resources to staff a boarding school. As they saw it, the physical strain of attending to students day and night would jeopardize the health of the Jesuits, a situation that tended to "disgust us with boarding colleges." From the viewpoint of the *magis*, Dzierozynski argued, an equal number of Jesuits could accommodate three times more day students than boarding students. If Worcester could be made into a day school, he promised, the Jesuits would accept. Otherwise, he suggested that the bishop draw up "a plan for a large College of day-Scholars on the plan of the Society in which our slender exertions may be employed to more advantage than in any boarding College no matter how large, or flourishing."[79] Only Boston was large enough to support the sort of day school Dzierozynski was suggesting, but his delicate sense of ecclesiastical courtesy precluded asking for something that had not been offered.

In a masterful response, Fenwick readily conceded the principal objection —an urban day school would "effect a greater amount of good with a comparatively smaller number of operators. But," he added quickly, "I am decidedly of opinion that these City establishments will not do *alone*, at least, in this country." He insisted that city schools exposed students to distractions that could jeopardize vocations to the priesthood. Moreover, he expected that day colleges would tend to attract students from "the lower order of society"; that being the case, economic necessity would force many parents to withdraw their sons before they could finish the humanities course. The Worcester college, exclusively Catholic, was "too remote even from the town of Worcester to admit day-scholars." But, he promised, a small staff would be sufficient at first: a rector, three teachers, and a prefect could manage the academic side. Domestic duties could be handled by a gardener, a procurator, and several laundresses. Finally, he conceded that he wanted a day college in Boston on the Jesuit plan, but he couldn't afford it at that time. He urged the Jesuits to accept the offer in Worcester to prepare the way for future work and establishments.[80] Like Dzierozynski, Fenwick could communicate by indirection: if

---

79. Dzierozynski to Fenwick [January 25, 1843], MPA, 214 Z 4. In opposing the concept of a boarding school, Dzierozynski was echoing the policy of the first Jesuits. John O'Malley notes that the early Jesuits "did not particularly favor schools that accepted boarders"; but they did accept some, especially in northern Europe "to protect boys from a Protestant environment." Bishop Fenwick based part of his argument for a boarding school on the same grounds. O'Malley, *First Jesuits*, 229.

80. Fenwick to Dzierozynski, Boston, February 4, 1843, MPA, 214 Z 5.

they wanted to establish a day college in Boston, the Jesuits would first have to accept the boarding school in Worcester.

In mid-March, the bishop's letter was forwarded to Father Roothaan, together with the province consultors' judgment. Dzierozynski had put three questions to them—one asking whether to accept a boarding school in Worcester for Catholics only, and two concerning the personnel to be sent there in case of acceptance. On the first question, the consultors were generally favorable, so long as Fenwick honored his pledge of financial support; but there was sentiment that the acceptance be provisional and subject to the availability of Jesuits for the school. The second and third questions asked whether the bishop's request for Thomas F. Mulledy as rector should be granted, and whether an assistant should be assigned to Mulledy. To these questions, the answer was positive. The decision now rested with the general.[81] As it turned out, the recommendations reached Rome at a favorable time. Roothaan was in the process of appointing John Ryder as provincial of Maryland in place of the aging Dzierozynski. He was also urging the Maryland Jesuits to redirect their efforts to the education of city youth, "which is the proper work of the Society."[82] Meanwhile, pending final approval of the enterprise, Father Mulledy was sent to Worcester.

Personal experience and an energetic temperament made Mulledy an acceptable choice as founding rector. Born in 1794 in western Virginia, he studied at Georgetown for several years before entering the Society in 1815. Five years later, he was sent to Rome to study philosophy and theology. The time in Italy afforded Mulledy greater familiarity with the Plan of Studies, and the European atmosphere enhanced his identity as an American and a republican. During his stay, he lampooned Archbishop Maréchal for his affected style while visiting the Eternal City:

His *Lordship* (God forgive me) is rigged off in Italian style . . . he wears also the cock hat, the purple stockings, etc. etc. . . . His lodgings consist of four or five rooms furnished in grand style. Chambers and anti-chambers all upon the high rope—I felt my republican simplicity a little ruffled when we visited his Lordship (o dear! relapsed again) to find that, according to the European style we had to take an airing of 10 or 15 minutes in the anti-chamber before we were admitted to an audience.[83]

81. Dzierozynski to Roothaan, Georgetown, March 14, 1843, ARSI, MD 7-VIII, 2.

82. John Grassi to John McElroy, Rome, March 31, 1843, MPA, 214 Z 8; Roothaan to Ryder, Rome, April 7, 1843, ARSI, MD Reg. I 207. See also Curran, "Troubled Nation," 16–18.

83. Fragment of a letter from Mulledy to [?], Rome [February or March, 1822], GUA, Mulledy Papers. In a letter to Francis Dzierozynski dated at Genoa, July 8, 1828, Mulledy

Thomas F. Mulledy, the first President of Holy Cross, 1843–1845. He also served as spiritual prefect between 1855 and 1857 and escorted the Know-Nothing "Nunnery Committee" on their visit of inspection to the College.

The same letter lamented the "ancient austerity of Roman lents . . . nothing but fish & oil & herbs & herbs & oil & fish—hard times." Like Bishop Fenwick, he relished a good table. After his return from Italy, Mulledy was named prefect of studies at Georgetown in 1828. The following year, he began an eight-year term as rector. Under his leadership, enrollment grew to nearly 200, and the college received authorization to expand its academic offerings upwards through the years of Philosophy and Theology. Although he was sometimes impatient, his hearty manner won friends for his projects; observers described him as "a jolly faced, big bellied man dressed in a cassock . . . ," and as "a marvelous salesman."[84] But Mulledy was also a weak financial

---

reported a five-month tour of Jesuit colleges in Italy and Savoy. GUA, Dzierozynski Papers, Catholic Historical MSS 3:2. For a summary of Mulledy's activities before 1834, see Curran, *Georgetown*, 1:68–69, 107–12; and Meagher and Grattan, *Spires*, 42–43.

84. Bernard C. Steiner, ed., "The South Atlantic States in 1833, As Seen by a New

manager; his building program encumbered the college with a substantial debt.[85]

In October of 1837, Mulledy was named provincial of the Maryland Province. In this position, he encountered serious difficulties when he sold the province's slaves. In fact, Maryland Jesuits had been slave holders since colonial times, when they, like the lay planters of the area, gradually moved from the use of indentured servants to the use of slaves as workers on the manors that served as their parish centers and economic support. In the nineteenth century, there was considerable opposition to slave holding and interest in deferred emancipation; but that option became problematic because of the declining status of free blacks under Maryland law. Late in 1838, Roothaan sent permission to sell the slaves, provided that their religious needs and family bonds be respected, and that the revenue be used for the province formation program. It fell to Mulledy to follow through; and by June 1838, he had reached an agreement with two Louisiana planters. The plan encountered angry resistance from some Jesuits for breaking "the bond that existed between the Society and its black families." Afterwards, it became clear that Roothaan's prohibition against the separation of families could not be enforced.[86] Besides the unspeakable harm inflicted on the individuals, the sale was an unmitigated disaster for Mulledy. Maryland Jesuits sent Roothaan heart-rending accounts of the round-up and described the magnitude of the "tragic and disgraceful" scandal.[87] By August 1839, Roothaan had become convinced that Mulledy should resign as provincial and be required to clear himself of the charges of promoting scandal and disobeying orders. By then, Mulledy had already sailed to Rome to explain himself. Under the circumstances, Roothaan judged it best to keep Mulledy in Europe; he assigned him to duties in Nice, where Mulledy was contrite and lonely. "You all seem to have forgotten me," he wrote, "but I must not complain of that—no doubt I deserve it."[88]

Englander," *Maryland Historical Magazine* 13 (1918), 289–90; and James Ryder to Roothaan, Georgetown, February 18, 1830, ARSI, MD 3-IV, 24, both cited in Curran, *Georgetown*, 1:109.

85. Curran, *Georgetown*, 1:109–19; Powers, *Catholic*, 161–65; Curran, "Troubled Nation," 9.

86. Curran, "'Splendid Poverty': Jesuit Slaveholding in Maryland, 1805–1838," in *Catholics in the Old South*, ed. Randall M. Miller and Jon L. Wakelyn (Macon: Mercer University Press, 1983), 125–43; the quotation is Curran's in *Georgetown*, 1:119.

87. Havermans to Roothaan, October 20, 1838, ARSI, MD 7-I, 9, cited in Curran, *Georgetown*, 1:120.

88. Mulledy to George Fenwick, March 15, 1841, MPA, 213 R 6. See also Francis Dzierozynski to John McElroy, Frederick, March 9, 1840, MPA, 213 Z 7a; Curran, "Troubled Nation," 10–11; Curran, *Georgetown*, 1:120.

By the winter of 1841–42 the controversy had subsided and a provincial congregation petitioned the general to send Mulledy back. The general acquiesced and, early in 1843, Bishop Fenwick asked for Mulledy to head the new college.[89] On Monday, March 13, Mulledy made his first visit to Worcester with the bishop and liked what he saw. He reported: "I was pleased with the situation of [the] future College—most of the materials brick & stone—are already on the ground. . . . The mere locality of the College is beautiful."[90] Mulledy laid out the building site and commissioned an engraving that was used for early notices of the opening. A late spring delayed construction; but extra workmen were hired to speed progress. On Sunday, June 18, Bishop Fenwick formally announced to his Boston congregation the establishment of the College of the Holy Cross, named after his cathedral in Boston.[91]

Wednesday, June 21, 1843, the day of the cornerstone-laying, dawned fresh and sunny. A special train conveyed Fenwick, twelve priests, and "a large concourse of the citizens of Boston and several distinguished strangers" to Worcester, where Fathers Mulledy and Fitton and a crowd of local parishioners greeted them. The local chapter of the Catholic Temperance Society, and young men's and young women's societies from Fitton's parish, joined the visitors in a procession nearly a mile long as the band played "Hail Columbia" and *"Adeste Fideles"* and cannons thundered. Ahead, one participant dreamily recalled, "the star spangled banner of America could be seen . . . waving triumphantly on the Alpine like heights of the romantic site." About noon, Fenwick gathered the group at a large wooden cross that had been erected on the grounds; then they processed to the corner of the building. In Latin, Fenwick intoned the prayer:

In the faith of Jesus Christ we lay this first stone on this foundation in the name of the Father and of the Son and of the Holy Spirit, that true faith may flourish here, and the fear of God, and fraternal affection; and may this place be devoted to invok-

89. Dzierozynski to John McElroy, Georgetown, February 26, 1842 MPA, 213 K 6; Dzierozynski to Fenwick [early January, 1843], Georgetown, MPA, 214 Z; Fenwick to Dzierozynski, Boston, January 11, 1843, MPA, 214 Z 3; Curran, "Troubled Nation," 18.

90. Mulledy to Dzierozynski, Philadelphia, March 18, 1843, GUA, Francis Dzierozynski Papers.

91. Mulledy's book of Mass intentions, April 25, 1843, GUA, Mulledy Papers; Mulledy to Dzierozynski, Boston, May 9, 1843, GUA, Francis Dzierozynski Papers; Meagher and Grattan, *Spires*, 40. Reporting to George Fenwick on the prospectus and the advertising campaign, Mulledy wrote: "We are on the cheap plan—not a heretic shall poke his nose, as a student, in the College." Mulledy to Fenwick, Boston, June 30, 1843, MPA, 214 W 8. Notices of the opening may be found in the Mulledy Papers, ACHC, 7.0-1.

Fenwick Hall as it appeared between 1869 and 1875, showing the east wing which survived the fire of 1852 and the amplified scale of the new central and west wings.

ing and praising the name of our Lord Jesus Christ, Who, with the Father and the Holy Spirit, lives and reigns, one God, forever and ever.

The stone contained coins and medals, newspapers, a copy of the oration given by Daniel Webster four days earlier at the dedication of the Bunker Hill monument, pictures of Webster and President John Tyler, and a document which began:

Ad Majorem Dei Gloriam
Deiparae Virginis Mariae Honorem
Hunc Primarium Lapidem
Collegii Sanctae Crucis
Prope oppidum Vigorniae
Posuit RR. Dominus Benedictus Josephus Fenwick
Episcopus Bostoniensis Secundus

The document included the names of Mulledy, President John Tyler, and Governor Marcus Morton, and was signed by all priests present, by the superintendents of the project, and by the carpenters.[92]

After the stone had been set in place, the participants turned their attention to the orator of the day, Charles Constantine Pise, a widely known preacher and author who had been the first Catholic chaplain of the United States Senate in 1832. As a young man, Pise had spent several years in the Jesuit order and had traveled to Rome with Thomas Mulledy in 1820. Later, he opted for the diocesan priesthood and in 1843 held a pastoral assignment in New York City.[93] Sensitive to the position of Catholics in New England, Pise directed his remarks more to the Yankees in the broader community than to the audience in attendance. Stressing the compatibility of freedom of conscience with the establishment of a Roman Catholic college, he discussed the "misgivings, not to say misapprehensions" about the Jesuits and their purpose. He spoke of Ignatius and his spirit, the Jesuit tradition in education, and the good work and patriotic records already achieved at Georgetown and St. Louis. Then, addressing the fears of incompatibility between Catholicism and free government, he asserted that students at Holy Cross would be "moulded into true Christians and sincere republicans" without "interference of any ecclesiastical power from abroad":

They will be instructed to recognize no temporal power over this free land, in any foreign authority, whether secular or ecclesiastic. They will be taught that even the Sovereign Pontiff, whose spiritual protection, as Catholics we admit and revere, possesses and claims, no right to exercise any sway over us as citizens of this republic. . . . While we constitute but one Church in dogmatical tenets, we are bound to embrace all the other communions in the universal national creed of equal liberty. . . . He who is not faithful to his country, will not be true to his God.[94]

Pise had done well to pitch his address toward the potentially hostile portion of the community. The following day, the *Boston Daily Advertiser* suggested

92. "To the Greater Glory of God / And in Honor of the Virgin Mary, Mother of God / This First Stone / Of the College of the Holy Cross / Near the City of Worcester / Is Placed by the Very Reverend Benedict Joseph Fenwick / Second Bishop of Boston." The description of the stone is taken from Mulledy to William Lincoln, Boston, June 24, 1843, American Antiquarian Society, Lincoln Family Papers, Box 5, folder 4. The rest of the account is from *U. S. Catholic Magazine* 2 (August 1843), 509–10 [Copy in ACHC 7.0-1]; and from Meagher and Grattan, *Spires*, 40–42.

93. Curran, *Georgetown*, 1:89, 114; John J. Delaney, *Dictionary of American Catholic Biography* (Garden City, New York: Doubleday and Co., 1984), 466.

94. Fitton reprinted the text of the speech in *Sketches*, 292–307; see also Thomas Mulledy's historical sketch of the College during his presidency, Mulledy Papers, ACHC, 12.1-1.

that Holy Cross would do no harm if it carried out Pise's program, but also asserted that the school was unnecessary because the region already had several good colleges. The Evangelical press was openly antagonistic; one editor warned readers to beware this "attempt on New England."[95] But Worcester historian William Lincoln published a friendly account in the *Worcester National Aegis:* "Whatever opinions we may entertain of the Catholic Faith, no diversity of sentiment can exist as to the expediency of good education." Lincoln urged his readers to practice toleration, allowing for the education of the growing Roman Catholic population, whose spread would be monitored by the laws of the nation. His conclusion offered a new benediction on Holy Cross and its prospects: "Long may the Institution now planted flourish, and never may ruthless violence invade the seat of learning!"[96]

The ceremony had been splendid, and the participants returned to their homes with an enhanced appreciation that the Worcester college was truly a "bold undertaking," as Bishop Fenwick had predicted. In a surprisingly short period of time, the long-delayed project had sprung to life. An imposing building was under construction; the energetic Mulledy was driving the process forward; and public notice had been given of an opening in October. But there were problems that still gave a tentative cast to the enterprise. Father Roothaan had not yet committed the Jesuits permanently to Holy Cross. The slender human and economic resources of the Maryland Province would somehow have to be stretched to staff a college in a location that must have seemed remote and even uncongenial from the headquarters at Georgetown. Many Jesuits were genuinely skeptical about a the wisdom of running another boarding school. Students had to be recruited. Books and other learning resources had to be gathered. And the question of whether an exclusively Catholic school could exist without violence in Massachusetts was still open.

On June 21, 1843, the misgivings were laid aside. Benedict Fenwick committed the resources of Catholic New England to Holy Cross. Afterwards, Francis Dzierozynski reported to the Jesuit general:

We have achieved prodigies! It pleases me to send you news of "the Catholic College of the Holy Cross of the Society of Jesus"—in the midst of *Yankees!*[97]

95. Lord et al., *History*, 2:326–27.
96. The article is substantially reprinted in an anonymous History of Holy Cross, 1843–1883, ACHC, 10.0-1.
97. Dzierozynski to Roothaan, Georgetown, August 22, 1843, ARSI, MD 7-VIII, 3.

PART ONE

"In the Midst of Yankees"

CHAPTER ONE

The Catholic College of New England, 1843–1851

A s a Massachusetts college, Holy Cross began its institutional life in a region whose educational traditions were the strongest in the nation. Four New England colleges had roots in the colonial period; in Cambridge, Harvard College celebrated its bicentennial in 1836. Massachusetts was also the home of Williams College (founded 1793) and Amherst College (1821). All three held charters that made them eligible for public funding; all were institutional expressions of the dominant values and traditions of New England. In their company, Holy Cross was an outsider, drawing inspiration and support from distinctive sources. Being different was a condition of life on Pakachoag; administrators and teachers had to put the enterprise in motion without paying undue attention to the perceptions of a Yankee society that tended to be as unfamiliar to most of them as they were to it. The *Ratio Studiorum* supplied the College's central paradigm, but the rectors, faculty, and students had to bring the plan to life. The Georgetown connection helped: books, money, even diplomas flowed northward along with the Jesuit personnel who constituted a renewable human resource and took only their livelihood as recompense. The winds of fortune blew gently on Holy Cross at first. Slowly, the College grew.

Growth, for ante-bellum American colleges, was calculated in surprisingly small units. Yale, whose enrollment reached 500 in 1859–60, was the largest American college. Faculties were correspondingly small: twenty was a large liberal arts faculty; small colleges had as few as four or five instructors, some of whom were ministers of the sponsoring denomination. College libraries also varied in size: Harvard had 100,000 volumes by the time of the Civil War, but

37

many small colleges had no more than a few hundred books.[1] Despite their size, colleges were a popular expression of the optimistic spirit of nineteenth-century America. The impetus to found colleges was part of the general expansion and improvement of education in the ante-bellum period; city and state rivalries, and the drive by religious sects to educate clergy, supplied additional motives. According to one study, there were 250 colleges in the United States in 1860, of which only nine predated the War for Independence. Hundreds more had been founded and failed; survival was often a function of denominational sponsorship. The number of college students rose steadily between 1800 and 1860, when the collegiate population increased three times faster than the population of 15- to 25-year-olds. There were interruptions during the hard times that followed the War of 1812 and the Panic of 1837, but by the late 1840s the growth rate was steady.[2]

In many of America's well-established colleges, the curriculum imitated the traditional offerings of English universities, with emphasis on classical languages, rhetoric, mathematics, logic, and moral philosophy. The goal was to render a college graduate "fit to conduct himself with dignity in any calling."[3] Curricular reform was difficult to effect. An attempt by the Amherst faculty in 1827 to introduce courses in American history and government, modern languages, architecture, and engineering was unsuccessful. The following year, the Yale Report endorsed the traditional curriculum in ringing tones.[4] For the time being, then, many of the eastern colleges followed a four-year curriculum that included three years of Latin and Greek, and two years of rhetoric and mathematics. Natural philosophy (chemistry and physics) was offered in the third year; logic, metaphysics, ethics, and moral philosophy were offered in the fourth. The academic level of these colleges tended to be close to that of a modern high school, with an approach to university studies to-

1. Colin B. Burke, *American Collegiate Populations: A Test of the Traditional View* (New York and London: New York University Press, 1982), 47–48; David F. Allmendinger, Jr., *Paupers and Scholars: The Transformation of Student Life in Nineteenth-Century New England* (New York: St. Martin's Press, 1975), 125; George Gary Bush, *History of Higher Education in Massachusetts* [Contributions to American Educational History, Vol. 13], ed. Herbert B. Adams (Washington: U.S. Government Printing Office, 1891), 110.

2. Frederick Rudolph, *The American College and University: A History* (New York: Alfred A. Knopf, 1962), 44–49; Burke, *American*, 35; Colin B. Burke, "The Quiet Influence: The American Colleges and Their Students, 1800–1860" (Ph.D. diss., Washington University, 1973), 16, 24, 29, 155–60.

3. George P. Schmidt, *The Old Time College President* (New York: Columbia University Press, 1930), 21–22.

4. Rudolph, *American College*, 118–20, 122–24, 131.

ward the end of the program. The range in ages of college students also varied considerably. At mid-century, students entered Harvard at an average age of sixteen; yet an increasing number of impoverished youth who deferred college plans to earn tuition money or to meet family obligations added an older group to the campuses. Between 1830 and 1860, at the time of their graduation 25 percent of all New England college graduates were older than 25.[5]

Social diversity promoted change in the pattern of college life. Dining commons gradually died out at New England colleges: some students couldn't afford the fee, while others disliked the food and/or the mandatory association with the poor. By 1860, New England colleges no longer assumed responsibility for feeding and housing their students in a self-contained community. In response to student preferences, strict rules mandating early rising, common prayer, and regular study periods and recitation yielded to a more easygoing approach. Another development was the emergence of debating and literary societies, often linked with a senior-year course that combined natural and moral philosophy with Christian doctrine. At some colleges, the literary societies had better collections than the school library. After 1830, literary societies gave way to fraternities that promoted a peer culture based on high spirits, insubordination, material success, and a diminished regard for the academic life. In time, freedom of thought also led to demands for free religious expression. The mixture of tradition and change in the curriculum and in student life signaled a transition from classical and sectarian traditions toward a new sense of purpose that emerged after the Civil War.[6]

In the early years at Holy Cross, the sense of purpose and the means of achieving it were never in doubt. Besides the existing colleges at Georgetown and Frederick, the Maryland Province assumed sponsorship of four other schools between 1843 and 1852 — Holy Cross, Washington College (Gonzaga) in the District of Columbia (1848), St. Joseph in Philadelphia (1851), and Loyola in Baltimore (1852). This educational network possessed enough corporate strength to constitute what Emmett Curran has called "a highly centripetal

5. Ibid., 25–26; Schmidt, *Old Time*, 95–97, 102–4; Burke, *American*, 7, 38.

6. Allmendinger, *Paupers*, 1–5, 8–9, 30, 83–85, 89; Schmidt, *Old Time*, 79–81, 102–4; Horowitz, *Campus Life*, 12–13, 29–33, 37; Rudolph, *American*, 36–40, 137–45. Excellent summaries of American higher education before the Civil War include Burton J. Bledstein, *The Culture of Professionalism: The Middle Class and the Development of Higher Education in America* (New York: W. W. Norton & Co., 1978), 238–86; and Oscar and Mary F. Handlin, *The American College and American Culture: Socialization as a Function of Higher Education* (Berkeley: The Carnegie Commission for Higher Education, 1970), 19–42.

intellectual endeavor. . . . With Georgetown, as the oldest and most presti-gious, at the center, the Jesuit network linked these colleges as more than local enterprises, even as higher education evolved throughout America."[7] The set-up afforded experienced leadership to Holy Cross and the other schools. Thomas Mulledy, who was rector in Worcester from 1843 to 1845, headed Georgetown College before and after his work at Holy Cross. James Ryder (1845–48) and John Early (1848–51) also served as Georgetown rectors.

Despite the problems associated with his term as Maryland provincial, Thomas Mulledy had long enjoyed Bishop Fenwick's confidence. Mulledy was a powerful preacher and a man of profound faith who offered frequent prayers for the College, for the Jesuit community, and "for my boys."[8] His wry sense of humor softened a tendency to be impatient with human imperfection and headstrong in his relations with others. He showed that side in 1844 in a description of the arrival in Worcester of a Jesuit brother:

On Saturday . . . Br. Finegan arrived safely. He ought to have arrived early in the morning, but he allowed the cars to leave Norwich without him, & was consequently obliged to wait for the evening train, from this *small fact* & some other passing obser-vations, I clearly perceive, that said Br. Finegan *is not* the inventor of gun-powder.[9]

Mulledy had enough wisdom to recognize his need for personal reform. Dur-ing the controversy surrounding the slave transaction, he struggled with a temptation to drink and committed himself to a year of abstinence. To a friend, he confided: "I hope that this will enable me to correct my other de-fects—which, I believe, took their origin from this—."[10] In defense of his causes, Mulledy was articulate, even emotional. Near the beginning of the College's second year, he pointedly asked Maryland Provincial James Ryder for help and companionship:

I . . . only ask you to reflect on what a life I lead [sic] last yr & whether you wish me to be submitted to such an ordeal for another year—A new College requires some fos-tering care—& I, if nothing else, at least am an object of pity and commiseration . . .

I am ready to suffer—I have proved it—I am willing to labour—you cannot doubt it. But the strongest back may be broken by overloading it. The strongest mind may be

7. Curran, *Georgetown*, 1:129–30.

8. Fenwick appointed Mulledy vicar general of the Boston Diocese in 1838, during Mulledy's term as provincial. Document of appointment, January 17, 1838, MPA, 212 R 2; Hughes to Mulledy, Philadelphia, November 17, 1837, and Mulledy Mass Book, GUA, Mulledy Papers.

9. Mulledy to James Ryder, Worcester, October 15, 1844, MPA, 214 H 1.

10. Mulledy to John McElroy, Georgetown, February 20, 1839, MPA, 212 H 4.

shattered in the midst of numerous & *solitary* perplexities. Let me entreat you to send me a father who can be spiritual father, minister, & at the same time give some little lesson in philosophy and Theology—Do not think me importunate—look only at my situation & ask your heart—if you would be satisfied to be thrown into a similar *solitary* position.[11]

Almost everyone recognized that Mulledy was a good choice to be the College's first rector—even Father Roothaan, who readily endorsed his appointment.[12]

During the summer of 1843, Mulledy visited Worcester regularly to inspect the new building. On September 28, he moved to the city permanently, offering Mass the next morning "for our new beginning (put under the protection of St. Michael)." At first Mulledy, together with Brother John Gavin and Jesuit candidate John O'Sullivan, lived in the farmhouse near the foot of the hill, a building that later became the washhouse and residence of the laundresses. On October 25, George Fenwick arrived to help open the school as prefect of studies and discipline. On the same day arrived Edward Scott, "a youth from Ireland and first student of the College."[13] Years later, Scott remembered those first days at Holy Cross, particularly the meals: "rice mush and milk for supper—the toothsomeness of which dish can never escape from the memory of man or boy enjoying it in earlier and happier days."[14] On October 30, the little group moved into the former academy building to prepare for the opening, now set for November 1.

In comparison with the cornerstone ceremony, the opening was a small affair. In the morning, Father Mulledy celebrated Mass; afterwards, Bishop Fenwick and James Ryder, who had recently replaced Francis Dzierozynski as head of the Maryland Province, toured the new building, which was not yet ready for occupancy. They did use the new dining room, however, toasting "the health of the Founder in a good glass of wine." Six students were present for the opening of classes on the following day. Students, faculty, and workers slowly gathered in the months ahead. By January, Mulledy counted thirty-four individuals in the "family." They included eighteen students and two other priests: Joseph Balfe, who taught classics and served as spiritual prefect and prefect of studies (after George Fenwick's re-assignment in January), and

11. Mulledy to Ryder, Worcester, August 10, 1844, MPA, 214 K 3.

12. Roothaan to Dzierozynski, Rome, August 20, 1843, MPA, 214.

13. [Thomas F. Mulledy], "History of the College of the Holy Cross, Worcester, Massachusetts," handwritten MS, ACHC, 12.1; Mulledy Mass Book, GUA, Mulledy Papers.

14. Ross to J. Havens Richards, Newberry, SC, May 24, 1890, GUA, Holy Cross, 1879–1912.

James Power, Fenwick's successor as prefect of discipline and the minister of the Jesuit community. There were also three lay teachers (two of whom departed later in the year to enter the Society of Jesus), three Jesuit brothers, two Jesuit candidates who worked in the dormitory and in the garden, and five lay employees—the laundresses (Miss Jane Agnes Angus and Mrs. Salvo) and hired men to work in the refectory and the farm. By the end of the academic year, enrollment stood at 26.[15]

The College building, as Fenwick Hall was first known, was completed on January 13, 1844, at a cost of $19,000, which Bishop Fenwick paid completely. The cupola was crowned with a six-foot-high gilt cross atop a ball measuring thirty inches in diameter. Its imposing appearance and its atmosphere delighted the bishop and he visited frequently, at times almost weekly. Years later, Boston Archbishop John Williams could remember Fenwick, relaxing on the portico and predicting that the school would soon be full.[16] The bishop promoted Holy Cross actively. To the bishop of New Orleans he wrote: "Do you know that we have at Worcester . . . a flourishing College already under way & under the direction of the Peres Jesuits?" Fenwick recommended the school for its "first rate education," moderate terms, and healthy location.[17]

Beneath the public display of satisfaction, problems were arising. The first was connected with staffing the school. According to his understanding with Dzierozynski and Roothaan, Bishop Fenwick was to supply several clerical or lay faculty members to supplement the Jesuits. Tension arose when both sides found the arrangement difficult to honor. The bishop kept importuning the Maryland Province leaders for at least three good Jesuits to staff the school:

My ambition was to have it a Jesuit College . . . , & preparing to become so, there should be at least two Priests of the Society in it & a Prefect, who should be at least a scholastick. These I easily imagined would be sufficient to give a first impression & a tone to the establishment. These two Priests of the Society should be of one mind & of one heart—without this, all would go wrong.[18]

Yet, Fenwick seemed in no hurry to keep his part of the bargain. Shortly before classes opened, Mulledy complained that "the good Bishop talks more

15. Ibid.; Meagher and Grattan, *Spires*, 43–44.

16. Benedict to George Fenwick, Boston, October 7, 1843, MPA, 214 F; George Fenwick to Samuel Barber, Worcester, December 25, 1843, MPA, 214 S 7; Annual Letter for 1845, MPA, 335 Z 2. Williams's comments were delivered at the 50th anniversary banquet, November 9, 1893, Worcester *Telegram*, November 10, 1893.

17. Fenwick to Blanc, Boston, August 10, 1844, UNDA, New Orleans Papers, V-5-b.

18. Fenwick to Ryder, Boston, October 5, 1843, MPA, 214 S 1.

than he acts—You know that he promised three efficient teachers—well he is beating about for a pair of beardless boys—who are not capable of managing a country school." The likeliest candidate lacked the personality to teach effectively; others, the bishop was reluctant to send to Worcester for fear they would be attracted to the Jesuits instead of the diocesan priesthood. Since teachers were expected to work for room, board, and clothing, potential seminarians were the most likely candidates for teaching positions. "The fact is," Mulledy concluded, "I see that we shall have as little help from the Bishop as he can, by quibbing and quirking, give us."[19]

As Mulledy sensed, part of the bishop's problem in hiring faculty was related to the handling of vocations to the priesthood, the very issue that had prompted Fenwick to insist so strongly upon Catholic exclusivity. Joseph O'Callaghan, one of the lay teachers recruited by Fenwick to open the school, was accepted for the Jesuit novitiate at Frederick, Maryland, in January 1844 and instructed to depart as soon as a Jesuit replacement arrived. Meanwhile, for fear of raising Fenwick's opposition, Mulledy advised O'Callaghan to "say nothing to the Bishop," or to anyone else, until he had arrived at Frederick. Mulledy finally discussed the matter with the bishop shortly before O'Callaghan's departure, and won the bishop's consent for the Jesuits to act independently in accepting candidates.[20] Yet Fenwick remained out of sorts about the school. In June, he visited the campus for the first time in five months, and, Mulledy reported, "he was cross—taciturn &—evidently wished me to feel the weight of his displeasure. . . ." He made certain arrangements and "studiously *scorned* to ask my opinion. . . . He went away as gruffly as he came."[21] The letter does not specify the source of the bishop's irritation. It may have been lingering irritation with the Jesuits' recruitment of O'Callaghan and a second lay teacher who had also left for Frederick; or it may have been his displeasure with Mulledy's financial management. But a larger problem was already straining the relationship between Bishop Fenwick and the Maryland Province Jesuits: the long delay in acceding to the bishop's wish that they accept trusteeship of the College.

Negotiations had been underway since January 1843, when Fenwick first offered the school to the Society. Jan Roothaan's response was cautious and his

19. Mulledy to Ryder, Worcester, October 19, 1843, GUA, Dzierozynski Papers. On terms of employment for lay teachers, see James Ryder to Orestes Brownson, Worcester, March 11, 1847, UNDA, Brownson Papers, I-3-h.

20. Mulledy to Ryder, Worcester, January 29, 1844, MPA, 214 P 3, and March 31, 1844, MPA, 214 N 7; Meagher and Grattan, *Spires*, 43.

21. Mulledy to George Fenwick, Worcester, June 15, 1844, MPA, 214.

approval only tentative: he desired further advice from Mulledy and province authorities before deciding.[22] Apparently unaware of the general's reservations, Bishop Fenwick hoped to convey the College to the Jesuits at the time of the formal opening. He proposed as much to James Ryder in September, suggesting that he formally accept the College on behalf of the Society at that time. But Ryder agreed only to attend the opening, citing the general's instructions. Fenwick accepted the setback with equanimity: "I see in this I must await the pleasure of Fr. General."[23] Less than three weeks after the formal opening, Mulledy sent his analysis of the situation to Jan Roothaan. Although he admitted "the force of objections" against a boarding school, he detailed three reasons for accepting Holy Cross. First, he was convinced that the Jesuits ought to be established in the Boston Diocese and that the bishop would ultimately assign a college in Boston to them if they didn't thwart his plans for Worcester. Second, it was "rather probable" that an exclusively Catholic boarding school would lead more young men to the priesthood. Third, accepting the college in Worcester would root the Society in the diocese so strongly that it could not easily be dislodged after Fenwick's death. He recommended acceptance of the school as "a great advantage."[24] About the same time, Roothaan delegated the final decision about accepting the College to Ryder and his consultors, urging them to forbear accepting the school until circumstances would justify it. The general himself had misgivings: "I cannot pretend that a better and greater good would have resulted if so large a College and boarding school had been erected in some large city and for externs only." Nevertheless, he urged the province authorities to do their best for the fledgling school.[25]

By the winter of 1843–44, then, the Maryland Jesuit authorities had received discretionary authority to accept Holy Cross, but apparently they withheld that information from Bishop Fenwick. The reason was largely economic. Within three months of the opening, Fenwick was begging Mulledy in writing to be more frugal, calling the college expenses "a nightmare." At this point the ink grows darker and the letters bolder: "**I have already borrowed two thousand two hundred Dollars on the college account—and they have dis-**

22. Roothaan to Dzierozynski, Rome, June 17, 1843, ARSI, MD Reg. I, 209.

23. Fenwick to Ryder, Boston, September 19, 1843, MPA, 214 T 8; Fenwick to Ryder, Boston, October 5, 1843, MPA, 214 S 1; Ryder to Roothaan, Georgetown, September 27, 1843, ARSI, MD 7-VIII, 4; Ryder's notes, September 27, 1843, on the back of Benedict Fenwick's letter of September 19, 1843, cited above.

24. Mulledy to Roothaan, Worcester, November 17, 1843, ARSI, MD 7-VIII, 5, and GUA, Dzierozynski Papers; Mulledy to Ryder, MPA, 214 S.

25. Roothaan to Ryder, Rome, November 10, 1843, ARSI, MD Reg. I, 214.

appeared—have been absorbed and they are no longer to be found— all—all have already been spent—and still heavy Bills remain staring me in the face!"[26] The bishop, Mulledy reported, "*appears* to be disposed not to buy one article of furniture more than he has bought—provided you had accepted the College. This, mind, is merely my opinion." Mulledy amplified his "opinion" by pointing out that Fenwick was unwilling to buy more than a few beds at a time, not to mention additional curtains to hang between the beds for privacy. His point was that the Jesuits couldn't afford the furnishings without running into debt, and he wanted Ryder to confront the bishop about bearing the expense:

You might then, when you think it prudent, inform the Bishop that you are ready to accept the College as soon as it is finished & *furnished*—& that the furnishing [of] the building & not merely erecting four walls—is what is understood in the Society by "founding a College."[27]

The impasse dragged on after Peter Verhaegen succeeded Ryder as Maryland provincial in January 1845. There is no documentary evidence that Ryder or Verhaegen ever told Fenwick that the decision about accepting Holy Cross lay with the Maryland Province, though the matter may have come up in personal conversations. A boarding school in a small city still seemed far less desirable than a day school in a large city, even given the arguments about promoting religious vocations. Holy Cross was tying up scarce manpower and preventing the province from being able to accept a day school in Philadelphia.[28] The result was a stalemate of sorts. The Jesuits, divided in their enthusiasm for the project, delayed accepting the College outright, hoping to use the situation to induce Fenwick to supply more of the school's material needs. Fenwick, now in his declining years, took such delight in the school—he visited fourteen times in the year before his death in August, 1846—that he seemed unwilling to risk driving the Jesuits away by forcing the issue.[29] So he reluctantly stretched the limited resources of the diocese for Holy Cross while awaiting an opportunity to make the transfer.

Like the bishop, Thomas Mulledy was finding the College a financial challenge. He struggled to balance operating expenses with revenues from tuition

26. Fenwick to Mulledy, Boston, March 2, 1844, MPA, 214 N 5.

27. Mulledy to Ryder, Worcester, April 11, 1844, MPA, 214 N 9.

28. Ryder to McElroy, Georgetown, April 22, 1844, MPA, 214 N 11.

29. The Boston archdiocesan history noted Fenwick's affection for Holy Cross: "It was the pride and joy of his later years . . . and undoubtedly it was his greatest creation." Lord et al., *History*, 2:328. Fenwick's visits are noted in the Jesuit House Diary [hereafter HD], ACHC, 19.3.

charges of $150 and income on the farm. Even higher enrollments were a mixed blessing, since some hard-pressed parents had negotiated with college authorities for reduced tuition and others were delinquent in payment.[30] "We can hardly scrape along—let alone pay high wages for workmen," Mulledy told Ryder early in 1844. Later that year, Holy Cross was still operating close to the margin. When Mulledy learned that Ryder was going to order classical texts from Europe, he could afford only a modest request for Worcester—"thirty dollars worth of books calculated for the three humanities with a few, say ten dollars' worth, for Rhetoric and poetry."[31] Under these circumstances, it was a real boon for the College to receive its first major gift in March of 1844, a contribution of $1000 from Boston philanthropist Andrew Carney, who expressed the hope that the College would be an instrument for promoting *"pure and undefiled religion."*[32]

As the debate about accepting the College continued, increasing enrollment was crowding the building. The original structure could accommodate about 90 students, plus the Jesuits. In the spring of 1846, when the enrollment reached 94, the bishop reached an agreement with Peter Verhaegen to erect an addition large enough to accommodate 100 more students. This wing, he promised, "will not in the least interfere with the establishment I intend for the Society in Boston."[33] On that condition, Verhaegen committed $5000 of Maryland Province funds to the new building. At about the same time, Fenwick decided to deed the College property to the Jesuits outright. In June, he asked Thomas Mulledy for procedural information and promised to follow through "in three jerks of a spider's leg."[34] Ultimately, it was decided that the George-

30. Thomas White of Ellsworth, Maine, had negotiated a tuition of $125 for his son. White to George Fenwick, March 19, 1851, MPA, 219 A. In 1850, a Jesuit faculty member wrote that "many do not pay, and others not the full price." James Clark to F. P. McFarland, Worcester, May 5, 1850, UNDA, Hartford, I-1-a.

31. Mulledy to Ryder, Worcester, April 11, 1844, MPA, 214 N 9, and October 15, 1844, MPA, 214 H 1.

32. Mulledy, "History." Carney arrived in Boston in 1816 as a penniless immigrant from Ireland. He worked for several years as a tailor, then became a pioneer in manufacturing men's ready-made clothing—a line which won him a lucrative contract from the United States Army. Lord et al., *History*, 2:343.

33. Benedict Fenwick to Thomas Mulledy, Boston, June 19, 1846, MPA, 215 R. Verhaegen had visited Worcester and Boston in May, 1846. HD. See also Edmond Fay, "History of the College of the Holy Cross, Worcester, Mass.," 15, ACHC, 10.0-1. Fay taught music at Holy Cross, 1891–93.

34. Benedict Fenwick to Thomas Mulledy, Boston, June 19, 1846, MPA, 215 R; Verhaegen to Roothaan, Georgetown, August 14, 1847, ARSI, MD 8-I, 27. Unknown to the Jesuits, he inserted a proviso obligating the school to lodge and educate free one student designated by the Bishop of Boston for every fifty students enrolled.

town College trustees should hold the Worcester property until a charter could be obtained from Massachusetts. Accordingly, on August 6, 1846, Benedict Fenwick signed the deed conveying the property of Holy Cross to the President and Directors of Georgetown. By then, the bishop was gravely ill; the conveyance of the deed was his last public act.

On August 10, Father James Moore, the community minister, journeyed to Boston to present the respects of students and faculty and to receive Fenwick's dying blessing for them. The bishop died the following day; on August 13 he was laid to rest on the College campus. A month later, at St. John's Church in Frederick, Jesuit Charles Stonestreet, destined one day to play a crucial role in the College's history, delivered a formal eulogy. Noting that the bishop had died on the anniversary of the destruction of the Ursuline academy, Stonestreet praised his courage in altering the educational profile of Massachusetts: "Harvard was too near the blackened walls of Mount Benedict, and the demon of prejudice had infused his blue spirit into the other Academies." Holy Cross itself would be Fenwick's monument, "a lasting trophy of his generosity and zeal."[35]

Bishop Fenwick died four weeks after visiting the College to pace out the area for the new wing, designed to add 80 feet to the length of the building. The addition was ready for occupancy in March 1847. Students were willingly pressed into service for the move, as a faculty member recorded:

After much talking and planning, . . . it was concluded that there should be no Greek class, consequently school went out at 3½. The boys then commenced to carry their desks to the new study-room, where they were arranged in order, the small boys being in front. As soon as things were fixed there, the boys marched down to the chapel, where the Litanies were Sung.[36]

There were sanguine plans for speedily completing Fenwick Hall, which now had a lopsided appearance, by raising an identical wing to the west of the original structure. There were even hopes for a separate college chapel as a memorial to Bishop Fenwick.[37] Then the debt became a serious issue.

35. For years afterwards, students recited the *De Profundis* in his memory on August 11. HD, August 6–13, 1846, August 11, 1847, August 11, 1848; a copy of the deed recorded at the Worcester Registry of Deeds on August 8, 1846, may be found in GUA, Holy Cross, 1843–47. Stonestreet delivered the address on September 11, 1846. Copy in ACHC, 7.0-1.

36. Details on construction of the east wing are in the Samuel Lilly Diary [hereafter Lilly Diary], GUA, Catholic Historical MSS, 5:6, and in HD.

37. Samuel Lilly to Joseph Lilly, Worcester, October 9, 1846, GUA, Holy Cross, 1848–1878.

Although the annual operating budgets for the early years are difficult to recover, the books make clear that the college debt stood at a manageable $2000 in October of 1846. A year later, the figure was $8000. The figures alarmed Peter Verhaegen, who traveled to Worcester in the summer of 1847 and examined the books. To Roothaan, the provincial reported that he couldn't understand how the school's indebtedness had risen so sharply in the course of a year, except through mismanagement on Ryder's part. He recommended the rector's removal; but Ryder remained at Holy Cross for another year and reduced indebtedness to $6000.[38] It was hard going, despite regular pleas for tuition payment.[39] The debt prevented further expansion for the time being, though by the fall of 1848 space was again tight, at least for the Jesuits. "If yr Reverance [sic] would only give us enough to build the other wing to the College," John Early wrote plaintively to the provincial, "we would most cheerfully receive more [Jesuits]; but at present we have no room for a single individual."[40]

In fact, the debt was a function of more than the cost of the east wing. By 1848, the school had reached a leveling-off point in students and revenues. Exact figures for the early years are impossible to determine, because students came and left throughout the course of the year; but the Matricula book offers clues about enrollments by making it possible to count the number of students admitted each year and to determine their average length of stay (Chart 1.1). The number of new students

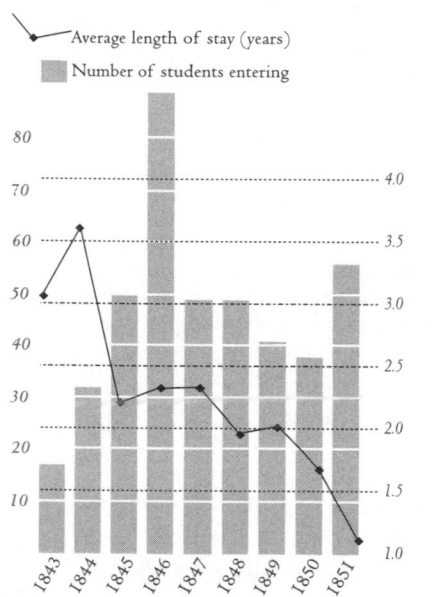

Chart 1.1 New Students and Average Length of Stay, 1843–1851

38. Verhaegen to Roothaan, Georgetown, August 14, 1847, ARSI, MD 8-I, 27; HD, October 23, 1846, October 14, 1847, March 10, 1848.

39. Ryder to Orestes Brownson, Worcester, May 16, 1848, UNDA, Brownson Papers, I-3-i. Brownson, a prominent Yankee publicist and Catholic convert, was considerably behind in covering his sons' tuition. In November 1848, he received a statement of $555 for his sons John and William; the following spring, the total had risen to $832. The total owed was down to $280 by the summer of 1850. Statements/letters from Peter Blenkinsop to Orestes Brownson, November 17, 1848; May 13, 1849; July 12, 1850; January 25, 1851, UNDA, Brownson Papers, I-3-i.

40. Early to Ignatius Brocard, Worcester, November 23, 1848, MPA, 216 D 11.

climbed steadily until 1846, then fell back to about fifty per year. The average stay of each student after 1844 was about two years; the falling-off in 1850 and 1851 is an aberration reflecting the closing of the college after the fire in 1852.

Obviously, the number of new students affected income. Relatively short stays and the inability of some of them to pay full tuition also made revenues uncertain. Tuition fluctuated considerably as a percentage of revenue during the early years, but seemed to stabilize at about 80 percent, in 1850.[41] The considerable shortfall in some years had to be addressed principally through fund raising and loans, which contributed to the slow rise in indebtedness beyond the initial borrowing for the east wing. The uncertainty of tuition and other revenues and the fluctuating size of the student population affected the size of the operating budget and made it difficult for the rectors and treasurers to manage the budget efficiently. Given the unevenness of contributions and the uncertainty of tuition revenue, it seems clear that the John Ryder, and especially John Early, were covering operating expenses through borrowing. Indebtedness rose to about $8500 between 1848 and 1851. Holy Cross was not paying its way; the sanguine predictions of continuous growth after the opening of the east wing were premature.

Although it was not fully paid for, the expanded Fenwick Hall accommodated a variety of activities and functions. An unidentified student offered a charming description of the building, floor by floor, in June of 1852: "The College is a very beautiful building. It is built of brick, all except the foundation, which is formed of large stones. There is before the door a beautiful piazza which is two stories high and is a neat piece of workmanship." The ground floor held a kitchen, dining rooms for students and the faculty, bathing and wash rooms, and a play room for use in inclement weather. The first story included a "very neat little chapel," classrooms, and a large library room. The second floor held a study hall and rooms for the Jesuits; and the third floor and garret were used as student dormitories. From the cupola on the roof, observers could see "nearly all over Massachusetts."[42]

After the completion of the east wing, Benedict Fenwick's successor, John Fitzpatrick, continued the policy of personal support for the College, even though financial responsibility now rested completely with the Jesuits. The bishop visited frequently, extended his personal support to individual Jesuits,

41. Fiscal year 1844 ran from April 1, 1843 to July 31, 1844. Fiscal year 1845 ran from August 1, 1844, to June 30, 1845. Subsequent fiscal years opened on July 1 and closed on June 30 of the designated year. Summaries of the annual operating budgets, compiled by James P. Heidbreder '94, are in ACHC, 16.0.

42. The letter is addressed "Dear Friend," Worcester, June 1852, MPA, 220 A.

and permitted the diocesan clergy to make retreats at Holy Cross.[43] But there were limits to Fitzpatrick's ability to favor the Jesuit presence in New England. Unlike Fenwick, he had never been a Jesuit; he lacked his predecessor's experience with Jesuit education and his familiarity with the men of the Maryland Province. Some Jesuits doubted his willingness to make a priority of Fenwick's pledge to set up a Jesuit day school in Boston, given his pressing pastoral concerns and fact that the Jesuits themselves fell under criticism for some of their customs.[44]

It was hardly surprising that the Jesuits at Holy Cross had critics. The members of the community were largely Southern men and European immigrants whose manners sometimes gave unintended offense. One critic was Paulist founder Isaac Hecker,[45] who visited the school in June 1844, shortly before his baptism as a Catholic. He found much to praise: the physical set-up of the College, the cleanliness, the students' daily schedule of study and play, and the food. But the Jesuits unsettled him. He found their knowledge of philosophy narrow, their intellectual method weak, and their lack of religious fervor upsetting. He was so dismayed that he had second thoughts about his impending baptism, as he confided to Orestes Brownson, the prominent Yankee publicist and Catholic convert:

These men *seem to me* are wanting that vital consciousness of divine eternal life and high spiritual aspirations which have animated so many of the children of the true

43. Joseph O'Callaghan to P. Duddy, Worcester, April 17, 1850, MPA, 218 T 7. Orestes Brownson dedicated his autobiographical book of 1857, *The Convert*, to Fitzpatrick and included this encomium: "I owe him more than it is possible for me to owe any other man. . . . I have never met a man of clearer head, a firmer intellectual grasp, a sounder judgment, or a warmer heart. . . . Though I have found men who made a far greater display of theological erudition, I have never met an abler or sounder theologian." *The Works of Orestes Brownson*, Collected and Arranged by Henry F. Brownson (20 vols.; Detroit: Thorndike Nourse, 1884), V: 164–65.

44. [?] to Peter Verhaegen, Boston, April 18, 1848, trans. J. McElroy, MPA, 216 S 10. The impression was misleading in the sense that Fitzpatrick was committed to the college in Boston, but lacked the means at first. John McElroy, a versatile Jesuit who was working in Boston, had been promoting a Jesuit school there since 1843. On October 31, 1847, St. Mary's parish in the North End was entrusted to the Jesuits, with McElroy as pastor. David R. Dunigan, *A History of Boston College* (Milwaukee: Bruce Publishing Co., 1947), 16–22; Lapomarda, *Jesuit Heritage*, 80.

45. Isaac Thomas Hecker (1819–88), a one-time associate of Thoreau, Emerson, and Bronson Alcott, became a Catholic in 1844, and in 1858 founded the Congregation of the Missionary Priests of St. Paul the Apostle (the Paulists), a group devoted to converting non-Catholic Americans to Roman Catholicism. See also David J. O'Brien's biography of Hecker, *Isaac Hecker: An American Catholic* (New York: Paulist Press, 1992).

church. I had to ask them repeatedly if that was the ground on which they based a true Christian life[,] the lowest and the least that the Church demands of us. Understand me I believe these very men have private virtues which if I knew would command my deepest respect and reverence for their individual characters[,] but I wish they did not take so much snuff and that even in the midst of that holy . . . Sacrafice [sic] the Mass. Oh my dear friend there must be something deeper[,] more eternal and invisible . . . that can attract a Soul to the Church as she now is in this country.[46]

Hecker's reaction did not deter Brownson from sending four sons to Holy Cross, or from giving public support to the College. But the impressions that Hecker had passed along were not completely false: Mulledy had written the provincial two months earlier to defend his policies of governance among the Jesuits. In the end, Mulledy achieved only mixed success in addressing the criticism of outside observers. At Holy Cross, the Jesuits tended to find him critical and impossible to please.[47]

John Ryder, who succeeded Mulledy in 1845, also encountered problems in leading the Jesuit community. Born in Dublin in 1800, Ryder had immigrated to the United States and was sent to Rome for Jesuit studies. Small of stature, with dark eyes and black hair, Ryder was a gifted speaker, described by one commentator as a man of "superb eloquence as also . . . wit and raillery [that] combined Attic expression with a dash of Irish flavor which made his discourses delicious." It was customary to read sermons in those days, but Ryder preached without notes, a technique that thrilled his audiences. Ryder was rector of Georgetown from 1840 to 1845 and, concurrently, Maryland provincial from late 1843 to early 1845.[48] In October of that year, he was assigned to Holy Cross. During his administration, the quality of religious discipline within the Holy Cross Jesuit community attracted notice in Boston and beyond. In 1848, Bishop Fitzpatrick confided that "he was very uneasy about the college of Holy Cross—that some of our fathers there had to be taken home quite intoxicated in a carriage from Worcester—that the Religious in the college,

46. Hecker to Brownson [New York, June 24, 1844], in *The Brownson-Hecker Correspondence*, edited and introduced by Joseph F. Gower and Richard M. Leliaert (Notre Dame and London: University of Notre Dame Press, 1979), 104–6.

47. Mulledy to Ryder, Worcester, April 11, 1844, MPA, 214 N 9; Peter Verhaegen to Jan Roothaan, Georgetown, August 14, 1847, ARSI, MD 8-I, 27; Thomas R. Ryan, *Orestes A. Brownson: A Definitive Biography* (Huntington, Indiana: Our Sunday Visitor Press, Inc., 1976), 400. In 1848, Ryder reported the community's relief that John Early would replace him as rector, not Thomas Mulledy—"something which will be appreciated by not a few." Ryder to Brocard, Worcester, August 11, 1848, MPA, 216 K 2.

48. Edward P. McAdams, "Historical Notes," *WL* 79:239–41; J. Fairfax McLaughlin, "Fenwick," in GUA, George Fenwick Papers; Meagher and Grattan, *Spires*, 45–46.

each one seems to do as he pleases—that the Scandal given, will injure the reputation of the house." From Rome, Jan Roothaan expressed similar concerns.[49] In this instance, a clash of cultures was clouding the issue of personal conduct. George Fenwick did enjoy a social drink, but he was also the product of Maryland's more tolerant culture. Evidence suggests that the episodes involved little more than congenial visits with the local pastor, Father Matthew Gibson. Yet, given the prominence of the temperance movement at mid-century and the moral weakness then associated with drinking, the authorities felt constrained to voice concern about the potential for injury to the reputation of the Catholic clergy and the College.

Ryder's successor at Holy Cross, John Early, was also Irish-born. He immigrated to the United States in 1833 at the age of nineteen with the goal of becoming a priest, entered the Society of Jesus in 1834, and studied at Georgetown. After his ordination in 1845, he taught philosophy at Georgetown and did pastoral work in Philadelphia. After leaving Holy Cross, he spent most of his life in college administration. He also lectured on geology, geography, and history. An affable man who delighted in hearty friendships, he was remembered for his competence, his "commanding presence," and his familiarity with the lives of great individuals.[50] Despite his feelings of being unprepared for the Worcester assignment, he liked the college and appears to have had fewer problems with discipline in the Jesuit community.[51]

The eight years encompassed by the terms of Mulledy, Ryder, and Early set the tone for the academic and student life of Holy Cross. Administrators and faculty organized the courses; students went about their tasks; and a pattern of campus life began to emerge. The faculty grew slowly, from five teachers in the first year to ten or more after 1846. The Jesuit scholastics—unordained men who were assigned to teach for a period of time after completing the Philosophy segment of the *Ratio*—brought diversity to the school because of their backgrounds and individual talents. Pennsylvanian Samuel Lilly taught as a scholastic from 1845 to 1849, covering classics, arithmetic, and French in addition to his supervisory duties. Joseph O'Callaghan, a native of Lowell, arrived in 1847 to teach mathematics and French, to head the Sodality and the li-

49. The quoted comments are in a confidential letter, evidently conveyed to Peter Verhaegen by John McElroy. Boston, April 18, 1848, MPA, 216 S 10. See also Roothaan to John Ryder, Rome, March 11, 1847, ARSI, MD Reg. I, 250.

50. Georgetown *College Journal* (Supplement), June, 1873, MPA, 354 V 12; *WL*, 19:112–13; GUA, Early Papers.

51. Early to Brocard, Worcester, September 1, 1848 MPA, 216, H 1; September 24, 1848 MPA, 216 G 6; Roothaan to Early, Rome, May 6, 1850, ARSI, MD Reg. I, 263.

brary, and to serve as prefect of discipline. Scholastics did much of the teaching and extracurricular supervision, while a dedicated local musician, Samuel Reeves Leland, gave individual lessons and directed the band.[52]

Among the priests, the giant of the early years was George Fenwick. First assigned briefly to Worcester to help Thomas Mulledy open the school, Fenwick was re-assigned to Holy Cross in 1845 as prefect of schools [studies], a position he held until 1852. He also taught algebra, classics, and philosophy. Fenwick's assignment to Holy Cross was, in part, an effort by the Jesuit authorities to please the bishop, for the two brothers were close; but his extended service in Worcester as an early-day academic dean and teacher provided a mature element to the Jesuits' presence. His personal gifts and pastoral sense gave him a strong influence on the spirit of the College. The youngest of the three Fenwick brothers to enter the Jesuit order, George had studied in Rome with Thomas Mulledy and James Ryder. He was a tall, gaunt man, plain of face, but with an affable, hearty manner that attracted people, especially students, to seek out his company and counsel. The students loved him, confided in him, confessed to him, appreciated the time he spent with them playing checkers for a piece of candy—all this despite the fact that he took seriously his responsibility to set and defend high academic standards for the new school. His room at Holy Cross, called the "Horse Guards" by those who frequented it, was a sort of club during recreation hours. "Dad" Fenwick, as he was called, was the first Holy Cross faculty member to be adopted by the students via a nickname.[53]

There was a quality to his presence that made him a classic instance of the bonding between students and teacher that the *Ratio* was attempting to foster. This was particularly true in his relationships with James, Patrick, Hugh, and Sherwood Healy. They were sons of Michael Morris Healy, an Irish immigrant and Georgia planter, and Eliza Clark, a mulatto slave. The couple had ten children in a committed union that lacked legal status and subjected the children to slavery so long as they remained in the South.[54] A chance meeting

52. Lilly Diary; *Catologus Provinciae Marylandiae,* 1843–1852; Meagher and Grattan, *Spires,* 63.

53. McLaughlin, "Fenwick," GUA, George Fenwick file; James A. Healy Diary [hereafter, Healy Diary], January 29, 1849, ACHC 8.0; Albert S. Foley, *Dream of an Outcaste: Patrick F. Healy* (Tuscaloosa: Portals Press, 1989), 14, 60. See also Edward Boone to George Fenwick, Washington, D.C., August 17, 1852, MPA, 220 N 6A.

54. Albert S. Foley has written biographies of James A. and Patrick Healy: *Bishop Healy: Beloved Outcaste* (New York: Farrar, Straus and Young, 1954), and *Dream of an Outcaste: Patrick F. Healy* (above). Martha Healy was also sent north, to Boston, where she lived with Bishop Fitzpatrick's sister's family, the Bolands. *Beloved Outcaste,* 18–19. See also James M. O'Toole, "Passing: Race, Religion, and the Healy Family, 1820–1920," University of Notre Dame,

with Bishop Fitzpatrick prompted Healy to send his four oldest sons to Holy Cross in 1844. Their diligence and their personal circumstances attracted Fenwick's attention. He became particularly close to James, who became a priest and bishop in New England, and Patrick, who joined the Jesuits. When Patrick was assigned to Worcester as a scholastic, Fenwick encouraged him: "Whatever may be your difficulties, however restive or lazy your boys may be[,] you are sure—yes infallibly sure that with prudence & patience you will finally gain your end." He advised him to take time for his own intellectual development: "Study hard . . . to keep crickets out of your head." He liked to joke about individual qualities in a kindly manner: "Tell [Fr. Mulledy] I miss him wonderfully. I cannot find any one to quarrel with now."[55] After many years, Fenwick's heartiness and good advice still ring true. No wonder the students appreciated him so well. By 1851, Fenwick's health was beginning to fail; he was relieved of his teaching duties to concentrate on his work as spiritual prefect and prefect of studies. "We should pray hard for his recovery—" Father Early wrote, "he is a most valuable member of the Society—one whose lose [sic] will be greatly felt."[56]

More than two dozen other scholastics and priests assisted in the classroom in the first decade. The most distinguished was Felix Sopranis, a former professor of philosophy and rector of the Jesuits' Roman College, who arrived in the fall of 1848 to teach the first Philosophy class.[57] Another European-educated faculty member was Father Philip Sacchi, who entered the Society in Russia in 1807 and came to the United States in 1821. At Holy Cross he was spiritual prefect from 1845 to 1850 and taught modern languages. Peter Blenkinsop, an Irish-born Georgetown alumnus, was assigned to Worcester in 1847. He taught bookkeeping and served three presidents as minister and college treasurer before assuming the presidency in 1854. Father James Clark, a Pennsylvanian and West Point graduate, taught chemistry and mathematics during the 1849–50 academic year and returned twelve years later as president. In addition to their classroom and administrative duties, all of the priests except the spiritual prefect, who remained at home to offer Mass for the students,

Cushwa Center for the Study of American Catholicism, Working Paper Series, 26 (Spring 1996).

55. George Fenwick to Patrick Healy, Frederick, September 28, 1853, and two undated letters [1853/54?], GUA, Patrick F. Healy Papers.

56. Fitzpatrick to Early, Boston, August 24, 1849, GUA, Early Papers; Early to Ignatius Brocard, Worcester, August 10, 1851, MPA, 219 R 4.

57. HD, November 22, 29, December 1, 1848; John Early to [Mulledy?], Worcester, November 27, 1848, MPA, 216 D 9.

regularly took parish calls and sick calls.[58] It was a strenuous life that stretched their time and their energy. Nevertheless, given the general condition of college education in the country at that time, the Holy Cross faculty could hold its own.

The first circular issued by Thomas Mulledy offered three courses of study: ecclesiastical, professional, and commercial. The commercial course was the most basic and involved writing, arithmetic, bookkeeping, English, French, algebra, geometry, the use of the globes, public speaking, and natural and revealed religion. The professional course included these courses, plus the traditional offerings of the *Ratio* in Latin, Greek, philosophy, ethics, ecclesiastical history, astronomy, chemistry, and natural science. This program contained the heart of the Jesuit approach—humanism as the *Ratio* prescribed it. An early prospectus recommended the professional course for "those who are intended for any of the learned professions." The ecclesiastical course proposed to add to the professional course the study of "sacred learning, biblical and theological." In fact, the ecclesiastical course indicated Bishop Fenwick's desire to develop a regional seminary at Holy Cross; but only two priests were ordained after pursuing the program in what amounted to private studies with the Jesuit faculty, and the program was dropped in 1858.[59] An extra charge was assessed for studying German, Spanish, Italian, music, drawing, painting, dancing, fencing, and medical aid.

The commercial course was introduced, not without misgivings, as a realistic concession to the desire of parents that the education be "practical." As early as 1846, Mathias Kramer, who had two sons at the College, requested Father Ryder to excuse them from classical languages and French and to direct their attention to English, arithmetic, bookkeeping, and writing, "which studies will be the most useful for them."[60] Arguments about the impracticality of studying classical languages varied according to the family. The father of Henry Collier was disturbed that his son was showing more aptitude for Latin than for English, because the latter "would be all important to his success in business." The paternal remedy was to direct Henry to give up Latin and concentrate on writing, arithmetic, bookkeeping, and mathematics.[61]

58. *Catologus Provinciae Marylandiae*, 1843–52; HD, 1843–52; *Holy Cross Purple*, III (1896), 360–69. A list of missions attended by Holy Cross Jesuits may be found in GUA, Holy Cross, 1843–1847.
59. Advertising flier, 1843, ACHC, 9.0-2; Meagher and Grattan, *Spires*, 58–60.
60. Kramer to President of Holy Cross, Boston, December 11, 1846, MPA, 215; Edward Power notes that commercial courses were common enough at Catholic colleges, where they were viewed by administrators as an expedient—not a desideratum. *History*, 56–57.
61. Martin Collier to George Fenwick, Boston, March 22, 1849, MPA, 217 B.

The curriculum combined an English and Latin high school with a rudimentary college—an approach that was something of an anomaly in New England, but consistent with the *Ratio Studiorum.* The lowest level, Second and First Rudiments, was designed for students who lacked the basics of Latin grammar and also covered geography, English grammar, and Bible history. The middle segment of the program was Humanities, broken up into classes or "schools" called Third, Second, and First Humanities. These years were given to the study of intermediate Latin grammar and literature, including Cicero, Ovid, Caesar, Sallust, Vergil and others. Humanities students also studied Greek and filled out the program with geography, history, mathematics, and composition. The top part of the humanities program also had three years, designated Poetry, Rhetoric, and Philosophy. As the terminology suggested, students in Poetry concentrated on composition and more advanced texts in Latin and Greek prose and poetry, while Rhetoric students devoted more time to classical orations. Students in Philosophy took their philosophy course work in Latin and also studied "Natural Philosophy," which at Holy Cross was basically a general physics course with some chemistry.[62]

The intellectual goal of the program, as Philip Gleason has pointed out, was to integrate faith and reason—a common characteristic of Catholic colleges at that time. As philosophers, students considered God, the human soul, human acts, the nature of reality, and the criteria of true knowledge under the headings of natural theology, psychology, ethics, ontology, and logic. These studies, in turn, were supposed to afford a foundation for intelligent faith:

Because God was the author of philosophical truth as well as revelation, correct philosophizing was congruent in its result with the teaching of the Catholic church, the divinely-instituted interpreter of revelation. But since philosophy reached its results by an intellectual process, rather than by the mere fideistic acceptance of dogmatical pronouncements, mastering the Christian philosophy was an appropriate academic mode of religious instruction for students who had advanced beyond the level of grammatical and rhetorical studies.[63]

This approach presented no difficulties for James Healy, who was held up as a model student because of his intelligence and application to study and because of his success in achieving the desired integration. Healy developed a broad interest in current events and the world of ideas and read a variety of historical and literary texts, and religious and secular news-

62. Holy Cross advertising circulars, 1848–51, ACHC, 9.0-2; David R. Dunigan, "Student Days at Holy Cross College in 1848" (M.A. thesis, St. Louis University, 1938), 43, 45–48.

63. Philip Gleason, "The Curriculum of the Old-Time Catholic College: A Student's View," in *Records of the American Catholic Historical Society of Philadelphia* 88 (1977), 112.

papers. At Holy Cross, Healy developed diction, values, a view of reality, and a sense of style.[64]

The academic program was gradually put in place from the bottom up as the student population grew. By the spring of 1846, there were fourteen courses, including Rudiments, all three years of Humanities, English, French, bookkeeping, and five mathematics classes. In the fall of 1846, the first Poetry class was convened, a group that subsequently became the first Holy Cross classes in Rhetoric and Philosophy. By the fall of 1848, the full program was finally in place. By 1850, in addition to the courses in the upper and lower divisions of the classics or Humanities sequence, there were at least fourteen other classes—six in mathematics classes, three in French, and two classes each in "writing" and "English" (second English included history, geography, and grammar, while first English also included composition). Bookkeeping, despite its appeal to practical-minded parents, was apparently omitted from the curriculum at times.[65]

School opened in mid-September with a Mass to invoke the aid of the Holy Spirit and a meeting in which the prefect of studies read the rules of conduct and assigned students to classes. Studies continued, with scheduled and unplanned holidays, until February, when mid-year examinations were held. The results were announced publicly on Ash Wednesday. The second term concluded with another round of examinations and an exhibition toward the end of July. Every month, students assembled for a reading of class standings, to receive academic awards, and to hear samples of outstanding work. It was a demanding program, and the close supervision connected with the living arrangements gave students little escape from the routine. Those who could not appreciate the discipline while they were at school sometimes missed it after they withdrew. Andrew McKenna, who must have struggled with spelling and grammar during the year he spent at the College, wrote later: "I used to think when I was their it was a hard place but now I do not think it was hard enough The teachers are most to easy with the boys to make them learn I remember when I left of saying that I never wanted to go to colledge again but I wish I was back again [sic]."[66] Academic fireworks occasionally erupted. On one occasion, eighteen-year-old John Brownson challenged

64. Ibid., 113–14, 118.

65. Reports of the Prefect of Studies, February 25, 1846 and February 13, 1850, GUA, George Fenwick Papers; Report of the Prefect of Studies, February 17, 1847, Lilly Diary. Boundaries between the subject matter of separate but related courses were flexible, with overlapping discussions—a by-product of the fact that one teacher would teach the same students in two related courses. Gleason, "Curriculum," 107.

66. Andrew McKenna to [George Fenwick?], Newark, February 27, 1851, MPA, 219 A.

Father Sopranis about his insistence that philosophy had to rest on reason alone. When the priest charged him with heresy and blasphemy, Brownson stormed out of the classroom. John corresponded about the encounter with his father, who backed his son's ideas and afterwards presented his thoughts in his journal, *Brownson's Quarterly Review.*[67]

The system of examining the students was formidable. The process took at least two weeks and included both a written and an oral component in most subjects. Faculty members took responsibility for examining each other's classes in individual oral examinations—a task that occupied the greatest amount of time. Students also wrote compositions, a procedure that moved along more quickly because the testing was simultaneous. No concessions were made to the weather: spring exams in 1851 ran from June 30 to July 18 and started on a day when the temperature stood at ninety. The examination periods were particularly strenuous for teachers, as Joseph O'Callaghan noted during the winter exams in 1852. After five days of written themes, oral exams started on February 9. O'Callaghan examined Geography, second English, first Mathematics, first English, second Mathematics, and Rhetoric, concluding his work on February 21.[68]

For the younger students, especially, the exams were an ordeal. In the winter exams of 1847, two lads in First English were "at times completely tongueless but not tearless." A classmate of theirs excelled in his history exam but struggled with grammar and catechism: "He seemed puzzled sometimes, then silence succeeded; at last he . . . sighed again; & tears began to flow." Roderick Masson, a student in Second Humanities, was honest enough to admit at the outset of the exam that he did not know his assigned memory work and was demoted to Third Humanities for "notorious negligence."[69] Parents were, of course, notified of their sons' performance. The report cards bristled with candid praise and criticism, as the parents of Thomas Jenkins, a Holy Cross student in 1845, learned. His grades ranged from "very good" and "favorable" to "good for nothing" and "horrible." In his classics courses, he ranked near the bottom but was praised for good conduct. In French he stood dead last and his conduct was labeled "rascally."[70]

But the most painful ordeal, at least for the students who were struggling

67. John Brownson to Orestes Brownson, Worcester, April 19, 1849, Brownson Papers, UNDA, I-h-3; Healy Diary, January 24, 1849; Gleason, "Curriculum," 105–6, 112–13.

68. The House Diary and the diaries of Samuel Lilly and Joseph O'Callaghan, ACHC, 9.0-2 [hereafter O'Callaghan Diary], are excellent sources on the administration of exams. See also HD.

69. Ash Wednesday Report of Prefect of Studies, February 17, 1847, Lilly Diary.

70. Report card of Thomas C. Jenkins, ACHC, 9.0-2.

with academics, must have been the reading of grades by the prefect of studies on Ash Wednesday. Copies of these reports survive in the papers of George Fenwick. Fenwick interspersed detailed comments about individuals and classes with general observations on the value and cost of education—all designed to motivate the students through comparison, praise, and shame. Father Fenwick used preliminary comments to set the proper mood. The 1846 address was a classic example:

It is related in the life of one of the most finished scholars England has ever produced, Dr. Sam. Johnson, that it was his opinion that, were a person of ordinary talent to spend four hours every day in study, he would in a short time become a learned man. This sentiment we believe to be proved by the experience of thousands. Now not reckoning the time you spend in school almost every day, you have more than four hours regularly dedicated to study and consequently have every opportunity to realize the object for which you were placed by your parents or guardians within the walls of this institution.

That you have every motive to urge you to realize this object you yourselves are aware. That you have every facility the result of our late examination sufficiently proves. The best authors are placed in your hands and whether you are engaged in the perusal of the classics, the study of your own language, or the exact sciences, I could not but witness every exertion made on the part of your teachers to facilitate and further your progress.

The object of our meeting today is to render an impartial account of your progress during the last five months and in the first place we can say that we sincerely congratulate you on account of the progress you have made. . . . There are some few whose advancement has not corresponded with the expectations of their teachers owing . . . especially we think to a want of study. These we must hold up for inspection of their companions. The contrast will also serve to convince them that whilst a diligent and docile student is one of the most engaging of objects a lazy, careless one is a disgusting, loathsome, tedious sight. Disgusting, loathsome, and tedious to his parents, friends, teachers and even to himself. But we are glad to say that the number of them is very restricted.[71]

There followed a class-by-class analysis, with the best and worst students singled out. Those who were deficient in their studies were chided for reflecting poorly upon their parents or home towns—Peter O'Donaghue "absolutely disgraced" the District of Columbia in 1846. The following year, an entire class was indicted for lack of application: "leeches that suck their [parents'] life's blood." In 1850, a nineteen-year-old student was threatened with expulsion for want of application and poor conduct: "He was entirely defi-

---

71. Report of the Prefect of Studies, February 26, 1846, GUA, George Fenwick papers. Punctuation supplied.

cient in everything. Yet he bore himself so insolently as to change our pity to disgust . . . for one of his *beard* to cloak his ignorance with the poutishness of a child, is not to be endured. . . . Let him consider whether there is not a more fitting object of his ambition, than the character of the most impudently ignorant and insulting of the class." For his performance, the student was demoted from First to Second English. Strong medicine, even for an older student; but he took it and remained at Holy Cross for three more terms. Demotions, and the humiliation associated with them, were regular occurrences. In 1847, eleven students were promoted on Ash Wednesday, while two went down; three years later, twenty-five were promoted, while six faced demotions.[72]

Students felt the competition keenly. In March 1848, Orestes Brownson Jr. sent his father a three-page letter devoted to his and his brothers' rankings and promotions. In tone and content, it resembles the letters sent over a century earlier by the Carroll boys from St. Omers to their parents in Maryland.[73] Some parents responded in writing to the academic reports. One blamed his son's poor showing on George Fenwick for advancing the lad too quickly; another asked him to tell his twelve-year-old son that his parents were very proud of a good report: "Give him my love and tell him how much pleased his Parents are, that he has been so good a boy."[74]

Besides the academic offerings, College authorities stressed the school's Catholic atmosphere as an inducement to parents to bear the cost of tuition. One Jesuit pointed out, "the absence of protestants is beneficial to discipline and to the practice of religious duties."[75] Evidently, parents subscribed to the approach. In a letter to George Fenwick, Bostonian G. W. Lloyd emphasized the importance of religious training. "I hope his pride and stubbornness may yield to the pious influences which now surround him," he wrote of his son

72. The records show one instance of resistance to the practice of public humiliation. In 1851 a member of the Philosophy class, writing under the name "Junius," took George Fenwick to task for the "severe blow" he had delivered in accusing the class of negligence. The writer called the attack unfair because the philosophy students had not been examined as others were: "They receive counsels gratefully when they come from a frank and open heart, but never when they are given in the form of a sarcastic hint." "Junius" to George Fenwick, Worcester, March 6, 1851, MPA, 219 A.

73. Orestes Brownson, Jr. to Orestes Brownson, Worcester, March 1, 1848, UNDA, Brownson Papers, I-3-i.

74. P. L. Syndon to George Fenwick, Boston, November 30, 1846, MPA, 215; W. Hickey to George Fenwick, Washington, March 17, 1848, MPA, 216 T 4a.

75. James Clark to F. P. McFarland, Georgetown, April 14, 1846, UNDA, Hartford, I-1-a.

in 1849. "My most earnest wish is that he may embibe [sic] the principles of St. Ignatius; and imitate the humility and purity of his companions & followers."[76] Another father spoke of sacrifice: "I will do my utmost to earn the means to educate my children in virtue and Religion. It is the only inheritance I expect to leave them."[77]

In addition to attending daily Mass and Sunday Vespers, students received regular catechetical instruction from the spiritual prefect. Joseph Balfe was the first to hold that office, and Thomas Mulledy reported that "all are pleased with his instructions . . . really excellent."[78] Balfe's successor, Philip Sacchi, was not always as successful—at least, not in the opinion of James Healy, who characterized one of Sacchi's talks in 1849 as "one of the most shabby exhortations . . . that I ever heard from him," and another as one "which few of the students understood." Yet Healy appreciated good preaching and religious instruction. He particularly praised George Fenwick's sermon against the tendency to give "our youth to the devil, our poor old age to God."[79] Doctrinal instruction was taken seriously, as George Fenwick pointed out:

We are known as Catholics, that is as persons fully persuaded that their religion is not a matter of opinion[.] We may be asked to give an account of it; we may be asked why we are so fully persuaded of its truth[.] That man who cannot answer these questions, must experience a deep sense of shame; & the one who pays little or no attention to the elements of Christian doctrine will never be able to do justice to his religion."[80]

Fenwick was only doing his duty in reminding the students of their obligations, but the faculty and administration seem to have been pleased with the devotional side of student life. With pardonable exaggeration, Father Ryder reported in 1846 that Holy Cross was "the land of the angels."[81]

Powerful influences in the religious formation of the students were the annual retreat and the liturgical observances. The retreat was typically given in November and lasted three and a half days. Students were required to maintain silence throughout the period. The retreat followed themes from

76. G. W. Lloyd to George Fenwick, Boston, January 19, 1849, MPA, 217 B.

77. Thomas White to George Fenwick, Ellsworth, Maine, March 19, 1851, MPA, 219 A.

78. Mulledy to George Fenwick, Worcester, April 1, 1844, MPA, 214 N 8.

79. Healy Diary, June 1 and 3, July 15, 1849, ACHC, 8.0.

80. Prefect of Studies Report, February 25, 1846, GUA, George Fenwick Papers; Dunigan, "Student Days," 71.

81. Annual Letter, 1846, MPA, 335 W 1. Evidently, a pious custom of the students was to recite the rosary at Bishop Fenwick's grave on the 11th of the month, weather permitting. On June 11, 1849, James Healy explained it in his diary: "This is the day of the month on which he died 11th of Aug. which was the very day on which the convent was burned."

Ignatius' Spiritual Exercises, adapted according to the insights and skills of the retreat director and the capacities of the students. In 1844, the retreat concluded with the baptism of four Healy brothers and two Brownsons.[82] Given the scarcity of Catholic clergy in the United States in the ante-bellum period, a relatively high proportion of students received Catholic sacraments for the first time at Holy Cross. In 1845, 33 of the 78 students received their first communion. The records give repeated accounts of baptisms, first communions, and confirmation ceremonies.[83] A further expression of religious activity was the Sodality of Mary, established in 1844 as the first student organization on campus. As at other Jesuit schools, the Sodality offered a program of regular devotional exercises and affiliation with like-minded individuals who met regularly for mutual encouragement. By 1848, 75 of the 108 students belonged to the Sodality and were regular in their duties. The Sodality library at that time held 200 volumes.[84]

Besides the goal, common to all Jesuit schools, of forming individuals who would conduct their lives according to the principle of the *magis*, Holy Cross was founded to encourage vocations to the Catholic priesthood. After the opening, the sponsors waited hopefully to see whether Bishop Fenwick's expectations would be borne out. In April of the first academic year, Thomas Mulledy watched with satisfaction as the first Holy Cross men—teacher Joseph O'Callaghan and student Hugh McCaffrey—set out for the Jesuit novitiate in Frederick: "the firstfruits of the College of the Holy Cross—God bless them—."[85] In fact, Holy Cross did produce a good number of vocations to the Catholic priesthood. Between 1843 and 1900, 523 individuals, about 13 percent of the College's matriculants, opted for a clerical career.

With the students deliberately isolated within the campus, the faculty and administrators shaped a distinctive lifestyle to foster academic and formational goals. The means had to be adjusted to the age group. Applicants between the ages of 8 and 14 were accepted; the average age at entry varied during the school's early years—from a low of 12 in 1844 to a high of 16 in 1848. Yet the spread in ages ranged from 7 to 31 (Chart 1.2). The tender age of some of the students necessitated careful supervision from the faculty, as anxious parents reminded them. In 1845, the mother of a ten-year-old asked George Fenwick to buy socks for her son and to attend to his dress: "You will oblige

82. Mulledy, "History," ACHC, 12.1.

83. HD, March 28–April 4, 1847; Annual Letter, 1845, MPA, 335 Z 2; Anthony Ciampi to Ignatius Brocard, Worcester, October 4, 1851, MPA, 219 P 12.

84. John Early to [?] Worcester, November 27, 1848, MPA, 216 D 9.

85. Mulledy, "History"; Early to [?], Worcester, December 11, 1848, MPA, 216 C 8.

me very much . . . if you will see that Ralph sleeps in the flannel drawers, which I have prepared for him—likewise that he does not go without his cotton drawers in the daytime. Boys are generally very careless about these things and I know by experience that he requires a great deal of looking after."[86] From New York, a father labored with grammar in asking Fenwick to look after a homesick son: "Sir You will please let me no if he got any change he being

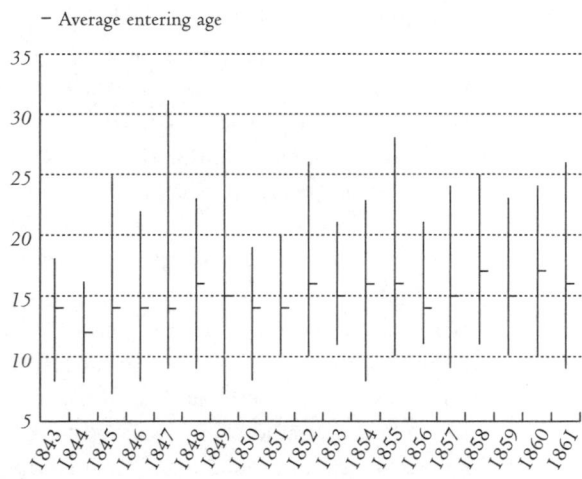

Chart 1.2   Age of Students at Registration, 1843–1861

– Average entering age

veary delicite his Mother is uneasy and if he gets Sick you will please write and let me no it is not my wish for him to see this letter."[87]

Campus life was hard, judged by the standards of later generations. The daily order sustained the notion that formal studies are a serious endeavor. On school days, students normally rose at 5:00, and descended to the basement washroom and then to the study room to complete their toilet. Mass was next, followed by two hours of study before breakfast. Classes met in the morning and in the afternoon after the mid-day meal. Supper was followed by more study, rosary at 8:00, optional study and then bed at 9 o'clock.[88] Winter made the routine more spartan. The windows were drafty; classrooms and dormitories could be cold. During a cold snap in January of 1852, the pipe to the washroom froze, forcing the boys to perform their morning ablutions in the snow.[89] Sanitation and hygiene were adequate. A privy behind Fenwick Hall ("the Necessary") accommodated the group; tub baths were available in the basement. Given the close quarters and the tendency to bathe infrequently, cleanliness sometimes acquired an urgent aspect. "O'Neil took a bath today

86. M. Symms to George Fenwick, Georgetown, October 2, 1845, MPA, 215.

87. Anthony Conron to George Fenwick, New York, April 12, 1848 MPA, 816. Punct. and spelling sic.

88. William D. Farren to parents, Worcester, October 6, 1851, ACHC, 17.3A-3.

89. Healy Diary, January 3, 1849; Lilly Diary, December 5, 1848; O'Callaghan Diary, January 24, 1852.

to our great joy," James Healy noted in his diary. Dental needs were addressed by Dr. Orville H. Blood; students became familiar with the shouts and groans of their classmates during his visits. There was also a campus infirmary, which sometimes became the target of official inspections by George Fenwick to roust out the slackers. In public, students were required to wear a college uniform—black coat or jacket, black vest, grey pants in winter, white pants in summer.[90]

Given the age group, disciplinary infractions and punishments were a regular occurrence. Most infractions were minor—smoking in restricted areas, drinking, "immoral" books, insubordination, oversleeping or falling asleep in class, fighting, and attempting to run away. Behavioral problems multiplied when inclement weather kept the boys indoors. "A great many punishments," Joseph O'Callaghan noted on one such day. February 12, 1849, was singled out by James Healy as a cold and comfortless day when the stove pipe fell down in the play room and "the boys stood looking over the bars of the windows like prisoners from the Old Bailey, shivering like a dog over a briar bush on a cold day." Kneeling during class or during a meal, rations of bread and water, loss of town privileges, and memorizing lines of Latin were the commonest forms of punishment; students could also be assigned to the "punishment room" during a recreation period. Sometimes the prefects resorted to corporal punishment, a practice that engendered some criticism. William Brownson complained to his father about being cuffed repeatedly on the side of the head, and James Healy once called the flogging of the youngest boy "a very unnecessary & unjust thing." But apparently, most students accepted the discipline in due course.[91]

Dining room order was maintained, in part, through the custom of reading at table. The more advanced students were assigned to be readers for a week at a time, and were served a late meal. In 1849, the selections included biographies of Martin Luther and Ignatius of Loyola and a history of Maryland. At times, the routine was varied to allow students to read original compositions, humorous pieces, and poetry in English and Latin. It is doubtful, however, that any of these materials were engaging enough to distract attention from the quality of the food. Sixty years out, George Lloyd, Class of

90. William L. Lucey, "College Life in Worcester, 1848–49," in *The New England Galaxy* 10 (Winter 1969), 58; John Ryder's College Circular, ACHC, 9.0-2. On February 1, 1849, Samuel Lilly described in his diary the new College flag, whose design included "two boys dressed in the summer uniform of the college."

91. The James Healy and Joseph O'Callaghan diaries are excellent sources on student discipline and punishment. See also William Brownson to Orestes Brownson, Worcester, April 1, 1847, Brownson Papers, UNDA, I-3-h.

1850, still remembered the "former continuous feasts of bread and coffee, with bean soup on Fridays, and old Brother Murphy's grease, gravy and hash thrown in."[92] James Healy's diary, kept in 1848–49, bristles with anguished expressions of gustatory disappointment: "bread soaked in turpentine," "dishwater for soup," and "meat tough enough to break a fellow's teeth." "It does very well to talk of a celebration," he wrote after a poor meal on Washington's Birthday, "but the anticipation is heaven, to the reality." Not all meals were bad. Healy appreciated pudding, pie on Sunday, and oyster soup on Saint Patrick's day—"a very strange thing for the College of the Holy Cross." Even the Jesuits realized that the fare could be meager. In 1847, Fr. James Moore, who was the business manager, endured a dinner that was "miserable to describe and to eat." To their credit, responsible parties did their best with limited means. The boys were fed ham and eggs (though not in sufficient quantity, according to James Healy) for Easter breakfast in 1849, and Washington Pie was established early as the dessert of choice at College feasts.[93] Campus visits by a local baker afforded students an opportunity to supplement campus fare.

Although students attended classes on Saturdays, afternoons on Tuesday and Thursday were free. The half-holidays, reflecting Ignatius's ideas about recreation, were savored by the students and their teachers. There were, in addition, frequent full holidays; Samuel Lilly recorded fifteen free days between January 7 and July 4, 1845. Some, like Independence Day and George Washington's Birthday, were civic holidays; others were granted by the bishop or the Jesuit provincial to mark their visits (to great acclaim, when announced to the boys in the dining hall). Holy days (including certain Jesuit feasts) were free; and holidays could also be granted by the rector when he judged that a break was in order, like the half-holiday Father Early granted in March of 1849 when the sun came out after a week of dismal weather.

Traditional holidays were readily integrated into the pattern of campus life. Thanksgiving Day, a Massachusetts holiday unfamiliar to many of the faculty and students, was readily adopted. And despite Samuel Lilly's disappointment that Christmas was "not much respected [in] Yankee land," Holy Cross faculty and administrators introduced some Catholic and Southern customs in keeping the feast. In 1846 the students were roused from sleep with a spirited rendition of *Adeste Fideles* by the College band. After Mass and

92. George Lloyd to Dr. J. W. Cahill, Boston, June 6, 1910, ACHC, 12.15.

93. HD, March 9, 1847; Lilly Diary; Healy Diary. Washington pie is a cream pie with fruit filling, somewhat similar to Boston cream pie.

breakfast, the students rushed to the rooms of priests and scholastics for small gifts to complement the boxes that had arrived from outside—mostly from the South. "The pictures and medals were shelled out by the wholesale," Samuel Lilly wrote in 1846; "I was soon freed from the few that I happened to have." In the evening and throughout Christmas week there was entertainment: minstrel shows and concerts, sometimes magic lantern shows or performances by the Dramatic Club. New Year's Day featured another rush for gifts, and the Jesuit table included wine for toasting the future.[94]

Independence Day brought additional celebratory opportunities. The indefatigable Mr. Leland and the College band provided wake-up music at 5 A.M. from the portico with a spirited rendition of *Hail Columbia*. Samuel Lilly remembered: "In a moment, like an electric spark, the fire of patriotism shot thro' every breast and glowed on every countenance:—the youth that slumbered no longer turned upon his pillow . . . bounded from his bed, and as his feet touched the floor they instinctively danced to the national air." Later in the morning, students and faculty gathered in the grove at the foot of the hill, where students read the Declaration of Independence and delivered patriotic addresses. In 1848, John Brownson was the orator of the day, subjecting his audience to an address that required 32 handwritten pages to argue that George Washington's ideals were superior to those of Henry VIII, Napoleon, and Jean-Jacques Rousseau. Afterwards, there was a picnic lunch with lemonade and sweets, followed by games and a good dinner. After dark, homemade fireworks concluded the celebration. In 1848, there were rockets, candles, and turpentine balls. In the finale, about twenty blazing balls were kicked down the bank: "For a few moments the whole playground was in a blaze with balls flying in every direction," Lilly reported. Other special events included a holiday for the Cattle Show (the annual autumn fair in Worcester), and St. Patrick's Day, when local Irish-American societies visited the campus with their bands.[95]

Many of the daily recreational activities were seasonal, and Samuel Lilly, in particular, enjoyed them. Ice-skating was highly favored in the winter. "I went frequently to enjoy this pleasing exercise, " Lilly wrote in 1845, "cut high-dutch and performed many other wonderful feats." So popular was ice-skating that the boys risked it even on the Sabbath, in violation of local custom. Lilly was also introduced to "another amusement very popular in this Yankey land, called coasting or riding down hills on sleds." The sleds, wrote Lilly, "will run so obstinately right on that [the rider] has to be very cautious if he run not

94. HD, November 27, 1845; Lilly Diary.
95. Lilly Diary, July 4 and October 6, 1846; March 17, 1847.

against the fence[,] a stone pile, tree or some other obstacle to the disadvantage of his shins." Snowball fights and day-long sleigh rides offered further outlets for youthful energy.[96]

Warmer weather held other possibilities, often involving the waters of the Blackstone or Lake Quinsigamond. Fishing was a favorite pastime in the spring and fall, generally involving cooking and eating the catch, though on one disappointing day in 1845 food had to be sent from the College to supplement the fish, and on another occasion in 1849, "the boys while cooking fish let the fire catch in the leaves and soon the whole island was overrun." Both Samuel Lilly and Joseph O'Callaghan sponsored student hikes. In 1849, Lilly took four students in the carriage to Mount Wachusett and enjoyed twitting Yankee farmers along the way with an empty molasses bottle. "They would ask if he was not dry[,] holding out the bottle; the answers and indications of desire to get a swig were various and laughable. . . . Various remarks were made by us on the *temperance* spirit that is so much held up in Massachusetts; here we saw everything to prove that they were very willing to take a drink whenever they could get it."[97] Swimming in the Blackstone and sailing on the lake were other popular warm weather events.

There were, of course, regular opportunities for recreation on campus. A playground was available for cricket, "duck on a rock" and other games. In 1849, two "volidores" were set up and a ball alley was installed for ten pins. Town ball, bow and arrow competitions, quoits, and "jumping" provided additional diversion. Indoors, the playroom in the cellar provided an alternate space for recreation. Debating societies grew up early—the Philomathian Society for less advanced students, and the Philodemic Society, which became the BJF Society shortly after Bishop Fenwick's death. By early 1851, the Dramatic Club was sponsoring a series of minstrel shows and plays.[98]

The ceremonial conclusion of the academic year was the exhibition, which took the place of a commencement in the years before students had qualified for the baccalaureate degree. Bishop Fenwick, Orestes Brownson, former Governor Levi Lincoln, and prominent Worcester citizens attended the first exhibition on July 29, 1844, and heard eleven readings and addresses, interspersed with piano selections. Bishop Fenwick dispensed the awards—silver crosses to the top-ranked student in each class, book premiums to those who stood second. By 1846 the college band had been organized and provided music for the

96. The best sources of information on recreational activities are the Lilly, O'Callaghan, and Healy Diaries, and Lucey, "College Life."

97. Lilly Diary, May 28 and July 30, 1849.

98. Healy Diary; Meagher and Grattan, *Spires*, 72.

James A. Healy, Class of 1849, the first Holy Cross valedictorian and alumnus, later Bishop of Portland, Maine (1875–1900), always an active supporter of his alma mater.

occasion. The 1848 Exhibition served as a leave-taking for Father Ryder and included a farewell address that Samuel Lilly described as "very touching":

He said that the three years which he spent here were almost the happiest ones within his recollection, that he had been seconded by a faculty united to him in the warmest ties of fraternal affection; he spoke of the prosperity of the college, he alluded to the discourses just declared by the boys as proof of the talent & energy of the students; he alluded to the sainted founder of the college as the one, under God, to whom the college owed its prosperity.[99]

The first baccalaureate exercises were held on July 26, 1849. The ceremonies introduced a College flag that featured two boys in the summer uniform of the College and an illuminated cross encircled by clouds under the words *In Hoc Signo Vinces*. On the eve of graduation, students walked around the campus singing "Home Sweet Home." "I was quite melancholy," wrote James Healy, "and walked about all alone until bed time thinking of tomorrow." In the morning, a crowd of over a thousand joined Bishop Fitzpatrick, Orestes Brownson, Irish temperance crusader Father Theobald Mathew and other distinguished citizens and clergy in the study hall, elaborately festooned with paper hangings, wreaths, and pictures. The ceremony ran for four hours; it included addresses by the degree recipients and representatives of the hundred students who were present in formal collegiate dress.[100] In his valedictory address, James Healy offered a spirited defense of his alma mater's distinctive mission. He and his classmates had selected Holy Cross, he said, "because, here we are taught to practice the faith of ages" rather than serving the spirit of the age—a seductive spirit he equated with "anarchy and licentiousness." Healy invoked the spirit of Bishop Fenwick and thanked the faculty for "the most uniform and unvarying kindness." Then he became personal, his tears matching those of his classmates:

Today I cease to be a student; I can no longer call myself the companion of those, who are endeared to me by the years of fellowship we have passed together. . . . Fellow-students (and it is the last time I shall ever address you by that endearing name) fellow-students, farewell! . . . *It will be a band of brotherhood through life, this companionship at college.* May it be so for us at least. Then once more farewell—a sound which makes us linger—yet farewell, forever!

Father Early conferred the degrees on top-ranked James Healy, then on John H. Brownson, John J. McCabe, and Hugh Healy in order of merit. After

---

99. Meagher and Grattan, *Spires*, 63–65; Lilly Diary, July 23–25, 1848. A full account of these first exhibitions may be found in Meagher and Grattan, *Spires*, 74–77.

100. Lilly Diary, February 1, 1849. The collegians dressed in black frock coats, and the others in black round jackets and vests. Healy Diary.

Bishop Fitzpatrick awarded the customary silver crosses, guests adjourned to an abundant banquet. The pattern, successfully established, was essentially repeated in the following years, drawing large throngs, as well as favorable notice in the Worcester and Boston press.[101]

Successful as they were, the ceremonies were a tangible reminder of the College's exceptional status in the educational network of Massachusetts, for, having failed to receive a charter from the state, College authorities were forced to award Georgetown degrees to the graduates. Bishop Fitzpatrick and Father Early discussed a charter application in the fall of 1848 in anticipation of awarding baccalaureate degrees in the spring. By December, Early had determined to press the process forward despite uncertain prospects: "I fear the exclusive character of the College will be a great obstacle in the minds of the Sapient Legislators."[102] In January of 1849, John Early and George Fenwick sought legal advice and were told that the institution's exclusively Catholic character would be a sticking point. Early raised this matter with Bishop Fitzpatrick, but the prelate insisted that Benedict Fenwick's policy should be formalized. Orestes Brownson drafted the petition, which was presented to the Massachusetts General Court on February 27. The preamble pointed out that Holy Cross had been in operation for five years as a "literary institution designed to teach a course of classical and scientific studies, taught in the higher class of colleges in the United States." The petition had five sections, covering the amount of property and real estate the trustees could hold, the right of the legislature to visit and inspect the school, and the ordinary powers and privileges of college corporations under the statutes of Massachusetts. Section Four incorporated the bishop's desire that Holy Cross be "a private corporation, for the benefit of one denomination only, and, therefore, having no claims whatever upon the Commonwealth." In March, Fitzpatrick and Early appeared before the Joint Standing Committee on Education in a meeting that was cordial enough to raise their hopes about the College's prospects, though they may have mistaken patronage for friendship.[103]

As expected, the petition encountered opposition within the legislature; on March 30, the full House accepted the recommendation of the Education Committee's majority of "leave to withdraw," a legislative nicety that directed

101. Graduation Scrapbook, ACHC, 9.0-2; Lilly Diary; Healy Diary; HD.

102. Early to Brocard, Worcester, October 27, 1848, MPA, 216 F 19; Early to [someone at Frederick], Worcester, December 11, 1848, MPA, 216 C 8.

103. John Early to Orestes Brownson, Worcester, February 2, 1849, UNDA, Brownson Papers, I-3-i; Early to [?], Worcester, January 15, 1849, MPA, 217 W 6; HD, January–April, 1845; Meagher and Grattan, *Spires*, 50–51. A copy of the 1849 charter petition is in ACHC, 11.0-1.

the petitioners to withdraw their request in order to avoid the humiliation of outright rejection. The recommendation was offered without explanation, but Bishop Fitzpatrick and others were convinced that the cause lay in Section Four. On April 4, the House debated the motion of Representative Charles Upham of Salem, the Chair of the Committee on Education and a supporter of the petition, to reconsider the vote of March 30. The motion carried, sending the petition back to committee. The following day, George Fenwick and Peter Blenkinsop testified before the committee for 2½ hours on "various points concerning the incorporation of the college and . . . dogmatic points of theology." On April 13, by a vote of 4 to 3, the committee again recommended "leave to withdraw." The majority spokesman was Erastus Hopkins of Northampton, a former Congregationalist minister.[104]

The issues were laid out in the two committee reports.[105] The majority argued that Section Four violated the nonsectarian principle that had been incorporated into the charter of Amherst College in 1824 and had acquired the force of precedent. In effect, the majority alleged, the Holy Cross petitioners sought a public charter for a college whose exclusivity made it essentially private. They wanted patronage rather than toleration. Although Section Four specifically excluded public funding for the College, the majority expressed skepticism that the prohibition would be maintained after the precedent of chartering sectarian schools had been established. The point about separation of church and state was exacerbated by the anti-Catholicism of the period— an issue the majority raised directly by describing the religious practices of the school in a fashion calculated to reinforce misgivings about Catholics. Students, the majority reported, were required to "kneel one half hour" at Mass and prayer; and the old shibboleths about freedom of conscience and sacramental confession were brought in:

All students, uniting themselves in full with the institution, must conform fully and strictly to the religious teachings and ceremonies of the Roman Catholic sect. . . . They are also required to attend the confessional, and receive absolution from the priests, according to the customs of the sect. This confession, we were told, extends to all thoughts and feelings, as well as acts.

The minority took the position that the free exercise of religion required that distinctive educational institutions, as amenable to Catholics as the current colleges were to Protestants, be permitted. The nonsectarian Amherst charter did not constitute a precedent against sectarian schools,

104. Meagher and Grattan, *Spires*, 51–52.
105. Copies of the reports, House Document No. 130, dated April 13, 1849, are in ACHC, 9.1-2.

they argued, because its non-sectarianism incorporated "the great distinguishing principle of Protestantism" and was agreeable to the Amherst petitioners as representatives of the dominant Congregationalism of western New England. Although the question of chartering a private, exclusively sectarian school had not previously been raised in Massachusetts, the state had chartered Andover Theological Seminary in 1825 to educate ministers "in such manner, as the trustees . . . shall direct." Meanwhile, one in seven residents of the Commonwealth were now Catholics, members of a church which "during the long night of Europe, kept alive the light of learning." The Catholics' own principles, the minority concluded, required them to seek a charter which, though innovative, was only seeking a legitimate exercise of equality.

The reports were debated in the House on April 25 and 26. Erastus Hopkins spoke on both days, mixing legal arguments with anti-Catholic cant, and adopting a "we" versus "they" approach to portray Holy Cross as an unwelcome institutional intruder. The case, he argued, devolved upon two questions: "Do they ask for more than others have? Do they ask for any thing inconsistent with the usages and principles of the Commonwealth?" His answer to both questions was yes; but even if the answers had been favorable to Holy Cross, he asserted, there was a further question of "whether a fourth College is needed in the state." Citing Orestes Brownson as his source, Hopkins asserted that there were no other exclusively Catholic colleges in the United States; nor, for all he knew, had any other sect founded an exclusive college in the United States: the very concept was un-American. In Europe, there were religious tests for certain colleges, but in the United States, a college applicant "need but be a MAN." In Worcester, he warned, a different issue was at stake: "They ask us to do for them *what we have done for no other sect;* what *no other sect have ever sought,* and what is at utter variance with our views of a college as a place of POPULAR EDUCATION."

Hopkins appealed to anti-Catholic fears, particularly on the second day of debate, when the charter's chances were enhanced after Section Four was stricken from the petition by the College's friends in an effort to save it.[106] The first line of this approach was to impugn the Jesuits:

We ought . . . to consider whether it is expedient to sanction a system of education which commits the entire training of youth, from the tender age of 8 years and even less, to *Celibates,*—men who, by their strongest religious views, have separated them-

106. Charles Upham moved the striking of Section Four to meet an objection from Hopkins that it could be construed as conferring a claim to public funding if Holy Cross ever dropped insistence on exclusivity. Meagher and Grattan, *Spires,* 54.

selves from all the refining and beneficial influences of social life. . . . Are we prepared to commit the youth of this commonwealth to the training of such a class?

Hopkins also objected to the educational philosophy of the *Ratio* as being in fundamental conflict with intellectual freedom:

Their purpose is not, like that of our colleges and academies, to teach and diffuse knowledge; it is not in accordance with the American idea, that Learning is to be broadcast throughout the community; but their purpose is to teach Religion *first*, and Knowledge *afterward*—to diffuse light, not to all, but only to the *faithful*. Their purpose is not like that of our churches, whose end is to promote religious culture; but it is a purpose remarkably blending Religion and Learning, and bringing the one into subjugation to the other.

Finally, Hopkins argued that the hierarchical organization of the Jesuits and of the Catholic Church was at war with the American spirit. To charter a school run under Catholic and Jesuit auspices would risk sanctioning a dangerous and un-American corporation that would be "really under the control, and absolute direction, of a foreign power, (substantially papal)" that was in league with tyranny. "They" were not entitled to the charter, he insisted, because "we cannot, in their behalf, disturb our settled policy, or accord to them any novel and peculiar privileges."[107]

Friends of the College attempted to deflect the attack. Charles Upham stated openly that anti-Catholicism was the principal objection to the charter and read an appeal from Bishop Fitzpatrick. Others chastised Hopkins for the tenor of his remarks, argued that the real question was the equality of Catholics with Protestants, and pointed out that the state's right to inspect the institution was willingly granted and that the petition reserved to the Legislature the right of alteration, amendment, and repeal.[108] Unfortunately for Holy Cross, these arguments did not prevail. The motion of incorporation lost by a vote of 84 to 117, with 52 absences. "*Tantum puritanorum sine viribus ist*," Philip Sacchi wrote with ungrammatical ire in the House Diary that day, lamenting the school's powerlessness against the lack of character of "Puritans."

Analysis shows that legislators from the urbanized, more heavily Catholic sections of the Commonwealth supported the measure, but could not overcome opposition from the agricultural areas. Much of the support came from Democratic legislators, though several Whigs, including Charles Upham, sup-

107. Hopkins published his speeches in pamphlet form. *Speeches of Mr. Hopkins of Northampton on the Bill to Incorporate the College of the Holy Cross in the City of Worcester, Delivered in the House of Representatives, April 24 & 25, 1849: With an Introductory Letter to the Members of the House.* (Northampton, 1849). ACHC, 9.1-2.

108. Boston *Daily Courier*, April 25, 26, 30, 1849.

ported the petition on principle. During and after the debate, newspapers in Boston and Worcester sprang to the College's defense. On May 2, a long editorial in the Worcester *National Aegis* expressed regret that Catholics had been "ungraciously singled out as a mark for intolerance" and asserted that "the intelligence of the Representatives" was on their side.[109] The most blistering analysis of the vote came from Orestes Brownson, in a 25–page article, "The College of the Holy Cross," published in the July, 1849 issue of *Brownson's Quarterly Review*. Brownson stressed the inherent right for religious denominations to exercise appropriate claims in Massachusetts. Since a common objection to Catholic schools was that they were used to proselytize non-Catholic youth, Holy Cross would be still more objectionable to many if non-Catholics were admitted. And, he argued, the right had to be conceded to every denomination to offer advanced education to youth unless infidelity were to be established as public policy.

The hard feelings generated during the charter effort left a residue of disagreement about the motives of the opponents. Despite the temptation to blame the rejection on anti-Catholic bigotry,[110] more was involved. The key to understanding the events of March and April, 1849 lies in appreciating the context of the institutional life of Massachusetts colleges at that time. As historian Akira Tachikawa has pointed out, in the 1840s enrollment in the state's three chartered colleges was not keeping pace with the general increase in population, a circumstance that raised questions about the amount of public funding the colleges could expect. In 1848, the year before the Holy Cross petition, the three colleges had asked the legislature for money for scientific apparatus. Erastus Hopkins had supported their petition by arguing that, because these colleges were *public* institutions, supporting them would benefit all the people. His opponents had contended that the colleges were class-oriented and exclusive and, hence, funding them benefited only a few. Eventually, the proposal was defeated, but Hopkins' argument, that colleges were public entities founded to serve all the people, was still fresh when Holy Cross submitted its petition to become a chartered "private" school.[111] Controversy

---

109. Worcester *Palladium*, May 2, 1849; Boston *Pilot*, April 28 and May 5, 1849; Meagher and Grattan, *Spires*, 54. See also research notes by G. F. O'Dwyer, ACHC, 7.0-1.

110. David R. Dunigan argued that the charter "failed through the religious prejudice of the Massachusetts legislature." *Boston College*, 6. Lord, Sexton, and Harrington offered a similar, but more nuanced, view that "opposition was to a large extent based on prejudice." *History*, 2:581.

111. Akira Tachikawa, "'Public' vs. 'Private' Colleges in 19th Century Massachusetts: The Ordeal of the College of the Holy Cross in 1849," in International Christian University *Educational Studies* 28 (1986), 3–10. Between 1834 and 1844, Amherst's in-state freshmen enrollment

relating to the chartered colleges erupted again in 1850, when a committee of the legislature charged Harvard with failing "to answer the just expectations of the people of the State" and recommended a number of stringent anti-elitist solutions.[112] The legislature was not in a particularly friendly mood toward any of the Commonwealth's colleges when it rejected the Holy Cross petition.

Thus, the Holy Cross petition failed for a combination of reasons. First, competition among Harvard, Williams, and Amherst for students, and their uncertain claim to public money, raised the practical question of the need for another college at that time. Second, the Holy Cross petition jeopardized the campaign in the legislature to identify and promote the state's colleges as public assets and public responsibilities, against the objections of those who alleged that the colleges were unworthy of public aid because, in practice, they benefited mainly a privileged elite. Finally, the traditional "anti-papal phobia" of the region and the intolerance of the times supplied a convenient, if regrettable, reinforcement for the anti-petition forces.

Nevertheless, public policy toward higher education rather quickly turned in a new direction. By the time of the Civil War, a broader public toleration of pluralism and the growing ability of colleges to survive without public assistance made private colleges an attractive option. Harvard obtained a private charter in 1865, the same year a new Holy Cross petition found success. Not long afterwards, Williams and Amherst followed suit.[113] But in 1849 there was no way of knowing whether and when the circumstances would change, and Holy Cross had to make the best of its disadvantaged position.

After the issue had been decided, John Early thanked Charles Upham for his support of Holy Cross. In response, Upham reiterated his belief that Catholics had been denied their civil and religious rights by the vote and urged perseverance in the fight. "No act of my life," he concluded, "gives me more satisfaction than the stand I have taken on this subject."[114] Eight months later, Early spoke with Bishop Fitzpatrick about renewing the effort for a charter. But Fitzpatrick resisted the idea, arguing that a new petition would encounter the same fate.[115] As Fitzpatrick's biographer has pointed out, his motives for refusing to compromise on exclusivity—whether loyalty to the wishes of

---

dropped over 40 percent, and the three Massachusetts colleges dropped from an enrollment of 5.8 freshmen per 100,000 population in 1835 to a figure of 2.5 in 1845.

112. Handlin, *American College*, 34.

113. Ibid., 17–20. See also, Edward I. Devitt, "College of the Holy Cross, 1843–1914," *WL*, 64:217–22.

114. Charles W. Upham to John Early, Salem, May 8, 1849, GUA, Early Papers.

115. John Early to Ignatius Brocard, Worcester, January 8, 1850, MPA, 218 Z 3.

Bishop Fenwick, a failure of his general good sense, or hostility to the prevailing spirit of anti-Catholicism—were never entirely clear.[116] But the fact is that the bishop's intransigence on the issue helped prolong the stalemate.

The charter failure had little impact on everyday life at the College; most faculty and students found the situation agreeable and the setting almost idyllic. Jesuit educational traditions and a Holy Cross style had been firmly established by the early 1850s. The academic program was fully in place and the first graduates had already departed after nostalgic farewells. Faculty and students who were far from home still marveled over the fact that, for better or worse, they were living among the Yankees. The social context of Worcester and New England amplified the charm of the location and accentuated the distinctiveness of those who belonged to Holy Cross. As their months lengthened into years, they became attached to the program, the place, and each other; and personal loyalty emerged as one of the College's most important characteristics. Samuel Lilly spoke for many when he described his feelings:

[I am] still among the Yankeys. . . . I retain an attachment and an affection for Packachoag, and I think that if things were to remain as they have been and still continue to be, I could happily spend my life on this hill; we have prospered so well & have been so much favored since I have been here that my attachment seems every day to grow stronger for this place.[117]

As the diaries and letters make clear, few would have disagreed.

Yet, for all its apparent success, the College was in a vulnerable position. Debt was delaying construction of the west wing. Enrollments and tuition revenues were flat. The lack of a charter compounded the difficulty of collecting debts. The refusal to admit Protestants made such a point of Holy Cross's special character that it placed the school beyond the philanthropic scope of most of the wealthier segment of the community. And the suspicion that Bishop Fitzpatrick was not as enthusiastic as his predecessor about establishing a Jesuit day college in Boston diminished the attractiveness of Holy Cross for some of the Jesuits. For the moment, the College was inching along—its survival a tribute to the human effort that had been invested, its problems serious but manageable. Then, on July 14, 1852, the vulnerability of Holy Cross became dramatically apparent when fire broke out in Fenwick Hall.

116. Thomas H. O'Connor, *Fitzpatrick's Boston, 1846–1866* (Boston: Northeastern University Press, 1984), 118–19.

117. Samuel Lilly to Joseph Lilly, Worcester, October 9, 1846, GUA, Holy Cross, 1848–1878.

CHAPTER TWO

A "Struggled" Success, 1851–1861

NTHONY F. CIAMPI, the College's fourth rector in eight years, arrived at Pakachoag in August 1851. Thirty-five years old, he was an alumnus of the Roman College who had volunteered for work in the United States in 1840 and completed his Jesuit studies at Georgetown. Youthful, almost boyish in appearance, he was elegant in his manners and tenacious in his resolve, a pious and generous man who could also, by his own admission, be imperious.[1] As rector of Holy Cross for eleven years in three separate terms of office (1851–54, 1857–61, 1869–73), he was destined to have a major impact on the College over more than two decades. Above all, he was called upon to solve a set of problems that nearly destroyed the College after the fire of 1852. Under less competent leadership, Holy Cross might have closed, as 81 percent of colleges in the Union states did in the years before the Civil War.[2] The survival of Holy Cross is a tribute to his leadership.

There were no obvious hints that a crisis was impending. When Ciampi took office, his biggest challenges were to monitor religious discipline among the Jesuits and to reduce the chronic debt. He addressed Jesuit discipline first, assuming the task of religious mentor for the ten lay brothers at the school. For the faculty, he instituted a "Council of Teachers" to discuss pedagogical problems, and a "Council of Prefects" to address disciplinary issues. He monitored requests for assistance from local pastors because of his concern that

1. Michael Earls described Ciampi as having "elegant manners and priestly deportment, every inch a princely Roman, yet with the humility of a child." *Manuscripts and Memories: Chapters in our Literary Tradition* (Milwaukee: Bruce Publishing Co., 1935), 153–54. In *Baltimore's Loyola, Loyola's Baltimore, 1851–1986*, (Baltimore: The Maryland Historical Society, 1990), Nicholas Varga described Ciampi as "a handsome man . . . [whose] speech always retained a delicate trace of his native Italy." P. 71. The late Maurizio Vannicelli of the Holy Cross Political Science Department described Ciampi's Italian letters as exquisite in style.

2. Bledstein, *Culture*, 242.

excessive pastoral obligations would compromise the quality of teaching.[3] Idealistic and energetic, he wanted the Jesuit community to be productively engaged in education and the students to be well taught and supervised. Among his other duties, Ciampi kept the community's House Diary, a daily journal ordinarily assigned to the community minister. These beginnings impressed Roothaan, who urged the young rector to stay the course.[4]

The college debt was a harder problem. When Ciampi took office, the figure stood at about $8500, with interest payments adding to annual expenses. The debt was a source of continual frustration. He found himself in an impossible position: creditors, with the force of law behind them, demanded payment of obligations; but the College was hampered in collecting its accounts because it lacked a charter, a circumstance that also made the school annually liable to over $200 in taxes. Ciampi's only recourse was to cajole and pressure individuals to pay what they owed, to borrow money, and to pray. To Ignatius Brocard, who was still the Maryland Jesuit provincial, he admitted that he had prayed to St. Francis Borgia for the welfare of the College: "I only hoped that he would inspire some fear of God in our debtors—if they paid us we would be able to satisfy our creditors."[5] Early in 1852, he was even more concerned and cast about for solutions. He contemplated a campaign through the Boston *Pilot* to create a fund for Holy Cross, "the Catholic College of New England." He requested power of attorney from Georgetown College to help collect debts. He sought permission to publish a letter reminding parents that students would be sent home after two months if no payment were received.[6] And he worried about the lack of funds to replace the hard-used furnishings of the school, as he told Brocard: "Not a single matress [sic] has ever been washed or redone. And then, the laundry and linen supply—the so called infirmary—. It is providential that the boys[,] coming from poor families, generally, adapt themselves."[7]

3. Ciampi to Ignatius Brocard, Worcester, September 16, 1851, MPA, 219 P 9, October 10, 1851, MPA, 219 N 5, February 2, 1852, MPA, 220 W 5; O'Callaghan Diary, December 17, 1851, January 20, February 25, and March 17, 1852.

4. Roothaan to Ciampi, Rome, April 16, 1852, ARSI, MD Reg. I, 291.

5. Early to Brocard, Worcester, October 27, 1848, MPA, 216 F 19; Ciampi to Brocard, Worcester, October 10 and 11, 1851, MPA, 219 N 5.

6. Ciampi to Brocard, Worcester, February 9, 1852, MPA, 220 W 5; March 4, 1852, MPA, 220 T 3, March 18, 1852, MPA, 220 T 3; Ciampi to Charles Stonestreet, Worcester, September 8, 1852, MPA, 221 W 12. A statement, dated January 13, 1853, contains a bill of $431 due to the College since 1848, and on which interest had increased the account to $548. At the bottom, Peter Blenkinsop wrote: "All the bills and items of bills have been sent frequently." GUA, Holy Cross, 1848–78. A copy of the document granting power of attorney, November 7, 1853, is in ACHC 11.0.

7. Ciampi to Brocard, Worcester, February 9, 1853, MPA, 220 W 5.

Anthony F. Ciampi, three-time president (1851–1854, 1857–1861, 1869–1873), energetic defender of Holy Cross after the fire of 1852, he struggled to rebuild and re-establish the College.

Father Brocard died of typhoid fever in April of 1852. His passing deprived the debt-laden Maryland Province of a capable and experienced leader. Joseph Aschwanden, one of 41 German Jesuits who had sought refuge in the United States after the upheavals of 1848, succeeded him as acting provincial, pending the appointment of a permanent replacement. In that capacity, Aschwanden visited Holy Cross in June. He liked what he saw. He was particularly fulsome in his praise of Anthony Ciampi, who was popular —even admired—among the Jesuits and seemed to have the College on the right track:

Everyone in the house . . . gave testimony that Fr. Ciampi was a marvelous superior. The large debt was being cut down. . . . In the whole Province there is not a man who, if some duty were placed on him, would be more faithful and more prompt in exact execution than this man.

Aschwanden was also impressed with the rector's authentic piety.[8] Ciampi would need all of his resources of mind and spirit in the month that followed.

In the afternoon of July 14, 1852, fire broke out on the third floor of Fenwick Hall. Father Ciampi claimed afterwards that "we are altogether ignorant of where the fire began," raising doubts about the persistent legend that it was caused by a negligent teacher burning discarded exam papers in his stove. The blaze spread through the laths and wooden beams within the walls of the section of the structure which dated to 1843. The fire department came quickly, but the cistern was nearly dry. A series of hoses and pumping engines had to be connected to draw water from the river up the slope of the hill—a distance of nearly a quarter mile and an elevation of 120 feet to the base of the blazing building. During the hour the men labored to gain a supply of water, the fire continued to spread; the sight of the burning building on the hillside attracted a considerable crowd. Among the on-lookers was Bishop Fitzpatrick, who had been passing through Worcester at mid-day and stopped to have lunch with Father Gibson. When they heard a boy in the street shouting that "the Catholic college" was on fire, they hastened to the disaster.[9]

As the spectators watched, furniture and books, religious statues, kitchen utensils, and personal items were thrown from the windows in advance of the spreading flames. Finally, the firemen completed the connection to the river and doused the fire, saving the east wing. But the original college structure and many of its contents were lost. The proprietor of the Worcester House and other hospitable townsfolk took homeless students in for the night. The next day they were sent home; many had lost everything but the clothes on their backs.[10] Underneath the blackened walls, the Jesuits gathered items that were strewn about the terrace and stored them away from the elements. Much of

8. Aschwanden to Roothaan, Georgetown, July 16 and August 12, 1852, ARSI, MD V, 18–28, 22; Curran, "Troubled Nation," 40.

9. Ciampi's account of the fire is in the House Diary; see also Worcester *Spy*, July 15, 1852; Meagher and Grattan, *Spires*, 85–87; and Lord et al., *History*, 2:611–13.

10. James C. Bergen, Class of 1852, told George Fenwick afterwards that the only personal items he had rescued from the fire were two essays and an empty trunk. He received his diploma from the College in November, even though he owed money to the school. Bergen to Fenwick, Cambridge, November 18, 1852, MPA, 220 A.

the furniture was damaged, but a good part of the library was saved. The loss in building and contents came to about $40,000. There was no insurance.

Whatever private agony the fire may have caused him, Anthony Ciampi was careful to attend to his public responsibilities. Two days after the fire, he published a "card" in the Worcester *Spy* to thank "those citizens of Worcester who assisted them in their late calamitous visitation." He called the public manifestation of sympathy "our best consolation in our sudden misfortune" and thanked in particular the sheriff, the fire companies, and those who had offered shelter to the students. He recorded more private thoughts in the House Diary. On July 15th, he was drawing solace from his faith: "What else will happen to us? God is with us. It is He who takes and gives life." The following day, he was still refusing to yield to the general gloom: "Everything uncertain and full of sadness—but all of us are chipper enough." On the 17th, he made his first mention of a new building; and on the 18th he noted that $600 had been raised for the College by Father Gibson and his parishioners.

At Georgetown, Joseph Aschwanden had other ideas, as he reported to Jan Roothaan on July 16, the day after receiving the news from Worcester. Although he praised Ciampi as a good man with "a heavy cross to bear," his concern about heavy province debts and his preference for colleges in large cities prompted an unfavorable conclusion: "I do not care about the rebuilding of the Worcester house."[11] A week later, in a much longer letter to the general, he presented his case against re-opening Holy Cross. Practical objections included the school's vulnerability to fire, its problems with solvency, its distance from the rest of the province, and the relatively high cost of operating in Worcester. Moreover, the province had just agreed to open Loyola College in Baltimore, where personnel from Holy Cross could be advantageously used. Aschwanden's goal was disengagement: "Why should this Province expose itself to the immediate threat of financial ruin for the sake of rebuilding this College? Certainly I shall never undertake the rebuilding of this College: (never, never:) even if it is rebuilt free from debt." His greatest fear was that the surviving east wing would furnish a pretext for a hasty and ill-considered rebuilding. For that reason, he admitted, "I would have wished that the whole place had burned down to its foundation." Aschwanden did admit that there were arguments on the

11. Aschwanden to Roothaan, Georgetown, July 16, 1856, ARSI, MD V, 18–20. Part of the reason for Aschwanden's panic about Holy Cross may have been his unfamiliarity with the condition of the Catholic Church in the United States. After leaving Germany, he had spent time in Missouri before being transferred to Maryland in 1850. He had previously served at several colleges in Germany, where Catholic institutions, presumably, were more firmly grounded and economically stable. Personal correspondence to the author from Emmett Curran, Washington, D.C., March 1, 1993.

other side, particularly the need to serve the growing Catholic population of New England, and Bishop Fitzpatrick's friendly disposition toward the Jesuits. On the main point, his consultors agreed with him, but they were trying to show even-handedness in a controversy already being characterized as the worst in the history of the Maryland Province. Meanwhile, Aschwanden wrote Ciampi twice to urge him to accept a new assignment in Philadelphia and to stipulate that no funds be collected for rebuilding.[12]

Aschwanden's prohibition against accepting money prompted friends of the school to mount a defense. On July 20, Father Gibson fired the first volley in a letter to the acting provincial, offering three points that became familiar elements in the case for Holy Cross in the months ahead: the generosity of New England's Catholics and Protestants would provide the funding; the school had become an asset and point of pride among Catholics of all the New England states; if the Jesuits abandoned a school that had been entrusted to them by Bishop Fenwick on behalf of the Church in the entire region, they would "place the fathers of the Society in a very bad light."[13] A week later, Anthony Ciampi also wrote to Aschwanden, stressing the costs associated with *not* reopening: lay employees whose services were being terminated would have to be paid; registration fees for the fall term would have to be refunded. He complained that, because of the prohibition against accepting funds, "we are prevented from enjoying the benevolence and liberality of the people." And he begged Joseph Aschwanden to visit Worcester to see the situation for himself.[14]

Ciampi and two of his local consultors, Augustine Kennedy and George Fenwick, also defended the College to Jan Roothaan. Writing on July 26th, Ciampi appealed his re-assignment directly to the general and reported Bishop Fitzpatrick's view that restoration was a matter of justice because the diocese had already expended a large sum of money on the College. Perhaps with an eye to John McElroy's insistent advocacy of a college in Boston,[15] he developed the argument that Holy Cross had been founded particularly to educate

12. Aschwanden to Roothaan, Georgetown, July 23, 1852, ARSI, MD 9-XVIII, 8; Ciampi to Roothaan, Worcester, July 26, 1852, ARSI, MD 9-XVIII, 9; Kauffman, *Tradition and Transformation*, 136–37.

13. M. W. Gibson to Aschwanden, Worcester, July 20, 1852, MPA, 220 P 14.

14. Ciampi to Aschwanden, Worcester, July 27, 1852, MPA, [220].

15. McElroy had been trying for nearly a decade to open a Jesuit college in Boston and subscribed fully to the general preference for Jesuit day schools in large cities. Inevitably, he saw Worcester's set-back as Boston's opportunity, a chance to re-think and, perhaps, renegotiate the *quid pro quo* by which the Society had reluctantly accepted Holy Cross. McElroy to Aschwanden, New York, July 24 and 24, 1852, MPA, 220 P 17, 220 P 18.

the sons of the Irish, who had suffered discrimination principally on account of their lack of formal education. He argued that the College had gained acclaim as "the only Catholic College in America, a College so advanced in its discipline and one that had from its very beginnings won respect for Catholics among the Protestants of New England." He repeated the argument that sympathetic Protestants saw the rebuilding as a chance to make amends for the burning of the Ursuline academy. And he asserted that the inflexibility of Aschwanden and his consultors rested upon their ignorance about the origins of the College and its current condition.[16] Augustine Kennedy contextualized the argument by pointing out that Maryland, with a Catholic population of about 112,000, had three Jesuit colleges, while the New England states, with 82,500 Catholics in Boston and Worcester alone, had only Holy Cross: "Is it not injuring the Catholic Religion here to suppress the only Catholic college in these six states?"[17]

Father Kennedy also sent Aschwanden a strong letter, characterizing his refusal to allow collections as "a virtual suppression of the College." He recommended re-opening the school in the fall to prevent losing the students, arguing that $500 would suffice to repair the east wing. The Jesuits, he insisted, could be "joyfully accommodated . . . with a little inconvenience" in the old academy building, freeing the entire east wing for dormitories and classrooms. For $10,000, the main building could be reconstructed, while the outstanding debt could be re-financed through a ten-year loan. Abandonment, on the other hand, would obligate the province for the debt. New England Catholics, Kennedy reported, were coming forward in great numbers to contribute their mite:

"Here Father are two dollars. I have no more now.—come to our village, our factory, our mission. there is not a Catholic who will not give you as much as he can afford." I wish you could see & hear them when we tell them that we can receive nothing for the College. . . . They cannot understand why we are not among them collecting.

Nor, Kennedy thought, was their interest misplaced. Holy Cross was the only "truly Catholic" college of the Society in the United States. It was a source of vocations for the Society of Jesus and the diocesan priesthood. It had removed a great deal of anti-Catholic prejudice in the region. Holy Cross was the fulfillment of Bishop Fenwick's dream; his remains rested on the campus. To return the campus to his successor after the fire would be disgraceful:

16. Ciampi to Roothaan, Worcester, July 26, 1852, ARSI, MD 9-XVIII, 9. The province consultors that summer were Charles Stonestreet (Georgetown rector), Benedict Sestini (Georgetown faculty), and James Curley (Maryland Province socius, at Georgetown).

17. Augustine Kennedy to Roothaan, Worcester, July 26, 1852, ARSI, MD 9-XVIII, 10.

"The College was freely, generously given. It was freely received. Can we now abandon it? . . . Shall we act so ungenerously as to present the ruins to his successor?"[18]

On August 2, Ciampi sent Roothaan a Latin translation this letter. By then, Joseph Aschwanden had been badgered into traveling to Worcester; but Ciampi was still frustrated by his "precipitous" eagerness to abandon Holy Cross. Ciampi was convinced that the province authorities couldn't grasp how crucial Holy Cross was for establishing a respectable Catholic presence in New England.[19] Early in August, Aschwanden visited Worcester and Boston. He told the general that his findings confirmed his judgment that the College should be closed: only the Worcester people wanted the College rebuilt; in Boston, the Jesuits and even the Protestants favored opening a day school. The fire damage was more extensive than he had been led to believe: losses totaled $45,000; and the old debt was at least $13,000. He was skeptical, moreover, of all the talk about willing donors, since Americans, in his experience, were not inclined to support institutions like Holy Cross, which "did not have much to offer for the good of Catholics." It was remote, expensive to operate, a waste of some of the best talent in the Maryland Province.[20]

Father Aschwanden and Bishop Fitzpatrick discussed Holy Cross on August 5. Two different versions of that meeting survive—Aschwanden's report to the general, and Ciampi's report to Rome with an Italian translation of Fitzpatrick's notes on the meeting. Aschwanden stressed the bishop's refusal to take the College back for the diocese—that is, to accept responsibility for the entire package: property, existing structures, and debt. If the Jesuits chose to withdraw, Fitzpatrick wanted them to sell the property, pay off the debts, and return the remaining money to the diocese. The acting provincial advocated that course, though he admitted Fitzpatrick was unhappy with it. Aschwanden fostered the impression that the meeting was business-like and devoted to resolving a problem that had an unattractive but inevitable solution.[21] Six years later, in a further account, Aschwanden added that he had countered the bishop's claim that the Jesuit commitment to Worcester was perpetual by

18. Kennedy to Aschwanden, Worcester, July 30, 1852, MPA, 220 P 4. Punctuation supplied in quotes.

19. Ciampi to Roothaan, Worcester, August 2, 1852, ARSI, MD 9-XVIII, 12.

20. Aschwanden to Roothaan, Worcester, August 6, 1852 ARSI, MD 9-XVIII, 13. After 1848, a substantial number of German and Italian Jesuits immigrated to the United States, where they helped staff Holy Cross and the other colleges. By 1851, 49 of the 213 Jesuits in the Maryland Province were immigrants and helped supply faculty for the new Jesuit colleges at Washington and Baltimore. Curran, "Troubled Nation," 30–36.

21. Aschwanden to Roothaan, Worcester, August 6, 1852, ARSI, MD 9-XVIII, 13.

arguing that "the Society does not obligate itself nor wishes to be obligated to anything to its own great harm."[22] Ciampi's report emphasized Fitzpatrick's frustration that Aschwanden was attempting to violate an understanding by which the diocese had invested $25,000 in the College in return for an "implicit promise . . . that the diocese of Boston would always enjoy the advantages associated with the existence of such a Catholic institution." The bishop wanted to be certain that responsibility for closing the school would rest in the public mind with the Jesuits; but he could not forbid the closing, since the school was not his responsibility.[23]

As the correspondence on Holy Cross was crossing the Atlantic, Jan Roothaan decided to appoint Charles Stonestreet to lead the Maryland Province. The son of a Maryland lawyer, Stonestreet was a Georgetown alumnus who had been the rector of his alma mater before his designation as provincial.[24] When he assumed office on August 15, he immediately set to work on the crisis at Holy Cross. More open-minded than Aschwanden, he was familiar with the details because he had been a province consultor. Before the end of the month, he journeyed to Worcester to discuss the issues in person.[25] He reassigned most of the twenty Jesuits who were still at the College. George Fenwick remained in Worcester, but failing eyesight necessitated his removal the following winter. That left Ciampi and Peter Blenkinsop, together with two Jesuit brothers to manage the farm and look after the house.

In Rome, Jan Roothaan was trying to make sense of the contradictory information. On August 18, he communicated his confusion to Stonestreet:

[Joseph Aschwanden] was so depressed of mind that he was unwilling to accept the spontaneous offerings of many people and from the Bishop himself with which the College might be rebuilt. This is a relief to us, especially if the College is completely destroyed. I do not wish a rebuilding such as this to increase the Province debt[,] but if by donations the College can be restored, then by all means let it be rebuilt.

22. Aschwanden to Peter Beckx, Georgetown, July 29, 1858, ARSI, MD 9-XVIII, 16.

23. Ciampi to Roothaan, Worcester, August 12, 1852, ARSI, MD 9-XVIII, 14. Despite their disagreement, Ciampi and Aschwanden preserved fraternal respect for each other. Aschwanden always defended Ciampi for respecting the prohibitions about reconstruction. Ciampi thought Aschwanden unqualified for leadership because of his youth and short residency in the country. Aschwanden admitted to Roothaan that the office was "too serious and impossible for me." A humble, pastoral man, he eventually found more suitable niches as pastor of Holy Trinity Church in Georgetown and as an instructor of theology. Aschwanden to Roothaan, Georgetown, August 12, 1852, ARSI, MD V, 22; Ciampi to Roothaan, Worcester, August 12, 1852, ARSI, MD 9-XVII, 14; WL, 33:318–22.

24. WL, 14:400–403.

25. Ciampi to Stonestreet, Worcester, September 8, 1852, MPA, 221 W 12.

He urged Stonestreet to proceed cautiously and told him that he had done well in leaving a skeleton crew at the College.[26] To help clarify the alternatives, Stonestreet asked Thomas Mulledy whether, according to the Jesuit Constitutions, it was permissible to abandon Holy Cross. Mulledy replied that, since the Society had "formally and explicitly" accepted the school, neither the provincial nor the general had the power to relinquish it on their own authority.[27] Having addressed the technical issue, Mulledy added his opinion: Holy Cross was "an honor to the Society," a far richer source of candidates for the order than Georgetown. Opponents of Holy Cross had argued that a boarding school required a prohibitively large number of Jesuit faculty, and that one boarding school, Georgetown, was enough for the province. But the efficiency argument worked in favor of Holy Cross: with the same number of students, Georgetown had many more faculty and staff. Mulledy gave his case a final twist by expressing his conviction that Roothaan would ultimately order a restoration. Under the circumstances, he advised Stonestreet to authorize reconstruction and submit his reasons to the general.

Less than two weeks after receiving that letter, Stonestreet wrote to Roothaan: "This is my mind: the College must absolutely . . . be rebuilt." In response to Roothaan's pointed question about whether reconstruction could be accomplished without increasing the province debt, he admitted that he didn't know; there was a "marvelous" division of opinion on the matter. His recommendation was based on Bishop Fitzpatrick's unyielding attitude and not on inflated claims about the College's record of accomplishment. To sell the property and remaining structures for repayment of outstanding debts would incur Fitzpatrick's opposition—something "odious and not even to be considered." The net indebtedness was actually $9000 and reconstruction costs would total $10,000, toward which the bishop was willing to contribute $6000 from the diocese. Stonestreet was willing for the province to assume a substantial portion of the debt to move the process forward. Meanwhile, he thought it best to proceed slowly, leaving a few men at Holy Cross to oversee collection of funds and reconstruction of the building.[28] Roothaan concurred, though he took a hard line on fiscal management: "Unless it seems probable that they can sustain themselves from their own funds or receive sufficient subsidies, they must do no building. I absolutely forbid it since mon-

26. Roothaan to Stonestreet, Rome, August 18, 1854 ARSI, MD Reg. I, 294–95.

27. Mulledy to Stonestreet, Frederick, September 6, 1852, MPA, 220 M 2. Mulledy cited Part IV, chapter 2, paragraph 3A, (Constitutions, 323) to the effect that once a college has been formally accepted, only the vote of a general congregation of the Society can authorize the general to abandon it.

28. Stonestreet to Roothaan, Georgetown, September 18, 1852, ARSI, MD V, 26.

eys for this purpose could ruin the province."[29] The general's economic concerns were offset only by the arguments that circumstances in the diocese permitted no alternative to saving Holy Cross. In March, after a further consultation in Rome, he delegated the final decision to Charles Stonestreet.[30]

While they waited for the Society's authorities to come to a decision, the small band of Jesuits in Worcester did their best to keep their spirits up. Father Roothaan's expressions of solicitude helped, but his cautious approach to rebuilding made the future uncertain.[31] In December, a Jesuit visitor stopped there "to see the gloomy ruins. . . . All around it is sad. There are the blackened walls, one of the inmates lame, another well nigh blind, amusing themselves with cats and dogs in the fault of more congenial company."[32] In Boston, John McElroy was insisting that his plans for a school in Boston not be ignored and implying that the actual state of Holy Cross was being deliberately misrepresented by its friends. His hostility to the restoration irritated John Early, who called McElroy "a deadly enemy of Holy Cross [who] would gladly see it at the bottom of the sea."[33] But Ciampi was hopeful enough that winter to insure the east wing for two years. And in Boston, Bishop Fitzpatrick remained optimistic because of his confidence in Stonestreet's judgment. "The rebuilding of Worcester seems the great hobby here," one visitor wrote; "all seem sanguine that it will be rebuilt."[34]

As soon as Stonestreet received authorization from Rome to act on Holy Cross, he moved quickly to a decision. In April of 1853, with the approval of his province consultors, he proposed to Bishop Fitzpatrick that the school be reopened on a reduced scale. He was willing to assign two Jesuits to raise funds in a campaign to be backed by a pastoral letter from the bishop. Reconstruction would be limited to the east wing and a portion of the original building. Admittedly, the plan was a compromise, but his consultors believed it would save Holy Cross, protect the good name of the Jesuits in New England, and furnish "a select school or college for the more smiled upon by fortune of yr. diocese and thereabouts." This arrangement, he estimated, would

29. Roothaan to Stonestreet, Rome, October 7 and December 24, 1852, ARSI, MD Reg. I, 295 and 297.

30. Roothaan to Stonestreet, Rome, January 17 and March 21, 1853, ARSI, MD Reg. I, 300 and 301.

31. Ciampi to Stonestreet, Frederick, September 15, 1852, MPA, 220 M 7; Roothaan to Ciampi, November 5, 1852, ARSI, MD Reg. I, 296.

32. John Blox to Stonestreet, Boston, December 12, 1852, MPA, 229 K 5A.

33. McElroy to Stonestreet, Boston, September 19 and December 10, 1852, MPA, 220 M 8 and M 8A; Early to [George Fenwick], Baltimore, July 1, 1853, MPA, 221 B 5.

34. John Blox to Stonestreet, Boston, December 12, 1852, MPA, 229 K 5A; HD.

accommodate about 70 students, with the Jesuits living in the old academy building. With good fortune, the College could eventually be enlarged.[35] In response, Fitzpatrick called the plan "the wisest you could have hit upon," and promised full cooperation. By May, the collectors had been designated—the College's old advocate, Augustine Kennedy; and John Moore, who had been at Holy Cross from 1845 to 1848 and in the Maine missions from 1848 to 1851. Moore's appointment was particularly welcomed by Fitzpatrick: "He has a pretty good cheek for such business and would pick up a good deal about— besides what might be had in the churches."[36] The decision to save the school raised spirits among the College's friends throughout the province. In Baltimore John Early was relieved: "All now stands fair for H. Cross."[37]

The plan was easier to formulate than to execute. Ciampi was under strict orders not to begin reconstruction until he had $4000 in hand, and collections moved slowly; some of the public sympathy generated at the time of the fire had been dissipated through delay. Still, the rector clung to the hope of reopening in September. On June 3, he sought permission to start cleaning the old bricks so that they could be used for reconstruction. On June 20, when the collection stood at $3151, Ciampi asked Stonestreet to waive the monetary restriction so that he could, at least, hire an architect. The money, he felt certain, would come: there had still been no collection in Boston, nor (as Ciampi pointedly reminded him) had Stonestreet yet remitted the money he had promised on behalf of the Maryland Province. Meanwhile, the delay itself was becoming a problem: the first phase of the reconstruction had to be completed before winter, and applications were starting to come in; yet the reopening could not be advertised. Ciampi was convinced that donors would be more numerous after the beginning of reconstruction convinced them that the project was actually moving forward.[38]

The summer of 1853 became a nightmare of frustration for Anthony Ciampi. Criticized on one hand for inactivity and secret opposition to the College, warned on the other that he was not to move beyond the limits that had been imposed by Jesuit authorities, and disappointed in the architect's slow progress after receiving authorization to begin, Ciampi barely persevered.[39] On July 14,

---

35. Stonestreet to Fitzpatrick (draft) [Georgetown, April, 1853], MPA, 221 W 1.

36. Fitzpatrick to [Stonestreet], Boston, April 9, 1853, MPA, 221 W 2.

37. Early to [Fenwick], Baltimore, April 24 and May 16, 1853, MPA, 221 B 3 and 4.

38. Ciampi to Stonestreet, Worcester, June 3 and 20, 1853, MPA, 221 W 4 and 221 W 5.

39. Within the province, John Early criticized Ciampi for the delay and maintained that Ciampi had opposed rebuilding Holy Cross at a province congregation in 1853 and was a "wet blanket" to the collectors. "The destinies of Holy Cross have been confided to strange

the anniversary of the fire, the project was still being delayed. On August 12 work had still not begun; but the monetary conditions had been met and he asked Stonestreet's approval of a plan covering reconstruction of the east wing and partial repairs to the main building to prevent further deterioration. Ciampi had engaged Captain Lamb, "a man of great reputation in the County for his honesty and workmanship," whose bid for the work was $7000. Of this, almost $5600 had been raised, with the collection still in progress. The east wing could be ready for the opening of schools in September. The main building could be completed in the spring, when labor would be cheaper. At the same time, Ciampi requested authorization to raise tuition from $150 to $170, and he asked for Jesuit brothers to repair broken furniture and to assist with other necessary tasks, including the farm—an asset the fire had left untouched. Again, Ciampi had to wait for authorization: "Every prudent economist would advise us to undertake the work; but obedience is our rule. Please answer me as quick as possible; for I have to give a definite decision to the builder."[40]

When the answer arrived, six days later, it drove Ciampi into a crisis. Although Stonestreet's letter has been lost, its contents can be inferred from Ciampi's reaction: evidently, the provincial raised further questions about projected outlays because of his fear that the plan would run ahead of the ability to pay. Ciampi's exasperation was evident in his reply. He found the provincial's letter confusing, and asked point-blank whether he had approval to start the project. He wasn't sure how to read Stonestreet's intentions: "Tell me one word only: Go on—or; Stop at the . . . west end." In response to the query about raising tuition to $170, Stonestreet had authorized $200; but that, Ciampi claimed, was too high for the working-class Irish boys who would be the school's principal clients because of the Catholics-only restriction. Obviously, Stonestreet wanted to proceed cautiously to avoid mistakes. But Ciampi was now at the end of his patience, as he made clear by referring to an earlier conversation: "In truth, if you had accepted my resignation when I offered, I would be a much better man. . . . There is no improvement, no magnificence, no grand style to be afraid of." To Stonestreet's credit, he recognized that he

---

hands," he wrote, "Ciampi, I fear, has fallen in with bad advisers." Yet, documentary evidence that was confidential at the time shows Ciampi to have been a steadfast supporter of rebuilding, though his discouragement sometimes prompted private second thoughts. In this case, the rumors were misleading, and Ciampi felt compelled to defend himself, pointing out that his lamented inactivity had only been obedience to the wishes of Aschwanden and Stonestreet. Early to [George Fenwick], Baltimore, August 7, 1853, MPA, 221 B 6.

40. Ciampi to Stonestreet, Worcester, July 11, 14 and August 12, 1853, MPA, 221 W 7, W 9, and W 18.

could press the beleaguered rector no further. At the bottom of Ciampi's letter, he wrote: "Answered in person at H. Cross. Chas. H. Stonestreet."[41]

The provincial visited Worcester sometime during the last ten days of August and authorized the project, more or less along the lines Ciampi had proposed. Delays necessitated that the re-opening be deferred until early October; tuition was held at $150 for the time being with the hope of attracting more students. By the time of opening, the collectors had raised $8000, but that was hardly sufficient to solve the financial crisis. At the end the year, Ciampi estimated that he needed $4000 more to meet further obligations for reconstruction. He tried to borrow $5000 from Georgetown or from the Maryland Province, pleading strongly with Stonestreet about the justice of his appeal: "Shall it be unjustifiable to invite Our Brothers to do charity, while we are calling on the people? . . . Holy Cross is to be restored, because justice was to be done to a Bishop, to his Diocese, to the Society.—Oh! may God inspire you and give you a strength equal to your feelings."[42] Eventually, Ciampi had to borrow the money from a Worcester bank, using College land as collateral. Meanwhile, Ciampi practiced strict economy. Well into the autumn, the furnaces were left unfired because, as Ciampi explained, "we cannot afford to be liberal. We have to live on a few hundred dollars for six months."[43] Remarkably, between October and December of 1853, the rector and treasurer paid off nearly $1500 of the old debt, an achievement that gave Peter Blenkinsop the hope that, with economy and larger enrollments, "we will gradually liquidate old and new debts, until the College may cease to be a Cross."[44]

The needs of Holy Cross were represented to New England Catholics principally by John Moore, since Augustine Kennedy left the campaign in 1854. Although Moore worked with good will and eventually raised a substantial sum, he was something of a free spirit who didn't work well with those in authority. Toward Ciampi he harbored a sense of mistrust about his aptitude for directing the College. He also resisted Ciampi's insistence that he have access to the collections. Moore feared that, if the money were held in Ciampi's name, College creditors would claim it for outstanding claims, whereas the money had been collected exclusively for rebuilding. He wouldn't even tell Ciampi how much money had been collected until the rector appealed to Stonestreet.[45] Not every pastor appreciated Moore's mission. Ciampi reported

41. Ciampi to Stonestreet, Worcester, August 18, 1853, MPA, 221 W 9.

42. Ciampi to Stonestreet, Worcester, December 30, 1853, MPA, 221 W 18.

43. Ciampi to Stonestreet, October 17, 1853, MPA, 221 W 15.

44. Blenkinsop to Stonestreet, Worcester, January 26, 1854, MPA, 222 T 1.

45. Moore to Stonestreet, Worcester, June 22, 1853, MPA, 221 W 6; Ciampi to Stonestreet, Worcester, July 14, October 17 and 31, 1853, MPA, 221 W 15 and W 18; *WL* 18: 129.

that John McElroy had virtually "killed the collection" at his parish in Boston. And in Bangor, Jesuit John Bapst was outraged that Moore, with Stonestreet's approval, had visited some of the churches twice, engaging in what Bapst called "brigandage":

With regard to collect[ing] money for Worcester College: Since (according to the elegant expression of F. Ciampi) since the collectors have once *Swept* the Maine Missions, I think that will do for a year at least. I am quite sure, that the same sweeping collectors, will not sweep to pay my debts or furnish my churches.[46]

In the fall of 1853, Moore journeyed to Quebec and northern Vermont. During the summer of 1854 he sailed to Ireland on the College's behalf on a trip that raised hackles with Jesuit authorities because it was undertaken without authorization.[47]

Although Stonestreet originally envisioned assigning John Moore to this work for a relatively brief period, he stayed at his work for almost three years, until the middle of 1856. By September of 1855, Stonestreet was asking Peter Blenkinsop, who had by then succeeded Ciampi as Holy Cross rector, to send him back to Georgetown; but Blenkinsop held on to Moore through the following winter and spring, even though by then the collections were "not very remunerative."[48] The exact amount collected during the rebuilding campaign is impossible to determine because of the inconsistency of the records, but the total exceeded $17,000.[49] Anthony Ciampi also tried his hand at fund raising, with admittedly dismal results. He found that Protestants withheld their generosity because of the school's sectarian character—"we exclude their children, and they refuse to help us." The collection outside the Catholic community gathered only $460, of which Steven Salisbury II, a local philanthropist, offered $50. Some prominent Catholics were even greater disappointments. Ciampi found Andrew Carney "inflexible" in refusing to contribute. Since 1851, the College had been in default in interest payments on a loan from him; by now, he had become a major contributor to John McElroy's projected school in Boston. Contributions from the bishop and many of the

46. Ciampi to Stonestreet, Worcester, July 11, 1853, MPA, 221 W 7; Bapst to Stonestreet, Ellsworth, Maine, October, 1853, MPA, 221 T 7.

47. Moore to Stonestreet, Quebec, September 10, 1853, MPA, 221 W 13; Moore to Stonestreet, Worcester, October 3, 1853 and November 17, 1854, MPA, 221 W 13 and 222 T 14; Stonestreet to Blenkinsop, Georgetown, June 5, 1855, MPA, 223 S 2a.

48. Stonestreet to Blenkinsop, Georgetown, September 11, 1855, MPA, 223 S 3a.

49. Blenkinsop to Stonestreet, Worcester, September 17, 1855, MPA, 223 S 3; Moore to Stonestreet, Worcester, August 8, 1856, MPA, 224 S 13; Account books, ACHC, 13.0, Book 12.

clergy were also thin.[50] Some of the generosity was unrecorded, particularly in the case of creditors whose contribution consisted in forgiveness of money owed on the pre-fire debt. In October 1855, Jesuit scholastic Patrick Healy became the campaign's largest donor by directing $2300, his share of the family estate, to Holy Cross.[51]

Despite the issues of personality and priorities, the fund-raising campaign did allow the reconstruction to go forward. When the school re-opened on October 3, 1853, students were lodged in the east wing; Jesuits lived in the old academy. Work on the main building ran late, but a mild autumn favored the project until its completion in December. Even so, the College's appearance was disappointing. When Jesuit Peter O'Flanagan joined the faculty in November, he wrote: "I could not help dropping a tear for the once noble, stately building so different from what I had seen it before." Rubble remained stacked about the buildings through the autumn.[52] In March, a severe gale blew down four chimneys and destroyed the roof and rafters that had been set in place for the main building; fortunately, Ciampi had not yet formally accepted the work from the contractor, so the College did not have to bear the expense.[53] These circumstances were the background for the third, and final, year of Ciampi's first term as rector. The school re-opened with only part of the lower portion of the *Ratio Studiorum* in operation, the years from Rudiments through Second Humanities. Fourteen students, including Michael Healy and five other pre-fire veterans, were present. Numbers rose very slowly, to a total of 26 in early December. That may have been just as well, since amenities were scarce, as Ciampi told Stonestreet: "Those who come to W^r . . . *must* make up their minds that they come for God—and to help a house that is still bearing either a punishment or a trial."[54] Library books remained in storage be-

50. Ciampi to George Fenwick, Worcester, October 4, 1853, MPA, 221 B 7; Ciampi to Stonestreet, Worcester, October 17 and December 30, 1853, MPA, 221 W 15 and 221 W 18; Meighan, "Nativism," 107; Charles F. Donovan, David R. Dunigan, and Paul FitzGerald, *History of Boston College* (Chestnut Hill: The University Press of Boston College, 1990), 24–25, 35–38.

51. ARSI MD, Litt. Ann., 1847–53; Stonestreet to Blenkinsop, Georgetown, October 14, 1855, MPA, 223 S 4; Foley, *Dream*, 71.

52. O'Flanagan to Stonestreet, Worcester, November 4 and December 3, 1853, MPA, 221 W 16; Ciampi to George Fenwick, Worcester, October 5, 1853, MPA, 221 B 7; Ciampi to Stonestreet, Worcester, October 17, 1853, MPA, 221 W 15.

53. Ciampi to Stonestreet, Worcester, March 26, 1854, MPA, 222 T 3.

54. Ciampi to Stonestreet, Worcester, October 4, 31, and December 7, 1853, MPA, 221 W 4, W 15, and W 19; Ciampi to George Fenwick, Worcester, October 4, 1853, MPA, 221 B 7; HD.

cause there was no place to put them. Cold weather sometimes necessitated that students be kept in the chapel, "the sole place where we can keep the Boys and have some fire for them." To meet operating expenses, Ciampi borrowed money from the rebuilding fund.[55]

At first, Ciampi had little help in running the re-opened school. Although one of the brothers slept in the east wing with the boys, it was Ciampi's responsibility to go to the dormitory at 6 o'clock and supervise the students as they washed and dressed. He then led prayers for them and celebrated Mass, after which he monitored the study hall until breakfast. He taught Rudiments and Third Humanities in the morning and Latin in the afternoon, then French for the entire school. Peter Blenkinsop assisted with classes in English and arithmetic. That left the boys without supervision after morning and afternoon classes and during night studies.[56] To relieve the situation, Charles Stonestreet sent scholastic Patrick Healy, an alumnus of the Class of 1850. He was to prove a godsend to the College during the next five years, a teacher and mentor who was capable and generous enough to do the work of several men. He taught Third and Second Humanities, French and algebra, and supervised meals, morning and afternoon studies, and some of the recreation periods. He was also *de facto* prefect of discipline.[57]

Given the general racism of the era and the immaturity of some students, it was inevitable that Patrick and his younger brother Michael became the butt of hurtful comments. The situation bothered Patrick, as he confided to the provincial:

Placed in a college as I am, our boys who were well acquainted either by sight or hearsay with me & my brothers, remarks are sometimes made (though not in my hearing) which wound my very heart. You know—to what I refer. The anxiety of mine caused by these is very intense. I have here with me a young brother Michael. He is obliged to go through the same ordeal. . . . I trust that all this will wear away; tho' I feel that whilst we live here, with those, who have known us but too well; we shall always be subject to some such degrading misfortune. Providence seems to have decided thus.[58]

George Fenwick's sympathetic counsel helped Patrick Healy to rise above the prejudice. He also drew strength from his older brother: "James desires that I

---

55. ACHC, 13.0, Book 12. At the end of his administration, Ciampi admitted to Stonestreet: "There is not so much as a quarter of a dollar in the Treasury; and already *too much* has been borrowed from the Collection funds." Worcester, August 14, 1854, MPA, 222 T 6. It was February 23, 1857, before a permanent library was in place. HD.

56. Ciampi to Stonestreet, Worcester, October 11, 1853, MPA, 221 W 4.

57. Ciampi to Stonestreet, Worcester, October 31, 1853, MPA, 221 W 15; Foley, *Dream*, 50–58.

58. Patrick Healy to Stonestreet, Worcester, November 23, 1853, MPA, 221 A.

should become a real Jesuit, . . . a man of interior spirit, of deep religious feelings, a model & leader of souls to God."[59] Common sense reinforced his resolve; he told Stonestreet he realized that his students in the College were "not very bright." On the latter point, Ciampi tended to agree. There was disorderliness, he maintained, mostly because Patrick Healy lacked the gift of ubiquity; but he also viewed the students with an unappreciative eye: "The Irish stock brings out the rudest & roughest kind of beings, that Mother Earth had ever to foster. It takes much to lop them and engraft them and make them live to fructify."[60]

Besides Healy, Ciampi, and Blenkinsop, the only other Jesuit teacher in 1853–54 was Father Peter O'Flanagan, a man who found the winter such a severe trial that Ciampi and Healy had to assume many of his duties. Four Jesuit brothers rounded out the community—one to manage the farm, and three to work in the house. Lay employees were few, as Ciampi reported to George Fenwick: Mrs. Kelly and Owen (her son?) managed the kitchen, while "Old Kate" attended to the dairy.[61] As the little group stretched themselves to cover the demands, the school survived the first academic year after re-opening, only a shadow of what it had been before the fire. Ciampi expressed the mood perfectly when he told Stonestreet: "This year success will be a struggled one; and nothing else."[62]

Throughout the final year of his term, Ciampi struggled to maintain his equilibrium and optimism. When fatigue and discouragement overtook him, he had little defense against self-pity, as he indicated to the provincial in November 1853:

It is an uninterrupted succession of days & hours, that makes me grieve and mourn over the burthen of my office. . . . There is none among the Rectors of our Province, who can say that he has had to encounter & sustain the hardship I had to meet with, and with which I must still contend.[63]

In February 1854 and again in April, he asked Stonestreet for help in opposing a movement to have him nominated bishop for Portland, Maine.[64] In March, he was in contact with Orestes Brownson about re-applying for a charter, but he found himself caught between Bishop Fitzpatrick's insistence on

59. Patrick Healy to [?], Worcester, December 24, 1856, MPA, 224 S 11.
60. Ciampi to Stonestreet, Worcester, February 10, 1854, MPA, 222 T 2.
61. Ciampi to George Fenwick, Worcester, October 4, 1853, MPA, 221 B 7.
62. Ciampi to Stonestreet, Worcester, January 9, 1854, MPA, 222 T 1.
63. Ciampi to Stonestreet Worcester, November 11, 1853, MPA, 221 W 18.
64. Ciampi to Stonestreet, Worcester, February 28 and April 4, 1854, MPA, 222 T 2 and 222 T 4.

exclusivity and the legislature's unwillingness to grant a charter on those terms.[65] The discussion about the charter must have seemed to Ciampi an apt symbol for all the frustration he had faced in the two years since the fire: there was heavy responsibility, yet authority interposed itself somewhat arbitrarily to deny him the desired means of carrying through. Under these circumstances, his success in reopening the school was truly "a struggled one." On his final day as rector, he summarized his experience with touching directness in the House Diary:

Do not be surprised, Dear Reader, that of the things done in the College up to this very day, I recall nothing like this. We have lived according to the rule, but that rule which depends on persons and places makes it practically different each day.

He concluded with a prayer for Peter Blenkinsop, who had been announced that day as his successor: "God grant that all good and happy things come upon him." As Ciampi well appreciated, Blenkinsop would need all the help he could get.

Peter Blenkinsop received word of his appointment during the third week of August 1854. In conveying the news, Charles Stonestreet sent a personal wish for "great courage in your difficulties," and stipulated several priorities. He wanted Blenkinsop to try to eliminate the English, or commercial, course from the curriculum as "humbuggery" that interfered with the traditional content of the *Ratio Studiorum.* He asked Blenkinsop to press Bishop Fitzpatrick to eliminate "the *excluding* clause against protestants. . . . This can only be done however with his full approbation & entire consent." And he requested Blenkinsop "kindly and effectually" to bear Ciampi's record and personal sensitivity in mind: "It will in future be your privilege to treat delicately the acts of him, whom you succeed[,] and to defend his honor. He deserves both favors at your hands."[66] In response, Blenkinsop could only point out that it was "perfectly useless . . . to assure you how unwelcome was the news," and to promise his best effort.[67] The new rector seemed uniquely qualified to succeed Anthony Ciampi. He had been at Holy Cross since 1847 as treasurer and sometime instructor of bookkeeping and English. His quiet, undemonstrative manner contrasted strongly with Ciampi's elegance and sensitivity. During his rectorship he had to spend a fair amount of time and energy raising funds, entrusting the hands-on operation of the school to the faculty and prefects. Patrick Healy found him an "even-tempered, straight-forward

65. Ciampi to Stonestreet, Worcester, March 26, 1854, MPA, 222 T 3.
66. Stonestreet to Blenkinsop, Georgetown, August 20, 1854, MPA, 222 T 7.
67. Blenkinsop to Stonestreet, Worcester, August 24, 1854, MPA, 222 T 9.

man. . . . Under his guidance, our little community goes calmly & cheerfully on." His mannerism and absences made him seen distant to some; yet, as a writer pointed out years later, people appreciated "the honesty of his purpose" and "the patient struggle of this self-sacrificing priest."[68]

The rebuilding project was well along when Blenkinsop took office. With the help of Father Moore's collections, a gift of 1000 francs from the Jesuit general, and the $5000 loan, the main building was completed in 1854, but the interior was left incomplete to avoid raising the debt. In place of the portico, the new structure had an even front, with a porch that jutted out in the center. Those who had seen the College before the fire generally pronounced the reconstruction a grand success. The building was four stories high and contained 42 rooms, plus a chapel, refectory, study room, and two common dormitories for students. The set-up resembled the floor plan of the earlier building, with a furnace room on the lowest floor for the new system of central heat. The absence of a cupola afforded space to accommodate additional students.[69] When the interior was completed in 1855, Patrick Healy praised the new and refurbished furnishings, and Blenkinsop reported that the facility could accommodate up to 150 students, "if we can only get them."[70]

Getting students was a problem for the remainder of the decade. Blenkinsop was disappointed to begin his first year as rector with 32 students, a number that rose only to 42 in October. Nevertheless, the general prosperity of the mid–1850s sustained a rising en-

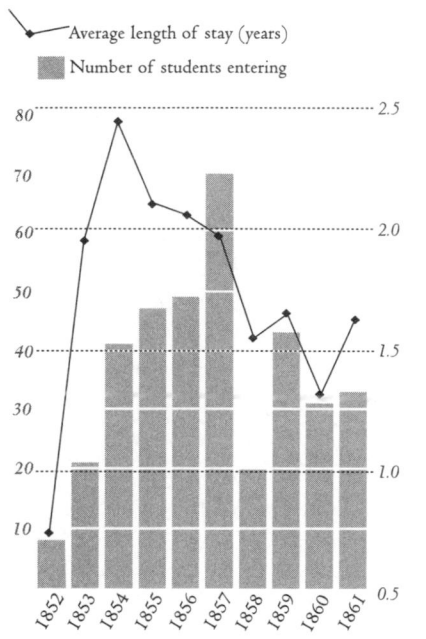

Chart 2.1 New Students and Average Length of Stay, 1852–1861

68. Patrick Healy to [?], Worcester, December 24, 1856, MPA, 224 S 11; *The Purple*, 3: 360–69.

69. Mulledy to [George Fenwick, Worcester, 1854/55], GUA, Holy Cross 1848–78; Peter Beckx to Ciampi, Rome, July 1, 1854, ARSI MD II: 3; Blenkinsop to Fr. Assistant, Worcester, January 14, 1855 ARSI, MD 9-XVIII, 15.

70. Patrick Healy to George Fenwick, Worcester, September 2, 1855, MPA, 223 B; Blenkinsop to George Fenwick, Worcester, May 30, 1855, MPA, 223 B 7.

rollment through 1857. Students in those years tended to reduplicate the pre-fire pattern of remaining at the College for about two years (Chart 2.1). Starting in 1858, a number of factors contributed to a decline in new enrollments, including the effects of the Panic of 1857 and the decline in students enrolling from the South as the Civil War approached. Beginning in 1857, the College published a catalog that included lists of students enrolled in the courses. That gives the first reliable estimate of actual enrollment which reached 114 in 1857–58, dropped to 64 the following year, and rose slowly to 81 in 1860–61. In these years, when the school was struggling to attract and retain students, low enrollments were devastating for the College budget. In the academic year which ended with the fire of 1852, the College had received $20,000 in tuition, room and board revenues to cover expenses of just over $24,000. In 1853–54, tuition revenues brought in only $5300. The $10,000 level of income from tuition was reached only in 1859–60; the pre-fire level was reached and surpassed only in 1864–65. Clearly, then, Blenkinsop had to spend an inordinate amount of time finding money to keep the College afloat. And he had to innovate. In 1857, for instance, he moved the date of the exhibition to early July, where it remained for the rest of the decade: "It will make a long vacation," he reported, "but in these hard times of high prices for all that we eat, a week of vacation will be of some service to our financial concerns."[71]

To his credit, he faced the situation coolly. During his three years as rector, he held total expenses, including interest on loans, below $20,000 per year; with the help of Father Moore, he raised substantial amounts of money to cover the gap between tuition revenues and expenses: $7900 in his first year; $8800 in the second year, when contributions accounted for 47 percent of income; and $4900 in the final year, when a spike in enrollment momentarily boosted tuition income. Total indebtedness fell slightly during his tenure, to $10,400 in the summer of 1857; yet the only actual decrease occurred in his first year, when the College received a windfall from the Healy legacy (Chart 2.2).

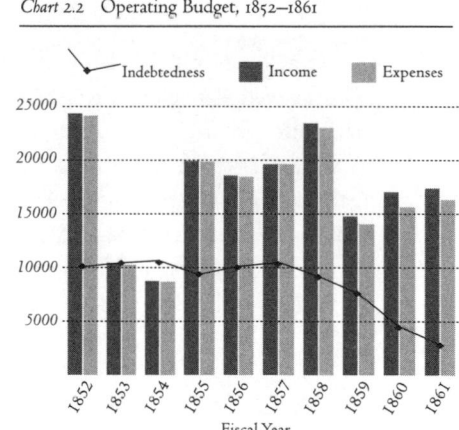

Chart 2.2   Operating Budget, 1852–1861

71. Blenkinsop to Stonestreet, Worcester, May 26, 1857, MPA, 225 S 3.

Meanwhile, the holders of the old debts were impatient, since the reconstruction gave the impression of abundant funds.[72]

During Blenkinsop's administration, campus life gradually picked up. The 1856 catalog promised that "watchful and anxious care" would be given to students during work and play, and much of the responsibility for the policy fell to the Jesuit scholastics who served as teachers and as disciplinary prefects. Despite the specification that students between the ages of nine and fifteen would be accepted for admission, the variation in students' ages remained similar to what it had been before the fire; but the average age, at 15 to 17, was somewhat older—only in 1856 did it slip to 14 (Chart 1.2). This demographic pattern made heavy demands on the prefects for supervision. By the fall of 1856, Patrick Healy was teaching a hard-working class in First Humanities and was president of the reorganized BJF Society for debating. The Philomathea Society for younger debaters and the Dramatic Club were defunct, with no prospect of an early revival. Ice skating again was popular; and other student activities were beginning to fall into a familiar pattern, as Healy reported to George Fenwick:

We have two play rooms. Fr. Blenkinsop has done all he could to make the boys pass their time agreeably, procuring chess, checkers, dice etc. So far it has succeeded admirably. We have had no disturbance of any kind so far—The large playroom is conducted more like a reading-room, than a playroom. The larger boys are very much given to reading & of course we encourage them & direct them. . . . In their spiritual duties they are very punctual—I admitted nine to the Sodality . . . , among them our lay-prefect. There are but few of the large boys, who are still out of its pale.[73]

The economic hardship affected the students directly. On January 19, 1857, classes were canceled during a cold snap because there was no money for coal; the following morning, students were allowed to sleep (and stay warm) until 7 A.M. Under these conditions, warm clothing was essential. Father Blenkinsop's catalog of 1856 specified that, in additional to the regular uniform, students have two suits, six shirts, six pairs of stockings, six handkerchiefs, three pairs of shoes or boots, and an overcoat or cloak. Discipline was generally satisfactory during the Blenkinsop years. The major exception involved a fifteen-year-

72. See the series of letters from Blenkinsop to Stonestreet, dated September 13, October 3, October 19, December 1, December 8 and December 29, 1854; and May 8 and June 23, 1856; MPA, 222 T 11, 222 T 12, 222 T 17, 224 S 3, 224 S 4. According to Albert Foley, a $500 contribution that warded off disaster in December, 1854, was raised with the help of three students who solicited friends and relatives. *Dream*, 71.

73. Healy to [George Fenwick], Worcester, December 24, 1856, MPA, 224 S 11.

old student expelled for wounding a prefect by throwing a piece of roofing slate at him. In 1856, students were allowed, if they wished, to visit their families for four days during Christmas week.[74]

The most noteworthy addition to the staff during Blenkinsop's rectorship was Thomas Mulledy, who was assigned to the College in the fall of 1854 as prefect of studies and spiritual prefect. Although Anthony Ciampi had speculated that "Fr. Mulledy will . . . find H.C. a Cross," Peter Blenkinsop reported that he was pleased with the assignment and the rebuilt school. Qualities of temperament and personality made Mulledy a large presence in a rather small place. He was sixty years old by then, and he took himself seriously enough to enjoy the attention he attracted. Patrick Healy reported that Mulledy rang the students' wake-up bell "in triumph," and that he had to be pulled out of a snowbank on one occasion after getting stuck. Age hadn't mellowed Mulledy; a certain feistiness had always been his trademark, and it intensified as he grew older.[75] In 1856, Mulledy pleaded incompetence when asked to teach Latin and Greek. He hadn't taught Greek for 37 years, and hadn't read 37 consecutive lines of Greek in that time: "I could not decline a Greek noun, or conjugate a Greek verb to save my life. . . . And I feel sure that your Reverence would never willingly expose an old man to be the laughing stock of a parcel of boys." He was willing to teach Latin, but only if released from the obligation to preach to the students.[76] Overextended himself, Patrick Healy complained about Mulledy's less taxing regime: "He spends the whole week preparing for delivery [of] a sermon and instruction written perhaps twenty-five years ago."[77] Later, Healy penned a caricature of Mulledy's routine:

Fr. Thomas, sits quietly in his room, reads over his sermons & hears confessions, with the assiduity of a saint & the patience of a martyr. It is wonderful to see how well he supports his many and difficult labours which he is every day called upon to undergo. They can better be imagined than described. He rejoices that he has run the good race, & can now sit down to table and eat his breakfast with a clear conscience on a fast day—He may be said to be one of those, who Xenophon asserts, to be called, & to be in reality *old men*.[78]

74. HD, November 20–December 1, 1856, January 19–20, 1857.

75. Ciampi to Stonestreet. Worcester, August 14, 1854, MPA, 222 T 6; Blenkinsop to Stonestreet, Worcester, August 24, 1854, MPA, 222 T 9; Patrick Healy to George Fenwick, Worcester, December 11, 1854, MPA, 222 A. Emmett Curran notes that, during his second term as rector of Georgetown (1845–48), Mulledy had a tendency to "alienate the faculty and drive students away by his despotic manner." *Georgetown*, 1:124.

76. Mulledy to Stonestreet, Worcester, July 28, 1856, MPA, 224 S 12.

77. Healy to George Fenwick, Worcester, September 2, 1855, MPA, 223 B

78. Healy to [George Fenwick ?], Worcester, December 24, 1856, MPA, 224 S 11.

Healy's description stressed Mulledy's concern with preaching. He kept a file of sermons, eighty-one of which survive in his papers at Georgetown. He wrote sermons in booklets resembling modern examination bluebooks, carefully noting the date and place of each delivery. The topics ranged from Love of Neighbor, the Mercy of God, and Sorrow for Sins, to Vainglory and "The Truth that Reprehends." "Devotion to the Passion of Christ," originally delivered in Nice in 1840, was offered in two parts to the students of Holy Cross in 1857. Though long (15 pages) by contemporary standards, it is an appealing and learned discourse, filled with allusions to both Testaments as well as to Bonaventure and Augustine. Mulledy reached a pinnacle of sorts at Holy Cross on January 27, 1856, when he presented a 40-minute assault against idleness to his young audience. The introduction offered a general principle: "It is absolutely necessary to give not only to every occupation its time, but also to every portion of time its occupation." Idleness, he warned, had dire consequences:

How many youths once seemed Angels in their morals, so respectful to their elders, so frequent at the sacred table, so modest in conversation, so fervent in piety, so assiduous in every practice of devotion. You now see them proud and haughty to their very parents, irreverent and disrespectful in the church, strangers to the sacraments, dissolute in their conduct, foul and filthy in their language; whence a catastrophe so mournful; whence? from idleness, my beloved friends, from idleness. Unemployed, unoccupied, they pass their days from visit to visit, from shop to shop[,] at one time walking at their ease in the public streets, at another associated with congenial spirits, murmuring against their neighbors: in the evening in parties until late in the night, the morning in bed asleep to a late hour. From a life so idle, so useless, what else can be expected but a flood of vices: gambling, debts, amours, detractions, dissoluteness, and whatever else is worse and more abominable.

Mulledy cited Thomas of Villanova's characterization of David—"in war a saint, in idleness an adulterer and a murderer." As a remedy, Mulledy proposed industriousness. The sermon concluded with a prayer to Jesus "that treating myself always—as the sinner that I really am, I may never seek any other repose, but that, which thou has prepared for every penitent heart in thy kingdom."

As Mulledy pored over his sermons, Peter Blenkinsop was trying to contend with an outbreak of anti-Catholicism associated with the overwhelming Know-Nothing victory in the state elections of 1854. Historian John Mulkern has argued that the movement was a populist reaction against the Bay State's "corrupt and unresponsive party system." The nucleus of the new party's leaders were nativist extremists, but the recruitment of so many to the standard tempered the movement, so that bigotry was "not the major part" of its character.[79] The political upheaval of 1854 elected an inexperienced, one-party leg-islature in which all of the senators and most of the representatives were in their first term. These were the men who created the "Joint Special Commit-tee on the Inspection of Nunneries and Convents" to examine Catholic insti-tutions in Massachusetts. Mulkern found that the motives for establishing the committee were varied.

A bizarre mix of concern for quality education, prurient curiosity piqued by centuries-old gossip, and a puritan penchant for minding other people's business, the Nunnery Committee, as it was popularly called, had a twofold mission: to assess the quality of parochial school education and to pry into Catholic institutions suspected of holding women against their will or of concealing "arms and instruments of war."[80]

Holy Cross felt the impact of Know-Nothingism in July of 1854, when a rumor circulated that weapons and ammunition were being sent by rail to the College "to be kept up to the day appointed for the revolution of the Cath-olics." Ciampi reported:

Some believed it, but the Mayor went to the Depot at the arrival of the Train, in order more solemnly to belie the Knownothings, I presume. —It is spoken of a general em-poisonment to be effected tomorrow by the Irish Servant Girls. Some ladies have al-ready protested, they will not drink any Tea.[81]

The following March, the Nunnery Committee visited Holy Cross. Since Peter Blenkinsop was away, the seven members were conducted through the building by Thomas Mulledy, who must have been in rare form for the encounter. Hav-ing found nothing suspicious, they "excused themselves for their silly visit, by saying that their tables were groaning under the weight of petitions about Catholics, and they wished to come and see and report to the Legislature." Be-fore leaving Worcester, they spent almost $100 of public money on food and en-tertainment. During another visit at a school run by the Sisters of Notre Dame in Roxbury, a committee member made indecent comments to one of the sis-ters. The committee's indiscreet junketing, no less than their violation of civil rights, helped to erode the party's popularity. In the elections of 1855, the Know-Nothing Party lost considerable support throughout the state.[82]

79. John R. Mulkern, *The Know-Nothing Party in Massachusetts: The Rise and Fall of a People's Movement* (Boston: Northeastern University Press, 1990), 86–87, 175, 178; Brooke, *Heart*, 385

80. Mulkern, *Know-Nothing*, 88, 103.

81. Ciampi to [Stonestreet ?], Worcester, July 2, 1854, GUA, Holy Cross, 1848–78.

82. Blenkinsop to Stonestreet, Worcester, March 3, 1855, MPA, 223 S 1; Meagher and Grattan, *Spires*, 96–97; Mulkern, *Know-Nothing*, 117; Brooke, *Heart*, 385; O'Connor, *Fitzpatrick's*,

Although Peter Blenkinsop suffered no further harassment from civil authorities, his administration eventually attracted criticism from Jesuits. At first, he seemed to be holding his own. He successfully resisted Stonestreet's requests to eliminate "the Commercial humbug" from the curriculum. Father Mulledy supported the resistance, citing personal remarks from Jan Roothaan that such courses could be justified "to prevent Catholic boys from becoming driven, by necessity, into protestant schools."[83] But Blenkinsop's frequent absences from the College, particularly to visit his brother in Chicopee, attracted criticism. Early in 1857 the general raised the matter with Stonestreet, along with a list of other complaints forwarded in annual letters written by the house consultors. The list included taciturnity, late sleeping, fiscal mismanagement, and an unwillingness to consult on College business.[84] Taken out of context, the comments seem harsh and out of step with the general favor Blenkinsop enjoyed among the Jesuits. But at this point, the criticism was probably intended as a signal. Blenkinsop was then in his third year as rector—the point at which, in ordinary Jesuit practice, a serious review is undertaken to decide whether to extend or terminate the appointment. In this case, it seems likely that the consultors were sufficiently concerned about Blenkinsop's capacity for leadership to believe that a change was in order, so they emphasized his weaknesses. The problems at Holy Cross were severe, and although Blenkinsop hadn't lost ground in addressing them, he hadn't made much headway.

In Rome, Peter Beckx was also concerned about Holy Cross, and his tentativeness about the school's future added to the general context of uncertainty. His election as Jesuit general in July 1853 took place just after the decision to re-open Holy Cross. Over the next few years, he kept himself posted on the College and on the ongoing interplay between the struggling college in Worcester and the prospective college in Boston. He considered the situation

---

153–57. Orestes Brownson derided the committee for hypocrisy. *Brownson's Quarterly Review*, 3:397–401. As far away as St. Louis, an anonymous letter in the press berated the committee for its ignorance: "as if to proclaim to the world the full extent of their school-boy ignorance, these men actually supposed that the good Fathers of the Society of Jesus were women!" Meighan, "Nativism," iii.

83. Stonestreet to Blenkinsop, Georgetown, August 14, 1855, MPA, 223 S 3a; Mulledy to Stonestreet, Frederick, September 6, 1852, MPA, 220 M 2.

84. Mulledy to Stonestreet, Worcester, June 7, 1856, MPA, 224 S 8; Beckx to Stonestreet, Rome, February 7, 1857, ARSI, MD Reg. II, 21–22. Apparently, many of the absences involved get-away visits to his brother, William, who was pastor of the Catholic parish in Chicopee from 1849 to 1864. William Byrne et al., *History of the Catholic Church in the New England States*, (2 vols.; Boston: The Hurd and Everts Co., 1899), 2:655.

in the summer of 1854, when Bishop Fitzpatrick called on him in Rome to discuss both projects and hear the new general's strong support for the projected school in Boston.[85] In 1856, the general considered the matter again. By then the Holy Cross situation struck him as a dilemma:

I strongly doubt whether this College can be preserved. The illustrious bishop wishes it preserved but Ours cannot too easily fulfill the desires of the bishop without foreseeing the evils and difficulties which our Society will have to endure in the future.

He could offer Holy Cross only an unenthusiastic endorsement: the Jesuits would have to stay if they would give offense to the diocesan clergy by abandoning the College so soon after collecting funds.[86] Later in 1856 and again in 1857, he stated his willingness to authorize a school in Boston only if Holy Cross would not be harmed; but he was still hesitant about sustaining Holy Cross. He had reports that some Maryland Province men regarded assignment to Worcester as a form of exile, even though they recognized that "no other college promises greater hope of vocations to the Society."[87] By then, the question of Blenkinsop's continuation in office was part of this larger picture.

In the summer of 1857, Anthony Ciampi was appointed to succeed Blenkinsop. According to one report, the Jesuit community was "rather gloomy and down-hearted at the prospect before them."[88] Father Blenkinsop was transferred to Philadelphia and Thomas Mulledy returned to Georgetown. The written records offer little information about the shake-up. Ciampi's personality had some controversial features, but he was valued in the province as a good Jesuit who dutifully complied even with directives he disagreed with, and who had engineered the school's revival under difficult circumstances. When his first term as Holy Cross rector ended in 1854, Ciampi had gone immediately to Chicopee, where he ministered to cholera victims until he contracted the illness himself. Afterwards, he had been assigned to Bangor for two years at his own request to do pastoral work, and then to Holy Trinity parish

85. Beckx to Stonestreet, Rome, July 1, 1854, ARSI, MD Reg. II, 2–3.

86. Beckx to Stonestreet, Rome, April 10, 1856, ARSI, MD Reg. II, 15.

87. Beckx to Stonestreet, Rome, October 31, 1856, January 3 and February 7, 1857, ARSI, MD Reg. II, 19–20, 22; Curran, "Troubled Nation," 41–42. Four postulants left Holy Cross for the Jesuit novitiate in Federick in the summer of 1856. Stonestreet told Blenkinsop that the event prompted him to "act generously" toward Holy Cross. In a postscript, he told him to "write a letter *soon* to Fr Genl & let him know of yr. postulants. . . . It will do him good." Stonestreet to Blenkinsop, Georgetown, June 27, 1856, MPA, 224 S 6.

88. B. F. Maguire to Stonestreet, Worcester, July 31, 1857, MPA, 225 S 6.

in Georgetown.[89] Now, he had been summoned back to Worcester to solve economic problems that his predecessor had found insoluble. He assumed office on August 15. Nine days later, the Panic of 1857 plunged the nation into a brief but frightening financial crisis.

Ciampi wrote to Stonestreet sixteen times before the end of the calendar year. Each letter was a little darker as he brooded about the possibility that the College would not survive. The institution's well-being was being jeopardized by two distinct problems: the size and quality of the faculty, and the ongoing financial crisis. Ciampi had some control over the first problem; the second he could only endure. Peter Blenkinsop had coped with vexing circumstances through physical absence and interpersonal distancing, but Anthony Ciampi was put together differently. Incapable of insulating himself emotionally from the problems and their consequences, he came to terms with his pain and frustration by confiding his misery to Charles Stonestreet as to a father. The intensity of the correspondence is evidence of the price he paid in guiding the school through such a difficult passage.

"The College needs fostering," Ciampi told Stonestreet in August; he couldn't achieve that goal without assistance. He needed Jesuits as proctors and teachers; but, with only eight dollars in the till, he needed money most of all. He couldn't even afford the fare of the three scholastics being re-assigned from Georgetown to Holy Cross.[90] As enrollment unexpectedly surged beyond 90 during September, he pleaded again for more teachers. Overworked Patrick Healy was the only qualified instructor in English. Several others were weak, even unqualified. Students in Rhetoric and Poetry were complaining about being combined into one class, and Bishop Fitzpatrick was insisting on "our obligation of doing justice to the Boys and Parents." That was a point Ciampi himself echoed: "For God's sake, do not throw this letter aside. I am in the greatest difficulty. The College name begins to be reestablished."[91] Ston-

89. Ciampi to Stonestreet, Chicopee, September 10, 1854, MPA, 222 T 10; Ciampi to Stonestreet, Bangor, December 17, 1854, 222 S 11.

90. Ciampi to Stonestreet, Worcester, August 26 and 29, 1857, MPA, 225 S.

91. Ciampi to Stonestreet, Worcester, September 6 and 20, 1857, MPA, 225 S. James Healy had voiced his misgivings about the caliber of the faculty three years earlier, when he returned to Boston after his ordination. To George Fenwick, he wrote: "Although I do not of course join in the hue and cry against your fathers, yet it does seem to me that the Holy Cross has been somewhat badly treated by your authorities. A College which had commenced so well, which the Bishop loved so much, to be left in ruins for two years, and to be left with so scant a faculty. It looks certainly rather hard. True, there are enough in numbers; but I should like to see a more experienced professor than Patrick there to form the course of studies, by leading up the first class." Boston, September 7, 1854, in Foley, *Dream*, 56.

estreet added two teachers and three lay brothers to the Holy Cross community, though Ciampi claimed that was not enough.

Disciplinary supervision of students was a chronic problem that year. Ciampi particularly clashed with two of the scholastics. One lacked the capacity to teach and had failed to gain the students' respect; the other was too harsh. "There is *number* beneath our roof"; Ciampi told Stonestreet, "there is no gladness. There is roughness, strictness, severity, punishing. I have no sufficient help."[92] By December, he was complaining that prefects were flogging students, against his orders and the wishes of their parents.[93] Always, he was mindful of Ignatius's strong stand against corporal punishment from Jesuits because it weakened the bonds of affection:

I dislike from my heart the constant severity & ungentleness, by which the Students are controlled. Under unkind disciplinarians the Boys must grow rough & unmannered. The prevailing principle seems to be, that the bad boys must be out of the College, and unfold its doors [sic] to only the good ones. I maintain that Colleges are instituted to *reform* & inform youths. Conseqly. that wayward ones are to be won & fostered in preference to the others. I began to object to such manners & rules, which I thought to disagree with the educational spirit of the Society. I desired & aimed that they should captivate to thems[elves] the love & not the fear of the Students.[94]

In February, a prefect "floored a Boy and hurt him very remarkably"; parents were beginning to express concern.[95] The stalemate persisted to the end of the year, when the offending scholastics were reassigned.

The problems with teaching and discipline emerged at the same time that the effects of the national economic crisis were being felt. In many of his letters, Ciampi turned from one set of problems to the other, descending hopelessly toward despair about the College's future and his capacity to lead. In October, he reported that "there is no money sent because there is no money in the market." He had been reduced to buying sugar and flour on a weekly basis, and already owed $1300 for coal. The prospect that the college would be "obliged to break up" was becoming very real.[96] Ciampi's gloom deepened as

92. Ciampi to Stonestreet, Worcester, October 24, 1857, MPA, 225 S.

93. Ciampi to Stonestreet, December 14, 1857, MPA, 225 S. The offending scholastic, Bernard Toale, was a 26-year-old Irish immigrant. He left Holy Cross in 1858 to complete his studies for the priesthood. After ordination, he was assigned to pastoral work in Virginia and Maryland. *WL* 18: 387–88.

94. Ciampi to Stonestreet, Worcester, January 7, 1858, MPA, 225 K; O'Malley, *First Jesuits*, 230.

95. Ciampi to Stonestreet, Worcester, February 24, 1858, MPA, 225 K.

96. Ciampi to Stonestreet, Worcester, October 24, 1857, MPA, 225 S.

winter approached. On December 8, he wrote another agonized letter about "my own cross on the hill. . . . I am penniless—and every source, where to draw money, is shut and dried against me."[97] By Christmas, Ciampi was desperate. He sent the boys home early to save the expense of boarding them. In describing the state of Holy Cross during that unforgettable winter, he disclosed his personal anguish:

In [an earlier letter], I spoke of my financial distress, and of my serious thoughts of proposing a dissolution. H.C. cannot stand. It has been plunged into debt too deeply to be raised out by the annual pension of even more than one hundred Boys. The Servants' wages are still unpaid—and so many old standing Bills. At present, we are supported by the charity of Protestant dealers. The Butcher, the Fishman, the Coalman cannot get one cent from us. I cannot do justice to the comm[unit]y. because I am *utterly unable.* There is *not a provision of any sort in the house*—Flour is nearly out.

I do all in my power to collect our dues — I quarrel — I make extra labor in answering missionary calls, to get a little profit for the College. Success is seldom encouraging. You allow me to borrow. From whom shall I borrow? Moreover, do you know they ask ten & twelve per cent? Raise the pension to $200 or 175. It will do us injury. The Colle[ge] has no dependance but on these poor Irish washerwomen & railroad & canal or factory & cart men. They can hardly pay $150 per ann[um]—and not without leaving their Boys as meanly supplied as can be tolerated. Perhaps, the admitting of Protestants would give us a strong life. But the Bishop objects to it. How[eve]r I shall urge my want with him at the first opportunity.

Meanwhile I am wearing out mind and body. I feel as miserable as man can ever stand. It grieves me to my heart's core to see the uncomfortable treatment dealt out to the Comm[unit]y—I know not what to do to relieve them.—My constant prayer is to beg bread for my family, and money to do justice to our Creditors.—Sheer necessity has prompted me to let the Boys (most of them at least) off at Christmas. The shutting of so many mouths will give us a chance to recruit a little. Three or four of us will have a Missionary Campaign—and may bring home some spoils, besides their own spiritual gain. Christmas in the College, will be as dreary as the bleak top of our hill.[98]

The New Year brought no relief. On January 7, Ciampi reported that, despite some monetary gains from pastoral work during the Christmas season, the treasurer had only $1.50 on hand and 25 cents in the bank. By the end of the month, he was beginning to fear that he would not be able to collect a large portion of second-semester tuition "because, all manufactures having been suspended, the Parents of most of my Boys, are out of funds. . . . I cannot squeeze one red copper from their hands. If I send them off, I shall lose

97. Ciampi to Stonestreet, Boston, December 8, 1857, MPA, 225 S.
98. Ciampi to Stonestreet, Worcester, December, 1857, MPA, 225 S.

still more." To save coal, he had stopped heating his sitting room, a gesture that seems to have been directed toward some of the Jesuits who were skeptical about the severity of the crisis. Meanwhile, notes were falling due. In January he had to ask Stonestreet for a new loan of $400; in February he borrowed $500 more from a local bank.[99]

Then, unexpectedly, the anguished letters came to an end. There were no more complaints about money, no further expressions of apprehension about abandoning the school. Gradually, the College benefited from the general economic improvement in 1858. Although tuition revenues dropped by more than $1600 from the previous academic year, Ciampi and the other Jesuits succeeded in raising $2700 more in collections and gifts. During the next three years, tuition revenues rose gradually, until they were providing more than 65 percent of the annual budget. During the same years, Ciampi achieved a major reduction in the college debt, from about $9300 in 1858 to $3100 in 1861 (Chart 2.2). Ciampi was a good manager and succeeded in a crucial area where his predecessors had failed. The record offers few clues about how he achieved the reduction; his comments about diminished lifestyle indicate one approach; longer vacations were another measure; and there were one-time helps, like the decision not to print a college catalog in 1857–58.[100] Clearly, Ciampi's method involved much more than pinching pennies; but just as clearly, he found no measure too small to be important in the struggle for solvency. By frugality, begging, apostolic labor, and hounding the College debtors, he brought the debt down.

Besides the slow improvement in financial standing, a second factor may have prompted Ciampi to alter his tone: in Rome and Georgetown, his alarming reports had prompted another discussion about closing the school. In the Maryland Province, Charles Stonestreet's term as provincial ended in April 1858, when Burchard Villiger, a Swiss immigrant, was designated to succeed him. The change provided another opportunity to re-examine the question of schools in Worcester and Boston. Peter Beckx took the initiative in March 1858, when he told Ciampi that his January report had caused "great grief of soul." He promised to seek remedies with the help of the provincial. Presumably he had the new provincial in mind.[101] In May, Beckx asked Villiger to investigate whether the College's general condition—the poverty of the house

99. Ciampi to Stonestreet, Worcester, January 7, 22, 31, and February 24, 1858, MPA, 225 K.

100. Devitt, "Holy Cross," *WL* 64:224.

101. Beckx to Ciampi, Rome, March, 1858, ARSI, MD Reg. II, 30–31.

and the overwhelming debts—warranted re-evaluation of the Society's commitment.[102] Villiger asked his province consultors to report their views directly to the general. Among them, Joseph Aschwanden offered a devastating analysis, even though he admitted that, when he had tried to close the school in 1852, Roothaan had written "in paternal admonition, disapproving my acting in this business." Nevertheless, he was convinced that his instinct had been correct. Holy Cross, he insisted, would be "a perpetual headache to this Province" because it had been "imposed on this Province" by Bishop Fenwick, "with such conditions and in such a location that it could only be good for the Diocese of Boston and no where else and not for Our Society." He saw no hope for improvement. The best solution was to close Holy Cross and transfer the operation to Boston, "but I have little hope the President would consent to this."[103]

By the end of the summer, Beckx had the impression that the new provincial and his consultors were inclined to abandon Holy Cross. Because their analysis clashed with earlier reports that Holy Cross and a day school in Boston could co-exist, he asked for more information, including the specific reasons why John Fitzpatrick was unwilling to release the Jesuits from their commitment to Holy Cross.[104] By November, his mind was almost made up: "I am becoming more and more convinced that the Worcester College must be closed down before the new Boston College opens."[105] But that was precisely the point Bishop Fitzpatrick had always refused to grant; moreover, Ciampi was beginning to turn the financial problems around. By the spring of 1859, he had reduced the debt by 25 percent. Ultimately, his hard-earned success and Bishop Fitzpatrick's good faith in promoting the establishment of Boston College[106] turned away this final threat to suppress Holy Cross.

As questions about the existence of the Holy Cross receded from consideration, Anthony Ciampi himself became an issue. Americans objected to his Roman manners, and his criticism of their pedagogical methods struck some as overbearing. His frequent absences on College business raised eyebrows. And there were questions about his association with women. The major cause of consternation on the latter point was his relationship with Clara G. Thompson of Pomfret Center, Connecticut, who was converted to Catholicism by

102. Beckx to Villiger, Rome, May 14, 1858, ARSI, MD Reg. II, 39.

103. Aschwanden to Beckx, Georgetown, July 29, 1858, ARSI, MD 9-XVIII, 16.

104. Beckx to Villiger, Rome, September 1, 1858, ARSI, MD Reg. II, 40.

105. Beckx to Villiger, Rome, November 27, 1858, ARSI, MD Reg. II, 43.

106. The college building in Boston was completed in 1859, and a charter obtained in 1863. The school opened in 1864, when the first Jesuits were assigned there as teachers. Donovan et al., *History*, 20–45.

Ciampi in 1864. He sustained her for a period of time against the opposition of many of her friends and relatives, encouraged her as a writer for Catholic periodicals, and wrote her many letters.[107] Whether fair or not, the complaints against Ciampi were real, and Beckx took steps to deal with them. He sent Ciampi a paternal letter in the fall of 1858, telling him that, despite his good intentions in making excursions, his first duty was to be present in the community and set an example; he was to offer charitable direction to poor teachers with an eye to their improvement.[108]

By the end of 1858, Villiger decided that Ciampi would have to be replaced. But Beckx defended him after receiving a personal letter from Ciampi to point out that Jesuits and externs all knew that the normal term of office in the Society was three years, unless the superior was performing poorly. At Holy Cross, he had worked very hard, and major difficulties had been overcome. He had put an end to his long absences, and he thought the community was happy. To replace him under these conditions would be an undeserved humiliation. Beckx summarized the letter for Villiger and asked whether "we should permit this companion and brother to be so afflicted and humiliated." Ultimately he left the decision to Villiger, but he had signaled his mind.[109] The Maryland provincial acquiesced. The fact was, Holy Cross was growing stronger. And almost everybody recognized that, whatever his human failings, Ciampi was indispensable in getting the college on its feet.[110] In the end, he even received an unexpected vindication when his second term as rector was extended to four years. Ciampi's final year was connected with the decision of Father Beckx in November 1859 to appoint Felix Sopranis to be Visitor[111] of all North American Jesuits. His authority superseded the normal governance structure in the various provinces until he completed his work early in 1861. Sopranis praised Ciampi's work and recommended that James Clark succeed him in due course. Beckx accepted the plan. After Father Sopranis concluded his work, Angelo Paresce, a Neapoli-

107. William L. Lucey (ed.), "A Letter to a Friend," *Records of the American Catholic Historical Society of Philadelphia*, 66 (December, 1955), 239–46.

108. Beckx to Ciampi, Rome, September 25, 1858, ARSI, MD Reg. II, 42–43.

109. Beckx to Villiger, Rome, December 18, 1858, February 26 and March 5, 1859, ARSI, MD Reg. II, 44, 48, 50.

110. Villiger to Beckx, Baltimore, April 16, 1859, ARSI, MD V, 37–38.

111. Within the structures of Jesuit governance, the general may appoint a "visitor" to inspect the houses and works of the Society personally and to make recommendations to Rome. The Constitutions (490) specify that the responsibility for selecting a college rector is vested "in the general or in someone else to whom he entrusts it, such as the provincial or a visitor; but the confirmation of the appointment will always belong to the general."

tan immigrant, was named to the office of provincial. He quickly facilitated the appointment of James Clark to Worcester.[112]

Life at the College during Ciampi's second administration continued the familiar pattern, with only minor changes. In 1858, a lengthy recess was introduced at Christmas. The following year, the school uniform was dropped because of the objections of parents who couldn't afford them. When one of the scholastics attempted to organize a military company among the students as "a fine chance to introduce the old uniform again," Ciampi forbade it.[113] During Ciampi's second term, Stonestreet's long-standing request that the curriculum be more exclusively classical was finally implemented. In 1858, the "ecclesiastical" course was removed from the catalog, and in 1860 enough stability had been achieved to drop the "commercial" course as well.[114] Henceforth, Holy Cross would stand as a liberal arts college patterned on the classical humanism of the *Ratio Studiorum*. The size of the faculty remained at about nine, with one or two lay professors supplementing the Jesuit staff. Because no students above Second Humanities had been admitted in 1853, no baccalaureate degrees were awarded until 1858. That year's five graduates were the first since 1852.[115]

Although circumstances often forced him to be penurious, Anthony Ciampi had strong paternal qualities, which he enjoyed displaying whenever he could. On holidays he delighted in stretching the budget for a feast: the boys were given cider, cake, and apples on the eve of Thanksgiving in 1858, and a "grand dinner" the next day; in June of 1859, Ciampi noted that the students were given peas, two kinds of meat, and ice cream to celebrate the confirmation of six students. Ciampi's fatherly sensitivity also appears in the account he wrote about the death and funeral of a student, August Seiberlich of Philadelphia, "the first who from the founding of this College was summoned as we hope from the buildings of the College to heaven." Seiberlich died in September of 1860 after a short illness with typhoid fever. To help the students come to terms with their grief, Ciampi arranged a meeting for the boarding students in the large study hall. They voiced their feelings, then signed a statement that was sent to their classmate's parents and also published in the paper. Faculty members also appreciated Ciampi's compassion. Fifty years afterwards, P. W. Boenisch, who served on the faculty from 1859 to 1861,

112. Sopranis to Beckx, St. Louis, July 28, 1860, ARSI, MD V, 48; *WL* 8: 186–90. Sopranis visited Holy Cross from December 2 to 11, 1859. HD.

113. HD, Edward Henchy to Buchard Villiger, Worcester, October 9, 1859, and Ciampi to Villiger, Worcester, October 18, 1859, MPA, 226 T 1.

114. Meagher and Grattan, *Spires*, 127–28.

115. HD.

called Ciampi "a fatherly friend of mine. His letters to me are my *most precious souvenir.*"[116]

During the first half of 1861, Ciampi fretted about the coming of the Civil War as he prepared for a new administration at the school. In April, he wrote that a late snowstorm was "as bad as Abe Lincoln to this country"; in July he complained about food prices and the scarcity of cider—"not a drop of it will remain for ours and scarcely enough to treat the second Division or Company of the Boston Regiment."[117] The change of rectors was announced on August 13. Noting the event in the House Diary, Ciampi added: "May he be blessed by the spirit with everything good, successful, and happy." To Paresce, he confided his regret that he had disappointed his community as rector: "I am gratified to hear from you that some satisfaction has been given to the Fathers & to the Scholastics. For myself, I have been fretting & heavy hearted all the time, thinking that they were no-wise contented."[118]

In fact, there was plenty of contentment on Pakachoag, whether Ciampi realized it or not. Among those who appreciated him was Father Edmund Young, who served on the faculty from 1859 to 1861. A native of Maine, Young was delighted to be in New England at Holy Cross:

There is no hill on which grass grows to be compared with Holy Cross Hill. Tis the gem of hills. You may talk till your tongue cleaves to the roof of your mouth about the South . . . and I will not believe you. Give me the laughing hills of New England and the pious Yankees with all their honesty[,] enterprise and unimpeachable integrity. Give me plenty of pork and beans and pumpkin pie by the square yard . . . a good library, good superiors and good boys such as we have here and the Union may slide for all I care. . . .

I wish you would say a hail Mary every day for me that I with meekness may bear the good fortune of dwelling among the everlasting hills of New England.[119]

A year later, his enthusiasm for the College was unabated. Young called Holy Cross "the best college in the Union" and praised it for its small size and Catholic atmosphere: "Oh how I pity those institutions who are doomed to afford spiritual and intellec[tual] pabulum [sic] to three hundred students some of whom have neither fear of God nor regard for man."[120]

116. P.W. Boenisch to Thomas Murphy, St. Paul, September 22, 1910, ACHC, 12.15; HD.

117. Ciampi to Villiger, Worcester, April 3, 1861, MPA, 226 J; Ciampi to Paresce, Worcester, July 12 and 24, 1861, MPA, 226 J.

118. Ciampi to Paresce, Worcester, August 2, 1861, MPA, 226 J.

119. Young to James Clark, Worcester, October 10, 1859, GUA, Clark Papers. On Edmund Young, see WL 69: 348–49.

120. Young to James Clark, Worcester, October 7, 1860, GUA, Clark Papers.

Exuberance notwithstanding, Young's letters are interesting on two counts. For one thing, they make no mention of the problems that had plagued Anthony Ciampi; the skies had brightened considerably in twenty months. Although Ciampi's self-effacing character prevented him from claiming credit, the happiness Young and others were experiencing at Holy Cross had come largely through his effort, his persistence, his economic skill, his impassioned management of the reopening. Appreciation of Ciampi's achievement was implicit in Young's letters: the province was small enough, the personalities familiar enough, and the gossip common enough to disclose what was being communicated when a mature Jesuit expressed his pleasure in being at Holy Cross. Apart from their content, the letters were important for another reason: their recipient was James Clark. He had the benefit of their optimism as he prepared to lead a school whose pains of rebirth were gone but not forgotten.

CHAPTER THREE

The First Holy Cross,
1861–1889

ON THE SURFACE, the Holy Cross that James Clark encountered when he assumed the rectorship in 1861 resembled the school he had known as a faculty member in 1850. The appearance of Fenwick Hall had been altered, but its proportions were essentially the same. The academic program and the daily routine were more or less as he had left them; tuition was still $150; graduates received Georgetown degrees; and Bishop Fitzpatrick remained adamant about Catholic exclusivity. But for all that, some things had changed. The end of the debate about keeping the school and the easing of economic problems gave Clark and his successors a freedom of action that their predecessors lacked. Free from the consuming burden of establishing and defending the College, they could develop the school according to the Jesuit model. James Clark's rectorship opened an era of fulfillment—a period of almost three decades during which the physical plant expanded, enrollment rose, the humanistic curriculum of the *Ratio* was successfully asserted, and the graduates, including the large number of priests, began to make their mark on the larger world. These years vindicated Bishop Fenwick's dream. Holy Cross came into its own at last.

James Clark was born in Pennsylvania in 1809 and attended West Point. After his graduation in 1829, he was posted to Louisiana, where he became interested in Catholicism. He resigned from the service in 1830, was baptized four years later, and joined the Jesuits in 1844.[1] Besides his year at Holy Cross

---

1. Biographical information on James Clark may be found in the *Official Register of the Officers and Cadets of the U.S. Military Academy, June, 1829*; and in *Biographical Register of the Officers and Graduates of the U.S. Military Academy* (Boston and New York: Houghton-Mifflin & Co., 1891). See also his obituary in the *Catholic Mirror*, ACHC, 12.6-1; William Barber, Father James

in 1849–50, Clark had spent most of his Jesuit days at Georgetown as a professor of mathematics, as college treasurer, and, from 1859 to 1861, as vice-president. A stern man who never lost his military bearing, Clark had a dark complexion and short black hair and spoke with a loud voice. According to one account, "a knock at his door was answered by a thunderous 'come in!' which sometimes startled the timid"; yet his kindness put visitors at ease.[2]

By the time Father Clark assumed his duties in Worcester, the Civil War was under way. A classmate of Generals Robert E. Lee and Joseph Johnston, Clark felt the presence of the war strongly. In 1862, he implemented President Lincoln's proclamation of a day of fasting. His first annual report to Peter Beckx included a reference to the country's "troubles . . . 700,000 men in the field, waging civil war with an other army nearly as large"; but the campus was tranquil and there were only two boys from the South.[3] Although Clark seemed relieved that war had not disrupted the routine, one Jesuit scholastic was surprised by the apathy of the students early in the war:

It really is striking what little interest the boys take in the war. They seem to have no enthusiasm at all. . . . I can assure you if you may judge of the sentiments of the parents by the sons, there are not many here who would prosecute this war.[4]

A year later, another observer commented on the "perfect charity" that prevailed among the students: "No North or South this year. Of course they are all for the Union." Among the Jesuits, there was little discussion of "politics." That was a hard necessity within the Maryland Province because of the mixed backgrounds of the members. When he assumed office as provincial, Angelo Paresce asked all members of the province to avoid "every spirit of party"; he even directed superiors to monitor outgoing mail in the interest of safeguarding harmony.[5]

The military aspects of the war finally caught the enthusiasm of the students during 1863, when plans were laid to form a military company known as the Holy Cross Cadets, with Father Clark as honorary major. The group studied the manual of arms and contacted Governor John Andrew about getting

---

Clark—Holy Cross' Civil War President," in *The Purple*, 55:482–91; and Meagher and Grattan, *Spires*, 99–100.

2. *Catholic Mirror* obituary [1885], ACHC, 12.6-1.

3. Clark to Beckx, Worcester, January 26, 1862, ARSI, MD 9-XVIII, 17.

4. Michael Byrnes to Edward Devitt, Worcester, October 4, 1862, GUA, Holy Cross, 1843–47.

5. William Scanlan to Edward Devitt, Worcester [Fall 1863], GUA, Holy Cross, 1843–47; Paresce to Beckx, Frederick, April 22, 1861, and Baltimore, November 26, 1861, ARSI, MD 8-V, 1 and 8-V, 7, cited in Curran, "Troubled Nation," 52–53.

muskets. When they learned that firearms could be issued only on condition that the group would be subject to mobilization, they voted to disband. Apparently, the young age of some of the members influenced the outcome.[6] The draft posed only a minor inconvenience, because so many of the students were underage. Brother Patrick Lynch was drafted, then excused because he was not a citizen; the other Jesuits were spared in the draft lottery of July 1863, as Clark reported: "None of the rest of our community drew a prize, and consequently we are spared the expense of paying $300."[7] One faculty member, Father Joseph O'Hagan, left the College in September 1861 to serve as chaplain of the Excelsior Brigade of New York. Of former Holy Cross students, 28 served in the Civil War. Five fought for the Confederacy, including Edward Scott, the College's first student. Eight Holy Cross men died in the war.[8]

Wartime conditions began to alter the composition of the student body, as Chart 3.1 indicates. About 91 percent of students fell within the graph's geographic categories before the Civil War, and about 96 percent afterwards. The proportion from the slaveholding part of the country stood at 19 percent before the war, with the largest numbers coming from Maryland, the District of Columbia, and Louisiana; after that date, the proportion shrank to about 2 percent. The proportion of students from three Middle Atlantic states—New York, New Jersey, and Pennsylvania—also declined, from 21 percent before the Civil War to about 14 percent in the 1870s and 1880s. Foreign students followed the same pattern. Before the war, they constituted about 11 percent, principally from Ireland, Canada, Cuba, and other Latin American countries; afterwards they declined to about 2 percent.[9] After the Civil War, Holy Cross drew most of its students from New England; the proportion of students from those six states rose above 75 percent after 1870. The tendency of the College to become more regional reflected both the effects of the war and the expansion of the Catholic and Jesuit educational network throughout the country.[10]

6. William Scanlan to Edward Devitt, Worcester [Fall, 1863], GUA, Holy Cross, 1843–47; William H. Rogers, "A Few Reminiscences of Holy Cross Days a Generation Ago," in *The Purple*, 5:64.

7. Clark to Paresce, Worcester, July 22 and 24, 1863, MPA, 227 T 5 and 6. Under the terms of the Enrollment Act of March 1863, a draft lottery was conducted in July of the same year. The legislation allowed those whose number was drawn to avoid service by paying a commutation fee of $300. James M. McPherson, *Battle Cry of Freedom* (New York: Ballantine Books, 1989), 600–601.

8. For lists of Holy Cross men in the Civil War, see Meagher and Grattan, *Spires*, 101–02, and *The Purple*, 3:20–45.

9. Meagher and Grattan, *Spires*, 78–79.

10. During the 1870s, the Jesuits opened new colleges or universities in Buffalo, Chicago, Jersey City, New York, Detroit, and Omaha. In the 1880s, Milwaukee, Cleveland, and Spokane

The economic prosperity that arose from the war sustained slow gains in enrollment, to 141 in 1866 (Chart 3.2). The trend developed despite the fact that Father Clark raised tuition three times, a result of the 80 percent inflation in the Union during the war.[11] By the fall of 1866, students were paying $250 for tuition, room, and board, an increase of 67 percent since 1861. It was a modest increase, prompted by the realistic assessment offered by a faculty member in 1863 that "this last year[,] the College has rather been supporting the boys, than the boys it."[12] He was not exaggerating; tuition income had slipped to 65 percent of total revenue in 1862, the lowest point in the Clark presidency. The impact of tuition increases was offset by Father Clark's will-

Chart 3.1 Student Origins, 1843–1900

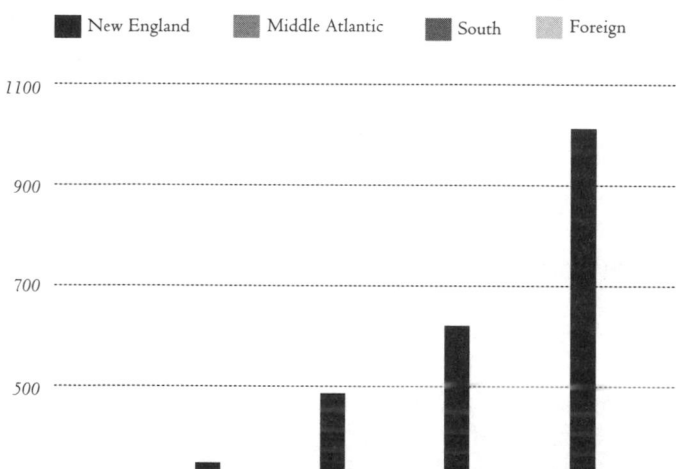

were added. For a list of 93 Catholic "colleges" founded in the United States between 1860 and 1890, see Power, *History*, 287–311.

11. McPherson, *Battle Cry*, 447.

12. Michael Byrnes to Debbs [Edward Devitt], Worcester, August 12, 1863, GUA, Holy Cross, 1843–47.

ingness to be flexible. Years later, an alumnus described the rector's reaction to his plea of poverty when he applied for admission in 1864: "Good Fr. Clarke [sic] . . . told me 'go on and mind my studies and *pay what*, I could & pay the rest afterwards.' . . . This was God's own deed through a noble man— as dear, *stern* Fr. Jas. Clarke . . . was well known to us."[13] Father Clark also bought property for the campus, the first land purchases since the Jesuits had assumed responsibility for the College. The first parcel, 48 acres of farm land adjacent to the lower part of the campus, was purchased in 1862. Four years later, Clark bought three more acres—one acre "next to our water land so as to square the piece," and two acres on the hill side, totally surrounded by college property.[14] Land purchases and the gap between tuition increases and inflation led to a modest increase in indebtedness during Clark's tenure in office. Yet, the farm was a boon, providing food at low cost. In the fall of 1863, the harvest yielded 800 bushels of potatoes, and a good amount of other produce as well.[15]

The conclusion of the war brought relief and jubilation. The few students from the South kept their feelings to themselves, particularly in the city, where "the stars and stripes were everywhere streaming to the breeze and the eagle was . . . glancing at the sun."[16] On the evening of Lee's surrender, there was an "illumination" of the college—a lighted candle was set in each window facing the city, with students posted to guard against fire. From a distance, the effect was impressive. Some campus residents had mixed feelings. Scholastic John Ryan, a Southerner, remembered: "We all, of course, thanked God for the long-wished-for dawn of peace; but some who, like myself, came from the sunny South, naturally felt sorrowful for the defeat of the other side." According to one account, James Clark spent the evening of victory alone, walking in the old back yard behind Fenwick Hall, reflecting and doubtless praying about the conclusion of that tragic conflict and its impact on his old comrades from West Point.[17]

13. Dennis F. McCaffrey to Thomas Murphy, Reuthven, Iowa, October 8, 1906, ACHC, 12.15.

14. Clark to Paresce, Worcester February 7, September 4, October 4, 1862, and November 17, 1866, MPA, 226 E 2, 3, and 4, 227 T 5.

15. Clark to Paresce, Worcester, November 6. 1863, MPA, 227 T 12.

16. Michael Byrnes to Edward Devitt, Worcester, October 4, 1862, GUA, Holy Cross, 1843–47.

17. Michael Byrnes to Edward Devitt, Worcester, October 4, 1862, GUA, Holy Cross, 1843–47; John J. Ryan, "Recollections of Holy Cross at the Season of the End of the War Between North and South," *The Purple*, 5:2–3; Meagher and Grattan, *Spires*, 101.

The spring of 1865 brought cause for undivided celebration when Holy Cross at last received a charter from the Commonwealth of Massachusetts. In contrast with the failed effort of 1849, the charter petition of 1865 passed with remarkable ease. Holy Cross enjoyed a powerful advantage in the support of Governor Andrew, who first accorded the College recognition of sorts by visiting the campus in March of 1862. The governor returned in July for the exhibition and remarked to Father Clark that "Holy Cross should be enabled to give her own degrees."[18] In the fall, Clark told Father Paresce that he had taken preliminary steps to apply for a charter. He was receiving encouragement on all sides because "a great and favorable change" had altered the public atmosphere; the governor, he was certain, would help. In seeking permission to move the process forward, he mentioned two possible objections: the possibility that a Holy Cross petition at that time would "diminish the chances" of a charter for Boston College; and the possibility that Paresce intended to *"give up"* Holy Cross.[19]

Clark's timing proved premature, and the process became stalled for two more years. Despite his concern about a possible Jesuit withdrawal, there is no other documentary evidence that reconsideration of the Jesuit commitment to Holy Cross was under way. The delay was probably strategic: with charter petitions pending for both Boston College and Holy Cross, the Jesuit authorities may have decided against acting concurrently. Of the two petitions, Boston College's would have taken precedence: it was less controversial because it explicitly prohibited the exclusion of students on religious grounds; in the meantime, Holy Cross could rely on its traditional association with Georgetown. The Boston College petition was approved in the spring of 1863.[20] A year later, the editor of *The National Quarterly Review* predicted that a renewal of the Holy Cross application would succeed because of the excellence of the academic program and because of the "increased liberality and cosmopolitan spirit" of Massachusetts legislators.[21] The petition, signed by "all the most prominent and influential men of the city of Worcester," was sent to the General Court in November 1864. The following January, Alexander H. Bullock, the Speaker of the Massachusetts House of Representatives, predicted an easy passage. He

18. W. H. Fitzpatrick [Class of 1862 valedictorian] to [?], Dorchester, June 30, 1904, ACHC, 10.0-1; HD, 1862.

19. Clark to Paresce, Worcester, November 15, 1862, MPA, 226 E 7.

20. Donovan et al., *Boston College*, 27–31.

21. Edward I. Sears, "College of the Holy Cross," in *The National Quarterly Review*, IX (June and September, 1864), 110–11, cited in Robert Mahlon Nicholson, "A Legacy in Transition: A Social Portrait of the Professoriate in a Liberal Arts College of the Catholic, Jesuit Tradition" (Ed. D. Thesis, Harvard University, 1991), 44.

was aware, since Father Clark had alerted him, that Holy Cross was still committed to Catholic exclusivity.[22]

Two days after meeting with Clark, Speaker Bullock, who had also signed the petition, introduced it to the House. The document, similar to the 1849 petition, had a few differences: the corporate property limit was raised; the likelihood of legislative interference was minimized; and a new section echoed the wording of the Boston College charter in allowing for an endowment. Like the Boston College charter, the Holy Cross charter specifically stated that the Commonwealth was not financially responsible for the College. The Holy Cross charter made no mention whatever of religious exclusivity. In effect, the new petition left the trustees free to maintain exclusivity by not forbidding it. The bill received final passage in the House on March 22. Even Erastus Hopkins held his peace. It was rapidly approved in the Senate and signed by Governor Andrew on March 24.[23]

The outcome occasioned gratitude and celebration. A faculty member captured the spirit shortly afterwards:

Holy Cross is no longer a secondary branch of Geo[rgetown]. It is now a chartered college. The charter was granted with . . . scarcely any opposition: although much was anticipated. The successful issue was in a great measure due to the exertions of Gov. Andrew (who by the by seems not only to be a liberal man towards all classes in general; but towards Catholics in particular.) It is reported that he had a private interview with all the members in order to place the passage of the bill beyond a doubt. . . . The consideration that Protestants are still excluded must enhance the value of the charter & also the liberality of the state. To many who doubted even to the last moment that the Charter would pass it seems that a total re-action has taken place.[24]

A grand banquet was held on April 27. Guests included Governor Andrew, prominent legislators, Bishops Fitzpatrick and Francis McFarland (Hartford), Provincial Angelo Paresce, John Early, and about thirty alumni. Father James Healy, who was now chancellor of the Diocese of Boston, delivered an address; afterwards, the Dramatic Club performed Edward Bulwer's *Cardinal Richelieu*.[25]

22. Lord et al. *History*, 2: 607; Clark to Paresce, Worcester, January 10, 1864, MPA, 227 P 1. Although this letter is dated 1864, it was almost certainly written in January of 1865, Father Clark having made the common error of confusing the year in early January.

23. A copy of the 1865 Act of Incorporation is in ACHC, 11.0-1. See also Meagher and Grattan, *Spires*, 103–5; and Lord et al., *History*, 2:606–7. A copy of the original Boston College charter, approved by Governor Andrew on April 1, 1863, is included in Donovan et al., *Boston College*, 30–31.

24. William Scanlan to Edward Devitt, Worcester, April 7, 1865, GUA, Holy Cross, 1843–47.

25. Ibid.; Ryan, *Purple*, 5: 5–6.

The five petitioners—Fathers Clark, Charles Fulmer, James Moore, Charles Kelly, and Livy Vigilante—met on April 24 "to consider whether they will accept said Act of Incorporation." Following unanimous approval, the trustees directed Charles Fulmer, the Jesuit minister and interim secretary of the trustees, to send formal thanks to public officials and prominent citizens who had assisted in the process. In his response, the governor expressed the hope that the charter would promote "mutual respect for the convictions of men, irrespective of their differences."[26] Throughout his term, Governor Andrew continued to attend the College Commencement unless public business prevented it. Alexander Bullock, who succeeded Andrew, continued the practice; after 1875, for nearly a century, their successors honored the custom.[27] On July 1, the trustees adopted by-laws to set a pattern of organization that was maintained for about a century. The rector became the president of the corporation and, following Jesuit procedures, held office for a term of three years. The community minister was generally the vice-president, while two other Jesuits at the school served as treasurer and secretary. In this way, the civil requirements were matched to the Jesuit method of governance, allowing the legal trustees of the College to function also according to the norms of the Society of Jesus. The trustees commissioned Fr. Benedict Sestini of Georgetown to design an official seal. Circular and somewhat cluttered, it featured a cross near the top, surrounded with rays and clouds—an adaptation of the logo that had been used since the founding of the College.[28] At the left of the circle was a hill which represented Packachoag, topped by an American flag. To the right at the foot of the hill was a train drawn by a grasshopper engine of the 1860s, a reference to the importance of railroads in Worcester's economy. Behind it were several ships sailing on the ocean, presumably a reference to commerce of the Bay State. The lower part of the circle included three books, a telescope, and a globe. Around the outer circle in Latin were the name of the school and the city. The seal was adopted by the trustees on April 24, 1867.[29]

Throughout his administration, James Clark insisted that he needed more help to run the school. At the beginning of his term, his request to Father

26. John Andrew to Fulmer, Boston, June 6, 1865, Trustees' Minute Book, ACHC, 11.0-1.
27. Meagher and Grattan, Spires, 106.
28. The early logo featured a large cross surrounded by rays and clouds and the Greek words, EN TOUTO NIKA [In This Sign You Shall Conquer], a reference to the legend that, before his victory over Maxentius at the Milvian Bridge in October 312, the Emperor Constantine saw a cross in the sky with a message in Latin [IN HOC SIGNO VINCES]. Afterwards, Constantine became a Christian.
29. Trustees' Minute Book, ACHC, 11.0-1.

Paresce was peremptory: "Until peace is restored I think you may as well consider this the principal boarding College of the Province; and provide for it accordingly."[30] Early in 1862, he pressed his claims to the general—and with justification, for he was badly overworked. He was teaching natural philosophy, chemistry, and two classes of mathematics while carrying the duties of rector: "I have more teaching to do than some of our fathers who have nothing to do but teach." He won a sympathetic response from Beckx, who urged the matter upon Paresce as a matter of justice, since Clark was "worn out with too much teaching so that he is carrying out the duties of his office less satisfactorily."[31] That argument prevailed: the number of Jesuit priests and scholastics at Holy Cross rose from ten to twelve in the fall of 1862 and remained at twelve or thirteen for the remainder of Clark's term. With this extra help, the academic program functioned smoothly.[32]

Father Clark was careful to see that the students had regular opportunities for recreation. There were free days for sleighing, skating, outings to Lake Quinsigamond, hikes to Mount Wachusett, and even apple picking. Washington's Birthday was observed with a special meal, a reading of the Farewell Address, and a party in the evening. On other occasions, the college band provided music under the talented leadership of George P. Burt, who had succeeded Samuel Leland. The spirit of the College during the war was captured by scholastic William Scanlan, who supervised outings with evident delight:

I take the boys to walk about two or three times a week. Now-a-days boys are allowed to smoke on walks, to call into stores & buy whatever they want. You may imagine how the boys enjoy their privileges. On evenings preceeding [sic] holidays [they] go into the refectory after supper & have a grand time there until 9 o'clock. dancing[,] singing[,] playing games &c. &c. I went to Leicester with the boys last-week. It is the greatest walk on record.[33]

An old alumnus described the students as "manly, frank, respectful to authority, and intensely loyal to each other." Philosophers had the privilege of wearing silk hats. Discipline was generally good, though on one occasion students found and buried the head prefect's record of infractions, the "jug book."[34]

30. Clark to Paresce, Worcester, [Fall, 1861], MPA, 226 J.

31. Clark to Paresce, Worcester, September 4, 1862, MPA, 226 E 3; Clark to Beckx, Worcester, January 26, 1862, ARSI, MD 9-XVIII, 17; Beckx to Paresce, Rome, March 22, 1862, ARSI, MD Reg. II, 79.

32. HD, 1862–63.

33. [William Scanlan] to Edward Devitt, Worcester, October 10, 1863, GUA, Holy Cross, 1843–47; James McDonough to [?], Worcester, March 10, 1864, GUA, Clark Papers; HD, 1861–64.

34. Rogers, *Purple,* 5:61–64.

As the students kept to their routine, Father Clark struggled to provide for them under wartime conditions. In 1863, he had trouble finding coal and contemplated heating with firewood. Early in 1864, he was trying to requisition bedding from Boston College, which had been used as a Jesuit seminary from 1860 to 1863. Water, on the other hand, was abundant on the Hill of Pleasant Springs; early in his term Clark had a well of "clear and good water" dug uphill from the building. Afterwards, he noted with satisfaction that the well was 30 feet above the highest point of the roof, "thus affording a very strong pressure even at that height" in case of another fire.[35] The war had little impact on the dining room. William Scanlan, who had been a student at the College during the terrible fall and winter of 1857–58, could hardly believe the change: "Butter morning & even[ing]. Meat—the very best—quality pie every day in the week. How different to our time! The boys think there is no man like Father Clark."[36]

Within the faculty, however, there was occasional criticism of Clark for being stern and unbending—too military, perhaps—in his leadership. Difficulties surfaced in 1863, when one of the priests confided to Paresce that Clark expected too much of the scholastics and showed them too little appreciation. To illustrate the point, he described an encounter in which Clark had offered him "a *mathematical* reason" why a certain scholastic ought to be able to meet his obligations.[37] During Christmas week of 1864, there were more problems when the scholastics voiced a formal complaint that they were denied permission to visit the city for concerts and lectures.[38] The fact was, much was demanded of the scholastics. They were expected to teach and also to work as prefects (supervisors) in the time that the ordained Jesuits on the faculty attended to pastoral and administrative duties. Michael Byrnes, who was teaching Latin and mathematics in 1862, described his duties with humor:

A prefect is the best and most jovial fellow on earth. He has to go through thick and thin, to work from morning till night like a pack-horse[,] to look pleasant now, now to transmogrify his phiz into an expression of most picolly [sic] sourness. He has to punish and be tortured whilst he is doing so, he has to rebuke, keep cool, have his ears

35. Clark to Paresce, Worcester, November 19, 1861, August 6, 1863, and January 1, 1864, MPA, 226 J, 227 T 8 and P 2; Donovan et al., *Boston College*, 25. The decision to move all seminarians in the United States to Boston was made by Felix Sopranis as Visitor. Curran, "Troubled Nation," 49–50.

36. [Scanlan] to Edward Devitt, Worcester, October 10, 1863, GUA, Holy Cross, 1843–47. Devitt had also been at Holy Cross in 1857–58.

37. Charles Kelly to Paresce, Worcester, February 13 and February 21, 1863, MPA, 227 T 2 and 3.

38. Joseph Ryan to Paresce, Worcester, December 31, 1864, MPA, 217 P 5.

cocked up for every sound, his eyes peeled and his nose blood-hound like, to smell out the "Cutty" or look for the "Quid." But although he has to go through such tough work, he has also sometimes his frolick and jollity. And I tell you he enjoys it hugely.[39]

The rector's task was to support such commitment and zest through encouragement, rewards, and patient correction. Too much austerity, even if well intended, destroys morale. Apparently, that sometimes happened under the rectorship of James Clark.

In 1865 and 1866, the complaints became chronic, and in November of 1866 Father Beckx told Clark that he would be relieved of administration before the end of the academic year. Three months later, Paresce told Clark that Robert Brady would succeed him in February and offered thanks for "the faithful & conscientious manner with which you promoted the interests of the Institution during your administration."[40] From the perspective of many years, the thanks seem more formal than warm. Apparently, that was how Clark struck some of his Jesuit associates. Like Anthony Ciampi, he encountered opposition because of his personal style. Although he had to endure the indignity of being removed in mid-year, he took his orders with soldierly acceptance. In 1869, at the age of sixty, Clark was appointed rector again, at Gonzaga College in Washington, D.C., a post he held until 1875.

Robert Brady was a native of Maryland who had served at Holy Cross as teacher and prefect from 1846 until the fire. During the first part of the Civil War, he was assigned to pastoral work in Washington and ministered to wounded soldiers in government hospitals. From 1863 to 1867, he was rector of St. Mary's in Boston—a good vantage point for watching Holy Cross during the Clark years. Brady spent almost all his adult life in leadership positions— an indication of the confidence and respect he won through his discretion, piety, and good management.[41] He remained at Holy Cross for two and a half years, then assumed the rectorship of Boston College. Brady's successors in Worcester were Anthony Ciampi, whose third term as rector ran from 1869 to 1873, and Joseph B. O'Hagan, who followed Ciampi and served until 1878. To these three rectors fell the challenge of expanding and completing Fenwick Hall.

39. Michael J. Byrnes to Edward Devitt, Worcester, October 4, 1862, GUA, Holy Cross, 1843–47. All spelling sic. "Cutty" may refer to whiskey; "Quid," to tobacco.

40. Beckx to Clark, Rome, November 2, 1866, and Paresce to Clark, Baltimore, February 17, 1867, GUA, Clark Papers.

41. *WL*, 20: 250–55.

Physical expansion was made possible by prosperity of the postwar years. Enrollment rose from 88 in 1861 to a peak of 177 in 1874 (Chart 3.2). The numbers fell to about 140 later in the decade, when tuition and board charges were lowered to $200 under the influence of the appreciating value of the dollar. The smaller enrollments of the late 1870s were almost certainly a reflection of the economic downturn that followed the Panic of 1873. During this period, the average length of stay fluctuated between two and three years; few students remained for the full seven-year program. Despite the fluctuations in enrollment, tuition and other revenues provided a steady surplus in the operating budget and helped justify the loans that supported additions to Fenwick Hall and the rest of the physical plant. At the end of 1867, the trustees delegated Father Brady to "make all necessary contracts for the enlarging and improving [of] the college buildings." Altogether, they authorized loans of $46,000 for a project that eventually cost about $50,000. Taking enrollment increases into account, they decided to make the new wing one story higher than the rest of the building, to raise the central wing by an additional story, and to add the now-familiar towers to Fenwick Hall. The construction work also afforded the opportunity to install steam heat. The west wing provided space for the library, meeting rooms for the debating societies, and rooms for Jesuits and senior students. The reconstruction of 1868–69 gave Fenwick Hall a lopsided appearance for six years; viewed from the front, the old east wing was dwarfed by the newly massive structure that now adjoined it on the right (see illustration, page 31).[42]

In 1875, after the trustees authorized a new loan of $30,000 to cover "extensive improvements and additional buildings," the east wing was expanded to the proportions of the rest of Fenwick Hall. The match with the rest of the building was not seamless, however. An interruption in the roof line on the back of the building still shows where the joining occurred; inside, the corridors on the upper stories bear signs of a builder's error that created a difference of about seven inches in the floor levels of the two struc-

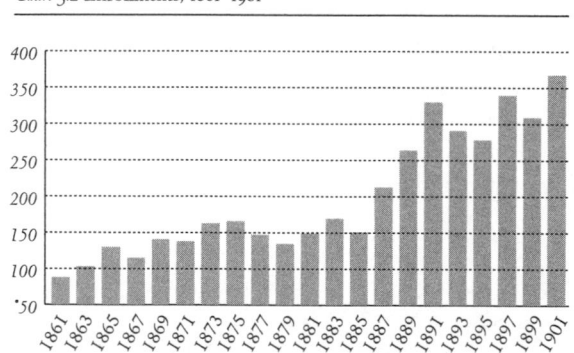

Chart 3.2 Enrollments, 1861–1901

42. Trustees' Minute Book, ACHC 11.0-1; Meagher and Grattan, *Spires*, 108.

tures.[43] The reconstructed east wing contained a dining hall on the ground floor, a study hall above that, and a large chapel with gothic windows on the second floor. In October, the chapel was blessed by Bishop Patrick O'Reilly, who had been named in 1870 to head the new Diocese of Springfield, which included the city of Worcester.

College catalogs touted the improvements and indicated that the amplified structure now had room for 230 students and better classroom space and new "Philosophical and Chemical Apparatus." In fact, the provincial had directed that a substantial sum of money be set aside to procure scientific instruments, a decision that recognized the enhanced importance of natural sciences in the curriculum of American colleges.[44] The years of the Fenwick Hall expansion also brought utilities to the campus for the first time: after a limited trial of electric light, college authorities settled for gas lighting in 1875, when gas pipes from the city reached the College; city water came in 1871; by the end of the decade indoor toilets had been installed near the dormitories for the students to use at night. "These and other improvements brought great relief to the students," noted an early historian.[45]

After the war, the College debt seemed more manageable (Chart 3.3). During the Clark years, indebtedness fluctuated between $8000 and $15,000, figures that reflected the land purchases and other capital improvements. That figure was to rise above $47,000 during the 1868–69 construction, and nearly as high again as a result of the east wing renovation; yet there was no sense of crisis. The debt was connected with major projects and purchases, and fell substantially between capital expenditures. In 1871, Father Ciampi and the trustees voted to build a new barn, stable, and carriage house and to purchase more land along the river.[46] Ciampi also improved the campus farm, as its manager, Father J. J. Tehan, gratefully noted:

43. Trustees' Minute Book, ACHC, 11.0-1; HD, 1875; "*Historia Collegii, 1877–83*," MPA, 325 M 3.

44. Provincial Joseph Kelleher directed that $1000 be used "to furnish the Cabinet with indispensable [scientific] instruments" in 1875, and that annual appropriations be budgeted thereafter "til the Department of Natural Sciences is well supplied." Memorial of October 28, 1875, ACHC, 19.1-2. Frederick Rudolph, *Curriculum: A Study of the American Undergraduate Course of Study since 1636* (San Francisco: Jossey-Bass, 1977), 104–8.

45. Devitt, "History," *WL* 64:228–31; Meagher and Grattan, *Spires*, 109; HD, 1871–75; *Historia Collegii, 1877–1883*, MPA, 325 M 3; Albert Peters, Handbook for Ministers, ACHC, 19.3; Holy Cross Catalogs, 1874–76. Trustees' Minute Book, February 13, 1871, ACHC, 11.0-1. Even after the improvements, bathing was less frequent than in later years. In 1888, the prefect of discipline noted in his diary on October 2: "Baths for the students began." School had opened on September 5th! ACHC, 15.2-2.

46. Trustees' Minute Book, ACHC, 11.0-1.

Chart 3.3 Operating Budget, 1862–1889

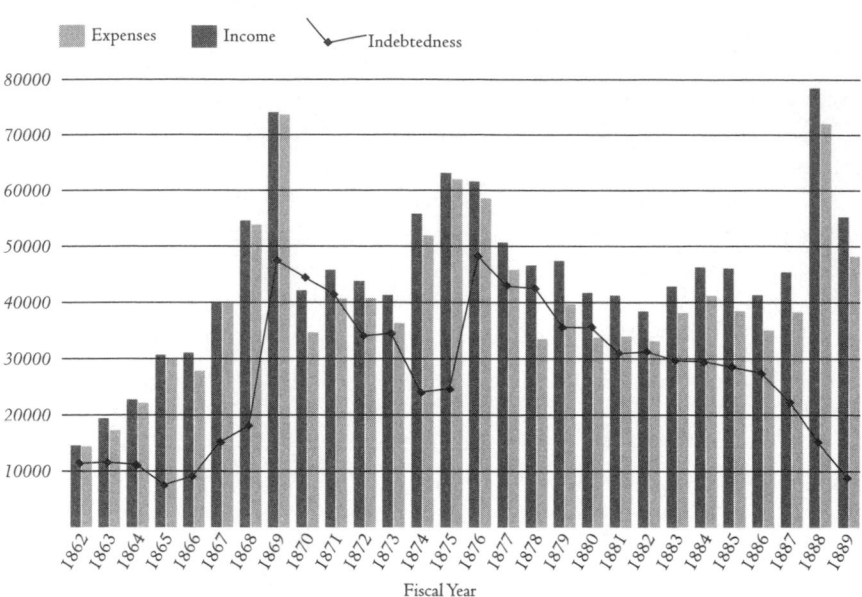

I deem it due to the character of Fr. Rector, A. F. Ciampi, to bear testimony to his liberality, in granting me the means to improve the condition and outworks of the farm and College. In two years, he added water-works, a convenient and costly privy—and above all, a first class barn—also bought a pair of horses, valued at 800 hundred [sic] dollars—a two horse cart—and everything that, by me was thought necessary for the farm. We found the farm in poverty, and by his generosity, we leave it well stocked and furnished.[47]

Not everyone appreciated Anthony Ciampi so well. During his third term he again reduced a heavy debt; but he was disinclined to delegate authority. In time, letters of complaint about his inability to win the affection and trust of the community flowed to the provincial and to the general; by 1872 they decided to replace him.[48]

The choice fell on Joseph B. O'Hagan, who had left the College faculty at the start of the Civil War to serve as an army chaplain. O'Hagan was born in Ireland in 1826 and came to Boston in 1847. There he met John McElroy, who influenced him to become a Jesuit. During the Civil War, he spent two years

47. Farm Diary, 1869–90, ACHC, 9.0-1. The entry is dated November 20, 1871.
48. Beckx to Joseph Keller, Rome, November 11, 1869, April 21, 1871, April 8, 1872, ARSI, MD Reg. II, 154, 174, and 193.

with the Army of the Potomac and was even captured and held briefly during McClellan's Peninsula Campaign. After an interruption for the final stage of his Jesuit training, he rejoined the army in early 1865 for the march to Richmond and Appomatox. A surviving fragment of O'Hagan's war diary makes clear that he was a sensitive man with a keen sense of justice who found military life difficult. "With some exception, everything corrupt, low[,] vulgar and debasing in our corrupt nature is rampant," he wrote early in 1863. On another occasion, he remonstrated with the Provost Marshall for his handling of deserters: "He is bent on having them shot—himself the greatest coward in the army."[49] Yet, his Protestant co-chaplain, Joseph H. Twichell, described him as a man with "a bright, happy wit; no discomforts could overcome his cheerful temper, and his generosity was boundless."[50] Even Mark Twain fell under his spell after Twichell introduced the two men in Hartford. Twain characterized O'Hagan as "a most jolly and delightful Jesuit priest."[51] After the war, O'Hagan was assigned to pastoral work in Boston until his appointment to Holy Cross.

During these years, the College was attracting students with its strictly classical curriculum; but the curriculum was something of an anomaly within the Jesuit network, where the commercial course was usually included.[52] Starting in 1867, the catalog specified that all students were obligated to follow the classical humanism of the *Ratio:* "It will be required of each one to pursue *the regular course*, as experience has proved exemptions in this regard to be a source of great inconvenience." In a first effort to create a division between the higher and lower courses, Father Brady grouped Rudiments and Third and Second Humanities under the heading "Preparatory Department"; First Humanities,

49. O'Hagan Diary, February 2 and 18, 1863, ACHC, 12.8-1. For general biographical information on O'Hagan, see *WL*, 8:176–183.

50. Hartford *Courant*, January 4, 1879, cited in William L. Lucey, ed., "The Diary of Joseph B. O'Hagan, S.J., Chaplain of the Excelsior Brigade," in *Civil War History* 6 (December 1960), 403.

51. Twain to C. W. Stoddard, February 1, 1875, Mark Twain Papers, in Kenneth R. Andrews, *Nook Farm, Mark Twain's Hartford Circle* (Cambridge, 1950), 250, n. 21. Cited in Meagher and Grattan, *Spires*, 109, n. 11.

52. Meagher and Grattan, *Spires*, 120. Historian Edward Power wrote: "In 1862 a uniform policy with respect to the commercial course was decided upon for all Jesuit colleges in the United States. First, the course was to be retained in all of the colleges to meet the needs of students and the demands of parents. It was a boon to the colleges financially. Second, it was to be strictly separate from the classical course, and Jesuit teachers were not to be engaged in it except for the teaching of philosophy." *History*, 85–86. Evidently Power was unaware that Holy Cross offered an exclusively classical curriculum by the time of the Civil War.

Poetry, Rhetoric, and Philosophy constituted the "Collegiate Department." Brady also wanted writing and public speaking to be emphasized—an essay or composition was to be assigned by each teacher every week, and elocution exercises were mandated for each class.[53] In 1868, Father Brady re-instituted the custom of reading compositions at the monthly assembly where grades were read, and he revived elocution in the refectory. In addition, the Philosophers were required to offer specimens and disputations, though on one occasion the Jesuit minister criticized the instructor for dominating the presentation: "We were all pleased, though we thought that the Professor did not give sufficient opportunity to the boys to get a word in now and then. . . . It was a Students' Specimen, not a Professor's."[54]

Father Ciampi revised the catalog slightly during his third administration. Rudiments was now billed as the "Preparatory Department"; Third and Second Humanities became the "Junior Department"; and the top four years were designated "Senior Classes." This division of the sequence of courses persisted until the 1890s. In the 1870s, grades were read on the first Tuesday of the month, with the first Tuesday in February replacing Ash Wednesday as the point of demarcation between the two semesters. Placement examinations in late August were introduced by Brady in 1868; but the exams were evidently administered as needed, since the school retained the policy of admitting students "at any time during the year."[55] After 1874, expanded facilities and new scientific apparatus made it possible to expand science offerings by adding a two-year program in chemistry for Rhetoric and Philosophy students to supplement the Philosophers' study of physics, astronomy, and geology.

Father Brady stipulated three sets of requirements for the Bachelor of Arts degree: rigorous examinations in moral and natural philosophy, astronomy, and chemistry; a good knowledge of Latin, Greek, French, and mathematics; and an original speech or essay on a literary, scientific, or moral subject as a final project. During the 1860s and 1870s, relatively few students completed the program: the College awarded ten A.B. degrees in 1865; it would be fifteen years before the number of degree recipients topped twenty. Conforming to the custom of the times, the College also awarded master's degrees. James Healy and John Brownson were the first M.A. recipients, in 1851. Qualifications for the master's degree were specified in the 1867 catalog: an extended

53. HD, October 2, 1868.

54. The comment was written by Charles Bahan, the Jesuit minister from 1872 to 1879. HD, February 14 and 15, 1879.

55. College Catalogs, 1868–70; HD, January 20, 1879. On the curriculum during the quarter century after the Civil War, see Meagher and Grattan, *Spires*, 128–38.

stay at Holy Cross for higher studies in moral and natural philosophy, or conclusion of a course "in any learned profession" after receiving an A.B. from Holy Cross. Apparently, only the second possibility was put into practice; and for the rest of the century, the trustees regularly debated the merits of M.A. applications from graduates. Honorary doctorates were awarded for the first time in 1874, when the Trustees voted honorary Doctor of Divinity degrees to two prominent alumni clerics, James Healy and John J. Power (Class of 1851).[56]

After 1856–57, the catalog no longer specified a minimum or maximum entrance age; instead, it offered the vague specification that "no student is admitted who has not made some progress in studies and who has not a good moral character." Nevertheless, the data show that during the 1870s the range of ages at entrance began to shrink; late in the decade, the youngest students were 12, and the oldest 25. Meanwhile, the average entrance age gradually advanced to 17 or 18, so that the student body was somewhat older and closer in age than before the Civil War. The students remained relatively cloistered on the campus; unlike other colleges where looser rules of conduct prevailed, Holy Cross stood *in loco parentis* in designating rules of conduct and penalties for violation. The catalog for 1869–70 specified memorization of lines as the normal penalty for "faults of ordinary occurrence, failure in recitations, or minor instances of misconduct." Expulsion was indicated for infractions that

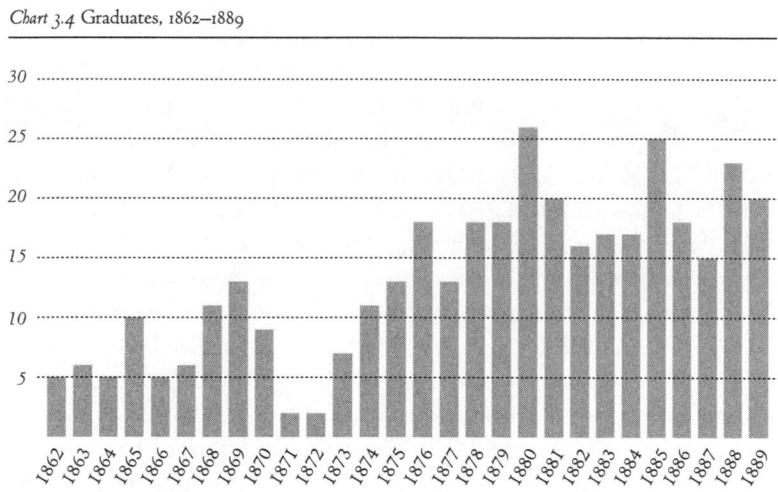

Chart 3.4 Graduates, 1862–1889

56. Trustees' Minutes, June 24, 1874, ACHC, 11.0-1; Foley, *Beloved Outcaste*, 47. Holy Cross did not award another honorary doctorate until 1892. Holy Cross Fact Book, College Archives.

threatened the reputation of the College or injured the welfare of fellow students. Students could also lose town privileges or forfeit recreation periods. Home visits were strictly limited; in the 1870s, students were permitted to visit their parents only during the Christmas holidays; students from Worcester were permitted overnight home visits on some other holidays and on the second Saturday of each month.

Although the disciplinary rules seem draconian by modern standards, most students accepted them in an age when internal and external constraints made American Catholicism a largely self-enclosed social network. The insular atmosphere of Holy Cross reflected the position of Catholics in American society, particularly in New England. Moreover, the process of application was largely self-selecting: those who came to the College were already disposed to conform to its values and approaches. During the 1870s, high spirits produced minor infractions and pranks. On one occasion, students smuggled a goat into the study room. In 1873, a general outbreak of misbehavior produced a blanket refusal of permission to attend Barnum's circus in the city. The rigors of the academic program produced at least one serious personal crisis, as a writer recorded with unintended humor in the House Diary early in 1873:

Manning left to-day entirely out of his mind. He returned after the holidays, apparently sane; when all at once four or five days ago—his madness began. He was completely prostrated physically and mentally—This morning he was very violent. His brothers took him away. Poor fellow—too great a desire to get an education.[57]

Two years later, several boys left on account of dissatisfaction with the program; but their departure was noted as an exception.[58]

Local students won an important concession during the 1870s, when the College began to accept day students. The first was James Conlin, accepted in the fall of 1870 as a "day scholar" for a tuition of $75. After a short interruption, the policy was reinstated in the fall of 1875, when nine non-boarding students were accepted. Thereafter, day students were a regular feature of campus life; in the latter decades of the century, about 20 percent of the students were day scholars. The written record offers only indirect evidence concerning the change of policy. Probably, various factors were involved—the fact that day students' tuition would add income without appreciably raising expenses; the availability of extra classroom space after the expansion of Fenwick Hall in 1875; and pressure from local families of slender means to provide instruction without the added charges for room and board. Day students were required to

57. HD, January 14, 1873.
58. HD, 1872–75.

be punctual for classes and to study in the study hall during the mid-day break if they stayed on campus. They were also forbidden to carry letters or perform errands for the boarding students. It is hard to see how the latter rule could be enforced, but it was probably connected with a new policy, announced in 1879, which subjected all outgoing mail, and incoming mail except letters from a student's parents, to inspection by the prefect of discipline. Presumably, romantic correspondence was the issue.[59]

During the 1870s, a surge of interest in billiards prompted the formation of a Billiard Room Association and necessitated that the use of the tables be restricted to noon and evening recreation. "Danger," then "Pluto," were the campus dogs of the 1870s; indoors, a canary named "Little Pete" serenaded students and faculty. Occasionally, students were allowed to take advantage of events in the city. Isaac Hecker's public lecture and a performance of Haydn's oratorio *The Creation* were two such events in 1867; in 1875, all the students went to the circus. Students who were unable to return home for the Christmas holidays—eight in 1879—enjoyed long recreation periods and a minstrel show in the city during the week.[60]

Difficult days occasionally interrupted the routine. In February 1876, Daniel Dowd died of typhoid fever at the age of 23, three months after arriving at the College. The Philosophers kept vigil with him during his illness and joined their schoolmates in reciting prayers after his death. Also moving was the death of Tom Connolly, an "old and faithful servant of the college," who died on November 3, 1869, at the age of 85. Connolly had worked on the construction of Fenwick Hall in 1843 and was afterwards hired by Thomas Mulledy to help in the kitchen and dining room. "Old Tom" was a venerable presence, who enthralled students with reminiscences of his "premeditated vengeance" after the burning of the Charlestown convent in 1834 and of Bishop Fenwick's role in averting the general desire for violent retaliation. Connolly's obituary in the Boston *Pilot* employed the florid sentimentality of those times, crediting him with ardent faith and loyalty to Holy Cross:

Fear of encroachment forbids us to chronicle the series of sarcastic and witty replies given by our old friend to the "Smelling [Nunnery] Committee" upon the occasion

59. The exact proportion of day scholars is difficult to determine, since enrollment in the latter part of the nineteenth century still lacked stability. The figure of 20 percent is derived from frequent reports on enrollment found annually in September and October in the House Diary.

60. College catalog, 1879; HD, 1867–80. On April 4, 1883, a mournful entry in the House Diary stated: "'Little Pete' the canary who had delighted many in the College for the past 10 years by his singing &c. died this morning and was sent to town to be stuffed."

of their visit to the College. Affectionate old man! Even now we can picture him . . . hat in hand, among the silent graves of the Jesuit dead, telling with tremendous voice of the noble deeds and the secret acts of charity often performed by these heroic sons of Ignatius, until tears and sobs choking his utterance, he would silently pray that these same saintly dead might plead for him at the bar of God's eternal justice.

Connolly was buried from the campus chapel, apparently the first lay employee of the College to be so honored.[61]

Toward the end of 1878, death deprived the College of its rector, Joseph O'Hagan, just as he seemed likely to become the first Holy Cross rector to serve a full six-year term. Early that year, persistent illness struck; ultimately, the doctors prescribed an extended sea voyage and a winter in the mild climate of California. On December 1, he set sail from New York, bound for Panama, with Patrick Healy as his traveling companion.[62] At first, he seemed to improve; but a terrible storm blew up after the ship docked at Panama, and it had to be cut loose from the docks to save it. While they were at the mercy of the tempest, O'Hagan's condition declined. When the ship re-docked, he had to be carried ashore. After crossing the isthmus on the train, O'Hagan was carried aboard the *Granada*, where he died on December 15, off the coast of Nicaragua at the age of fifty-one. His body was embalmed, and four days later he was buried at Acapulco. Later, his remains were sent back to Worcester, where in March of 1879 he was laid to rest in the campus cemetery. As late as 1891, there were reports of grey-haired Civil War veterans limping to his grave on Memorial Day with flowers and a flag, then kneeling in the grass with bowed heads.

Father O'Hagan's death occurred just as external circumstances were altering the context of the College's institutional life. For one thing, the summer of 1879 brought the "astonishing news" that Jesuit authorities in Rome had decided to join the Maryland Province with New York, formerly a portion of the Canadian Jesuit province. The new province, Maryland-New York, had well over 500 Jesuits; its administrative offices were moved from Baltimore to New York City. Robert Brady, who had been provincial of Maryland since 1877, now became the head of a more extended province that lacked the intimacy and common historical experience of the old Maryland Province.[63]

61. HD, November 3 and 5, 1869. Fr. Mulledy noted that Connolly was one of three hired persons in 1843. "Fr. Mulledy's Diary," January 23, 1844, ACHC, 12.1-1. The *Pilot* obituary was signed by B.J.D. and appended to the house diary.

62. The best source on the final journey and death of Joseph O'Hagan is Patrick Healy's diary of the trip. ACHC, 9.0-1. See also O'Hagan's obituary, *WL*, 8: 176–83; and Foley, *Dream*, 189–92.

63. Curran, "Troubled Nation," 65–66; HD, August 8, 1879.

Outside the Society, other developments began nudging Holy Cross toward the character it would assume in the twentieth century. At Harvard, Charles William Eliot, who had assumed the presidency in 1869, prevailed in his campaign to introduce the elective principle to the curriculum by the mid–1880s. Electivism and the abandonment of required courses—the very antithesis of the *Ratio*—gained popularity in some quarters and generated controversy about the principles, means, and goals of higher education. Meanwhile, the growth of white-collar professions in the Gilded Age gave colleges and universities a more prominent role as the principal means of access to professional careers. College educators began to base their requirements and academic programs on the German system of education, with the Ph.D. as the culminating academic degree and academic professionalism as the distinguishing feature of faculties.[64] In distinction from the Jesuit goal of educating the whole individual in the humanistic tradition, the emerging academic culture of the late nineteenth century sanctioned a separation between academic life as the proper sphere of educators, and the students' private lives, which were not regarded as a primary institutional concern. By 1880, the movement to privatize colleges and universities that had once been public emphasized the importance of fund raising and the value of the alumni as loyal supporters of alma mater. At about the same time, under the leadership of Harvard and Yale, intercollegiate athletic competition was gaining popularity.[65]

Many of these movements were still tentative in the 1880s and their interconnectedness was not fully apparent, but they were profoundly altering the educational patterns of the nation. The emerging academic culture, with its emphasis on "practical" and pre-professional learning, was less congruous with the spirit of the *Ratio Studiorum* than older, more prescriptive approaches. At first, the effects of these changes on Holy Cross were slight, but they were noticeable: intercollegiate athletic competition made its first appearance; fund raising became more formal; the integrity of the traditional academic program was defended and strengthened; and student conduct was monitored with determined conviction even as students tested the limits of the rules. The Holy Cross of the 1880s was still a proud expression of the *Ratio Studiorum*, but the tranquillity of the 1870s was becoming harder to sustain in the midst of the new academic culture.

Three rector/presidents served at Holy Cross between 1879 and 1889: Ed-

64. Rudolph, *American College*, 290–306; Rudolph, *Curriculum*, 191–96; Bledstein, *Culture*, 269–90, 303, 318–31.

65. Horowitz, *Campus*, 39, 41–42; Rudolph, *American College*, 428–30; Ronald A. Smith, *Sports and Freedom: The Rise of Big-Time College Athletics* (New York: Oxford University Press, 1988), ix, 56–61, 80, 107–09.

ward Boone (1879–83), Robert Brady in his second term (1883–87), and Samuel Cahill (1887–89). This dedicated triumvirate brought the College a period of competent leadership. Boone, who traced his roots to an old Maryland family, had graduated from Holy Cross in 1851 and was the first alumnus to head the school. A mild-mannered man, he had served as a vice-president of Loyola College in Baltimore before assuming office in Worcester after O'Hagan's death. His tenure as Holy Cross rector was ended at his own request. In the winter of 1883, he petitioned Father Beckx to be relieved because of poor health. The general seemed reluctant to lose Boone's leadership, and he counseled patient endurance:

The weight of the Cross that a new Superior must bear is a heavy one, but almost invariably it happens that through these very Crosses of the Superior, borne with patience and resignation and received in the spirit of obedience, many blessings are conferred upon the whole community.

Nevertheless, Beckx took the request seriously and by June had agreed to assign Robert Brady to head Holy Cross for the second time.[66] Father Brady was nearly 58 when he returned to the College in 1883, the oldest man to assume office up to that time. During his second term at Holy Cross, his manifold administrative gifts were again fully engaged. The termination of his appointment after four years was probably because of poor health; he lived less than four years after leaving Worcester.[67]

Samuel Cahill, Brady's successor, was born in Ireland in 1844 and was brought to the United States as a child during the famine. He entered the Society in 1868 and was ordained in 1880. During the 1880s, he served at four different colleges, gaining broad experience. A gifted administrator and an austere but kind man, he achieved unprecedented success in reducing the college debt; but he lacked physical stamina for the job. Almost immediately after assuming office, he was complaining about a lack of energy. By the beginning of 1889 it was clear that he could not continue, and Anton Anderledy, who had succeeded Peter Beckx as general, initiated the search for a successor.[68]

Holy Cross grew solidly under the leadership of Fathers Boone, Brady, and Cahill. Enrollment rose from 135 at the beginning of Boone's presidency

66. Beckx to Boone, Fiesole, February 15, 1883, ARSI, MD Reg. II, 406; Beckx to Robert Fulton, Fiesole, June 1, 1883, ARSI MD Reg. II, 416; HD, 1879, 1883, 1886. For a biographical sketch of Boone, see *WL*, 45: 254–55.

67. *WL*, 20: 250–55.

68. Anderledy to Cahill, Fiesole, October 19, 1887, ARSI, MD Reg. III, 27; Anderledy to Robert Fulton, Rome, April 19, 1888, ARSI, MD Reg. III, 38; Anderledy to Thomas Campbell, Fiesole. February 17, 1889, ARSI, MD Reg. III, 58.

to 223 during Cahill's last year (Chart 3.2). The momentary dip in enrollment in 1885–86 was attributed by Father Brady to the attractiveness of less expensive alternatives at Boston College (a day school) and the Canadian colleges (lower tuition charges).[69] Few students took advantage of the whole program during those years, but the average length of stay did rise above three years several times during the 1870s and 1880s.

During the 1880s, fund raising assumed more prominence than at any time since the drive after the fire. The catalog of 1879–80 was the first explicitly to thank supporters of the College. During Father Boone's presidency, the catalog solicited gifts as large as $50,000, with specific designations and naming privileges connected with the size of the contribution. Between 1880 and 1884, there were specific pleas to "friends of Catholic Education, throughout our New England States" for donations for a new three-story building. Throughout the decade, the catalog named individuals who donated money, books, artwork, or other gifts to the school. But the gifts, when they came, were discouragingly small. For a contribution of $100 in 1884, Mr. and Mrs. Patrick Quinn were designated benefactors of the school. In 1887, Governor Oliver Ames became the first substantial non-Catholic donor, with a surprise announcement at Commencement that he was contributing $1000.[70] The following year's catalogue highlighted Ames's munificence by announcing that the money had been designated by the trustees to establish the Governor Ames Scholarship for students from Worcester.

Annual gift totals were generally less than $1000 throughout the 1880s, except for 1887–88 when, stimulated by the governor's contribution, the College received over $5300 in gifts. The Alumni Association that was founded in 1869 was another disappointing source of monetary support. In 1885, the $200 remaining in its treasury was transferred to a new organization, the "Alumni Association of the College of the Holy Cross," then being organized.[71] Tuition revenues were a more dependable source of revenue. Reflecting the changing value of the dollar, tuition was lowered to $200 in 1878, then raised to $225 in 1886. With these rates, tuition income rose from $26,000 to $43,000 during the 1880s and furnished over 70 percent of revenue and an operating surplus that facilitated debt reduction.

Contributed service by the Jesuit community was another major factor in the College's economic health. Although no monetary value was placed on these professional services, the amount was significant. By 1888–89, seventeen

69. Holy Cross annual letter, February 21, 1886, MPA, 325 M 4.
70. HD, September 7, 1884 and June 30, 1887.
71. HD, 1879; Trustees' Minute Book, November 17, 1885, ACHC, 11.0-1.

teachers and administrators were working for little more than room, board, and clothing. Perquisites received for pastoral ministry on weekends and during the summer added over $25,000 more between 1881 to 1889. Jesuit lay brothers also kept expenses down by doing much of the manual labor in the school and the farm. During the 1880s, the number of brothers rose gradually from nine to twelve. In 1881, the job description for the brother assigned to keep the wardrobe in order indicated that the man had to be a jack-of-all-trades. He locked up at night and saw to the fires and lights; in the morning he extinguished the lights and unlocked the doors. In cold weather, he had to close windows and turn off the water in the dormitory wash room. He pumped the organ at Sunday Vespers and swept the student chapel weekly. At mealtime, he waited on tables in the Jesuit dining room, substituted when needed for ill waiters in the student dining room, and carried meals to the sick. During his spare time, he was to paint, clean, and mend bedding.[72]

The campus farm was another important asset. The old academy building served as the residence of the farm and campus laborers. Some were young immigrants who lived on campus before getting married; others, like Tom Connolly, lived at the College for a major part of their lives. Father Albert Peters, Holy Cross minister for eleven years in the 1870s and 1880s, designed a blank contract that offered a laborer board, lodging, washing, and a small salary in return for faithful service.[73] During the 1880s, the farm was managed by a "boss farmer," whose importance to the College was indicated by the output of the operation. The fall harvest in 1879 brought nearly 1000 bushels of potatoes and 105 barrels of apples. By May of 1883 the dairy herd was producing over 100 gallons at the morning milking; in the same month, the dairy produced more than 300 pounds of butter. Other livestock included a bull, heifers, oxen, hogs, work and transport horses—including "Charley Horse," whose name was recorded in 1871. Campus workers made sausage, ham, and lard. While potatoes and apples were the principal crops, the farm also produced rhubarb, corn, rutabaga, turnips, carrots, cabbage, rye, and beets, in addition to hay and oats for the livestock. In the winter, the workers cut ice at Coes Pond and transported it to the campus, where it was stored for use in the warmer months.[74]

A combination of factors, then, sustained the school's fiscal security dur-

72. Albert Peters, Handbook for Holy Cross Ministers, ACHC, 19.3.

73. Ibid. A note in the farm journal from 1870 indicates that a worker named Scully was hired at $25 per month; the following year, Michael Dennison, who made an X in place of a signature, was given a monthly wage of $22. Farm Diary, 1869–1890, ACHC, 9.0-1.

74. Peters, Handbook for Holy Cross Ministers, ACHC, 19.3; Farm Diary, 1869–71, ACHC, 9.0-1; HD, 1879–83.

ing the 1880s and made it possible to pay most of the debt incurred for the completion of Fenwick Hall. By 1889, the figure had fallen to $9000 (Chart 3.3). Father Cahill even purchased two more pieces of property along College Street in 1887.[75] By the end of the decade, when increasing enrollment was creating a need for expanded facilities, the school was on a solid footing. But, as their record of poor health and short terms indicates, the three rectors of the 1880s paid a personal price for institutional progress.

The academic side of campus life during the 1880s was marked by an intensified commitment to the methods and goals of *Ratio Studiorum*. Positioning himself with those who opposed electivism, Provincial Robert Fulton (1882–89) appointed a commission to "improve and unify" the Jesuit colleges' approach to classical studies. The commission worked under the leadership of Father James Ward, the prefect of studies at Holy Cross, and issued a report in 1886 that emphasized "the paramount necessity of following the Ratio Studiorum in every particular," and opposed "the effects of innovation, which always threaten when private judgment is the only rule."[76] In their determination to present a united front, the commissioners designated a common set of names for the years of the seven-year Jesuit course: Lowest Grammar, Middle Grammar, Highest Grammar, Prosody, Humanities, Rhetoric, and Philosophy. The recommendations spelled out the subjects, goals, and texts involved in each of the six years from Lowest Grammar to Rhetoric. Students in Lowest Grammar, for instance, were to learn Latin and Greek grammar and to use the easier texts of Cicero. They were also expected to study spelling, letter writing, and grammar in English, plus sacred history and geography. Students in Rhetoric read Cicero, Juvenal, Horace, and expurgated texts of Plautus and Terence in Latin and Demosthenes and Thucydides in Greek. Further recommendations included seven years of training in mathematics, to be taught five hours each week. Latin instructions started at ten hours per week and diminished to six hours by the end. History, catechism, chemistry, English, and French were also mandated. Philosophers were to devote eight hours to science each week, plus studies in history, catechism, and declamation.

75. HD, December 22, 1887; Holy Cross Annual Letter, 1887, MPA, 325 M 6; Devitt, "History," WL, 64:232–33. The two tracts of land, separated from each other by College-owned property, were uphill from Linden Lane. Brady to Robert Fulton, Warwick, November 23 and 26, 1887, ACHC, 13.0-2.

76. "A Summary of the Proceedings of the Commission appointed . . . to help towards Improving and Unifying the Studies In the Classes Below Philosophy, of the Colleges of the Maryland-New York Province" (Boston: Frank J. McQueeney, [1886]), MPA, 520 D. For a discussion of the reaction against electivism see Rudolph, *Curriculum*, 188–96.

As he had done in his first term, Robert Brady moved to bind the academic program of Holy Cross as tightly as possible to the *Ratio*, even before the commission's recommendations came out. Oddly enough, he did not adopt the provincial nomenclature for the seven years of the academic program. Meeting with the faculty in 1885, he facilitated the introduction of two courses in declamation. The same meeting agreed to use maps extensively in history and geography classes. Dates and procedures for mid-year and final examinations were fixed, and the teachers agreed to add First Mathematics to the list of courses required for graduation. In 1888, renovations in Fenwick Hall made it possible to open a new laboratory for applied chemistry.[77]

Outside the Jesuit system, the astonishing growth of high schools after 1870 incorporated priorities that placed a low emphasis on classical languages. At Holy Cross, adherence to the classical curriculum meant that some otherwise qualified students lacked a sufficient proficiency in Latin and Greek to study even at the level of Rudiments. For such applicants, "Special" classes were added in 1880 as an auxiliary course outside the regular curriculum to bring students up to the requisite level.[78] These courses found a ready audience. Enrollment rose to ten students in 1882–83 and to 54 in 1887–88, when Samuel Cahill defended the courses as a necessity if the *Ratio* was to be fostered in the midst of the contemporary American educational network: "Certainly it would be better if all of them from the start were formed into our system, but this is impossible under present circumstances."[79] By then it was clear that, to preserve the integrity of the curriculum, Holy Cross would have to offer introductory Latin and Greek.

During the 1880s, the academic routine went on much as it had since the Civil War, except for the better science laboratories and the new emphasis on mathematics and elocution. Beginning in 1881, the essays written by graduating seniors were listed in the annual catalog. Semesters ran eighteen weeks, with 90 to 95 class days each term. Tuesday and Thursday afternoons were free; grades were read on the first Tuesday of the month. During the 1884–85 school year, holidays included Washington's Birthday, St. Patrick's Day, Pentecost Monday, and Memorial Day. There was even a special sports holiday in

77. Minutes of Faculty Meeting, September 21, 1885, ACHC, 12.7-1; Annual Letter, 1888–89, MPA, 325 M 6.

78. *Historia Domus*, 1885–86, copybook, ACHC, 19.0. Between 1870 and 1900, the number of American high schools grew from 1026 to 6005. The number of students rose from 72,000 to 519,000 during the same years. Rudolph, *Curriculum*, 211–12.

79. Annual Letter, November 1, 1888, MPA, 335 J. Catalogs show the number of "Special" students as follows: 1880–81: 4; 1881–82: 0; 1882–83: 10; 1883–84 and 1884–85: 18; 1885–86: 35; 1886–87: 28; 1887–88: 54; and 1888–89: 33.

September.[80] The exhibitions, or commencement ceremonies, of the 1880s were held indoors in the large study hall. Guests found elaborate decorations that included banners with the names of western authors—Milton, Shakespeare, Plato, Cicero, and others. The dais featured a large oil portrait of Bishop Fenwick, an American flag, and the papal arms. In 1885, four essays were publicly declaimed, and the governor offered remarks before distributing the prize medals. Although the commencement exercises themselves were paragons of decorum, Albert Peters worried about the ancillary celebrations on the eve of graduation. In 1885, a band concert and fireworks drew a large crowd from the city: "These night entertainments have great inconveniences —the people come from town & the boys' morals are much exposed—two officers were on duty and could hardly keep back the crowd." After graduation, the scene on campus was nearly as bad—"drinking and eating and perambulating the whole college without any or very little regard to 'enclosure.'" In 1886, the eve-of-commencement celebration was halted, and Father Peters was relieved to note that students spent the evening "in quiet conversation— interrupted now and then by bursts of hilarity."[81]

Late in the 1880s, enrollment surged past 250; by then the upward trend in the age of the student body was confirmed. The youngest student was eleven years old and, despite an occasional registrant in his mid-twenties, the pattern shows a consistent mean age at entry of seventeen or eighteen. The older age of the students had an impact on social life and discipline, especially in the area of sports. Interest in athletics started with intramural baseball. The first formally recorded game was played on September 30, 1868, between "picked nines from the sides of the house."[82] The rapid development of intercollegiate competition during the 1870s and 1880s, and the comparatively large proportion of students in their upper teens and early twenties, gave team sports and athletic competition increasing prominence.[83] For the students no less than for interested faculty and alumni, the emerging popularity of sports was one of the most striking developments of the 1870s and 1880s.

After intercollegiate competition entered college campuses, athletic associations became necessary. Historian Ronald Smith has found that such orga-

80. HD, 1880–89; Academic Calendar, 1884–85, ACHC, 15.2-1; Prefect of Discipline Diary, 1882–83, ACHC, 15.2-2.

81. HD, 1884–86; Worcester *Gazette*, June 26, 1884; Commencement Files, ACHC, 14.3B.

82. Rudolph, *American College*, 154; HD. Nearly two decades earlier, on July 28, 1849, diarist James A. Healy recorded an informal campus game of "town ball," an early form of baseball. Evidently, baseball (in some form) was a campus pastime almost from the beginning.

83. Smith, *Sports and Freedom*, 119–24.

nizations were organized at most colleges between 1870 and 1900. They were usually founded as student organizations "to provide financial assistance to relieve athletes of the entire expense of their sports and to give moral support for college athletics." Often founded to support one sport, they evolved into general organizations operating on behalf of all sports. Dues were generally one dollar per year or less, and at some places students were under "severe social pressure" to join. Members of the athletic association also began to collect gate receipts to supply revenue for the athletic program. At most schools, the faculty became involved only after academic life was affected; in time, some associations were broadened to include alumni. In this way, college athletic committees functioned as "buffers between the students who wanted complete faculty hands-off and the faculty, many of whom wanted severe restrictions or abolishment of intercollegiate sports."[84]

At Holy Cross, the first athletic association emerged in 1874. Like other student organizations, the Holy Cross Athletic Association was headed by a Jesuit faculty member, scholastic Henry J. Sandaal. Students held the other offices, and the membership was about thirty. The organization was listed in the catalogs of 1874 and 1875, then disappeared until 1894. Little information exists about this group, but the fact that it folded after Sandaal's re-assignment suggests that it may have been mostly an expression of his personal enthusiasm. In 1883, there is an isolated reference to the Holy Cross "Baseball Association" as the beneficiary of a benefit performance of *The Merchant of Venice* at Mechanics Hall;[85] so, presumably, a campus organization for the support of interscholastic baseball continued to function, at least sporadically, between 1875 and 1894.

Enthusiasm for baseball grew rapidly in the 1870s and 1880s. The nature of competition varied; team managers arranged games as they could. The fact that the Jesuits followed the teams and savored the victories implies that the development was approved by College authorities. The House Diary is a rich source on those early seasons. A disappointed entry in May of 1876 recorded a defeat to a local club: "College boys whipped again—haven't had much this year. All the rising young Arabs of the town seem to have congregated to add to our humiliation." A year later, the players were given ice cream and cake after beating Brown, 3–2. By the mid 1880s, there were two teams—designated as the "first" and "second" nine; possibly they were separate squads from the higher and lower academic divisions.[86] Worcester Academy, North

84. Ibid., 119–33.
85. Prefect of Discipline Diary, ACHC, 15.2-2.
86. Prefect of Discipline Diary, October 17, 1883, ACHC, 15.2-2; HD, 1876–89.

Brookfield, and Holden were among a set of opponents that included high school and college teams and some amateur clubs. In 1886, enthusiasm built to a peak when the college team achieved an undefeated season with a defeat of Cherry Valley on June 19. The students' supper was delayed for the game, and the players were allowed to dine at a local restaurant. "It was a little *contra legem* [against the rule]," the prefect of discipline noted, "but they enjoyed the supper."[87] Baseball was not the only form of athletic competition. Records mention an intramural game of rugby football in 1880; and in the fall of 1885, 24 Boston College students came to Holy Cross "for an athletic contest with our boys"—presumably track and field events, and baseball. A partisan observer recorded only the outcome: "Our boys won in everything."[88]

Apart from the emphasis on competitive sports, the social life of the students of the 1880s resembled that of earlier decades. There were sleigh rides in winter; in warm weather, excursions for boating and swimming. Despite efforts at supervision, a student drowned on one such outing in 1883. On campus, the Dramatic Club offered *William Tell, Rip van Winkle, Richard III*, and other shows billed as operettas. Sometimes, individual classes offered an entertainment for the entire college; one such offering by the Rhetoric class in 1889 lasted so long (perhaps by design) that prayers had to be canceled. Debating remained popular. In 1882, a campus debate on the question "Is the increasing power of the moneyed corporations a danger that should be averted by legislation?" attracted favorable notice in the local press. The reporter praised the students for their "graceful and spirited manner" of dialogue and found the debate "remarkable for clearness of statement, force of argument, propriety of diction, and attractive elocution." Singing and dancing on special holidays also relieved the tedium of study. In 1883, the Shrove Tuesday party lasted until 10:45; afterwards, the students who had arranged the entertainment were allowed to enjoy their own feast until 11:30.[89]

During the 1880s, college authorities attempted to foster class spirit through class outings and the system of rules and privileges. The seating plan in the chapel, study hall, and dining room distinguished "senior" students from the others. Rhetoricians, poets, and first humanities students were seated by class; others were seated by size, regardless of class; philosophers, as the ranking class, sat in the rear. "Larger boys" were allowed to smoke twenty

87. Prefect of Discipline Diary, June 19, 1886, ACHC, 15.5-2.

88. Diary of John J. McAuley, May 30, 1884, and October 24, 1885, ACHC, 9.0-1; HD, 1876–89.

89. HD, 1880–89; Prefect of Discipline Diary, February 6, 1883, ACHC, 15.2–2; Worcester *Spy*, April 12, 1882.

minutes after breakfast and dinner and in the evening; but "small boys" were forbidden to smoke or to "lounge around among big boys." The categories of large and small may have depended upon age, or they may have followed the rule used in athletics that divided groups by height. By the 1880s, the custom of class dinners was also well established. The philosophy class held an annual banquet at the Bay State House, with invited guests from the faculty. The rhetoricians' banquet was held on campus during the 1880s. In 1885, the dinner included oysters and a special desert, followed by dancing that attracted unfavorable notice from the prefect of discipline: "It was a romping party and nothing else. If they do not get up something better next year, 'twould be just as well to abolish it. The principal part of the entertainment consisted in knocking one another down."[90]

The high spirits of the rhetoricians may have been connected with a sense of liberation from the disciplined atmosphere of the dining room that distinguished Holy Cross from most contemporary colleges and universities. At the start of the decade, the room held eleven tables in two rows, plus a carving table, a portable lectern, and two napkin cases at the end of the room. White tablecloths were used for the principal meal at mid-day; red tablecloths functioned for breakfast and supper. Waiters were cautioned about personal cleanliness, excessive haste, and "useless talking with the boys." There was still reading at table. In 1883, students heard a biography of Louis XVII of France, and *Tour of Both Hemispheres* by Jesuit Eugene Vetromile. On Holy Thursday and Good Friday, devotional readings were substituted.[91] During the 1880s, students ate relatively well, especially on feast days. In 1880, the 95 students who spent Thanksgiving Day on campus enjoyed a traditional turkey dinner. The following Easter, they were given stuffed ham. St. Patrick's Day presented a particular challenge because of the strict Lenten rules: one year, the menu featured oyster soup, boiled cod, peeled potatoes, sauerkraut, apple pie, an orange, and "store cakes." The workmen were given the same food, plus a "horn."[92]

The school's exclusively Catholic character and manner of operation was reinforced in the 1880s by the emphasis on hierarchical authority associated with Vatican Council I (1870) and the Third Plenary Council of Baltimore (1884), and by the religious devotionalism that characterized Roman Catholi-

90. Prefect of Discipline Diary, October 30, 1885, ACHC, 15.2-2; HD, November 25, 1879, and October 19, 1889.
91. Minister's Handbook, 1881, ACHC, 19.3; Prefect of Discipline Diary, February and March, 1883, ACHC, 15.2-2.
92. HD, 1880–89.

cism during that era.[93] Routinely, on the first Saturday of the month, all students were obliged to go to confession. Students received communion the following morning. The liturgical seasons were observed with appropriate and careful solemnity. Retreats were held every year in the fall. The Sodality continued to be a major campus organization in two branches—the Sodality of Mary for older students, and the Sodality of the Holy Angels for younger students; inductions were conducted with great ceremony. In 1888, 90 of the 204 students were in the Sodality of Mary; 20 more belonged to the Holy Angels Sodality. In addition to the catechetical lecture presented to students in the chapel every Thursday morning, religious instruction was given on Saturday afternoons by the various teachers. Albert Peters noted in 1882: "It is customary for the Professor of each class to devote the last half hour of class on Saturday afternoon to a Catechetical instruction or explanation: for this the bell is rung . . . at 4:30." The pervasive religious atmosphere was still fostering vocations to the priesthood: between 1884 and 1886, 31 students entered diocesan seminaries and seven entered the Jesuit novitiate.[94] Small wonder that, in his annual report for 1888, Samuel Cahill claimed that, because the students were all Catholic, there was "a good spirit of piety and obedience among the students."[95]

As a general claim, Cahill's boast was fair enough, but the 1880s brought their share of disciplinary problems and occasionally led officials to maintain the "good spirit of piety and obedience" by expelling uncooperative students. The greatest danger to the carefully cultivated campus atmosphere was the proximity—and attractiveness—of the city. Students could obtain "town permission" from the rector during his office hours. They walked in groups and were subject to elaborate rules:

Walks in charge of one or more prefects, according to number of boys, are taken to the Country or City on Tues., Thurs., and Special Holidays; ordinarily one walk to the City during the week. On walks smoking is never permitted within the City limits (Providence Railroad Crossing). During the walk no one is allowed to go ahead of the two leaders appointed, without the permission of the Prefect. At the option of

93. On the emphasis on authority within the Catholic Church see Gerald P. Fogarty, *The Vatican and the American Hierarchy from 1870 to 1965* (Wilmington: Michael Glazier, Inc., 1985), 1–35, and James Hennessey, *American Catholics: A History of the Roman Catholic Community in the United States* (New York: Oxford University Press, 1983), 160–71. On the devotional expression of religion during the late nineteenth century, see Jay P. Dolan, *The American Catholic Experience: A History from Colonial Times to the Present* (Garden City: Image Books, 1985), 208–40.

94. Holy Cross Annual Letter, November 1, 1888, MPA, 335 J; Instructions for 1882–83, Prefect of Discipline Diary, ACHC, 15.2-2; HD, 1880–89.

95. Latin copy, inserted in HD.

the 1st Prefect a "scatter" is given in the city for thirty or forty minutes: this, as well as length of time, must be fixed by the 1st Prefect before the walk starts. A boy goes round before the walk and collects the names of those wishing to go; two lists are made out, one is kept at home; the other is kept by the Prefect who takes the walk. Before starting, the Prefect of walk assembles the boys at the West end of College and calls off the names on the list, each boy answering to his *own* name; the names of those not answering are checked off on both lists; a roll call is also had on returning at the entrance to the Grounds.[96]

Students could also receive an "Out of Bounds" permission to stroll around on the farm for 90 minutes. In January of 1887, seventy students were allowed to go home for three days during the mid-year recess. No doubt, the students valued these short interruptions in a routine that subjected them to so much scrutiny and afforded so little privacy.[97]

The tight restrictions governing absence from campus and prohibiting the use of alcohol were sometimes broken, with disastrous results for the offending party. Early in the fall term of 1880, a student returned to campus *"hors de combat"* after attending a concert. The following day, he was sent away. "This College stands up for temperance," wrote Father John Murphy, the prefect of discipline. Later that year, five students came home late, of whom two were "manifestly out of trim." The reaction was unambiguous: "Those five boys were expelled. That is the only way to strike terror into the others with regard to drinking."[98] Father Murphy may have inclined toward severity, but his concern about student drinking sprang from the general desire to maintain a good image in the local community.[99]

While isolated incidents of drinking represented individual challenges to the authority structure of the College, a group of students mounted a more serious test of the power of the prefect of discipline in 1885 by staging a strike. The episode started on Sunday, November 1, when the members of the choir went to the refectory before Mass seeking breakfast, but were offered only coffee. Although they sang for Mass and also for evening service, on the next day all but three struck for an early breakfast for the choir, refusing to chant at the

96. Prefect of Discipline Diary, ACHC, 15.2-2.
97. HD, January 29, 1887.
98. HD, September 23, 1880, and January 12, 1881.
99. In April 1885, three Irish Catholic pastors in Worcester, including 1869 alumnus Thomas Conaty of Sacred Heart Parish near the College, publicly attacked the liquor trade and the local saloons. Despite such opposition, by 1900 over 75 percent of the Worcester Irish who were small proprietors were in the liquor trade. Roy Rosenzweig, *Eight Hours for What We Will: Workers and Leisure in an Industrial City, 1870–1920* (New York: Cambridge University Press, 1983), 49, 62.

customary services for All Souls Day. "Trouble in camp," wrote the prefect of discipline, Father Michael Hughes. The following Sunday, the strike continued: the choir refused to sing at Mass, and the evening service was moved to mid-afternoon, in order to pre-empt daylight hours ordinarily reserved for recreation. "This is the order to be followed during the strike," Hughes noted. The situation threatened to become a lengthy impasse; then tragedy struck the campus twice in a short period of time. On November 14, Father Francis Sadlier, a popular teacher and moderator of the Holy Angels Sodality, died. In response, some of the strikers requested to declare a moratorium so that they could sing at his funeral "to show their affection and esteem for . . . Sadlier." Hughes granted the request. Then, on December 2, Father John McAuley, who taught Latin and French and headed the Marian Sodality, suffered a fatal heart attack. This second faculty funeral in three weeks prompted the students to end the strike. On December 7, Hughes noted that the "choir boys returned on condition that they are not to dictate anything and to sing whenever requested." The following day, liturgical music was back to normal.[100]

The choir strike of 1885 was the first recorded instance of an organized challenge to authority. That it was put down is not surprising, particularly considering the two faculty deaths. Father Hughes was resolute in his resistance to their demands, and even brought peer pressure to bear by moving the Sunday devotions to a recreation period. What is more interesting is that the strike occurred. Although the only account of the episode was kept by Hughes and reflects his point of view, the unity of the strikers and their ability to hold to their course for as long as they did indicates that the Holy Cross students of the 1880s were not completely docile. Like their contemporaries at other campuses, some, at least, could be actively critical in response to an alleged grievance. The choir strike strained the system for five weeks, but did not break it. Nevertheless, the episode was a signal, whose meaning is clearer in retrospect than it must have been when it occurred, that the spirit of the times could not be completely excluded from the campus by the exercise of authority.

Like the student body, the faculty was also reflecting the changing times as the older generation of Jesuits gradually yielded to the new. A symbol of the process was Charles Stonestreet, who had played such an important role in re-establishing the College after the fire. In the fall of 1880, at the age of 66, he was assigned to Holy Cross as spiritual prefect. In August of 1883, he cele-

100. Prefect of Discipline Diary, November 1 to December 8, 1885, ACHC, 15.2-2; HD, November 14 and December 2, 1885.

brated his Golden Jubilee as a Jesuit with a special banquet, followed by songs and speeches.[101] His guests included two former Holy Cross rectors—Robert Brady, and James Clark, who, at 74, was living in retirement at Georgetown. The archives hold no copies of the speeches given that day, nor are there any accounts of the conversations among the old timers. But Stonestreet had been in the Society since 1833, had known and consulted Thomas Mulledy, had co-operated with John Fitzpatrick in resurrecting the College and consoled Anthony Ciampi in his darkest hours. His knowledge of Holy Cross and its founders was personal and detailed, and the reminiscences he shared that day were ones that nobody else could duplicate. He and his contemporaries represented the continuity of commitment that had wedded the Society of Jesus to the College and to its founder's purposes.

Father Stonestreet's celebration was a culminating moment of the first Holy Cross—the still small Holy Cross of the *Ratio Studiorum*, proudly and independently, perhaps defiantly, planted "in the midst of the Yankees" by men from another region. After the Civil War, when the College finally gained its financial footing, the system thrived in every way, producing priests and loyal Catholic laymen exactly as Bishop Fenwick had intended. The revelers on that summer afternoon could take justifiable satisfaction in what they had accomplished: as an institutional expression of the Ignatian system of education, Holy Cross was at a pinnacle, the achievement of a generation whose personal sacrifice gave life and prosperity to the College. To the next generation fell the responsibility of coming to terms with an altered academic context whose challenges could no longer be avoided.

101. HD, November 20, 1880, January 23 and August 22, 1883.

CHAPTER FOUR

Problems and Promise, 1889 – 1901

T HE LAST DECADE of the nineteenth century proved to be the most challenging time for Holy Cross since the Fenwick Hall fire. High enrollments were straining the facilities and fostering an eagerness to expand the physical plant quickly, even precipitously. The emergence of a national collegiate culture, with its assumptions about student life, was making inroads on the settled traditions of campus life. The modern educational pattern of elementary school, high school, and college did not correspond readily to the seven-year course of the *Ratio Studiorum*. The vogue for electivism raised questions about the set curriculum of the Jesuit system. Expansion, student life, the curriculum: each issue posed a challenge; each prompted movement toward unfamiliar terrain. At first, it was hard to tell which of the problems were disguised opportunities and who among the challengers were really friends. These were years of trial and error, a period when Holy Cross encountered larger problems than anybody had anticipated and was in a stronger position than many people realized.

The first of the three rectors between 1889 and 1901 was Michael O'Kane. Forty years old when he assumed office, O'Kane was born in Ireland and raised in Spencer, Massachusetts. He attended Holy Cross from 1865 to 1867, when he joined the Jesuits. After his ordination in 1883, he served as minister and prefect of studies at Georgetown, then as director of the novice program for the Maryland–New York Province. O'Kane's sonorous voice and friendly manner made him an effective preacher; his personality was magnetic, as a contemporary characterization indicated: "His genial, kindly face, always lit up by a smile, was well known to everybody and his warm 'God love you' was enough to bring gladness to any heart."[1] Anton Anderledy had a more balanced assessment, asserting that O'Kane was "more diplomatic than strict" in his governance.[2] But his diplomacy was a helpful asset, and at first the enterprise thrived under O'Kane's administration.

Surging enrollment was the most striking indication of the College's prosperity. The number of students rose above 200 for the first time in 1887 and passed 300 in 1892 (Chart 4.1). The extra students strained the capacity of Fenwick Hall and forced Father O'Kane to refuse some applicants and to divide classes, with some sections meeting during night studies. The Jesuit community, with 33 members, was using every available room. Meanwhile, tuition revenues increased by 21 percent between 1890 and 1892 without a tuition increase.[3] Under these conditions, College authorities revived the question of a new building—a topic that had lain dormant since 1880, when Edward Boone had plans drawn up for "a *new Building* at the West end of the College," with a gymnasium, a large hall, billiard rooms, a laboratory, lecture room, and library.[4] In January of 1890, Father O'Kane informed the general that he planned to set aside $14,000 for the project that year. In response, Anderledy expressed his pleasure at the successful reduction of the debt and at the "safe condition" of the College's finances.[5] The statement may have been read as a friendly signal toward the projected addition; in any case, the idea at Holy Cross was to have a new building ready for the golden jubilee in 1893.[6]

The project moved ahead smoothly at first. Architectural plans were drawn up by the local firm of Fuller and Delano, and by the spring of 1891 workmen were readying the site. In May of 1891, the trustees authorized O'Kane to borrow $100,000 for the project, using College land and buildings as collateral. In late June, well after work had begun, the trustees voted Father O'Kane "full powers to proceed in the matter of providing the buildings aforesaid at his discretion." The following day, the contractor assembled a steam shovel at the site and began to excavate the twenty-five million square feet of earth that were moved downhill for a new athletic field.[7] By

1. *WL*, 47:359–61.

2. Anderledy to Thomas Campbell, Rome, April 10, 1890, ARSI, MD Reg. III, 87.

3. HD, 1889–92; *WL*, 19:437.   4. HD, December 12, 1880.

5. O'Kane to Anderledy, Worcester, January 31, 1890, ARSI, MD 12-XXV,1; Anderledy to O'Kane, Rome, May 26, 1890, ARSI, MD Reg. III, 98–99.

6. Report of William Singleton, S.J. in *WL*, 20:310. Singleton's report, which appeared in 1891, stated that plans had been sent to Rome.

7. Trustees' Minute Book, June 25, 1891, ACHC, 11.0–1; HD, May, 1891 to December, 1892; Annual Letters, 1890 and 1891, MPA, 326. Other Fuller and Delano buildings include the

December, the lower floor was complete with windows and a temporary roof for protection against winter weather. The expansion also necessitated construction of a new steam plant at a further cost of $20,000.[8]

Oddly enough, approval from the Jesuit general was still pending. Thomas Campbell, who headed the Maryland-New York Province from 1889 to 1893, submitted the final plans to Father Anderledy with the unanimous approval of his consultors in October of 1891. He urged quick approval because of the pressure of space and the quality of an academic program that held "first place among all of our colleges."[9] Then misfortune intervened. On January 18, 1892, Anton Anderledy died at Fiesole, the temporary headquarters of the Society of Jesus after the Jesuits, with all religious orders, were ousted from Rome in 1873. These conditions delayed the process of choosing a successor, but Luis Martin was elected to the office of general at Loyola, Spain, in October 1892.[10] Issues of governance and location, and the urgency of electing a new leader under difficult conditions, absorbed the time and energy of the upper echelon of Jesuit leadership throughout most of 1892, delaying approval for the new building. Under these circumstances, on March 6, 1892, Thomas Campbell sent a preemptory note to Holy Cross, forbidding any further work on the project "until word comes from Fiesole."[11]

That order stopped work during 1892. In March of 1893, Father Martin was able to focus his attention on the problem. In his first directive, he faulted Michael O'Kane for acting before securing approval:

The Rector is not to agree to any contract so that the work once begun is not to proceed without proper approval[,] and let him note precisely that the lack of due caution . . . will not be tolerated in our Superiors. Before any further commitments are made, let him send us the plans.

Worcester Armory, North High School, and several buildings at Worcester Academy. Elliott B. Knowlton (ed.), *Worcester's Best: A Guide to the City's Architectural Heritage* ([Worcester]: Worcester Heritage Preservation Society, 1984), 80–81, 96–100.

8. HD, May 14–17, 1891; McGurk to Martin, Paris, July 18, 1894, ARSI, MD 12-XXV,9. Permission to complete the boiler house "beyond the lower terrace" was received on August 4, 1893. Consultors' Minute Book, ACHC, 19.0. The boiler house, with four large steam boilers, a coal furnace, and an electric dynamo, was completed on November 8, 1893. Annual Letter, 1893, MPA, 326.

9. The letter included an unrealistically low estimate of $90,000 for the project, of which $25,000 was on hand. Campbell to Anderledy, Worcester, October 21, 1981, ARSI, MD 12-XXV, 2.

10. In January, 1895, Martin succeeded in returning the headquarters to Rome. Bangert, *History*, 438–39, 441.

11. Provincials' Memorials, March 6, 1892, ACHC, 19.1-2.

Martin also raised the question of removing O'Kane from office. He asked Campbell for a quick recommendation so that, if change were indicated, "an early succession" could be arranged.[12] The general was not alone in questioning O'Kane's capacity for administration. From South Carolina, Edward Scott complained that O'Kane had neglected to acknowledge a reminiscence he had composed for an alumni banquet, calling the slip-up the first ill treatment he had ever received from a Jesuit. Another alumnus complained that O'Kane had failed to acknowledge a $50 prize provided for the commencement "till I had written to . . . [the Jesuit] Provincial about the unaccountable delay."[13] Father O'Kane had a great heart and engaging personality, but the details of the job could elude him. In the end, Campbell decided to replace him before coming to a decision about the unfinished building.[14]

The choice fell to an experienced administrator, Edward A. McGurk, who was born in Philadelphia in 1841 and entered the Society of Jesus in 1857. He taught as a scholastic at Holy Cross during the rectorship of James Clark, was ordained in 1872, and served at Holy Cross as prefect of studies from 1874 to 1876. Afterwards, he served full terms as rector of Loyola College in Baltimore (1877–84) and Gonzaga College in Washington (1884–90), markedly improving the financial condition of both schools.[15] In the summer of 1893, he returned to Worcester for the third time, an experienced trouble shooter whose skills were sorely needed and whose reputation for sound judgment became a factor in reaching a solution.

As Father McGurk was familiarizing himself with the situation, the province consultors were trying to devise a solution. They met in New York in September to discuss whether the College could afford to finance the additional $150,000 that was now the estimated cost of completing the project. Afterwards, the consultors, whose number included McGurk, urged Father Martin to approve completion. Joseph Jerge, the province socius (the executive secretary and second-in-command to the provincial), cited McGurk's considered opinion that the College could eventually repay the debt. The consultors

12. Martin to Campbell, Fiesole, March 3, 1873, ARSI, MD Reg. III, 164.

13. Edward Scott to J. Havens Richards, Newberry, SC, May 24, 1890, GUA, Holy Cross, 1879–1912; Lewis Drummond, S.J., to Edward McGurk, St. Boniface, Manitoba, October 22, 1893, ACHC, 12.12-1.

14. O'Kane was assigned to give parish missions and retreats from 1893 until 1906, when his health broke down. After his recovery, he was assigned to parish work until his death in 1917. *WL*, 47:359–61.

15. *WL*, 25:480–83; Varga, *Baltimore's Loyola*, 96–97; typed biographical sketch of McGurk by Walter Meagher [copy], ACHC, 12.12-1.

were also swayed by the fact that most of the building materials had been purchased and were deposited on the campus. Jerge also argued that the College's reputation would be harmed if the project were abandoned. Another consultor, Fordham rector Thomas Gannon, stressed McGurk's competence as grounds for optimism.[16] In response, Luis Martin authorized partial completion:

Since the building has been begun, in order that greater evils be prevented, I am permitting for the present that the exterior parts (namely the walls and the roof, that is, the shell of the building) be completed—but the interior is to be omitted until I am sure that they have sufficient money to pay for the exterior. Once this is accomplished, I will then judge what is to be done about the interior.[17]

Resumption of construction was now assured for the spring of 1894, but McGurk was not content with the restrictions and petitioned the general for total completion—a course, he argued, that would forestall damage to the new structure from winter weather and would also induce alumni and friends to contribute to the school. But Martin held firm, pending reconsideration by the provincial.[18] While he was working to change the general's mind, McGurk canvassed the alumni for contributions in letter that included a candid statement of the financial condition of the school and a straightforward appeal to alumni loyalty: "While we are warmly grateful to our benefactors, it will not seem amiss to say that their name is not legion."[19] Despite the appeals and the seriousness of the need, contributions were slow. In June of 1893, a financial panic had plunged the American economy into a four-year depression.

In New York City, William Pardow succeeded Thomas Campbell as provincial in November 1893. The following March, he visited Holy Cross for a personal assessment. During his stay, after a delay of twenty-seven months, workmen began to prepare the incomplete structure for further work. By the end of March, a revised contract had been signed, with alterations that brought the cost of completing the shell down to about $76,000, not including steam fittings, plumbing and gas fixtures, or furnishings.[20] Credit for mov-

16. J. M. Jerge to Martin, New York, September 19, 1893, and Thomas Gannon to Martin, New York, September 22, 1893, ARSI, MD 12-XXV, 3 and 4.

17. Martin quoted this passage directly in letter written the following June. Martin to William Pardow, Fiesole, June 4, 1894, ARSI, MD Reg. III, 217.

18. McGurk to Martin, Worcester, January 14, 1894, ARSI, MD 12-XXV, 6; Martin to McGurk, Fiesole, February 10, 1894, ARSI, MD Reg. III, 203.

19. Undated letter [January, 1894 ?], ACHC, Chronological Scrapbooks; HD, January 23, 1894.

20. Consultors' Minute Book, March 28, 1894, ACHC, 19.0; HD, March, 1894.

ing the stalled project forward belonged mostly to Edward McGurk, whose health was beginning to break down under the strain. Sometime during the second week of April, he left for the Jesuit house at Keyser Island, off the Connecticut coast, to make his annual retreat. There, he suffered "a slight stroke of paralysis." When he returned to Holy Cross on April 21, his speech was "quite thick"; after a few days he began to improve. When a vacation in the South failed to produce a complete recovery, he departed on June 2 for an ocean voyage and a three-month rest in Europe, returning to campus on September 3 "much improved in health."[21]

Remarkably, Father McGurk kept pressing for the completion of the building during his convalescence. On May 5, he penned a 4 ½ page letter to the general, formally requesting approval for the entire building. His only concession to illness was to write in English. McGurk invested his case with clarity and urgency that were astonishing under the circumstances. One set of arguments was financial: debt already stood at $100,000; the debt for a complete building would be $190,000, while a shell alone would involve a debt of $160,000. But by erecting only a shell, the college would be unable to accept additional students whose tuition could support the debt. Moreover, the structure had sustained $2000 in damages by standing through two winters. Subjecting the building to another winter without heat would risk "great damage" to the unprotected walls. McGurk reinforced economic arguments with a plea for the well-being of the students:

> The present building does not accommodate our students. The class-rooms are small and badly ventilated. We have had very much sickness during the winter among the students, which could have been avoided, were the ampler space at our disposal: for there are only five rooms for an infirmary, in which we have had to accommodate as many as thirty sick at one time. Those who could not be accommodated in the infirmary were obliged to stay in the common dormitory, in which the beds are so close that one boy could stretch his hand and touch his neighbor. . . . As for bathing facilities, there is only one small room in which four bath-tubs are partitioned off and these must do for the whole college. We have noticed that this deficiency is a cause of much uncleanliness.
>
> The boys have been patient with their lack of accommodations during the past two or three years in the hope of speedy relief. They have been comforted by the sight of the actual effort to relieve them by building, and would now be rendered impatient by another delay.

McGurk cited the effect of his fund-raising appeal to the alumni and friends of the college and the danger of communicating the impression of failure.

21. HD, April–September, 1894.

"We are now committed to the building and we must trust to Providence for means to finish it," he concluded. Later, in a subsequent letter, he confided his frustration with the miscalculations that had produced the crisis: "I would not have begun these improvements had I been rector, but I was appointed when it was *too late* to stop."[22]

In response, the general formally requested a new recommendation. He wanted Father Pardow to send specific information about costs and a detailed plan for repayment of the debt.[23] In July, the province consultors met as requested, endorsing McGurk's arguments unanimously. To retire the anticipated debt, they were counting on higher enrollments and a prospective increase in tuition from $225 to $250. These expedients would generate a surplus of $13,000 per year, which, they predicted, would cover the interest on the debt and leave some money for repayment of the principal.[24] Clearly, the debt would encumber the College for many years, but they were convinced that the best chance of managing it lay in completing the project. Acceding to this advice, Father Martin removed his restriction. He also directed that as much of the money as possible be borrowed from other Jesuit institutions.[25] Throughout the Maryland-New York Province, there was sympathy and financial assistance to prevent Holy Cross from extending its commercial loans beyond the $100,000 already contracted. Loans totaling $40,000 came from St. Joseph's Parish in Philadelphia; other institutions added what they could.[26] Holy Cross students were also set to work as fund-raisers for equipment for the new gymnasium. And in January of 1895, a fund-raising committee was set up under the chairmanship of Judge Joseph Fallon (Class of 1858).[27]

Meanwhile, the new building rose quickly. On September 19, 1894, the students were given a half-holiday to celebrate the erection of the metal cross on

22. McGurk to Martin, Worcester, May 5, 1894, and Paris, July 18, 1894, ARSI, MD 12-XXV, 7 and 9.

23. Martin to Pardow, Fiesole, June 4, 1894, ARSI, MD Reg. III, 217.

24. William Pardow to Luis Martin, New York, July 10, 1894, ARSI, MD 12-XXV, 8.

25. There is a gap in the documents relating to Holy Cross between June 1894 and March 1895—the period during which the Jesuit headquarters was returned to Rome and during which the general would have sent his response to the letters of July 1894. In a letter to McGurk of March 17, 1895 (ARSI, MD Reg. III), Martin speaks sympathetically of the heavy debt burden, implying that he had consented to it. The quoted passage is from the House Diary, August 23, 1894. On April 3, 1895, McGurk informed the Holy Cross consultors of Martin's wish that money be borrowed from other Jesuit institutions. ACHC, Consultors' Minute Book, 19.0.

26. John A. Chester to McGurk, Baltimore, September 20, 1894, ACHC, 12.12-1.

27. HD, January 17 and 21, 1895. The students' collection netted $615 for the school. Prefect of Discipline's Diary, ACHC, 15.2-2.

the tower. "The Cross tops everything in the city," Father Lehy wrote in the House Diary. The grounds were prepared under the direction of Brother Francis X. Horwedel, the general supervisor of buildings and grounds, who had begun more than a half century of service to Holy Cross in the summer of 1891. Finally, in April of 1895, the building was formally dedicated.[28] The O'Kane Building, as it was being called in generous recognition of the man who started it, substantially relieved the cramped condition of the College. Its dimensions were 220 feet by 110 feet by 95 feet high. The ground floor had a swimming pool[29] and a gymnasium (139 feet by 50 feet) with an elevated running track and dressing rooms with bathtubs. On the first and second floors were the rector's office, physics and chemistry laboratories, a museum, classrooms for Humanities, Rhetoric, and Philosophy, and a large meeting hall named Fenwick Hall (later, Fenwick Theater), which seated 800. The third floor had two-man rooms for the Philosophers, and the top floor contained an open dormitory. The new building also made space available for a College-sponsored student library of 2000 volumes donated by the student organizations that had formerly kept libraries for their members. The total cost was $182,000. Institutional indebtedness peaked at about $187,000 in early 1894, and interest payments constituted as much as 10.5 percent of annual expenses.[30]

The pressure of completing the building and paying for it took a heavy toll on the fragile health of Edward McGurk. Generous to a fault in addressing the crisis, McGurk was under a great deal of strain—as events proved dramatically on commencement day in 1895. Shortly after the start of the ceremonies, held outdoors that year, a downpour interrupted the program. As Father McGurk bustled about to facilitate resumption of the proceedings in the new hall, he collapsed with another stroke. Two doctors from the audience attended to him until he regained consciousness in the late afternoon. But his health was broken, and he had to be relieved of office. He clung to life for one more year, on one occasion expressing the hope to be buried "on the hill at

28. HD, 1894–95; Prefect of Discipline Diary, September 19, 1894, ACHC, 15.2-2.

29. The planned swimming tank could not be opened. On April 3, 1895, Father McGurk informed the consultors that an additional $3000 to $4000 would be required to open the pool because "a deep drain ought to be built on the south side of the new wing to catch up the water which[,] coming from the numerous springs on the hill, is trickling through the walls of the tank." Consultors' Minute Book, ACHC, 19.0. Apparently, the deep drain was never built. Late in 1901, Father Hanselman proposed that "the room set apart for swimming tank be filled up to accommodate three billiard tables." Consultors' Minutes, December 15, 1901.

30. Meagher and Grattan, *Spires*, 114, 138–39; Annual Letter, January, 1894 to September, 1896, MPA, 326; College Catalog, 1900–1901.

Holy Cross College." Two days after his death on July 3, 1896, his remains were laid to rest as he wished.[31]

Father Pardow appointed John F. Lehy to act as vice-rector until the formal procedures for the choice of rector could be implemented. Known among the Jesuits as "Jeff" after his first two initials, Lehy was born in Royalston, Massachusetts, in 1850. He entered the Society of Jesus in 1874 after two years at Holy Cross, and taught at his alma mater as a scholastic from 1879 to 1884. During the six years following his ordination in 1887, he had a new assignment every year, including two separate stints on the Holy Cross faculty (1887–88 and 1890–91), and assignments as prefect of discipline at Georgetown, and minister at Gonzaga College in Washington. A versatile young Jesuit, he was given a variety of experiences to broaden his expertise. In 1893, he was assigned to Holy Cross as minister, and he headed the school during McGurk's convalescence in 1894. The general approved the temporary appointment, writing tersely: "I . . . approve that Father Lehy be appointed Vice-Rector of Holy Cross College until the investigation is held to appoint a new Rector."[32] But there is no evidence that the investigation was held, nor did there seem to be any urgency about altering Lehy's status. For three years, he was designated as vice-rector; only in 1898 was he named rector.

The records hold few clues about the reasons. It is possible that Lehy's relative lack of administrative experience made Jesuit authorities cautious on his behalf; if he had blundered in managing the debt, he could have been replaced with the face-saving excuse that his appointment had been only temporary. There was a hint of that thinking in the general's response to Lehy's first annual report: "The state of financial affairs is extremely serious and demands the greatest prudence. . . . Take care, therefore, to avoid all unnecessary expenses."[33] The point was a critical one, not only for Holy Cross, but for the entire Maryland-New York Province—particularly during the economic depression. Shortly after Lehy assumed office, William Pardow entreated a benefactor to divert a bequest from Georgetown to Holy Cross, "the real damper for the province." The provincial stressed the precariousness of a situation that threatened to place the College, and even the province, on "the verge of bankruptcy." Father O'Kane, he confided, "was to collect $20,000 this year for Worcester [but] has really collected $1500."[34] The point is not so much that

31. HD, June 27–July 6, 1895 and July 4–5, 1896; *WL*, 25:481–83.
32. Martin to Pardow, Rome, July 27, 1895, ARSI, MD Reg. III, 292.
33. Martin to Lehy, Rome, March 11, 1896, ARSI, MD Reg. III, 323–24.
34. Pardow to Francis A. Barnum, New York, April 14, 1896, Pardow Papers, MPA.

John F. Lehy, College President, 1895–1901, whose administration slowly retired the debt on O'Kane Hall and sponsored modifications in the curriculum in response to criticism from Harvard President Charles W. Eliot.

contributions were scarce but that J. F. Lehy's management was terribly critical for the well being of the College and of the whole Jesuit operation. Besides his gift for administration, Lehy communicated a sense of generous concern to students and alumni. For graduates, he constituted a personal link with alma mater and was a highly popular speaker and guest at alumni gatherings.[35]

35. *The Purple*, 31:163–68; biographical sketch, ACHC 12.13. Michael J. Costello, Class of 1900, eulogized Lehy in the following terms: "He stood for Holy Cross to his friend Michael

These personal assets he put to good use as the first to serve a full six-year term as head of Holy Cross. Father Lehy served at the College again from 1906 until failing health necessitated his reassignment in 1917.

The return of economic prosperity in the later 1890s aided in stabilizing the College budget by supporting a rise in enrollment. In 1896, the figure surged to 357 and remained above 300 for the rest of the decade. Faculty and administrators watched these statistics with a worried eye every autumn, noting almost daily the rising number of students, whose tuition would help avert catastrophe. New milestones prompted celebrations—a holiday in September 1899 to mark a new record for the size of the Philosophy class; a special dinner in November 1900 when enrollment reached 337, which was thought (mistakenly) to be a record.[36] The length of stay, computed by year of entry, was generally shorter than three years—an indication of the sort of turnover that made enrollment figures unpredictable and helps explain the worried concern as students arrived each autumn. Despite the fluctuations in average length of stay, the number of graduates during the 1890s was generally above thirty and reached a peak of 49 in 1893.

Apparently, most students paid full tuition. Records for the years 1890–95 provide information on 596 of 610 matriculants. Of those whose records are known, nearly 98 percent paid full tuition; the remainder were on reduced tuition or defaulted. Tuition revenues rose above $60,000 for the first time in fiscal year 1897, when the consultors raised tuition from $230 to $250 with the proviso that, "if the old students should plead great difficulty in the payment . . . , Fr. Rector might readily grant them board and tuition at present terms."[37] By 1900, tuition revenues were consistently providing two-thirds of the operating budget; operating surpluses were above $15,000, thanks to Jesuit perquisites that added between $7000 and $8000 per year. Records are less clear about contributions to the school during this period, but in most years they tended to be fairly low.

The operating budget for the period from fiscal year 1890 to fiscal year 1901 (Chart 4.1) shows the dramatic rise in indebtedness connected with O'Kane Hall. In 1896, the debt was more than twice as high as total income.

Costello from the day he met the lonesome lad from Scranton, through all the years of college and the days that came after. . . . No one was more widely known and better loved by Holy Cross men." Costello to Fr. [Donnelly], Scranton, North Dakota, ACHC, 12.13. In 1917, Lehy suffered from mental weakness or senility. J. N. Dinand to Fr. Himmel, Worcester, November 24, 1917, ACHC, 12.13-1.

36. HD, 1895–1901.
37. Consultors' Minute Book, May 30, 1897, ACHC, 19.0.

Predictably, interest payments absorbed most of the operating surplus at first. Only in his last year in office was J. F. Lehy able to reduce the principal by $10,000.[38] In 1901, indebtedness still stood at $166,500, but Lehy had incurred other expenses during his term of office. In the summer of 1900, the fourth-floor dormitory in the O'Kane Building was converted to 25 double rooms for juniors. Later in the year, the College bought a small parcel of land at the lower end of College Street to demolish several dilapidated structures and to square off the corner where a new baseball field was being planned.[39]

The golden jubilee of the College's founding occurred in 1893 in the midst of the crisis precipitated by the new building. When Edward McGurk raised the issue of a formal jubilee with his consultors, they agreed, after two uncertain discussions, to "attempt a celebration if a sufficient response from the alumni be received."[40] They need not have worried. Enthusiasm for the plan was spearheaded by Thomas Beaven, Class of 1870, who had been named bishop of Springfield in 1892. The date of the celebration was set for November 9, 1893. On the 8th, students were given a holiday to assist with preparations. Professional decorators from the city draped the study hall chandeliers and placed potted palms on the platform to frame the portrait of Bishop Fenwick.[41] On the 9th, 300 alumni guests wended their way past the halted construction project to enjoy a celebration that became a resounding vote of confidence in Holy Cross. Bishop Beaven presided at a solemn High Mass. Bishop

Chart 4.1 Operating Budget, 1890–1901

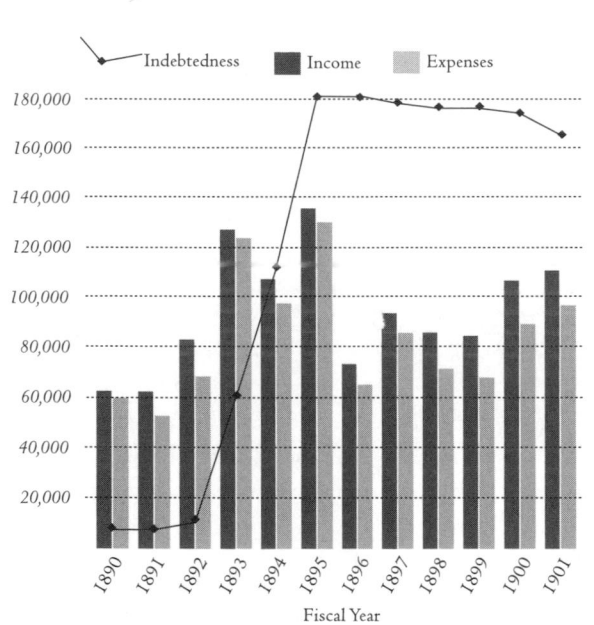

38. Consultors' Minute Book, September 9, 1900, ACHC, 19.0.
39. HD, July-December, 1900; Consultors' Minute Book, December 2, 1894, ACHC, 19.0.
40. Consultors' Minute Book, August 14 and 16, 1893, ACHC, 19.0.
41. Prefect of Discipline Diary, November 8–10, 1893, ACHC, 15.2-2.

Dennis Bradley of Manchester, New Hampshire, also an alumnus, offered a sermon that was noteworthy for its thoroughness and its characterization of Holy Cross students as "the race of men by whom salvation will come to Israel." At mid-day, the students enjoyed a banquet, with menus printed in Latin. The alumni and honored guests repaired to the study hall for their banquet at 3:00. Archbishop John Williams of Boston held the place of honor. He was flanked by Bishop Beaven, Worcester Mayor H. A. Marsh, and three other alumni bishops. Over cigars and *café noir*, guests listened to a warm memoir of Bishop Fenwick from the archbishop. Bishop Beaven, Mayor Marsh, Provincial Thomas Campbell, and Georgetown President J. Richards Havens also spoke, and there was a humorous address by Dr. Walter Corcoran, Class of 1878. Before the program ended at 7:30, the guests sang the Jubilee Ode, later attributed to Father Lehy, to the tune of *Maryland, My Maryland*. The beginning and conclusion capture the spirit of the entire composition:

> On this day of jubilee
> Sweet songs of praise we sing to thee.
> For all we have or hope to be
> O Holy Cross, we owe to thee. . . .
>
> Tonight we pledge our loyalty
> To God, to Country and to thee
> Holy Cross,—Old Holy Cross.

Afterwards, students supplied entertainment, followed by a bonfire and fireworks. A local reporter summarized the day in a single word: "glorious."[42]

Besides its function of affirming the College, the golden jubilee attracted attention to the accomplishments of the alumni and to their potential as benefactors of the school. After the celebration, Father McGurk issued a general appeal for contributions for the new building. The largest gifts came from the clergy, who gave more than $10,000 to the school in 1895.[43] At about the same time, college officials began collecting and publicizing statistics about graduates. The scorebook for the 1894 baseball season carried a brief history of the school and offered the information that, of 514 graduates, 242 had opted for the priesthood; 92 were in medicine, 90 in business, 65 in law, 18 in teaching, and 7 in journalism. Starting in 1894, the college released information about the career plans of graduating seniors. As the school grew larger, the priesthood was slipping in proportion to the other choices. Six of the 30

---

42. Worcester *Telegram*, November 10, 1893; for the Jubilee Ode, see ACHC, 12.13-1.
43. Annual Letter, 1895, ARSI, MD *Litt. Ann.*, 1502.

graduates in 1894 chose the seminary, compared with nine going to medical and dental schools and six more to the study of law.[44]

Efforts to organize the alumni gained momentum after the jubilee. For many years, the commencement had provided an occasion for a reunion. Apparently, the gatherings were somewhat haphazard, as the house diarist noted disapprovingly in 1892: "The Alumni meeting was a protracted awkward affair—the proceedings do not amount to a row of pins."[45] Although his appeal for the O'Kane building indicated Edward McGurk's willingness to cultivate the graduates, poor health deprived him of energy for advancing the matter; it fell to J. F. Lehy to promote formal organizational efforts. In February of 1896, the Class of 1885 held an "anniversary banquet" in Worcester, apparently the first individual class reunion. The following day, Lehy and the prefect of studies, Father Joseph Hanselman, journeyed to Hartford for the first alumni meeting for the state of Connecticut. Attendance was described as "not large but enthusiastic." Two years later, the Worcester County Alumni Association was organized. In January of 1900, the senior class was invited to add "numbers and noise" at this annual dinner.[46]

After 1895, the College was large enough to attract notable visitors. The first was Cardinal-designate Francesco Satolli, the first permanent papal delegate to the United States, who stayed from June 1 to 3, 1896, shortly before returning to Rome to receive a new assignment.[47] When he arrived, each class gave its cheer in succession as Satolli's coach passed among them along Linden Lane. The welcome was followed by a major feast with Bishop Beaven and the local pastors in attendance, and then a general gathering at which Satolli gave a "most appropriate, beautiful, and eloquent address." He also gave the students a two-day holiday, which must have impressed them even more. On the second day of his visit, he attended a campus baseball game (Newport 2, H.C. 1), and spoke to the Philosophers on Thomas Aquinas. Prior to his departure, Satolli imparted his blessing from the O'Kane porch as the students knelt on the grass.[48]

Among the visitors was Irish leader John Redmond, who paid a brief visit to the campus and addressed an assembly in the large hall. Henry Adams came to dinner and recreation with the faculty early in 1900 and spoke to the stu-

44. Worcester *Post*, October 6, 1894. *The Purple* (June 1895) noted that "one-third of all the priests in the diocese [of Springfield], bishop and vicar-general and all but two of the permanent rectors . . . are alumni of Holy Cross."

45. HD, June 30, 1892.

46. Alumni Scrapbooks, ACHC, Locker 8; HD, February 12–13, 1896, January 22, 1900; Worcester *Telegram*, April 13, 1898.

47. On the circumstances surrounding Satolli's appointment, see Fogarty, *Vatican*, 115–42.

48. HD, June 1–3, 1986; Annual Letter, 1896, MPA, 326.

dents about education. In 1899, there was a visit and formal address from "Bishop Meerscharr, the Vicar Apostolic of the Indian Territory," who afterwards turned out to be an impostor and a convicted felon.[49] Fortunately, the College found legitimate bishops to entertain, particularly Thomas Beaven, who had spent eight years on the hill as a student. Shortly after his designation as bishop of Springfield, he dropped in unexpectedly for dinner, then spent the afternoon playing billiards with the Jesuits and "charmed us all by his unassuming manners," in the words of the house diarist. In October of 1892, the College staged a three-day celebration to honor Beaven and his fellow graduate of 1870, John Michaud, who had been named coadjutor bishop of Burlington, Vermont. The following summer, Beaven agreed to head the arrangements committee for the golden jubilee.[50]

The celebration for Bishops Beaven and Michaud, a three-day holiday that gave the students a personal stake in the event, underscored the fact that College authorities were still consciously fostering the religious atmosphere of the school and the loyalty of the students to Roman Catholicism. The conviction that the College should open its doors to non-Catholic youth was no longer voiced; religious exclusivity was enforced without external pressure. In 1895, a non-Catholic father who brought his son from Ohio was advised to apply to Fordham.[51] The devotional mentality of the period found expression in the fall of 1890, when a shrine in honor of the Sacred Heart of Jesus was built outside the chapel door on the second floor of Fenwick Hall. In April of 1894, wooden grill work was put in place around the shrine. "It is beautiful and completes the work of the Shrine," Father Lehy noted.[52] The annual retreat was still an important part of the program, with a strenuous daily routine; and in the spring of 1896, Father O'Kane returned to the campus to offer a special retreat to the Philosophers as "a new departure to give the philosophers a chance to decide their vocation." The effort was evidently in response to a critique from the general, who pointedly asked Father Lehy "why there are so few vocations to the Society from the College."[53]

49. HD, November 24, 1899, December 1899, and February 19, 1900. On Bishop Theophile Meerschaert, see Delaney, *American Catholic*, 385–86.

50. HD, August–October, 1892 and August 29, 1893.

51. HD, March 13, 1895.

52. HD, September 1890–June 1891, April–June, 1894. In 1996, the original statue outside the new Brooks Concert Hall was replaced by a bust of Bishop Fenwick, the gift of John W. Spillane '54.

53. Prefect of Discipline Diary, April 20, 1896, ACHC, 15.2-2; Martin to Lehy, Rome, March 11, 1896, ARSI, MD Reg. III, 324. In 1897, Father Martin was still pressing Lehy on

The general's query was part of his more general concern about the direction of the Maryland-New York Province. In 1897, he took the unusual step of replacing William Pardow with Edward Purbrick, a member of the English Province. A year, later, the general admonished Lehy again on the primacy of spiritual matters:

Some people think that much more care is desirable. What does it profit if the minds of students are developed in the sciences and worldly topics and their hearts are left destitute of solid religious doctrines and true religious principles? If this defect exists among you, I beg you to try to correct it by every means possible.

Lehy believed that the religious education of the students was being conscientiously addressed.[54] Catholic exclusivity and the schedule of mandatory religious devotions and catechetical instruction guaranteed that students would be exposed to the tenets and practices of Catholicism; effectiveness was another question. Doubtless some faculty members were more effective preceptors and preachers than others. At its best, the system did inculcate mature Catholic piety and the spirit of the *magis*. One example is a sermon preached early in 1899 in honor of the seventeenth-century Jesuit Peter Claver, who labored among African slaves in the South American port of Cartagena. Claver's life was extolled as a call to action, "action at all times, . . . action on the part of all. When you see anyone in need of your assistance, either for body or soul, do not ask yourself why some one else did not assist him, but think to yourself that you have found a treasure."[55]

Spiritual formation, like the other areas of student life, was supposed to be adapted to the age and experience of the students. Following the pattern that was developing across the country during the 1890s, the average age of Holy Cross students at the time of matriculation was about 18; with a few exceptions, the great majority of students were in their upper teen years when they arrived; very few were younger than fourteen.[56] The variety of ages became an issue dur-

---

the issue of vocations to the Society because "it seems incredible that the students are not attracted to the religious life by the good example of our Scholastics." Martin to Lehy, Rome, April 9, 1897, ARSI, MD Reg. III, 368.

54. Martin to Purbrick, Rome, March 2, 1897, ARSI, MD Reg. III, 364; Martin to Lehy, Rome, April 13, 1898, ARSI, MD Reg. III, 409, and August 26, 1898, ARSI, MD Reg. III, 421.

55. The homily is accompanied by an editor's note, attributing it to Edward Devitt, who was prefect of studies at Holy Cross. GUA, Holy Cross, 1879–1912.

56. Colin Burke notes that, during the 1890s, the average entering age for college undergraduates became standardized at 18 to 20. High schools were proving to be a dependable supplier of students, and older potential students were now less likely to attend college. *American*, 230.

ing the 1890s, as emerging concepts of adolescence and sexual development[57] and Catholic teaching about sexual morality prompted concern. At the direction of the general, Father Pardow suggested in 1894 that the new building be set up so as to create a division between younger and older boys. Evidently, he was dissatisfied with the arrangements after O'Kane opened, for he repeated his concern in 1896: "It is to be feared that harm is done the smaller boys by contact with the larger ones."[58] In 1897, Father Martin also challenged Lehy to act:

It is reported to me that there are 282 boarding students, but that there is no separation between junior and senior students, and that the boys committed to our care are thereby exposed to danger: to which defect your Reverence should bring about a remedy most promptly, lest our College, which is morally obligated to be a certain fortress of innocence, be turned into a source of scandal, which God forbid. A one-time student of the College of the Holy Cross tells certain secular priests that in the College many indecent things are seen and heard which formerly were done in the Public School: which surely should fill us with horror. Therefore you are to safeguard the innocence of the boys.[59]

Lehy offered a measured response, admitting the lack of a "real separation" between younger and older students, but arguing that there was an "imperfect" division: "The younger who are few in number, have their own dormitory and have their own section in study halls. They are not permitted to mingle with the older students at recreation time."[60] Father Joseph Hanselman, doubling as prefect of studies and prefect of discipline, had already reviewed the norms for prefects, directing them to keep "a watchful eye . . . especially on Bath Room and Closets (those in the Yard as well as those in new building)."[61] At the end of July, Lehy told the general that all but a few students were fourteen or older and pledged that, henceforth, "I will not accept boys younger than 14." Apparently, these answers satisfied Father Martin, who urged again vigilant discipline and consistent guidance according to religious norms of modesty.[62] A related

57. Joseph F. Kett, *Rites of Passage: Adolescence in America, 1790 to the Present* (New York: Basic Books, 1977).

58. Provincials' Memorials, March 23, 1894, and June 3, 1896, ACHC, 19.1-2. In 1894, Father Martin wrote to Pardow: "It is greatly to be desired that the College be separated from the Preparatory School lest morals be subjected to danger." Rome, March 25, 1894, ARSI, MD Reg. III, 213.

59. Martin to Lehy, Rome, April 9, 1897, ACHC, 19.1.

60. Lehy to Martin, Worcester, April 30, 1897, ARSI, MD Reg. IV, 24.

61. Consultors' Minute Book, May 2, 1897, ACHC, 19.0; Prefect of Discipline Diary, March 31, 1897, ACHC, 15.2-2.

62. Lehy to Martin, Worcester, July 31, 1897, ARSI, MD 13-XXV, 2; Martin to Lehy, Rome, September 2, 1897, ARSI, MD Reg. III, 387.

question arose on the topic of inviting guests from the city to public functions in the large hall. The objection was that girls and young women would come "and thus students [would] become acquainted with them." The consultors resolved the question by agreeing to charge admission for public events so that the number of younger female guests "would be considerably diminished."[63]

As the authorities pondered the consequences of intermingling among ages and genders, they were careful to provide healthy outlets for youthful energy. The Sodality remained strong. Public performance was facilitated by the Dramatic Society and the Glee Club. Other non-athletic organizations included the Camera Club, Reading Room Association, Scientific Circle, Philharmonic Society, and the Mandolin, Banjo, and Guitar Club. Debating gave students practice in public speaking and kept participants in touch with contemporary issues; judges included the presidents of Clark University and Worcester Polytechnic Institute.[64] Some campus events were closed to the public. On the eve of Thanksgiving in 1891, the students who spent the holiday on campus entertained each other. The program opened with solos from several singers. "Professor" William Glasgow of the Poetry class next gave an exhibition with Indian clubs. Stanley Clinton of Rudiments then boxed John Jordan, the freshman football center, in a bout of four rounds. Two sentimental songs followed the boxing: "The Song that Reached My Heart," and "In Days of Old." After a comical speech by one of the students "in imitation of a Dutchman," the program concluded with community singing.[65] It was homespun entertainment with some jarring changes of pace, but a happy reflection of an age when people were accustomed to providing their own amusement.

The Purple originated in April 1894 when a general assembly of students voiced support for a College journal. In the first issue, in June 1894, the editors explained their goals: to be "a representative journal containing notes of interest, gathered from every pathway of Holy Cross life, a journal filled with useful articles and official college news," and to serve as a source of information to the alumni. The cost of subscriptions was one dollar per year for ten issues. *The Purple* carried essays on campus life, student fiction and poetry, editorials, social commentary, editorials, biographical sketches, and obituaries. Two thousand issues of the first number were printed.[66]

63. Consultors' Minute Book, September 27, 1896, ACHC, 19.0.

64. HD, 1894–1899; "The Freshman," March, 1891, ACHC, 10.0-4; *The Purple*, 1894–1901; Meagher and Grattan, *Spires*, 172–79.

65. "The Sophomore," December 1891, ACHC, 10.0-4.

66. Prefect of Discipline Diary, April 16, April 24, May 18, and September 14, 1894, ACHC, 15.2-2; HD, June 24, 1894; Worcester *Post*, May 19, 1894; *The Purple*, June 1894 and following.

By the end of the century, certain privileges and traditions were associated with the upper academic classes. In 1896, the Philosophers received permission to hear William Jennings Bryan speak in the city. Philosophers also received extra holidays: St. Catherine's Day on November 22, and extra free days at Christmas and Easter.[67] The Rhetoricians had a moment of glory in 1895 when they presented *Eutropius*, an original play in Greek and English, to "a large cultivated and appreciative audience." Father Lehy could hardly contain his delight: "To say that the rendition was a success would be but faint praise —it was eminently so."[68] By then, the Rhetoricians' Banquet—later called the Juniors' Banquet—was an annual tradition. The event originated about 1883, when the students in that class raised a fund to sponsor a festive evening "spread" on Halloween. In 1886, when the celebration was separated from Halloween, the collection supported a special student dinner, followed by entertainment. Members of Rhetoric class waited at table. By the 1890s there was a formal, catered dinner, sponsored and served by the Rhetoricians to all students, even day students. The host class decorated the refectory, and the students keenly appreciated the respite from the routine—in 1899, the sophomores (as Poetry was starting to be called) exhibited their high spirits when they entered the dining room "singing their class song and giving their class cheer." The meal that year was described as "well served and unstinted in quantity—all were satisfied." After dessert, the younger students were given boxes of candy and the older students, cigars, as the Rhetoricians presented a play. At 10:30, after the other classes had retired, the Rhetoricians sat down to their own supper with guests from the faculty. Well after midnight, when speeches and cigars had come to an end, the group retired. All students enjoyed a holiday the following day in honor of the Rhetoricians. The custom, one member of the faculty claimed, was "certainly a unique feature of Holy Cross."[69]

67. Prefect of Discipline Diary, December 22, 1893, ACHC, 15.2-2; HD, September 25, 1896; College Schedule, 1900–1901, ACHC, 14.0-3.

68. HD, June 19, 1895. The play was written by scholastic Terrence J. Shealy. The lines were in Greek, but the chorus spoke English, explaining the action. An English translation was distributed to the audience. Worcester *Telegram*, June 24, 1895.

69. HD, November 30, 1895, November 23, 1896, November 21, 1899. In 1896, the cost of sponsoring the dinner was between $6 and $7 for each member of the Rhetoric class. The after-dinner play that year was *Rob Roy*. HD, November 23, 1896. The 1896 event was covered as a favorable feature of life at Holy Cross by the Boston *Globe*, and the *Telegram* and *Spy* in Worcester. For a history of the Rhetoricians' Banquet, see the Worcester *Spy*, November 17, 1895. See also *The Purple*, June 1894, and December 1896.

Not unique at all was the widespread interest in sports. On campus, that involved individual and class competitions, especially in baseball and track and field events. The faculty well understood that physical activity was a benefit to morale, and they exercised discretionary judgment in releasing students from the classroom. Father O'Kane granted a holiday in September of 1890 "because the rain had lasted so long that everybody was getting the blues. The boys played ball all day." Four days later, a half-holiday was stretched to a full holiday for "a match game of ball" because of "the loveliness of the weather [and] the fact that there are more than two hundred boys in the house."[70] The following month, students participated in a campus-wide track and field competition; prizes were awarded in more than a dozen events. Weather permitting, two tennis courts received heavy use during recreation periods; in the winter, a skating rink was set up in front of Fenwick Hall.[71] The opening of the O'Kane gymnasium provided new possibilities. In September of that year, a teacher was engaged to offer four classes of "gymnasium drill," plus training in track events. The new facility could accommodate up to 1500 observers for track meets. The space proved to be less satisfactory when basketball became popular, because two rows of steel pillars interrupted the open floor space. "One played basketball at the risk of breaking one's bones," an alumnus remembered.[72]

Despite the popularity of other sports, it was intercollegiate baseball that became a craze at Holy Cross during the 1890s. Between 1888 and 1891, the number of scheduled games rose from eight to fourteen; starting in 1894, about 24 games were played every spring. Students and local residents followed the Holy Cross nine enthusiastically; even the faculty and administrators succumbed to the passion. Game details filled in the house diary, and baseball talk sometimes supplanted Cicero in the classroom, as a student noted in 1891:

During the latter part of the morning we were treated to a delightfull [sic] discourse on the advantage of base-ball by our professor. He pictured to us the many advantages which were derived from this game, and said we were improved by it, both intellectually, and physically, and that proficiency in the science of base-ball was absolutely necessary in order to become a "Sport."[73]

70. HD, September 19 and 23, 1890.
71. Worcester *Telegram*, October 11, 1890; HD, 1891–92.
72. Prefect of Discipline Diary, September 17, 1895, ACHC, 15.2-2; HD, February 22, 1897; Raymond J. Swords, Remarks at the dedication of the Hogan Campus Center, October 13, 1967, ACHC, 12.24.
73. Dennis J. Murphy, Class of 1894, Class of '94 Diary, May 7, 1891, ACHC, 10.0-4. See also Worcester *Post*, February 19, 1894.

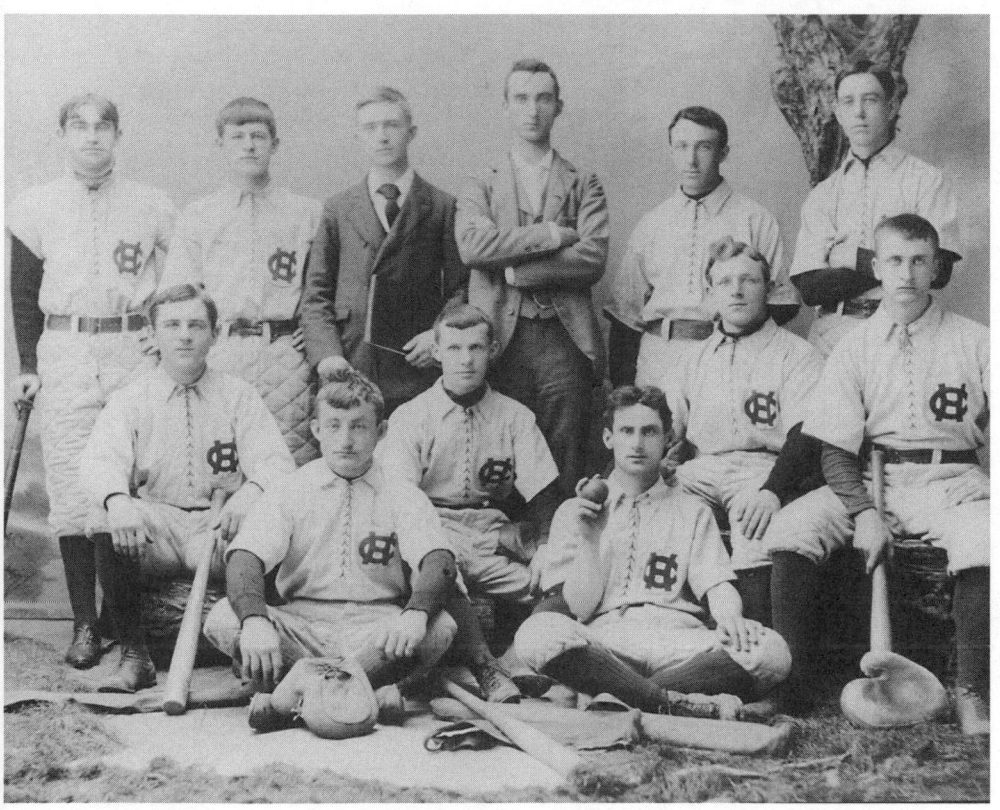

When baseball reigned supreme, this Holy Cross team in 1893 compiled a record of 11–5, including defeats of Harvard, Brown, and Georgetown.

It was a topic on which the students needed no persuasion. They followed the team avidly, particularly the contests with intercollegiate powerhouses like Harvard, Yale, and Brown. The 10–2 win at Brown in 1891 incited pandemonium: "The students seemed to have lost all control of themselves when they heard the result of the game. Bonfire—Fireworks—drums and music— shouts & yells—parades etc.—were the order of the night until the witching hour."[74] That celebration proved to be only a warm-up for the following week,

74. HD, June 6, 1891. The season scorecard for 1894 included seven "College Yells at H.C.C.," another indication of the zaniness of baseball mania during the 1890s. The options included: (1) "Hobble gobble, razzle dazzle; Sis boom bah; Holy Cross, Holy Cross, rah-rah-rah." (2) "Hooki, eyki, Kai-ai-ai; Hooki, eyki, Kai-ai-ai; Ho-o, ho-o-o; Hollobaloo, Holy Cross." (3) "Rickety rack, come back, come back; Rickety rack, come back, come back. Mia,

when Holy Cross defeated Harvard for the first time. A reporter noted that the Holy Cross and Boston College students attending the game in Cambridge "went wild. They threw their hats into the air and yelled until they were black in the face." Back in Worcester, there was no studying that evening as students, faculty and local citizens caught the spirit.

The air of this city was full of enthusiasm, last evening, which was inspired by the students of Holy Cross college. They were celebrating a victory of their ball team over the crack Harvard university club. A bon fire [sic] of large dimensions on the hill illuminated the southern section of the city, while groups of students paraded the streets, cheering and blowing horns while their breath lasted. M. J. Whittall of South Worcester illuminated his grounds in honor of the victory.

Whittall, whose carpet mills were close to the College, also provided fireworks.[75]

Throughout the country, the phenomenal popularity of baseball, the new vogue for school spirit, and the general willingness to accept the association between intercollegiate sports and the reputation of the school, promoted the practice of awarding athletic scholarships and fostered competition among schools for the best players. Athletic scholarships were awarded to baseball players as early as the 1870s; by the 1890s, Holy Cross had adopted the practice, though the number of scholarship athletes at first was small.[76] Only one full athletic scholarship is recorded before 1900; 21 other individuals received reduced tuition between 1880 and 1899, and it is likely that some of these involved athletes. Unregulated by rules, competition for players flourished. Holy Cross fell victim to Notre Dame in 1896, as the minister recorded:

Michael Powers, the *great* Captain of H.C.C.B.B. Nine for some years past & as a consequence a free scholar, recd. Indirectly . . . I believe, a bribe from The Notre Dame University & had too small a spirit to refuse it. He left College at 3 *this* afternoon. Instead of injuring, as we do not believe was intended, it will rather improve our *College Nine* & the College itself, though indeed other . . . small spirits, may imitate ex-Captain Powers.

The fear proved true. Two days later, shortstop Lou Sockalexis, a Native American from Old Town, Maine, also left for Notre Dame. Part of the blame was assigned to a student who had left for South Bend a year earlier be-

---

mia, Holy Cross, rah-rah-rah." (4) "Boom-a-lacka, boom-a-lacka, boom-a-lacka, boom; Boom-a-lacka, boom-a-lacka, boom-boom-boom."

75. HD, June 11, 1891; Worcester *Spy*, June 11, 1891.

76. Smith, *Sports*, 184–87;

cause Holy Cross would make no further reduction on his tuition.[77] Notre Dame had raided well. Powers went on to a major league career as catcher; Sockalexis played for Cleveland, where he allegedly inspired the team's designation as "Indians."

To keep pace with the interest in baseball, a playing field was built on the lower terrace, at the present-day sites of Carlin and Edith Stein Halls, using earth from the excavation of O'Kane. It was dedicated in the spring of 1893. The team drew well—a crowd of 4000, including the Jesuit provincial, watched Holy Cross defeat Dartmouth in 1895. In 1897, more seating was added; gate receipts were used to cover the cost.[78] Interest in the sport was so intense on all sides that the schedule of classes was altered in the spring of 1891, when the half-holidays were moved from Tuesday and Thursday to Wednesday and Saturday, freeing students and faculty for games. On another occasion, classes were advanced to allow faculty and students to attend the Dartmouth game. The 1895 team compiled a record of 17–5–2; Sockalexis batted .436 and his teammate William Maroney compiled an average of .376. At the conclusion of the 1895 season, the players, plus reporters from the *Spy* and *Telegram*, were feted at "a grand banquet" hosted by Father Hanselman.[79]

As baseball's popularity soared, football was gaining a place as well. It was first mentioned in the College annals in November of 1884, when students received a holiday for a game against Worcester Tech. Holy Cross won, 36–6. Despite that promising start, seven years elapsed before Father John Collins proposed a football association to the students in the fall of 1891. A committee drew up a constitution, and 194 students voted in the election for manager. That year, a single game was played against Dean Academy.[80] The following year, the players elected a manager and a captain, and played two games. In 1893 season, when the sport might have come into its own, Father McGurk imposed control by revoking the students' right to elect managers in baseball and football. At the start of the 1894 season, he disbanded the varsity football team because he was unwilling to let them play outside the city. "Everyone is pleased that Fr. Rector has taken this stand," Father Lehy wrote, for the record. With this restriction, football continued on a limited basis for two seasons: there were "junior" games between players from the lower classes and local rivals, and also intramural games.[81]

77. HD, December 16 and 18, 1896. See also Smith, *Sports*, 182–84.
78. HD, May 30, 1893, May 30, 1895, and May 2, 1897.
79. HD, April 27, June 6, and June 18, 1895.
80. HD, November 22, 1884; "The Sophomore," October, 1891, ACHC 10.0-4.
81. HD, 1891–1895; Worcester *Post*, October 20, 1894.

After Lehy assumed office in 1895, he discontinued the prohibition against away games, and the first regular season of six games was set up in 1896. Dr. A. C. N. Peterson, a Worcester resident who had played for Penn State, was hired as coach. That season included the only disputed game in the College's history, the contest against Boston College on November 14. The game ended with a disputed play involving a 4-point touchdown, as the game was then scored. Father James Gardiner recorded the "facts" for posterity:

Fr. Cryan with 24 students—the Foot-Ball Eleven—left on the 11 o'clock train for Boston, where they are to play the return Boston College game this afternoon. The team ret'd at 9:30 this evening—Score 6 to 4 in favor of Holy Cross team. A great row at end of 2nd half: Boston Team acted disgracefully & after our team had left, got the Umpire to reverse his decision, allow them a count of 4 for carrying ball across H.C. line after latter team had left field, & declaring game against H.C. by score of 8 to 6. No one, however, doubts the record, i.e., H.C. 6 to 4. In consequence of Boston College uniform dishonest & ungentlemanly conduct—Holy Cross will not, either in Foot or Base, Ball again contend with Boston College.[82]

Already, football was engaging strong feelings, and the long athletic rivalry with Boston College had begun.

Financial support and student loyalty to the College teams were organized through the Holy Cross Athletic Association, revived in the fall of 1894 under the leadership of Father Joseph Gorman, a professor of mathematics, who held the title of director. Annual dues were fifty cents, and the goal was "to furnish the students of the college with the best possible facilities for the promotion of general athletics, as well as moral and financial support for the maintenance of representative Baseball, Football, and Track Teams." Supplemental associations were formed specifically for baseball and football. By 1896, Father Lehy had instituted the practice of having members of the association elect team managers for the varsity teams. In the same year, the College secured membership in the Intercollegiate Association of Amateur Athletes of America, a regulatory group that had originated as a track and field organization in 1875.[83] Two years later, the Athletic Association voted to withdraw from the ICAAAA and join a regional group. Such affiliations enabled Holy Cross athletes to participate in intercollegiate meets. The Athletic Association

82. HD, November 14, 1896; Holy Cross Athletic Association, 1992 Gridiron Guide.

83. Smith, *Sports and Freedom*, 107–9; College Catalogs, 1894–97; Prefect of Discipline Diary, 1894–96, ACHC, 15.2-2. The Worcester *Post* (September 18, 1894) reported that baseball players had *elected* a manager, marking "the revival of the old rule, whereby the students instead of the faculty shall elect the officers of the athletic association." Apparently McGurk's intervention in baseball lasted only one year.

also drew up rules to determine lettermen in each sport. In baseball and foot-ball, team managers still set up the schedules and "engaged" coaches.[84]

The Athletic Association managed the costs of varsity sports by setting the price of admission and handling the gate receipts. Two thousand people attended a track meet at the Worcester Rink in March 1896, paying admissions of fifty and seventy-five cents—a price deliberately set high "to keep out [the] rough element."[85] Baseball produced the largest crowds and gate receipts; after construction of the new bleachers in 1897, there were 1825 seats in the ballpark. Students paid fifteen cents for admission; the general public paid a quarter. Receipts covered the cost of umpires, police, and other expenses. In a pre-game exhibition in 1895, Lou Sockalexis threw a ball 131 yards, 8 inches to set a new amateur record; and William H. Fox (ex-1900) rounded the bases in 13 $^2/_5$ seconds. Visiting teams sometimes played for a guarantee, at other times for a percentage of the gate. Profits for the College Athletic Association var-ied according to the weather. The 6000 who attended the game on Patriots' Day in 1899 generated a profit of $830 for Holy Cross; in 1900, Brown's share of the Patriots' Day receipts was almost a thousand dollars.[86]

The enthusiasm for intercollegiate sports raised the red flag of athleti-cism in the minds of the Jesuit provincials. In 1892, Thomas Campbell warned against admitting students "merely for the purpose of helping athletic sports[,] especially those who[,] although well on in age, are compelled on ac-count of their backwardness to enter the classes of younger students. . . . It de-stroys the name of the College and in reality injures the sports."[87] In 1896, Fa-ther Pardow warned the Jesuits against singling out athletes for attention by offering them "more than their share of interest and time." The following year, Edward Purbrick forbade the admission of students solely on the basis of athletics.[88] By the mid-1890s, the general was also concerned about the mania for sports:

I have been informed that in the College, athletic games are indulged in with too much ardor and that too much time, labor and money is expended in these games.

---

84. *The Purple*, February, 1898; Prefect of Studies Diary, September 17 and 24, 1899, ACHC, 15.2-2. To earn a letter in baseball, a player had to be on the starting team or a regu-lar substitute; football letters required participation in four regular college games; in track, a student had to score at least one point in competition.

85. HD, March 12, 1896.

86. Records of profits and losses were kept in the Prefect of Discipline Diary, ACHC, 15.2–2. The House Diary contains some financial information and many other details.

87. Memorial of Thomas Campbell, March 6, 1892, ACHC, 19.1-2.

88. Memorial of Pardow, June 3, 1896, and Memorial of Purbrick, June 14, 1897, ACHC, 19.1-2.

The minds of the students become too excited; it promotes distractions and students are turned from their studies.[89]

Lehy replied blandly that there was no excess in sports, but the general was not to be deterred. He asked that the matter be debated formally among the community consultors, "lest a frivolous and worldly spirit should undermine the College." The mandated discussion was held in May 1897; after an apparently perfunctory review of the issue, no change in policy was indicated.[90] In fact, Lehy had been trying to hold the line. In 1897 he refused permission for the baseball team to take a four-day trip to Princeton during the Easter recess. In opposition to his dean of discipline, he also refused permission for five or six students to compete in team races at the University of Pennsylvania, because "such a trip would be looked upon unfavorably by the bishop and priests and many of the boys' parents, as it makes us too prominent in athletics, and apt to convey the impression that our discipline is being relaxed and prejudicial to study."[91]

The tug-of-war between Rome and Worcester about athletics involved the character of the schools and the nature of the educational process, as the participants in the debate surely sensed. At Harvard, Charles Eliot was worried enough about the impact of sports to propose a ban on intercollegiate athletics.[92] In her study of Jesuit colleges in New York City, Christa Klein argued that intercollegiate sports altered the character of the institutions. School officials tended to endorse athletics because team sports fostered loyalty to the school and appealed to the Catholics' desire to prove social equality. But at the same time, the movement for big-time campus sports was "a step towards secularization" for the Jesuit colleges because it opened the schools to a wider network of educational contacts.[93] That point was certainly valid for Holy Cross. Athletic competition decisively interrupted the older, largely self-enclosed routines. Contact with other schools and students introduced students and faculty to values and options whose sources lay outside the *Ratio*.

89. Martin to Lehy, Rome, September 1, 1896, ARSI, MD Reg. III, 334.

90. Martin to Lehy, April 9, 1897, ARSI, MD Reg. III, 368; Lehy to Martin, Worcester, July 31, 1897, ARSI, MD 13-XXV, 2. The minutes of the discussion on athletics read as follows: "Rev. Fr. Rector asked the consultors about the opinion that there was too much athletics in the college, & all were unanimous that there was no excess in this matter." Consultors' Minute Book, May 2, 1897, ACHC, 19.0.

91. Consultors' Minute Book, October 29, 1896, and March 28, 1897, ACHC, 19.0.

92. George E. Peterson, *The New England College in the Age of the University* (Amherst: Amherst College Press, 1964), 84; Smith, *Sports*, 215–16.

93. Klein, "Jesuits and Catholic Boyhood," 239–43, 255–58.

Evidence suggests that Jesuit authorities were aware of the implications of intercollegiate competition, and they argued about the proper place of college sports. But like it or not, the changes occurred, and they provided an avenue of interactive contact with the wider world.

The exuberant mood of the students sometimes strained campus discipline. In 1892, the students were temporarily grounded after returning late from the Harvard game. In 1896, 79 students—nearly half of the boarders—left campus without permission and "paraded in nightshirts" to meet the baseball team at the depot after a major victory over Brown. In 1899, 140 students ran off campus without permission after a victory over Yale at New Haven. The offenders lost town privileges for an extended period and were made to pay for broken band instruments.[94] Being out of bounds without permission and inebriation—sometimes in connection with athletic victories, and sometimes not—were the most frequent violations during the decade. The effort to hold the line on student drinking was unrelenting. Students who returned to campus under the influence of alcohol were almost always expelled. Less frequent were punishments for insubordination and other failures to accept the still heavily-ordered routine of campus life. Violations of the norms of sexual conduct always produced drastic consequences. In 1896, a student was expelled when he was caught writing "immoral letters." And in 1893, a student named Wood was expelled after being accused of "enticing students to visit bawdy houses[,] frequenting such places himself and . . . strong suspicion of more infamous conduct." Father O'Kane delivered the sentence in a dramatic confrontation in his office, inviting a city policeman to be present for the interview. "He ordered Wood to leave the State at once and never return," the record states.[95]

Often enough, efforts to enforce the disciplined quality of campus life created a contest of wills between students and administrators. "It is difficult to govern and direct the boarding students," Father Lehy reported to the general in 1899.[96] The difficulty was not for want of trying. When double rooms for Philosophers became available in O'Kane Hall, the rules required permission for students to visit between rooms; students were forbidden to cover transoms or to lock doors from the inside; lights-out was set at 9:50 P.M.[97] In 1892 and 1893, at the order of Michael O'Kane, boarding students were refused permis-

94. HD, May 4, 1892, May 19, 1896, May 20, 1897; Prefect of Discipline Diary, April 26, 1899, ACHC, 15.2-2.

95. HD, 1891–1901. The Wood episode occurred on March 22 and 23, 1893.

96. Lehy to Martin, Worcester, January 31, 1899, ARSI, MD 13-XXV, 8.

97. Prefect of Discipline Diary, ACHC, 15.2-2.

sion to go home for Thanksgiving. "The boys ought to be grateful," the Jesuit minister wrote; "90 per cent of them got a better dinner here than they would have got at home." The older students sometimes resented the extent of control: in 1893, the Philosophers declined to attend a public lecture because they didn't want to be out in public under the guidance of a prefect.[98]

The academic schedule at the turn of the century showed little change from earlier days. Students still arrived during the first week of September. The school year opened with religious exercises and the reading of class lists. In 1900–1901, grades were still read monthly, on the second Thursday of the month. After the monthly assembly, students adjourned to their respective classrooms to learn their class standing. The many hours spent in those rooms left indelible impressions in the students' minds. In the First Humanities classroom, the walls were crowded with pictures of the Roman world, oriented toward drama and death: a chariot race in the Circus Maximus, Julius Caesar's assassination, gladiators saluting the emperor in the arena (with the legend *"Ave Caesar Imperator, morituri te salutant"*), a picture of Death surrounded by a variety of its victims, and a crucifix. The room also held library books— mostly classical authors and Shakespeare. The large study hall had north-facing windows, from which students could see Mount Wachusett. The supervisor sat in the rear, on an elevated platform for better visibility.[99]

The rising enrollment of the 1890s necessitated the division of some classes. During the 1896–97 academic year, there were two sections of Poetry and two of First Humanities, called A and B sections. Poetry A prepared 1860 lines of Latin, 1185 lines of Greek, and 200 lines of English and Latin memorization for the end of year exams. Poetry B prepared less Latin and Greek. Rhetoricians memorized 150 lines of Juvenal and the final scene of *Hamlet*, in addition to learning texts from Cicero, Juvenal, Perseus, Demosthenes, and Aeschylus. All students studied mathematics, with Father Lehy teaching the advanced classes. The curriculum also retained three years of French, and physical sciences in the later years.[100] Special classes in Latin and Greek remained an important part of the academic program; peak enrollments were 84 in 1897, and 75 in 1892; the low point was 1895, when 31 students enrolled.

Examinations continued to be a strenuous ordeal. They were preceded by 21 days of review in each class. Written exams were given first, then the orals.

98. HD, November 26, 1892, and November 30, 1893.

99. W. C. Leary, "Our Study Hall," and F. M. Phelan, "A Journey around Our Classroom," in "The Freshman," March 1891, ACHC, 10.0-4; J. P. O'Brien, 1894 Class Diary, ACHC, 10.0-4.

100. Prefect of Studies Record, 1891–97, ACHC, 14.0-2.

Students were examined in alphabetical order by a board of two examiners. In Third Humanities and above, students were questioned for 13 minutes each in Latin, Greek, and English. Mathematics orals ranged from 8 to 12 minutes in length.[101] The fullest account of grading procedures appears in documents from the 1893–94 academic year. Mid-year grades were read on February 3. Students whose grades were above 95 percent were given a ticket of merit. Those who failed one or more exams were required to attend "free studies" until they remedied the deficiency by a make-up exam. 120 students (46 percent) fell into this category. Half of those students earned passing grades in a second examination in mid-February; the others were given a third chance later in the month. Some students received February demotions. Report cards were sent four times during the academic year.[102]

Fidelity to the norms and methods of the Ratio Studiorum concealed the fact that, by the late 1890s, the program as it existed in its relatively pristine state at Holy Cross was in trouble. A major source of difficulty was the influence of Charles William Eliot. He had largely accomplished his plan of transforming Harvard from a liberal arts college to a university of specialized professionals by blending the undergraduate college with the university via the elective system for college students. By the early twentieth century, the only universally required course for Harvard undergraduates was English composition in the first year. Lecture and seminar courses had replaced recitation and memorization as the method of learning. A new generation of students, products of the system, were being channeled to professional careers through graduate schools in law, medicine, and other academic fields. In time, every American college was affected by these changes, because of the power Harvard (and comparable universities) held in setting admission standards for their professional degree programs.[103] A case in point is the Harvard Law School, which pioneered the reform of legal education after President Eliot appointed Christopher Columbus Langdell to be its head in 1870. Langdell and his successor, James Barr Ames, transformed the school between 1870 and 1910: the program was lengthened to three years, and the case method was adopted as the "scientific" approach to legal studies.[104] The goal was to accept only highly

101. Prefect of Discipline Diary, 1894–96, ACHC, 15.2-2.
102. Prefect of Discipline Diary, 1894–97, ACHC, 15.2-2.
103. Horowitz, *Campus*, 70–71.
104. Robert Stevens, "Two Cheers for 1870: The American Law School," in *Law in American History*, ed. Donald Fleming and Bernard Bailyn (Boston: Little Brown and Co., 1971), 426–37.

Holding the line on Latin and Greek: the Special B class in 1892, with their teacher, Patrick M. Collins, who was then a Jesuit scholastic.

qualified applicants. Mediocre students, it was argued, lessened the value of the degree and weakened the atmosphere of study and learning, since "slate in coal impedes combustion."[105] By 1909, a B.A. had finally been established as an absolute requirement for admission to Harvard Law School; also, the prior question of what a given institution's baccalaureate actually signified had been raised, and Holy Cross did not fare well under scrutiny at Harvard.

The question came up for the first time in 1893, when the Harvard Law School faculty voted that, beginning in the fall of 1896, only persons qualified

105. Arthur E. Sutherland, *The Law at Harvard: A History of Ideas and Men, 1817–1967* (Cambridge: Harvard University Press, 1967), 167–68; Stevens, "Two Cheers," 426–27.

for the senior class in Harvard or graduates of 106 approved colleges would be admitted. No Jesuit colleges were on the approved list. Immediately, J. Havens Richards, the president of Georgetown, objected that many Catholic colleges were "at least comparable" to schools on the list and supplied evidence that tended to sustain the value of a Georgetown degree. Eliot added Georgetown to the list; whereupon, at the provincial's request, Richards wrote again, asking that all Jesuit colleges be included, since their curriculums were essentially the same. Eliot added Holy Cross and Boston College, but would go no further.[106] For the moment, the value of the Holy Cross curriculum had been sustained, but issues had been raised concerning the academic level of the *Ratio* and its compatibility with the Harvard concept of college education. Since Harvard students were deemed capable of admission to the law school at the start of senior year, the basic question was: could a *graduating senior* from a given college be successfully admitted *into the senior class* at Harvard? The affirmative answer accorded to Georgetown, Holy Cross, and Boston College in 1893 did not betoken a recognition that their graduating seniors were equal to Harvard's, only that they were no more than one year behind.

At first, Jesuit educators tried to meet the challenge without sacrificing the traditional features of the *Ratio*. When Edward Purbrick was designated to head the Maryland–New York Province in 1897, one of the reasons offered was that his predecessor, James Pardow, had failed to enforce conformity to Jesuit educational norms, even though he had authorized a province-wide review of the program.[107] One of the easier modifications involved terminology. In 1895, the Jesuit colleges in New York City abandoned the archaic designation of the various years in favor of freshman, sophomore, junior, and senior.[108] Holy Cross held out for a few years longer, but by 1897, Father Hanselman was using the old and new terminology indiscriminately. In the fall of that year, the Rhetoricians' Banquet became the Juniors' Banquet and the language in the catalog was changed. At that time, the upper four years were designated according to the modern terminology; the lower three years kept the traditional names.[109]

Maintaining a prescribed course of studies challenged administrators and

106. Kathleen Mahoney, "Fin-de-Siècle Catholics: Insiders and Outsiders at Harvard," in *U.S. Catholic Historian* 13 (Fall 1995), 22–24.

107. Notes on the 1896 Committee, MPA, 520 D; Martin to Pardow, Rome, March 22, 1896, ARSI, MD Reg. III, 331–32; Martin to Purbrick, Rome, March 2, 1897, ARSI, MD Reg. III, 357–58.

108. Klein, "Jesuits," 183.

109. Prefect of Discipline Diary, March 18 and November 15, 1897, November 14–16, 1898, ACHC, 15.2-2.

faculty to make the case that their alumni compared favorably with graduates of more open curriculums. The 1895 Holy Cross catalog provided a philosophical defense of the system: "The student at the end of his college course will not have mastered any special profession, but his mind will be so disciplined as to enable him to pursue a professional or business career with a more vigorous mental activity, with more painstaking care, order, method, energy and perseverance, and therefore with greater ease and more pronounced success, than if he had spent his years without any systematic training whatever, or in pursuing a course other than the one here prescribed." At the same time, academic quality had to be examined critically at all Jesuit schools, as Father Havens was insisting. In the fall of 1897, the Holy Cross consultors debated the best means "to elevate the standard of studies." The need for "elevation" was apparent in both senses of the word—tightening admissions and standards for promotion, and raising the academic level of the curriculum itself. The consultors mandated strict adherence to the entrance examination and laid down the policy that "we do not admit students who come simply for athletics." Concerned that standards for promotion had been too lax, they launched a new effort to define and sustain high standards. They also agreed on the need for increased emphasis on non-classics courses—French, mathematics, and chemistry. And, perhaps more telling than any other change, they voted that henceforth high school graduates would be admitted only to First Humanities (freshman year) and not to Poetry (sophomore year) as had hitherto been the case (Chart 4.2).[110] In effect, the consultors were groping toward a compromise that would harmonize the *Ratio* with the American plan of organization. The issue of the comparative value of a Holy Cross degree was clearly in the background. By accepting high school graduates only into First Humanities, the consultors were attempting to redefine Holy Cross as a modern four-year college by shifting the curriculum upwards one notch. As events were to prove, stricter standards and semantic alterations could not accomplish that goal.

As the reforms of 1897 were being instituted, the Harvard Law faculty was reviewing its list of selected schools. In February of 1898, Dean Ames informed Boston College rector, Timothy Brosnahan, that the review was under way because so many colleges with questionable standards were seeking placement on the list. Necessarily, this review included a re-examination of the Jesuit colleges. In time, Ames received an opinion from the chair of Harvard's Committee on Admission from Other Undergraduate Colleges, that

110. Consultors' Minute Book, September 17, 1897, ACHC, 19.0; Mahoney, "Fin-de-Siècle Catholics," 25.

Chart 4.2 The Holy Cross Curriculum, 1897–1901

1897–98	1899–1900	1900–1901
Collegiate Department	*The College Course*	*College Courses*
Senior Class (Philosophy)	Senior	Philosophy (3 Sr.; 4 Jr.)
Junior Class (Rhetoric)	Junior	Political Economy (Sr.)
Sophomore Class (Poetry)	Sophomore	Latin (4 yrs.)
Freshman Class (First Humanities)	Freshman	Greek (Jr., So., Fr.)
		English (4 yrs.)
		History (2 yrs.)
		Mathematics (Jr., So., Fr.)
		Sciences (Sr., Jr., So.)
		Christian Doctrine (4 yrs.)
		Modern Languages (2 yrs.)
Preparatory Department	*The Academic Course*	*Preparatory Department*
Second Humanities	First Academic	First Academic
Third Humanities	Second Academic	Second Academic
Rudiments	Third Academic	Third Academic
	Fourth Academic	Fourth Academic
[Special Classics]		
	[Special Classics]	[Special Classics]
		[Rudiments]

Holy Cross and Boston College graduates were at least two years behind Harvard graduates in academic achievement. Despite Father Brosnahan's pleading, both Holy Cross and Boston College were dropped from the preferred list in 1898. Of the colleges under Catholic sponsorship, only Notre Dame and Georgetown were accorded preferred status. Georgetown's inclusion prompted Fathers Brosnahan and Lehy to appeal the decision on the grounds that the curriculum at their schools was identical to Georgetown's —the argument that had proven successful in 1893. Once again, Harvard officials relented and reinstated Holy Cross and Boston College; but when Fordham appealed its exclusion, Eliot and Ames reversed themselves again. Ames asserted, in a letter to Eliot, that Boston College graduates were "two years below our standard," and that "we did not discover any considerable difference between the value of the Holy Cross and Boston College degrees. The graduates of these colleges, who have come to the Law School, have made poor records as a rule. Only one of the Holy Cross men has approached the honor mark."[111]

Charles Eliot corresponded with J. F. Lehy about the decision, citing evi-

111. Mahoney, "Fin-de-Siècle-Catholics," 26–28. The passage from the letter of Ames to Eliot, Cambridge, October 10, 1898, is quoted on page 28.

dence about the disappointing record of Holy Cross graduates at Harvard; he indicated his willingness to assist in bringing the Jesuit colleges up to grade by meeting with Lehy to discuss "the whole matter of the relations of the colleges in charge of the Society of Jesus to our professional schools." He also admitted that keeping Georgetown on the list may have been a mistake, but the point was relatively unimportant because so few Georgetown alumni then applied to professional schools at Harvard. That was not the case for Boston College and Holy Cross:

Boston College and Holy Cross have sent a considerable number of graduates to our schools of Law and Medicine, and we shall be very sorry to lose them, although, as I have stated above, they as a rule do not make high scores. We should, of course, be very sorry to do any injustice to the Catholic colleges in general, and particularly to those situated in Massachusetts; and we should be very glad to promote the tendency of the graduates of Holy Cross to go into secular professions, for we believe that the tendency will be very wholesome for Holy Cross College itself in the future.[112]

To W. G. Read Mullen, the new rector of Boston College, Eliot wrote: "The Law School adheres to its opinion that Georgetown is the best of the Jesuit colleges, and is entitled to stand in the Law School list if any Jesuit college is to be admitted to the list. . . . I am inclined to believe that Georgetown was originally placed in the list, lest it should seem to some persons that the Catholic colleges had been excluded on religious grounds."[113] It was hardly an endorsement of Georgetown or of the Jesuit plan. In fact, Eliot was urging that the Jesuit colleges upgrade their programs to the level of the schools on Harvard's list. His views on the *Ratio Studiorum* as the antithesis of electivism he saved for another day.

That day arrived on July 10, 1899, when Eliot addressed the American Institute of Instruction. His remarks were published in the October 1899 issue of *The Atlantic Monthly* under the title "Recent Changes in Secondary Education." Most of the piece described the rising prominence of American high schools and advocated an elective curriculum at that level. Toward the end, he delivered the blow that nettled Jesuit educators and their alumni:

There are those who say that there should be no election of studies in secondary schools,—that the school committee, or the superintendent, or the neighboring college, or a consensus of university opinion, should lay down the right course of study for the secondary school, and that every child should be obliged to follow it. This is precisely the method followed in Moslem countries, where the Koran prescribes the

112. Eliot to Lehy, Cambridge, October 24, 1898 [copy], MPA, 520 D.
113. Eliot to W. G. Read Mullen, Cambridge, December 8, 1899 [copy], MPA, 520 D.

perfect education to be administered to all children alike. . . . Another instance of uniform prescribed education may be found in the curriculum of the Jesuit colleges, which has remained almost unchanged for four hundred years, disregarding some trifling concessions made to natural science.

That these examples are both ecclesiastical is not without significance. Nothing but an unhesitating belief in the Divine wisdom of such prescriptions can justify them; for no human wisdom is equal to contriving a prescribed course of study equally sound for even two children of the same family, between the ages of eight and eighteen. Direct revelation from on high would be the only satisfactory basis for a uniform prescribed school curriculum. The immense deepening and expanding of human knowledge in the nineteenth century, and the increasing sense of the sanctity of the individual's gifts and will-power, have made uniform prescriptions of study in secondary schools impossible and absurd.

We must absolutely give up the notion that any set of human beings, however wise and learned, can ever again construct and enforce on school children one uniform course of study.[114]

Thirty years after beginning his campaign for electivism, the Harvard president had assaulted the educational philosophy that sustained the *Ratio*. Now, Jesuit educators had no alternative but to react.

One avenue of response was undertaken by Read Mullen, who engaged Eliot in lengthy correspondence that Read published early in 1900 in the *Boston Globe* and the Catholic press. A more elaborated response was prepared by Timothy Brosnahan, now on the faculty of the Jesuit seminary in Maryland. Acting at the request of Edward Purbrick, who found Eliot's comments offensive, he published his answer in January of 1900 in the *Sacred Heart Review*, after being refused by the editors of *The Atlantic Monthly*.[115] The opening criticized Eliot for inaccuracy in asserting that the curriculum had made only "some trifling concessions to natural sciences." Citing the Georgetown curriculum, Brosnahan noted that nearly half of school hours were devoted to subjects other than Latin and Greek, including a substantial amount for the sciences. At Harvard, it was possible under the elective system to graduate without any study of natural science. "It would seem that in such cases Harvard has made no concession at all, either trifling or important, to natural sciences."

The second part defended Jesuit education as an enlightened approach to the problem of educating students both as individuals and as members of the human community. Brosnahan accused Eliot of extremism in addressing the

114. Charles W. Eliot, "Recent Changes in Secondary Education," in *The Atlantic Monthly* 84 (October 1899), 433–44.

115. Mahoney, "Fin-de-Siècle Catholics," 34–41.

problem: "He banishes unity from college education and bows down before individuality." In Brosnahan's view, a comparison between the Harvard approach to collegiate education and the Jesuit system worked to the advantage of the latter because electivism abandons "the doctrine of unity in education" and "would tend to lower the standard of education, to lessen the intrinsic value of a college degree, to give onesided formation, to unfit men for effective University work." On the main point, Brosnahan had a great deal of support, and he cited President William Rainey Harper of the University of Chicago as one of several allies.[116] Students need guidance, he asserted, to counter the tendency to work "like electricity, along the line of least resistance." Brosnahan distinguished between the task of a college and that of a university, using Columbia University President Seth Low's definition: "A college is conceived of as a place of liberal culture, a university as a place for specialization based upon liberal culture." Under this definition, electivism was appropriate to graduate and professional schools, but not to colleges. Ultimately, only the college, as the opponents of electivism defined it, could properly form the mind and character of the student:

By the constant exercise and concordant enlargement of many faculties, by an introduction to many sciences, by grounding in logic, in the general principles of philosophy, and in ethics, it preserves any faculty in the formative period of life from so abnormally developing as to stunt or atrophy others; it widens the outlook, warding off the conceit and self-sufficiency of the boy specialist; it lays before him in large outline a map of the realm he may afterwards traverse in part and in detail, and it coordinates and relates his after specialty to other learning.

Brosnahan borrowed an analogy from President Melancthon Woolsey Stryker of Hamilton College, that a college makes iron into steel, while a university makes steel into tools; therefore, "specialization not based upon a liberal culture attempts to put an edge on pot-iron."

It was a striking defense of the Jesuit approach to liberal humanism; it positioned the amplified Ratio of the late nineteenth century with an emerging concept of liberal education that distributed undergraduate study among the humanities, social sciences, and physical sciences. Eliot and his allies were not moved by these arguments; nor were there any concessions from the considerable group of non-Jesuit American educators who opposed electivism. The debate endured. But "Brosnahan's Reply to Eliot," as

116. Yet Harper was not a defender of traditional humanistic studies. Frederick Rudolph argues that "the curriculum at the University of Chicago was quite as chaotic as elsewhere, but it did not seem so, and that was an achievement not just for public relations but also for institutional unity." *Curriculum*, 199.

the article was popularly known, was studied by American Jesuits and their students for decades as a clear statement of their educational philosophy and method.

At Holy Cross, Eliot's attack became the *cause célèbre* at the Third Annual Worcester County Alumni Banquet in January of 1900. Alumni were invited from all of New England and from New York, making it the largest alumni gathering in history. James B. Carroll, Class of 1878, a Springfield lawyer, set the tone by defending Jesuit concepts of formation and liberal education. Msgr. Conaty returned from Washington to remind the alumni that the Holy Cross diploma was "our passport to the professions, upon it our standing as college men rests." In the main address, a Boston College professor, Francis J. Barnes, himself an alumnus of Boston College and the Harvard Medical School, accused Eliot of educational megalomania and anti-Catholicism. In Barnes's view, Eliot was "determined to destroy" Catholic schools by "branding our colleges with the stigma of inferiority":

Take off the mask of liberality which our opponents wear in public and you will see that it is used to cover the black visage of bigotry. Even the liberal, broad-minded president of Harvard University, in his venomous sneers at the Jesuit colleges, now displays a spirit of intolerance which up to this time he has wisely restrained. For years, he has posed as an unprejudiced observer and fair-minded critic of educational methods, but now, when he deems the time is ripe for putting his schemes into execution, he appears in his true character—a dogmatizing bigot.

Although the speakers were interrupted more than a hundred times with applause, Father Lehy offered an oddly downbeat response, stating merely that the speakers "had given him something to consider."[117] In backing off from engagement in the debate, Lehy was running true to form; preoccupied with other problems, he was content to let Brosnahan, Mullen, and others confront Eliot in public; perhaps he also wanted to distance himself from the intemperate tone of remarks that caused a sensation in the press. Asked by a Boston reporter to respond to Barnes, Eliot held his ground, maintaining that the Jesuit schools were "not advancing." Of Barnes, he said, "Let him talk. It won't hurt me any. And I only hope that things will be so stirred up by what he says that the Jesuit colleges will be bettered thereby."[118]

Despite the condescending tone of his article, Eliot did Holy Cross and the other Jesuit colleges a service by forcing a re-examination of the level of

117. Worcester *Telegram*, January 23, 1900.
118. Boston *Journal*, January 24, 1900; Mahoney, Fin-de-Siècle Catholics," 39.

their academic programs and the relationship between their seven-year curriculum and the standard educational pattern in the United States. On the
issue of classical humanism versus electivism, there was too much disagreement among American educators for the point to be settled according to
Eliot's design. Classical humanism, and the Jesuit notion of character formation, had influential friends beyond the slopes of Pakachoag and the Society
of Jesus. Those elements of the College program could weather the storm. By
1900, the catalog was extolling the *Ratio Studiorum* as "a body of rules and suggestions [that] has been elaborated by centuries of experience and . . . judged
worthy of attentive study and hearty approbation by the ablest scholars." The
graduate of the program would be "possessed of trained and cultivated faculties" and "so disciplined as to enable him to pursue any professional or business career."

But the questionable value of a Holy Cross degree called for change; it was
up to College authorities to upgrade the degree to enhance the reputation of
the school and promote the careers of its almumni. Even friends of Holy
Cross had reservations about the rigor and the level of studies. In 1899 Edward
Purbrick noted that six of the eighteen Jesuits listed as full-time teachers were
"more or less invalids."[119] Two years later, Bishop Bernard McQuaid of Rochester offered a mixed review on the College alumni in his seminary: "All the
Holy Cross boys . . . have been fine, manly, and honorable young men. They
are not of equal merit intellectually. . . ."[120] In Rome, Father Martin stressed
the importance of academics after learning of Eliot's attack. To Lehy, he suggested that there was not much to worry about "as long as the studies are promoted with strong emphasis."[121]

The general tightening of academic requirements and admissions standards in 1897 were genuine efforts to position Holy Cross more favorably in
the contemporary academic world. By 1899 it was clear that those efforts had
been insufficient. And so, in his final years as rector, J. F. Lehy made further
attempts at "elevation." In the fall of 1899, the Holy Cross curriculum was
lengthened to eight years by adding an extra year, "Fourth Academic," to the
lower division, or "Academic Course" (Chart 4.2). The College years were designated according to the American terminology—freshman, sophomore, junior, senior, with a prescribed curriculum at each level. Freshmen and sophomores took Latin, English, Greek, history, mathematics, and Christian doctrine.
Juniors took less Latin, Greek, and English, and more classes in the physical

119. Purbrick to Martin, New York, February 17, 1899, ARSI, MD 13-XXV, 9.
120. McQuaid to Lehy, Rochester, August 21, 1901, ACHC, 12.13-1.
121. Martin to Lehy, Rome, April 7, 1900, ARSI, MD Reg. III, 454.

sciences. They also studied philosophy of history and political economy. Seniors concentrated heavily on philosophy (twice each day) and on the physical sciences. In addition to classics, students in the Academic Course studied history, modern languages, "science," and Christian doctrine. Supplementary classes in Special Classics were maintained outside the regular curriculum for otherwise qualified students.

The 1900 Catalog re-defined the preparatory department as "a Classical High School" and treated it as a separate entity rather than as a downward extension of the college program. Applicants needed eight years of "pre-academic work, or its equivalent." Preparatory students took four years of Latin, English, history, and mathematics, 3½ years of Greek, and 2 years of French or German. Rudiments, which was not listed in 1899, reappeared in 1900 as a special class in which applicants who were "not prepared to meet the requirements for entrance in the first-year courses . . . will be taught the branches in which they are deficient." Sixteen students fell into that category in 1900–1901. Although there were no modern academic departments in 1900, college courses were arranged by subject for the first time, each course carrying a description of contents and a designation of the year in which it was taken. Under Philosophy, seniors studied psychology, natural theology, and ethics, while juniors took cosmology and metaphysics. College science courses included optional physics for seniors planning on medical school, physics and analytical chemistry for juniors, and general chemistry and geology for sophomores. In History, seniors studied the history of philosophy; juniors took the philosophy of history; sophomores learned church history and United States history; and freshmen studied world history. By then, college students could elect a few options in mathematics, natural science, and modern languages. The *Ratio Studiorum* was clearly evident in the content of the curriculum, but the organization had become recognizably American. It was a step toward making Holy Cross degrees comparable with those of other schools; experience and outside reaction would indicate the next move.

Besides the furor associated with Charles Eliot, the end of the century brought an important milestone to the College: the fiftieth anniversary of the first graduation. The sole surviving member of the Class of 1849 was James Healy, who had been bishop of Portland since 1875. It was his practice to attend commencements whenever possible, but in 1899, he was invited "in a special way" to be honored as the school's first golden jubilarian. The center of attention, as he had been fifty years earlier when he delivered the valedictory, Healy addressed the last commencement to be attended by the entire student body as a requirement.[122] He offered realism rather than optimism to the 43 graduates: "When our class went into the world we thought well of ourselves, but we were but four, and no doubt you young men, who are over forty, must think that there will be a great commotion and the world will be stirred; but it won't. It will be the same world tomorrow."[123] Like most words of wisdom offered to graduates, Healy's were useful, up to a point; the young men, whose active lives would span the first half of the twentieth century, did well to take the his advice to heart. But the graduates of 1899 were encountering a world very different from the one James and Hugh Healy, John Brownson, and John McCabe had found a dozen years before the Civil War. Administrators, faculty, and alumni were aware of the magnitude of the educational challenges they faced. On the brink of a new century, they were laboring to sort out the legitimate claims of tradition and those of progress. Whether the source of the difficulty was Charles Eliot's abrasive caricature of the *Ratio*, or the admitted need to raise the academic level of the school, the challenge was to utilize the Ignatian spirit of adaptation in shaping Holy Cross to be faithful to the spirit of the *magis* and responsive to the needs of the times.

Bishop Healy did not witness the outcome of the upheavals that rocked the College during his latter years; on August 5, 1900, he died at the age of seventy. With his passing, an era came to an end. One of his eulogists praised his "piety and learning" and noted with poignant understatement that his death was a loss for the College, "not alone for the material benefits which it gained but for the influence which he exercised on its behalf."[124] More than a loyal alumnus, Healy had become a symbol of the first Holy Cross—its particular learning and piety, its human dimensions and achievement and spirit. He aspired to that role for over fifty years, and he played his part well. At his request, the small crucifix he had brought from Holy Cross in 1849 was placed in his hand as he lay in state.[125]

---

122. In June 1900, J. F. Lehy decided to allow students to leave school after they finished their examinations, without the customary obligation of remaining for Commencement. The idea that the exercises functioned partly as an "exhibition" of academic talent for all classes was now outmoded. HD, June 15, 1900.

123. *The Purple*, July, 1899; Consultors' Minute Book, May 2, 1899, ACHC, 19.0.

124. HD, August 5 and 8, 1900.

125. Foley, *Beloved Outcaste*, 238

PART TWO

"To Maintain This Splendid Tradition"

CHAPTER FIVE

The Emergence of the Second Holy Cross,
1901—1911

B Y 1901, HOLY CROSS had made substantial progress in adapting to contemporary academic standards, but the process was still incomplete. The curriculum had been expanded to eight years, with a separate college segment; but the comparative value of a Holy Cross degree still had to be established. The opening of O'Kane Hall accelerated the rise in enrollment, and facilities were again being strained; but a heavy debt impeded further expansion. The tightness of space raised the fundamental question of whether it was desirable to drop the high school to create more space for the college. The popularity of varsity sports stimulated school spirit but vexed administrators, who struggled simultaneously to foster alumni loyalty and to raise the academic reputation of the school. After Father Lehy stepped down, these issues—the unfinished agenda of the 1890s—challenged a new group of administrators and faculty. Under their guidance, in the space of a decade, Holy Cross addressed these issues and became an authentic modern college, the second Holy Cross in which the traditions and content of the *Ratio Studiorum* were cast into contemporary American form.

More than anyone else, Joseph Hanselman was the architect of the new Holy Cross. The son of Swiss and German immigrant parents, he was born in Brooklyn in 1856. He entered the Jesuits in 1878 and taught as a scholastic at St. Peter's College in Jersey City and at Fordham University. He was ordained in 1892 and assigned to Holy Cross in 1893, serving simultaneously as prefect of studies and prefect of discipline until he was assigned to Tertianship (a final year of ascetical training for Jesuits) in 1897. When he departed, the two offices were separated for good. Hanselman returned in 1898 as prefect of discipline and earned the nickname "Honest Hans" for his even-handedness. Hanselman succeeded J. F. Lehy as president and rector of Holy Cross in 1901.

In 1906 he began a six-year term as provincial of the Maryland-New York Province. In that capacity, he worked carefully with his Holy Cross successor, Thomas Murphy, to carry forward the plans and projects he had initiated. By 1912, when his term as provincial ended, Hanselman had been involved in some way with the administration of the College for most of the eighteen years of its evolution into a modern college. His capacity for work, his compassion, and his unassuming forthrightness made him an outstanding administrator, as an alumnus of 1905 recognized:

His personality was always dominant—It found expression in his spirit of great seriousness and austere integrity. He was unvaryingly amiable and simplicity itself. He said little but there was something about his presence that spoke constantly. In discipline he was strict—some thought hard at times but no one ever thought him unjust. Aside from the splendid achievements that he wrought for the college . . . , the men of Holy Cross will always revere his memory as the *vir justus* of eloquent silence.[1]

When Hanselman became rector of Holy Cross, his Jesuit provincial, Thomas Gannon, offered advice that rang with the spirit of the *magis:* "Great courage. Go slowly; our good God is with you and will give you great aid with certain success for his glory."[2] The sentiments were still echoing when Hanselman, collaborating with Thomas Murphy, his prefect of studies, initiated a period of unprecedented development. The physical plant, the curriculum, the alumni, the athletic program, the status of the preparatory division—every aspect of campus life was altered by Joseph Hanselman. By the fall of 1905, the pace of activities prompted him to hire a recent graduate as "a sort of secretary" to assist him in the office.[3] And when, at the mid-day meal on February 5, 1906, students and faculty received the unexpected announcement that Hanselman was being re-assigned that very day, the sadness was genuine. A few hours later, students and faculty stood in the cold as he bade them farewell from Fenwick porch. One observer remembered: "Many a tear filled the eyes of all who witnessed the departure of the one they loved so much."[4]

As rector from 1906 to 1911, Thomas Murphy carried the momentum forward. A native of New York City, Murphy entered the Jesuits in 1875 and

1. Joseph C. Fleming, S.J. '05, *The Purple*, 35: 407. In 1912, he was appointed rector of the Jesuit seminary at Woodstock, Maryland; and from 1918 until his death in 1923, he was a general assistant to Jesuit General Wlodimir Ledochowski—a position at the Society's headquarters in Rome that made him the general's principal advisor on the personnel and works of United States Jesuits. On Hanselman, see *WL*, 52:382–97.
2. Gannon to Hanselman, August 31, 1901, Provincial's Correspondence, ACHC, 19.1.
3. HD, August 24, 1901 and October 18, 1905; *The Purple*, 52:401–3.
4. Prefect of Discipline Diary, February 5, 1906, ACHC, 15.2-2.

Joseph F. Hanselman, College President, 1901–1906, was a primary influence in adjusting the traditional curriculum to contemporary patterns and establishing the pattern of campus expansion.

taught at Georgetown as a scholastic. After his ordination in 1890, he was assigned to pastoral work and then, in 1894, to the presidency of St. Francis
Xavier College in New York City. That responsibility took a toll on his health,
and his assignment to Worcester in 1900 was designed to give him a chance to
recover. Scholarly in temperament, a defender of the importance of the classics, he worked hard and conscientiously. During his term as rector, the burden of office again affected his health; in 1908 and again in 1910, at Hanselman's insistence, he took long vacations to recover from neuralgia, neuritis,

and heavy colds. Despite his ailments, he proved to be a resolute leader, and Hanselman had enough confidence in his leadership and judgment to keep him in the post for 5 ½ years, completing a ten-year collaboration that set the basic pattern of the College for a half century.[5]

When Joseph Hanselman assumed office, the re-organized curriculum had been in place for one year. The new approach amplified and "elevated" degree requirements by the addition of new courses at the high end of the old plan.[6] Now there were two years of philosophy at the top of the academic ladder where formerly there had been a single year.[7] As prefect of studies, Father Murphy won limited recognition for the revised curriculum. In 1902, the New York State Board of Regents included Holy Cross among the schools whose graduates could use their senior year credits toward the first year in the professional schools run by the state of New York.[8] Harvard, on the other hand, still required Holy Cross students to take entrance examinations for its professional schools. But the difficulty of getting alumni into Harvard's professional schools slowly eased: in 1900, no Holy Cross graduate was admitted to a graduate program at Harvard; five members of the Class of 1903, however, graduated from the Harvard Medical School, and two members of the Class of 1904 completed studies at Harvard Law.[9] Undoubtedly, the reputation of Holy Cross was also enhanced by the reaction against electivism that gained strength after 1900. In 1909, Abbott Lawrence Lowell, an opponent of electivism, succeeded Eliot in the Harvard presidency and initiated curriculum reforms featuring distribution requirements and academic "concentrations."[10]

5. Murphy biographical sketch, ACHC, 12.15; HD, 1908–10; Hanselman to Murphy, New York, October 22, 1908, Provincial's Correspondence, ACHC, 19.1; *WL*, 36: 202; Meagher and Grattan, *Spires*, 196; *The Purple*, 35:401–3.

6. Laurence Andrew Dorr argues that the movement to add a year at the bottom of the *Ratio* and a year at the top started at St. Louis University in 1903, spreading to the other Jesuit schools by 1910. Evidence suggests, however, that that approach was essentially in place at Holy Cross by 1900. Dorr, "Academic Deans in Jesuit Higher Education: A Comparative Study of Deans, Jesuit and Lay" (Ph.D. Dissertation: University of Michigan, 1966), 50–51.

7. Curriculum Report, 1899–1909, ARSI, MD 15-XXII, 4 bis. Administrators were aware of the changes. Answering the request of an alumnus for a transcript of the work he had done at the College in 1898, Fr. Murphy pointed out that "what was then Fresh. is now 4th year Prep." John B. Purcell to Murphy, New York, June 8, 1910, [Murphy's notation] ACHC, 12.15.

8. Worcester *Telegram*, July 31, 1902.

9. Donovan et al., *Boston College*, 109; *The Purple*, October 1900 and October 1902; Worcester *Post*, June [?] 1907.

10. Rudolph, *Curriculum*, 207. In 1904, Harvard English Professor Barrett Wendell called electivism "doing what everybody likes best . . . the principle of the kindergarten." "Our National

A number of constraints, including the uneven academic skills of some students, served as brakes on further curricular reform. Because Greek and the more rigorous science courses created difficulties for some students, College officials decided in 1902 to offer a Bachelor of Philosophy degree, the Ph.B.,[11] to students who were unable to pass mandatory A.B. courses. "Thus we will hold for philosophy some young men who will otherwise leave," they reasoned. In 1903, one student was awarded a Ph.B. after failing chemistry and mathematics, but two seniors who failed philosophy (and presumably passed in science and mathematics) were refused degrees. The number of Ph.B. recipients remained very low for several decades. Between 1903 and 1911, twelve graduates received Ph.B. degrees, while 428 earned the A.B.[12]

The concession of a Ph.B. for students who could not master Greek, mathematics, or science was the absolute limit of compromise for the time being. Father Murphy and others continued to resist appeals to weaken the classical curriculum by dropping Greek. In the fall of 1906, in fact, "Special Greek" was replaced with a new course, "Elementary Greek for Freshmen." The change was mostly a semantic shift that acknowledged the declining status of Greek in American high schools and integrated beginning Greek more tightly into the Holy Cross curriculum. Because of the declining popularity of classics at other schools,[13] Father Hanselman was careful to advertise the classical orientation of the curriculum in the context of the natural and physical advantages of the school:

Situated magnificently on the "Hill of pleasant springs," . . . thoroughly modern in equipment, with large well-ventilated class and lecture halls, students' rooms and dormitories, and fitted with a first-class gymnasium, shower-baths, running track etc.,

---

Superstition," *North American Review* 179 (1904), 388–401, cited in Phyllis Keller, *Getting at the Core: Curricular Reform at Harvard* (Cambridge: Harvard University Press, 1982), 8–9.

11. The Ph.B. was introduced at Brown in 1850 for graduates of non-humanistic programs as a way of reserving the B.A. for graduates with demonstrated competence in the classics. Other schools adopted the B.S. and Litt.B. degrees for similar reasons. By 1914, the percentage of American college graduates receiving the B.A. degree had shrunk to 55 percent. About 23 percent of graduates received B.S. degrees; 4 percent received the Ph.B., and 2 percent earned Litt.B. degrees. Rudolph, *Curriculum*, 138, 210, 214.

12. Consultors' Minute Book, 1902–1909, ACHC, 19.0; College Catalogs, 1903–1911. The number of Ph.B. degrees awarded in 1904 (if any) was not published.

13. Consultors' Minute Book, May 6, 1906, ACHC, 19.0; R. Markey to Thomas Murphy, November 30, 1907, ACHC, 12.15. By 1915, the Greek requirement had been suppressed at most American colleges and universities; fewer than 15 secular schools still required four years of Latin for the B.A. degree. Rudolph, *Curriculum*, 213–14.

supplemented outside with delightful walks, tennis and hand-ball courts and a large athletic field,

HOLY CROSS COLLEGE

offers to the young man about to enter college, conditions and surroundings designed to keep him in good healthy condition for the hardest kind of mental work and study, and a course of studies improved and perfected by over three hundred years of teaching experience which will give him

A BROAD LIBERAL CLASSICAL
EDUCATION.

Only in the second paragraph were the prescribed and elective courses detailed.[14] Father Murphy revised the advertisement in 1908, rejecting a version which emphasized "STRICTLY CLASSICAL," in favor of another lead-in: "Terms Reasonable." The promotion was forthcoming about the place of classics: "Holy Cross makes a specialty of the classical course, while furnishing courses in mathematics and the sciences and modern languages equal to the best. No special COMMERCIAL course."[15]

Despite the differences in emphasis, both Joseph Hanselman and Thomas Murphy marketed the College by asserting the advantages of the classics. Their fullest rationale and defense of the Holy Cross approach appeared in the catalog for 1902–3, under the heading "Educational System." The passage characterized the *Ratio* as a time-tested approach that enjoyed "hearty approbation by the ablest scholars" and was characterized by uniform, effective teaching methods. Although President Eliot was not mentioned by name, the section attacked programs based on "ever-changing theory and doubtful experiment" and emphasized classics, mathematics, and philosophy as the "essential trinity of courses" that provide the grounding for liberal education. The graduates of the program would be "profound thinkers, safe guides, clear writers, and cultured gentlemen." Each alumnus would be "sent out from his college so uniformly equipped and harmoniously developed in character that he is prepared to take up and prosecute any career, or even get more pleasure out of a life of leisure than a man who has missed such a preparation." The statement remained in the catalog until the end of Murphy's presidency, a confident assertion of priorities that drew a line of judgment across the terrain of American higher education.

14. ACHC, 12.14. The advertisement was carried in the summer of 1905 in fifteen Catholic newspapers in cities including Pittsburgh, Providence, New Bedford, New York, and Boston. William Lawler to Hanselman, New York, June 27 and August 3, 1905, ACHC, 12.14.

15. The advertisement, prepared by the Richard A. Foley Advertising Company, included a picture of Fenwick/O'Kane and was carried in papers in Boston, Philadelphia, Buffalo, Providence, Hartford, Newark, and New York. ACHC, 12.15.

Catalog statements can be verified only in the record and accomplishments of students and graduates. Despite the claims that its graduates departed for medical school with "some knowledge of physics and chemistry," the evidence for graduates of Holy Cross and other Jesuit schools was unconvincing. That reality prompted Charles Eliot to make another effort—this time privately and in a friendly manner—to alter the modified Jesuit Plan of Studies. Early in 1906, he wrote to Thomas Gannon with the "confidential suggestion . . . that you, with your authority and influence over the colleges maintained by the Society of Jesus, could cause to be introduced into their programmes a larger representation of the laboratory method of teaching sciences." The central problem was that graduates of Jesuit colleges had "great difficulty" in the first-year medical school courses because of their lack of laboratory experience.[16] It was a fair criticism. Eliot may have been aware that Gannon was already trying to upgrade the curriculum at the province's schools. In 1903, he had directed that all schools implement the *Ratio* according to the formulation then in use at Holy Cross.[17] The following year, he had appointed a permanent advisory committee on the revision of the Plan of Studies, mandating that the group devise a plan for achieving "a proper standard of solid excellence." Gannon was particularly concerned that the committee pay attention to science. But the group's report, delivered in 1905, gave heavy weight to modernizing classics instructions and to the further separation of the high school and collegiate programs.[18]

Part of the problem in upgrading the science offerings at the Jesuit schools was the strong preference for a Jesuit faculty, many of whom were unskilled in the new methods. In 1903, Father Hanselman admitted to the general that it was difficult to find competent teachers beyond the classics, English grammar, and ordinary mathematics. English, French, German, and Spanish literature, history, natural science, mathematics, political economy, and the history of philosophy were understaffed fields among the Jesuits; in his view, "unless such studies are more fostered, we will not be equals of non-Catholic schools, in which these studies are emphasized." Although compulsory Greek turned many students away, he was convinced that improved science offerings would enhance the College's attractiveness.[19]

Slowly, the curriculum was amplified with advanced courses and more

16. Eliot to Gannon, Cambridge, February 6, 1906, MPA, 520 D.

17. Gannon to Hanselman, New York, January 20, 1903, Provincial Letter File, ACHC, 19.1.

18. Gannon to committee members, New York, October 20, 1904, MPA, 520 D; Committee Report, August 21, 1905, MPA, 520 D.

19. Hanselman to Martin, Worcester, July 30 and November 24, 1903, ARSI, MD 13-XXV, 12 and 13.

electives. By 1907, there were new pre-professional senior electives in jurisprudence, pedagogy, experimental physics, biology, and organic chemistry; new laboratories had been opened. Courses in comparative literature and history of education enhanced the preparation of graduates for teaching. By then, entrance requirements to the College had also been tightened.[20] Standards were enforced through a system of penalties for substandard work. Students whose grades dropped below 60 in regular course work were suspended from most extra-curricular activities. Those who dropped below 60 in mid-year examinations were "conditioned," that is, required to re-take the examination several weeks later and to attend "free study" in the late afternoon until they passed. Those who failed a second examination faced a prolonged limbo of supplementary study and restricted activities until they raised their standing. Father Murphy enforced the rules rigorously. In March of 1908, a number of "conditioned" students were forbidden to attend the final basketball game; those with season tickets were given back their 15 cents.[21]

Despite the tighter standards and improved facilities, some graduates still did poorly in medical school. From the Harvard Medical School, Dr. John Bottomley, Class of 1889, reported in 1911 that the performance of Holy Cross alumni was "very disgraceful." Five of the seven failures in anatomy the previous semester were Holy Cross men, as were four of eight failures in histology. Characterizing them as "good fellows" who were inclined to be lazy and too interested in playing cards, Bottomley warned that they were giving the College a bad reputation.[22] It is possible that the graduates of 1910 were unusually weak in sciences, since Bottomley's reports were isolated within a single month. If that was so, the situation emphasized the precariousness of the academic progress the school had made. With a faculty of 24 Jesuits and one layman to cover the expanded curriculum, individual pedagogical strengths and weakness were magnified. A report on the Holy Cross faculty in 1904 pointed out several problems: the pedagogical method tended to overload teachers with the time-consuming task of correcting papers—one freshman teacher had 216 each week; some of the classics professors were openly biased against mathematics, suggesting to students that they pick it up in class without additional study.[23] In 1907, the College was exceptionally fortunate to ob-

20. Murphy to Franz Wernz, Worcester, January 12, 1908, ARSI, MD 15-XXII, 2; *WL*, 36: 426–27.

21. Prefect of Discipline Diary, 1901–08, ACHC, 15.2-1 and 15.2-2; *WL*, 32: 288–89; Worcester *Telegram*, November 12, 1905.

22. Bottomley to Murphy, Boston, February 26, 1911, and undated memo [1911] from Bottomley to Murphy, ACHC, 12.15.

23. Comments on 1904 schedule at Holy Cross, author unidentified, ACHC, 14.0-3.

tain the services of the German Jesuit historian and writer Robert Swickerath (also spelled Schwickerath) to teach pedagogy and history. His level of public intellectual accomplishment was rare on the faculty, and his presence emphasized the point so often mentioned by Hanselman and Murphy that a principal obstacle between their aspirations for the College and its actual condition was the lack of qualified instructors.

Problems with academic achievement notwithstanding, Holy Cross was more than holding its own in enrollment. By 1902, the total enrollment stood at 340, of whom 212 were enrolled in the college division. That made Holy Cross the largest Jesuit college in the nation by a substantial margin; Boston College, in second place, had 139 in its college department.[24] Because about 80 percent of the students were boarders, the O'Kane-Fenwick complex was soon crowded, a situation that prompted Hanselman and his consultors to discuss a new building. In 1903, Hanselman reported to the general that, despite the heavy debt, rising enrollment justified expansion of the physical plant for the sake of additional accommodations, classrooms, and science laboratories.[25] The pace of planning accelerated during the autumn, when the number of boarding students rose beyond the ideal maximum of 300. Under these circumstances, Father Gannon gave preliminary approval for a new structure. Meanwhile, the consultors approved the idea of appealing directly to the alumni to fund the project, and of naming the building for the alumni. Nothing could be said publicly until Luis Martin had approved the plan. In soliciting his preliminary approval, Hanselman stressed the possibility that qualified applicants would have to be turned away.[26]

The crucial element in finalizing the decision was alumni response. To gauge what it would be, Father Hanselman invited one representative of each class, starting with the Class of 1865, to a meeting on campus on January 26, 1904, to discuss the project.[27] As everyone sensed beforehand, the meeting was to be an important milestone. Joseph Hanselman and Thomas Murphy prepared the ground carefully. Already, the organization of regional clubs connected the alumni more tightly to their alma mater. By 1902, regional dinners were scheduled in Worcester, Boston, Hartford, and New York, in addition to the graduation reunion and banquet. In 1903, Father Murphy compiled the

24. Worcester *Post*, November 17, 1902; *WL*, 1901.

25. Hanselman to Martin, Worcester, July 30, 1903, ARSI, MD 13-XXV, 12. In 1901, the original loan of $100,000 for O'Kane Hall was re-negotiated with the State Mutual Life Assurance Co. of Worcester for five years at 4 percent. Trustees' Minutes, December 21, 1901, ACHC, 11.0-1.

26. HD, September 18, 1903; Consultors' Minutes, October 11 and November 1, 1903, ACHC, 19.0; Hanselman to Martin, Worcester, November 24, 1903, ARSI, MD 13-XXV, 13.

27. Consultors' Minutes, January 17, 1904, ACHC, 19.0.

first alumni directory of addresses and occupations. In the same year, when the junior class found itself unable to maintain the traditional junior banquet, "Holy Cross Night" emerged as a substitute evening that brought alumni back to campus to address the college men and socialize with them. The event served the dual purpose of putting students in touch with graduates and amplifying bonds of loyalty and responsibility among the alumni. By 1904, the event was held on the eve of a football game; as it grew in popularity with alumni and students, it foreshadowed the later tradition of Homecoming.[28]

Thirty-three of the thirty-nine invited class representatives attended the special meeting in 1904. Father Hanselman laid the case before them directly. The College was again overcrowded; it was likely that students would have to be turned away unless a new building was put up. He was not asking for help with the O'Kane Hall debt—that was under control. The question was whether that debt would be allowed to prevent expansion:

Shall we let well enough alone or . . . forge ahead, and take a more conspicuous, a more commanding, a more influential position among the institutions of the country, and especially of New England? Shall the first Catholic college of New England lag behind when a little more material encouragement will give her an opportunity to get nearer to being absolutely the first college in New England?

The problem could be addressed by building a dormitory with 100 student rooms and six to eight classrooms. The projected cost was $100,000. Hanselman estimated that 500 of the 714 living alumni were sufficiently advanced in their careers to pledge $10 annually for ten years to raise a fund of $50,000 for the building; non-graduates would also be solicited. This plan, he insisted was practical and would rally the alumni to erect "a lasting monument of their loyalty." The disappointing record of previous fund-raising appeals did not mean that failure was inevitable, because all classes would be represented in this drive and class representatives would help set the procedures. "I know that we have no Carnegies, no Rockefellers in our ranks," Hanselman said, "but we have amongst us men just as devoted, nay, more so because really more sacrificing. . . . Cannot, I say, all the classes of Holy Cross erect this ALUMNI HALL?"[29]

The response was as gratifying as he had hoped. The delegates accepted his proposal enthusiastically and instituted a plan of organization, with class officers and an executive committee. The representatives also endorsed the idea of an annual alumni meeting on the eve of Commencement Day.[30] On that mem-

28. For the last insight, I am indebted to a research assistant, Edward O'Donnell '86. Worcester *Post*, August 11 and October 12, 1903; HD, 1902

29. Address of January 26, 1904, ARSI, MD 13-XXV, 14.

30. Hanselman's report on the alumni meeting of January 26, 1904, ibid.

orable evening, Joseph Hanselman achieved a double success: the alumni association was re-founded, with an organizational framework to sustain its efforts, and the Alumni Hall fund was established. In February, Hanselman agreed with his consultors to commit the school to an "architect of established reputation" for the new building.[31] After the press was informed about the alumni meeting, the College received a half dozen unsolicited letters of inquiry from architects, including one from Charles D. Maginnis of Boston. When Hanselman met with Maginnis, he asked whether his firm, whose previous work had involved mostly churches, was prepared to design a purely utilitarian building. The affirmative response stressed the concept that such a building could be "artistic and dignified so as to be worthy of its relation to a seat of learning."[32] Toward the end of February, Maginnis was awarded the contract and returned to the campus to examine possible sites. In March, the lower terrace site was selected for a building that would assume the shape of a capital I, and be positioned to leave room for a projected dining hall and chapel, thus initiating the eventual conformation of the lower quad.[33]

The choice of architect was inspired. Charles Maginnis became the College architect; his firm designed every major building over the next half century, plus Commencement Porch and the gates and fence along College Street. A native of Ireland, Maginnis emigrated to Boston in 1885. In 1898, he helped form Maginnis, Walsh, and Sullivan (later, Maginnis and Walsh), a firm that specialized in churches, convents, schools, and hospitals.[34] In a short book published in 1898, Maginnis defined his artistic standards as a rejection of excessive Victorian ornamentation in favor of harmonies of color and form, and coordinated means and ends for the sake of "style." Later, a promotional brochure advocated, not lavishness, but "a refined and structural beauty . . . [to perpetuate] those great artistic traditions which so dignified and enriched the whole art history of Europe."[35]

31. The first advisory committee was chaired by Hanselman, and included John B. Ratigan '79, and Frs. William Foley '85, Richard Neagle '73, and a non-alumnus, Fr. Kettridge. HD, January and February, 1904; Consultors' Minutes, ACHC, 19.0.

32. Maginnis, Walsh, and Sullivan to Hanselman, February 8 and 13, 1904, ACHC, 16.1BB-1.

33. HD, February 12 to March 9, 1904; *Historia Domus*, 1903–4, ACHC, 19.0; Consultors' Minutes, February 21, 1904, ACHC, 19.0. According to Brother Horwedel, there had been a strong possibility that the new building would be added to the east end of Fenwick Hall, balancing O'Kane at the west end. Joseph J. LaBran, S.J., personal interview, May 1, 1993.

34. R. Andrew Richards '87, "The Ideals of Holy Cross as Expressed through Architecture" (unpublished MS in the possession of the author); Maginnis, Walsh, and Sullivan, *Recent Catholic Architecture* (Boston: The Everett Press, 1900), contains illustrations of their early buildings.

35. Charles D. Maginnis, *Pen and Drawing: An Illustrated Treatise* (Boston: Bates and Guild Co., 1898), 3; *Recent Catholic Architecture*, vii–viii.

Architect and rector met regularly to plan a structure in the style of the Italian Renaissance. The early success of the fund drive heightened the optimistic atmosphere; by mid-April, $18,000 had been pledged. Approval for the project arrived from Rome in early June. On June 21, the trustees authorized Hanselman to borrow $100,000 for construction and furnishings. The following day, on the eve of commencement, the seniors, in cap and gown, led a procession to the site of the new building for a ceremonial ground breaking.[36] Excavation started in mid-September, and the race was on to have the structure ready for the opening of school in 1905. Father Hanselman presided at a second groundbreaking on September 14 with all the students present. In January, the decision was made to mix pink sand with the mortar to give the building a softer look.[37] Bishop Beaven blessed the cornerstone on May 20, 1905. The inscription[38] stressed the generosity of the alumni who gave the building its name:

ALUMNORUM SANCTAE CRUCIS
PIETATEM
IN ALMAM MATREM
HIC LAPIS PRIMUS
TESTATUR
1904

The summer brought good news on alumni pledges and speedy progress on the building; and a crew of college workers built a wooden bridge from the upper terrace. When Alumni Hall opened on September 13, Joseph Hann, the Jesuit minister, reflected the general sentiment: "Everything is fine—beautifully lit up—Corridors bright as day—Everyone delighted and proud of it. We could fill another if we had it."[39]

The five-story building had 92 student rooms on the upper floors, plus large classrooms for philosophy, physics, history, and English on the lower floors, which also held an instrument room, reference library, and laboratories for physics and physiological psychology. The floors were assigned by class:

36. Gannon to Hanselman, New York City, April 23 and June 6, 1904, Provincial Letter File, ACHC, 19.1; Consultors' Minutes, April 17, 1904, ACHC, 19.0; HD, June 1904; Trustees' Minutes, June 21, 1904, ACHC, 11.0-1; Prefect of Discipline Diary, June 22, 1904, ACHC, 15.2-2.

37. HD, August 1904–May 1905; Consultors' Minutes, January 22, 1905, ACHC, 19.0; Prefect of Discipline Diary, September 14, 1904, ACHC, 15.2-2; Richards, "Ideals."

38. The inscription may be translated: "This first stone testifies to the devotion of the alumni of Holy Cross towards alma mater, 1904." The cornerstone's contents and the ceremony are described in HD, May 20, 1905.

39. HD, May–September, 1905.

college sophomores on the top floor, juniors on the middle floor, and seniors on the lowest floor; freshmen were given leftover rooms on all three floors. Room fees were higher for Alumni Hall. Six Jesuits were assigned to prefects' quarters, two per floor; electrical switches in their rooms controlled the corridor lights and the lights in the students' rooms.[40] The opening of the building made possible the conversion of large Fenwick Hall dormitory into student rooms. After 1906, the large study hall below the chapel was no longer needed, because bedrooms with desks now accommodated so many students. The old study hall became a dining room for the college students; students in the high school used the old dining room.[41]

The only disappointing facet of the project was the inability of the alumni to meet the goal of $50,000. Almost $4400 was contributed in 1905, but the collection fell off in subsequent years. The story behind the figures is difficult to discern. Class representatives sent reminders, and Father Murphy sent a general letter to the "Sons of Holy Cross" early in 1911, with disappointing results.[42] In April of 1912, the seven-year total reached $25,800, or 74 percent of a goal of $35,000 at that point in the ten-year campaign. The final report, published in April 1920, set the total collection at $34,750.[43] Under the impact of the Alumni Hall project, the College debt peaked at $263,000 in 1906; despite the economic bump associated with the Panic of 1907, it was steadily reduced (Chart 5.1).

Throughout the period, tuition revenue continued to supply about 60 percent of operating revenue. Loans offset the building expenses incurred in 1905 and 1906. The Alumni Hall drive, the contributed income of the Jesuits, and individual contributions from benefactors supplied much of the rest. When Clark University received an unsolicited gift of $100,000 from Andrew Carnegie for a new library, the house diarist could only observe, "What a contrast!" In 1908 an unusual gift of $8000 came in to establish a scholarship. Sometimes the smaller gifts, like the offering of $300 from "Old Miss Peggy

40. B. W. Feeney '09 to Raymond Swords, Bronx, September 23, 1965, ACHC, 16.1BB-1; D. D. Kimball to Hanselman, Boston, June 23, 1905, ACHC, 16.1BB-1; Consultors' Minutes, May 28, 1905, ACHC, 19.0.

41. Historia Domus, 1906, copy in ACHC, 19.0; Consultors' Minutes, June 3, 1906, ACHC, 19.0; Worcester *Post*, August 28, 1905; College catalog 1907–8.

42. Consultors' Minutes, November 4, 1906, ACHC, 19.0; Murphy to "Sons of Holy Cross," Worcester, January 16, 1911, copy in ARSI, MD 15-XXII, 7; form letters from Alumni Class Representatives are in the Holy Cross scrapbooks, ACHC.

43. Worcester *Telegram*, April 6, 1912; Holy Cross *Bulletin*, April 1920.

Callahan, a former laundress of the College and very much interested in H.C.C.,"[44] were important for morale.

In 1904, with the Alumni Hall plans pending, Father Hanselman received authorization to raise charges for tuition, room, and board above $225. The tuition fee of $60 was separated from room and board charges of $200. Extra charges of $40 to $75 were levied upon those who desired private or semi-private rooms. In 1910, Father Murphy sought to raise room charges again, as a justifiable surcharge for students whose means allowed them to pay for rooms that were, after all, "in the nature of a luxury." He opposed raising fees for tuition because "that is payment for our own services and most of our students can ill afford to pay any more and we do not need more."[45] Even with the cost-saving option of lodging their sons in the common dormitories, some families found the expense difficult to bear. Father Murphy received many requests for tuition reduction and granted exceptions regularly. By 1907, he was also receiving requests from students for assistance in finding part-time employment in the city; but few firms were willing to hire students for the few, scattered hours they were free. On rare occasions, the College was able to employ one of the students for work on campus. In the spring of 1911, Murphy hired Thomas F. Curran '15, an 18-year-old student who had previously completed a year in business college, to work as a stenographer and typist during the summer for a set wage. When classes resumed, Curran worked during his free hours for room and board. But that was an exceptional case; for the most part, the academic schedule made part-time work difficult to arrange.[46]

Chart 5.1 Operating Budget, 1902–1911

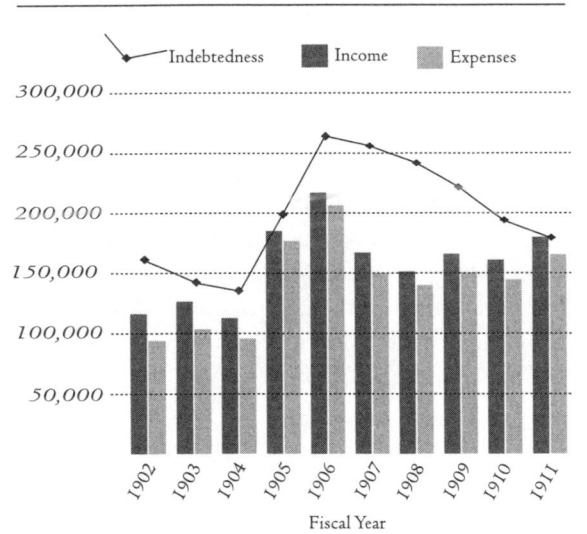

Fiscal Year

---

44. HD, January 14, 1904, January 19 and June 30, 1908.

45. Murphy to Hanselman, Worcester, October 18, 1910, ACHC 14.0-3; College Catalogues, 1905–11.

46. Curran to Murphy, Adams, April 12, 1911, ACHC, 12.15; Worcester *Post*, September 30, 1907.

Despite the disappointments of the Alumni Hall drive, the first decade of the century brought great progress in alumni organization and activities. In March 1905, the *Holy Cross College Bulletin* was initiated to publish an alumni directory and disseminate information about the alumni activities independently of *The Purple*. By 1911, three standing committees were furthering the work of the Alumni Association, and there were eleven regional clubs: Connecticut (organized 1896), Worcester County (1898), Bristol County (1900), New York (1901), Berkshire County (1903), Northeast Pennsylvania (1906), Boston (1907), Rhode Island (1908), Philadelphia (1908), and Connecticut Valley (1911). Pride in the distinctiveness of Holy Cross was a carefully fostered theme at all meetings. Describing the 1905 Holy Cross night, a reporter noted that "the exercises brought out considerable enthusiasm and college spirit because of their nature and again because of the fact that Dartmouth is met today at the oval."[47] A year later, alluding to the brutality and corruption in intercollegiate athletics, Father Murphy warned the guests at Holy Cross Night that "dishonorable conduct" in the name of school spirit is intolerable:

I see every reason to hope that Holy Cross, while, if not leading, keeping at least abreast of her sister colleges in scholarship and in athletics, will be among the first to raise the standard of high ethical ideals in student life. . . . Better a thousand times that we should lose in athletic contests than that we should win through tactics which, even though adopted by all other colleges, are in the light of reason and conscience, unfair and dishonorable.[48]

As subsequent events were to show, not all alumni endorsed these priorities.

The opening of Alumni Hall spurred another rise in enrollment, to 465 in 1905, the first year the building was in use. In 1910, attendance passed 500 for the first time. By then, there were 391 boarding students and over 100 day students, and the latter category had increased to about 25 percent of the student body. Although Holy Cross was still primarily a boarding school, it was clearly popular with local students and others who were able to board with family and friends in the vicinity. Throughout the period, Holy Cross remained the largest Jesuit college in the United States; in 1910 the 414 students in the col-

47. Worcester *Telegram*, February 11 and October 22, 1904; HD, 1905–11. Father Hanselman also attended the New York City dinner in February 1907. John G. McTigue to Murphy, New York, January 19, 1907, ACHC, 12.15.

48. Worcester *Post*, November 18, 1905. The comments were intended to defend athletic policies during a season in which the Holy Cross varsity compiled a 6-3 record, with losses to Yale, Dartmouth, and Syracuse at a time when Yale, in particular, was under attack by muckrakers for abuses in its athletic program. Smith, *Sports and Freedom*, 191–208.

lege division represented over 17 percent of all college students enrolled in the 24 American Jesuit colleges.[49]

The pattern of surging enrollment that quickly filled and exceeded the capacity of two new buildings gave rise to a new question: was it desirable to sponsor a classical high school and a college on the same premises? The question had been raised in a variety of contexts as Holy Cross and its associated Jesuits schools struggled to reform their curricula and to keep their programs attractive to prospective students. In a report to the Catholic Educational Association in 1899, Boston College President W. G. Read Mullan had suggested four steps: separation of the college from the preparatory department; modification of disciplinary rules for college students; enrichment of the curriculum; the conversion of open dormitories to private or double rooms.[50] At Holy Cross, all the steps had been addressed by 1906. In that year, besides the separation of the dining rooms, the prep students took over O'Kane Hall, while many of the college students were occupying Alumni Hall. Throughout the decade, administrators held the prep school students to a stricter regime of curfews and town permissions.[51] The heavy debt and the costliness of maintaining boarding facilities made the decision about a separated prep division more weighty than at day schools, where separate high school facilities could be constructed less expensively. As Father Hanselman noted in 1908: "There is no doubt that it would be wise to separate [the] Prep. Dept from the College. . . . It always comes back to a financial difficulty. If we had plenty of revenue, we could quickly enough solve the question."[52]

Financial constraints, the numerical strength of the college division, and the desire to keep educating college men through an ambitious humanistic curriculum: these issues created the context for evaluating the status of the prep school. The lower division was pared down slightly in the spring of 1903, when Rudiments was dropped as a pre–high school year. In its final year, 22 students were enrolled.[53] In the fall of 1906, the question of cutting the pro-

49. In 1905, after the opening of Alumni Hall, the number of boarding students rose by 59, while the number of day students rose by 15. Attendance figures were recorded annually in *Woodstock Letters*.

50. James Howard Plough, "Catholic Colleges and the Catholic Educational Association: The Foundation and Early Years of the CEA, 1899–1919," (Ph.D. Dissertation: University of Notre Dame, 1967), 85–86.

51. Prefect of Discipline Diary, 1907–1910, ACHC, 15.2-2; Worcester *Republican*, June 18, 1906.

52. Hanselman to Murphy, New York, August 19, 1908, Provincial Letter File, ACHC, 19.1.

53. Consultors' Minutes, May 3, 1903, ACHC, 19.0; HD, May 7, 1903; *WL*, 33: 127. Hanselman

gram further came up again because of rising enrollment; Joseph Hanselman authorized the rector to drop Fourth Academics "if you are pressed for room."[54] The announcement was made in the summer of 1907 and created confusion by giving the impression that the entire preparatory division was being phased out.[55] The situation concerned Father Hanselman, who cautioned Murphy to be clear that "we gave up not the high school, but only one year of it":

To precipitate the giving up of our high school would be ill advised. If want of room and other circumstances compel us to do so, well and good, but in the meantime we can feed our college from our own high school as well as from others. As we become more independent as regards numbers and finances we can adopt more exclusion measures for the interests of the college proper. The mischief is that reports and rumors get abroad about any move we make and being unintentionally misinterpreted, may do us harm.[56]

Murphy did his best to correct the impression. Yet, in January of 1908, he told the Worcester County alumni that the question of closing the prep school had not been settled and was dependent on the growth of the college department. "If you desire, therefore, to be able to say that Holy Cross is the one Catholic college to which . . . a [prep] department is not attached, then send us a large freshman class next year."[57]

Behind the scenes, Murphy was actively pressing for authorization to drop the high school. The first step was to bring the issue to the attention of the new Jesuit general, Franz Wernz, who had been elected general of the Society in September 1906 after the death of Luis Martin. During the summer of 1908, Father Murphy proposed gradual elimination of the lower school, citing familiar arguments about separation, the growth of the college division, and the popularity of a college-only setting for undergraduate work. Wernz concurred that the question had to be faced, and he asked Murphy to conduct a formal review.[58] In January 1909, Murphy sent his first report to the general. He and his consultors, who included the prefect of studies and the College

---

informed students that Rudiments would be dropped at the reading of grades in May 1903. The news was "enthusiastically received" by the college men. Worcester *Post*, May 7, 1903.

54. Hanselman to Murphy, New York, November 23, 1906, Provincial Letter File, ACHC, 19.1; Consultors' Minutes, December 2, 1906, ACHC, 19.0.

55. Boston *Post*, August 4, 1907.

56. Hanselman to Murphy, New York, December 31, 1907, Provincial Letter File, ACHC, 19.1.

57. Worcester *Gazette*, January 21, 1908.

58. Murphy to Wernz, Worcester, July 10, 1908 [Latin draft], Wernz to Murphy, Rome, July 27, 1908, ACHC, 14.0-3.

treasurer, were monitoring the effect of dropping Fourth Academic and were in favor of dropping Third Academic "when the needs of our College classes and two special classes, as to classrooms, study rooms, etc. demand it."[59] It was a preliminary discussion and there was considerable sentiment for waiting longer to monitor the growth of the college division. Nevertheless, by the beginning of 1909 it was clear which way the wind was blowing.

The moment of decision came in the fall of 1910, when 418 students were enrolled in the upper division, 118 more than in 1908. Enrollment in the prep school, meanwhile, had dropped below 20 percent of the student body (Chart 5.2).[60] On October 9, Murphy put to his consultors the question of whether to have a prep school in another location or to close it. This time the vote was unanimous for dropping the lower division by phasing it out as current students graduated.[61] In explaining the vote to Father Hanselman, Murphy cited the lack of space, the availability of alternative schools, and the fact that the prep school at Holy Cross did not really feed students into the College. Murphy also pointed out that Holy Cross would require fewer teachers under this plan. He argued that the best alumni of the school favored the change and were even "indignant" with Jesuit authorities for holding onto the prep division for so long. Another argument involved the prestige of the College and its attractiveness to young Catholic men who favored colleges without attached preparatory divisions. Meanwhile, some of the larger double rooms had already been converted into triples; if the plan to accept no new applicants into the preparatory school were granted, the returning students in Third and Fourth Academic in 1911 plus the "special" college students would "tax our present accommodations to the limit." A final argument was the forthrightness owed in justice to prospective prep students: "I have to urge that we be allowed now to state definitely what we propose to do as we can not any longer give a reasonable reply to reasonable in-

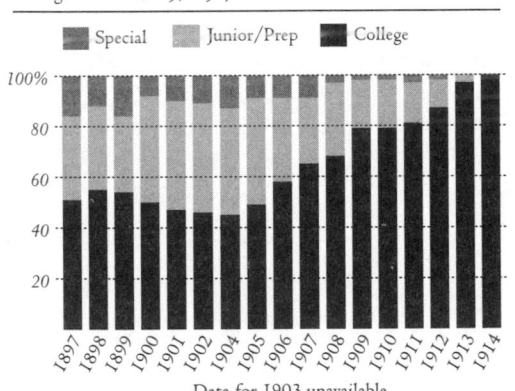

Chart 5.2 Fall Term Distribution of Prep and College Students, 1897–1914

Data for 1903 unavailable

59. Murphy to Wernz, Worcester, January 17, 1909, ARSI, MD 15-XXII, 3.
60. Murphy to Wernz, Worcester, October 23, 1910, ARSI, MD 15-XXII, 6.
61. Consultors' Minutes, ACHC, 19.0.

quiry by evasive answers." A few days later, Murphy repeated his appeal in a letter to Franz Wernz.[62]

The clarity of the arguments masked their audacity: if granted, the petition would make Holy Cross the only American Jesuit boarding college to adapt its curriculum by dropping the preparatory division completely, instead of merely separating it from the college. In the Maryland–New York Province, both Georgetown and Fordham, as boarding schools, organized separate schools for high school students. Holy Cross was seeking to be different. Although Joseph Hanselman was well informed about the issues and the facts, he took his time in resolving the matter. His immediate response to Father Murphy was a compromise: "I approve of dropping the second year of high school class and shall refer the matter to Rev. Fr. General. No formal announcement of the change need be made in the Holy Cross College Bulletin or other publications."[63]

Murphy was satisfied with the response, since it moved the process forward while keeping the final option open for a while longer.[64] In fact, the compromise of retaining two years of high school classes was maintained through the 1912–13 academic year—perhaps because, with Thomas Murphy's term of office coming to an end in 1911, it was thought better to allow his successor, Joseph Dinand, to make the final decision. In the fall of 1912, Dinand reported that at least 150 applicants for the Fourth and Third Academic had been turned away and that Bishop Beaven and others were interested in building a boarding prep school associated with Holy Cross.[65] But nothing came of the proposal: there were already five high schools for day students in Worcester, two of which were Catholic; Beaven soon turned his attention to the task of providing an additional dormitory for the College. In the fall of 1913, the last nineteen prep students enrolled in First Academic; when they graduated in June 1914, the prep school era came to an end. By then, 532 students were enrolled in the College.

62. Murphy to Hanselman, Worcester, October 18, 1910 [copy], ARSI, MD 15-XXII, 5, and draft, ACHC, 14.0-3; Murphy to Wernz, Worcester, October 23, 1910, ARSI, MD 15-XXII, 6.

63. Hanselman to Murphy, New York, December 7, 1910, Provincial Memorials, ACHC, 19.1-2.

64. Murphy to Wernz, Worcester, January 23, 1911, ARSI, MD 15-XXII, 8.

65. Dinand to Wernz, Worcester, November 24, 1912, ARSI, MD 15-XXII, 12. There is little indication of resistance to the prep school closing in Father Murphy's correspondence. One correspondent praised the decision and the excellent quality of the "strictly college curriculum" and the reputation the school enjoyed within the Catholic Education Association: "With the 'prep' gone, HC will be in a class by itself among the Catholic colleges with which I am acquainted." M. V. Carney [?] to Murphy, Chicago, September 19, 1911, ACHC, 12.15.

Financial considerations contributed to the elimination of the prep division, but they did not impede ongoing improvements to the existing physical plant, especially during Hanselman's administration. Electricity, which had been installed for outside lighting in 1890, was gradually brought indoors. In 1904, electricity was in use in the chapel, study halls, bathrooms, and junior and senior rooms; by 1907, even the barn had been electrified after the installation of poles to carry the "electric fluid" to that part of the campus.[66] During the same period, the College constructed a new residence—now Campion House[67]—for the laymen who worked on the farm under Brother Horwedel's direction and a new house for the family who operated the laundry. In the summer of 1907, the small bakery on the hillside behind Fenwick Hall was abandoned in favor of a larger unit in the main building.[68]

Apart from Alumni Hall, the largest construction project during the Hanselman years was the new athletic field at the foot of the hill. The project had been initiated by Father Lehy in 1899, when he began to accumulate a fund. Bishop Healy gave $100 shortly before he died, and one of the larger donors was Governor G. Murray Crane, who contributed $200 anonymously. In the spring of 1901, a contract was signed to excavate and grade a new field in the area adjacent to the river at the northwest corner of the campus, the present site of the baseball field at the foot of the hill. The work of filling and leveling was completed that summer.[69] In September of 1903, the new field was grid-ironed for practice, and on October 31, in the first varsity football game on campus, spectators stood around the field as Holy Cross defeated the Aggies from Amherst, 36–0. Meanwhile, pending the construction of new stands, the older grandstand and field on the lower terrace continued to be used for baseball games.[70]

66. HD, 1890–1907.

67. Popular belief has it that Campion House is a reconstruction of Fr. Fitton's academy. Apparently, however, the old academy building was torn down during the late 1890s, having been relocated from its original site where Fenwick Hall now stands, to spot later occupied by the Millard Art Center. Memorandum of W. L. Lucey, April 25, 1965, from an interview with Fr. Thomas White, Holy Cross student, 1883–86, and College chaplain, 1937–40. ACHC, Fact File. The House Diary (September–October, 1901) calls the workers' house "new." Yet it bears a resemblance to an archival photograph that shows the relocated academy building.

68. HD, September 1901–January, 1902; Hanselman to Martin, Worcester, February 10, 1902, ARSI, MD 13-XXV, 10.

69. Fitton Field publicity brochure, ACHC, 16.1BL–1; Worcester *Telegram*, April 30, 1901; Worcester *Post*, July 9, 1901; Thomas Murphy to A. G. Bullock [undated], ACHC, 12.15.

70. HD, 1901–3; Holy Cross Athletic Association, *1992 Gridiron Guide.*

At the end of 1903, Father Gannon authorized completion of the field in a two-part project that included construction of a grandstand and bleachers on the present baseball field and extension of the field to the east, for football. In November 1904, work started on the new stands, which had reserved seating for 2000 and bleacher seats for 2500. Money was borrowed by the Athletic Association, not by the College directly, to be repaid from revenue generated by the athletic program.[71] In April 1905, the name "Fitton Field" was chosen "to perpetuate the memory of Old Fr. Fitton," who had died in 1881. About 7000 people attended the first baseball game on Fitton Field in 1905, an 8–5 victory over Brown University. The formal dedication took place on Saturday, May 20. Before the game, the Holy Cross and Yale teams marched to the flag-pole at the end of the field and watched as the two captains hoisted a new emblem, a large purple banner that carried the words FITTON FIELD in large letters. In August, the old grandstand on the upper field was demolished.[72]

Meanwhile, plans were under way for the football field. In August of 1904, Father Hanselman reached an agreement with the American Steel and Wire Company, located on the opposite bank of the river, which produced cinders as a by-product of manufacturing. The company agreed to pay one dollar for the right to dump cinders in the low area where the field was to be constructed, up to a depth of six feet, according to set specifications. Eventually, 35,000 cubic yards of cinders were transported across a temporary bridge constructed by the school. In 1905, loam was stripped from a meadow at the foot of the hill to cover the cinders. By 1908, with the construction of wooden stands, the new field was ready for use. It was inaugurated on September 26, when Holy Cross defeated Norwich, 5–0.[73]

The opening of Fitton Field promoted interest in varsity athletics; it also required some adjustments in the campus routine to accommodate the athletes and fans. In 1902, the long mid-day recess was shortened so that team

71. "*This is not a college debt,*" Joseph Hann wrote in the House Diary, November 9, 1904. See also Prefect of Discipline Diary, April 19, 1905, ACHC, 15.2-2. In September 1899, when plans for the development of the lower athletic field were just getting underway, the Athletic Association took the unusual step of publishing its budget for the previous academic year. There was a net gain of $857.95. Losses in football and track were offset by a profit of nearly $2300 on baseball. *The Purple,* 9:124.

72. HD, April 17, May 20, and August 18, 1905; Worcester *Telegram,* April 20, 1905; Prefect of Discipline Diary, May 20, 1905, ACHC, 15.2-2.

73. H. G. Stoddard to Hanselman, Worcester, July 18, 1904; and signed agreement, August 4, 1904, between Hanselman and H. G. Stoddard of American Steel and Wire, ACHC, 16.1BL-1; Consultors' Minutes, September 4, 1904, 19.0; HD, August 1905 Holy Cross Athletic Association, 1992 *Gridiron Guide.*

practice could begin earlier. Soon, training tables were instituted for athletes, and the baseball team won permission to make a southern trip prior to the start of the regular season.[74] In the stands, the enthusiasm of the late nineteenth century exploded into the twentieth. On April 26, 1902, after a defeat of Yale, students and even the local citizenry erupted into a celebration that was recorded by the House Diarist:

The College walls rocked from the cheers of the Boys as they came out of the Chapel from the Rosary. Immediately a brass band was organized with some old windbroken instruments and down they walked in procession to the city. On the city hall square one of the Boys addressed a crowd of about 2000 people[,] inviting them to be up at the College at 10:30 P.M. to witness the fire works. The whole city is in an uproar. . . . [The bonfire] was lighted at 10:30 P.M. The fireworks were a great success. The red lights were prepared by Father Ulrich, professor of Chemistry.[75]

In addition to evincing school spirit, such episodes reflected growing support for Holy Cross athletics within the local community. Newspapers promoted their interest; so did many Catholic pastors. During good seasons, the crowds were large; on Memorial Day in 1906, 10,000 spectators attended the Dartmouth game.[76]

After the turn of the century, there were keenly felt rivalries with Boston College and Fordham, and sometimes trouble on this account. In 1901, when the Holy Cross prep and varsity teams played a home double-header against their football counterparts from Boston College, both games were terminated early amid acrimonious dispute. The return match was canceled and, the prefect of discipline reported, "all athletic relations with B.C. severed. Every effort was afterwards made to patch up but the students would not have it."[77] In fact, Holy Cross played a football game at Boston College in 1902; then the series was halted until 1910. In 1903, a baseball game at Fordham also ended in a "wrangle," but there was no talk of dropping the series. Rivalry for star players raised a complaint from Fordham in 1910 that Holy Cross had undercut their efforts to recruit players from Boston: "We can understand a Protestant College doing this, but is it fair for us to fight our own colleges?"[78]

74. Prefect of Discipline Diary, April 10 and October 3, 1905, ACHC, 15.2-2; Worcester *Post*, August 19, 1902; Worcester *Telegram*, January 21, 1908.

75. HD, April 26, 1902.

76. Rosenzweig, *Eight Hours*, 227.

77. Prefect of Discipline Diary, November 9, 1901, ACHC, 15.2-2.

78. HD, May 23, 1903; Charles A. Mulally, S.J., to Joseph Dinand, S.J., Bronx, September 10, 1910, ACHC, 12.16. Trouble of a different sort emerged in 1902, when a home game against Villanova was canceled after a half inning, because Villanova allegedly attempted to use two profes-

Intercollegiate basketball made its debut during the 1900–1901 academic year and was so popular by 1902 that all but fifty students attended a game against Harvard at Mechanics Hall. By 1905, however, attendance had fallen; in 1906, basketball was disbanded because it was "not . . . self-supporting." The sport was revived again for two years in 1907, then suspended indefinitely by Father Murphy before the start of the 1909–10 season.[79] The records offer no explanation for the decision except the inability of basketball to cover its expenses. Certainly the faculty were not opposed to increasing the number of intercollegiate sports: in 1910, they arranged a game of soccer on campus "to get an idea of the game as most likely it will have to be adopted within a year or two," and in 1911, a varsity team competed in a tennis match against Amherst.[80]

Like their counterparts at most other campuses, students had a participatory role in the varsity program through the Athletic Association.[81] Students elected association officers and team managers of football, track, baseball, and basketball, who were *ex officio* officers. Managers were responsible for setting up schedules and, at the start, for choosing the coaches. Captains and managers chose team members. In 1904, the College adopted the widely established procedure of appointing a graduate manager to supervise team managers and have oversight over the association's finances. The graduate manager and Jesuit faculty moderator were appointed by the president, and the moderator had veto power over the association's actions. In 1906, the association initiated a system of choosing graduates as coaches and designating the coaches as officers. The officers (students and non-students) constituted the Athletic Association's advisory board and had oversight of activities. The Holy Cross Athletic Association was the agency through which Fitton Field and its spectator stands were built—a hybrid organization through which the administration and students collaborated in the direction and management of

sional players who were not students. Money was returned to the spectators, and Holy Cross refused to pay the guarantee. "If we did not effectually protest[,] we might be considered as being in the same class as they and consequently afraid to object," the prefect of discipline noted. Prefect of Discipline Diary, May 7, 1902, ACHC, 15.2-2; HD, May 7, 1902.

79. HD, January 21, 1902; Prefect of Discipline Diary, February 11, 1905, ACHC, 15.2–2; *The Purple*, 19:151 and 21:579; Worcester *Telegram*, June 15, 1909; unidentified press clipping, December 19, 1910, ACHC, Locker 8, Scrapbook 7; Holy Cross Athletic Association, *1992–93 Basketball Media Guide*. J. Fred Powers was the basketball coach 1901–5 and 1908–9; John Smith coached in 1907–8. Andrew W. Sullivan '93, "Historical Sketch of the Holy Cross Athletic Association" (unpublished MS in the possession of the author).

80. Prefect of Discipline Diary, 1910, ACHC, 15.2-2; Worcester *Telegram*, May 13, 1911.

81. Smith, *Sports and Freedom*, 118–20.

the athletic program.[82] In practice, however, the rector had considerable influence over the operation of the athletic association. In 1909, the football manager admitted to Father Murphy: "I could not think of doing anything without first consulting you."[83] In 1911, when Murphy removed a junior from the position of assistant baseball manager, his classmates demanded his reinstatement and threatened to withdraw support from the Athletic Association and to have juniors withdraw from teams. The controversy was settled by appointing a different member of the junior class to the position.[84] Such disputes were rare between 1901 and 1911, and easily resolved. Two broader issues, however, required considerable attention, patience, and judgment from Fathers Hanselman and Murphy: the problem of violence in intercollegiate football, and the effort of the alumni to win a broader role in the direction and management of College athletics.

Wanton violence in college football prompted Theodore Roosevelt to invite representatives of Harvard, Yale, and Princeton to the White House in 1905 to discuss the problem.[85] At Holy Cross that year, a varsity player was deliberately kicked in the face by an Amherst opponent. At the end of the season, Father Hanselman added his voice to those insisting on reform. He was careful to criticize, not the game, but the rough manner in which it was then being played—the "overwhelming ambition to win" that destroyed sportsmanship and produced injuries that were not accidents. Holy Cross, he pledged, "would join in a general movement for a radical reform of the game. Such a reform is necessary, for means must be found . . . to make the game less dangerous to life and limb."[86] Hanselman kept his word, sending the prefect of discipline, Father Ferdinand Rousseau, to join the representatives of 67 other colleges at the organizational meeting of the National Collegiate Athletic Association in December.[87]

The controversy with alumni over the direction of the College's athletic policy was connected with Father Murphy's effort to ensure that players were academically qualified. He was forthright on the point during his first year in office, when he told students at the November assembly for reading grades

---

82. College catalogs, 1902–1905; *The Purple*, February 1898 and October 1906. The first Graduate Manager was William M. Welch '04. Worcester *Telegram*, June 18, 1904. See also Sullivan, "Historical Sketch." On the practice of using professional coaches in college football, see Smith, *Sports and Freedom*, 147–64.

83. Joseph G. Pyne '10 to Murphy, Lowell, [July, 1909], ACHC, 12.15.

84. Worcester *Post*, June 14, 1911.

85. Smith, *Sports and Freedom*, 191–98; Rudolph, *History*, 375–77.

86. Worcester *Post*, November 6 and December 1, 1905.

87. Worcester *Post*, January 3, 1906; Smith, *Sports and Freedom*, 202–3.

that the College fully supported its athletic teams but scholarship had to come first. The following January, he made the same point at the annual alumni banquet in Worcester.[88] To be eligible for participation, athletes had to maintain an average of at least 60 percent in every class; those falling below the mark were ineligible until the deficiency was made up. College authorities enforced the policy conscientiously: in 1904, two football players were declared ineligible on academic grounds; in 1905, only twelve of the fifteen football players were allowed to play at Syracuse; and in 1910, a baseball player was expelled for keeping "late hours" and ignoring his studies. The track team tested the rules, to their regret, in 1907, when they took a conditioned student to a meet in violation of orders. The manager and the captain were told afterwards to cancel the rest of their schedule, and the offending student was expelled.[89] By then, the catalog stated unambiguously: "The students are not permitted to neglect their studies no matter how proficient they may be in any branch of sports." Clearly, Fathers Hanselman and Murphy worked hard to maintain priorities in a world which even then was willing to compromise the ideal of the student/athlete. As a local reporter put it, "'Study and play' seems to be the shibboleth at the college, but great emphasis is placed on study."[90]

The problem with maintaining standards was that the policy did not readily afford a winning record; in the view of some of the alumni, that was the rub. The chief critic of the policy during Father Murphy's administration was a former member of the baseball team, Father John J. Harkins, Class of 1887, a pastor in South Boston. An enthusiast of Holy Cross sports, Harkins attended home games regularly. In the fall of 1907, he turned his attention to football during Timothy F. Larkin's '05 first year as head coach, when the team won only one game. Harkins told Murphy: "Oh, Father, how I wish I had authority to get about five players around here—all with necessary scholarship—and all good fellows." A year earlier, he claimed, two star players from his "list" had been lost to Brown and Harvard. He proposed hiring a certain coach who had a "system" and recommended a talented young athlete for a scholarship.[91] Murphy asked Harkins to temper his enthusiasm

88. Worcester *Telegram*, November 12, 1905; Worcester *Post*, January 31, 1906.

89. Worcester *Post*, October 14, 1904, November 9, 1905, and October 11, 1906; Worcester *Telegram*, April 30, and June 11, 1910; Prefect of Discipline Diary, February 22, 1907, ACHC, 15.2-2.

90. "A Word As To Athletics," ACHC, 12.15; Worcester, *Telegram*, September 17, 1905.

91. Harkins to Murphy, South Boston, November 6, 1907, and [*circa* December 1, 1907], ACHC, 12.15; HD, May 14 and 28, 1903. The 1907 record was 1-7-2. In six seasons, Larkin's record was 18-25-8.

and received a humble reply: "I thank you, for the gentle reminder, that I probably take things athletic, too seriously. In my future conduct, I intend to be guided by your advice."[92] After a season of 1–7–2, that resolve proved difficult to keep.

Tensions between the rector and the alumni flared into the open on January 15, 1908, at the dinner of the Holy Cross Club of Boston. Father Murphy had been warned beforehand that Harkins and his allies in the club "intend to make it disagreeable for you if they can."[93] The force of the assault became clear during the evening, when William P. Kennedy '00, a former star athlete and a journalist, stated that many alumni had been ashamed of Holy Cross during the past football season. He called three of the defeats "a blot upon the honor of Holy Cross that will take years to wipe out" and argued that "it was in football that Holy Cross suffered her humiliation and it is in football that we must win back our lost prestige and even greater glory." Kennedy blamed the poor season on "faculty restrictions which aim at raising the standard of scholarship at Holy Cross." He could not understand why athletes rejected by Holy Cross could attend Fordham, Georgetown, and Princeton. To solve the problem, Kennedy advocated more alumni involvement in recruitment, a more cooperative attitude from the faculty, a board of "conservative alumni" to replace the graduate manager (who was too responsive to the faculty), and the introduction of an English-scientific academic program to attract a greater number of qualified athletes. After all, he pointed out, the school's purpose was not to inculcate classical languages but to teach a way of life with sound moral values. In his response, Father Murphy corrected some of the allegations and received a vote of confidence from the club. But it was Kennedy's speech that drew most of the attention.[94]

Kennedy's address was reprinted the following day in the Worcester *Telegram* under the headline, "Boston Holy Cross Club Blames Faculty For Poor Football Team." The beleaguered rector suspected that Kennedy had supplied the speech to the paper, but Kennedy denied it, admitting only that the reporter had received a tip beforehand. He told Murphy that he spoke for many alumni and that the 1907 team was "the rankest aggregation of quitters I ever saw." His intent, he claimed, was honest criticism. Murphy rejected this explanation and insisted that Kennedy was working "to create a false impression and do injury to Holy Cross' interests." Signing his second response "with re-

92. Harkins to Murphy, South Boston, December 5, 1907, ACHC, 12.15.

93. Thomas J. Burke to Murphy, Boston, undated, ACHC, 12.15.

94. From Murphy's address to the Holy Cross Club of Worcester, January 21, 1908, Worcester *Gazette*, January 21, 1908.

newed esteem," Kennedy again held his ground: "I said it, I am willing to shoulder all the blame, I thought I was right."[95]

Thomas Murphy responded publicly on January 23, in a speech to the Holy Cross Club of Worcester. He held the press responsible for distorting the proceedings of the Boston meeting by downplaying all but the sensationalistic comments of the evening's youngest speaker. He held certain alumni responsible for seeking "some exceptional concession which, if granted, would imply favoritism in college administration"; at the same time they declined to support efforts like the Alumni Hall fund. He also resented the unfairness of the attack for singling out football while discounting the achievements of the baseball and basketball teams. He pointed to concessions already made for the sake of athletic success—permission for a southern trip for the baseball team and a special tutorial program for freshmen deficient in Greek. He concluded somewhat disingenuously with a plea for constructive suggestions.[96] Murphy distributed press accounts of his speech to his allies, prompting Kennedy to express his irritation that Murphy was attempting to put him in the wrong: "Sometimes even the president of Holy Cross can be unjust."[97] Other alumni disagreed. From Fall River, Judge John McDonough, Class of 1880, reported that most alumni approved the College's athletic policy; he dismissed the criticism as "whispered mutterings of young graduates."[98]

Conspicuous by his silence during the flare-up of January 1908 was the intrepid Father Harkins, who was secretary of the Boston alumni club. Harkins tipped his hand during the 1908 football season when he criticized the new graduate manager, Thomas J. Faherty '08, for ineptitude in handling a recruit, Frank Craig. Harkins also twitted Faherty about his scheduling policies, writing that the Executive Board of the Boston Club had considered contacting Harvard themselves to schedule a game with Holy Cross: "Is this interference, and should we have consulted H.C. people first?"[99] Eventually, Frank Craig did attend Holy Cross and graduated with a Ph.B. in 1912, but Harkins was still unsatisfied. In November, at the end of a 4–4 season, he sent Father Rousseau a list of eight prime candidates and argued against entrusting their recruitment to Faherty, "a zany graduate—with no experience." His advice was to appoint an alumni advisory board; meanwhile, Harkins himself had hired a coach to help the team before the Dartmouth game; he was certain

95. Kennedy to Murphy, Boston, January 19 and 22, 1908, ACHC, 12.15.

96. Worcester *Gazette*, January 21, 1908.

97. Kennedy to Murphy, Boston, January 23, 1908, ACHC, 12.15.

98. McDonough to Murphy, Fall River, January 28, 1908, ACHC, 12.15.

99. Frank Craig to Faherty, Boston, October 9, 1908, and J. J. Harkins to Faherty, South Boston, October 13, 1908, ACHC, 12.15.

that other alumni would be willing to subsidize players' College costs—as he was doing with Craig—if their suggestions on the athletic program were taken seriously.[100]

Thomas Faherty and Father Rousseau kept Father Murphy posted about Harkins's efforts. In December, with the annual banquet of the Boston Club again pending, Murphy decided to act. In a pointed letter to Harkins, he attempted to clear the air about Harkins's criticism of athletic policy. Harkins had become a point of irritation on campus: "The only trouble which the Rev. Moderator of Athletics and the Graduate Manager have felt obliged to make a subject of complaint to me has been the insistent interference—of Fr. Harkins—in the name of the Alumni and the Boston Club in particular."[101] A stunned Harkins called the letter "positively insulting. . . . I resent your writing very much." He defended his motivation in helping the athletic program and disassociated himself from the "narrow-minded interpretations" Murphy had received.[102] It took another exchange of letters in January to clarify that Murphy would be welcomed at the annual dinner of the Boston Club. There would be no formal speeches, Harkins stated, but Murphy would be asked to make a few remarks. The Club had taken no action "to take issue with you on matters going on by letter between us." He admitted that there were complaints about College athletic policy from other members of the club; but the executive board, to which Harkins belonged, had expressed only the sentiment that "they might have suggestions to make, but they felt, that they might not be well received, because of the traditions of the Jesuits." For his own part, Harkins still felt unfairly treated, and he resolved to offer no further financial support to any members of the football, baseball, or track team.[103] On that note, the effort of John Harkins to involve the alumni more directly in the management of the athletic program came to an end. There would be no alumni advisory board; compromises with athleticism would be resisted. But there was a cost. The football team posted losing seasons for ten more years; the basketball program was suppressed; even the baseball teams posted an aggregate record of only 40–34–5 during the last three years of Murphy's rectorship.

The College's athletic profile was balanced in those years by the effort to involve the faculty in public lectures. Father Hanselman set up the first six-

100. Harkins to Rousseau, South Boston, November 8, 1908, ACHC, 12.15.

101. Murphy to Harkins, Worcester, December 21, 1908, ACHC, 12.15.

102. Harkins to Murphy, South Boston, December 18, 1908, ACHC, 12.15.

103. Murphy to Harkins, Worcester, January 11, 1909 (notes), and Harkins to Murphy, South Boston, January 13, 1909, ACHC, 12.15.

week series in 1902, with an advertisement that set the tone: "To gratify the frequently expressed desire of many friends of Holy Cross College and the large number of teachers in this city and county, the college professors of history and literature are prepared to offer them, as well as to the students and their friends, a course of lectures." The talks, which were free, were offered in the Fenwick Lecture Hall. The 1902 speakers focused on European history and English literature, and were so successful that the series was maintained throughout the decade. Father Murphy inaugurated the 1903 season to a standing-room-only audience with a defense of the classics entitled "Popular Errors about Classical Studies," later reprinted as a pamphlet. Over the years, the series broadened out into science and theology, and lecturers were brought in from beyond the campus. In 1908, Father Swickerath delivered five lectures on the topic of education to record-breaking crowds.[104]

Despite the innovations of the early twentieth century, the basic pattern of campus life remained comparatively monastic. Martin Tiernan, Ex-'06, who arrived in the fall of 1901, remembered ringing the doorbell and being enrolled personally by Father Murphy. Lacking high school Greek, he was placed in a special class of about a dozen students. The daily order began with Mass at 7 A.M. and a half hour of study before breakfast. There were recreation periods after lunch and before dinner, with a two-hour study hall in the evening. Tiernan slept in a large dormitory which held 75 to 100 beds; at night, clothing went on the chair next to the bed and "we slept on our pants, between the mattresses, to keep them pressed." He described the food as "simple and fairly wholesome" and the lifestyle as "very simple and primitive."[105] The dormitory was purely for peaceful rest—"not a word should be spoken," the prefect of discipline noted in 1905; there was a penalty for leaving clothing on the floor. Students were given 20 minutes after the wake-up bell for dressing, morning toilet, and morning prayer.[106]

Father Hanselman introduced a demerit system to enforce discipline. The highest penalties were incurred by missing Mass or class (10), and going AWOL to town during the day (15) or at night (25). Parents were sent a warning at 75 demerits; when the total reached 125, a student was suspended for a month; at 200, he earned "expulsion for habitual insubordination." Students needed permission for late sleep, early bed, or late study; they needed a note from the Jesuit corridor prefect to visit another corridor during study hours,

104. HD, 1902–11. The pamphlet of Thomas Murphy's address of March 1903 is in ACHC, 12.15.

105. Martin F. Tiernan, *Memoirs* (privately printed, 1956), 19–20.

106. Prefect of Discipline Diary, 1905, ACHC, 15.2.

and another note to return. Only the prefect of discipline could give town permissions and authorize absence from class and study hall.[107] Students were still expelled for returning to campus under the influence of alcohol. The prohibition against smoking received new emphasis in December, 1903, when two students were expelled for starting a fire by tossing a lighted butt into the wastebasket of their O'Kane room. "This danger is ever present," the Jesuit minister wrote, "and unless heroic measures are taken the College will surely be burned down." When students returned from their Christmas holidays that year, they were informed of a special regulation against cigarettes.[108] But the students winked at the rule, willing to take the consequences if they were caught, as one convicted smoker (who eventually became a Jesuit) pointed out to Father Murphy: "There is hardly a room in Alumni Hall in which the fellows, at some time or other, do not use cigarettes."[109]

Although his concern about fire prompted Father Murphy to enforce rules severely, he was fundamentally sympathetic to the needs of the older students, as his dispute with Franz Wernz over night permissions made clear. In 1907, Father Hanselman, as provincial, formally asked Murphy to work toward reducing night permissions "to a minimum consistent with prudence." A year later, Hanselman renewed the request, recommending a severe sanction for those who returned late.[110] By the summer of 1908, it was clear that the impetus for tightening the rule was coming from Franz Wernz, who specifically requested a report on night permissions at Holy Cross with an eye toward abolishing them completely.[111] Murphy pleaded for their retention, arguing four points. First, acting *in loco parentis*, the College was only granting the same permissions the parents ordinarily granted to their sons at home. Second, college students were distinguished from prep students in this regard; only college students received night permission. Third, night permission was refused to students who were academically weak. Fourth, students would move off campus if the prohibition were set in place "and greater evils might be feared."[112]

To Murphy's disappointment, the general directed all rectors of boarding colleges in the United States to move gradually and "prudently" toward the abolition of night permissions because of the "grave danger" associated with

107. Prefect of Discipline Diary, 15.2-1.

108. HD, 1903; Prefect of Discipline Diary, January 21, 1904, ACHC, 15.2.

109. Charles Roddy to Murphy, Fitchburg, May 8, 1908, ACHC, 12.15.

110. Provincials' Memorials, March 11, 1907 and March 18, 1908, ACHC, 19.1-2.

111. Hanselman to Murphy, New York, June 27, 1908, ACHC, 19.1.

112. Hanselman to Murphy, New York, March 23, 1909, ACHC, 19.1. Hanselman quotes Murphy's response to Wernz in this letter.

the practice. Students freely chose a school knowing its rules, Wernz argued; therefore it was no deprivation of their freedom to enforce the policy. The challenge was to inculcate "family spirit"; after all, a Jesuit college was not a hotel.[113] When Murphy appealed to Hanselman, the provincial admitted the matter was delicate, but that his hands were tied—Wernz had given him no discretionary authority in the matter. He could only suggest that Murphy appeal directly to Rome.[114] Murphy did so in a nine-page letter that was significant not only for the case it built for retaining night permissions but also for the vision it offered of Holy Cross, as he and his immediate predecessors had re-fashioned it during the previous decade.[115] They wanted the College to be attractive to Catholic undergraduates, with administrators who were trusting rather than suspicious of the student body and students who had opportunities to acquire social poise.

Making the College attractive to Catholic youth was an important advance, Murphy argued, because the school had formerly had the reputation of resembling a seminary or a reform school. That approach had induced many Catholic youth to prefer non-Catholic colleges. In recent years, however, the pattern had changed:

We are now . . . attracting larger numbers of such students by making our curriculum, our boarding and lodging accommodations and our system of discipline, as far as possible, attractive rather than repulsive for such young men. Many of our graduates have spoken in the highest praise of these changes as improvements, and to these they attribute our increase in . . . students.

To Wernz's suggestion that the collegiate community should resemble a family, Murphy responded that Holy Cross was a family, but an *American* family, with evening privileges parents approved of. Fifty-five parents, in fact, had petitioned for evening privileges for their sons: if the student was trusted at home, why not trust him at school? The fact was, Murphy insisted, Wernz did not understand contemporary American students and he sought to bind them with rules that did not take into account American patterns of living and relaxation, including parish activities, alumni banquets, and other activities held in the evening. These were "an excellent training of the students in that self respect, self control and 'savoir faire' which fits him for social life among educated gentlemen and which he will need when he goes out from us . . . in our large cities." College authorities had found that withholding the privilege of

113. Wernz to [Hanselman], Rome, October 20, 1908 (copy), ACHC, 12.15.
114. Hanselman to Murphy, New York, April 3, 1909, ACHC, 19.1.
115. Murphy to Wernz, Worcester, April 18, 1909, ARSI, MD 15-XXII, 4.

night permissions was a better inducement to study and good order than negative punishments had been in earlier times. Why introduce stricter rules, he asked in conclusion, when there were currently no abuses to be corrected?

But the general held firm; Murphy's arguments he found "not . . . persuasive." If parents lacked good judgment and allowed their sons to be out at night, that hardly obligated Jesuits to do the same. Nor were Jesuits obliged to imitate non-Catholic colleges in establishing such policies. To Wernz, the danger of attending the theater and visiting women in the evening was self-evident, since trusting young men does not remove temptation. Moreover, students were at school to study, not for social life: efforts to join the two only imperiled studies. Again, the general expressed his regret that the custom had been introduced, and he held to his directive that it be gradually abolished. Nevertheless, he was willing, for the time being, to allow college students in higher classes to go out at night for a special reason; the matter rested on the rector's conscience. Ultimately, Murphy had to agree to a gradual withdrawal of night permissions for boarding students, but the fact that no deadline was imposed left him enough discretion in the matter to allay his alarm.[116]

Under Hanselman and Murphy, the religious tone of campus life remained unchanged. Mandatory Mass attendance and the annual retreat were rigorously enforced. In 1905, Father Rousseau introduced a "no Mass, no breakfast" rule; a few years later, a mother who requested that her son be sent home during the retreat, received a telegram from Father Murphy: "Retreat next few days far more important than studies. Harold may go on Thursday."[117] During these years, Catholic piety was expressed through May devotions in honor of Mary, the mother of Jesus. Prayers were recited at her statue, erected in 1904 opposite the O'Kane porch; seniors delivered short May Talks on "the titles and privileges of Mary"; all wore small medals throughout the month on their lapels.[118] Senior retreats before graduation continued, and the Jesuits still emphasized Ignatian ideas of character formation. In a circular letter issued in 1909, Father Hanselman reminded the faculty of the obligation to model and foster mature piety among their students. Jesuit teachers were exhorted to be "masters in profane sciences . . . but . . . also models and teachers of spiritual truths. . . . Be always masters of yourselves in patience and self-

116. Wernz to [Hanselman], Rome, May 6, 1909 (copy), Wernz to Murphy, Mondragone, August 24, 1909, ACHC, 12.15.

117. Prefect of Discipline Diary, November 21, 1905, ACHC, 15.2-2; Clara Terwilliger to Murphy, October 22, 1909, ACHC, 12.15.

118. Drafts of annual letters, 1905 and 1909, ACHC, 19.7B-1. The statue was later moved to a spot near the campus cemetery, opposite Campion House. Meagher and Grattan, *Spires*, 227.

control, be spiritual men, men of prayer and self-denial; all for the one great cause, the love of Our Lord and the salvation of souls."[119]

After the establishment of the annual Holy Cross Night in 1903, each college class began to host its own off-campus dinner. Soon, the routine was established: the freshman dinner was held in December; the sophomores gathered in February; the juniors, in May; the senior class sponsored a prom on the night of commencement and a class banquet on the following day at the Hotel Edgemere on the lake.[120] Meanwhile, Holy Cross Night became increasingly elaborate as students staged masquerades. In 1910, prep students wore white shirts with purple ties; the freshmen wore colored pajamas; the sophomores sported togas; the juniors came as red devils; the seniors, as always, wore caps and gowns. After that, the expense of renting or fashioning costumes became a negative consideration, and the masquerade was dropped.[121] Holy Cross Night acquired an academic aspect in 1909, when Father Murphy invited the alumni to attend morning or afternoon classes and to eat with students or faculty at noon and six P.M. That year, twenty arrived before the evening meal and thirty more arrived for the evening events and a late lunch.[122] Another indication of class spirit was the initiation of the *Purple Patcher* in 1907, as a supplement to *The Purple* and a memory book for the graduating class.

During the Hanselman and Murphy years, distinguished alumni were invited to campus for festive visits designed to honor the visitors, supply role models for the students, and indicate the success of the institution in the careers of its graduates. In December 1901, the College hosted a reception for Thomas Conaty shortly after his elevation to bishop.[123] His reception served as a prelude to a "Bishops' Day" in May 1902, when all seven "mitered sons" of Holy Cross returned for a celebration. At Mass, Bishop Conaty preached in praise of Holy Cross and in defense of its academic quality and moral values. The bishops attended an intramural baseball game and then a banquet in

119. Circular letter of Joseph Hanselman, New York, September 3, 1909, Provincials' Letters, ACHC, 19.1; HD June 12, 1902, and June 7, 1907.

120. Worcester *Post*, May 12, October 20, and December 15, 1903; Worcester *Telegram*, September 5, 1903; HD, 1910–11. Prefect of Discipline Diary, December 13, 1910, and February 14, May 18, and June 23, 1911, ACHC, 15.2-2. Despite their popularity, there were problems with the class dinners. In 1910, thirty freshmen found the $2 ticket to be beyond their means, while those who did participate straggled in until 2 A.M.

121. Prefect of Discipline Diary, November 1, 1907, October 27, 1910, October 9, 1911, ACHC, 15.2-2.

122. Murphy to Alumni, Worcester, October 1, 1909, ACHC, 12.15; HD, October 21, 1909.

123. HD, November 22 and December 1–4, 1901.

the large study hall with invited guests and seniors. In the evening, the guests ventured outdoors for an illumination of the front of Fenwick Hall with purple lights prepared by the resident pyrotechnist, Father Albert Ulrich.[124] Alumni success along a different line of endeavor was celebrated in 1905, when Dr. John Duggan, Class of 1880, was elected mayor of Worcester. Father Hann grasped an institutional meaning of Duggan's success when he recorded, *"May he bring more credit* to H.C.C. by a grand administration of his duties." The mayor was feted at a formal reception in April of 1906. The orchestra and glee club performed; the presidents of each of the college classes made remarks.[125] Honorary doctorates were instituted by Father Murphy at the 1906 commencement, when Massachusetts Governor Curtis Guild, Jr., and Mayor Duggan accepted the LL. D. and Charles G. Herbermann, chief editor of the *Catholic Encyclopedia,* received a Litt. D.[126]

Recognition on a far grander scale was at stake when Theodore Roosevelt and Cardinal James Gibbons visited Holy Cross in 1905 and 1907. The president came to the city primarily to deliver diplomas at the first undergraduate commencement of Clark University. He had agreed to do so partly because he owed a debt of gratitude to Clark College President Carroll D. Wright for help in resolving a coal strike. When Father Hanselman learned in February 1905 that the president was coming to Worcester, he contacted President Wright, who readily agreed to share the glory with Holy Cross, if Roosevelt was willing. Hanselman's ease in broaching the subject was itself a measure of the distance he had come in accepting the necessity of establishing friendly links with schools outside the Catholic network. Only two and a half years earlier, a general invitation to the Holy Cross faculty and students to attend the opening of Clark's undergraduate branch had posed a dilemma for the Jesuit consultors: on the one hand, the alumni and other Catholics might criticize such contact; on the other hand, "to hold aloof after a formal invitation would put us in opposition from the beginning and expose us to unfavorable comments in the newspapers."

124. HD, May 20, 1902. The Worcester *Post,* May 20, 1902, gave extensive front-page coverage to the event and reprinted Conaty's talk. The bishops were Thomas Beaven (Class of 1870) of Springfield; Mathew Harkins (1862–63) of Providence; Michael Hoban (1868–71) of Scranton; Elphege Gravel (1858) of Nicolet, Canada; John Michaud (Class of 1870) of Burlington, Vermont; Dennis Bradley (1864–67) of Manchester; and Thomas Conaty (Class of 1868) of The Catholic University of America.

125. Duggan was defeated in 1907 after serving two one-year terms. HD, December 12 and 15, 1905, April 4, 1906, December 10, 1907.

126. Annual Letter, 1906, ARSI, MD 1502. College sources claimed that this was the first time any Catholic college presented an honorary degree to a governor. WL, 35:177–78.

President Theodore Roosevelt speaking in 1905 at the first commencement to be held on Fitton Field. In the midst of a rainstorm, he praised Holy Cross for its commitment "to train not merely the body and mind, but the soul of man."

In the end, Fathers Hanselman, Murphy, and a number of Jesuit faculty attended.[127]

Hanselman extended the invitation to Roosevelt through Worcester Congressman John R. Thayer, who communicated the president's acceptance on February 24. "Hurrah, for Teddy" wrote Father Hann in the House Diary. Roosevelt's acceptance required Holy Cross authorities to advance the commencement by one day, to June 21. The planning took into account that the

127. Consultors' Minutes, September 30 and October 9, 1902, ACHC, 19.0. G. Stanley Hall, president of Clark University from 1888 to 1924, was a friend of Bishop Conaty and the only non-Catholic educator to speak at the Silver Jubilee of The Catholic University of America in 1915. He said that Conaty's appointment as rector there made papal infallibility more believable to him! Paul Julian Schuler, "The Reaction of American Catholics to the Foundations and Early Practices of Progressive Education in the United States, 1892–1917" (Ph.D. Dissertation, University of Notre Dame, 1970), 288–91.

president would be in Worcester only five hours, with two commencements and a private reception. His appearance at Holy Cross would therefore be brief, but it was the only event open to the general public. For that reason, the commencement was held for the first time on Fitton Field, with a special platform for honored guests and speakers. Since Roosevelt would clearly be unable to be present for the entire ceremony, the beginning was set at 11 A.M. with the usual array of speeches, music, and awards; the president would arrive at 12:30 to deliver an address and pass out the diplomas.[128]

Heavy rain fell all morning on Commencement Day. Nevertheless, 6000 people gathered in the stands and waited with the 37 graduates for the guest of the hour. Finally, a telephone call from Clark brought word that the president was on his way. Fathers Hanselman and Murphy greeted him and escorted him from his car to the platform. As he came into sight, the students gave a college cheer: HOIAH HOIAH, CHOO CHOO RAH-RAH, CHOO CHOO RAH-RAH, HOIAH ROOSEVELT RAH! In an enthusiastic introduction that was interrupted frequently by applause, Father Hanselman called Roosevelt "the most popular president that ever claimed the allegiance of the people . . . the typical soldier of the 20th century, he seeks to make peace." Roosevelt spoke for about fifteen minutes, starting with a humorous comment that "Holy Cross had taken the summa cum laude in baseball" by defeating Harvard that year. Next, he saluted Holy Cross:

It is eminently characteristic of our nation that we should have an institution of learning like Holy Cross, in which the effort is made to train not merely the body and mind, but the soul of man (loud applause) so that he shall be made a good American and a good citizen of our great country.

He described Americans as a new nationality made up of various races with a variety of contributions to make, and he encouraged more scholarship at Holy Cross in Celtic literature. To the crowd in the stands, he advocated active citizenship that combined "the power of efficient action with the power of fealty to lofty ideals . . . , the spirit which makes a man decent, and sends him out into actual life, able to hold his own." Then, pleading the tightness of his schedule, he turned to the awarding of degrees. He shook each graduate's hand heartily, saying "Delighted to meet you"; and "Glad to know you." As he

128. Sources on Roosevelt's visit include HD, February 24–26 and June 20–21, 1905; Consultors' Minutes, February 19, 1905, ACHC 19.0; the Worcester *Post*, June 21, 1905; the Worcester *Gazette*, June 22, 1905; Historia Domus, 1904–5, ACHC 19.0; Annual Letter, 1905 (draft), ACHC, 19.7B-1; and Charles Nutt, *History of Worcester and Its People* (4 vols.; New York: Lewis Historical Publishing Co., 1919), 2:751.

returned to the car, he planted an elm which Brother Horwedel held in place. He shook Horwedel's hand, saying: "God bless you, Brother, and may the *tree grow!*" He had been on campus for thirty minutes, and the campus had been his. It was a masterful performance. As Father Hann noted afterwards, Roosevelt had "made himself all to all—a grand man—he has won the hearts of all. . . . This really marks the *golden era* of H.C.C."[129]

What Theodore Roosevelt represented in the political life of the United States, Cardinal Gibbons, Archbishop of Baltimore, represented in the ecclesiastical life of American Catholicism. He was the unofficial leader of the nation's Catholics, a role he had filled since the time of the third Plenary Council of Baltimore in 1884. Early in 1906, Father Murphy approached him to speak at that year's commencement, stressing Bishop Beaven's enthusiasm for the idea and mentioning that twelve alumni had been bishops. By visiting Holy Cross, Murphy emphasized, the cardinal would promote the College's seasoned enterprise:

Holy Cross College as the oldest Catholic college in New England, has been battling vigorously for sound Catholic higher education for over sixty years against heavy odds in the shape of the best equipped and most influential Protestant institutions. Encouragement will therefore give new zest to our efforts.[130]

Joseph Hanselman also promoted the idea, and reported in January of 1907 that the cardinal was ready to come.[131] Gibbons arrived at Union Station on June 16, the day before commencement. He was greeted by a large throng of local dignitaries and representatives of Catholic parishes and societies. The parade from the depot to campus was triumphal; it included thirty marching bands, representatives of Irish, French-Canadian, Polish, Italian, and Lithuanian societies, the alumni sodality, and Holy Cross graduates in cap and gown—3000 people in all. Along the line of march were thousands, some shouting, "Long live the cardinal!" Even non-Catholic spectators doffed their hats respectfully when he raised his hand in blessing—an indication, in the mind of one reporter, of "change in spirit of a people once intensely anti-Catholic."[132] On campus, the presidents of Clark University, Worcester Polytechnic Institute, Worcester Academy, and the State Normal School, and other honored guests participated in a public reception and were presented to the cardinal.

129. HD, June 21, 1905.
130. Murphy to Gibbons, Worcester, January 5, 1906, ACHC, 12.15.
131. Hanselman to Murphy, New York. January 30, 1907, ACHC, 12.15.
132. *WL*, 36:268–74, contains a full account of the visit. See also, Worcester *Post*, June 19, 1907; Annual Letter, 1907 (draft), ACHC, 19.7B-1.

At the alumni banquet in the evening, Gibbons expressed his great appreciation of the public reception: "It seems a trifle short of marvelous that a Cardinal of the Catholic Church should come into this old Commonwealth . . . , where fifty years ago he would hardly dare to venture, and find on his reception committee a Catholic Mayor to extend to him the greetings of this beautiful city." The commencement ceremonies took place outdoors, at the Fenwick Hall porch. Gibbons urged the graduates to seek Christian manhood, to be "sturdy men, endowed with courage of their convictions, . . . controlled by conscience rather than by expediency," and to take an interest in public affairs. For Father Hann, it was the "greatest day in the history of the College."

When President Roosevelt and Cardinal Gibbons pronounced their separate benedictions on the College, they offered an affirmation of the changes that produced the second Holy Cross. Between 1901 and 1911, Joseph Hanselman and Thomas Murphy achieved a durable balance by adapting the *Ratio* to contemporary trends in American higher education. Rudimentary pre-medical, pre-legal, and pedagogical programs enhanced the curriculum and confirmed the College's upward climb on the ladder of academic achievement; but resolute maintenance of the classics nucleus wedded Holy Cross firmly to the traditional Jesuit plan. The expansion of athletic facilities acknowledged the modern spirit, but academic restrictions on the players and the willingness to drop varsity basketball indicated that the priority was less to win and so promote school spirit than to stand upon the primacy of academics and to be realistic about expenses. The construction of Alumni Hall, the formation of the modern Alumni Association, and the introduction of annual Holy Cross Nights emphasized the importance of alumni to the well-being and reputation of the College; but the confrontation between Fathers Murphy and Harkins over the formation of an advisory committee for athletics drew the line between helpful participation and "interference," and the line was drawn by the rector. The debate about night permissions indicated how far a Holy Cross rector was willing to go in adapting the Jesuit spirit of discipline to the American context. The willingness to phase out the prep school, unusual as it was, significantly altered the nature of the enterprise. And the public response to the College's athletic programs, lecturers, and prominent guests indicated unambiguously that Holy Cross was a source of civic pride, a valued participant in the life of the community. By the time Thomas Murphy relinquished the rectorship in 1911, Holy Cross had become a modern college—an American, Catholic, Jesuit college whose curriculum and pattern of life successfully harmonized the *Ratio Studiorum* with contemporary educational norms. That was no small achievement.

CHAPTER SIX

Halcyon Years, 1911–1927

B Y 1911, THE PRINCIPAL COMPONENTS of the second Holy Cross were in place. In the space of two decades, College officials had responded to modern challenges by introducing the most significant changes in curriculum, student life, and physical plant since the founding of the school. Now the largest Catholic undergraduate college in the nation, Holy Cross had an academic program that was gaining broad acceptance. Under the circumstances, Joseph Dinand and James Carlin, whose rectorships covered the period from 1911 to 1927, chose to enhance the school's advantages. The curriculum, with its emphasis on the classics and philosophy, required adjustment but not wholesale reform. The growing student body needed more space—dormities, a chapel, and a library. Student life continued to be disciplined, oriented toward religion, and under the supervision of the Jesuits. After 1911, the second Holy Cross came into its own.

When Joseph M. Dinand assumed office, he was only 41 years old, but he brought a great deal of experience to the job. A native of Boston, he had attended Boston College before entering the Society of Jesus in 1887. Before his ordination in 1903, he taught at St. Francis Xavier College in New York City. Afterward he worked in Jamaica and then served as minister at St. Andrew-on-Hudson, a Jesuit house of formation. Dinand was installed as rector on October 9, 1911. Before the month was out, he had met with Bishop Beaven in Springfield and called on local Catholic pastors. A hearty, outgoing man with a gift for public speaking, Dinand enjoyed friendships with Bishop Beaven and David I. Walsh, an alumnus of 1893 who was a rising Massachusetts Democrat. These leaders of church and state became Dinand's allies in achieving his vision of an expanded campus.[1]

Father Dinand's first term lasted almost seven years and was the longest up to that time. Documents shed little light on the reasons for extending his term

1. HD, 1911–1916; Dinand to David I. Walsh, Worcester, September 1, 1915, ACHC, 12.16; *Jesuit Seminary News*, 8:2-3; *Holy Cross Alumnus*, 2:1.

beyond the customary six years. The explanation may have been connected with unusual circumstances during World War I, or with the fact that in 1917, when his sixth year ended, Dinand was in the midst of a fund drive. At that time, Father Dinand figured strongly in plans for the development of Jesuit life in the Northeast. When he left Holy Cross, he was assigned to be *socius* to Joseph Rockwell, who became head of the Maryland–New York Province in July 1918. By then, the province had grown so large that a division was indicated. In 1921, the New England Vice-Province was established under the jurisdiction of the Maryland–New York provincial, as a preparatory stage in the erection of the independent New England Province in 1926.[2] Rockwell proposed Dinand as the first vice-provincial—his appointment as *socius* may even have been intended as preparation for that office; but Dinand was unacceptable to Cardinal William O'Connell, the crotchety archbishop of Boston, and Patrick O'Gorman was chosen instead.[3]

James Carlin succeeded Dinand at Holy Cross in 1918. Born in 1872 in Peabody, Massachusetts, Carlin studied at Boston College for three years before entering the Society of Jesus in 1892. He taught at Georgetown for four years and was ordained in 1907. Afterwards he served as prefect of discipline at Georgetown and then taught philosophy at Holy Cross for two years before becoming *socius* of the Maryland–New York Province in 1912. A quiet, compassionate man who was methodical and reserved, he declined to join a citizens' committee in 1920 for the commemoration of the Pilgrim Tercentenary because of the Pilgrims' antipathy toward "those who differed with them, especially in religious opinions. . . . They had many good qualities, but in as much as I cannot give whole-hearted approval to all their doings, I am constrained to forego active cooperation in doing them honor."[4] Yet Carlin enjoyed human company: in 1919, he hosted a campus luncheon for Rotarians; two years later, he bought the first automobile for the Jesuit community—a seven-passenger Buick sedan—and gladly took passengers on his errands. In

2. James L. Burke, *Jesuit Province of New England: The Formative Years* [Boston: Society of Jesus, New England Province, 1976], 1–2, 8–12.

3. Patrick O'Gorman to Ledochowski, [Chestnut Hill], April 4, 1922, NEPA, Correspondence to General. The October 1991 issue of *The Catholic Historical Review* (vol. 77, no. 4) carried two excellent articles on O'Connell. James M. O'Toole, "The Role of Bishops in American Catholic History: Myth and Reality in the Case of Cardinal William O'Connell," (77:603–5) explains how Boston College officials thwarted the cardinal's attempt to slow down their plans for expansion. On O'Connell's near-removal from office, see Douglas J. Slawson, "'The Boston Tragedy and Comedy': The Near-Repudiation of Cardinal O'Connell," 77:616–43.

4. James Leo Burke, S.J., Personal interview, June 17, 1988; Carlin to Francis C. Holmes, Worcester, August 19, 1920, ACHC, 12.17; biographical sketch of Carlin, ACHC, 12.17.

1923 the Jesuit minister inserted an editorial note about Carlin in the House Diary: "I want to insist on one point here—the excessive thoughtful kindness of Rev. Fr. Rector to the sick."[5]

Carlin's term was associated primarily with fund-raising and expansion of the physical plant. Jesuit authorities worried that his preoccupation with financial matters left him disinclined to attend to the intellectual and spiritual formation of the students and to issues of discipline. Father O'Gorman considered replacing him with Joseph Dinand as early as 1922, but held back because he feared the reaction of Boston's archbishop.[6] When the change was announced in 1924, it was sudden. On July 24, Carlin was designated on the annual list of assignments as rector of Holy Cross for the coming year; one week later, Dinand was read in as the new rector, while Carlin was sent to the vice-province's novitiate as business manager and spiritual director.[7] As it turned out, Dinand's second term lasted for three years, extending to 1927 the era of expansion he initiated in 1911.

Overcrowding was the most serious problem when Joseph Dinand assumed office the first time. Thomas Murphy and his consultors had focused on the issue in 1910, when their thinking moved toward the construction of an "Executive Building" that would house the Jesuits and furnish space for a library and large lecture rooms. The old Jesuit rooms in Fenwick Hall would have then become available for students. In the summer of 1911, Father Murphy had Maginnis and Walsh draw up plans for such a building, at an estimated cost of $80,000.[8] Dinand took up the matter immediately, holding consultations on the proposal after school opened in 1911. The need was clear: at 406, the number of boarding students was up fifteen from the previous year and offered convincing evidence that the increase in enrollment over the last few years had not been a fluke.[9] Only the College debt was standing in the way of expansion.

Then, unexpectedly, Bishop Beaven came to the rescue with a plan by which he and the clergy of the Springfield Diocese agreed to contribute a new

5. Holy Cross Consultors' reports to O'Gorman, April 1, 1922, March 24, 1923, March 26, 1924, NEPA, Consultors' Excerpts; HD, May 5, 1919, September 30, 1921, February 26, 1923.

6. O'Gorman to Ledochowski, [Chestnut Hill], April 4, 1922, NEPA, Correspondence to General.

7. HD, July 1918, July-September 1924.

8. Murphy to Hanselman, Worcester, October 18, 1910 (draft), ACHC, 14.0–3; Consultors' Minutes, 1910–1911, ACHC, 19.0; Worcester *Post*, October 30, 1911. Correspondence with Maginnis and Walsh, and sketches of the proposed building (never built) are in ACHC, 16.1BN-1.

9. Consultors' Minutes, September 17 and October 1, 1911, ACHC 19.0; Jesuit minister's note book, 1911–35, ACHC, 19.3-4.

building. Beaven was friendlier with Joseph Dinand than he had been with Thomas Murphy; together, bishop and rector consulted about the needs of the school. In November 1911, Bishop Beaven met with the priests of his diocese to propose a plan that, he insisted, was entirely his own: "I have broached it to no one, and no one has suggested or mentioned the matter to me: I alone am responsible for this initiative."[10] He spoke, not as a Holy Cross alumnus, but as the head of a diocesan clergy who benefited from the College's "prosperous usefulness . . . [as] a well-spring of benefaction and blessing for the diocese of Springfield." Now Holy Cross needed help; its facilities were overcrowded; indebtedness prohibited growth. The time was ripe for Catholic leaders to join a "Catholic educational crusade" that would signal their intentions to secular educators. By offering $100 annually for three years, the more than 300 diocesan clergy could raise $90,000 to sustain the progress of "the first and best Catholic educational institution in our New England garden of Catholicity." Each priest was asked to signify his willingness to pledge the money, or not; but clearly, the expectation was on the side of participation. On November 23, the bishop assured Father Dinand that he could count on $90,000.[11] Beaven and Dinand soon agreed that the new structure would be a student dormitory, with classrooms on the ground floor. The building was to be known as the "Memorial of the Clergy of the Diocese of Springfield," but soon everyone was calling it Beaven Hall.[12] The decision to locate it west of O'Kane Hall on the upper terrace, instead of using the more obvious site on the lower terrace opposite Alumni Hall, was probably a function of the amount of funding. A building large enough to match Alumni Hall would have cost more than the available sum. In the spring of 1912, Charles Maginnis's plans for a five-story building received speedy approval from Rome. Because the bids were far above the budgeted amount, Maginnis scaled down the plans by removing one floor.[13]

The groundbreaking in May provided the occasion for another Bishops' Day. Bishops Matthew Harkins (Providence), Michael Hoban (Scranton), and Louis Walsh (Portland, Maine) joined Beaven for a Mass that was fol-

10. Address of Right Reverend Thos. D. Beaven, DD. to The Clergy of the Springfield Diocese, Worcester, November 21, 1911, ARSI, MD 15-XXII, 9; Prefect of Discipline Diary, December 12, 1911, ACHC, 15.2-2.

11. HD, November 23–29, 1911; Dinand to Holy Cross alumni, Worcester, November 25, 1911, ARSI, MD 15-XXII, 10.

12. Beaven to the Clergy of the Springfield Diocese, December 1, 1911, ARSI, MD 15-XXII, 10; Dinand to Wernz, Worcester, November 24, 1912, ARSI, MD 15-XXII, 12.

13. Maginnis and Walsh to Dinand, Boston, May 23, 1912, ACHC, 16.1BC-1; HD, April–June, 1912; Meagher and Grattan, *Spires*, 200. The final contract was set at $96,670. HD.

lowed by the groundbreaking and a lavish banquet. Afterwards, the guests enjoyed a Victrola concert arranged by a member of the faculty, then repaired to Fitton Field, where the Holy Cross nine capped the day by defeating Wesleyan. Work commenced on June 10. During the autumn months mild weather favored the project, and the bishop sent enough money to cover the bills without borrowing.[14] Beaven Hall was completed in the summer of 1913 and opened as the senior dormitory. The building could accommodate 140 students in double rooms, plus Jesuit prefects. The lower floor contained a large lecture room, a classroom, the biology laboratory, the geological museum, and the senior class library. Bishop Beaven and his clergy honored their pledges; in 1918 the books were closed when the collection reached $100,000.[15]

After the completion of Beaven Hall, Father Dinand focused on smaller campus improvements that could be sustained without raising the debt. A formal gate at the principal entrance on Linden Lane came first. In 1914, Charles Maginnis agreed to design one whose object would be "to impart as much stateliness as possible . . . [because] a good deal of psychology is mixed up with architectural gateways."[16] In 1917, representatives of the Class of 1907 agreed to fund the project for their tenth anniversary. With the seals of church and state on the two main pillars and the College seal at the top of the wrought-iron arch, the structure served, as Father Dinand put it, to "proclaim the purpose of the Institution, namely, education for both Church and State."[17] In 1918, Maginnis was contacted about a second ornamental gate for the entrance to Fitton Field. The new gate, Maginnis replied, should echo but not duplicate the first, because it led to an athletic field whose "spirit of festivity" required "a certain vivacity of ornament." The war and other campus priorities interrupted this project until 1923, when the Fitton Field gates and an iron fence "really worthy of a high grade educational institution" were completed along College Street to link the two gates.[18] Father Dinand introduced another campus trademark by facilitating the installation of the first pillar clock on the terrace in front of Fenwick Hall. Complete with illuminated

14. Jerome Towne Diary, May 21–22, 1912, ACHC, 19.4-1; HD, May 22, 1912; Dinand to Wernz, Worcester, November 24, 1912, ARSI, MD 15-XXII, 12; Meagher and Grattan, *Spires*, 200–201.

15. HD, June–October 1913; Consultors' Minutes, February 25, 1913, ACHC, 19.0; Treasurer's Records, Beaven Hall Fund book, ACHC, 13.0; Meagher and Grattan, *Spires*, 200.

16. Maginnis and Walsh to Dinand, Boston, February 28, 1914, ACHC, 16.1BS-1; HD, February 24, 1912.

17. Dinand to William J. Cahill, Worcester, February 24, 1917, ACHC, 12.16; HD, July–October, 1917; Worcester *Gazette*, February 19, 1917.

18. Maginnis and Walsh to Dinand, Boston, July 1, 1918, ACHC, 16.1BS-1; HD, June 16, 1923. In voting to construct the fence, the consultors decided that "the price should not be a deterrent."

face and a water font at its base, the clock was donated in 1916 by the Union Institution for Savings on Tremont Street in Boston, where it originally stood.[19]

Throughout his administration, Father Dinand promoted the College widely within the Catholic community. The advertisements emphasized size ("The Largest Catholic College in America"), location, facilities, and academic standards ("Extensive and Beautiful Campus. Fully Equipped Gymnasium and Athletic Field. Beneficial Athletics Encouraged, but Subordinated to Study, Ennobling College Spirit"). And the faculty was "exceptionally able."[20] Ever larger numbers of students found such publicity attractive and found the means to attend Holy Cross, whose tuition charges rose from $60 to $200 between 1911 and 1927. The largest increases came after 1922, when tuition doubled from $100 to $200 over a period of three years. The basic room and board charges also rose, from $200 at the beginning of the interval to $400 by 1925 ($375 for students who lived in Fenwick or O'Kane), when the complete package for most students cost $600. The opening of Beaven Hall ensured that the number of boarding students could continue to expand. By the fall of 1915, there were 462 boarding students on campus; after the war, in the fall of 1919, 561 boarders matriculated, raising the total enrollment to 688.[21]

The College's reputation also attracted political candidates. Early in the presidential campaign of 1912, Woodrow Wilson and his secretary, Joseph Tumulty, a graduate of the Jesuits' St. Peter's College in Jersey City, visited Holy Cross after attending a local political rally. The New Jersey governor gave a brief talk to the students and met the members of the faculty. In October, Wilson's running-mate, Governor Thomas Marshall of Indiana, also came to campus and visited several classes.[22] Although the visits were not overtly po-

---

The cost of the 1923 project was $30,600. Consultors' Minutes, June 26, 1922, ACHC, 19.0; Father Minister's Note Book, 1911–35, ACHC, 19.3-4. The true completion of the project occurred in 1985, when the chain-link fence above Linden Lane along College Street was replaced with a new fence that copied the 1923 design.

19. Thomas J. Kelly, Class of 1880 and treasurer of the donor institution, arranged the gift. F. S. Atkinson to Dinand, Boston, July 25, 1916, and Dinand to Thomas J. Kelly, Worcester, July 29, 1916, ACHC, 12.16; *Historia Domus*, 1916, ACHC, 19.7A-1.

20. Advertising copy, ACHC, 12.16.

21. Enrollment figures for boarding and day students were published annually, except 1918 and 1926, in the October issue of *Woodstock Letters*. The 1926 figures come from the College catalog and the Jesuit minister's note book, 1911–35. ACHC, 19.3-4. 1918 figures are irregular due to effects of World War I.

22. HD, April 27 and October 3, 1912; unidentified press clipping, ACHC, Locker 8, Scrapbook 7, p. 214.

litical, their context was: a stop at the nation's largest Catholic college was good politics and did the candidates no harm among Catholic voters.

The candidates' visits may have been arranged by David I. Walsh, who was elected lieutenant governor of Massachusetts in 1912. Interest in Walsh's career intensified in the fall of 1913, when he secured the nomination for governor. On election day, many ventured into the city to watch the posting of returns by local newspapers. Walsh's victory, as the first Catholic and first alumnus to win the Massachusetts State House, brought enormous satisfaction. Joseph Dinand could hardly contain his delight when he wired congratulations: "Alma Mater rejoices from her heart and congratulates with warmest affection her noble son on his personal victory and the unmistakable confidence and appreciation of the citizens of the Commonwealth." To a prominent alumnus, he remarked:

I know how the heart of every Holy Cross man must feel today over Dave's success, for his glory is ours and every one of us participates in his happiness. . . . In him the Catholic cause has triumphed, and may he be the leader of many a Catholic Governor in the old State of Massachusetts.[23]

A special celebration, dubbed "Walsh Night," was set for January 12, 1914, with all of the living former presidents of the College—Fathers Murphy, Hanselman, O'Kane, and Boone—invited. Not even subzero weather cooled the excitement that day. Classes ended at 2:30, after which the governor received a noisy ovation at the O'Kane porch. Inside, Walsh greeted the students as they filed past him into the lecture hall for a formal program. In the evening, 400 alumni gathered at the Bancroft Hotel. Their sentiments sprang from a shared sense that Walsh's election signified a more honored place in the Bay State for Roman Catholics, Irish-Americans, and Holy Cross. They celebrated with delight and spoke from the heart. In thanking the speakers afterwards, Father Dinand basked in the warmth of his memories. To one, he wrote that January 12 was "a night on which we were glad we were Holy Cross men."[24]

David I. Walsh's special standing as a symbol of the College's success and its spirit of loyalty endured for the rest of his life. There was another campus

23. Telegram to Walsh, and Dinand to James B. Carroll, Worcester, November 5, 1913, ACHC, 12.16. On Walsh's career see Dorothy G. Wayman, *David I. Walsh: Citizen-Patriot* (Milwaukee: Bruce Publishing Co., 1952).

24. Dinand to Michael F. Fallon, Worcester, January 14, 1914, ACHC, 12.16. For an account of Walsh's campus visit, see Prefect's Diary, January 12, 1914, ACHC, 15.2-2, and HD, January 12, 1914. Speeches given at the alumni gathering were reprinted in *The Purple* 26:239–78.

celebration when he was re-elected in November 1914. That evening, he began his toast with a wry observation: "If the old Puritans could see [their] governor sandwiched between two live Jesuits in a Jesuit refectory . . . what a howl!"[25] A year later, Walsh was defeated, but he was still a campus hero. He responded warmly to a consoling letter from Father Dinand: "Let me again tell you . . . how dearly I prize your friendship. You have been, even without your knowing it, a tremendous source of encouragement to me."[26] After his gubernatorial term ended, Walsh set his sights on Washington. He ran successfully for the U.S. Senate in 1918, becoming the first Democratic senator from Massachusetts since 1851. On election day, the Jesuit minister noted, "most of us voted for the first time." Throughout his term, Walsh maintained his contact with Holy Cross and the Jesuits when he was at home in Clinton. Defeated for re-election in 1924, Walsh staged a successful comeback in 1926, an event celebrated with a campus bonfire and fireworks. Walsh remained in the Senate for twenty more years, an active and influential friend of his alma mater.[27]

As David Walsh pursued his political plans, Joseph Dinand was preparing for the College's Diamond Jubilee. He set 1918 as the target for the liquidation of the Alumni Hall debt, hoping to use the anniversary to launch a new era of campus expansion. Dinand discussed his plans with alumni representatives in 1915, covering the possibilities—a library, a science building, an athletic clubhouse at Fitton Field, a new gate and brick wall along College Street, and a new chapel. The proposed chapel won strong endorsement; in April 1915, the Worcester County chapter of the Alumni Association announced a campaign to raise $250,000 for that purpose by seeking $100 contributions from 2500 of the 4500 former students who were then alive.[28] But the organizers of the campaign seemed unaccountably oblivious to the lessons they might have learned from the failure of the Alumni Hall drive. Little was done to promote the effort during the remainder of 1915. In October, when Charles Maginnis expressed his interest in drawing up a plan for the new chapel, Father Dinand replied that the question was premature and suggested that he "influence

25. HD, November 5–7, 1914.

26. Walsh to Dinand, Boston, November 5 and 11, 1915, ACHC, 12.16.

27. HD, 1918–1947; John J. Delaney, *Dictionary of American Catholic Biography*, (Doubleday & Co.: Garden City, 1984), 580–81; Wayman, *Walsh*, 98–102, 152–350. Walsh was defeated for re-election in 1946 by Henry Cabot Lodge, Jr., and died on June 11, 1947. Edward B. Hanify '33 offers a vivid memoir of Walsh in *Memories of a Senator: Recollections of The Honorable David I. Walsh, Holy Cross Class of 1893* [Privately printed, 1995].

28. Dinand to George Linnehan, Worcester, May 8, 1915, ACHC, 12.16; unidentified press clipping [1915], ACHC, Locker 8, Scrapbook 8, p. 200; Worcester *Telegram*, April 3, 1915.

some of your wealthy friends to donate such a needed building."[29] The following month, Governor Walsh sent a gift of $1000, indicating his disappointment that the drive had not made much headway, but the following February, the officers of the Alumni Association offered only a lukewarm appeal: "Each alumnus should do his part and contribute his mite that this event may be a grand success, and thus bring honor and credit to the college, and its alumni."[30] Much of the burden for raising money fell on Father Dinand, who promoted the Diamond Jubilee Fund in meetings with the alumni and through letters of encouragement to presidents of local chapters.[31] In the end, the effort was largely campus-centered, directed by individuals who added the drive to already crowded schedules, trusting that good intentions and hard work would suffice.

The campaign brought mixed results. There was good news in November 1916, when Richard Healy, a Worcester merchant and friend of the College, offered a gift of $20,000—half for the Jubilee Fund and half for a scholarship. Yet, by January of 1917, the fund, including the Healy contribution, stood at only $25,000—ten percent of the goal. The following month, an anonymous pledge of $50,000 provided a major boost and was followed by several other large gifts.[32] Then, in April, the United States entered the European war. At first, there were efforts to keep the drive going. Near the end of the year, Father Dinand reported that many donors were contributing Liberty Bonds to the fund. And in June of 1918, Irish tenor John McCormack, who had accepted an honorary degree the previous year, sang a benefit that was touted as "the biggest concert ever given in Worcester."[33] By then, Dinand's notes showed a total collection of about $105,000, well over half of which ($60,000) had come from two large gifts; but the figures were misleading, be-

29. Maginnis to Dinand, Boston, October 18, 1915, and Dinand to Maginnis, October 28, 1918, ACHC, 12.16.

30. Walsh to Dinand, Boston, November 15, 1915, ACHC, 12.16; Edward Fitzpatrick and John Gannon to Alumni, Worcester, February 5, 1916, in *The Purple* 28:387–88.

31. These letters are scattered throughout Dinand's 1916 correspondence, ACHC, 12.16. See especially letters to John Dore (February 17), John Cullion (June 3), John P. O'Brien (December 6), and James F. Rockett (December 13).

32. HD, November 9, 1916, and January–March, 1917; Edward Fitzgerald and John Gannon to Alumni, Worcester, January 16, 1917, and Dinand notes on Diamond Jubilee Drive, ACHC, 12.16; Fall River *Herald*, February 5, 1917.

33. Dinand to James J. Fitzgibbon, Worcester, November 13, 1917, ACHC, 12.16; HD June 16, 1918. McCormack was nominated for the degree by Dr. John Bottomley '89. The singer first visited the College in February 1917 and stayed for a meal. In June 1917, he attracted a record crowd to the alumni banquet, at which he spoke and sang. Consultors' Minutes, February 17 and May 25, 1917; HD, February 19 and June 19, 1917.

cause the $50,000 pledge was never paid. In all, about $66,000 was collected for the Diamond Jubilee Fund.[34] It was a disappointing outcome but hardly a disaster. The College had raised more money than in the Alumni Hall drive, and in a shorter period of time. The Diamond Jubilee Drive was also valuable for the lessons it taught about effective fund-raising.

Meanwhile, public preoccupation with the war forced cancellation of the diamond jubilee. Although he had drawn up plans for a major celebration, Father Dinand was having second thoughts by the start of 1918. "The country seems to be ready for anything but a celebration of this kind," he told an alumnus; "It may be better for us in the long run to put off anything like a really big affair."[35] Early in the spring, he decided to cancel the event because of the war. The commencement in 1918 was held quietly; but in recognition of the institutional milestone, 366 attended the alumni banquet and the largest crowd ever was present to honor the graduates. After the armistice, Father Carlin faced the question of a deferred celebration in 1919. But the moment had passed; by common consent of the senior class and the faculty, the jubilee was quietly laid to rest.[36]

The relative brevity of American involvement in World War I made its impact only a blip in the College's development. Nevertheless, the months between April 1917 and the end of 1918 were a time of intense feeling that brought out the best and worst in individuals associated with the school. Although the opening of hostilities in August 1914 passed unnoticed in the official diary, the war came closer in 1915. In March, the students heard a talk on preparedness, and in May, after the sinking of the *Lusitania*, Father Dinand wired President Wilson: "We the Faculty and Students of Holy Cross are earnestly praying God to direct you in these hours of anxiety and doubt."[37] Two years later, the president delivered his war message just as students were departing for their Easter recess. When they returned, they voted unanimously to establish a temporary student military corps. Father Dinand engaged Major Joseph W. O'Connor '03, a member of the 9th Massachusetts Infantry and a

34. Treasurer's Records, 1918 Fund (Book 62), and Statement for Fiscal Year, 1924–25, ACHC, 13.0; Dinand notes on Diamond Jubilee Drive, June 15, 1918, ACHC 12.16. The likeliest possibility as the anonymous donor was Bishop Beaven, who once offiered the Jesuits $50,000 to start a high school after the Holy Cross prep division closed. He died in 1920. Dinand to Wernz, Worcester, November 24, 1912, ARSI, MD 15-XXII, 12.

35. Dinand to Frank P. Craig, Worcester, January 26, 1918, ACHC, 12.16.

36. Dinand to Patrick F. Hussey, Worcester, May 16, 1918, ACHC, 12.16; HD, June 18–19, 1918; Carlin to Ledochowski, Worcester, April 27. 1919, ARSI, MD 1017, *Fasc.* "Ex Officio" (1919).

37. HD, March 9, 1915. The wire was sent May 10, 1915. ACHC, 12.16.

veteran of General Pershing's expedition into Mexico, to organize a military drill with 90 ceremonial rifles borrowed from Sacred Heart Parish.[38] The activity had no official connection with the Department of War and imposed no direct obligation upon the students. The point was to communicate a sense of involvement and to help students to secure officer's commissions if they were called to serve. In the main, Father Dinand admitted, the novelty of the activities made them attractive to students.[39] Then O'Connor departed for France with the Allied Expeditionary Force, leaving Dinand to search for a new commanding officer throughout the 1917–18 academic year. He told officials in Washington that the College, with 600 mostly able-bodied men, all high school graduates between the ages of 17 and 21, was "prepared to make whatever changes in our schedule would be deemed necessary for the accomplishment of better results in the Military training of our students."[40] But for the time being, the government had nothing to offer.

The failure to maintain a military program notwithstanding, students and faculty entered into the spirit of the war effort in positive ways. The baseball game at Fitton Field on Patriots' Day in 1917 provided an occasion for patriotism. Before the start of the game, three flag-bearers and the Worcester Brass Band led the whole student body, grouped by class, down Linden Lane and College Street to the centerfield flagpole, where a sixteen-gun salute was given. Struck by the solemn mood of the record-breaking crowd, Dinand observed that "people were as reverential . . . as if they were in Church."[41] In May, College authorities released students from school for essential summer work on farms or in shipbuilding, subject to certain conditions that included an average of 60 or higher in all courses. Within a week, civilian war work and military enlistments had reduced the number of students on campus by half. The baseball team played out the schedule and worked on the College farm to assist the war effort. All students were exempt from final exams.[42] In the autumn of 1917, the war permeated campus life, de-

38. A graduate of the Harvard Medical School, Dr. O'Connor had a long association with Holy Cross. He played football, ran track, and managed the baseball team during his senior year, and taught biology (1913–14). Worcester *Telegram* (Peace Edition), July 31, 1919; *Holy Cross Alumnus*, May 1959.

39. Dinand to John F. Duston, Worcester, April 27, 1917, and Dinand to Brig. Gen. William E. Crozier, Worcester, May 1, 1917, ACHC, 12.16. The rifles had been used by a parish organization, the Sacred Heart Cadets. Unidentified press clipping [spring 1917], Locker 8, Scrapbook 11, p. 37.

40. Dinand to Commissioner of Education, Worcester, April 26, 1918, and Dinand to Major Kendall Banning, Worcester, June 29, 1918, ACHC, 12.16; HD, January 9–15, 1918.

41. Dinand to Mary F. Healy, Worcester, April 21, 1917, ACHC, 12.16; HD, April 16–19, 1917.

42. Dinand to Robert Swickerath, Worcester, May 19, 1917, ACHC, 12.16; Consultors' Minute Book, May 7, 8, and 14, 1917, ACHC, 19.0. Dinand's address to the students about early release for

spite the absence of a military unit. In October, a new flagpole was erected on the O'Kane tower. In November, a weekly Mass was instituted for the Holy Cross men "with the colors." On Holy Cross Night, November 20, Holy Cross soldiers from Camp Devens were the guests of honor. In December, the freshman class substituted a smoker for the traditional banquet. Fundraising efforts like choral concerts and plays, lectures in Fenwick Lecture Hall, and clothing drives kept students involved in the war effort. In May 1918, the wartime labor shortage hit home when, at Dinand's urging, the students "agreed to help out as a war measure and to *make their own beds.*" Father Dinand made himself available regularly to speak at patriotic rallies and to preach at Masses at military bases in New England: the House Diary records twenty such engagements between mid-February and the end of June 1918.[43]

Despite a large enrollment in the fall of 1917, Dinand worried about the potential effects of the draft and voluntary enlistment on the student body. On October 4, there were only 220 seniors and juniors, compared with 493 in the two lower classes.[44] In November, President Wilson promulgated Selective Service regulations without exemptions for liberal arts students. A few weeks later, Dinand reported: "The boys are getting quite anxious about the next Draft and I fear that quite a number of the Seniors may not return after the Thanksgiving holidays, since many prefer to enlist in some branch of the service, rather than wait to be drafted into the Army."[45] In December, he wrote to Massachusetts Senator Henry Cabot Lodge, urging that the official policy of exempting seniors in technical colleges from the draft be extended to seniors in classical colleges. Like their counterparts in the technical schools, he argued, the classical seniors would be able to render greater service to the nation if they were allowed to finish the course. In reply, Lodge enclosed a letter he had received from Colonel Hugh Johnson of the War Department regarding Dinand's request. He was struck, the senator said, by the "great force" of Johnson's position that military necessity justified allowing medical, dental, veterinary, and engineering students to finish their academic programs and

---

civilian war work over the summer, May 11, 1917, was reprinted in *The Purple* 29:524–26. Dinand reported to Food Administrator Herbert Hoover that 290 of the 580 students had gone to work on farms for twelve weeks; 90 more were at work in munitions factories or in the Navy (shipyards). Dinand to Herman [sic] C. Hoover, Washington, June 28, 1917, ACHC, 12.16.

43. HD, 1917–18; Bishop M. J. Hoban to Dinand, Scranton, October 24, 1917, ACHC, 12.16; unidentified press clipping, ACHC, Locker 8, Scrapbook 11, p. 84.

44. Dinand to James Q. Purcell, Worcester, October 4, 1917, ACHC, 12.16.

45. Dinand to J. F. Lehy, Worcester, November 28, 1917, ACHC, 12.16.

precluded exemptions for students in "Cultural Colleges."[46] That ended the effort.

By January, Dinand was reporting that the war "is making severe inroads on our number and every day finds one or two leaving for some branch of the Service." In April, there were about 400 stars on the College service flag, representing past and present students who had gone to war.[47] The circumstances lent urgency to Father Dinand's efforts to expedite the establishment of a campus Student Army Training Corps (SATC) program after college presidents were notified in May of its establishment in all schools of higher education with enrollments of 100 or more. Its purpose was to enroll all able-bodied male students above the high school level as army privates in what one historian called "a vast network of pre-induction centers where young men could be temporarily held prior to call-up for active military duty."[48] To provide assistant instructors for the program, military authorities authorized 62 Holy Cross students to attend a summer training session at a military camp near Plattsburgh, New York; 28 were commissioned as lieutenants and assigned to SATC programs at schools throughout the East. Meanwhile, just before changing offices with James Carlin on July 25, Dinand traveled to New York and Washington to conclude arrangements for beginning the program when school opened.[49]

From the day he assumed office, Father Carlin directed his attention toward the military program. At the request of the Army, the opening date was set for September 26, presumably to allow extra time for preparation; but soon after they arrived, the students were sent home again, on orders of the War Department, because of the epidemic of Spanish influenza. The induction was finally set for October 22, with classes beginning the next day. Arriving able-bodied students were given the option of enlisting voluntarily in the SATC unit, under the command of Captain John G. Meem, or in an associated Navy unit, whose establishment was still pending. Ultimately, 639 students were inducted into the Army unit and 114 into the Navy unit, which was

46. The entire correspondence on exemptions—Dinand's letter of December 8, Lodge's replies of December 13 and 21, and Johnson's letter to Lodge on December 14—were reprinted in *The Purple* 30:260–62, 362–63.

47. Dinand to John P. Gallagher, S.J., Worcester, January 28, 1918, and Dinand to John Wickham, Worcester, April 24, 1918, ACHC, 12.16.

48. Newton D. Baker to Presidents of all institutions of collegiate grade, Washington, May 8, 1918, ACHC, 14.7K-1; David M. Kennedy, *Over Here: The First World War and American Society* (Oxford and New York: Oxford University Press, 1980), 57.

49. HD, July 4–5, 1918; Joseph S. Dineen, ed., *Holy Cross College Service Record, War of 1917* (Worcester: Harrigan Press, 1920), 465.

formally separated from the SATC as the Naval Unit of Holy Cross College on November 21, when Ensign Arthur F. Anderson assumed command. There were also 134 civilian students, who followed the traditional College course and raised the total enrollment in the fall of 1918 to a record-breaking 887. Throughout the fall, bedsteads, shoes, woolen uniforms, guns and "army sacks" arrived from Camp Devens. Student Corpsmen were paid $30 per month, subjected to military discipline, and given military drill and special courses that added eleven hours per week to the 42 hours spent in traditional academic pursuits. They were even assigned to duty in the kitchen and "mess hall," as the dining room was now called. The curriculum was adjusted to conform to military norms, and the Maryland-New York Province catalog that year listed eighteen Jesuits as teaching "in the military course." Their subjects included English and French, mathematics and topography, organic and analytical chemistry, physics and mechanics, biology, and military history. The military and civilian units attended separate Masses on Sunday mornings; and after the armistice in December, the SATC unit was given a separate retreat.[50]

The long-term effect of the military units on campus life was negligible, because the war ended less than three weeks after their formal establishment. Mostly, the units lent a tone to the local celebration of the Armistice, as the house diarist noted on November 11:

A Great Day—Peace declared to-day. The city went mad. Full Holiday. The Students assembled in front of porch where Fr. Rector, the Captain and Fr. Earls [instructor of English and French in the military program] addressed them. The S.A.T.C. received their over-coats and with sailors in uniform made a fine showing as they paraded thro' city with Rev. Fr. Rector and Faculty leading.

Both units were mustered out by December 19. In the spring of 1919, over 300 of the SATC and Navy students who were otherwise unaffiliated with Holy Cross left the College, reducing the enrollment to 562 at the start of the semester.[51]

In addition to the military units on campus, 960 students and former students and seven former professors of Holy Cross served in the armed forces during World War I. Many answered the call to arms early in the war; in the spring of 1917, 450 Holy Cross men—including more than half of the Class of 1916—were enrolled. Twenty-four Holy Cross men died in action; twenty-

50. Consultors' Minutes, July 31, 1918, ACHC, 19.0; Dinand to James E. Grady, Worcester, July 18, 1918, ACHC, 12.16; Carlin to Ledochowski, Worcester, January 21, 1914, ARSI, MD 1017, *Fasc. "Ex Officio"* (1919); HD, September–November, 1918; Meagher and Grattan, *Spires*, 202–3.

51. Carlin to Ledochowski, Worcester, January 21, 1919, ARSI, MD 1017, *Fasc. "Ex Officio"* (1919); HD, November–December, 1918; Dineen, *Service Record*, 465; Meagher and Grattan, *Spires*, 203–4.

three more were wounded. The last American officer killed in the war was Fr. William F. Davitt '07, who was killed while attending to pastoral duties just ninety minutes before the armistice.[52] During the war years, *The Purple* listed the names of the Holy Cross men in the service and published a number of their letters. Faculty members and administrators corresponded with former students at American bases and at battle lines "somewhere in France." For many, life under Army discipline had a certain familiarity. As Father Dinand told one alumnus, "You are not the first of our Alumni to remark the great similarity between discipline in a Jesuit College and in the Army."[53]

The jingoism that was part of the national spirit during World War I also left its mark at Holy Cross. The principal victim of intolerance was the most outstanding member of the faculty, Father Robert Swickerath, who had come to Holy Cross in 1907 to teach history and German and to initiate a course in pedagogy that was afterwards widely imitated. He had published books and pamphlets in the United States and in Germany on the Middle Ages, Christian education, and Martin Luther, and was a popular lecturer. Because he had not become an American citizen, he was forced to register as an enemy alien after the declaration of war. Dismissed from the faculty in the fall of 1918 so that the College could qualify for the SATC program, he was sent to St. Mary's Church in Boston for pastoral work; but even there he encountered the anti-German hysteria that persisted after the armistice in the xenophobic campaign for "100% Americanism." By early 1920, discouraged by so much hostility, Swickerath asked the Jesuit general to assign him to another country. Despite his absolute silence about the conflict and his respectful attitude toward the United States, he had endured "many humiliations." Some Jesuits and Catholic lay people refused to accept him or his scholarship, denigrating the latter as "made in Germany," and there was no place for him at the College, where he was regarded as "undesirable." The bitterest pill was the opposition he faced within the Society from men who were sympathetic to the spirit of "intense nationalism." Even the rector, he alleged, presumably referring to Joseph Dinand, had given "a violent speech against the Germans," and afterwards smilingly remarked, "I don't really believe a lot of what I said, but at present we are obliged to speak this way."[54]

In war, the first casualty is truth. Robert Swickerath's experience verified the observation. Apart from his letter, the written record holds only fragmen-

---

52. Dineen, *Service Record*, 15–459, contains pictures and service records of Holy Cross men in World War I. An unidentified press clipping (ACHC, Locker 8, Scrapbook 11, p. 88) offiers the figures from the spring of 1917.

53. Dinand to James G. Russell, Worcester, March 1, 1918, ACHC, 12.16.

54. Swickerath to Ledochowski, [January, 1920], ARSI, MD 1017, "Prov. Marylandiae Particularis, 1920."

tary indications of jingoism at Holy Cross during World War I; but what evidence there is, tends to support his complaints. An entry in the House Diary on July 18, 1918, notes that the community enjoyed a mint julep "to celebrate the victory of the Yanks and French over against the Huns near Soissons." A press account of Father Dinand's "Thrilling Patriotic Address" at the dedication of the service flag at Immaculate Conception Parish indicates abundantly his capacity for patriotic cant.[55] The spirit of the times was intolerant, and, like other Americans, some Jesuits were vulnerable to it. Father Swickerath was re-assigned to war relief work in Austria, where he distributed thousands of dollars of offerings from his friends in the United States. By 1923, times had changed; he returned to the Holy Cross faculty for two years to teach his former subjects; then he served as a professor of ecclesiastical history at the Woodstock and Weston Jesuit seminaries.[56]

As conditions on the campus returned to normal in 1919, Father Carlin turned his thoughts to expansion of the physical plant. In April, he told the Jesuit general of his plans for a chapel large enough for 1000 worshipers, at a cost of at least $150,000, nearly half of which had been raised in the Diamond Jubilee Drive. During the second half 1919, as the College's fiscal situation improved, Carlin's thinking about campus expansion grew bolder.[57] He indicated his new frame of mind in his correspondence with Wlodimir Ledochowski, who had become General of the Society of Jesus in 1915. He hoped to construct a new chapel and to ease overcrowding by building the previously planned residence for the Jesuits. Carlin argued that the growing movement for higher education among Catholic youth required the expansion of Catholic colleges; otherwise, these youth would attend non-Catholic colleges, "where their faith partly or completely vanishes." In that light, expansion became a moral obligation.[58] In the fall of 1920, former Boston College rector Thomas Gasson reported that he had spoken with the pope and the general. Both were

55. Unidentified press clipping [1918], Dinand Papers, ACHC, 12.16.

56. *Holy Cross Alumnus*, 23:15. Swickerath's letters on his work on postwar Austria were published in *WL*, 50:214–16, and 51:159–62. In 1945, College trustees voted an honorary degree to Swickerath, but he declined the honor. Trustees' Minutes, February 15, 1945, ACHC, 11.0.

57. Carlin to Ledochowski, Worcester, April 27, 1919, ARSI, MD 1017, *Fasc. "Ex Officio"* (1919). Despite its debt, the College had a considerable war chest for campus expansion by the summer of 1920. The annual financial statement, July 1, 1919, to June 30, 1920, prepared for Roman authorities, showed loans and investments of $275,000 as against a debt of $142,000. The assets included the money raised in the Diamond Jubilee Drive. ARSI, MD 1017, *Fasc. "Ex Officio"* (1920).

58. Carlin to Ledochowski, Worcester, September 12, 1919, ARSI, MD 1017, *Fasc. "Ex Officio"* (1919), and January 22, 1920, ARSI, MD 1017, *Fasc. "Ex Officio"* (1920).

favorable toward the expansion of colleges, and Holy Cross particularly. The general's main concern was to ensure that "the new boys can be housed comfortably and educated thoroughly."[59]

Anticipating approval for expansion, Carlin moved forward. In 1920, plans were finalized for a major fund drive covering five new buildings and renovations to the existing plant, at a projected cost of over one million dollars. The Building Fund Campaign, also called the Million Dollar Drive, was headed by a committee of 25 alumni under the chairmanship of Senator Walsh. The College hired a professional fund-raising firm and drew up aggressive plans.[60] Father Carlin announced the drive at regional alumni meetings in the winter of 1920. At the 1920 Commencement, he developed points that became the major themes of the campaign: unless the College made a "supreme effort to enlarge our plant," many applicants would be shut out; contributed service from Jesuits kept student costs low and within reach even for students of slender means; and "a universal, systematic campaign" had never before been attempted. Acknowledging the "Red Scare" that was sweeping the country at the time, he stated that the drive was animated by the desire "to give to the Church and to the state Christian young men, who can be relied upon to give intelligent, loyal service."[61] The plans included four new buildings: a 200-student dormitory (at $300,000); a science building/lecture hall with 25 classrooms (at $350,000); a dining hall and assembly building (at $300,000); and a memorial chapel (at $200,000)—in total, $1,150,000.

As a case statement, the College issued a 16-page pamphlet that opened with a quote from Theodore Roosevelt, closed with another from David Walsh, and included architects' sketches of *five* proposed buildings, adding an administration building to the four whose need had already been represented. Three of the sketches depicted buildings that were eventually built—Carlin Hall, Kimball Hall, and the Memorial Chapel; the proposed science and administration buildings were not built according to the 1920 plan. The case statement stressed the College's ideal location for the large Roman Catholic population of the Northeast, its high academic standards, and the cramped facilities. Jesuit contributed service offered a further angle, because their labor made endowment funds unnecessary: "Her instructors ask nothing but the privilege of serving for the greater glory of Alma Mater and Holy Church."

59. Gasson to Carlin, en route [from Rome], October 28, 1920, ACHC, 12.17.

60. HD, 1919–20. The firm, Fund Raisers, Inc. eventually earned $90,000 on the Holy Cross drive. Joseph R. N. Maxwell to W. D. O'Leary, Worcester, February 4, 1941, ACHC, 12.20.

61. Boston *Herald*, January 27, 1920; Carlin speech text, 1920 Commencement, ACHC 12.17.

The latter point overlooked the fact that seven of the thirty-two full-time faculty members were laymen, but it was effective salesmanship.[62]

The campaign organizers set goals for various areas and concentrated on them at specific times over a four-month period starting in September, using district committees. The minimum goal for the pledge campaign was $780,000, with an additional $250,000 to be raised among wealthy Catholic donors by Senator Walsh and a special committee. Worcester and eastern Massachusetts were targeted in October; by the end of the month, that part of the drive "went over the top with glory." In Boston, Cardinal O'Connell contributed $5000; the Worcester County collection alone exceeded its $200,000 goal by $101,000. At the beginning of December, organizers announced that Berkshire County, with a quota of $10,000, had collected $34,278, raising the grand total past $800,000.[63] In its final month, the drive centered on New York City and New Jersey. At first, the results there were so disappointing that Joseph Dinand sent a melodramatic letter to the local alumni, appealing to them in the name of personal and collegiate loyalty: "I personally, with all the love in my heart for Holy Cross and her interests, call on your love for Holy Cross, to come to her aid now. . . . Before God, I tell you this is the hour in which Holy Cross stands or falls!"[64] By the end of the year, the pledge total reached $960,000. The following June, Father Carlin told the alumni that the million dollar goal had been achieved, and construction of a new dormitory, designed to match Alumni Hall on the lower quad, would begin that summer.[65]

The decision to build another dormitory followed both from Father Carlin's desire to accept as many students as possible and from Father Ledochowski's stipulation that expanded enrollment be linked with adequate housing. While the drive was still in progress, Carlin asked Charles Maginnis to design a mate to Alumni Hall. By January of 1921, the trustees had approved the general plans for a new I-shaped building, and in August the building con-

62. The pamphlet is in the Carlin papers, ACHC, 12.17.

63. HD, 1919–20; Worcester *Telegram*, October 28, 1920; *Berkshire Evening Eagle*, December 2, 1920.

64. Dinand to Holy Cross alumni, New York, December 8, 1920, ACHC, 12.16. As of December 2, the New York City/New Jersey collection had raised only $15,000 toward its $100,000 goal. *Berkshire Evening Eagle*, December 2, 1920.

65. HD, December 27, 1920; Worcester *Telegram*, June 22, 1921; Meagher and Grattan, *Spires*, 208. To the $960,000 in pledges, the College added an additional $89,700 from the Diamond Jubilee Fund and memorial chapel collection, raising the total building fund to about $1.05 million, if every pledge were paid. *Holy Cross College Bulletin* (April, 1921), p. 1; Financial Statement, FY 1925, Treasurer's Records, Box 1, ACHC, 13.0.

tract was accepted.[66] The project acquired new urgency in June, when the general, still concerned about overcrowding, limited Holy Cross to 600 boarders in the coming year.[67] Work progressed satisfactorily and Loyola Hall (renamed Carlin Hall in 1941) opened on schedule in September of 1922. Its cost, $414,000, reflected the inflation that had occurred since Beaven Hall was raised; but its five stories provided 60 percent more space than Beaven. The top three floors contained 91 student rooms; the lower floors held eleven classrooms.[68]

The opening of a new dormitory relieved overcrowding somewhat by raising the ideal number of places for boarding students to 695, including rooms in O'Kane 3 and 4, and in open dormitories in the Fenwick Hall Annex. In the fall of 1922, there were 686 boarding students, who filled almost every available space. In 1925, when 750 applicants were turned away, the number of boarding students climbed to 771, including those who lived in Regis Hall, a small residence for 40 students, opposite the main gate on College Street.[69] By the fall of 1927, there were 781 boarders in a student population of 1126, and, even with Regis Hall, the dormitory population was about 50 over capacity. The number of day students increased in the same period, rising from 148 to 345 between 1921 and 1927. Some of the latter lived in boarding houses like the one run by Mary Fitzgerald on Claremont Street, where as many as 19 students were housed. The increase in off-campus living arrangements prompted official warnings in 1925 and 1927 to discontinue the practice, except in cases where students could board with their own relatives.[70] After 1927, enrollment was stabilized at about 1100 for a number of years.

While the new dormitory was under construction, plans were drawn up for a chapel. After the war, when Father Carlin was promoting the chapel as a memorial to the College's war dead, Charles Maginnis claimed priority of interest in the structure's design: "We are intensely interested in Holy Cross, and have been so much identified with it of late years, that we have become very jealous of the association."[71] Before long, Maginnis was commissioned

66. Carlin to [Fund Drive] Advisory Committee, December 22, 1920, and contract with Maginnis and Walsh, December 22, 1920, ACHC, 16.1BD-1. Consultors' Minutes, January 8 and August 21, 1921, ACHC, 19.0.

67. Memorial of Joseph Rockwell, June 21, 1921, ACHC, 19.1-2.

68. HD, 1921–22; Jesuit Minister's Note Book, 1911–35, ACHC, 19.3-4; Maginnis and Walsh to Joseph R. N. Maxwell, Boston, May 25, 1943, ACHC, 16.1BJ-1; Meagher and Grattan, *Spires*, 208.

69. Wheeler to Carlin, St. Marys, Kansas, July 21, 1923, ACHC, 12.17; *Tomahawk*, September 28, 1926.

70. Memorials of J. M. Kilroy, May 9, 1925, and May 25, 1927, Provincial Memorials, ACHC, 19.1-2; HD, March 18, 1940.

71. Maginnis to Carlin, Boston, August 15, 1919, ACHC, 12.17; Richards, "Ideals," 16–18.

to draw up plans for a church in the form of an Italian Renaissance basilica, incorporating features of Jesuit architecture first expressed in the church of the Gesu in Rome.[72] In February 1922, Carlin submitted the plans to the Jesuit provincial officers. They approved the design but raised questions about the site. Maginnis and Carlin favored a location on the main terrace to the east of Fenwick Hall because it was convenient for the students and had a long vista to set it off. But Joseph Dinand, as *socius*, objected that the plans "do not show any big development centralizing in some group, but show a scattered lot of buildings put up with an idea of convenience.... The chapel at H.C. ought to be the focus or heart of the entire scheme of future development."[73] Dinand was upset because the proposed location overturned the campus plan he had developed as rector, with a chapel occupying the location where the library was eventually built. To meet Dinand's objections, Maginnis developed an alternate plan, but a committee of Holy Cross Jesuits, appointed by Father O'Gorman to settle the matter, eventually endorsed the Carlin arrangement.[74]

On November 29, 1922, a building contract was signed for $291,000. Work began the following June.[75] In recognition of its patron, the dedication of the St. Joseph Memorial Chapel was set for April 7, 1924, the Solemnity of St. Joseph, even though many of the finishing touches had yet to be added. Bishop O'Leary consecrated the structure in a solemn ceremony that lasted from 7 A.M. until past midday. In the afternoon, the guests returned for a recital on the Cassavant organ.[76] While the dignitaries attended to the solemn duty of consecrating a church, the students enjoyed a holiday crowded with more mundane pursuits. In the opinion of the house diarist, their activities, like the rituals of their elders, made it a day of triumph:

Great day for Holy Cross: Dedication of Chapel, splendid organ recital, Holy Cross took a number of events in the dual meet with Boston University here, we won from Clark in tennis, the Freshmen won from Brown [in] baseball 11 to 0, and the Holy Cross team beat Princeton at Princeton 3 to 2 in fourteen innings.

72. Bangert, *History*, 59–60; Richards, "Ideals," 20–21.

73. Rockwell to Carlin, New York, February 28, 1922, and O'Gorman to Carlin, Chestnut Hill, March 31, 1922, ACHC 16.1BE-1; Burke interview, June 17, 1988.

74. Maginnis to Carlin, Boston, February 23, 1922, and O'Gorman to Carlin, Chestnut Hill, March 31, 1922, ACHC, 16.1BE-1; *WL* 48:292–93.

75. The final cost was just under $300,000. HD, November–December, 1922; Consultors' Minutes, November 29, 1922; Building Contract with John P. Keating of Westboro, November 29, 1922, ACHC, 16.1BE-1; *The Purple* 35:45, 50; *Historia Domus*, 1920–1924, ACHC, 19.0; list of construction dates, ACHC, 16.1BG-1.

76. *Historia Domus*, 1920–24, ACHC, 19.0.

The architectural inspiration of Charles D. Maginnis: St. Joseph Memorial Chapel, about 1925.

After the dedication, another month was required to complete the work. Finally, on Sunday, May 11, Father Carlin opened the chapel permanently by celebrating the first student Mass. They found a place of worship that was a masterpiece of design. The front façade featured four Corinthian columns and a sculpted pediment with a figure of the risen Christ. The interior followed the plan of a basilica in the Jesuit tradition—a plan designed around a middle axis and vertical ascent to draw the worshipper forward and upward toward the altar. The nave was 45 feet wide and 132 feet long, set off at each side by a row of marble columns that separated the side aisles, where confessionals were located. Over the nave were large windows; a semicircular vault, decorated with octagonal forms, rose 57 feet above the floor. The interior proportions, Maginnis wrote, were designed "to create an effect of great dignity in simplicity of line." The altar, of Botticino marble, stood within a carved and richly painted wooden baldachin whose supporting columns were of red Verona marble. The baldachin was topped with the characteristic Jesuit design of a cross breaking through the pediment. The fourteen large stained glass windows—seven dedicated to martyrs and seven to doctors of the Church—were designed by Walter G. Ball of Boston and installed in 1926 at a cost of $20,000. The thirteen small windows along the side aisles were designed by Joseph Tierney of New York City in 1939–40. The windows on the left carry symbols associated with the Eucharist; those on the right are dedicated to the Sacrament of Reconciliation. Downstairs was an auditorium large enough to accommodate the student body.[77]

While the chapel was being constructed, several smaller projects were also underway. Commencement Porch was reconstructed, because, as one Jesuit put it, "the present steps obscure the view of the new chapel." To improve the vista, Maginnis and Walsh designed stairways for each side of the porch, curving forward at the bottom. At the same time, a small porch was added to the east end of Fenwick Hall, facing the chapel.[78] Soon afterwards, wood paneling was installed in the president's office and along the first floor corridor of Fenwick Hall, the gift of a friend of Joseph Dinand.[79] Discussion about expanding the football stadium arose in the fall of 1923, when local alumni requested expansion of the Fitton Field stands—baseball, football, or both. In December, the trustees voted to expand the football stands, using "whatever money the Athletic Association has on hand" (a sum that proved to be $110,000), plus whatever revenue would be generated during the 1924 baseball season. The new stands, with steel structure and wooden seats and flooring, raised the capacity to about 18,000 and lasted for over sixty years.[80]

77. Charles D. Maginnis, "The New Chapel," in *The Purple* 36:828–30; "Chapel—Incidental Expenses," and Joseph Tierney to B. W. Feeny, NYC, June 26, 1939, ACHC, 16.IBE-1; Tierny to Feeny, NYC, January 29, 1940, and Feeny to Maxwell, NYC, January 30, 1940, ACHC, 12.20; William Sprout, "Windows Recount Lives of Fourteen Saints," *Crossroads*, November–December, 1982; *Tomahawk*, September 28, 1926; Richards, "Ideals," 21.

78. Consultors' Minutes, March 2, 1924, ACHC, 19.0; Contract of June 20, 1924, 16.IBG-1; Contract of August 19, 1924, ACHC, 16.IBF-1; HD, September 1924–June 1925. The main porch was completed in time for commencement in June, 1925.

79. The donor was the father of James Buckhout '21. The date was about 1926. Gene Flynn to Joe Perotta, August 20, 1970, ACHC, 16.IBF-1.

80. Consultors' Minutes, October 15 and December 6, 1923, March 2, March 20, May 25, and August 4, 1924, ACHC, 19.0; College catalog, 1928–29. The cost of the project was about $150,000.

The central portion of the campus about 1925, shortly before the construction of the library. Note the old barn beyond the chapel and the original baseball diamond near Carlin Hall.

When Joseph Dinand assumed office for the second time, in the summer of 1924, two buildings projected during the 1920 fund drive had been erected at a combined cost of $714,000, not counting furnishings and equipment. With the likelihood in mind that further expansion would require the College to borrow money, James Carlin had made efforts in 1923 to persuade the donors to fulfill their unpaid pledges.[81] Facing the same prospect, Joseph

81. Carlin to Benefactors, Worcester, May 21, 1923, ACHC, 12.17. The 1920 drive actually produced about $700,000 in paid pledges by June 1925. Statement for FY 1925, Treasurer's Records, Box 1, ACHC, 13.0.

Dinand tried unsuccessfully to interest the Carnegie Foundation in providing a library building. But Dinand was determined to keep the expansion program moving, regardless of how the new buildings were funded. In fact, a library facility was badly needed. For a time, the circulating library was located on Fenwick I; it was moved to two rooms in Beaven Hall in 1921, a haphazard solution to a pressing academic need. Immediately after his return to Holy Cross, Dinand opened discussions regarding a combined library and auditorium building. But the consultors of the New England Vice-Province authorized a library only, whose cost was not to exceed $350,000 —a figure that could be covered by the current balance of $300,000, plus surplus income.[82]

On September 23, 1924, Father Dinand met with an architect from Maginnis and Walsh to discuss preliminary plans; the following day, a groundbreaking ceremony was held. Dinand's haste to begin while plans were still incomplete indicated his energetic determination to keep the expansion moving. Other motives included the need for extensive excavation to prepare the hillside location and the possibility of attracting contributions by having a work in progress.[83] When the plans were finalized early in 1925, they encompassed a building far more expensive than the limit set by province authorities. Through the new vice-provincial, James Kilroy, Dinand requested Roman approval to borrow up to $200,000 for a $500,000 building. The loan, he confidently predicted, would be paid off in a few years. Father Ledochowski endorsed the plan, but he was irritated that no explanation had been offered for the higher cost. And he worried whether so splendid a structure was in accord with the spirit of poverty at Jesuit colleges. As the building neared completion in 1927, plans were drawn up for a terrace in front of the library, at the top level of a massive stairway.[84]

The library was another example of Charles Maginnis's architectural inspiration. The exterior featured a classical façade with eight Ionic columns, 35 feet high. The entablature quoted a line from the Gospel of John that summarized the College's mission: UT COGNOSCANT TE SOLUM DEUM VERUM ET QUEM MISISTI JESUM CHRISTUM [That they might know you, the one true

82. Henry L. Banzhaf to Dinand, Milwaukee, January 26, 1925, and Carlin correspondence book, January 28, [1925], ACHC, 12.16; Consultors' Minutes, September 1924, ACHC, 19.0; Dinand to American Assistant, July 22, 1924, Dinand Correspondence Book, ACHC, 12.16; HD, September 23, 1924; Burke interview, June 17, 1988; *Tomahawk*, January 26, 1926.

83. Excavator's contract, 1924, ACHC, 16.1BO–1; HD, September–November, 1924.

84. Kilroy to Ledochowski, Chestnut Hill, June 30, 1925, NEPA, Correspondence to General; Ledochowski to Kilroy, Rome, July 31, 1925, NEPA, Correspondence from General; HD, May–July, 1927.

God, and Jesus Christ, whom you have sent]. Around the perimeter of the main reading room, beneath a clerestory that helped illuminate an elaborate ceiling, were inscribed "an imposing roster of immortal names in Catholic culture." The library enclosed almost 1.1 million cubic feet of space, and the stacks could accommodate over 300,000 books—more than six times the number they held when the library opened.[85] The library's final construction cost, including the terrace, was $415,000. Between 1925 and 1933, an additional $300,000 was spent on books and furnishings. The responsibility for organizing and managing the move and building up the collection lay with Foster Stearns, former state librarian of Massachusetts, who was hired in 1925. Stearns was succeeded in 1930 by Irving T. McDonald '15, who defended library expenditures as an extension of the College's mission and goals.[86]

As it moved forward, the project only whetted Joseph Dinand's desire for expansion. In the fall of 1925, following a suggestion from Senator Walsh, Dinand and his advisors began discussing the construction of a gymnasium. A $10,000 gift for that purpose from T. T. Ellis, a local newspaper publisher, added impetus to the plan.[87] In November 1926, Dinand received authorization to borrow another $800,000 to construct two buildings: a gymnasium and a dining hall. The approval carried a condition from Rome. The general warned against operating on the assumption that the Jesuits were obligated to educate all youth. To that end, he imposed on Holy Cross an absolute limit of 800 boarding students as a guide for further planning.[88] The new plan never came to fruition. Father Dinand was appointed to be the bishop in Jamaica, and the future of the College fell into other hands.

The availability of additional loans in 1926 was partly a function of the College's solid financial status throughout the 1920s (Chart 6.1). In 1921, income rose past one million dollars for the first time; furthermore, the success of the Million Dollar Drive enabled the college to retire its debt for the first time since 1846 and to accumulate a fund for future construction. Loyola (Carlin) Hall and the Memorial Chapel were built without additional borrowing; not until fiscal year 1927 did the loan for the new library add a sub-

85. Irving McDonald, "The Dinand Library" [1933 pamphlet], ACHC, 16.1BO-1; HD, 1926–27.

86. Maginnis and Walsh to John Fox, Boston, April 26, 1928, and Irving McDonald, "The Dinand Library," ACHC, 16.1BO-1; Meagher and Grattan, *Spires*, 257.

87. Consultors' Minutes, October 1925–January 1926, ACHC, 19.0; unidentified press clipping [late 1925], Locker 8, Scrapbook 16, p. 123.

88. Dinand to American Assistant, February 28, 1926, Dinand Correspondence Book, November 8, 23, and December 14, 1926, ACHC, 12.16; Ledochowski to Kilroy, Rome, November 14 and 24, 1926, NEPA, Correspondence from General.

Chart 6.1 Operating Budget, 1912–1927

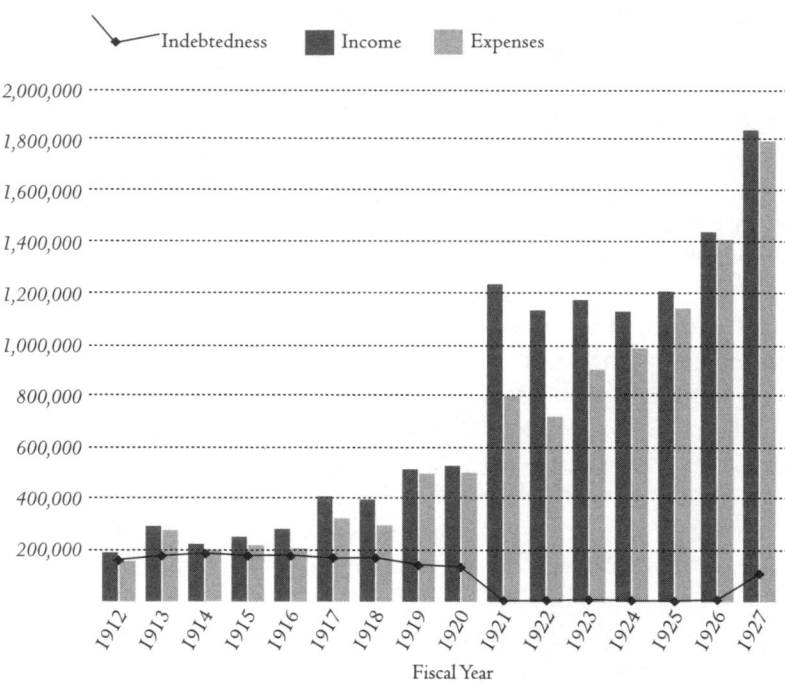

stantial debt to the college accounts. Sources of revenue as a percentage of the total budget varied widely between 1912 and 1927. Payment of pledges in fiscal year 1921 made contributions the largest single item and created a balance that was carried over in successive years until the construction of the library depleted it. Tuition, room, and board revenue rose from $122,000 in 1912 to $510,000 in 1927, yet declined dramatically as a proportion of income, well below 50 percent after 1920.

In the years before the library opened, the College was still struggling to establish and defend its academic reputation. Father Dinand faced the issue in 1912, when the U. S. Bureau of Education prepared a ranking of American undergraduate colleges. Holy Cross was rated with the best 103 undergraduate programs, but in a middle category—a point that raised sensitivities about discrimination, because all schools with classical curriculums were excluded from the top rank. Dinand and other Jesuit college rectors joined many other educators in an appeal to have the study dismissed as arbitrary and unfair. In this instance, the effort succeeded; President Taft ordered the book suppressed.[89] Another controversy erupted five years later when an alumnus applying for the Junior Chemist examination with the U.S. Civil Service Commission had his application canceled because "he was not a graduate of a recognized college." The episode prompted an appeal to the state's Congressional delegation. Quickly, the head of the federal Civil Service Commission explained that the language had been misleading: the action had been prompted by the lack of a regular chemistry major at Holy Cross.[90] Holy Cross officials were mollified, but the episode indicated that the practice of enhancing the traditional curriculum with junior and senior elective courses was reaching its limit. Academic departments and majors were becoming a necessity.

For the time being, Holy Cross administrators left the curriculum as it was. Father James Mullen, who served as prefect of studies from 1908 until 1924, subscribed to the *status quo*. He was backed up by the Jesuit provincial who, in 1914 and 1916, exhorted the faculties of colleges in the Maryland-New York Province to stress proficiency in Latin and Greek "which is supposed to be implied in the A.B. Degree conferred by the classical colleges of the Society of Jesus."[91] Although Jesuit administrators prided themselves on the curricular independence associated with their own traditions, their colleges existed in an active relationship with other American educational institutions and had been influenced by them since at least the 1890s. After World War I, the relationship became less adversarial when a conservative reaction against electivism at many leading colleges led to the introduction of core courses and general education curricula.[92] That may have helped delay reform at Holy Cross.

89. E. McDonnell to Anthony Maas, Washington, November 26 and December 3, 1912, MPA, 520 D. The booklet was written by a Dr. Babcock for the Bureau of Education and appeared under the title, "A Classification of Universities and Colleges with Reference to Bachelor's Degrees." P. P. Claxton, "An Explanatory Statement in regard to 'A Classification of Universities and Colleges . . . ," ACHC, 14.0-2. Judge James B. Carroll, a Holy Cross alumnus, complained about Babcock in a letter to Senator W. Murray Crane: "He has put Holy Cross College and every other Catholic college in America in the second class, and he has made this artificial arrangement without consulting anybody, except a few presidents of colleges in America, without any opportunity to be heard, an entirely ex-parte and star chamber proceeding." Carroll to Crane, Springfield, December 2, 1912, MPA, 520 D. See also Rudolph, *Curriculum*, 220–21; and David S. Webster, "The Bureau of Education's Suppressed Rating of Colleges, 1911–1912," in *History of Education Quarterly* 24 (Winter 1984), 499–511.

90. Dinand to Rep. Samuel E. Winslow, Worcester, June 19, 1917; John A. McIlhenny to Dinand, Washington, July 6, 1917; George L. Coyle to Dinand, Philadelphia, July 13, 1917, ACHC, 12.16.

91. Burke interview, June 17, 1988; Memorial of Anthony Maas, November 10, 1914, ACHC, 19.1. See also memorials dated November 13, 1916, and November 8, 1917, ACHC, 19.1.

92. Rudolph, *American College*, 452–61; Rudolph, *Curriculum*, 236–44.

After 1914, the only Holy Cross students with exceptional status were "Sub-Freshmen"—individuals who came to the College with three years of high school Latin instead of the required four. The designation was introduced in 1916, apparently as a substitute for the category of "Special" students, which was discontinued after 1913. The Sub-Freshman program was maintained for five years, with numbers equaling roughly 10 percent of the student body. In the fall of 1921, the program was dropped because rising applications supplied a sufficient number of students who were fully prepared in Latin. Until 1924, the classical curriculum, with its heavy accompaniment of prescribed courses and a few electives, remained the norm. In 1922, Father Carlin explained that the greatest difficulty was to find students with the required three years of high school Greek; those with little or no Greek were required to take it as a "compulsory elective" during junior year. Carlin was convinced that the College was on the right track: "Our principle should be to place our standards high and to lift the high schools up and not allow them to pull us down."[93] Pre-medical students met the same standards, though after 1920 the College catalog noted that additional hours of biology, laboratory physics, and chemistry were required by the American Medical Association. Apparently most students at the College came to terms with the Latin and Greek requirements: between 1912 and 1924, the highest number of Ph.B. degrees conferred in a single year was five. In the same period, the number of A.B. degrees rose to a high of 167 in 1923.

Prompted by the desire to raise educational standards, the rectors and prefects of studies of the schools in the Maryland–New York Province held a conference at Fordham University in the summer of 1922. They agreed upon uniform procedures, including greater emphasis on student use of the library. The first changes were noted at Holy Cross in the fall of 1922, when for the first time the catalog arranged the academic offerings in fifteen groups that began to resemble modern academic departments. A year later, the required curriculum was adjusted by reducing the number of required courses and requiring students by the end of sophomore year to choose majors that committed them to at least eighteen credits in a single academic discipline or in a set of related disciplines. During senior year, candidates for the A.B. were required to write a thesis. Elective courses outside the prescribed core and major requirements were chosen with the help of academic advisors. A total of 136 credits was required for graduation.[94]

93. Carlin to James McCabe, Worcester, [December 30, 1922], ACHC, 12.17.

94. Meagher and Grattan, *Spires*, 240–42. The 1922–23 catalog clustered courses in the following groups: Philosophy, Political Economy, Pedagogy, Jurisprudence, Latin, Greek, English, History, Mathematics, Science, Physics, Chemistry, Evidences of Religion, Modern Languages, and Oratory and Elocution.

The pace of change accelerated in the fall of 1924, when Francis X. Downey became prefect of studies at the start of Joseph Dinand's second term. So extensively did Father Downey transform the curriculum during the five years he held the post that one observer credited him with bringing Holy Cross into the modern era. Immediately after assuming office, Downey added new elective courses in Latin pedagogy, advanced pedagogy, journalism, and jurisprudence. In 1925, he initiated a further departmentalization of the curriculum by listing faculty members, designated as professor or assistant professor, under the eighteen departmental headings in the catalog. The same catalog defined the Holy Cross as a "School of Arts and Sciences," and indicated that the School of Arts was intended for those who desired the traditional Jesuit system of classical training, while the School of Sciences existed for those more interested in scientific training. Applicants to the School of Arts needed four years of high school Latin. A preference (not a requirement) was also indicated for three years of Greek. Prospective students could take the regular college board exam, the Holy Cross exam, or the intercollegiate exam offered for students at Jesuit high schools.[95]

The Arts curriculum was broken down into the A.B. degree program, which included two years of Latin and two to three years of Greek, and the Ph.B. program, which required only Latin but added a course in the history of philosophy. Students in the School of Sciences received a third degree, the B.S., by completing prescribed courses in chemistry, mechanics, physics, mathematics, English, psychology, and German. Accompanying the introduction of the B.S. degree was the opening of a master's degree program in chemistry, under the direction of the Committee on Graduate Work composed of the rector, the prefect of studies, and Father George Strohaver, the "Dean of the Chemistry Department." In the fall of 1926, eight students were candidates for the Master of Science degree in chemistry.[96] The new pattern put Holy Cross in step with many other schools, where a varied curriculum accommodated students who chose to by-pass Latin and Greek altogether.[97] The area of common courses emphasizing English, philosophy, and religion was still extensive, and only juniors and seniors were allowed electives. By 1928, the graduation figures were beginning to disclose the new pattern as the first students graduated with B.S. degrees and the number of Ph.B. graduates began to rise (Chart

95. Burke interview, June 17, 1988; *Tomahawk*, November 24, 1925.

96. 1926 Report of Academic Dean, ACHC, 14.0; Meagher and Grattan, *Spires*, 242–43, 246; College catalog, 1925–26.

97. By 1923, only Amherst and Williams still required Latin of all graduates. Other schools, including Holy Cross, were using the Ph.B. and B.S. degrees to minimize or eliminate classical language requirements. Rudolph, *Curriculum*, 214.

6.2). During the start-up period, the overwhelming majority of students still entered the arts program. A freshman class staging of Euripides' *Hecuba* in Greek drew over 5000 spectators to Fitton Field in 1926 and was a stunning display of the persistent strength of the classics at Holy Cross.[98]

During the Dinand and Carlin years, the familiar pattern of academic life remained unchanged. Grades were still read monthly at an assembly conducted by the rector. Father Carlin's approach was merely to salute the top students and encourage those at the bottom to do better—a weak echo of George Fenwick's thunderings eighty years earlier. Perhaps Carlin was only defending himself against the boldness of the new generation: in the fall of 1924, students hissed the lay professors as they marched to the platform for the reading of grades; despite his efforts, Father Dinand was unable to learn the cause. Each month the weaker students were "conditioned" until they restored their standing. Oral and written exams remained a part of the routine, and there were strict rules—nine were listed in 1914–15—to prohibit cheating and enforce good order. Failure was still relatively common. In 1912, ten of fifty students failed trigonometry. In October of 1925, two juniors, including the basketball captain, were dismissed for failing to remove their "condition" from the previous spring. They fell under a policy instituted in 1921 that required dismissal of any student who failed two months in succession. In a sense, the school's popularity reinforced its commitment to high standards; the place of a student dismissed for academic reasons would soon be filled by another. But Carlin was also convinced that high standards supplied motivation to study: "We must sacrifice the individual for the universal good of the College, although we may thereby, through a lack of appreciation of our position on the part of those affected, lose dear and influential friends."[99]

The disciplined routine of student life changed very little during and after

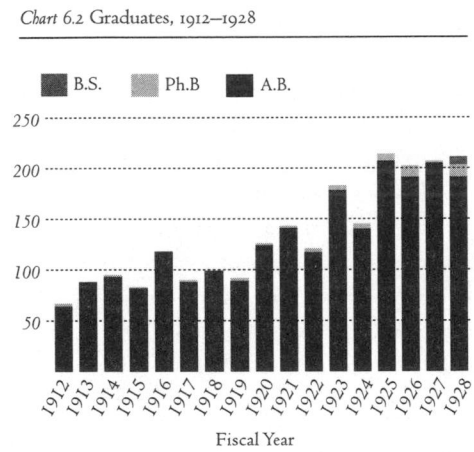

Chart 6.2 Graduates, 1912–1928

B.S.   Ph.B   A.B.

Fiscal Year

98. Worcester *Post*, May 29, 1926; Meagher and Grattan, *Spires*, 243–44.

99. Carlin to Father Flynn, Worcester, January 15, 1923, ACHC, 12.17; HD, 1919–25; Diary of Jerome Towne, January 19, 1912, ACHC, 19.4-1; Academic Dean's Diary, October 1, 1925, ACHC, 14.0-5.

the war: the rules conceded no more than necessary to modern times. In 1927, students still rose at 6:25 for Mass, to face a regimented schedule until lights out at 10:00. Classes ran from 9 o'clock until 2:45, with a mid-day break for dinner and a brief rest. After supper, students had a mandatory chapel visit, followed by a long study period that was interrupted by a twenty-minute break. Wednesday and Saturday afternoons were free. In the 1920s students readily obtained permission to go into the city on free afternoons; night permission was granted on Saturday to those in good standing—freshmen had to report to campus by 10:15, all others by 11:15. Another set of rules enforced good order in the dormitories through the system of demerits. Although the exact numbers changed somewhat from year to year, there was always a maximum after which a student was sent home.[100] Occasionally, the faculty intervened before a student reached the point of suspension for misconduct. In 1925, Father Downey invoked help from a parent: "Your son absented himself from class this morning with absolutely no permission to do so. He is being punished for it but I want you to have a clear understanding with him as to why you are sending him here to college."[101] The faculty realized that the rules were strict. A chemistry teacher who moved from Holy Cross to Georgetown in 1915 reported that "application of the Holy Cross rules and ways of doing things causes a howl against the severity."[102] Night permissions, limited though they were, continued to raise the opposition of higher Jesuit authorities. The Maryland–New York provincials sent five letters between 1915 and 1921 in an effort to force compliance with Roman policy.[103] The evidence suggests that Fathers Dinand and Carlin were realistic about legitimate student desires, but they took the system seriously.

By the 1920s, lay teachers and administrators were playing an increasingly important role in the life of the school. Twenty-two lay teachers, the athletic trainer, and the school doctor met in 1924 with the Jesuit teachers about the new semester—an early day faculty meeting. The number of lay faculty members reached 31 in 1925; they were hired principally to teach mathematics, modern languages, and the sciences (Chart 6.3).[104] The increase in the non-Jesuit proportion of the faculty, a result of the growth of the school and the broad-

100. Student handbooks, 1920s; Burke interview, June 17, 1988.

101. F. X. Downey to Stephen Fleming, Worcester, January 20, 1925, Dean's Records, ACHC, 14.0.

102. Murray Cummings to Dinand, Washington, November 3, 1915, ACHC, 12.16.

103. Provincial Memorials, 1915–1921, ACHC, 19.1-2.

104. The College catalog for the 1925–26 academic year listed 31 lay professors. Nine taught chemistry, including the new master's degree program; three taught Greek, and two each taught biology, mathematics, music, and physics.

ening of its curriculum, caused concern in Rome that the student body had expanded beyond the ability of the Society of Jesus to provide competent teachers. That fact was a strong consideration in 1926 when Father Ledochowski limited the number of boarding students.[105] In the 1930s, the proportion of Jesuit professors increased temporarily, and the goal was clearly to maximize their number. Nevertheless, by the 1920s, lay professors and professional administrators had become a familiar and permanent part of school's life. The Jesuits maintained administrative control, but they could no longer carry the enterprise forward without significant help from lay associates.

The self-contained atmosphere of the campus promoted the student-teacher bonding that was supposed to be a hallmark of Jesuit schools. Students may have feared some Jesuits and lay professors, but they also acquired warm memories of mentors. Father Charles Kimball, who joined the faculty in 1915 as a popular professor of Latin and Greek, was sometimes called "The Roper," for his efforts to "rope" students into the priesthood. Father Michael Earls, professor of English, introduced himself as "a singular man with a plural name." He enjoyed walking with students and, on at least one occasion, taught College songs to freshmen before a Harvard game. One section of freshmen who enrolled in 1919 studied Latin with scholastic George Bull, a gifted teacher who expanded their horizons and brought current events into the classroom. Bull was representative of a talented group of scholastics brought to Holy Cross by Joseph Dinand in his first term. He knew the younger Jesuits because of his prior work at St. Andrew-on-Hudson, and he asked for the best when he moved on to the College.[106]

The human dimension of campus life tempered the rules' harshness and lent warmth to individual experience. The 1920s were rich in school spirit, despite all the rules, and most students and faculty thrived on the experience. An idyllic portrayal of campus life appeared in three novels for Catholic youth published by Irving McDon-

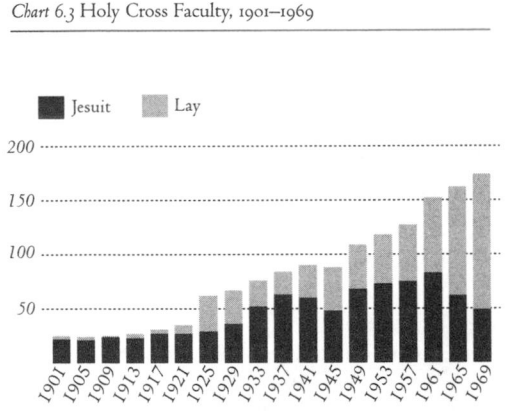

Chart 6.3 Holy Cross Faculty, 1901–1969

■ Jesuit   ▨ Lay

105. Ledochowski to Kilroy, Rome, November 14, 1926, NEPA, Correspondence from General.
106. Ibid.; Harold L. Moran to Raymond Swords, Bay Shore, NY, May 25, 1969, ACHC 12.24; Dean of Discipline Diary, October 15, 1925, ACHC, 14.0-5; Burke interview, June 18, 1988.

An institutional family portrait: James J. Carlin (College President, 1918–1924) and the Faculty in 1919. All but three were Jesuits.

ald in 1926 and 1928. The plot details the improbable exploits of campus hero Andy Carroll, with a depiction of school spirit that is still endearing:

Loud shouts of noisy greeting; confused dartings here and there; eyes dancing with excitement; sudden, surprised explosions of delighted laughter; resounding slaps on backs; hearty, anxious inquiries for missing chums as old-timer meets old-timer; sighs of rapturous relief when lost ones are found. . . . Prefects welcoming roomers to their quarters. . . . Sun smiling benignly through leafy arches, and insects droning the only monotonous note of the whole symphony. . . . Holy Cross in September![107]

107. Irving T. McDonald, *That Second Year (At Holy Cross)* (New York: Benziger Brothers, 1928), 7–8. The first two volumes, entitled *HOI-AH! Andy Carroll's First Year at Holy Cross* and *SCHOONER AHOY! Holy Cross Boys with the Cape Cod Fishing Fleet*, were published by Benziger Brothers in 1926. Doubtless, the Andy Carroll figure was modeled on Owen Carroll '25, a star pitcher for Holy Cross.

School spirit was supported by familiar traditions like class dinners and the pancake supper on Shrove Tuesday. Students stood before meals until grace was said and good manners were obligatory; the dean of discipline held himself ready "to remedy any defect that may need correction." Student morale was lifted in 1923 when a second telephone booth was installed for their use. Meanwhile, the custom of greeting others in passing—even those who were not acquaintances—was a campus tradition that was regularly promoted.[108]

Fathers' Day, the predecessor of Parents' Weekend, started in May 1925. In his invitation to the fathers of students to attend the two-day event, Father Dinand stated the goals: "It will afford the fathers of our students a very opportune occasion of visiting the College, coming closer to the lives of their own sons, and associating with the members of the faculty." On Saturday afternoon, the 160 fathers who accepted the invitation joined 20,000 spectators at Fitton Field as Holy Cross defeated Boston College. On Sunday morning, Father Swickerath celebrated Mass and preached. After breakfast, all adjourned to Fenwick Lecture Hall where Father Dinand described his vision of the College and appealed for generous cooperation. The event concluded with a faculty reception and a band concert.[109]

Debating, which involved more than 25 percent of the students, remained the most popular extracurricular activity, followed by regional student clubs, varsity athletics, and Sodality. Intramural debates were held in English, Latin, German, French and Spanish; intercollegiate debates, in English and French. New opportunities for student journalists opened in February 1925, when the first issue of *The Tomahawk* appeared. Founding editor John O'Shea '25 adopted the name from the newsletter that had circulated during the most recent fund drive. Predecessor of *The Crusader*, *The Tomahawk* concentrated on the daily affairs of the school, including sports, while *The Purple* became a literary magazine for student writers.[110] The Sodality maintained its place as the primary religious organization for students; the obligation of daily Mass, complete with pew check, and the evening chapel visit inserted a hefty religious component into the life of every student. Predictably, the practice was appreciated by some, tolerated by others. In 1914, Father Dinand reported that 250 students received communion every morning; but by the winter of 1927, punctuality at Mass had become such a problem for many seniors that the class con-

108. Student handbooks, 1920s; HD, 1912–18; *The Purple* 35:704; *Tomahawk*, February 6, 1926.

109. Circular letter from Dinand to students' fathers, May 20, 1925, ACHC, 12.16; *Tomahawk*, May 25, 1925; HD, May 30 and 31, 1925.

110. Report of the Academic Dean, 1926, ACHC, 14.0; *Tomahawk*, February 17, 1925; Meagher and Grattan, *Spires*, 146.

templated the use of bells, drums, and a trumpet in Loyola (Carlin) Hall to facilitate the wake-up process. To promote the Ignatian spirit among the alumni, Father Dinand introduced a three-day summer retreat in 1914. By 1922, about 1000 laymen had availed themselves of the opportunity.[111]

In 1924 the College acquired a new official seal. The change was Father Carlin's idea, since the old design had become archaic. The new seal was prepared by "an authority on the subject," Pierre LaRise of Cambridge, Massachusetts. The lower ⅔ contained a gold cross on a field, representing Worcester, England; an open book, standing for education, was superimposed across the center of the cross. The words *In Hoc Signo Vinces* were placed in the book. The upper ⅓ carried at its center the IHS of the Society of Jesus; a European martin on each side was taken from Bishop Fenwick's coat-of-arms. The inscription around the circle of the seal was retained from the Sestini design of 1867.[112] In 1925, another College symbol was adopted when students chose the cognomen "Crusaders" for their teams, in place of the unofficial former designation, "Chiefs." The symbol of a crusader mounted upon a horse went back at least to 1884, when the design was used on the menu of an alumni banquet in Boston; but the immediate impetus came from Boston *Herald* sportswriter Stanley Woodward, who used it in early 1925 in a story on Holy Cross baseball. Woodward later credited players Owen Carroll '25 and Walter "Doc" Gautreau '25 with suggesting the name. The new name became popular among the students, who chose "Crusaders" over "Chiefs" by a large margin in a campus vote.[113]

In baseball, the Dinand and Carlin years were a time of spectacular success: from 1912 through 1927, College teams compiled a record of 306–73–4, won the Eastern Intercollegiate Championship five times (1914, 1917, 1919, 1921, 1923), and sent eighteen players to the major leagues. The successful era was identified with Jesse Burkett, hired as head coach in 1917, and his successor, Jack Barry, who was head baseball coach from 1921 to 1961. Barry attended Holy Cross from 1904 to 1908, the first two years as a prep student. His success at shortstop was so notable that Connie Mack signed him to play for the Philadelphia Athletics in 1908 as a member of the "$100,000 Infield." During the 1920s, when there was no theoretical limit on the number of baseball

111. Worcester *Telegram*, May 28, 1914; *Catholic Messenger*, August 10, 1922; *Tomahawk*, February 8, 1927.

112. Consultors' Minutes, May 25, 1924, ACHC, 19.0.

113. *Tomahawk*, September 29 and October 6, 1925; J. Alfred Belisle, "Athletics at Holy Cross," in *The Harvard A.A. News*, November 16, 1929; *The Purple* 49:404–5.

scholarships, Barry's program attracted gifted athletes and large crowds, including the record-breaking Memorial Day crowd of 22,000 for the Boston College game in 1922.[114] Barry's best player in his early years as coach was pitcher Owen "Ownie" Carroll '25, whose college record was 52–2, including fifteen shutouts. In 1924, Carroll helped his team achieve the only undefeated baseball season in the history of the College. Among Carroll's teammates was a three-sport athlete, Albert D. "Hop" Riopel '24, who won eleven varsity letters in baseball, basketball, and football.[115] Afterwards, Riopel coached all three sports at his alma mater.

While the baseball program was riding a crest of popularity, the football program held its own, especially after 1919, when Cleo O'Donnell '08 started an eleven-year career as head coach and posted the most successful record since the departure of Frank Cavanaugh in 1905. Fathers Dinand and Carlin were more enthusiastic about football than Father Murphy had been. In his first year, Dinand authorized the team to travel to St. Louis University; in 1920 the Boston College game was moved to Braves Field in Boston.[116] Earlier fears about violence on the field diminished gradually, although a Norwich quarterback died in 1913 as the result of a tackle from a Holy Cross defender. Father Dinand visited the player at St. Vincent's Hospital and complied with his request to be baptized.[117] Great enthusiasm characterized the Boston College rivalry, but beating Harvard in football became a passion during the 1920s, because it had never been done. Before the 1924 game, students held an enthusiastic pep rally at which Father Dinand and Coach O'Donnell spoke. Harvard took the victory, however, the only Holy Cross defeat of the season. Fortune changed in 1925, when 43,000 spectators at Soldiers' Field watched Holy Cross win, 7–6. After the game, Purple supporters "marched under the goal posts . . . , many hatless, some coatless, all frenzied with the memory of a victory over mighty Harvard."[118] The enthusiasm for sports was part of the hoopla of the 1920s, an opportunity for the local citizenry to revel in the excitement of college athletics. Seven thousand people were waiting at the depot in November 1922 when Holy Cross returned to Worcester after defeating Georgetown. The mayor gave a "wonderfully good speech" at a campus victory rally the

114. Raymond F.X. Cahill, *The Quiet Crusader: Holy Cross Baseball Coach—John J. Barry, 1921–1961* (Worcester: Privately printed, 1976), 7–16.

115. HD, May 30, 1922, April 30, June 4 and 13, 1925; *Tomahawk*, June 15, 1925; *Purple Patcher*, 1924.

116. HD, November 25–30, 1911; William Devlin to Carlin, Chestnut Hill, January 15, 1920, ACHC, 12.17.

117. HD, September 26 and 28, 1913.

118. Richard O'Brien to Dinand, Chestnut Hill, November 2, 1917, ACHC, 12.16; HD, October 17–18, 1924, *Tomahawk*, October 20, 1925, October 8, 1926.

next day. In 1924, 400 students—over half of the boarders—traveled to New York City to see the Fordham game.[119] Sports revenues reflected the trend: during the 1922–23 school year, Athletic Association revenues reached $122,800, with expenses of $104,200—profits that helped finance the new football stands.[120]

Although baseball and football held the preeminent position before 1930, intercollegiate tennis, track, basketball (in 1922), and golf (in 1926) rounded out the varsity athletic program. Track, for fifty years beginning in 1912, was coached by Bart Sullivan. The most prominent runner was Andy Kelly '17, who set a new world record in the indoor 300-yard dash during his senior year.[121] Basketball returned on a trial basis in March 1921, when James A. Buckout '21, student manager of the resurrected team, arranged a set of home-and-home games with Boston College. The coach was William J. Casey '10, who had been captain of the basketball team when it was disbanded in 1909. Two Holy Cross victories set the basketball program back on track, and Casey was named coach for the 1921–22 season, when the team complied a record of 14–3. In 1924, Casey was succeeded for one year by Ken Siemendinger '24, and then by John M. Reed, who had played football at Holy Cross between 1900 and 1905. Reed held the coaching job from 1925 to 1931, compiling a record of 60–41.[122]

As in the past, the prominence and popularity of varsity sports required regular attention to priorities and the danger of athleticism. The question acquired a new aspect after 1915, when the University of Pittsburgh initiated the practice of putting numbers on players' uniforms to stimulate the sale of programs—a sign, in the view of one historian, of "the degree to which the game had fallen beyond the control of those who played it, the degree to which it now belonged to the paying customers and to the treasurer of the athletic association. . . . Before very long many Americans would be acting as if *the* purpose of an American college or university were to field a football team."[123] Holy Cross administrators, under scrutiny from Jesuit authorities in New York and Rome, attempted to keep athletics under control. In 1911, they imposed their own candidate for student manager upon the baseball team; in 1926, three football stars "withdrew" from the College after they were dropped from the team for staying out all night; and in 1924, the College adopted the policy of awarding varsity letters to members of the BJF and Philomathic de-

119. HD, November 5–6, 1922; Prefect of Studies Diary, November 6, 1925, ACHC, 14.0-5.

120. Anthony Maas to Patrick O'Gorman, Tusculi, July 11, 1923, NEPA, Correspondence from Rome.

121. Kelly's time was 31.4 seconds. *Crusader*, January 30, 1962; Worcester *Telegram*, April 11, 1982.

122. *The Purple* 33: 512–13, 675; *Holy Cross 1992–93 Basketball Guide*, 74–75.

123. Rudolph, *American College*, 386–87.

bating societies. In 1925–26, when a number of students played at least two sports, the number of varsity athletes was small: football had 40; baseball, 16; basketball, about 10; and track ranged from 9 to 28.[124] Yet, in their eagerness to foster the athletic program, the rector-presidents occasionally pressed the limits. In 1916, for instance, Father Dinand confided to an alumnus that Frank Cavanaugh, now coaching at Dartmouth, was secretly helping the College varsity prepare for the Boston College game.[125] When Holy Cross lost the game by three points, Dinand wrote an impatient letter to the press in response to "the very glib spirit of criticism which arises whenever defeat falls to the lot of one of the teams." Dinand explained the 4–5 season in terms of the school's "stringent and exacting requirements in Studies," and "the plain statement of fact" that representatives of other schools had lured some of College's best athletes away. "The college authorities insist upon their standards in scholarship and discipline, preferring honorable defeat upon an athletic field to victories won at the expense of collegiate requirements."[126]

The other side of the case emerged in 1924, when the Jesuit consultors (acting as trustees) justified the construction of the new football stands in terms of the intrinsic value of sports on a college campus and public support for the game:

There is some agitation in the country against giving undue prominence to athletics and taking up too much time of the students, but it was pointed out by the Consultors that athletics is a necessity at a boarding college to keep the boys interested and moreover athletics at Holy Cross does not take any time from studies nor is it any more prominent here than it ever was. The same number of games were formerly played as now, but the public is taking more interest in them and are willing to pay to see them. The stands will be put up with revenue from the sale of tickets.[127]

They were brave words, but they were not completely true. Athletics had gradually became more prominent at Holy Cross; the Athletic Association's receipts topped $168,500 in 1927; tens of thousands of spectators came to Fitton Field; hundreds of students left campus for away games; and the student-athletes, many holding athletic scholarships and under pressure to succeed in the classroom and on the field, were competing for higher stakes than their predecessors. All this was a condition of full participation in the contempo-

---

124. Jesuit minister's note book, 1911–35, ACHC, 19.4-3; Worcester *Post*, September 21, 1911; HD, October 29–30, 1926; unidentified press clipping [1924], ACHC, Locker 8, Scrapbook 15, p. 106.

125. Dinand to John F. Dore, Worcester, November 23, 1916, ACHC, 12.16.

126. Dinand to Worcester *Telegram* (copy), December 5, 1916, ACHC, 12.16.

127. Consultors' Minutes, March 20, 1924, ACHC, 19.0.

rary American educational system. At Holy Cross, athletics served the additional function of providing an outlet for the students' exuberance within a tightly disciplined pattern of life. In this context, Father Dinand's efforts to defend the athlete as scholar and to render defeat palatable because it was honorable were not universally appreciated. And when the College consultors consoled themselves with the idea that nothing had really changed in the athletic program, they were ignoring the fact that the whole context of intercollegiate sports, and of College life in general, was evolving in ways that were beyond their control. By 1927, several of the consultors were privately expressing their fear that athletics were being overemphasized.[128]

Prominent campus visitors also provided students and faculty with diversion from their ordinary routine. One of the best known was Irish Sinn Fein leader Eamon de Valera, who visited Holy Cross in February 1920 as part of his American tour. Aware that de Valera would be visiting the city to raise funds for Irish Bonds, Carlin extended a formal invitation: "In as much as a large majority of faculty and students belong to that class of people which our distinguished alumnus Senator David I. Walsh has . . . described and defended as 'descendants of a subject race,' it would be . . . a pleasure to welcome to our halls the duly-elected representative of such a 'subject race.'" When de Valera agreed, Carlin received "a joint petition of Alumni and friends of the College" to offer the Irish leader an honorary degree. But de Valera was as controversial as he was famous, and the Million Dollar Drive was pending. After "a long and serious discussion," the trustees rejected the proposal, 4–1, Carlin abstaining. Three days before the visit, Carlin offered "new reasons" to the trustees, who then voted to award the degree, 5–1.[129] In 1927, controversy again interrupted the normal pattern of granting honorary degrees, when sociologist Jane M. Hoey and poet Katherine Bregy became the first women so honored. Once again, a split vote determined the outcome; not all the trustees were pleased about this first breach of the gender barrier. Other campus visitors included Red Wing and his wife Morning Star, New York Governor Alfred E. Smith, and magician Harry Houdini, who lectured on the fraud of spiritualism.[130]

128. Consultors' reports, May 5, 1927, NEPA, Excerpts of Consultors.

129. Carlin to DeValera, Worcester, January 23, 1920, ACHC, 12.17; Trustees' Minutes, January 30 and February 4, 1920, ACHC, 10.0. On the circumstances and controversies of DeValera's visit, see Tim Pat Coogan, *Eamon DeValera: The Man Who Was Ireland* (New York: Harper-Collins, 1995), 134–96.

130. Dean of Studies Diary, June 15, 1927, ACHC, 14.0-5; Trustees' Minutes, 1912–1927, ACHC, 11.0-1; HD, December 16, 1924, and July 1, 1925; James Carlin's notes for 1920 commencement, ACHC, 12.17; Worcester *Telegram*, December 14, 1925; Meagher and Grattan, *Spires*, 250.

When Joseph Dinand returned to Holy Cross in 1924, there was every expectation that his new administration—with all his plans for further expansion and hearty bonding with alumni, faculty, and students—would last until 1930, given the full six-year term that was customary for successful rector-presidents. True, he was hospitalized in June of 1926 with *angina pectoris*, but he returned for the new academic year with renewed vigor. The new library was under construction; he and Charles Maginnis were working on plans for a new gymnasium to be built in the pine grove west of Loyola (Carlin) Hall overlooking Fitton Field, and bids had already been solicited.[131] Then, to his astonishment, on July 28, 1927, a radiogram arrived from Father Ledochowski: "Dinand appointed Vicar Apostolic Jamaica." Immediately, Dinand radioed back: "Earnestly implore withdrawal appointment, urge unfitness, age, health." A second message went to Fr. Emil Mattern, the general's chief advisor for America: "Implore personal intercession withdraw appointment." On July 30, at 9:15 A.M., he radioed Ledochowski again with an urgent request to delay acting until he received Dinand's letter of explanation. The letter represented at length his personal unfitness for the office, his age, and his health. But that very evening, Mattern's reply arrived: "Fr. General appreciates your feeling. Church demands sacrifice: God will bless generous acceptance." The next day, the general wrote a personal letter, imposing the obligation upon Dinand. He received this final word on August 17.[132]

The new assignment was sudden and, apparently, unexpected. Dinand had been nominated early in 1927 by the head of the Maryland–New York Province; by the end of April, the process of inquiry was so favorable to Dinand that he became the top choice for the office.[133] Dinand's Jesuit superiors kept him in the dark for reasons of their own. They may have wanted to allow him for as long as possible to foster the momentum he had generated at Holy Cross; or, considering the needs of the Church in Jamaica, they may have wanted to forestall whatever delays his anticipated resistance might have introduced into the process. This much is clear: Jesuit authorities wanted him to accept the office. In Rome, Father Ledochowski was influential enough to have blocked the appointment if he had wished. Closer to home, Father James Kil-

131. HD, 1926–27; Gymnasium Blueprint, June 9, 1927, ACHC, 16.1BU-1; *Tomahawk*, September 8, 1926.

132. Documents pertaining to the episcopal appointment are in Dinand's papers, ACHC, 12.16.

133. In a letter to James Kilroy, Wlodimir Ledochowski attributed the initiative for Dinand's appointment to Patrick Kelly of the Maryland–New York Province. But Patrick Kelly, long assigned to pastoral work at St. Joseph's in Philadelphia, died in May 1925. The general clearly meant Lawrence Kelly, the Maryland–New York provincial. Ledochowski to Kilroy, Rome, February 2 and April 30, 1927, NEPA, Correspondence from General.

roy had been named provincial of the independent New England Province in 1926, when it was formally separated from the Maryland–New York Province. The new province had joint responsibility for mission work in Jamaica. Dinand, who had worked in Jamaica from 1905 to 1908, including two years as Headmaster of St. George's College in Kingston, was an experienced administrator with personal knowledge of the island. In that sense, he was a logical choice. But he turned 58 in 1927 and had developed some medical problems; he was well positioned at Holy Cross to foster its further expansion; and he was happy and effective in his assignment. Clearly, Fathers Kilroy and Ledochowski found the weightier considerations to be on the side of reassignment. Possibly, they were concerned that Dinand was pushing the College plans ahead too quickly and was too willing to borrow money.[134] Within the Catholic community, there were a finite number of potential donors; Boston College was also expanding; and the New England Province had to face its own financial need as Father Kilroy sought the means to construct a school of philosophy and a major theological seminary, and assumed the further expense of supporting a novitiate, retreat house, and other facilities ordinarily associated with the life and work of Jesuits.[135] Whatever reasons impelled the change, Father Dinand's appeal was refused; when students returned for classes in the fall of 1927, he was bishop-designate and Father John M. Fox, formerly a professor of ethics, political economy, and sociology, had assumed responsibility as vice-rector.

On October 30, 1927, Joseph Dinand received episcopal consecration in the campus chapel from Bishop O'Leary of Springfield. The following day, John Fox assumed office as rector and eighteenth president of Holy Cross. On the afternoon of November 2, the new library was dedicated on the anniversary of the opening of classes in 1843. In the evening, the departing rector was feted at a farewell dinner that became an affectionate celebration of the College and Joseph Dinand. The toastmaster was Judge Edward F. Hanify '04 of Fall River; among the speakers were Senator Walsh, who offered a personal tribute to Dinand ("A master of speech, he is yet more a master of hearts"), and Father Fox, who announced for the first time that the new library would bear Dinand's name. Bishop Dinand was modest in his response: he was surprised at the announcement — it had been his intention to name the building for Joseph Hanselman.[136] A few more weeks for good-byes, and it was time to depart. On the afternoon of November 30, students lined Linden Lane to bid

134. The general told Father Kilroy that Roman authorities might question the wisdom of such an accumulation of debt at Holy Cross. Ledochowski to Kilroy, Rome, November 24, 1926, NEPA, Correspondence from General.

135. Burke, *Jesuit Province*, 53–69, 94–100, 104–19.

136. Worcester *Post*, November 3, 1927; Meagher and Grattan, *Spires*, 255–56.

An enduring friendship: Senator David I. Walsh (Class of 1893) with Joseph N. Dinand (College President, 1911–1918, 1924–1927) about 1925. Their partnership of interest promoted the expansion of the interwar years.

him farewell, the seniors in caps and gowns at the end of the drive, the faculty on the O'Kane porch. Bishop Dinand wept as he responded to the applause. It was hard to leave Holy Cross, he said; the College had been his home; and he told the students that he had requested a holiday for them. They all knelt down to receive his blessing, then resumed their cheers as his car passed slowly through their ranks.[137]

137. Group interview by James Phalen '88 with members of the Class of 1931 (Edmund P. Keleher, John P. Connolly, Richard F. Hegarty, and Robert G. Friedrichs), June 10, 1988; Worcester *Telegram*, December 1, 1927.

That parting gesture, his hand raised in blessing, was a striking symbol of Joseph Dinand's importance to Holy Cross. As leader of the College for ten years, he had advanced the institution in a multitude of ways that enhanced its academic quality, its reputation, its physical environment. With James Carlin, Dinand had probed the potential of the second Holy Cross and developed many of its best features. In sixteen years, the two rector-presidents had strengthened and enriched the curriculum; they had raised well over a million dollars for campus development; they had increased the physical plant through the addition of four buildings, including a chapel and a library that stood the test of time for their architectural inspiration; they had broadened the athletic program and built up the Fitton Field stands; and, in the midst of the Roaring Twenties, they had kept Holy Cross, with all its discipline, attractive to more students than could be accommodated. Very different in temperament, Dinand the exuberant expansionist and Carlin the practical planner were a well-matched pair who were wise enough—and bold enough—to take advantage of a period of unprecedented opportunity. Theirs were halcyon years.

CHAPTER SEVEN

Depression and War,

1927–1946

DECEMBER 1, 1927, opened a new chapter in the life of the College. Joseph Dinand was gone. His passion to build, his affectionate bonding with alumni and friends, his driving enthusiasm that made every outpouring of energy a labor of love—these assets were no longer at the service of Holy Cross. But he and James Carlin left a legacy of momentum. That was an advantage their successors were careful not to squander. The challenge of the thirties was to maintain enrollment and enhance the physical plant during the years of economic turmoil. In the early forties, the preparedness movement and then the war challenged all-male Holy Cross with the frightening prospect of a depopulated school, until Navy programs filled corridors and classrooms again. Fathers John Fox and Francis Dolan guided the College through the Depression; leadership during the war fell to Joseph R. N. Maxwell. In addition to the particular problems connected with their years as rector, they each faced continuing issues of academic standards and faculty status. Their solutions were generally conservative; they steered a safe course through uncertain times.

John Fox was born in Dorchester, Massachusetts, in 1881. He entered the Society of Jesus in 1902 after graduating from Boston College, and was assigned to the faculty at Holy Cross in 1917, with a teaching specialty in economics and ethics. In those days before academic departments, he also taught philosophy, classics, and theology and moderated the athletic program, debating societies, and the dramatic association. A kind man, he found Holy Cross a less consuming interest than his predecessor had. The alumni liked him and appreciated his talks, though at times his rhetoric abounded with platitudes. The editor of the *Holy Cross Alumnus* described him succinctly in a eulogy published in 1940: "A conservative by nature, he governed in like manner."[1]

The principal campus project during the Fox administration was a new dining hall. The building had been under discussion since 1923, when Father Carlin decided that the structure would be placed on the lower quadrangle and include a boiler house, bakery, and laundry, besides the kitchen and dining room.[2] When Joseph Dinand returned to Holy Cross in 1924, he built the library instead, and then turned toward construction of a gymnasium. John Fox was closer to Carlin in his sense of priorities; soon after assuming office, he revived the idea of a dining hall. Early in 1929, he announced a campaign to raise $300,000 for the project. Then the stock markets collapsed, and contributions flowed in slowly. By September of 1933, $221,000 had been pledged, of which $138,000 had been paid.[3] Toward the end of 1930, he commissioned Maginnis and Walsh to draw up plans for a dining hall and auditorium. But the estimated cost of $350,000 to $400,000 was deemed "prohibitive," and discussion turned temporarily to a smaller building. By the summer of 1932, however, monetary deflation and the strong economic condition of the school again favored the larger plan, at a projected cost of $330,000.[4] But Father Ledochowski had other ideas: he stopped the project cold, explaining that the times had changed since 1926, when he had approved the $800,000 loan for Holy Cross. He didn't doubt that the dining hall was needed; but with so many schools on the brink of financial ruin, he was concerned that the College might mortgage its future foolishly at a time when any surplus could be better utilized to assist less prosperous apostolates. Approval was withheld.[5] Only after the trustees appealed the refusal, pleading "urgent need," did the general soften his opposition, insisting only that no money be borrowed.[6]

1. WL, 69:220–29; Burke interview, June 17, 1988; *Holy Cross Alumnus*, March 1940; Sermon at installation of Archbishop John G. Murray, Class of 1897, ACHC, 12.18.

2. Consultors' Minutes, December 6, 1923, ACHC, 19.0.

3. Worcester *Gazette*, January 10, 1929; WL, 63:138.

4. Consultors' Minutes, November 20, 1930, March 31, 1931, and August 22, 1932, ACHC, 19.0; HD, March 1931-August 1932; Contract with Charles Logue Building Co., August 25, 1932, ACHC, 16.1BN-1.

5. Ledochowski to Kilroy, Rome, October 13, 1932, NEPA, Correspondence from Rome. Among Jesuit schools, Marquette University almost experienced bankruptcy in 1932, and the University of Detroit defaulted on loans of $3.5 million in 1933. William P. Leahy, "Jesuits, Catholics, and Higher Education in Twentieth-Century America," (Ph.D. Dissertation, Stanford University, 1986), 230.

6. Consultors' Minutes, December 4, 1932, ACHC, 19.0; McCormick to Ledochowski, Chestnut Hill, June 23, 1933, NEPA, Correspondence to General; Ledochowski to McCormick, Rome, May 23, 1933, and Tusculi, July 24, 1933, NEPA, Correspondence from Rome.

In retrospect, it seems astonishing that the College could afford an expensive building at the height of the Depression, after an unsuccessful fund drive. But in fact, the College budget was generating a surplus, partly because the salaries of employees had been cut. In 1931, several of the athletic coaches had their salaries reduced—Jack Barry's by 20 percent, from $5000 to $4000. That fall, at the direction of Father Kilroy, teachers and clerical assistants earning more than $2000 were given a 5 percent cut; those earning over $2500 were reduced by 10 percent.[7] In 1933, James McCormick, who had succeeded Father Kilroy as provincial, insisted that "more could be done . . . to reduce considerably the salary budget of each office. The saving thus effected would materially hasten the day of the completion of the much-needed dining-hall."[8] That summer, citing a "marked decline" in athletic revenues, Father Fox broached the issue of a "very large cut" in the pay of salaried members of the Athletic Association: "We must make . . . extraordinary efforts to continue safely."[9] Yet, despite the salary reductions for faculty and staff, tuition was held at $280 from 1928 to 1941; and basic room and board charges were *raised* from $370 to $420 in 1931, and to $445 in 1935.

The result of these efforts was a budgetary surplus during the Depression (Chart 7.1). Before fiscal year 1938, the surplus was computed on the basis of *ordinary* income and expenses, a set of figures that excluded the Athletic Association, building projects, and gifts. On that basis, the College accumulated a surplus of about $880,000 between 1928 and 1937. Excess revenue peaked at $167,400 in 1934, a year characterized as "one of the most successful in the history of the College." The surplus was accumulated despite the fact that some students were on reduced tuition and others were unable to pay their bills. A list of delinquent accounts from 1934 carries 250 names, with figures ranging as high as $1673; in 1935, the trustees established a policy of withholding grades until a satisfactory agreement was reached. Beginning in 1938, a new accounting procedure computed the surplus only in terms of the *general* operating budget, which included all items of income and expense. Under this system, the surpluses continued, totaling over $368,000 from 1938 to 1941. A good part of the surplus came from room and board charges: in fiscal year 1938, the school made a profit of $123,000 on its board charges and about $60,000 on

7. Consultors' Minutes, May 28, 1931, ACHC, 19.0; Trustees' Minutes, April 29, 1932, ACHC, 11.0; Memorial of J. M. Kilroy, May 22, 1932, ACHC, 19.1-2; HD, September 29, 1932.

8. Memorial of James McCormick, May 30, 1933, Provincials' Memorials, ACHC, 19.1-2.

9. Fox to Cleo O'Donnell, Worcester, July 8, 1933, ACHC, 12.18. Baseball revenues alone declined from $26,500 in 1930 to $7000 in 1933; the program suffered a net loss of $29,300 during those four years. Annual Statements, 1930–33, Trustees' Records, Series 4: Financial Records, ACHC, 11.0.

Chart 7.1 Operating Budget, 1928–1946

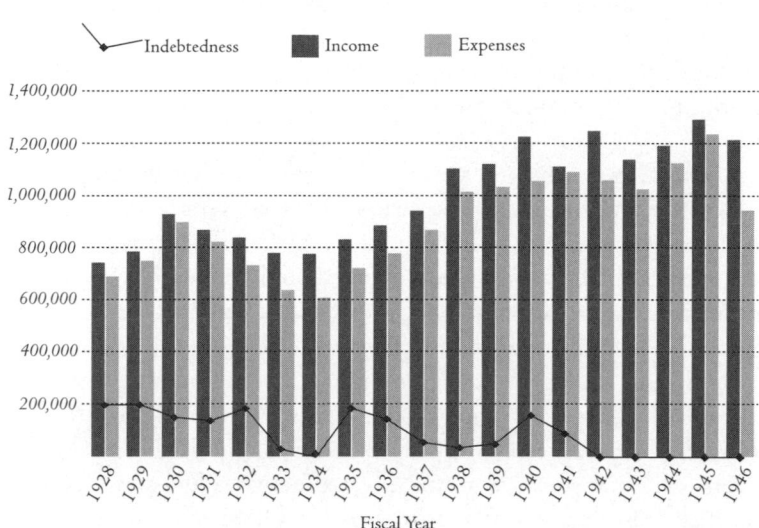

Fiscal Year

room charges to offset a loss of about $107,000 on tuition charges for instructional and administrative expenses.[10] The maintenance of tuition and student fees at or above pre-Depression levels, and the salary cuts introduced in the early 1930s, meant that boarding students and their parents, as well as College employees on reduced salaries, contributed substantially to campus expansion.

Work on the dining hall started in August of 1933 and continued for over sixteen months. The building was named Kimball Hall after Father Charles Kimball, who died in May of 1934. He had served the College as a teacher and librarian since 1915.[11] The building opened in January 1935. With 1.3 million cubic feet of space, Kimball Hall was the largest—and costliest—structure built between the two wars. The first floor held a dining room designed to seat 900, plus the kitchen and bakery. In the basement were administrative offices, the campus post office, a day students' room, and the laundry. The sub-basement held a cafeteria, bowling alleys, a billiard room and a workmen's dining room; the ground floor at the north (downhill) side of the building held a visiting team locker room, graduate manager's office, the boiler room, and a garage. The building also contained a large auditorium. A Renaissance

10. Summary statements of annual profit and loss, 1930–41, Trustees' Records, Series 4: Financial Records, ACHC, 11.0; Treasurer's Records, 1934–45, ACHC, 13.0; Consultors' minutes, May 11, 1935, ACHC, 19.0.

11. HD, May 1–3, 1934.

design, with red brick and limestone, harmonized with the other buildings on the quad. The new building freed space in Fenwick Hall for more classrooms and new dining and recreation rooms for the Jesuits.[12] With furnishings and equipment, the final cost came to $627,750. The trustees had to borrow about $195,000 to complete the project, but the loan was short-term and repaid in three years.[13]

As Kimball Hall was taking shape, another project was engaging Father Fox's attention: the termination of the farm and the conversion of the barn, located at the present site of Loyola Hall, into a makeshift gymnasium. The matter came up in 1932, when the trustees "agreed on the advisability of doing away with the farm, owing to the financial loss, as well as the poor health of Bro. Horwedel." In fact, the farm had not been profitable for some time; from 1924 through 1933, the net loss totaled over $13,500.[14] In the spring of 1933, after receiving a favorable report from a contractor, the trustees voted "that the red barn should be remodeled in such a way as to make physical exercises etc. available there." The transformation was effected between July and October, and the football team held its first drill there on October 17. In time, the structure also housed billiard tables and bowling alleys.[15]

Father Fox's term came to an end in July of 1933, before the Kimball Hall plans were finalized. He was succeeded by Father Francis J. Dolan, who had just turned 40. Born in Boston, Dolan was an athlete in track, baseball, and football at Boston College High School and Boston College. He entered the Society in 1912 and taught classics at Loyola College in Baltimore and at Holy Cross before his ordination. He returned to Holy Cross in 1930 and served as academic dean until he succeeded to the presidency. Dolan sometimes found his office burdensome; yet the Jesuits liked him and praised his governance as "accurate and paternal."[16] More questionable was his ability to foster academic development. Late in his rectorship, a newspaper reported that he at-

12. Kimball Hall description, ACHC, 16.1BN-1; Consultors' Minutes, January 3, 1935, ACHC, 19.0.

13. Kimball Dining Hall, Expense Report, December 21, 1934, Treasurer's Records, ACHC, 13.0; Annual Financial Report, 1935, Trustees' Records, Series 4: Financial Records, ACHC, 11.0; HD, October 1934–June 1935; Maginnis and Walsh to Joseph Maxwell, Boston, May 25, 1943, ACHC, 16.1BJ-1.

14. Consultors' Minutes, December 4, 1932, ACHC, 19.0; Financial Reports, 1924–33, Trustees' Records, Series 4: Financial Records, ACHC, 11.0.

15. Consultors' Minutes, December 4, 1932, ACHC, 19.0; Trustees' Minutes, May 26, 1933, ACHC, 11.0; HD, April–October, 1933; Raymond Swords, Remarks at Hogan Center Dedication, October 13, 1967, ACHC, 12.24.

16. *WL*, 69:104–7; Consultors Excerpts, May 18, 1934, NEPA, Consultors' Excerpts; Boston *Post*, July 23, 1933.

tended football practice "almost daily"; one astute observer characterized his administration, on balance, as "not great." Yet, he was young for the responsibility; and his term was extended to a seventh year to allow him to complete the construction of the new dormitory, which had been begun late in 1938 and was the second major accomplishment of his administration.[17]

The project had been under discussion for three years, the result of the overcrowding of freshman students in Fenwick and O'Kane Halls and the fire hazard associated with utilizing those structures as dormitories. In June of 1936, Father Dolan announced that construction would begin shortly; by September, Charles Maginnis had drawn up plans for a 3½ story building in "modified Georgian style," large enough to accommodate 192 students, with eight classrooms on the lower floor. The estimated cost was $293,000.[18] Then, with the plans apparently on track, the enterprise came to a standstill. The records offer little evidence for the delay, but it may have been connected with the economic downturn of 1937 or with a desire to retire the debt incurred for Kimball Hall. On campus, overcrowding was relieved slightly in the summer of 1936 by converting the house that formerly lodged the farm laborers, into Campion House, a 12-room residence for 48 students.[19] Delay proved costly for the dormitory project. In the fall of 1937, a Maginnis and Walsh architect warned Father Dolan that the cost of labor and materials had increased by about 15 percent in the previous year. But the interval had given architects and college authorities time to reconsider campus needs, and new plans were drawn up for a larger building, in which more space was allocated to student quarters and less to classrooms.[20] In the spring of 1938, plans were approved for a dormitory with a student capacity of 240. The cost was to be repaid over three years from the annual operating surplus.[21] Strikes and a flooded foundation delayed the opening from September of 1939 to January of 1940. Meanwhile, the largest freshman class in history (400 students, including 290 boarders) was straining facilities, with seniors temporarily housed in O'Kane III and IV. Named for the late Father John D. Wheeler, who had served at

17. J. H. Dolan to Zacheus Maher, Boston, August 22, 1939, NEPA, Correspondence to General; Worcester *Gazette*, September 6 and 7, 1939; Burke interview, June 17, 1988.

18. Consultors' Minutes, November 14, 1935, ACHC, 19.0; Wendell T. Phillips to Dolan, Boston, September 17, 1936 and October 21, 1937, ACHC, 16.1BJ-1; HD, June 9, 1936, and July 27, 1939.

19. HD, August, 1936; unidentified press clipping [fall, 1937], ACHC, 16.1BL-1.

20. Wendell T. Philips to Dolan, October 21, 1937, ACHC, 16.1BJ-1.

21. Dolan to J. H. Dolan, Worcester, April 20, 1938, and Zacheus Maher to J. H. Dolan, Rome, May 20, 1938, NEPA, HC-Rector; Ledochowski to James H. Dolan, Rome, May 20, 1938, ACHC, 16.1BJ-1.

Holy Cross for 22 years in a variety of jobs, the building was occupied on January 2, 1940—seniors on the lower four floors, juniors on the fifth floor. Wheeler Hall added 610,000 cubic feet to the physical plant at a cost of $415,000, including $15,000 for furnishings.[22]

An element of sadness tempered the joy connected with the completion of the dormitory when Francis Dolan died on September 6, 1939, following minor surgery for a throat infection.[23] Within days, Father Joseph R. N. Maxwell, who had been academic dean at Boston College since 1935, was appointed successor. Born in Taunton, Massachusetts, in 1899, Maxwell had attended Holy Cross for one year before entering the Jesuit novitiate in 1919. As a scholastic, he taught Latin and English at his alma mater from 1926 to 1929. He had an academic mindset and had published works in biography and poetry. Over the next six years, Holy Cross consultors praised his capacity for governance and his hard work—qualities that served the College well, particularly during the war.[24] Maxwell was a popular speaker and a strong advocate of high standards of teaching. As rector, he practiced what he preached, striving to upgrade the academic program. He was willing, when necessary, to retire ineffective teachers and to assert the pedagogical needs of the College with Jesuit authorities. At the end of his term, a friend praised him for "your insistence on high academic standards, the scholarly qualifications of your faculty and your willingness to expend money and all the necessary time to reach these standards and maintain them."[25] Those were important points at a time when the condition of the school might have induced a spirit of complacency.

As Fathers Fox and Dolan guided Holy Cross through the Depression years, they had the advantage of generally rising enrollments. The College had 1040 students when Fox assumed office in 1927, and 1276 in the fall of 1939, the last normal year before the war. Small declines in 1930–32 and again in 1937–38, were almost insignificant echoes of the financial catastrophe that had

22. *Tomahawk*, October 10 and December 8, 1939; HD, December 1938–January 1940; Memo [Maginnis and Walsh–? to Joseph Maxwell], April 4, 1940, and Maginnis and Walsh to Maxwell, Boston, May 25, 1943, ACHC 16.1BJ-1

23. HD, September 5–8, 1939; Worcester *Gazette*, September 6, 1939.

24. Biographical summary, Maxwell papers, ACHC, 12.20; Meagher and Grattan, *Spires*, 214–15; Worcester *Telegram*, September 13, 1939; Holy Cross Consultors' Excerpts, 1940–45, NEPA, Consultors' Excerpts.

25. Maxwell to Provincial, Worcester, July 18, 1944, NEPA, HC-Rector; Maxwell's Commencement Address, Worcester State Teachers' College, May 19, 1942, ACHC, 12.20; Burke interview, June 17, 1988; Phil Donnelly to Maxwell, Weston, August 27, 1945, ACHC, 12.20.

Chart 7.2 Student Origins, 1901–1960

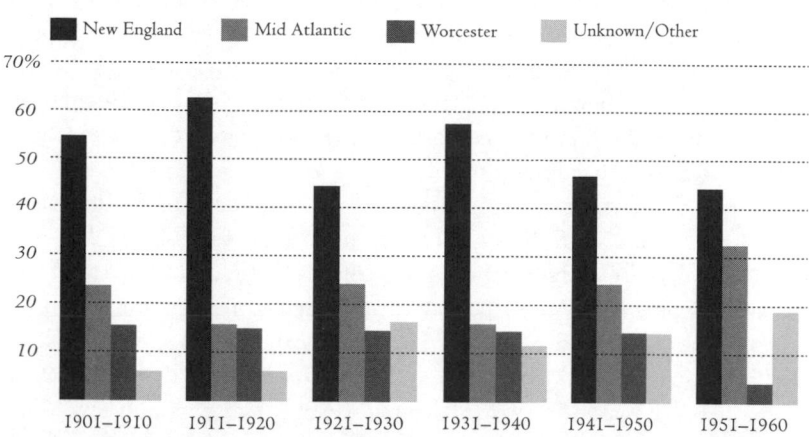

stricken the country. The proportion of boarding students held steady through the 1930s at about 75 percent. The pattern was sustained despite the decision to hold the line on tuition and fees, partly because some students were offered reduced tuition and campus jobs to help cover expenses. The College treasurer's records from September 1934 show that 149 upperclassmen (18 percent) received some sort of assistance exclusive of athletic scholarships. A majority worked in the dining hall for room and board; others had reduced tuition or Lehy Loans (from a fund established by Father Wheeler in 1923), or combined dining hall jobs with another form of assistance. Among the upperclass day students, 27 had loans from the Lehy fund, and 25 were on reduced tuition.[26] Even so, many students left the College as their parents' financial standing declined.

Their places were filled in a variety of ways. Some Depression-era students attended Holy Cross instead of Georgetown to save traveling expenses, temporarily raising the proportion of New Englanders (including Worcester area students) to 72 percent (Chart 7.2). The College also accepted less gifted students, described by a faculty member as "a goodly number of slow coaches . . . , people who would normally never have been admitted, but in those

26. "Help Received by Students Now In School," September 5, 1934, Treasurer's Records, J. Joseph Reilly, S.J., ACHC, 13.0; *Holy Cross Alumnus*, October 1929. A list dated October 26, 1933, indicated $23,000 in aid to 79 students (including freshmen) by way of "gift reductions," and $17,380 to 69 students in the form of Lehy Loans. An additional 71 students received $41,500 from the Athletic Association. Treasurer's Records, 1933, ACHC, 13.0.

straightened days . . . the rooms had to be filled so that the doors could be kept open."[27] In the fall of 1940, it was the draft that caused concern; by September, newspapers reported that most schools had dropped by 10 to 18 percent. With Wheeler Hall less than a year old, Father Maxwell watched the enrollment anxiously, relieved at the end of September that enrollment was down only 70 from the previous year; all student rooms except those in Campion House were fully occupied.[28]

Under the circumstances, it was a struggle to maintain the College as a stronghold of the classics in the strict tradition of the *Ratio Studiorum*. The unwillingness or inability of high schools to promote Latin and Greek, and the need to accept some less gifted students during the Depression years, favored relaxation of the rigorous curriculum. Many American colleges and universities dropped specialized courses during the 1930s in favor of broad preparation to enable graduates to make the most of limited employment possibilities.[29] The Jesuit general was also urging educational reform. In the fall of 1927, under pressure from Roman authorities, Father Ledochowski directed the American provincial leaders to assert the Catholicity of their institutions. Three years later, the general turned his attention to points of academic weakness. He was concerned about the comparatively new movement to certify standards through the process of accreditation. Catholic and Jesuit schools were not faring particu-larly well in evaluations; in 1930, only sixteen Catholic schools, among them Holy Cross, stood on the approved list of the prestigious Association of American Universities, which accredited schools nationally.[30] Determined to address this problem, Father Ledochowski appointed a Commission on Higher Studies in 1931 to recommend changes in the curriculum and in the training of Jesuit faculty. Their report, delivered in August of 1932, rebuked the spirit of inertia that tended to make many of the Society's academic programs problematic to outsiders. To follow up on the report, Ledochowski sent a delegate to inspect colleges and universities and make specific recommendations. When he visited Holy Cross in the fall of 1934, the delegate found much to praise, but he recommended constructing several new buildings, limiting enrollment to avoid overcrowding, and dropping Greek to the status of an elec-

27. William J. Leonard, *The Letter Carrier* (Kansas City: Sheed and Ward, 1993), 60; Burke interview, June 17, 1988; Phalen group interview, members of Class of 1931, June 10, 1988.

28. Maxwell to James H. Dolan, Worcester, August 14, September 17 and 25, 1940, NEPA, HC-Rector.

29. Rudolph, *Curriculum*, 248.

30. Ledochowski to Kilroy, Rome, October 18, 1927, and Ledochowski to American Provincials, Rome, December 8, 1930, NEPA, Roman Correspondence; FitzGerald, *Governance*, 8–9, 41; Leahy, "Jesuits," 77–8.

tive, "since having so many disinterested students does not conduce to scholarship."[31]

The following year, New England Provincial James McCormick appointed a committee to recommend curricular revisions. At Holy Cross, the consensus was to drop compulsory Greek for the A.B. degree for the reasons advanced by the general's delegate.[32] The new recommendations went beyond Francis Downey's program, last altered in 1932, which offered ten degree tracks:

Bachelor of Arts
Bachelor of Arts, Pre-Law or Pre-Medical
Bachelor of Philosophy
Bachelor of Philosophy in Latin or English
Bachelor of Science in Chemistry, Physics, Metallurgy, or Pre-Medical

In 1936, the degree program was re-organized into four basic degree programs:

Bachelor of Arts with Honors (Latin and Greek required)
Bachelor of Arts (Latin required)
General Bachelor of Science (no required Latin or Greek)
Bachelor of Science in Economics, Education, or History (no required Latin or Greek)

Under this scheme, the Ph.B. was discontinued. Only the Honors A.B. program maintained the classics requirements of the old *Ratio*; students lacking high school Greek could complete the Honors A.B. at Holy Cross with three years of Greek. The non-Honors A.B. degree contained three tracks: a general liberal arts program, and pre-legal and pre-medical programs. Candidates for the general B.S. degree majored in physics, chemistry, or biology; the other B.S. programs incorporated majors in economics, education, or history. Between 1938 and 1941, the number of graduates with a A.B. degrees dropped to about half of the total; among the B.S. candidates, students in economics (business, after 1940) held the largest share: 55 of 115 in 1940, and 61 of 110 in 1942 (Chart 7.3). The changes were consistent with what the *Tomahawk* called "changing educational conditions that pervade our country today," and compatible with the principle of adaptation Ignatius had desired for his schools; some Jesuits, however, had grave misgivings about this further departure from tradition.[33]

Problems associated with the new curriculum were discussed in the re-

31. Notes on Holy Cross, Daniel M. O'Connell File, Boston College Archives, cited in FitzGerald, *Governance*, 41; Leahy, "Jesuits," 93–98.

32. McCormick to Ledochowski, Chestnut Hill, July 29, 1935, NEPA, Correspondence to General.

33. *Tomahawk*, May 19, 1936.

Chart 7.3 Graduates, 1928–1942

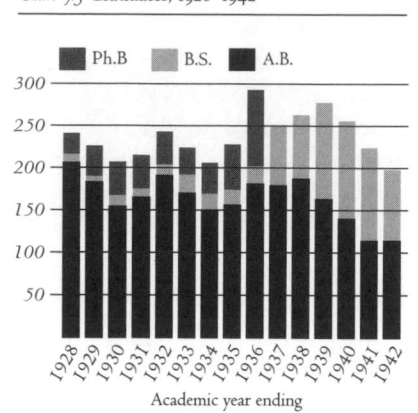

Ph.B   B.S.   A.B.

Academic year ending

ports prepared by the prefect of studies of the New England Province. Each year, from the interwar years until the 1960s, he made a formal visit to each Jesuit school and drafted an evaluation after dropping in on classes, examining requirements, and holding discussions. After his visit to Holy Cross in 1938, Father William Murphy indicated problems with the popular program in economics:

There is always the tendency of certain courses to become the lumber room of the college[,] and it would seem that the Economics course is becoming just such. It is to be hoped that the members of the faculty will refrain from any slighting remarks or from assuming an attitude of disdain towards the course or towards the students who choose that course. Such remarks are often damaging to the morale of the students and seriously interfere with the work of the professors. On the other hand[,] the members of the department must not furnish grounds for adverse criticism.[34]

Murphy himself was biased toward the traditional curriculum. In 1938, he urged "a very great effort" to maintain "the fine tradition of Holy Cross as a classical college."[35]

Such encouragement could not conceal the fact that the classics slipped considerably after the curriculum reorganization of 1936. In the first two years, freshman enrollment in the arts program dropped from 221 to 150. By 1939, Father Murphy was showing his concern. He praised the strong classics program: "It is reassuring to note that special effort is being made to preserve the fundamental character of the Ratio and of the Holy Cross tradition. . . . We have a great responsibility to maintain this splendid tradition." In the same year, Father James H. Dolan, who succeeded James McCormick as New England provincial in 1937, cited the "alarming decrease in the Arts Course matriculation at Holy Cross" as a justification for opening a new Jesuit prep school in the Berkshires, where candidates for Holy Cross could be properly prepared in the classics.[36] The *Tomahawk* echoed those sentiments. In the fall of 1939 its editors noted that "Holy Cross has ever stood Gibraltar-like in its

34. The statement, dated February 7, 1938, carried Murphy's name and appeared under the heading "Economics." It may have been posted on a faculty bulletin board. ACHC, 19.8-1.

35. Prefect of Studies Report, February 2, 1938, ACHC, 19.8-1.

36. Prefect of Studies Report, March, 1939, ACHC, 19.8-1; J. H. Dolan to Assistant, Boston, April 9, 1939, NEPA, Correspondence to General.

defense of true humanistic education which is gleaned chiefly from the pages of the classics." The following spring, thousands of visitors gathered on the lawn west of Loyola (Carlin) hall for two performances of *Oedipus at Colonus*—an endeavor that won high commendation from Father Zacheus Maher, who had been overseeing Jesuit activities in the United States since the outbreak of World War II.[37] Clearly, Jesuit authorities preferred the traditional curriculum and deplored the declining importance of classical humanism; they expanded the curriculum reluctantly and out of necessity.

Although the effort to work out the academic implications of the College's Jesuit heritage evoked some ambivalence during the 1930s, the Roman Catholic component of the institutional identity stirred hardly a ripple. Holy Cross existed within a Catholic community that was an identifiable American sub-community. Although the Jesuits evinced some interest in the "back to basics" ideas advocated by University of Chicago President Robert Maynard Hutchins in *The Higher Learning in America* (1936), they joined with other Catholic educators in rejecting Hutchins's belief that theology could not serve as an integrating force in modern education. Still less did they accept John Dewey's plea for progressivism in education.[38] Jesuit William McGucken summarized the difference in aims between Catholic and non-Catholic colleges and universities in an influential article published in 1942:

The university deals with things of the mind; education is an intellectual and spiritual process which has to do with the opening of the windows of the human mind, the enrichment and ennobling of the human soul. Therefore, the university must place humane values, spiritual values, above material values; training of men in thinking is more important than training in techniques.

. . . . .

For the Catholic university there is another grade in the hierarchy of values. Above the material, above the spiritual, there exist supernatural values [connected with] those facts which give meaning and coherence to the whole of life. . . . In a Catholic university there should always be on the part of all the faculties an awareness of these supernatural facts and values.

. . . . .

There is in the Catholic a singular unity of thought that springs from his totality of outlook that is particularly irritating to the non-Catholic.

37. *Tomahawk*, October 3, 1939; HD, May 17 and 19, 1940; Zacheus Maher to Maxwell, Poughkeepsie, May 12, 1940, ACHC, 12.20.

38. Rudolph, *American College*, 468–82; William J. McGucken, "The Philosophy of Catholic Education," in Nelson B. Henry (ed.), *Philosophies of Education* (Chicago: University of Chicago Press, 1942), 256; Philip Gleason, "American Catholic Higher Education: A Historical Perspective,

In this system, the primary purpose of Catholic schools was to subordinate academic subjects to the main goal, which McGucken defined as the inculcation of the "eminent knowledge of Jesus Christ our Lord."[39]

Within the Catholic context, the Jesuit curriculum of the 1930s represented an appealing approach because it harmonized so well with the Catholic intellectual revival of the 1930s—a broad movement that promoted the notion of a distinctive Catholic culture, superior to modern culture and expressing itself in Thomistic philosophy, intense spirituality, and Catholic Action. The movement expressed itself in a number of ways, including a Catholic literary revival and the establishment of professional organizations like the Worcester County Catholic Alumni Sodality, founded at Holy Cross in 1945.[40] Historian Philip Gleason has argued that the Jesuit pedagogical plan was "in practice [the] most satisfactory" educational approach within the Catholic system because it was "a systematically arranged progression of analytical and stylistic study of literary models that not only 'trained the mind,' but also gave the student mastery of language." Literature courses were designed to illustrate and promote the highest and best human conduct. Philosophy courses brought academic disciplines together in "an intellectually integrated vision of the natural order and its relation to the order of transcendental truth." The curriculum contained a strong religious dimension and emphasized character formation through contact between student and instructor. The system, Gleason concluded, was "religious, literary, and humanistic in spirit, synthetic in vision, rigid in approach, liberal in aim, and elitist in social orientation." Its goal, a Jesuit lecturer suggested at Fordham in the 1930s, was to impart Catholic culture as a "comprehensive organic unity"; and the meaning of research was deeper penetration into reality "as *Catholics possess it.*"[41] That spirit was abundantly evident at Holy Cross. Every College catalog from 1931 to 1941 proclaimed the understanding unambiguously:

The whole system rests on the principle that men cannot truly advance in knowledge unless they advance more closely to God. . . . Rightly, therefore, does Holy Cross in-

---

in Robert Hassenger (ed.), *The Shape of Catholic Higher Education* (Chicago and London: University of Chicago Press, 1967), 45; William J. Murphy, Report of March, 1939, ACHC, 19.8-1.

39. McGucken, "Philosophy," 264, 2734, 287.

40. Philip Gleason, "American Catholic Higher Education, 1940–1990: The Ideological Context," in George M. Marsden and Bradley J. Longfield (eds.), *The Secularization of the Academy* (New York: Oxford University Press, 1992), 235–38.

41. Gleason, "Historical Perspective," 45–48. The lecturer was George Bull, who had taught at Holy Cross as a scholastic during the Carlin years. Gleason cites his statement from "The Function of the Catholic Graduate School," in *Thought* 13 (1938), 364–80. See also Gleason, *Contending with Modernity: Catholic Higher Education in the Twentieth Century* (New York: Oxford University Press, 1995), 124–66.

sist that in every stage of intellectual development religious instruction be interwoven with training in the secular branches of knowledge.

It was a lofty statement of principles, though not surprisingly the reality sometimes fell short of the ideal. In 1933, province prefect of studies found ample room for improvement: one professor of philosophy was "nervous in conducting the prelection and far from tactful in a manifestation of disapproval"; a historian needed to be "more careful, while lecturing, about careful pronunciation"; and a Jesuit chemist was "orderly and practical, but too lifeless in the method of presentation to command the continued attention of this large class." Others were better; one teacher won praise for his "very practical and profitable" class.[42] Alumni of that period verify Dolan's analysis. Some teachers were fundamentally incompetent—like the religion professor who told his class in 1940 that it was a mortal sin to vote for Franklin Roosevelt. But other teachers offered enthusiasm and rigor that opened minds and changed lives.[43] The evidence suggests that most students were happy, and grateful for what they received. But, by aligning the academic program so tightly with the spirit of the Catholic subculture, Jesuit leaders ran the risk of ignoring or underemphasizing developments in the broader world of higher education.

The issue was raised pointedly in November 1938 in the first formal report prepared on Holy Cross by evaluators from the Association of American Universities. Although accreditation was readily accorded, Father Maxwell described the report as "far from flattering." Not a single Jesuit faculty member possessed a Ph.D., and the general credentials of the faculty were described as sub-standard for "an institution of the standing of Holy Cross." The situation prompted a recommendation that faculty pursue further studies "in leading graduate and professional institutions, including at least some not connected with the Catholic Church."[44] This suggestion gained a sympathetic hearing from Father Maxwell; within a month of taking office, he was devising plans to put the recommendations into effect. The desirability of having Jesuit professors obtain doctorates had been recognized as early as 1922; yet, there seems to have been relatively little urgency about the matter until the ac-

42. Prefect of Studies Report, 1933, ACHC, 19.8-1.

43. John McCarthy to William McCarthy, Karachi, Pakistan, December 23, 1969 (copy) ACHC, 12.24; Phalen interview with members of the Class of 1931, June 10, 1988.

44. Frank Bowles to Dean John F. Cox, November 8, 1938, Dean's Records, ACHC, 14.0; Maxwell to J. H. Dolan, Worcester, July 18, 1944, NEPA, HC-Rector. The Association of American Universities was founded in 1900 to foster common educational standards. Rudolph, *American College*, 438. Apparently, the early accreditation of Holy Cross by the AAU had been determined by a more informal method.

creditation report. During his first year in office, Father Maxwell found an ally in Father Edward Rooney, who was the National Secretary of the Jesuit Educational Association, an agency established at the request of Father Ledochowski in 1934 to foster cooperation among Jesuit schools. After visiting Holy Cross in the winter of 1939–40, Rooney urged better professional training for all faculty and recommended set standards for rank and tenure because "faculty members are designated as professor, assistant professor, etc., but there does not seem to be any fixed method of determining rank."[45]

Rooney's report and the 1938 accreditation review prompted College authorities to draw up a curious policy statement entitled "Tenure," covering rank and tenure and faculty salaries. The statement may also have been an effort to align the school somewhat with the Statement of Principles on academic freedom and tenure, issued in 1940 by the American Association of University Professors in reaction to the loyalty oaths prescribed in some schools during the 1930s.[46] Undated, it was inserted among the pages of the House Diary for March 1940. The document stated that Holy Cross had no policy of absolute tenure, but "a definitely reasonable expectation of continuance in service dependent upon satisfactory discharge of duty and proper conduct within and without the College." Grounds for dismissal included moral turpitude, mental disability, poor teaching, serious irregularity in the discharge of duties, and "serious failure to cooperate with the policy of the college department." Instructors received annual contracts for a maximum of four years; assistant, associate, and full professors received three-year contracts, renewable indefinitely. Tenure, "a reasonable expectation of permanency," was reserved to those in the upper two ranks. Promotion depended, not merely on length of service, but on "the quality of work done in the classroom, the individual's interest in his profession as evidenced by scholarly work at educational conventions, in publications, advanced degrees, etc." Ordinarily, the Ph.D. would be required for future promotion to associate or full professor.

College records offer few clues about the origins of the 1940 statement. The

45. O'Gorman to Ledochowski, [Chestnut Hill], April 4, 1922, NEPA, Correspondence to General; Maxwell to James H. Dolan, Worcester, October 16, 1939, NEPA, HC-Rector; Edward B. Rooney, "The Jesuit Educational Association," in *Jesuit Educational Quarterly* 3 (June 1940), 7. Rooney's report on Holy Cross was dated January 25, 1940, ACHC, 19.8-1.

46. Christopher J. Lucas, *American Higher Education: A History* (New York: St. Martin's Press, 1994), 197–200. The academic dean, John Cox, reported that Holy Cross had no tenure policy for lay faculty members: "Our policy always has been that of retaining those teachers permanently who are contented and do the required work satisfactorily." Cox to Frank Bowles, Worcester, April 29, 1938, Dean's Records, ACHC, 14.0.

titles of professor, assistant professor, and instructor were used for the first time in the catalog for 1924–25, presumably on the initiative of Francis Downey. The faculty were grouped according to the subjects they taught. Jesuit faculty were listed, simply, with S.J. after their names; the names of lay faculty indicated their highest academic degree. In 1924, one lay faculty member held the Ph.D. Starting in 1925, the faculty were listed alphabetically; in that year, lay faculty with master's degrees and one with a bachelor's degree held ranks as high as full professor. In 1931, the rank of associate professor appeared for the first time. During the late 1930s and early 1940s several lay faculty with master's degrees were full professors; and in 1945, two faculty members with bachelor's degrees were listed as full professors. (Both had received their initial appointments before 1940.) In 1945, the number of Ph.D. degrees among the lay faculty reached ten for the first time, of whom four held the rank of full professor.

Toward the end of the war, College trustees wrestled again with policies for tenure and promotion, prompted in part by the American Jesuit provincials, who, in 1942, had endorsed norms for governance, tenure, and promotion that differed somewhat from Holy Cross policy and were less protective of academic freedom—there was no tenure, and the grounds for termination included "a grave offense against Catholic doctrine or morality."[47] The Jesuit trustees took the matter up in 1945, when they adopted a new policy statement. It has disappeared from the trustees' files, but presumably it was similar to the standards published in 1949, when a master's degree was required for the rank of instructor; assistant professors were expected at least to be candidates for the Ph.D. with five years of teaching experience; associate professors were to hold the Ph.D., have nine years of teaching experience and "moderate eminence" in their field of scholarship; full professors needed thirteen years of satisfactory teaching, plus scholarly "eminence." Decisions on rank and tenure were made by an all-Jesuit committee chaired by the dean of the College and including the dean of admissions, the College treasurer, and a Jesuit member of the faculty. By 1949, the policy on academic freedom had been tightened to encompass loyalty to both Church and state: "Faculty members may not advocate in their teachings or publicly espouse doctrines or policies contrary to or subversive of either the Roman Catholic Religion or the American form of government."[48]

These efforts to define faculty status formalized the bifurcated pattern

47. Statutes for a Jesuit College of Liberal Arts approved by Provincials, May 1942, ACHC, 19.8-1.

48. Trustees' Minutes, September 22, 1944, April 11 and May 2, 1945, ACHC, 11.0; Rank, Tenure, Promotion Procedures, 1949–57, ACHC, 12.24.

that separated Jesuits from their lay associates. On the one hand, Jesuits were assigned and transferred at will by the provincial after consultation with the college rectors. In the catalog, the S.J. after their names, signaling a certain competence within the *Ratio Studiorum*, was presumed to be an adequate designation of academic credentials. With respect to the traditional curriculum, the presumption was logical, but it became less reasonable as the academic program expanded. In the administration of the school, Jesuits were firmly in control. From their perspective, Holy Cross was part of a family network owned and operated by themselves according to their own ideas. On the other hand, lay faculty members worked in an enterprise they were not allowed to manage. A different set of norms determined their status in the organization; although their contribution was valued, it was also circumscribed by rules and procedures beyond their control, and they were marginalized by their lack of familiarity with Jesuit ways. The situation, as one analyst described it, was partly a function of clericalism within a paternalistic Church and partly the result of a Jesuit fear that "laymen [might] contravene, even unwittingly, the goals and particular spirit of the Society of Jesus."[49]

Besides the initiation of procedures for faculty standing, the interwar years brought the introduction of academic departments. In 1938, for the first time, the College catalog listed academic departments, each with a designated "head."[50] There were fourteen departments: ten in the Division of Liberal Arts (Religion, Philosophy, English, Classics-Greek, Classics-Latin, Modern Languages, Economics, Education, History, and Sociology and Political Science), and four in the Division of Science (Biology, Chemistry, Physics, and Mathematics). Lay professors were eligible to serve as heads of departments: the Department of Mathematics had a lay head in 1938, and by 1945 three departments were directed by lay professors. Departments were supposed to meet quarterly and to file minutes in the dean's office. The faculty showed little enthusiasm in the matter, presumably because of the lack of authority invested in the departments. Although departments had been envisioned as an "effective way of facing and solving many problems which the changing character of the students is presenting,"[51] the fact was that most academic deci-

49. Laurence Andrew Dorr, "Academic Deans in Jesuit Higher Education: A Comparative Study of Deans, Jesuit and Lay," unpublished Ph.D. dissertation (University of Michigan, 1966), 19–21.

50. The impetus behind this development is not clear. It may have come from Edward Rooney and the Jesuit Educational Association, or from the province prefect of studies; it may have been a further result of the 1936 committee on New England Province schools; and/or it may have been connected with the accreditation in 1938.

51. Province Prefect of Studies Report, 1939, NEPA, HC-Varia; Province Prefect of Studies Reports, March 1941 and March 1950, ACHC, 19.8-1.

sions were still made at the level of the Jesuit province, or by the Jesuit administrators of the school, or in individual meetings between department heads and the rector-president.

Student life between 1927 and 1941 changed very little from the pattern of earlier years. The routine of campus life still placed heavy emphasis on academics, religion, discipline, and sports. Yet, standards could have been stronger: the 1938 accreditation report criticized the practice of "conditioning" students and allowing re-examination. The evaluators were concerned that the policy was "too liberal" because it afforded a second opportunity even to students who hadn't come close to passing. Soon policies were tightened: 29 students received academic dismissal between September of 1938 and March of 1939, and in 1940, for the first time, academic norms were defined in the student handbook.[52] Grades of A and B+ merited honors, and C+ or higher was required for a recommendation. Below D (60 percent), students failed; those receiving 55 to 59 percent received an E, or "conditioned failure," and those below 55 percent received a grade of F, "unconditional failure." Students who failed in three of their five courses were subject to review by the Committee on Standards composed of the academic dean and professors in the appropriate department.

Student handbooks, issued annually from 1924 (except for 1931, 1937, and 1938), listed the daily order and the rules of conduct and penalties for infractions. Until the Second World War, the pattern of daily life maintained the routine that had been in place for decades:

7:00	Rise	1:15	Class (All)
7:15	Mass	3:00	Classes End
7:45	Breakfast	5:55	Supper
9:00	Class	6:25	Chapel
11:50	Dinner	7:00	Study Period
12:20	Class (Freshmen only)	10:00	Lights Out (11:00, 1940–41)

Thursday and Saturday afternoons were free. Morning wake-up was assisted by student "callers," whose job was to move along the corridors after the bell, knocking on each door until they heard a response. The pew check at Mass was a further inducement for rising; those who missed Mass were refused town permission on Saturday. Lights out was enforced by corridor prefects,

52. Frank Bowles to John F. Cox, [November, 1938], NEPA, HC-Varia; Consultors' Minutes, March 5, 1939, ACHC, 19.0.

though students sometimes repaired to the lavatories for late study. Other rules about boisterous conduct, playing ball in unauthorized areas, smoking, and leaving the corridor during the evening remained essentially unchanged. Night absences were still a sore point during the late 1920s. Father Kilroy lamented the "serious nuisance" caused by "the ease with which boarders go out at night." He asked for an extra watchman and recommended room-by-room checks on a rotating basis. For decades afterwards, alumni laughingly described the atmosphere of those years as a "police state." Yet their characterizations were fond: the circumstances promoted friendships and mentoring relationships. The atmosphere did not suit everybody, but for those who survived, it was a "glorious crucible," as Evan Thomas put it.[53]

The students gained a new place to relax in 1929, when part of the old O'Kane gym was converted into a "social and recreational hall." A brochure urged students to respect the uses and cleanliness of the space and to conduct themselves appropriately: "Only the workmen, for instance, may wear their hats; and slouching attitudes, etc., are relegated to places remote from the college and to men who do not attend our school."[54] Forms of entertainment varied. Movies were popular, especially after 1930, when the first sound projector was installed on campus. During Prohibition, some students socialized at a speakeasy in the old Warren Hotel.[55] By 1930, class dinners were being held in the Bancroft Hotel. Menus were printed in Latin, French, Greek, or Gaelic, a different language for each class. In April, the seniors celebrated "Senior Day"—not a holiday, just a special day on which seniors received communion in caps and gowns and ate supper as a class, enjoying cake, cigars, and entertainment afterwards. Dances were also popular.[56]

Patterns of student participation in organized campus activities exhibit some significant changes after 1930, when intramural athletics became the single most popular extracurricular activity.[57] The Sodality enjoyed a revival during the Depression and war years, and regional clubs based on the geographic origins of the students also remained popular, while debating dropped in

53. J. M. Kilroy, Memorial of Visitation, May 20, 1929, ACHC, 19.1-2; Phalen group interview with members of the Class of 1931, June 10, 1988; Holy Cross College "Rules and Regulations," (September 1928), ACHC, 15.2; Evan Thomas, *The Man to See: Edward Bennett Williams, Ultimate Insider; Legendary Trial Lawyer* (New York: Simon and Schuster, 1991), 29.

54. HD, January 26, 1929.

55. Consultors' Minutes, November 30, 1929, ACHC, 19.0; *Tomahawk*, January 14, 1930; HD, January–March, 1930; Phalen group interview with members of the Class of 1931, June 10, 1988.

56. Diary of the Academic Dean, January–April 1930, ACHC, 14.0-5; *Tomahawk*, October 11, 1938.

57. Only the general pattern is known because the data program covered only two extracurricular activities, while many students participated in three or more; the percentage of students

popularity. The data indicate that, apart from academics, campus life during the 1930s and 1940s was dominated by sports and religion: by 1940, 72 percent of resident students and 28 percent of the non-residents participated in at least one intramural sport; varsity sports retained their following; and a large number of students had also undertaken the regular commitment of prayer, reception of the sacraments, and social action associated with the Sodality. That impression is confirmed by alumni of the period, who speak frequently of the twice-daily chapel obligation and of the near-universal attendance at home games.[58]

Even apart from worship in the chapel, religion and Catholicism pervaded campus life during the 1930s and 1940s. All classes began and ended with prayer—until 1947, the teacher was expected to kneel while the students stood.[59] The Crusader Council No. 2706 of the Knights of Columbus was organized in 1929 by John J. Spillane '22, a teacher and assistant dean of discipline. Under his leadership the Knights sponsored dances, dinners, debates, and even a radio play.[60] In 1939, a Passion Play written by Irving McDonald attracted 10,000 spectators to four performances during Lent; at the same time, Marian devotion remained strong, particularly during May.[61] The religious atmosphere reinforced Catholic teaching on sexual morality and created what has been called "an air of cultivated innocence." In 1939, a senior's lecture to the Sodality on "Ethics of Collegiate Mixed Company" repeated the Church teaching that deliberate sexual pleasure outside of marriage was seriously sinful, and that avoiding the urge to kiss made a boy into a man. And in 1938, when Governor Eurith Rivers of Georgia, at Holy Cross for a football game, told an off-color joke, none of the students laughed.[62] When Pius XI died in 1939, the *Tomahawk* carried a full-page drawing of the deceased pontiff. During the Spanish Civil War, the paper's editors sent congratulations to Franco in 1939 for his "brilliant offensive against those hordes

---

whose extracurricular activities are known rises dramatically after 1930, to 85–90 percent. See unrevised draft for details.

58. Phalen group interview with members of the Class of 1931, June 10, 1988; Edward F. Danowitz '43, personal interview with James Phalen '88, June 11, 1988; *Tomahawk*, March 5, 1940. Regional clubs were designed to provide students from given geographic areas an opportunity to associate at school with a further goal of maintaining the reputation and interest of the College when they were at home. *Tomahawk*, October 11, 1938.

59. Student Handbooks, 1920s–1947.

60. Vincent A. Lapomarda, program notes for 50th anniversary of the Crusader Council, April 7, 1979, ACHC, 15.1Q-1; *Tomahawk*, October 11, 1938.

61. *Tomahawk*, April 4 and May 2, 1939.

62. Thomas, *The Man to See*, 30; HD, October 22, 1938; *Tomahawk*, January 17, 1939.

of Atheistic communists. . . ." The editors characterized Hitler and German society as the doomed victims of a Godless system, which stood as a warning that America could avoid tyranny "only through *Christ's education.*" And they warmly supported the campus peace demonstration held on May 1, 1940, in response to Pius XII's plea for world peace.[63] The first honorary societies were also Catholic: Alpha Sigma Nu, introduced at Holy Cross in 1940, recognized students at Jesuit colleges who distinguished themselves in scholarship, service, and loyalty to the school. Delta Epsilon Sigma, organized in 1941, recognized students at Catholic colleges for "good character, liberal culture, and high-ranking scholarship." Even debating had a Catholic inflection. In 1939, when weekly debates were broadcast over a local radio station under the title "Crusader Forum of the Air," a stated goal was to "reflect the culture of a Catholic liberal arts education."[64]

For the most part, Holy Cross men wore their religious identity proudly, but they were robust Catholics, as the increase in campus athletics so clearly indicates. Intramural athletics was organized formally during the 1930–31 academic year, when Father Maurice Dullea was appointed the first moderator. The following year, a formal organization was set up under the direction of the students and faculty moderator. Contests between floors, dorms, and classes were an old feature of campus life, but the enthusiastic response to Father Dullea's efforts showed that organized intramural competition was an idea whose time had come. By 1931, there were tennis matches and track meets plus class teams in soccer, football, hockey, and handball, and corridor teams in basketball (16 teams) and baseball (14 teams). During the 1930s, intramural competition extended to bowling, swimming, horseshoes, pool, and even contract bridge.[65] In 1933, Father Francis Hart was named associate director of the program; he held that office intermittently until 1943, when he was appointed director of intramural athletics. In that position he became a beloved campus figure until his death in 1986.

Intercollegiate sports fell under the management of the Holy Cross Athletic Association. The HCAA was re-organized in 1928 and 1929 under the leadership of the prefect of discipline, Father John Wheeler, who was also the moderator of athletics. Before the reorganization, student officers retained a considerable amount of influence in the organization; but the new HCAA Constitution, adopted in 1929, shifted most of the responsibility and man-

63. *Tomahawk*, January 10, February 7, March 21 and 28, 1939, April 30, 1940.
64. *Tomahawk*, March 14, 1939, February 6 and March 19, 1940, May 13, 1941.
65. *Purple Patcher*, 1931, 1938, 1939.

agement to professional administrators.[66] The reorganized Athletic Association was managed by the director of athletics as an executive officer who reported to the College president. In 1929, Cleo O'Donnell became the first full-time director of athletics, at the end of eleven years as head football coach. Other officers were the faculty moderator, secretary, and the treasurer. The athletic director held responsibility for financial and business matters (with the assistance of the College Treasurer) and for scheduling. The Athletic Committee, consisting of the faculty moderator of athletics, director of athletics, assistant director of athletics, and the equipment manager of the HCAA, supervised intercollegiate athletic activities under the authority of the president.[67] The new system centralized control in the hands of the College administration. Students lost influence and power in the HCAA; yet the alumni, at least initially, were formally consulted on some decisions. There was precedent for the policy, thanks to Joseph Dinand, who had softened Thomas Murphy's policy on alumni influence in the athletic program.[68] The first two head football coaches chosen after the reorganization of 1929 were selected in collaboration with the alumni. In 1930, Father Fox met with the Alumni Athletic Committee to consult about Cleo O'Donnell's successor and, "with unanimous consent" of the Alumni Advisory Committee, hired Captain John McEwan, a West Point alumnus. The Alumni Advisory Athletic Board was consulted again about the hiring of Doctor Eddie Anderson as McEwan's replacement in 1933; but in 1942, Father Maxwell hired "Ank" Scanlan as head football coach "without consulting with any of the authorities connected with the H.C.A.A."[69] If anything, the record of the HCAA before and after the 1929 re-organization indicates that alumni were as active in the association as the president of the College permitted them to be.

On the field, baseball retained its popularity during 1930s and early 1940s, despite hard times early in the Depression. Jack Barry's program was well es-

66. Unidentified press clipping [October, 1928], ACHC, Locker 8, Book 22, p. 104; John D. Wheeler, Personal File, ACHC 14.8-1; College catalogs, 1920–28.

67. The early treasurer of the HCAA was Francis L. Miller, who was also named bursar of the College in 1933. *Crusader,* February 3, 1961; HCAA Constitution, 1929, ACHC, 18.0-1; John Wheeler, Personal File, ACHC, 14.8-1; Sullivan, Short History of HCAA.

68. Dinand to John B. Dore [head of H.C. Alumni Club of Boston] Worcester, December 19, 1916, ACHC, 12.16.

69. HD, March 9, 16, and 23, 1930, and March 5, 1933; "Sports" by Bill Grimes in the Boston *American,* n.d., ACHC, Director of Athletics, 1942–43, 18.0-1. Administration members of the Alumni Advisory Committee in 1933 were Fathers Fox, Phelan (Moderator of Athletics) and Wheeler, plus alumni John Creamer '13, Fr. George Connor '07, George Hughes '94, John Dunphy '17, James Crotty, '11, Peter Dulligan '07, and Charles Strome '23, who was executive secretary. Press release, March 6, 1933, ACHC, 18.0-1.

tablished and survived the national crisis; thirty of his players signed major league contracts between 1929 and 1945. Attendance at home games was nearly universal among the students; most sat on the slope to save the cost of a seat. Another sign of the program's success was the establishment, in 1934, of an annual exhibition game at Fitton Field with the Boston Red Sox. The series was interrupted by the war after the 1942 game, and concluded with a final game in 1947.[70]

Intercollegiate basketball fell victim to the Depression in 1931, when the consultors agreed, as a cost-cutting measure, to substitute intramural basketball for varsity competition. Their decision was also influenced by the lack of proper campus facilities for practice or games. But the trustees retained the services of the head basketball coach, John Reed, for the College coaching staff until his death in 1934. In that year, varsity basketball enjoyed a brief revival under the coaching of "Hop" Riopel, but the sport was dropped again at the end of the season after the team compiled a 3–12 record. Late in 1939, Father Maxwell authorized another revival of intercollegiate basketball and hired assistant football coach Edward "Moose" Krause, a former all-American basketball player at Notre Dame, as head coach. Krause's aim was to start the program slowly, building up to the status of a major sport by 1943, when a projected gymnasium was due to be completed. Krause remained at Holy Cross for three short seasons, posting a record of 11–14. The program remained low-keyed under his leadership; his last two seasons, after American entry into the war, had eleven and nine games, compared with seasons of sixteen to nineteen games in the program's last few years under Coach Reed.[71] During the interwar years Crusader athletes also participated in intercollegiate golf, hockey, and tennis. One of the most successful College competitors was varsity golfer Willie Turnesa '38, who won the U.S. Amateur Championship in 1938. Turnesa also won the British Amateur Championship in 1947, and repeated as U.S. Amateur Champion in 1948.[72] Hockey gained popularity in the late 1920s and was instituted as a varsity sport in the winter of 1927–28. Varsity tennis, dropped between 1937 and 1940, was revived for one season in 1941 and restored permanently as a varsity sport after the war.[73]

Apart from the continuing success of baseball, the most striking development in intercollegiate athletics at Holy Cross during the 1930s and early

70. "Baseball, 1876–1969," ACHC, 18.3A; HD, April 14, 1938; *Tomahawk*, April 25, 1939.

71. HCAA, Basketball Media Guide, 1991–92; *Tomahawk*, December 8, 1939 and January 23, 1940; Worcester *Telegram*, November 27, 1939.

72. Associated Press story, September 18, 1938, ACHC, Locker 8, Scrapbook 29, p. 5; unidentified press clipping, February 27, 1979, in William Turnesa '38, Alumni Files, ACHC, 17.3A.

73. *Tomahawk*, December 6, 1927, and April 29, 1941; *Purple Patcher*, 1937–47.

1940s was the rise of the football program. More than anyone else, Dr. Eddie Anderson was responsible for the change. A native of Iowa and a product of Knute Rockne's program at Notre Dame, Anderson had coached at DePaul University and played professional football for the Chicago Cardinals while he worked on his medical degree. Through a long coaching career, he continued to practice medicine. Anderson stayed at Holy Cross from 1933 to 1938, compiling a record of 47–7–4, including undefeated seasons in 1935 and 1937. He was a devout Catholic whose ideas influenced many of his players; one called him "a fine man who simply practiced virtue while most of my generation was still trying to define it."[74] Anderson was offered an initial contract of $5000, with potential raises to $7000 in the third year—a remarkable concession, given the salary cuts then in force. After the 1938 season, Anderson left Holy Cross for the University of Iowa.[75]

Anderson was succeeded by Joseph Sheeketski, another Rockne veteran. Sheeketski had come to Holy Cross in 1933 as an assistant coach; Father Dolan suggested he apply for the head coach's job because he was "a fine coach and tremendously popular with the players and students."[76] Coach Sheeketski had a successful year in 1939 (7–2), but disappointing seasons the next two years, when his record was 8–9–3. At the end of the 1941 season, Maxwell hired Anthony J. "Ank" Scanlan, who had been a highly successful coach at St. Joseph's High School in Philadelphia. Over three years, Scanlan's teams compiled a record of 16–8–3, but the outbreak of war just after he signed his contract severely limited his availability. He was an executive and part owner of the Philadelphia Asbestos Company, a firm which was a supplier in the war effort. To meet his responsibilities, Scanlan commuted to Worcester on weekends, leaving his assistant coaches to run the practices during the week. By the end of the 1944 season, he could no longer maintain the demanding pace and so resigned.[77]

In excitement and public interest, the football program of the 1930s and 1940s echoed the baseball program of a half century earlier. In 1931, almost the entire Jesuit community joined 58,000 spectators in Cambridge for the Harvard game; in 1933, Senator Walsh addressed the team before the game with Boston College; in 1934, a record crowd of over 23,000 filled Fitton Field for the Colgate game; in 1938, the Crusaders, with a record of 8-1, lost a bid to the Sugar Bowl only because of a one-point loss to Carnegie Tech in mid-season;

74. Tim Cohane, *Great College Football Coaches of the Twenties and Thirties* (New Rochelle: Arlington House, 1973), 6, 9–10. The quotation is from Bob Noble '66.

75. Ibid., 6, 9; Consultors' Minutes, November 13, 1933, ACHC, 19.0.

76. Worcester *Telegram*, September 7, 1939; HCAA, Football Media Guide, 1991.

77. HD, November 28 and December 1, 1941; Trustees' Minutes, November 30, 1944, ACHC, 11.0; Worcester *Telegram*, December 9, 1941, and December 12, 1944.

and in 1939, 41,000 spectators crowded Fenway Park for the Boston College game. In 1941 there was a "glorious triumph" for Holy Cross, 19–13, at LSU in the opening game of the season. The Purple Key Society, the student service organization, relayed scores of the game via telephone, from the teletype at a local radio station to students gathered at Kimball Hall. When the team returned to Worcester two days later, 30,000 people witnessed the victory parade.[78] The greatest individual star in the era was fullback Bill Osmanski '39, who won All-American honors during his senior year and later played for the Chicago Bears. A crowd estimated at 38,000 cheered his last game on November 26, 1938, a 29–7 victory over Boston College. "Osmanski finishes in a blaze of glory," was the general consensus.[79]

Glory is an elusive goal, but "Ank" Scanlan's 1942 team achieved it during an unforgettable game against Boston College at Fenway Park on November 28. As the contest approached, it seemed to be a mismatch. Boston College, favored by fourteen points, was undefeated and had outscored their opponents by 249–19; they were ranked first in the nation and seemed assured of a bid to the Sugar Bowl. Holy Cross had a mediocre record of 4–4–1, but the team had talented players and had improved during the season. The victorious home game against Manhattan on November 21 had drawn a small crowd, but late in the contest, the crowd began chanting "We're gonna beat the Eagles on the 28th," accompanied by the drumbeat of a member of the College band. They continued their chant through the week as many students, and the persistent drummer, attended the practices. In the locker room before the game, Coach Scanlan said, simply, "This is my first visit to Fenway Park. You seniors have been here before." (The seniors had lost three times to Boston College.) Then he led his assistant coaches to the field. For a minute there was absolute silence; then the players erupted with high spirits. There were ample grounds for enthusiasm: besides the traditional rivalry with Boston College and the strong display of support from their classmates, many members of the team, even non-seniors, knew this would be their last game because they had enlisted in the military reserves and expected to be called to active duty within weeks.[80]

That afternoon, Holy Cross achieved a decisive upset, 55–12. Five players scored touchdowns; and captain Ed Murphy kicked seven extra points while providing inspiring leadership on offense and defense. John Grigas also

78. HD, 1931–41; *Tomahawk*, September 30, 1941; unidentified press clipping [1941], ACHC, Locker 8, Scrapbook 36, p. 71.

79. HD, November 26, 1938.

80. Worcester *Telegram*, November 28, 1942. Many details about the 1942 Boston College game may be found in an interview with team manager Edward F. Danowitz '43, conducted by James Phalen '88 on June 11, 1988.

Coach "Ank" Scanlan and the Crusaders celebrate the 55–12 upset victory over Boston College in 1942. Many of the players were about to depart for the war.

played both ways, and was particularly adept at batting down B.C. passes.[81] In the end, their loss proved to be a blessing in disguise: that evening, the Cocoanut Grove, the night club where the canceled Boston College victory celebration was to have been held, burned with a loss of 492 lives.[82] For Holy Cross, the victory brought talk about in bowl games in Chicago or Birmingham. But the loss of players to the armed forces during the Christmas vacation and official requests that non-essential travel be curtailed aborted the effort.[83] Perhaps that was just as well. The victory of November 28, 1942, stood

81. New York *Times*, November 30, 1942; Worcester *Telegram*, November 28, 1942. Football, photocopies of press clippings, 1919–42, ACHC, 18.0-1. The Holy Cross Archives has two scrapbooks of press clippings on the game. ACHC, 18.2.

82. Boston *Globe*, December 1, 1942, and November 28, 1972; Boston *Post*, December 1, 1942.

83. Worcester *Telegram*, November 29, 1942; Phalen interview with Edward Danowitz '43, June 11, 1988; unidentified press clipping [1942] ACHC, Locker 8, Scrapbook 37, p. 128.

alone as a landmark in the school's athletic tradition, a spectacular finale to the football program of the interwar years.

The prominence of athletics re-opened concern in some quarters about athleticism. By the 1935–36 academic year, when Crusader teams were New England champions in football, baseball, track, and golf, the College's public image was strongly connected with its athletic program. In keeping with the spirit of the times, College authorities fostered (or at least tolerated) an atmosphere that associated school spirit with varsity sports. The monetary cost of supporting intercollegiate athletics on such a successful scale made Father Kilroy uneasy. In the spring of 1928 he warned that expenses associated with the athletic program were "quite out of proportion," especially in the number and salaries of coaches. Yet, a few months later, the football coaching staff totaled five and there were plans to involve sixty players.[84] Apparently, the increasing prominence of football and the general excitement about varsity sports posed no further problems for Jesuit authorities until 1940, when provincial James H. Dolan commended the "special effort" being made "to regulate student athletics and other extra-curricular activities."[85] The comment implies that Father Maxwell was taking a more active role than his two predecessors in managing the athletic program. Father Maxwell clarified his athletic policies in the fall of 1941, when, with the peacetime draft in effect and war pending, he limited the number of full athletic scholarships to twenty, at an annual cost of $16,000. No student was to receive more than the cost of room, board, and tuition. The policy allowed the directors of the HCAA to distribute the money as they saw fit, but only with the rector's approval, "since all scholarship grants are under his control."[86] Father Maxwell was also unwilling to bend academic standards for the sake of athletics, determined, he asserted, "to keep our standards where they belong," even at the risk of poorer athletic results.[87] Because of the war, it is impossible to know what the long-term impact of Maxwell's policies might have been.

When war broke out, Holy Cross students echoed other Americans in favoring neutrality. A campus poll taken in the fall of 1939 indicated overwhelming opposition to entering the conflict (98 percent) and strong support for a national referendum before committing troops to Europe, though about 40 percent believed the nation would eventually be drawn into the conflict. About

84. J. M. Kilroy, Memorial of May 13, 1928, Provincial Memorials, ACHC, 19.1-2; Worcester *Gazette*, [Fall, 1928] Locker 8, Scrapbook 22, p. 42

85. J. H. Dolan, Memorial of April 20, 1940, Provincial Memorials, ACHC, 19.1-2.

86. Policy Statement of Joseph Maxwell, September 1, 1941, NEPA, HC-Rector.

87. Maxwell to John Moran, Worcester, November 7, 1941, ACHC, 12.20.

38 percent said they would declare themselves conscientious objectors in the event of a draft.[88] The poll was followed by a lively debate in the *Tomahawk*, arguing the merits of conscientious objection and the issues of the war. The debate became far less hypothetical a year later, when a preparedness coalition in Congress passed the nation's first peacetime draft, requiring all men between the ages of 21 and 35 to register on October 16, 1940, for a year of military training. By then, Father Maxwell had already tried—and failed—to obtain a ROTC program for Holy Cross by seeking assistance from Senator Walsh, who chaired the Naval Affairs Committee of the Senate.[89] In the summer of 1940, funding for the Naval ROTC programs was comparatively meager; and although the senator appealed personally to Naval authorities and received "much encouragement," the effort proved fruitless. Holy Cross, Walsh reported, "would be considered next year."[90] After April of 1941, student deferments were no longer guaranteed. That summer, 21 Holy Cross students were drafted.[91]

These developments heightened the sense of urgency about obtaining a military program. In April of 1941, Senator Walsh approached the Navy Department several times in the interest of Holy Cross. Massachusetts Representative John McCormack, Majority Leader of the House, also promoted the College. Such advocacy helped: on May 22, Holy Cross was included in a group of 22 schools whose applications were accepted.[92] About a month later, C. Julian Wheeler was named to head the Holy Cross program and serve on the faculty as Professor of Naval Science and Tactics. Wheeler's arrival on July 14 constituted the official start of the program, which was designed to qualify college students for commissions in the Navy upon graduation.[93] Participants took courses designated by the Navy Department, including gunnery, ordnance, seamanship, communications, engineering, naval history, military law, naval tactics, Navy regulations, and military drill. All textbooks, uni-

88. *Tomahawk*, November 1, 1938, and October 31, 1939.

89. Navy Reserve Officer Training Corps programs had been established in 1926 at six colleges and universities. As the preparedness movement gained impetus, the Navy Department made inquiries to learn which other schools would be willing and able to host NROTC units. Meagher and Grattan, *Spires*, 216.

90. Maxwell to Walsh, Worcester, June 15, 1940, Walsh to Maxwell, Washington, June 24, 1940, Maxwell to Secretary of War and Maxwell to Secretary of the Navy, Worcester, June 28, 1940, Walsh to Maxwell (telegram), Washington, August 20, 1940, Walsh to Maxwell, Washington, September 6, 1940, ACHC, 12.20.

91. *Tomahawk*, May 6 and October 14, 1941.

92. Walsh to Maxwell, Washington, April 16 and 24, 1941, and McCormack to Maxwell, Washington, June 14, 1941, ACHC, 12.20; Meagher and Grattan, *Spires*, 216.

93. Chester Nimitz to Walsh, Washington, June 26, 1941, ACHC, 12.20; Maxwell to J. H. Dolan, Worcester, July 18, 1941, NEPA, HC-Rector.

forms, and equipment were supplied by the Navy, and Naval officers assigned to the College received faculty appointments. Only freshmen were eligible for admission, but other students could take Naval Science courses by application.[94] By mid-September, the campus was ready: an antiaircraft gun was in place in the basement of the chapel, which had been transformed into an armory and a drill area for use in inclement weather; Campion House and Fenwick Hall were re-opened as dormitories; and a flagpole, complete with signal arms, was erected near Wheeler Hall. A rifle range was later added in lower Carlin Hall. A full quota of 115 students enrolled in NROTC, raising the number of students to 1223, including 939 boarders (Chart 7.4). Before long, a drum and bugle corps and a drill team had been organized within the unit, and an informal mimeographed newsletter, *Salvo* (later, *Beacon*) made its first appearance on October 28.[95]

"War with Japan," Father Francis Toolin wrote in the House Diary on December 7, 1941. A few days later, Father Maxwell addressed the student body on the relationship between education and leadership: "The country is in need of educated men, and you are destined to be leaders." He told the students that they would eventually be needed in the war effort, but that they would serve the country best at present by staying at Holy Cross. Clearly, he was worried that voluntary enlistments and the draft would depopulate the school; but there was also wisdom in his words: full-scale mobilization would take time, and an educated officers' corps is an asset to a fighting force. Just before Christmas, Maxwell sent every student information on the V-5 and V-7 military programs: V-7 allowed recent college graduates to join the Naval Reserve, making them draft exempt until they could be assigned to midshipmen's schools; V-5 allowed students to continue academic work as reservists before entering the Naval Air Corps.[96] Among the students, enthusiasm for the war effort was genuine, but, to judge from the *Tomahawk*, the abrupt change in the national mood did not completely displace previous interests. Two days after Pearl Harbor, the headline announced Coach Scanlan's appointment and the issue contained considerable speculation about the war's impact on intercollegiate sports. Faculty and administrators had more pressing concerns, as Father Toolin recorded on the last day of the year: "The outlook for 1942 looks grim. We shall feel the effects of war during the coming year. . . . May God in His Providence

94. Meagher and Grattan, *Spires*, 216–17.

95. HD September-October, 1941; *Tomahawk*, November 4, 1941; Worcester *Telegram*, February 22, 1942; Meagher and Grattan, *Spires*, 217.

96. *Tomahawk*, December 12, 1941; HD, December 22, 1941.

be good to Our Country and Our Society, to our schools and our loved ones."[97]

The war's effects were swift in coming. In January of 1942, the chauffeur's position was eliminated; a few months later, the Jesuit community's small Buick was put in storage, and the large Buick was traded for a station wagon to transport servicemen to the Grafton airport for flying lessons. Sugar rationing was introduced in March, and gasoline rationing in May. By October, an Honor Roll of Holy Cross men in the armed forces had been posted in the O'Kane lobby. When classes resumed after Christmas of 1941, about thirty freshmen responded to a call for more NROTC members and Father Maxwell added two young Jesuits to the faculty to cover the increased need for mathematics instructors.[98] Meanwhile, students continued to enlist in the armed forces and to be called to active duty. Enrollment in the spring of 1941 dropped by about ⅓, and Campion House and the Fenwick dormitory were closed again as student residences. Many students joined the reserves. In one ceremony in March, 31 students (including seven football players and the student manager) enlisted in the Marine reserves, with the understanding that they would be trained as officers as soon as they finished their degrees. By June, eighty students were participating in the V-7 program; by the fall of 1942, over 200 students belonged to the NROTC unit.[99]

The academic calendar was quickly revised to accelerate progress toward graduation. Four days after Pearl Harbor, the trustees also voted that "financial adjustment in student tuition fees and other expenses be provided and[,] without relaxing academic standards and requirements, such changes be made as deemed necessary in the war emergency."[100] Father Maxwell shortened the Christmas vacation to nine days and advanced graduation for the Class of '42 to May 5th. A summer session, running from May 7 to July 3, was designed to allow members of the Class of 1943 to graduate at the end of the fall semester; the current sophomore and freshman classes were similarly advanced, and incoming students had their course compressed to three years. Students in the summer session attended classes on an 18-hour per week schedule; able-bodied students were also required to participate in calisthenics and intramural sports for 7½ hours per week.[101] In the fall of 1942, seniors were given oral exams be-

97. HD, December 31, 1941.   98. HD, 1942; *Tomahawk*, January 13, 1942.

99. HD, February 3 and 6, 1942; *Tomahawk*, January 13 and March 24, 1942; Worcester *Telegram*, March 24, June 2, and October 13, 1942.

100. Trustees' Minutes, December 11, 1941, ACHC, 11.0.

101. C. Julian Wheeler to Chief of Naval Personnel, Worcester, July 9, 1942, ACHC, 12.20; *Tomahawk*, December 16, 1941, January 13 and 27, 1942; Worcester *Telegram*, June 2, 1942.

fore Christmas, in the expectation that some would be called to active duty almost immediately. By the time of their advanced graduation date on February 13, the Class of 1943, which had begun with about 400 members in fall of 1939, had only 220 members at school. The College awarded degrees to all who had completed at least half of the final semester's work, but the graduation was canceled at the request of the Office of Defense Transportation. For the graduates still at the College, the only ceremony was a banquet in Kimball Hall, which featured speeches reminding them that the discipline they had learned at Holy Cross would serve them well against the enemy. In 1968, a commemorative graduation was conducted at their silver anniversary reunion.[102]

By February of 1943, more than half of the College's students were on active military duty in the ROTC and V-7 programs. Meanwhile, in February of 1942, the Navy started the V-I program to remedy deficiencies that had cropped up in the V-7 plan. Participants were required to take one year each of college mathematics and physical science and to participate in physical training. Holy Cross was authorized to open the V-1 program to sophomores who passed an exam on May 1, 1942.[103] These programs led to extensive curricular revision. For juniors in war-related programs, philosophy was cut from seven to four hours per week; third-year Greek was dropped in cases where it conflicted with the new courses; in some instances, seniors took only six hours of philosophy instead of the usual ten. The daily order was also adjusted to accommodate 8:30 A.M. classes; students now rose at 5 A.M.[104] Meanwhile, *Tomahawk* editors devoted abundant space to the war effort: campus recruiting, the College military units, Holy Cross men in the armed forces, and other stories about the war. The paper ran a weekly feature, "Army-Navy News," with information about the armed forces—dates of physical examinations, changes in enlistment regulations, and other items touching on the war and the draft.

Father Maxwell and Captain Wheeler cooperated in setting high academic standards for the military program. In January 1942, Wheeler formally recommended that Maxwell disenroll fifteen ROTC students with low grades and another student who had cheated during a quiz. Afterwards, Wheeler addressed the Navy men like a latter-day George Fenwick on the importance of application: "Neither you nor anyone else can learn enough to win a com-

102. *Tomahawk*, February 9 and 16, 1943; Worcester *Telegram*, February 13, 1943, and June 9, 1968; unidentified press clipping [1943], ACHC, Locker 8, Scrapbook 38, p. 1; Danowitz interview, June 11, 1988.

103. James G. Schneider, *The Navy V-12 Program: Leadership for a Lifetime* (Boston: Houghton Mifflin Co., 1987), 1–2; *Tomahawk*, January 13 and March 31, 1942; unidentified press clipping [1943], ACHC, Locker 8, Scrapbook 38, p. 1.

104. HD, September 10 and October 25, 1942; *Tomahawk*, January 13 and 27, 1942.

mission in the Navy by simply wanting it. You have got to work for it, and if you don't work for it you won't get it. Lead is a vital war material, but it is useless in the seat of your pants." Their work at Holy Cross, Wheeler insisted, was vital to the war effort because the armed forces badly needed officers: "Your life and the lives of all the members of your crew will be dependent upon how well you learned the subjects which we are doing our best to teach you."[105] After nearly a year and a half of service at Holy Cross, Captain Wheeler was relieved on December 18, 1942, by Captain Guy E. Davis.[106]

As national mobilization intensified throughout 1942, college administrators everywhere worried about enrollment. At Holy Cross, the number stood at 1142 in September, down about 70 from the previous year; but the February graduation in 1943 meant that Wheeler Hall would soon be vacant. In October, Father Maxwell corresponded with Senator Walsh about his desire to "interest some branch of the Armed Forces in a building or two at Holy Cross.[107] There were negotiations about using Wheeler Hall to train Military Police, but the plan fell through. In November, Navy officials inspected the campus as a possible site for an Aviation Ground School, but that plan was rejected because Holy Cross lacked a swimming pool. By then, Father Maxwell had been hospitalized with a bleeding ulcer.[108]

As he mended, the College's fortunes improved, thanks to President Roosevelt, who had requested the War and Navy departments in October to "have an immediate study made as to the highest utilization of the American colleges" by the armed services.[109] In Washington, Representative McCormack lobbied the president about the plight of colleges without large endowments, and John J. Hagerty '18, a lawyer who worked at the Boston office of the Reconstruction Finance Corporation, pressed the need of Holy Cross with Marvin MacIntyre, the president's appointment secretary and general assistant.[110] In December, Hagerty confided to Maxwell that a new, still unnamed

105. Captain C. Julian Wheeler, address on discipline and study, undated [1942], ACHC, 12.20; Wheeler to Maxwell, January 10 and January 23, 1942, ACHC, 12.20.

106. Meagher and Grattan, *Spires*, 217.

107. HD, September 11, 1942; Maxwell to David I. Walsh, Worcester, October 19, 1942, ACHC, 12.20.

108. Memo of Julian Wheeler to Chief of Naval Personnel, November 13, 1942, QR4/NC1 (HC) P11-1, no. 482, and Maxwell to John McCormack, Worcester, November 16, 1942, ACHC, 12.20; HD, October 21–31, November 30, and December 8, 1942; confidential memo from Maxwell to J. H. Dolan, [n.p.], December 11, 1942, NEPA, HC-Rector.

109. Roosevelt's letter was dated October 15. Cited in Schneider, *Navy V-12*, 3.

110. John McCormack to John J. Hagarty [sic], Washington, November 10, 1942, and John J. Hagerty to Maxwell, [Boston], November 13, 1942, ACHC, 12.20.

program was in the works to "put high school graduates on active duty in colleges with pay, and their tuition would be paid [by the government], and arrangements would be made with the colleges for instruction in courses as laid down by the Navy Department, leading to officers' commissions." Participants would study languages, American history, mathematics, physics, chemistry, and specific Navy courses.[111] The V-12 Program was formally announced on December 17. Two days later, Navy Secretary Frank Knox noted: "We will give special consideration to the smaller colleges whose financial resources are so meager that their existence may be threatened by war."[112]

Over 1600 institutions applied for V-12 programs, stimulating intense competition. In January, Father Maxwell reported his anxiety to Senator Walsh as he faced the prospect of an enrollment below 700. But he needn't have worried. In this instance, the College fit the program's categories and it was well connected politically. During the spring, 131 schools were selected for Navy V-12 units; but Holy Cross was one of five schools (the others were Baylor, the University of California, the University of North Carolina, and Notre Dame) that received early notification in February. The program was slated to begin on July 1, with about 600 participants at Holy Cross: high school graduates from the enlisted ranks, transfers from the old V-7 and V-1 programs, and Marine reservists who had become eligible for active duty when the draft age was lowered to 18 in November 1942.[113] The program's goal was to build upon existing programs at the selected institutions, making substitutions only to include subjects essential for Naval officers' training. Within broad guidelines, schools were allowed to select textbooks and course contents and to determine a student's academic standing. The Navy established a uniform calendar for V-12 schools: four-month terms would begin on July 1, November 1, and March 1. Students carried a workload of 17 hours in a work week of 5½ days, plus regular physical training. Candidates for deck officer were allowed no electives. Holy Cross was designated to offer a basic program for deck officers, plus a program for pre-medical and pre-dental candidates.[114]

111. McCormack sent a confidential memo he had received from Captain Forrest Lake of the Navy Department's Bureau of Personnel, dated December 11, to John Hagerty on December 11 as "personal and confidential." Hagerty then forwarded the information to Maxwell on December 14. ACHC, 12.20. By then, Maxwell was already aware of the program. Maxwell to Dolan, December 12, 1942, NEPA, HC-Rector.

112. Schneider, Navy V-12, 5. Knox was quoted in the Des Moines Register, December 19, 1942, cited in Schneider, Navy V-12, 10.

113. Maxwell to Hagerty, Worcester, May 19, 1943, ACHC, 12.20; Schneider, Navy V-12, 10–14; HD, February 13, 1943; Tomahawk, February 16, and March 2, 1943.

114. Schneider, Navy V-12, 7, 57; Tomahawk, April 20 and May 18, 1943. For an outline of the V-12 curriculum, see Schneider, Navy V-12, 58. According to Schneider, the program drew from a

A contracting committee from the Navy visited the campus in June to inspect the premises and settle the rate of reimbursement; eventually the parties agreed on a monthly maintenance fee of $35.49 per man for room and board, physical training instruction, and medical service. Salaries of instructors, including Jesuits, were set at about $3500 per year; the Navy would pay a percentage of the salary based on the faculty member's teaching load and his ratio of Navy to civilian students. The contract provided the College with income of $670,000 in fiscal year 1944 (including $259,000 in student maintenance fees and $247,000 in instructional fees), and contributed to a budget surplus of $67,000. Income from Navy contracts declined in subsequent years as the program was gradually reduced toward the end of the war.[115] The trustees agreed that students who completed eight semesters of the V-12 program would receive a B.S. degree, with a Naval Science major; students in the pre-medical and pre-dental programs who completed six semesters at Holy Cross would receive the appropriate degree after presenting evidence of successful completion of one year of medical school. Father Maxwell insisted that the traditional Jesuit pattern of character formation would apply to the Navy men.[116] Yet, there was one change: the religious diversity of the Navy men precluded compulsory Mass. The Navy adjusted its schedule to leave Catholic students free to attend morning Mass at 7:00. Religious services were held for non-Catholics at the same time, probably for the first time in the history of the school. Balfour Brickner, later rabbi at Steven Wise Congregation in New York City, was among the Jewish students at Holy Cross.[117]

The program opened formally on July 1, 1943, with 621 trainees living in Wheeler, Carlin, and Beaven Halls. A quota of 300 was assigned to the Basic (Deck Officer) training program, 133 to the Pre-medical/Pre-dental program; and 188 to the NROTC program. All took physics, chemistry, mathematics,

---

variety of sources. Most of those who would eventually become V-12s were formerly in V-1 or V-7 programs, or in the Marines' III (d) reserve program. While they had originally been promised that they would be able to remain in college until graduation, the reduction in the draft age from 20 to 18 made these reservists candidates for active duty. Other men were drawn from the V-5 aviation cadet program, and from 17–19 year-old high school graduates, some of whom were enrolled in college, but not in a reserve program. Ibid., 67.

115. HD, June 24 and November 8, 1943; Schneider, *Navy V-12*, 31–35. Income from the V-12 program was $517,000 in FY 1945 and $369,000 in FY 1946. Trustees Records, Series 4: Financial Records, Box 2, ACHC 11.0. In 1943, the Navy proposed a flat-rate salary of $3500 per faculty member, or a sliding scale ranging from $5500 for department heads to $2000 for instructors, the Navy percentage to be computed as indicated above. The documents do not specify which formula was used at Holy Cross. Maxwell to J. H. Dolan, Worcester, October 9, 1943, NEPA, HC-Rector.

116. *Tomahawk*, May 25, 1943; Trustees' Minutes, May 17, 1944, ACHC, 11.0

117. Schneider, *Navy V-12*, 370.

The Naval V-12 Program during World War II: the Holy Cross unit parades through the gate on Linden Lane in 1945.

mechanical drawing, U.S. Naval history, Naval administration, Naval organization, and a modern language—Japanese, German, or French. Japanese was taught by Father F. Everett Briggs, a Maryknoll priest who was one of the few professors of Japanese in the entire V-12 program. Some of the Jesuit faculty, especially the younger men, studied new topics so that they could teach courses in mathematics, mechanical drawing, and science that were outside their customary fields. The Jesuit catalog for 1944 listed ten scholastics at Holy Cross, all but one of whom were assigned to teach mathematics and/or to work as laboratory assistants in chemistry and physics. Every evening, Father Thomas Quigley, a professor of physics and mathematics, and scholastic James J. Dolan prepared the young Jesuit instructors for the next day's lessons. After two four-month semesters, the V-12 trainees took a comprehensive exam to determine which of three possible tracks they were to follow: remaining at Holy Cross, transferring to another school, or (if they tested poorly) transferring to the fleet. Very weak students were dropped from the program after the first four-month session.[118]

Four days after the first V-12 students reported to Holy Cross , they were joined by 250 civilians, including about 60 freshmen; all non-military students lived in Alumni Hall and pursued the traditional course of studies on the accelerated basis instituted by the Navy. At the end of October 1943, 117 members of the Class of 1944 graduated, anticipating their normal graduation by more than six months. Their places were filled in the November term by 75 new V-12 students and 30 new civilians. The pattern continued in 1944: on June 29, the 27 civilian members of the Class of 1945 graduated almost a year ahead of schedule; and in October over 100 members of the original V-12 class departed for midshipman and pre-midshipman schools.[119] The calendar created a pattern of frequent arrivals and departures, but overall enrollment stayed between about 750 and 850 for most of the war. The number of students reached a low point early in 1945, when the Navy began phasing the program out, then rose as the first veterans began to arrive (Chart 7.4).

Despite the continuance of the civilian program, the Naval programs dominated the campus atmosphere. Military inspections and commissioning ceremonies became important events. Father Maxwell beamed with pride after a successful inspection in September of 1943. A few days later, there was a Naval review on Fitton Field, followed by a military ball at the Bancroft Hotel.[120] The commissioning ceremony on February 27, 1944, was preceded by a Solemn Military High Mass with sermon by a military chaplain. Senator

Chart 7.4 Enrollment, 1941–1946

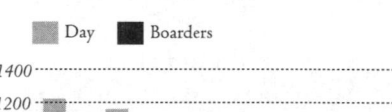

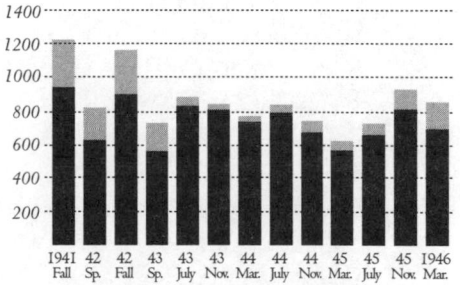

118. Worcester *Telegram,* October 3, 1943, and undated clipping [July, 1943], Locker 8, Scrapbook 32, p. 91; Joseph J. LaBran, Personal Interview, August 14, 1993; Eugene Harrington and Gerald Kinsella, Personal Interview, August 29, 1993; Fr. Thomas Quigley, Faculty File, ACHC, 14.8-1; Schneider, *Navy V-12,* 182; Meagher and Grattan, *Spires,* 218. Father Maxwell reported that it took a week to adjust the faculty teaching load for the November 1943 term. Maxwell to Dolan, Worcester, October 9, 1943. NEPA, HC-Rector.

119. HD, July 1 and November 11, 1943, March 1, 1944; *Tomahawk,* November 3 and 10, 1943, March 22 and October 18, 1944, and June 1944 Commencement Issue.

120. Maxwell to J. H. Dolan, Worcester, September 8, 1943, NEPA, HC-Rector; HD, September 11, 1943.

Walsh spoke at the ceremony, and Captain Davis was awarded an honorary Doctor of Naval Science degree as he departed for a new assignment. Davis was succeeded by Captain F. C. Sachse, who remained for a year, until relieved by Captain E. P. Hylant in March of 1946. Two Navy WAVES, Yeomen [sic] third class Eleanor M. Walsh and Mary E. Tobin, lived off-campus and helped administer the program from offices in the library.[121] Even the *Tomahawk* caught the spirit: events were listed by the 24-hour clock; stairways became ladders; students were referred to as hands. But the paper's editors did not neglect the needs of civilian students. A "Commencement Issue" of the paper took the place of a yearbook for the Class of 1945 in June of 1944, carrying pictures of the 27 graduates, the class history, and several stories about the graduation.

Since they were eligible for varsity teams, the V-12 men rescued the 1943 baseball season, which had originally been canceled. The following year, the team had a season of nine games; in 1945, they played a much fuller schedule, compiling a record of 14–2.[122] In basketball, "Hop" Riopel coached during three jury-rigged seasons that ranged from six to fourteen games and included opponents representing the Norton Company, the Southbridge Knights of Columbus, Camp Edwards, and Cushing General Hospital, in addition to traditional collegiate rivals. Alvin "Doggie" Julian came from Muhlenberg College to succeed Riopel as head basketball coach in 1945. The Crusaders compiled a record of 12-3 in Julian's first year and George Kaftan received All-American honors.[123] The V-12 program also provided a boost for Holy Cross football. John "Ox" DaGrosa, at Holy Cross since 1942 as backfield coach and chief assistant of "Ank" Scanlan, was named head football coach in 1945 and took his 8–2 team to the Orange Bowl against the University of Miami on January 1, 1946. But the excitement of being the first Crusader bowl team was dampened by the outcome. With the scored tied at 6-6 and two seconds left, Holy Cross gambled on victory with a pass play. The pass was intercepted and run back 89 yards for a touchdown as the time ran out. Final score: Miami 13, Holy Cross 6.[124]

As the war drew to a close, the number of V-12 students shrank from 423 in the March term of 1944 to 102 in March of 1946. Shortly after V-J Day, the College's NROTC quota dropped from 550 to 362; Carlin Hall was now re-

121. *Tomahawk*, February 16, 1944; HD, February 27, 1944; Schneider, *Navy V-12*, 370.
122. *Tomahawk*, March 16 and May 25, 1943; Worcester *Gazette*, July 23, 1943; Holy Cross Baseball Media Guide, 1993.
123. Holy Cross Basketball Media Guide, 1991–92.
124. *Tomahawk*, January 9, 1946; HD, January 1, 1946.

opened to civilian students.[125] By then, the first war veterans were trickling into the College—seven among the 170 who enrolled in July of 1945. The accelerated schedule officially ended with the formal de-activation of the V-12 program on July 1, 1946. Until then, the annual pattern of three graduations and three incoming classes continued. On June 26, 1946, the 138 civilian students and officers who participated in the College's 100th Commencement were the largest class to graduate under the accelerated program.[126]

Inevitably, the celebrations at war's end had an edge of sadness: of the 3900 Holy Cross alumni, students, and faculty who served in the war, 109 gave their lives. The dead included Leo W. Shields, a former Assistant Professor of Economics, and Lt. John Vincent Power '41, who was posthumously awarded the Congressional Medal of Honor for "a remarkable feat of daring and heroism" in which he single-handedly destroyed a Japanese pillbox in the Marshall Islands. President Roosevelt presented the medal to Powers's mother at the White House in August 1944; later, a statue was erected in his honor near the Worcester City Hall.[127] Twenty-two former Jesuit faculty members served as military chaplains; among them, Father Joseph T. O'Callahan, a member of the Mathematics Department before the war, received the first Congressional Medal of Honor ever awarded to a chaplain, for heroism aboard the aircraft carrier *U.S.S. Franklin*, after it was struck by a Japanese dive bomber. Father O'Callahan was honored again in 1968, when the Navy commissioned a destroyer escort, the U.S.S. *O'Callahan*.[128]

Despite the war's enormous impact on the College, there were opportunities that could be exploited without jeopardizing the military programs. In September 1943, seeing a need to bring local union and management representatives together "to help them in collective bargaining relations," Father Thomas Shortell opened The Holy Cross Institute of Industrial Relations. A veteran teacher of courses in ethics and in labor problems, Shortell was convinced that Holy Cross could provide a public service at a time when labor-management relations were new and representatives on both sides were uncertain about productive approaches. At first, the institute offered evening classes

125. Schneider, *Navy V-12*, 370; William Healy to McEleney, Worcester, October 11, 1945, NEPA, HC-Rector; HD, October 10, 1945. The latter source fixes the ROTC quota at 312.

126. *Tomahawk*, September 13, 1944, and March 14, 1945; unidentified press clipping [June, 1946], ACHC, Locker 8, Scrapbook 41, p. 104; Meagher and Grattan, *Spires*, 218–19.

127. *Tomahawk*, September 13, 1944; Meagher and Grattan, *Spires*, 219.

128. *Tomahawk*, May 23, 1945, and January 23, 1946; Worcester *Telegram*, July 14, 1968; Meagher and Grattan, *Spires*, 219. Father O'Callahan published an account of his experiences under the title, *I Was Chaplain on the* Franklin (New York: The Macmillan Co., 1956).

in three groupings: principle courses (Ethics and Applied Logic), fact courses (Current Labor Problems, Elementary and Applied Economics, Labor Law), and instrument, or tool, courses (Public Speaking, Parliamentary Procedure, Correct English). Instructors volunteered their time and were drawn from the College faculty and from the business, labor, and government sectors of the community. The Institute remained a part of the College's outreach to the local community until 1984.[129] The latter years of the war brought two guest lecturers to campus, participants in a program sponsored by the Carnegie Endowment for International Peace to promote international understanding. Professor Ignacio M. deLojendio of the University of Seville visited several classes in April of 1944 and offered a general lecture, "In the Face of a New Era." Prince Hubertus zu Loewenstein, described by a Carnegie representative as "the ablest foreign scholar resident in the United States," taught history from September 1945 until the following spring.[130]

The urgency of the military programs deprived Holy Cross of two important opportunities during World War II: the celebration of the College centennial, and the successful conclusion of an associated fund-raising campaign to keep the building program alive. Father Dolan had initiated discussion of a celebration and fund drive with his consultors in 1938: the drive would support a new building program encompassing a gymnasium, faculty residence, and science building. The plan was made public in June 1939; the three buildings were to be the gift of the alumni association in honor of the centennial. The drive was formally opened in January of 1940, with a goal of raising $1 million by 1943. Instead of hiring professional fund raisers, Maxwell chose to work through alumni chairmen. The plan was ambitious, but the prospect of constructing three buildings for one million dollars was unrealistic: in 1939, Maginnis and Walsh estimated that a gymnasium alone would cost $729,000.[131]

Maxwell, to sustain the campaign, undertook an alumni tour that brought him as far as St. Paul and Washington, D.C. The initial organizational phase,

129. "The Holy Cross Institute of Industrial Relations" (undated pamphlet), ACHC, 12.24; HD, September 6 and 14, 1943. In its latter years, the Institute was administered by Professor Jerome J. Judge of the Economics Department, who retired in 1980 but continued to direct the program until 1984. ACHC, Institute of Industrial Relations, 14.6-1.

130. *Tomahawk*, April 5, 1944; Nicholas Murray Butler to Maxwell, New York, March 10, 1945, ACHC, 12.20; "Loewenstein," Individual Faculty Files, ACHC, 14.8; HD, September 15 and November 22, 1945.

131. Consultors' Minutes, November 13, 1938, ACHC, 19.0; Maginnis and Walsh to Maxwell, Boston, November 29, 1939, ACHC, 16.1BU-1; HD, January 7, 1940; Worcester *Telegram*, January 8, 1940; *Tomahawk*, March 21, 1940; unidentified press clipping [June 1939], Locker 8, Scrapbook 29, p. 124.

which lasted through 1940, was beset at times with resistance from alumni who would have preferred that some of the proceeds be reserved for scholarships.[132] Collection and solicitation began in earnest in 1941. By May, Worcester donors had pledged $93,000 toward a goal of $165,000. But elsewhere, results were disappointing: in July, Father Maxwell admitted that the drive "has not met with the success . . . we anticipated."[133] Undoubtedly, preoccupation with preparedness, and then American entry into the war, hampered the organizers in generating momentum. The fund drive limped along for a while after Pearl Harbor. Late in 1942, Judge Hanify persuaded Joseph Kennedy to contribute $5000 "to be credited to his family"; and William O'Neil '07, head of the General Tire and Rubber Company, sent $5000, asking that there be no publicity. Eventually the drive netted $240,200.[134]

By the summer of 1941, steel was scarce and it seemed unlikely that building materials would be available for some time. To salvage part of the plan, the trustees sought approval to build only the "most useful" part of the building—a swimming pool, with handball and squash courts—that would require less steel. The College had $105,000 at hand for the project; since building costs were rising at an annual rate of 6 percent, moving ahead with what was possible at the moment would save money in the future. But approval was withheld: the times were deemed too uncertain. At the end of August, Father Maxwell informed Charles Maginnis of the decision to halt the project "in order that we may await for [sic] further funds and more auspicious times."[135] Afterwards, the centennial of the College passed almost unnoticed. On Tuesday, November 2, 1943, the house diarist wrote, simply: "The College is 100 years old today." Two days later, the Jesuits held a feast to commemorate the milestone.[136]

The opening of the V-12 program revived hopes for a new gymnasium. In September of 1943, Father Maxwell explored plans to build a cement block building west of Carlin Hall large enough to house two basketball courts. It would also serve as an indoor drill area for the military units. The need, he told

132. HD, 1940; John Gilmartin to Charles Strome, [Waterbury], October 31, 1940, Strome to Maxwell, November 4, 1940; Maxwell to Gilmartin, Worcester, November 14, 1940, ACHC, 12.20. In the last letter, Maxwell requested the Holy Cross Club of Waterbury to "confine all alumni activities of the next three years, which are held under the auspices of the College, to the Building Fund."

133. HD, May 1941; Maxwell to Thomas Markham, Worcester, July 17, 1941.

134. HD, December 24, 1942; O'Neil to Maxwell, Akron, December 23, 1942, ACHC, 12.20; Financial Statement, June 1953, Trustees' Records, Series 4: Financial Records, ACHC, 11.0.

135. Maxwell to J. H. Dolan, Worcester, August 5, 1941, NEPA, HC-Rector; Maxwell to Maginnis, Worcester, August 30 and September 19, 1941, ACHC, 16.1BU-1.

136. HD, November 2 and 4, 1943.

Jesuit authorities in seeking approval for the plan, was "very keen"; and he wanted to hold the confidence of the alumni: "I have always said that it would be the next building because it is so much needed." Jesuit approval arrived in early 1944, authorizing construction on a pay-as-you-go basis.[137] But nothing further was accomplished that year. The records offer no explanation for the delay; perhaps building materials were again the issue. With the war's end approaching in 1945, Father Maxwell made his final effort to erect the gymnasium. He again asked Senator Walsh for help, disclosing how intent he was on bringing the project to fruition: "If this project could be accomplished, I feel that my six years as Rector would not have been in vain."[138] But his hopes were frustrated again; the gymnasium became the responsibility of his successor, William J. Healy, when the rectorship changed hands on August 19.

No doubt, Father Maxwell was keenly disappointed at his inability to construct a gymnasium, but his service as rector had hardly been "in vain," as he suggested so disconsolately. He provided competent, imaginative leadership during the war years and earlier in his term, when the accreditation report of 1938 was still on the table. His immediate predecessors, John Fox and Francis Dolan, had constructed two buildings and kept the College prosperous during hard times; but to Maxwell fell a different set of challenges: representing the spirit of the College to students on the verge of being drafted, to Navy men assigned to Holy Cross, to military officials in Washington and in Worcester, to alumni at war, and to faculty whose contribution to the war was an exhausting commitment to learn day by day the subjects they taught on the morrow. As head of the College, Father Maxwell also had to articulate a vision for the future. He had to find a way to draw the old classical humanism into the broader context of the liberal arts and to define that approach as a necessary component of the nation's educational pattern in the coming postwar world. Speaking on the topic in 1943 to the New England Classical Association, he reminded his audience that, beyond the immediate advantages offered by the sciences during times of war, the humanities defend and preserve "the essential America" by conveying aesthetic and moral values that stand in contrast to totalitarian ideology. The liberal arts, he asserted, provide a richer life, tolerance for other people and cultures, and the "highest development of self" in service to others.[139] In the years ahead, that affirmation of liberal education became a defining standard for Holy Cross.

137. Maxwell to J. H. Dolan, Worcester, September 19, 1943, and January 3, 1944, NEPA, HC-Rector; Dolan to Maxwell, Boston, February 19, 1944, ACHC, 16.1BU-1.

138. Maxwell to Walsh, Worcester, February 12, 1945, ACHC, 12.20.

139. Joseph Maxwell, "Address to the New England Classical Association," March 26, 1943, ACHC, 12.20.

CHAPTER EIGHT

Postwar Challenges, 1946–1960

W HEN WILLIAM J. HEALY assumed the presidency of Holy Cross in September of 1945, he anticipated that his first major task would be to return the campus to a normal peacetime operation.[1] Yet, during his administration—and those of his successors, John A. O'Brien (1948–54) and William A. Donaghy (1954–60)—the question of what constituted a normal operation proved difficult to answer. The crush of returning veterans and the burgeoning popularity of undergraduate education necessitated expansion of the physical plant, and, despite misgivings, prompted a permanent increase in enrollment. The growing professionalization of American college and university faculties challenged administrators to upgrade the largely Jesuit faculty and to extend more responsibility to the laymen who were being drawn into the operation. For a time, success in athletics, the easy connection between active Catholicism and anti-communism during the Cold War, and enduring alumni loyalty fostered during four years on Mount Saint James, promoted the assumption that minor adjustments could meet any challenge. But the difficulties increased: the quality and morale of the faculty became a serious issue; the inability of the Jesuits to sustain a larger, more sophisticated enterprise became clear; and the context that supported the College's self-confident Catholic identity began to shift. By 1960, thoughtful observers were suggesting that the old approaches were themselves inadequate to maintain the tradition of excellence. Contrary to expectation, there was no return to normal after the war, only a slow accretion of evidence that the second Holy Cross had about run its course.

William Healy was only 38 when he assumed office. A native of Boston,

1. *Tomahawk*, September 19, 1945.

Healy entered the Society in 1925 and was ordained in 1935. After ordination, he taught English and served as prefect of studies at the Jesuit house of formation in the Berkshires, where a four-year program of academics and spiritual formation was given to most new Jesuits. He also helped launch the Cranwell School in 1939 and Fairfield Prep a few years later.[2] In 1945, he enrolled in the summer school at Cornell University, responding to the situation in letters sprinkled with humor. "The level of the classes is quite a bit under the floor," he wrote; one teacher was "an old geezer . . . , departing, I wouldn't be surprised, for a date with the embalmer." As a Jesuit, he felt his clerical status keenly: "It's a funny place here for a priest (and I'm not sensitive). Not exactly hostile, at least not openly. But I count my change carefully, all the time." At Cornell, his commitment to Jesuit education was re-awakened: "No doubt I am reactionary and narrow-minded but every contact I have with these other systems of education fills me with pride for our own. All they have is money."[3] By the time he wrote those letters, he was the first choice to succeed Joseph Maxwell at Holy Cross. Healy's personal qualities made him a popular leader, and his youthfulness made him energetic. During the first year of his presidency, Navy programs provided most of the agenda, but he was planning for an influx of veterans and hoping to construct the long-postponed gymnasium.[4]

The enrollment of veterans was related to the passing of the Servicemen's Readjustment Act of 1944, commonly called the GI Bill of Rights. Its educational features gave a monthly stipend and full tuition at any approved school to academically qualified veterans who had served at least 90 days and had not been dishonorably discharged. Primarily intended as a response to the veterans' lobby and as a means of cushioning the economic impact of demobilization, the GI Bill nevertheless had a dramatic impact on higher education, providing what one analyst called "an unprecedented Federal subsidy to education."[5] Altogether, 7.8 million people, or just over half of World War II veterans, took education or training under the GI Bill. This influx altered the tone of campus life, because veterans were the majority of college students in the United States between 1946 and 1948; as David Riesman remembered,

2. Autobiographical sketch in Healy's hand, ACHC, 12.21.
3. Healy to John J. McEleney, Ithaca, [undated] and July 6, 1945, NEPA, HC Rector.
4. *Tomahawk*, September 19, 1945.
5. David Riesman, *On Higher Education: The Academic Enterprise in an Era of Rising Student Consumerism* (San Francisco: Jossey-Bass Publishers, 1980), 45; Lawrence A. Cremin, *American Education: The Metropolitan Experience, 1876–1980* (New York: Harper and Row, 1988), 250. See also David B. Ross, *Preparing for Ulysses: Politics and Veterans during World War II* (New York: Columbia University Press, 1969), 89–124.

they "brought to the classroom a kind of sober realism," and forced some bending of regulations in recognition of their status.[6]

Beyond the GI Bill, other factors were driving college applications up-wards—the egalitarian spirit associated with the New Deal and the war, the economic value of college degrees, and the general prosperity of a society that could spare more of its young adults for additional education. In 1946, Harry Truman appointed a commission to study higher education. Its report, *Higher Education for American Democracy*, argued that higher education should no longer be conceived of as the province of the intellectual elite, but as an avenue of opportunity that would permit each American to be educated to the full extent of his or her capacity. The commission proposed a national goal of raising undergraduate enrollment from 2.3 million in 1947 to 4.6 million in 1960. The short-range impact of the report was slight, since Congress ignored proposals for federally backed, need-based scholarships and for the elimination of discrimination in education; but the long-range impact was important enough to make it "a turning point in American conceptions of higher learning," in Lawrence Cremin's estimate. College enrollments in the United States climbed to 3.2 million in 1959 as the percentage of college students within the eligible age group rose, and then to 12.1 million by 1980. By then, many Americans had accepted the notion of higher education as a reasonable expectation for qualified persons.[7]

At Holy Cross, the effort to prepare for the veterans began in the fall of 1944, when the trustees authorized Father Maxwell "to sign the contract with the U.S. Veterans Administration for the education of veterans of World War II at Holy Cross."[8] The 1945 catalog specified that veterans with three years of high school (including three years of English and two of mathematics) could submit to a series of tests and interviews to demonstrate their capacity for college work. Veterans with course deficiencies were given a "matriculation course" of remedial and refresher work before being placed in the appropriate curriculum. In February of 1946, the province prefect of studies directed that admissions preference was to be given to previously enrolled veterans and to incoming non-transfer freshmen, with particular attention accorded to the

6. Riesman, *Higher Education*, 46–47; Horowitz, *Campus Life*, 185; Ross, *Ulysses*, 124. The quotation is from Francis J. Brown, "Post-War Development," in P. F. Valentine, ed., *The American College* (New York: Philosophical Library, Inc.), 41.

7. Cremin, *Metropolitan Experience*, 251–52; Oscar and Mary Handlin, *The American College and American Culture: Socialization as a Function of Higher Education* (New York: Mc Graw-Hill, 1970), 72–73. The report of the President's Commission on Higher Education was published in six short volumes in December 1947.

8. Trustees' Minutes, October 4, 1944, ACHC, 11.0.

latter group as "a foundation on which to re-build scholastic standards, activities and traditions."[9]

In the fall of 1946, the impact of demobilization became clear, when about 1500 students registered for classes. Over 1000 of the students were veterans, including a large number of sophomores and about half of the freshman class. To accommodate them, 150 double rooms were converted into triples. By the middle of the academic year, Father Healy was reporting that the College was in a "crisis that is a direct result of the war." There were four applicants for every available space; he was looking for surplus barracks for extra housing; the need for additional teachers had become acute.[10] Enrollments surpassed 1700 in the fall of 1947 and reached 1838 in the fall of 1948, an increase of 50 percent over pre-war years. What seemed at first a "crisis" gradually came to be accepted as normal. The dining hall and chapel, it turned out, could accommodate the increase through flexible scheduling; before long, administrators were contemplating new classrooms and dormitories.[11]

As enrollment stabilized at 1800, the number of veterans declined gradually from 1033 in 1946 to 24 in 1953, the last year such a figure was recorded. The proportion of day students declined from a peak of 27 percent in 1947 to 18 percent in 1960.

Meanwhile, the gymnasium project had acquired new urgency. In 1945, one of Father Healy's advisors pointed out that a gym would enhance the school's popularity with students and help safeguard their moral lives because, he reported, there was "an astonishing drop in temptations and sins of impurity" after a gymnasium opened at another Catholic college.[12] Healy's first instinct was to follow through on the plans Maginnis and Walsh had drawn up earlier. In April of 1946, he received an estimate that the building would cost $1.18 million; but by then, the increase in applications had prompted second thoughts about priorities.[13] Healy became con-

9. Report of the Province Prefect of Studies, February, 1946, ACHC, 19.8-1.

10. Healy to McEleney, Worcester, February 28, 1946, ACHC, 16.1BU-1; Worcester *Telegram*, August 18, 1946. Enrollments at Holy Cross were reflected in rises at the country's 24 other Jesuit colleges and universities. Total enrollment rose from 28,100 in 1944 to 98,500 in 1948. Paul A. FitzGerald, *The Governance of Jesuit Colleges in the United States, 1920–1970* (Notre Dame, Indiana: University of Notre Dame Press, 1984), 79.

11. John O'Brien to Forrest Donahue, Worcester, January 17, 1952, NEPA, HC-Rector.

12. Unidentified memo [1945], [Fr. Leo O'Connor-?], ACHC, 16.1BU-1.

13. Gymnasium blueprint, May 8, 1945, Maginnis and Walsh to Healy, Boston, September 7, 1945, Healy to Maginnis and Walsh, Worcester, September 10, 1945, Estimate from Vermillya-Brown Co, New York, April 26, 1946, ACHC 16.1BU-1; HD, October 16, 1945; Healy to McEleney, Worcester, April 18, 1946, NEPA, HC-Rector.

vinced that the greatest need was not a gymnasium but more housing and more recreational and instructional space. He was also concerned that the federal government's priority on housing construction would delay or freeze less vital projects. Early in 1946, he began to explore the possibility of securing a surplus building from one of the military installations in New England for use as a fieldhouse. That would have the advantage of quickly securing a structure for indoor recreation, and of freeing reserve funds to provide another space, perhaps a new dormitory. The permanent gymnasium he considered to be a "luxury" that would have to wait; besides, the $1 million cost was "a very classy neighborhood for us."[14] In September, Maginnis and Walsh confirmed that federal restrictions against non-residential structures made it "a safe assumption that the construction of the gymnasium must be postponed."[15]

At that point, Healy intensified his search for a hangar as "a temporary structure that would tide us over the emergency of next Fall and Winter and would be a good stop-gap . . . until the gymnasium emerges."[16] In January 1947, he received word that the Public Works Agency had committed to the College a surplus hangar from Camp Endicott, Rhode Island, that had been used as a drill and recreation hall. The government would bear the cost of taking the building down and reconstructing it on the campus.[17] He announced the plans in April. The 100 × 300 foot structure, which cost about $35,000 for site preparation, was built with a protruding lip on the base for the bricking that was added to the outside walls in 1955.[18] The fieldhouse was placed along College Street, leaving open the possibility of a gymnasium behind Kimball Hall. When it opened in March 1948, the facility held four courts for intramural basketball, handball courts, athletic offices, and a refreshment stand. Although it was intended primarily for intramural sports, the building also contained a full basketball court, temporary grandstands for 2000 spectators, and a permanent balcony that could accommodate about 100 more. Besides its

14. Healy to McEleney, Worcester, February 28 and April 18, 1946, NEPA, HC-Rector.

15. Maginnis and Walsh to Healy, Boston, September 12, 1946, ACHC, 16.1BU-1.

16. Healy to Maginnis and Walsh, Worcester, June 18, 1946, ACHC, 16.1BU-1.

17. Healy to James E. FitzGerald, January 24, 1947, ACHC, 16.1BU-1; HD, January 23, 1947; *Tomahawk*, April 23, 1947. For the part they played in facilitating the transfer, Healy thanked House Minority Leader John McCormack, George F. Hines (Special Representative of Massachusetts in Washington), and Frank C. Nash '31 (a Washington attorney). ACHC, 16.1BU-1. At the dedication of the Hogan Campus Center, Fr. Swords stated that Fr. Joseph O'Callaghan had helped acquire the hangar. ACHC, 12.24.

18. William A. Donaghy to William E. FitzGerald, Worcester, March 10, 1955, NEPA, HC-Rector. The total cost of rebuilding the field house was $92,200, of which the U.S. government covered the construction contract of $67,200. Trustees' Records, series 4, ACHC, 11.0.

athletic use, the fieldhouse provided the location of commencement, the junior and senior balls, and other large events.[19]

As plans for the fieldhouse took shape, Father Healy decided that a new biology building should come next. In February of 1948, he submitted plans for a three-story, I-shaped building designed by Maginnis and Walsh. He justified the expense by citing a survey conducted by the University of Chicago, ranking the College's pre-medical program sixth in the nation and the best at a Catholic school. The estimated cost of $300,000 was on hand and no loan would be necessary. Meanwhile, the new structure would free space in Beaven Hall for more classrooms. Instead of approving the plan, however, New England Provincial John McEleney sent a list of questions that implied Healy was moving too quickly, not fitting the pieces into a general plan of expansion. How would a biology building affect plans for a new faculty residence? A gymnasium? A dormitory? A classroom building?[20] Healy responded that the building was needed to avoid compromising "perhaps the best course offered by the College." He admitted the lack of a general plan and acknowledged that many alumni were disappointed that the College was willing to make do with a war-surplus fieldhouse while developing the campus along other lines: "There is do doubt about it: the Alumni will scream in anguish *whatever* building is started before the Gym. The Gym is an *albatross* hung right around our necks."[21]

By February and March of 1948, frustrated with delays in gaining approval, Father Healy had lost a good deal of his confidence and jaunty humor. The irritation that started with alumni opposition was intensified when John McEleney and his consultants persisted in raising theoretical objections to the proposed biology building. Wasn't the need for a new dormitory greater than the need for a biology building, they asked. Wouldn't it be better to address the cramped living quarters and the "hazardous congestion and condition of Fenwick Hall?"[22] Healy responded with strained impatience. Of course the school needed dormitories, but building one would not solve the problem of protecting the excellence of the biology program; meanwhile, housing three men per room did solve the room shortage. He was leaving soon for an extended trip on College business, he said, and the expansion would have to wait: "It will be impossible for me to do anything, now, on either building until mid-June. Considering how long it takes plans etc. to get drawn[,] it

19. *Tomahawk*, April 23, 1947 and March 10, 1948; HD, June 9, 1948.

20. Healy to McEleney, Worcester, February 6, 1948, and McEleney to Healy, Boston, February 10, 1948, NEPA, HC-Rector.

21. Healy to McEleney, Worcester, February 17, 1948, NEPA, HC-Rector.

22. McEleney to Healy, Boston, March 6, 1948, NEPA, HC-Rector.

would be better for me to forget the entire project."[23] The journey afforded
Healy the time to consider his position, his state of mind and heart, and his
readiness to continue to lead. When he returned to Worcester in April, he
bared his soul to John McEleney in a long letter written "with extreme reluctance and heartfelt apologies," but he was "pretty much at the end of my rope
and filled with a kind of desperation." He was willing to continue in office
until the end of the academic year, but not longer, because nagging "personal
problems" were preventing effective leadership. The thought of remaining in
office was "so frightening I can no longer sleep nor work nor pray." The time
had come to step down: "After much agonized wrestling with myself and in
prayer made as well as I could, I believe for my own sake and some others, for
the good of Holy Cross and the Society and . . . for the greater glory of God,
I should leave this office and this place."[24]

The provincial was reluctant to grant the request, because of Healy's performance and his high esteem among the Jesuits. During his rectorship, the
faculty surpassed 100 for the first time, including 42 lay professors; the size of
the Jesuit community increased from 68 to 84. Father Healy installed an insurance and annuity plan for lay faculty, established the postwar NROTC
program, and started the campus radio station, WCHC. He was a thoughtful
administrator, attentive to the influence associated with his position, and sometimes strong in his positions. He showed that side of himself in 1947 when
he resisted McEleney's proposal for an honorary degree. Healy questioned the
ethics of recognizing someone who "never lifted a finger to bar salacious literature from his news-stands," asserting that "our Catholic colleges do not
better their academic prestige by conferring Honorary Degrees upon [per-
sons] who have never proven any ability except to make a quick dollar." He argued that such recognition would be nothing more than a bribe to obtain a
contribution.

It has been my hope . . . to confer degrees that would not cause ripples of amusement
or guffaws of incredulity in the academic world. We are only a small College and perhaps our degree does not cut much ice: but since it is all we have to give, we should
be jealous about it and try to dignify it by the reflected glory of bestowing it upon a
worthy candidate. If no worthy candidates can be found, we ought to call it off.[25]

Healy's straightforwardness was appreciated among the Jesuits. The local consultors praised him in their annual evaluations, and despite the tension over

23. Healy to McEleney, Worcester, March 9, 1949, NEPA, HC-Rector.
24. Healy to McEleney, Worcester, April 14, 1948, NEPA, HC-Rector.
25. Healy to McEleney, Worcester, February 8, 1947, NEPA, HC-Rector; Healy's autobiographical notes, ACHC, 12.21.

the proposed biology building, the provincial also appreciated his leadership and told the general that the school and Jesuit community were thriving.[26]

Father McEleney finally agreed to the resignation in June, when he reported to Rome that Healy had asked three times to leave office, despite the fact that "his rectorship at Holy Cross has been marked by success in administration and singular happiness in the [Jesuit] Community." At McEleney's request, he had postponed his decision; now the provincial felt compelled to act: "While I cannot come to the same conclusion as Father Healy . . . , I feel forced to yield to his personal plea which is very sincerely and urgently made."[27] Father John Baptist Janssens, the Jesuit general since 1946, acceded to Healy's wishes because of the "urgent motives," and authorized McEleney to nominate a new rector.[28] William Healy's tribulations, and the process of finding a replacement, were kept private. Assignments for the coming year were ordinarily announced in Jesuit communities in July; but the timing of Healy's request and the general's authorization for a change came too late for that deadline. At Holy Cross, people expected that Healy would serve for three more years, and the July lists did nothing to unseat that assumption. When notice of the change was made public on September 8, the Jesuits were astonished. Even Francis Toolin, the community minister, was taken by surprise. Later, in the House Diary, he reflected the views of many:

The community was stunned by the change of Fr. Healy after three years. The general comment was—"I have never lived under a Superior who *was* his equal." This was not an isolated comment but the well nigh universal opinion of all his subjects. It is a matter of wonderment about the change. . . . It will be a long time, if ever, before this Province has a Rector who is as competent, representative, efficient[,] self-effacing and humble as Fr. Wm. J. Healy, S.J.[29]

Healy's successor was John A. O'Brien, a native of Chicopee who graduated *cum laude* from Holy Cross in 1918. Entering the Society after graduation, he taught at Holy Cross between 1924 and 1927. He was ordained in 1930 and, after earning a doctorate at the Gregorian University in Rome, was assigned to Boston College, where he was a Professor of Ethics and Chair of the Philos-

•
    26. Holy Cross Consultors' Excerpts, April 22, 1946, May 24, 1947, and March 28, 1948, NEPA, Consultors' Excerpts; John Baptist Janssens to McEleney, Rome, April 19, 1948, NEPA, Roman Correspondence.

    27. McEleney to Janssens, Boston, June 10, 1948, NEPA, Letters to General.

    28. Janssens to McEleney, Rome, June 26, 1948, NEPA, Roman Correspondence.

    29. Father Healy worked in the formation program for two years, then served as dean at Sofia University in Japan and at Fairfield University before returning to Holy Cross as an Associate Professor of English in 1962. Healy autobiographical notes, ACHC, 12.21.

ophy Department.[30] Father McEleney described O'Brien as a defender of tradition and a good speaker who was well regarded outside Jesuit circles: "Able, prudent, and successful . . . , he is particularly strong in his stand for keeping philosophy and all our old Jesuit traditions in their wonted place of honor in our Colleges."[31]

Immediately, O'Brien turned to expansion of the physical plant. During his first year, he received approval for a building for the Biology Department, with classrooms for chemistry and physics and a library for the natural sciences. The structure was positioned to complete a quadrangle sided by the library and Beaven and Wheeler Halls.[32] The building was dedicated in October 1951 by Bishop John J. Wright, the first head of the Worcester Diocese after its establishment in 1950. It was called the Biology Building until 1959, when the trustees voted to re-name it O'Neil Memorial Hall, in honor of the family of a generous benefactor, William F. O'Neil '07, founder of the General Tire and Rubber Co.[33]

With plans for the biology building on track, Father O'Brien turned to the problem of overcrowded dormitories. In the fall of 1948, when the number of boarding students climbed above 1350, three-man rooms were the norm, and students were being accommodated in barracks-style quarters in Fenwick Hall. Both situations needed attention, especially the Fenwick open dormitory. In 1951, a visitor lamented the "very crowded" conditions on 4th O'Kane and 4th Fenwick, where bunk beds were used. The most serious objection to housing students there was the antiquated construction of the buildings that made them fire hazards. As a stopgap, Father O'Brien had a sprinkler system installed in 1950.[34]

30. O'Brien vita, ACHC, 12.22; HD, September 8, 1948.

31. McEleney to Janssens, Boston, July 15, 1948, NEPA, Letters to General.

32. O'Brien to McEleney, Worcester, December 6, 1948, NEPA, HC-Rector; Janssens to McEleney, Rome, June 15, 1949, NEPA, Roman Correspondence. The final cost of the building was $616,000, including $104,000 for furnishings. Trustees' Records, series 4, ACHC, 11.0.

33. Construction and occupancy data, ACHC, 16.1BG-1; Worcester *Gazette*, October 11, 1951; Trustees' Minutes, September 15, 1959, ACHC, 11.0; HD, February 1, 1950 and October 11, 1951. In 1957, William A. Donaghy reported that William O'Neil "two years ago said he intended to do something for Holy Cross." Donaghy to James E. Coleran, Worcester, February 2, 1957, NEPA, HC-Rector. In 1962, the O'Neil family pledged $1 million in memory of William F. O'Neil. It was the largest gift to the College up to that time. Records of Ass't Director of Development, ACHC, 17.2A-1; *Crusader*, September 21, 1962.

34. Joseph FitzGerald, Annual Report, March 23, 1950, ACHC, 19.8-1; O'Brien to Charles Maguire, Worcester, January 17 and May 12, 1950, ACHC, 16.1BF-1; Report of visitation, Forrest Donahue [province socius], January 22, 1951, ACHC, 19.1-2.

The question of additional housing involved the very nature of Holy Cross. The careful decisions of the prewar years to limit the size of the College for the sake of academic quality and an intimate college atmosphere had to be reconsidered in view of postwar enrollments. Essentially, the question was whether to let enrollments decline to prewar levels after the surge of veterans had gone by, or to accept 1800 students as the norm. To construct new dormitories was to choose the second option. In 1948, Father Healy attempted to defer the decision by concentrating on the biology building, but he understood what was at stake. "So much depends on what is wanted at Holy Cross," he told the provincial. If the priorities were to be low student fees, the admission of hardship cases, bowing to pressure for the admission of students, and a major athletic program, then the boarding population would have to be held at its postwar level and the number of day students increased, because low fees require high numbers. On the other hand, if the priority was to "make Holy Cross a genuine College" with high admissions standards, enrollment should be reduced to 1000, with higher tuition and a comparable reduction in the size of the faculty.[35]

Now the responsibility for determining enrollment had fallen to Father O'Brien, and he had no hesitation. In 1950, he contacted Maginnis and Walsh about residence halls; by 1952, he had settled on two buildings with a combined capacity of 360 students. In requesting authorization, he made it clear that practical reasons necessitated holding the enrollment at its postwar level. The dining facilities and chapel had proven adequate for 1300 boarding students. Meanwhile, the College had become dependent on the additional revenue, which had risen from about $1.5 million in fiscal year 1946 to $2.3 million in 1949, a figure that held steady for the next few years and then rose gradually to $3.8 million in 1960 (Chart 8.1). The additions would increase the College's capacity for boarding students to 1330, which, with approximately 500 day students, would keep enrollment at 1800 without overcrowding. The dormitories would be built on the site of the hillside apple orchard "which has lost its need and usefulness."[36]

In Boston, Jesuit authorities objected to the proposal as a questionable commitment to a permanent increase in enrollment, with the risk of altering the very nature of the school. One observer questioned "whether the great force that Holy Cross has been (due to the almost family spirit of the students and alumni) does not suffer when the student body grows so large that many go through the college course strangers to one another and to many of the Jesuit Faculty." There was concern that pressure would prompt even more

35. Healy to McEleney, Worcester, February 17, 1948, NEPA, HC-Rector.
36. O'Brien to Eugene Kennedy, Worcester, October 6, 1950, ACHC, 16.1BJ-1; O'Brien to Forrest Donahue, Worcester, January 17, 1952, NEPA, HC-Rector.

expansion and further weaken the spirit of the school.[37] Another objection involved the plan's boxy architectural style. In Rome, the general's principal advisor for the United States, who had taught at Holy Cross from 1910 to 1912, worried that the school would not be able to hold the line even at 1800. Holy Cross, he argued, "should be our ideal boarding school. . . . We do want to hold to and protect the Society's traditional college, where young men are formed, not only informed."[38]

Undeterred by the opposition, Father O'Brien pressed forward. He acknowledged that the proposed buildings were "quite different" in style; but, remarkably, he claimed to be pleased by the difference: "They are . . . , in my opinion, an improvement over the appearance of our present dormitories and yet do not clash too violently with them." Moreover, they were designed with weary Jesuit corridor prefects in mind, avoiding long hallways "that make an excellent dash course for running races." He quoted the architect's opinion that rising costs made it impossible to construct buildings in the earlier style: "Although Mr. Maginnis said that our group is all Classical or Georgian, recently he also said it would be 'immoral' to build a building like the Library today. The Georgian or Classical, with all their trimmings, run into impossible sums nowadays." O'Brien pleaded his case in person with the provincial and his consultors in February 1952 and overrode the objections.[39] Construction was started in 1953, and the buildings, named for J. F. Lehy and Joseph Hanselman, opened to seniors in the fall of 1954.[40]

Besides his decisions about enrollment and expansion, John O'Brien influenced the College in other ways. In 1951, Holy Cross was in a group of 62 colleges and universities designated to receive Air Force Reserve Officers Training Corps units. Within a year, there were 271 men in the program, who, together with the 322 students in the NROTC unit, maintained a strong military presence on the campus and involved nearly a third of the students. O'Brien started two traditions that endured: a recognition dinner for employees with 25 or more years of service, and the outdoor nativity scene, a gift of the Class of 1952, that was placed on the steps of the library.[41] His most sig-

37. James E. Coleran to William E. FitzGerald, Weston, January 18, 1952, NEPA, HC-Rector.
38. James H. Dolan to FitzGerald, Chestnut Hill, January 31, 1952, NEPA, HC-Rector; Vincent A. McCormick to FitzGerald, Rome, April 5, 1952, NEPA, Roman Correspondence.
39. O'Brien to FitzGerald, Worcester, February 7 and 13, 1952, NEPA, HC-Rector; Janssens to FitzGerald, Rome, April 11, 1956, NEPA, Roman Correspondence.
40. FitzGerald to O'Brien, Boston, April 15, 1952, NEPA, HC-Rector; *Tomahawk*, May 1, 1952, and October 29, 1953.
41. Meagher and Grattan, *Spires*, 222; Application to National Production Authority, February 14, 1952, ACHC, 16.1BJ-1; *Tomahawk*, May 14, 1952; HD, December 15, 1952, and January 22, 1953.

nificant innovation may have been the establishment in 1954 of a board of Associate Trustees. According to their by-laws, they were appointed by the Jesuit trustees to "render assistance to the President and to the Trustees of the College . . . in connection with the finances of the College, the business management of the College, and the general advancement of the aims and purposes of the College and its students and alumni." There was an expectation that, in time, the group would develop beyond its advisory role so that "certain definite elements of authority can be delegated to it." The first group of seventeen included representatives from the fields of medicine, law, business, publishing, politics, and the Church. All were alumni or honorary degree recipients. They organized themselves into committees on public relations, investments, and development and considered such issues as enrollment and the new gymnasium.[42] William A. Donaghy, who succeeded John O'Brien in 1954, failed to grasp the group's potential; during his administration the associate trustees became largely dormant.[43]

Father Donaghy was a native of New Bedford and had attended Holy Cross from 1927 to 1929 before joining the Society. As a scholastic, he pursued graduate studies at St. Louis University and also taught at Holy Cross for two years. The author of two devotional books and a contributor to several Catholic periodicals, Donaghy was best known as a public speaker who was remembered as a "profound and eloquent orator," whose speeches were "ever-so-faintly marbled with theatricality."[44] In the six years prior to his assignment to Worcester, he had been a retreat director. The new president set the tone for his administration in an interview on his first day in office. The purpose of education, he stated, was to educate students about "what to be as well as what to do." Donaghy advocated the liberal arts "to acquaint a man with the best thoughts of the noblest minds of the past, to have him estimate the present in timeless terms and so enable him to face the future with intelligent determination." He found Holy Cross well equipped to follow his model: "With academic, administrative and athletic personnel of such

42. Associate Trustees' By-Laws, 1954, ACHC, 11.1. The first board of associate trustees included William Leahy (chair), James Crotty (secretary), Dr. Alexander Carson, Msgr. George Connor, William Earls, Hon. Edmund Flynn, Msgr. Richard Haberlin, John Maguire, Michael Morrissey, Hon. Matthew McGuire, Richard Reid, Dr. Arthur Wallingford, Thomas Dignan, William Doyle, Henry M. Hogan, William F. O'Neil, and Foster Stearns.

43. Donaghy stated privately that the meetings hadn't accomplished much and he would welcome a pretext to disband the group. Donaghy to Andrew McFadden, Rome, September 1957, ACHC, 12.23-1.

44. Wesley Christenson to Sid McKeen, Worcester, January 24, 1975, ACHC, 12.23-1; *Boston Globe*, January 25, 1975.

stature, Holy Cross's future, if anything, may be brighter than her glorious past."[45]

After he assumed office, Father Donaghy turned to the urgent need for another science building. His first decision related to an architect. He did not admire the design of the biology building and hill dorms, and so he abandoned the fifty-year partnership with Maginnis and Walsh and turned to a local architect, Cornelius W. Buckley '29. Donaghy was impressed with Buckley's design of the Worcester airport terminal and hired him to design the facade of the fieldhouse at the time it was bricked in.[46] By early 1957, Buckley had drawn up plans for a science building that would be 50 percent larger than the biology building, and plans were sent to the Jesuit provincial for approval. The need was clear. The Chemistry Department was then located on the first floor of O'Kane Hall—a location that risked fire in a building that was also a student residence. The Physics Department was in the basement of Alumni Hall; the Mathematics Department, also destined for the new building, had no specific space.[47] Before the plans were put out to bid, the interested academic departments were consulted about the layout; their requests so squeezed space that the width of the stairways had to be reduced. Formally dedicated in December 1959, the building had fifteen classrooms, including a lecture hall for 210 and two other large classrooms. The final cost, including furnishing and supplies, was $1.6 million.[48] Father Donaghy took his time in naming the building. His first idea was to induce local industries to fund the project as Worcester Hall, with individual laboratories named for the city's "great Companies"; but the plan never came to fruition. In April of 1959, the trustees decided to honor Mgr. Richard J. Haberlin '06, the former vicar-general of the Boston Archdiocese, who had been the president of the General Alumni Association at the time of his death in March and had made Holy Cross the beneficiary of a $25,000 insurance policy.[49]

45. Worcester *Telegram*, August 1, 1954. For biographical material on Donaghy, see ACHC, 12.23-1.

46. Donaghy to FitzGerald, Worcester, March 26, 1955, NEPA, HC-Rector; contract for fieldhouse renovation, June 24, 1955, ACHC, 16.1B.

47. Buckley to Donaghy, Worcester, January 14, 1957, Donaghy to Coleran, Worcester, February 2, 1957, Coleran to Donaghy, February 28, and undated memo [early 1957], NEPA, HC-Rector.

48. Donaghy to Coleran, Worcester, July 17 and 18, 1957, NEPA, HC-Rector; copy of contract, ACHC, 16.1BH' program for dedication of Haberlin Hall, December 8, 1959, ACHC 16.1BH; HD, December 8, 1959.

49. Donaghy to H. G. Stoddard, Worcester, September 26 and December 2, 1958, ACHC, 16.1BH-1; Donaghy to Coleran, Worcester, March 16, 1959, NEPA, HC-Rector; Trustees' Minutes, May 15, 1959, ACHC, 11.0. The main entrance carries an inscription *Deus Scientiarum Dominus* [The Lord is a God of Knowledge], a phrase from 1 Sam. 2:3, used by Pius XI in a document of 1931.

The opening of Haberlin Hall fit into a larger scheme of expansion that had been developed by Father Donaghy and Cornelius Buckley. Although he considered a building for art and music, he quickly decided that a campus center, including recreational facilities for students and a larger replacement for the theater in Kimball Hall, should come next.[50] He explained to James E. Coleran, who had become New England provincial in 1956, that the need was "definite and vital because when a blizzard confines the boys . . . in their rooms . . . , they do not always talk about Our Lady. It would, therefore, be a solution to a moral and a morale problem." His principal hope was to attract students away from "pool rooms and bowling alleys and (I hate to admit it) beer parlors downtown to which they are driven by sheer boredom in those gray and snow-laden months."[51] He envisioned financing the project with the fund of $283,000 that had been contributed for a gymnasium, supplemented by a low-interest loan through the federal Housing and Home Finance Agency. In the fall of 1959, Buckley was commissioned to draw up plans.[52]

Then, in the spring of 1960, Father Donaghy abruptly reversed himself, postponing the project indefinitely. Several factors entered into the decision. The preliminary estimate of $2.9 million was high; the federal loan was on hold pending new funding; and, with only a few months remaining in his term of office, Donaghy had reservations about committing his still unnamed successor to a project so large. In April, he convened the Jesuit trustees and laid the matter before them. They voted unanimously to drop the project for the time being, leaving the next president free to study the options and make a final decision.[53] Like his predecessors, Father Donaghy had failed to bring to fruition the plans for a gymnasium, even in modified form as a campus center. But he left his mark on the campus in other ways. In addition to Haberlin Hall and the chapel and fieldhouse renovations, he widened Linden Lane,

50. HD, July 26, 1956; O'Connor memo to Donaghy [1956], and undated memo of Raymond Swords, ACHC, 16.1BP-1. *The Crusader*, December 15, 1955, carried a sketch of Buckley's campus plan, which featured a cross-shaped esplanade whose lengthwise component extended from Linden Lane to the chapel. Fenwick and O'Kane Halls, whose weak construction was thought to limit their further usefulness, would have been razed.

51. Donaghy to Coleran, Worcester, March 3 and June 1, 1959, NEPA, HC-Rector.

52. Donaghy to Horgan, Worcester, June 1, 1959, and contract with C. W. Buckley, November 24, 1959, ACHC, 16.1BP-1; Donaghy to Coleran, Worcester, June 1, 1959, NEPA, HC-Rector; Coleran to Donaghy, September 4, 1959, ACHC, 16.1BP-1.

53. Preliminary estimate of C. W. Buckley, February 3, 1960, and Donaghy to Buckley, Worcester, April 29, 1960, ACHC, 16.1BP-2; undated notation written by R. J. Swords on the letter from Coleran to Donaghy, dated September 4, 1959, Ralph Cornell [Regional Director, Housing and Home Finance Agency] to Donaghy, November 5, 1959, ACHC, 16.1BP-1; Worcester *Gazette*, November 17, 1959.

Chart 8.1 Operating Budget, 1947–1960

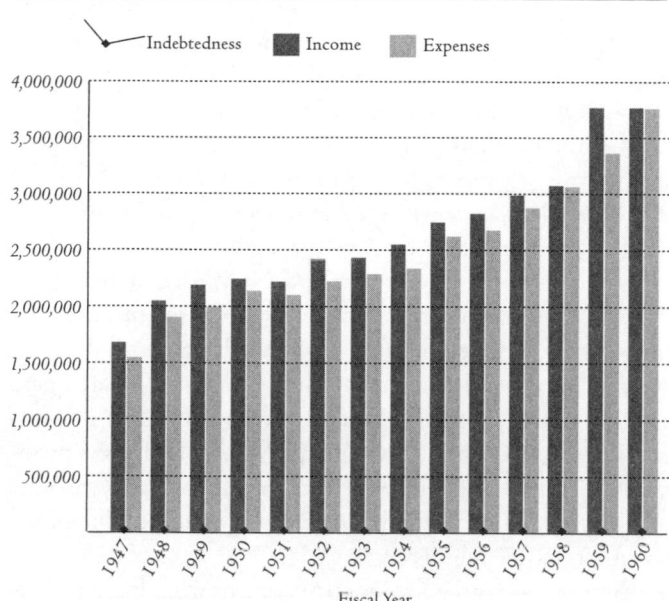

set the crucifixion group in the campus cemetery, and in 1958—concerned that historical materials were "lying about in closets neglected and uncatalogued"—he organized the College Archives.[54]

As the operating budgets during the postwar years indicate, the expansion in the physical plant was achieved without borrowing money. Tuition and boarding charges doubled between 1947 and 1960. Tuition was raised in five stages, from $380 in 1947 (when it accounted for less than a quarter of total income) to $775 in 1960 (when it supplied about one-third of the school's revenues). Boarding charges were raised seven times, from $900 in 1947 to $1750 in 1960, and they contributed about 60 percent of revenue during this period. These figures, reflecting the rise in enrollment to 1800, contributed to an annual surplus and helped finance the science buildings and the hill dormitories.

During the second half of the Donaghy presidency, the location of the College itself became an issue when, in October of 1957, the Massachusetts

54. Memo of visitation of province socius [Peter McKone], April 17–20, 1958, and Donaghy to Coleran, Worcester, February 4, 1959, NEPA, HC-Rector; HD, 1958–60; Trustees' Minutes, May 16, 1958, ACHC, 11.0.

Department of Public Works (DPW) disclosed a plan to build an interstate highway through the lower part of the campus, taking the athletic fields by eminent domain. Shortly after the announcement, College representatives met with highway planners in Boston, and both parties staked out their positions. There was reason for concern, as the Jesuit minister recounted: "The route on the map ran 20 yards behind Kimball Hall. After some discussion, agreement was arrived at, that the college would prefer a route around the edge of the football field." Father Donaghy was convinced that resistance would be "fruitless and impolitic." He hoped only that the College would be fairly compensated.[55] To protect its interests, the College hired a New York architectural firm, Eggers and Higgins, to draw up an estimate of replacement costs, exclusive of actual land-taking. The report indicated that, because of the hilly character of the campus, the new athletic fields would have to be located near the river, at a cost of $2.3 million. The architect also warned that the proximity of the proposed highway to Carlin, Kimball, and Alumni Halls was problematic: "Its high speed traffic, noise from trucks, headlights and gasoline fumes could be a most undesirable neighbor." And, there would be the problem of maintaining an attractive campus entrance.[56]

During 1959, the discussions reached an impasse, due to what Father Donaghy called "the tergiversation of the authorities." Only in November, two years after the original announcement, was College architect C. W. Buckley shown the actual land-taking plans; even then, he was refused a copy for College use, because state authorities had not yet approved them.[57] For Father Donaghy, that was the last straw: the failure to submit plans confirmed his opinion that the DPW was inefficient and incompetent.[58] In December, he retained Edward B. Hanify '33 of the Boston firm of Ropes and Gray to represent the College, telling Hanify that the DPW had been "thoroughly weird."[59]

55. HD, October 16 and 21, 1957; Donaghy to Coleran, Worcester, January 8, 1958, NEPA, HC-Rector.

56. Theodore J. Young to Michael Pierce, New York City, November 30, 1959, ACHC, 16.1B-5; C. W. Buckley to J. Leo Sullivan, Worcester, February 5, 1959, and Buckley to De Leuw, Cather and Co., Worcester, November 19, 1959, ACHC, 16.1B-5; memo of Francis J. Vaas to Hanify, November 9, 1962, Ropes and Gray Papers, CHCB-2, in ACHC, 16.1.

57. Edgar F. Coppell to C. W. Buckley, Brookline, October 15, 1959, ACHC 16.1B-5; [E. B. Hanify], Chronology, Proposed Land Taking, Holy Cross Property, Ropes and Gray files, CHCB 2, in ACHC, 16.1; C. W. Buckley to Edgar F. Copell, Worcester, November 20, 1959, and Copell to Buckley, Brookline, November 27, 1959, ACHC, 16.1B-5.

58. Donaghy to C. W. Buckley, Worcester, November 19, 1959, ACHC, 16.1B-5. The Copell plan was not filed until May 26, 1960, Hanify Chronology, ACHC, 16.1.

59. Donaghy to Hanify, Worcester, December 2 and 7, 1959, ACHC, 16.1B-5. Hanify's papers on the land-taking from Ropes and Gray are deposited in the College Archives, ACHC, 16.1.

By then, Donaghy had received the Eggers and Higgins estimates and had an idea of what was at stake.

In January of 1960, Hanify learned that no definite plan had yet been made for taking land. The information came to light in a conversation with E. J. McCarthy, Chief Engineer of the Massachusetts DPW. Hanify told McCarthy that the College lacked an adequate place for a new stadium and "as to a location on land now owned by the College I was curious as to how the Commonwealth proposed to exercise eminent domain . . . by taking land from one private citizen to mitigate the damages of another." "This comment," Hanify reported, "stopped [him] dead" by overturning his assumption that the College had a satisfactory alternative site. Hanify finally obtained McCarthy's agreement to furnish the College with a copy of tentative plans and asked "why it was necessary to go through or interfere with the College's property in the first place." McCarthy replied that the DPW had assumed, on the basis of very early estimates furnished by Cornelius Buckley, that alternative land takings would be more costly than building the road through the campus. Hanify countered that the costs of the Holy Cross route were "greatly in excess of any previously envisaged." That information led McCarthy to conclude that a public hearing was needed to consider expenses and costs. Hanify was pleased that the process was still open. "Let us keep our sword in the silken scabbard," he advised, "and indulge to all external appearances in the assumption that there still remains a cooperative attitude by the Department, without getting maneuvered into acquiescence in what they are doing. This way we learn more."[60]

By this time, uncertainty about the expressway was hindering plans for campus expansion. Hanify advised C. W. Buckley to bear in mind that the proximity of the proposed highway would affect the beauty and utility of the proposed campus center and recommended that federal authorities be told that "the present vague status of the expressway is hampering . . . this vitally needed improvement," and to use that point for a speedier resolution of the plan.[61] That argument may have been partly responsible for Father Donaghy's decision to defer construction. The level of irritation rose again in February of 1960, when a Boston sportswriter alleged that the College was selfishly holding out for $500,000—twenty times the alleged value of the land—and offered false information that a new stadium was being planned for the "upper terrace" near Kimball Hall.[62] To the provincial, Donaghy reported privately that "the Department of Public Works in the whole affair has been in-

60. Hanify to Michael Pierce, Boston, January 16, 1960, ACHC, 16.1B-5.
61. Hanify to C. W. Buckley, Worcester, February 11, 1960, ACHC, 16.1B-5.
62. The author was Arthur Siegel, Boston *Globe*, February 12, 1960.

efficient and, in at least two instances, dishonest." He was inclined to bring the matter to court. "We started out in a spirit of civic cooperativeness but, when we encountered political chicanery, we invoked legal and architectural aid."[63] The delay placed Holy Cross representatives on guard and motivated them to raise the stakes on giving up the lower campus. But as his term came to an end, Father Donaghy still expected the College to lose the land.[64]

In the summer of 1960, responsibility for managing the controversy fell to a new rector, Raymond J. Swords. A member of the faculty since 1952, Swords was aware of the complexity of the problem. By the time he took office, the expressway had been built as far as Brosnahan Square, but the exact placement of the Holy Cross link was still uncertain. College administrators knew that the DPW had an alternate plan—the "northerly route"—that featured a curve around the lower campus, but no specific details were available. Swords and his advisors had an idea of the cost of replacing the stadium, and they had begun to realize the extent of the "consequential damages"—the reduced value of the portion of the campus that would be close to the proposed highway. Accordingly, Swords set his strategy along three lines: first, getting another estimate from an assessor to set a figure for full reimbursement for loss of land and structures (including the football stadium) and for the diminished utility of buildings and lands near the planned road; second, finding and including acceptable land for a new stadium in the plan of compensation; and third, using public relations to clarify how much was actually at stake for the College. The goal was less to prevent a land-taking that seemed to be inevitable than to ensure that the College would be fully reimbursed.

By then, delays were causing frustration on all sides. Local wags were calling the incomplete highway "the expressway to nowhere," and College officials were stymied in their plans for further development. No further meeting was held until April of 1961, when the interested parties gathered at Holy Cross. Public Works Commissioner Jack P. Ricciardi told Father Swords that, despite the alternative plan, the Holy Cross route was the only acceptable alternative because the northerly route involved industrial property and jobs. For its part, the state agreed that reimbursement to the College should include consequential damages.[65] Afterwards, Father Swords confided to the provincial: "Even though we did not tell them this, we feel that we have no choice but to acquiesce in their decision, and we must now begin to marshal our facts and figures and to obtain an equitable financial repayment." He was retaining

63. Donaghy to Coleran, Worcester, February 23, 1960, NEPA, HC-Rector.
64. Donaghy to C. W. Buckley, Worcester, May 9, 1960, ACHC, 16.1B-5.
65. Memo by Ed Hanify on meeting of April 17, 1961 in Swords's Office, ACHC, 16.1B-5.

C. W. Buckley to advise him on the latter point.[66] As he ruminated about the meeting, Ed Hanify suspected chicanery and warned Father Swords that he thought the DPW approach was "pretty crass," an effort to foster the appearance that they were forced by business interests to choose the Holy Cross route, thereby affording the College an enormous windfall. "We have time to work out a careful statement [for the public hearing in July] which neither welcomes the taking of our property nor urges the taking of someone else's property," he advised.[67] But, besides his mistrust of the DPW, Hanify had another reason for caution: the College might succeed. In that case, the road would be built close enough to the boundaries of the campus to have a negative impact, but the College would be unable to claim reimbursement.[68]

The public hearing took place on July 25. The announcement included, for the first time, a detailed description of the northerly route and indicated that the cost of building the road through Fitton Field would be $6.3 million, while the northerly route would cost $9.4 million. The former figure incorporated an estimate from a state-sponsored appraiser that the College was entitled to replacement costs of $877,174, plus the value of the land. No allowance was made for consequential damages.[69] Meanwhile, Worcester realtor Francis Bailey had conducted an independent appraisal for the College, placing the damages between $3.2 and $4.9 million, depending on whether new land for the stadium was included in the settlement. On that basis, Hanify was prepared to claim $3.8 million, plus land costs—a figure nearly $3 million higher than the DPW was prepared to offer.[70]

More than 150 persons attended the hearing. A representative of the Chamber of Commerce emphasized the value to the local economy of fourteen businesses that would be displaced by the northerly route. Hanify's statement combined sentimentalism and fact in an appeal that reflected his strategy of avoiding a stand on the specific route while asserting the College's claims.[71] The statement included a brief history of Holy Cross, of Fitton Field and the football stadium, and a description of the sports programs.

66. Swords to Coleran, Worcester, April 18, 1961, ACHC, 19.2-3.

67 Hanify to Swords, Boston, April 18, 1961, ACHC, 16.1B-5.

68. Hanify to J. Leo Sullivan, Boston, July 6, 1961, ACHC, 16.1B-5.

69. Notice of Public Hearing of July 25, 1961, Jack P. Ricciardi, Commissioner of Public Works, and Hanify to J. Leo Sullivan, Boston, June 23, 1961, ACHC, 16.1B-5; Edward B. Hanify, "Holy Cross Land Taking," Ropes and Gray Papers, CHCB-2, in ACHC, 16.1.

70. Hanify to J. Leo Sullivan, Boston, May 23, 1961, and estimate of Francis S. Bailey, undated [1961], ACHC, 16.1B-5.

71. Worcester *Telegram*, July 26, 1961; Holy Cross statement on the proposed expressway, July 25, 1961, ACHC, 16.1B-5.

Hanify speculated darkly that the land-taking would "probably" lead to the elimination of intercollegiate athletics and harm the "laudable campus spirit" that was connected with sports. He cataloged other consequences: the reduced value of property, and the diminished quality of campus life (a disruption of the nine-month academic routine and of "the tranquillity of the cloister"). The proposal also frustrated the master plan for campus development. ("The College will bear for all time the scar of this taking . . . a grave and irreparable injury.") The land-taking, Hanify concluded, would considerably reduce the value of the campus: *"Any well-considered evaluation of the College's damages . . . must include this marked reduction in the value of its total remaining property as well as the damages resulting from . . . the actual taking."* Estimates provided by the DPW had sidestepped those realities, and Hanify warned against planning to take property "with an inadequate or unrealistic appreciation of the damage inflicted upon the College." Even so, the local press reported that the northerly alternative had "no takers." Father Swords admitted as much: "It is very certain that we will lose our property." The best hope was to hold out for full compensation.[72]

That hope became brighter shortly after the public hearing, when the DPW expressed willingness to reimburse Holy Cross for "actual, severance and consequential losses."[73] That summer, College agents prepared a contingency plan to secure industrial land near the campus for a new stadium from the United States Steel Company.[74] The DPW hired another appraiser, Matthew O'Regan, to determine consequential damages.[75] By mid-August, O'Regan had concluded that the College was entitled to $1.08 million. In reaching the figure, O'Regan rejected the claim that the hilltop site was unacceptable for a new stadium.[76] In September, Commissioner Ricciardi called a confidential meeting with representatives from Holy Cross and the Federal Bureau of Roads. He disclosed that the state would offer Holy Cross the amount indi-

72. Swords to Coleran, Worcester, July 26, 1961, ACHC, 19.2-3.

73. J. Leo Sullivan to Hanify, Worcester, August 3, 1961, ACHC, 16.1B-5.

74. H. F. McCloy to C. W. Buckley, Pittsburgh, July 28, 1961, and Buckley to Swords, Worcester, August 3, 1961, ACHC, 16.1B-5. J. Leo Sullivan and Ed Hanify agreed not to publicize the proposed agreement because of the possibility that U.S. Steel, the owner of the American Steel and Wire Company property in Worcester, was "under pressure from the local businesses to secure public credit for saving the adjoining business area." Sullivan to Hanify, Worcester, September 7, 1961, and Hanify to Sullivan, Boston, September 8, 1961, ACHC, 16.1B-5.

75. Hanify to J. Leo Sullivan, Boston, October 24 and 27, 1961, and Francis S. Bailey to Hanify, Worcester, December 8, 1961, ACHC, 16.1B-5. O'Regan's papers on the Holy Cross land taking are deposited in the College Archives, 16.1.

76. "Appraisal Report, College of the Holy Cross, Worcester, Massachusetts, Interstate 290," Matthew O'Regan Papers, in ACHC, 16.1.

cated in the O'Regan appraisal and admitted that the revised estimates now made the costs of the two routes nearly equal. In this circumstance, he suggested, Holy Cross would have to lose its property to protect the threatened industries. Hanify entered a strong protest, alleging that the DPW was still failing to come to terms with consequential damages. He told Ricciardi that the College would be "liable to severe criticism from our Alumni when they would be asked to supply the $1 million or more which the State should have paid us"; and he threatened to sue.[77]

In October, the offer to Holy Cross was formally set at $1.008 million, a figure that was $72,000 lower than the O'Regan appraisal and put the total costs for the Fitton Field route only $50,000 below the northerly route. Since the offer to the school was the maximum sum that would allow the Fitton Field route to win out on the basis of cost, Holy Cross representatives suspected that the figure had been artificially adjusted. In a dramatic confrontation, Commissioner Ricciardi pointed out that the DPW was being criticized for slowness and accused Holy Cross of "standing in the way of progress." But Hanify defended the College's conduct and its claim to fair compensation. Present at the meeting was John A. Hanson of the Federal Bureau of Roads, the official who held authority to make the final decision. His principal concern was cost. Hanify's reaction made a strong impression on him.[78] By the end of the month, Hanson had decided to secure yet another appraisal from Thomas Horan, of the Boston real estate firm Meredeth and Grew. Horan had earlier purchased land for M.I.T. and presumably understood the issues involved. Father Swords was pleased at the news: "Here is a man who really understands the College's position and who thinks along the same lines as Ed Hanify."[79]

The appointment of Horan proved to be the turning point in the process. Almost immediately, he communicated his sense that John Hanson would give College authorities the option of accepting the offer from the state or vetoing the entire campus land-taking. His judgment was that they ought to do

77. Swords to J. V. O'Connor, Worcester, September 17, 1962, ACHC, 19.2-3.

78. The meeting was held on October 8, 1962. A detailed account was kept by J. Leo Sullivan, ACHC, 16.1B-5. A week after the meeting, he told Fr. Sullivan that "O'Regan's appraisals were, in my judgment, somewhat forced" in order to make the Fitton Field route less expensive. Hanify to Sullivan, Boston, October 15, 1962, ACHC, 16.1B-5. See also Sullivan to Hanify, Worcester, December 28, 1962, ACHC, 16.1B-5.

79. Swords to J. Leo Sullivan, Worcester, October 3, 1962, and J. L. Sullivan to James J. Ritterskamp, Jr., Worcester, September 22, 1966, ACHC 16.1B-5. Afterwards, J. Leo Sullivan characterized Horan as "probably the only person in Massachusetts who could resolve this matter in favor of the College in such a short time." Sullivan to Francis Bailey, Worcester, January 10, 1963, ACHC, 16.1B-5.

all in their power to hold out for the northerly route: the cost of relocating the stadium would be "most expensive"; the school would not be awarded enough to reconstruct comparable athletic facilities; and the presence of a highway through Fitton Field would render all the land below Linden Lane useless to the school. He characterized the affected factories on the northerly route as "quite old and . . . not worth too much," and he accused the factory owners of being selfish, because they *could* relocate—an option that was not available to Holy Cross. He pointed out that the alternate route would eliminate the necessity of paying a high price to U.S. Steel for "very poor land" purchased under duress. Ultimately, the College had everything to gain from holding out for the northerly alternative:

It will keep the noise, fumes, dust and dirt farther away from the College. It will eliminate a very poor appearing highly elevated stretch of heavily travelled roadway from running very close to our existing buildings. It will help to remove some sub-standard housing and factory areas from very close to the College. It will eliminate the need of defacing the landscape very close to the center of our College campus. It will also make it possible for us to retain our athletic plant as a buffer between the College campus and the new Highway.[80]

Horan's advice was sensible; he convinced Raymond Swords to reverse the expectation that the lower campus would be lost.

There was general astonishment on December 10 when John Hanson announced that "excessive land damage costs" had prompted the Federal Bureau of Roads to choose the northerly route. Thomas Horan had set the replacement cost of Fitton Field between $2.3 and $3 million dollars, a cost that now made the Fitton Field alternate substantially more expensive than the northerly alternative. As expected, the Chamber of Commerce co-ordinated a protest, but reversed itself quickly when an adjustment was made to spare seventeen concerns initially marked for land-taking.[81] Edward Hanify's strong rejection of the DPW offer in October 1962 had turned the tide by convincing John Hanson to seek a new appraisal; Thomas Horan had sealed the case by convincing College authorities that the stakes were far higher than they had thought. Another factor in the outcome was the failure of the Massachusetts DPW to factor consequential damages into the proposed settlement, an approach that eventually doomed the initial, rather thoughtless preference for the Fitton Field route.[82] Ultimately, the state took two small

80. Hanify to Swords, November 5, 1962, and J. Leo Sullivan to Hanify, November 14, 1962, ACHC, 16.1B-5.

81. Worcester *Gazette*, December 11 and 27, 1962; Worcester *Telegram*, December 14, 1962

82. Hanify told the Associate Trustees that the College position had been "one of remarkable

parcels of college land for the project, forcing a re-orientation of the base-ball field.[83]

On the surface, the quality and pace of student life during the postwar years resembled the traditional pattern. The Student Handbook for 1951–52 prescribed a rising time of 6:45 and Mass at 7:00. Students were allowed an hour's break at midday for dinner; they attended chapel after supper, had an evening study period, and retired at 11:00 (10:30 for freshmen). The schedule was enforced by pew checks and evening room checks. Weekend out-permissions were extended to 1 A.M. in the mid-fifties, and students were liable to probation or suspension for absenting themselves after the check-in. Repeat offenders could be placed on "Dawn Patrol," a series of periodic check-ins to ensure their presence on campus. Dormitory regulations still forbade students to bring women, even their mothers and sisters, to their rooms; intoxication and the keeping of intoxicating beverages in the dormitories was punishable by ex-pulsion; beginning in 1956, the handbook specified that "room decorations should be consonant with Christian modesty and good taste." Guests were en-tertained in the large O'Kane Lounge, which is presently the site of the Can-tor Gallery; but after 1956 seniors were allowed to receive guests in the lounges of Lehy and Hanselman Halls.[84]

Postwar College catalogs openly stated that life at Holy Cross was subject to "a closer supervision . . . than is usual at the present day in most large col-leges," but added that "every harsh feature" was excluded by professors who "live with the students, mingle with them constantly, direct their studies, in-terest themselves in their sports and in every way assume the relation rather of friend than taskmaster." One 1952 graduate called his memories of campus life "uniformly fond," despite the fact that "discipline was by present standards unconstitutionally cruel and unusual. . . . Of course, we found out quickly how to sneak out at night to go to the . . . diner or to get a beer."[85] Tolerant corridor prefects allowed some latitude; and students were naturally deter-mined and inventive in flaunting rules. By 1960, student drinking was open

---

restraint and forebearance [sic]." Holy Cross "avoided all semblance of recourse to any political influence . . . and simply presented . . . the nature and extent of its prospective damages." Minutes of Associate Trustees, December 15, 1963, WDA, Holy Cross, 1956–1960 [sic].

83. Sullivan to Hanify, Worcester, December 12, 1962, and notes on the land-taking of De-cember 29, 1965, ACHC, 16.1B-5.

84. Student Handbooks, 1945–60; John O'Brien's regulations for corridor prefects, 1949–50, ACHC, 12.22.

85. Joseph A. Califano, Jr., "A Jesuit Education Revisited," *America* (May 20, 1989), 470–71.

enough to provoke a complaint that "scores of beer cans" were in evidence on Sunday mornings.[86]

Some of the disciplinary infractions involved pranks—in the late 1940s a Worcester city bus was found parked on the library stairs early one morning; in 1953, an "unauthorized student football rally downtown" turned rowdy and several students were arrested; in 1955, there were episodes involving the cows pastured on college property; and there were regular efforts—sometimes successful—to paint the Boston College eagle mascot purple.[87] Father Jeremiah Donovan, who became minister of the Jesuit community in 1955, took a dim view of free-spirited behavior. One warm afternoon, students frustrated his refusal to allow "medleys" to be played over the Fenwick tower amplifiers by using the Air Force amplifiers in Beaven Hall. "After running out of 'medleys,'" he moaned, "they played other records including rock and roll." A month later, he found freshmen "annoying the faculty by relaxing in the sun."[88] At its best, the disciplinary system fostered self-discipline and contributed a certain *esprit de corps*. At its worst, the system made the prefects into enforcers of laws that were deemed unreasonable, and the students into unwilling victims who resisted to the fullest possible extent. In 1955, the prefect of discipline asked to preside at the students' weekday Mass because he craved a relationship with the students that was pastoral and not disciplinary.[89]

The College catalog of 1960 carried the statement that the educational approach was "uncompromisingly intellectual and intransigently Catholic." For Catholic students, theology courses, annual retreats, and daily Mass were still mandatory. Father Donaghy even converted the chapel basement to a second student chapel because the upper church was too small to accommodate the entire student body. When the new Mary Chapel was completed in 1955, the daily obligation, which had been commuted to alternate weekdays after the war, was re-imposed.[90] Beginning in 1960, two Jesuits, designated as "Spiritual Counselors," assisted by Jesuit corridor prefects, assumed primary responsibility for chaplaincy work. Other specifically religious activities, like the Sodality, the Mass of the Holy Spirit at the start of the school year, and the Fitton Field Mass at the beginning of May, kept the Catholic profile high.

86. Unidentified memo, April 18, 1960, NEPA, HC-Varia.

87. HD, October 30, 1953, May 2 and 12, 1955. The episode involving the bus on the library stairs has been re-told on many occasions by John E. Brooks, S.J., '49.

88. HD, April 29 and May 22, 1956.   89. HD, April 16, 1955.

90. Donaghy to FitzGerald, Worcester, March 10, 1955, NEPA, HC-Rector; FitzGerald to Janssens, Boston, March 23, 1955, NEPA, Roman Correspondence; HD, May 21, 1956. Student Handbooks, 1954–57, ACHC 15.2.

Special events, like the convocation to award an honorary degree to Cardinal Spellman in 1954, intensified the spirit. *Tomahawk* editors accepted the Cold War characterization of communism as an evil monolith and supported Senator Joseph McCarthy. But beyond the rhetoric and pageantry and imposed obligations, there were signs that some of the Catholic students were growing restive. In 1960, an observer reported that many students returned to their rooms as soon as the pew check was concluded, and that others who remained were inattentive to worship.[91]

Innovations between 1946 and 1960 included the start of student government in 1948, when Father Healy signed a constitution recognizing the Student Congress as the official representative of the student body. Parents' Weekend, which originated as a one-day event in 1954, was expanded to two separate weekends in 1957.[92] Late in 1948, the campus radio station, WCHC, developed as an outgrowth of the amateur radio club.[93] In 1955, *The Tomahawk* became *The Crusader.* Beyond their statement that the new name was in "the true tradition of Holy Cross," the editors offered few clues about their motivation; apparently they intended to alert their readers to a new seriousness of purpose and a more professional style. "The *Crusader* attempts to be a newspaper, not an art brochure," they wrote; in the *Tomahawk* "the most interesting news was always buried."[94]

During the postwar era, Holy Cross became a less regional school (Chart 7.2). By the 1950s only about half of the students traced their origins to New England, while the number of matriculants from the Middle Atlantic region (including New York City) increased to about one-third. New patterns were also emerging in the pattern of extracurricular activities.[95] The percentage of varsity athletes shrank as enrollments rose, but the number of students participating in intramural sports continued to increase—a phenomenon that is partly explained by the availability of the field house for winter sports.

After the war, varsity athletics resumed their prewar pace and propelled Crusader teams to national prominence in the last years before television rev-

91. Unidentified memo, April 18, 1960, NEPA, HC-Varia; Convocation Program, December 8, 1954, WDA, Holy Cross, 1950–55; *Tomahawk,* March 20, 1952, October 16 and 29, 1953.

92. *Tomahawk,* January 8, 1948; HD, October 27, 1956, November 2 and 16, 1957; press release, November 9, [1963], ACHC, 12.24. In 1957, there were separate weekends for parents of freshmen and seniors, and parents of sophomores and juniors.

93. *Tomahawk,* October 29, 1947, December 10, 1948; *The Catholic Free Press,* March 20, 1953; unidentified clipping [December, 1948], scrapbook 42, page 7.

94. *Crusader,* January 13, 1955. The editor who facilitated the change was Laurence O'Donnell '57.

95. See unrevised draft, Chart 7.4.

The Holy Cross basketball team in 1947, winners of the NCAA Tournament after victories over Navy, CCNY, and Oklahoma at Madison Square Garden.

enue altered the nature of intercollegiate sports. In football, John "Ox" Da Grosa completed a three-year term as head coach in 1947, with a record of 8-9-2 in his last two years. In 1948, former football star Bill Osmanski '39, returned to Worcester as the first alumnus since Cleo O'Donnell to coach the sport. His two years as head coach yielded a record of 6-14, including only a single victory in his second season.[96] To rebuild the football program, Father O'Brien brought Eddie Anderson back to Holy Cross as head coach in 1950. Anderson held the job for the next fifteen years. Although the winning per-

96. Worcester *Gazette,* December 13, 1951; *Tomahawk,* January 8, 1948; Holy Cross Football Media Guide, 1993.

centage of his postwar teams (.577) was lower than the record accumulated between 1933 and 1938 (.870), he established and sustained a winning program under circumstances that placed Holy Cross, with its comparatively small enrollment, in competition with larger rivals.[97] Varsity baseball also maintained its winning tradition during the postwar years and several new varsity sports were introduced. Jack Barry continued as baseball coach until 1961. The 1952 team compiled a record of 21-3 and won the national NCAA championship at Omaha in the double elimination tournament. A number of Barry's players, including Johnny Turco '52 and Ron Perry '54, excelled at several sports.[98] Meanwhile, in 1949, Thomas Gallagher '51 and Father Francis Hart established swimming as a varsity sport; and in the spring of 1959, thanks to the efforts of Father Maurice Reidy, lacrosse was adopted as a varsity sport.[99]

Above all, it was the varsity basketball program that enjoyed a golden era during the postwar years. The team's rise to prominence began with the hiring of Alvin "Doggie" Julian as head coach in 1945. In his three seasons at Holy Cross, the Crusaders compiled a record of 65–10, including a national championship in 1947, when they achieved a record of 27–3 and won the NCAA Tournament. George Kaftan '49 was named the tournament's outstanding player, but the victory was a team effort that included outstanding play by Bob McMullen '50, Dermott O'Connell '49, Joe Mullaney '49, and Frank Offtring '50. A crowd of over 10,000 greeted the team when they arrived in Worcester and escorted them to City Hall for a public rally. On May 9, proclaimed Holy Cross Day by Mayor Charles Sullivan, the city sponsored a civic celebration, including a dinner, and a "monster parade" that attracted 30,000 spectators. That evening, 5000 persons attended a dance at the auditorium in honor of the players. Holy Cross played in the 1948 NCAA Tournament, too, but lost in the semifinal found. After the season, Coach Julian left Holy Cross to coach the Boston Celtics.[100]

The successful era in basketball continued under Lester "Buster" Sheary, head coach from 1948 to 1955. Besides the holdover players from the Julian era, Sheary coached Bob Cousy '50, Togo Palazzi '54, and Tom Heinsohn '56. Cousy was named AP and UPI Player of the Year for the 1949–50 season and was

97. *Tomahawk*, February 9, 1950. General statistics and records are listed in the annual Holy Cross Football Media Guide, issued through the office of the Sports Information Director.

98. *Tomahawk*, September 25, 1952. For details about the 1952 team and other highlights of Barry's career, see Cahill, *Quiet Crusader*, 32 and passim.

99. *Tomahawk*, December 7, 1949; *Crusader*, October 17, 1958; Maurice F. Reidy, Report on Lacrosse, June 25, 1957, ACHC, 18.3.

100. *Tomahawk*, March 5, 26, 31, May 7, and 14, 1947; HD, March 20–26, and May 9, 1947; March 18–22, 1948; Holy Cross Basketball Media Guide, 1991–92.

named All-American; Heinsohn was named a first-team All American in 1956. Sheary, who had assisted Coach Julian earlier, led his teams to a record of 155–36, including five seasons with twenty or more victories. Sheary's teams played in the NCAA Tournament in 1950 and 1953, and in the first National Invitational Tournament in 1952. The high point for Sheary's teams was the 1953–54 season, when the team achieved a record of 26–2 and won the NIT. Togo Palazzi was named the tournament's Most Valuable Player.[101] Sheary was succeeded in 1955 by Roy Leening, former head coach of St. Peter's Prep in Jersey City. Leening remained for six years, compiling a record of 106-48, including three seasons with twenty or more victories. Leening's teams kept Holy Cross in the national spotlight, with trips to the NCAA Tournament in 1956 and to the NIT in 1961 and 1962, when Jack "The Shot" Foley '62 was compiling a career average of over 27 points per game, the best in College history.[102]

The prominence of athletics raised old suspicions among Jesuit authorities. In 1948, New England Provincial John McEleney insisted that the schools limit the travels of their athletic teams. The following year, he again called attention to the "excessive inroads upon study being made by athletics and to the increasing number of extracurricular activities detrimental to classwork" and directed the dean to approve travel plans "so that the present distracting trends away from study may be checked."[103] After 1950, that sort of concern declined, and Father O'Brien publicly defended the concept of athletic scholarships, despite the fact that varsity football and basketball lost money during the postwar years. Football earned a net profit during five of the fourteen seasons (1947, 1948, 1954, 1955, 1959), and showed a loss during the period of over $230,000. The basketball program earned a profit in three seasons (1946/47, 1947/48, and 1949/50), with a net loss of about $121,000 between 1946 and 1960.[104]

As thoughtful observers understood, the success of the College's athletic program enhanced its profile but could not guarantee its academic reputation.

101. *Tomahawk*, October 15, 1948, March 16 and 30, 1950, February 29 and March 13, 1952, March 5 and 19, 1953, March 19, 1954; *Crusader*, March 1, 1956; Worcester *Telegram*, March 15, 1954; Holy Cross Basketball Media Guide, 1991–92.

102. Holy Cross Basketball Media Guide, 1993–94.

103. McEleney to John Tiernan, Boston, April 6, 1948, NEPA, HC-Varia; memorial of visit, February 13, 1949, ACHC, 19.1-2.

104. Worcester *Gazette*, December 13, 1951; Boston *Advertiser*, December , 1952 [ACHC, scrapbook 42, p. 119]. The financial statements may be found in the Trustees' Records, series 4, ACHC, 11.0. Average game attendance for football was gathered from press clippings in the sports publicity scrapbooks, ACHC, 18.3.

Provincial William FitzGerald discussed the school's standing with the general in 1953: "One is constantly hearing it referred to as the best Catholic College in the Country. This is probably true." He based his judgment on the fact that there were about 3000 applications that year for 500 openings. Yet, he was worried: 200 of those accepted did not enroll, and he was unwilling to blame the loss entirely on the availability of scholarships from wealthier institutions. Part of the responsibility rested with the school: "Not enough is done to produce first class scholars.[105] Two years later, the province prefect of studies found most of the classes adequate, but was convinced that "the number of specially trained and eager teachers at Holy Cross is too low in view of its national reputation." He had been told that, in addition to the loss of bright students to schools well endowed with scholarship funds, applications from the best high school seniors were generally down.[106] The common line in both letters was a conviction that the academic program and the largely Jesuit faculty needed improvement.

The merit of the academic program instituted in 1936 came to be taken for granted by many of the Holy Cross faculty and administrators during the postwar years, when they contented themselves with minor adjustments. In 1956, the College opened a language laboratory and was using the Institute for European Studies in Vienna as a beginning to the Study Abroad program.[107] In the same year, Saturday classes were dropped by tightening up the weekday schedule.[108] In 1959, Father Donaghy accepted a recommendation to revoke the required senior thesis that had been part of the curriculum since 1936. The requirement was not working out well: it was unspecific, created extra paperwork and, in the opinion of some faculty members, "by no stretch of language or imagination could their students write an essay which might be called a thesis."[109] In place of the thesis requirement, the catalog now emphasized the oral exam in philosophy for juniors and seniors.

105. FitzGerald to Janssens, Boston, March 6, 1953, NEPA, Roman Correspondence.

106. James Leo Burke, Memo on Holy Cross visit, March 29, 1955, ACHC, 19.8-1. Burke received his information about applicants from Raymond J. Swords, who was then admissions director. The number of distributed applications was down, from 3517 in 1948 to 2332 in 1952. In 1958, 1462 students applied to Holy Cross, of whom 887 (61 percent) were accepted to get a class of 552 (a yield of 63 percent). The following year, applicants rose to 1657, of whom 885 (53 percent) were accepted for a class of 549 (a yield of 62 percent). Holy Cross admissions reports, 1948, 1953, 1958, NEPA, HC-Varia.

107. The first director of the language laboratory was Fr. Alfred Desautels. *Telegram*, October 7, 1956. Donaghy to FitzGerald, Worcester, December 16, 1955, NEPA, HC-Rector.

108. Donaghy to FitzGerald, Worcester, July 23 and September 11, 1956, Donaghy memo of September 7, 1956, ACHC, 12.23-1.

109. John Long to Donaghy, Worcester, June 11, 1959, Dean's Records, ACHC, 14.0; Report of the Committee on the Advisability to Drop the Thesis as a Requirement for Graduation, Dean's

Chart 8.2 Graduates, 1947–1969

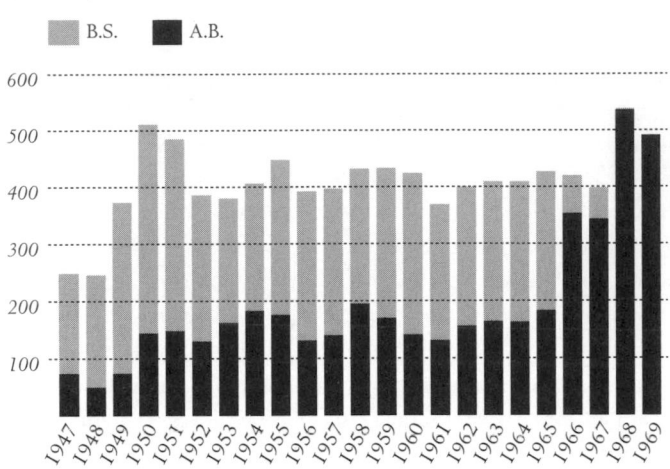

Graduation statistics and archival records contain other clues about the academic situation during those years. Immediately after the war, the number of students taking Latin so as to qualify for the A.B. dropped below 30 percent (Chart 8.2). At first, Jesuit authorities persisted in their loyalty to the power of the classics. In 1950, Father Janssens praised the American provincials for keeping Latin as a requirement for the A.B. There was some success at Holy Cross in reviving the tradition of classical humanism after veterans' enrollments dropped off. In 1954 and 1958, 45 percent of the graduates studied Latin; and during the 1950s, outside examiners attended a public final examination in translation and interpretation by Greek Honors graduates.[110] But in the spring of 1959, following nationwide discussions, the New England provincial authorized an A.B. without Latin, with requirements that included two years of a foreign language, traditional courses in philosophy, theology, and courses for the major. Holy Cross moved slowly to implement the changes; discussions were still underway when Father Donaghy left office.[111] The

Records, Committee Records, ACHC, 14.12. On the thesis requirement, see a report by John Cox in *The Alumnus,* April 1936, and College catalogs.

110. Janssens to McEleney, Rome, January 24, 1950, NEPA, Roman Correspondence; Program for 1958 Greek Honors Examination in Thucydides, WDA, Holy Cross, 1956–1960.

111. In addition to philosophy and theology and requirements for the major, the A.B. without Latin required one year each of science, mathematics, and social science, and two years each of English, a foreign language, and history. Memo of James E. Coleran, May, 1959, ACHC, 14.12; John Long to Coleran, Worcester, March 23, 1960, and Coleran to John Long, Boston, March 24, 1960, NEPA, HC-Rector.

brightest academic development in the late 1950s was the establishment of an Honors program, the work of an ad hoc committee, which selected sixteen students to begin an interdisciplinary Sophomore Honors colloquium on the Renaissance in September 1959. The program featured colloquia, oral and written examinations, and a senior thesis, now revived on a limited basis.[112]

A complicating factor in adjusting the postwar curriculum was that students were choosing different careers than their predecessors (Chart 8.3).[113] The data disclose some striking changes. Early in the century, when the basic academic pattern of the second Holy Cross emerged, a large percentage of alumni chose the priesthood, law, and medicine as careers, with small business enterprise and education trailing behind. After the First World War, law supplanted the ministry as the most favored choice; alumni of the Depression and war years gravitated toward medicine, law, and middle management positions. In the postwar period, ordained ministry was attracting only a small percentage, while an overwhelming majority opted for careers in management, medicine, and law. Within this pattern of preference, classical languages and

Chart 8.3 Alumni Occupational Choices, 1901–1960

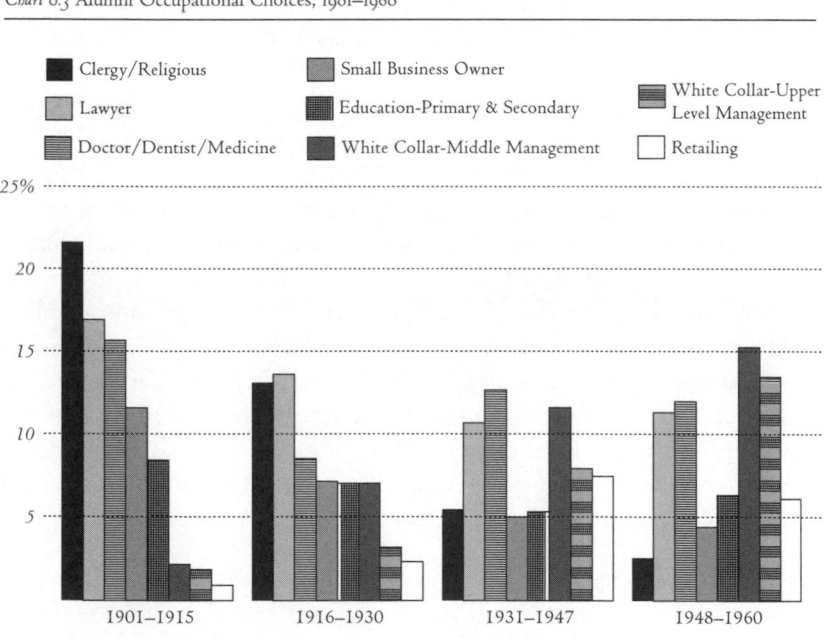

112. Honors Committee files, 1959–60, ACHC, 14.12; College catalog, 1959.

113. Figures are available for 68 percent of alumni between 1901 and 1915, 82 percent between 1916 and 1930, 83 percent between 1931 and 1947, and 87 percent between 1948 and 1960.

philosophy were becoming less attractive. In 1951 College authorities responded to changes by opening four separate concentrations under the B.S. in Business Administration—Accounting, Economics, Industrial Relations, and Marketing.

After the war, the required courses in religion presented their own set of challenges. An effort in 1948 to promote departmental initiative came up against the practice of centralized decision-making, as the dean admitted to Father FitzGerald: "Flo Gillis [Department Chair] is ready to call the Religion teachers together but wants to know what the official policy is. i.e. can they make suggestions concerning the course, textbooks, etc, or must they accept the status quo."[114] In 1949, when delegates at a meeting of the Jesuit Educational Association of New England were offered a choice between orienting college religion courses toward intellectual knowledge of faith and religion or toward formation for Catholic life, they favored the latter.[115] Until 1958, Holy Cross offered only the eight required courses (including the life of Christ, ecclesiology, sin and redemption, American church history, and Christian social principles) in the Department of Religion. In 1959, the department was re-named Theology, with essentially the same offerings. The following year, several of the courses were reorganized and re-named; a statement of purpose, combining intellectual and formational goals, was added to the catalog. All the instructors were Jesuits.

Part of the reason for complacency about the curriculum was that it wasn't under attack during most of the period. The postwar years were easy ones for Catholic advocates of the liberal arts. As Philip Gleason points out, religion had become respectable in America; the liberal arts revived generally, and progressivism in education was in decline. In these circumstances, Catholic intellectuals continued to offer neoscholasticism as a unifying agent for knowledge, contemporary culture, and religious faith.[116] One of the most ardent popularizers of this line of thought was the French intellectual Jacques Maritain, who was widely studied in the United States. Maritain incorporated the Thomistic distinction between the senses and the intellect into his view of the educational process as a liberating quest for truth. The goal of liberal education, he asserted, is "not the acquisition of science itself or art itself, along with the intellectual virtues involved, but rather the grasp of their *meaning*" and

114. James Fitzgerald [HC Dean] to Joseph Fitzgerald, Worcester, October 13, 1948, ACHC, 19.8-1.

115. "Discussion Agenda," JEA of New England, September 22, 1949, ACHC, 19.8-1.

116. Gleason, "American Catholic Higher Education," 239. On the resurgence of religion in the United States during the 1950s, see Will Herberg, *Protestant, Catholic, Jew*, revised ed. (Garden City: Anchor Books, 1960).

the insight they yield about truth and beauty. Liberal educators, therefore, had a noble task: "to see to it that the young person grasps this truth or beauty through the natural intuitive energy of his reason backed up by his whole sensuous, imaginative, and emotional dynamism."[117] At Holy Cross, Jesuits who had themselves been schooled in Thomistic philosophy offered to young people virtually unchanged what had earlier been given to them. The required courses in philosophy were designed to communicate a timeless system of thought that meshed with required courses in religion and the other mandatory and elective studies. Under the heading "Educational System," Holy Cross Catalogs from 1947 through 1959 set the goal of intellectual and moral development by interweaving "religious instruction with training in the secular branches of knowledge."

By the end of the 1950s, the consensus about that approach was fading. Part of the reason lay in the intrinsic difficulty of sustaining excellence in a system that was largely self-enclosed, the by-product of a mentality whose limits became more evident as the years went along. New Catholic spokespersons like John Courtney Murray promoted the goal of openness to the broader world by stressing the ideals of freedom, tolerance, and pluralism. Historian John Tracy Ellis startled his co-religionists in 1955 by asserting the lack of an authentic Catholic intellectual tradition in the United States. And, as Philip Gleason points out, by the end of the decade, Catholic institutions of higher learning were hiring a new generation of lay faculty, largely Catholic, "who had imbibed more of the atmosphere of secular higher education than earlier cohorts of Catholic academics." For them, scholarly excellence took precedence over Catholic distinctiveness. The new spirit of the times was reflected in the public careers of John XXIII and John F. Kennedy and gave rise to tension between a hard-line group of educators, who resisted the altered context, and a growing group who were more concerned about quality and reputation in the broader academic world.[118]

The gradual shift from the tranquil spirit of the early postwar years to the more dynamic mood of the late 1950s affected Holy Cross profoundly. At first the concerns addressed form rather than substance. In 1949, the province prefect of studies called the Holy Cross faculty "competent," but suggested that they could ask more of their students.[119] By 1952, the criticism was stronger;

117. Jacques Maritain, "Thomist Views on Education," in *Modern Philosophies and Education*, ed. Nelson B. Henry (Chicago: University of Chicago Press, 1955), 58–60, 79–80.

118. Gleason, "American Catholic Higher Education," 239–44.

119. Report of Prefect of Studies Joseph FitzGerald, March 23, 1949, ACHC, 19.8-1.

the prefect characterized the classes as "not poor, but too many were pedestrian." "I doubt very much if much inspiration is taken away from many classes," he wrote; "some teachers cover very little in a period, and have a way of following distractions that may temporarily amuse, but do not particularly instruct."[120] The following year, Provincial William FitzGerald told the general that many Jesuit teachers at Holy Cross were "psychologically old." FitzGerald was disappointed that, despite the esteem he enjoyed among benefactors and alumni, Father O'Brien himself tended to resist change.[121] In 1954, during O'Brien's last semester in office, FitzGerald attempted to animate the faculty himself with an admonition "to attain excellence in the field of teaching, to achieve and maintain progress in scholarship, and, above all, to exemplify in a high degree the virtues of religious life and character in all their dealings with the students." The stakes, he told them, were high: "The Professors of this College have, as it were, a ready-made field of national influence,—if they would but enter it."[122] To the general, FitzGerald explained: "I have tried to urge upon them . . . the pressing need of a more intense realization of the potentialities not only in greater spiritual influence but also in greater scholarly attainments." Part of the problem, he believed, was comfortable familiarity with old routines:

A large segment of this Community has grown old in the more pleasant aspects of the traditions of the Community and College: there is a definite spirit of complacency, on the part of older men, with things as they were. There is an inertia in the face of the need of closer organization of the institution, of stimulation of their methods and programs of teaching, of renewed zeal for personal guidance of students.[123]

Such documents suggest a reason for the urgency that was implied: the second Holy Cross depended primarily on Jesuits for its academic standing. Following custom, the word "faculty" usually applied only to Jesuit teachers. The rest of the teaching staff were generally designated as "lay faculty"—in some documents, the words were even capitalized. The sense of Holy Cross as a corporate enterprise of the Jesuits carried the implication that Jesuits were the principal faculty—they were the corporate sponsors; they lived on corridor; they had pastoral as well as pedagogical responsibilities. Until 1959, the catalog characterized them as "men long-trained in the world's best wisdom, whose consciences have been formed to the law of God by years of self-discipline . . . ,

120. Report of Prefect of Studies James Leo Burke, March 1952, ACHC, 19.8-1.
121. FitzGerald to Janssens, Boston, March 5, 1953, NEPA, Roman Correspondence.
122. William FitzGerald, Memorial of Visit, February 2, 1954, ACHC, 19.1-2.
123. FitzGerald to Janssens, Boston, March 2, 1954, NEPA, Roman Correspondence.

expounders of the eternal truths." Beside them, the qualifying adjective implied that the "lay faculty" were assistants, no matter how considerable their scholarly or pedagogical accomplishments. The point was not explicitly stated; it didn't have to be, because the institutional set-up expressed the two-tiered approach.

During the 1950s, the efforts of Jesuit authorities to rally the "faculty" were an effort to preserve institutional influence and control without compromising the school's high reputation. Besides worrying about complacency, American provincials had to prepare younger men for college teaching by supporting them in a course of studies that included the Ph.D. In doing so, they were following the lead of Father Janssens, who believed strongly that Jesuits in the educational apostolate should commit themselves to study and academic discipline. Modern circumstances, he argued, indicated that generalists could no longer sustain the enterprise; he desired more men to become specialists in their chosen fields. By 1952, 191 American Jesuits were in graduate studies.[124] For those who were already assigned to teach, there were distracting outside obligations, particularly corridor prefecting and the requests for pastoral assistance from nearby pastors. In the early 1950s, at least ten and sometimes close to twenty Jesuits were assigned on weekends to render such assistance.[125] Additional problems in motivating men to academic excellence were connected with the quality of modern life. When the first television was placed in the community recreation room, Jeremiah Donovan was disturbed by its impact: "Many fathers spend the whole evening in the recreation room two or three nights a week. Reading is curtailed. Troy's wooden horse is an apt symbol."[126] But the television remained, a Trojan horse indeed for those who found its lure irresistible.

Starting in 1954, it was William Donaghy who bore the responsibility for motivating the "faculty." That year, the American Chemical Association made an issue of the low number of faculty doctorates before extending recognition to the Chemistry Department.[127] The following year, Father FitzGerald was still concerned about the overall competence of the teaching Jesuits and told the general bluntly that, as a group, they lacked the scholarly interest and productivity of their lay colleagues. He pinned his hopes on Donaghy's ability to

124. FitzGerald, *Governance*, 75–77; Janssens to John McMahon, Rome, April 25, 1952, NEPA, Roman Correspondence.

125. HD, 1952–54. During the 1951–52 academic year, 63 faculty priests helped, at times, with outside weekend Masses. John Wright to Paul F. Barry, Worcester, May 27, 1952, WDA, Holy Cross, 1950–1955.

126. HD, April 24, 1955.

127. Donaghy to FitzGerald, Worcester, September 13, 1954, NEPA, HC-Rector.

succeed where his predecessor had failed.[128] In 1956, James E. Coleran succeeded William FitzGerald as provincial. By then, it was clear that the faculty problem could not be solved by exhortation. Father Donaghy had become convinced that the fundamental problem was "an aging faculty," as he explained to Coleran: "It takes young men to negotiate these hills, young men to prefect corridors with the noisy youngsters and the long hours. We have many who have grown weary and, as a result, discipline on the corridors as well as intellectual stimulation in the classes have suffered." To back his contention, he pointed out that the average age of the Holy Cross Theology Department was over four years higher than their counterparts at Boston College. There seven Jesuits were under 40; Holy Cross had none so young.[129] But it was easier to request talented young instructors than to supply them. Father Coleran admitted it in the summer of 1958, when he was discussing assignments for the coming year at Holy Cross: "If Fr. . . . is waiting for men with spectacular abilities, I am afraid we will not have too many of them."[130]

Even as the postwar rectors fretted about the competence of Jesuit instructors, they were coming to terms slowly with the fact that the lay faculty were an increasingly important part of the operation—in sheer numbers, and in their ability to uphold the academic reputation of the school by their teaching and scholarship. Faculty statistics made the point clearly enough (Chart 6.3). Until 1961, the decision to keep enrollment at 1800 held faculty growth to a slow but steady rise, a circumstance that helped prolong the numerical preponderance of Jesuits far longer than at most Jesuit schools.[131] In 1961, the number of full-time Jesuit instructors reached a peak of 83 (including two administrators who taught part-time); full-time lay faculty by then had risen to 69. Lay faculty constituted 45 percent of the teaching staff, and 26 of the 39 positions that had been added to the faculty in the previous twelve years had been filled by lay persons. The quality of the faculty, measured by the proportion of teachers with the Ph.D., remained relatively static during the 1950s. As the faculty grew larger, its academic quality was not rising. The number of

128. FitzGerald to Janssens, Boston, February 19, 1955, NEPA, Roman Correspondence.

129. Donaghy to Coleran, Worcester, March 1, 1957, NEPA, HC-Rector. The average age of the teaching Jesuits at Holy Cross rose from 45.6 in 1950, to 49 in 1955, and 49.6 in 1960. In 1954, the province prefect of studies noted that 32 percent of the Holy Cross Jesuits were over 55; 73 percent were over 45. James Leo Burke, memo to William FitzGerald on Holy Cross visitation, April 1, 1954, ACHC, 19.8-1.

130. Coleran to Donaghy, Boston, July 9, 1958, NEPA, HC-Rector.

131. The average percentage of full-time Jesuit faculty members at all the U.S. Jesuit colleges and universities stood at 31.1 percent in 1948, 27.5 percent in 1958, and 16.3 percent in 1968. William Patrick Leahy, "Jesuits, Catholics, and Higher Education in Twentieth Century America," Ph.D. Dissertation (Stanford University, 1986), 180.

Ph.D.'s stood at 32 percent in 1946 (29 percent of the Jesuits and 35 percent of the lay faculty), then declined to 24 percent in 1948 and remained between 22 percent and 24 percent throughout the 1950s. In 1960, only 25 percent of the lay faculty and 23 percent of the Jesuit faculty held the doctorate, and the proportion of faculty with doctorates had not risen for over a decade.[132]

Early efforts to promote solidarity between Jesuits and lay colleagues involved social contact. In the fall of 1946, Father Healy hosted a dinner that drew 30 of the 42 laymen on the faculty. The event proved so successful that it was repeated annually until 1958, when it became a banquet and reception for lay faculty and their wives.[133] These gatherings were a step in the direction of collegiality; but they also cast lay persons in the role of guests of the Jesuits, a situation that reinforced the subsidiary position assigned to them by tradition and custom. As the number of lay faculty increased, they were offered a weekend religious retreat at the start of the academic year, followed by another dinner with the Jesuits. Attendance was not mandatory but, under the circumstances, absence would have been noticed. During his first year as rector, Father Donaghy personally conducted the retreat.[134]

The lay instructors at Holy Cross were at first too few and too powerless to have much impact on the policies and governance of the school. A 1948 effort to organize a "Lay Professors' Association" was approved by the trustees with a vote of *"tolerandum sit,"* but it seems to have achieved little, possibly because the leadership of the College passed from Father Healy's hands soon afterwards.[135] Despite the lukewarm endorsement of the laymen's group at Holy Cross, some influential Jesuits welcomed the growing number of lay professors. Edward B. Rooney, President of the Jesuit Educational Association from 1937 to 1966, argued that lay faculty could make a contribution that Jesuits couldn't duplicate. Others doubted that lay people could communicate institutional goals or sustain the Catholic and Jesuit identity of the schools.[136] In 1955, the provincial corresponded with Father Donaghy about a plan to extend collaboration with lay professors by familiarizing them with Jesuit concepts:

132. Data on Ph.D.'s were obtained by correlating information in the annual catalogs with faculty files, ACHC, 14.81A-1. A study of the faculties at five Jesuit universities (Fordham, Georgetown, Loyola of Chicago, Marquette, and St. Louis) disclosed an average of 44 percent holding the doctorate in 1957. John P. Raynor, "The Encouragement of Research in Five Jesuit Universities," Ph.D. Dissertation (University of Chicago, 1957), 130.

133. HD, October 20, 1946, March 2, 1947, June 9, 1958.

134. Donaghy to FitzGerald, Worcester, September 13, 1954, NEPA, HC-Rector; HD, September 14–16, 1956, September 13–15, 1957.

135. Trustees' Minutes, February 19, 1948, ACHC, 11.0.

136. FitzGerald, *Governance*, 151; Leahy, "Jesuits," 169.

[The lay professors] should be those whose character and educational background are such as to make them apt members of a team striving for the aims of Jesuit education. To assure this unity of spirit, a program of indoctrination in the history, aims, and methods of Jesuit education should be provided for lay-members of our faculties.[137]

That was the culmination of one line of Jesuit thinking about lay collaboration: in effect, to commission their lay colleagues to be something like deputy Jesuits.

Neither Father O'Brien nor Father Donaghy succeeded completely in winning the lay faculty over to this approach. When O'Brien left office, Father FitzGerald admitted to the general that the lay instructors had held "considerable latent discontent" against him; Donaghy, near the end of his term, was defending himself from allegations that he was "not sufficiently interested in the academic."[138] The best Father Donaghy could do was to raise wages. A Ford Foundation grant of $551,000 in 1956 assisted in the effort. In 1959, he boasted that he had raised salaries between 33 percent and 40 percent during his time in office.[139] Yet faculty members were soon pointing out that the pay scale at Holy Cross was substantially lower than at comparable schools, particularly for associate and full professors.[140]

The context of the salary discussions was the College's first reaccreditation process since 1938, a development that afforded the lay faculty their first significant opportunity to participate in the direction of the school. To prepare the general report, Father Donaghy appointed a Committee on Re-Evaluation that included four lay and five Jesuit members.[141] The Eastern States evaluators vis-

137. FitzGerald to Donaghy, Boston, July 12, 1955, ACHC, 12.23-1. Roman authorities endorsed this idea in 1960 when, according to Paul FitzGerald, they "insisted . . . that lay professors understand the broad objectives of the Jesuit apostolate of education and, to the extent possible, contribute to them." *Governance*, 153.

138. FitzGerald to Janssens, Boston, February 19, 1955, NEPA, Roman Correspondence; Donaghy to John Long, Worcester, March 11, 1959, ACHC, 12.23-1.

139. Donaghy to John Long, Worcester, March 11, 1959, ACHC, 12.23; Treasurer's Memo, September 20, 1960, ACHC, 12.24.

140. Memo to Donaghy from Committee on Re-Evaluation, February 23, 1960, ACHC, 14.12. Salaries at Catholic colleges and universities were lower throughout the postwar period. In 1947, maximum salaries at Catholic institutions of higher learning averaged $3838, compared with $4225 at non-Catholic institutions. William Leahy argues that salary levels and lack of status were the principal grievances of lay professors at Jesuit schools during this period, with status often being the more serious issue. "Jesuits," 166–67, 194–96. In 1960–61, on a graded scale ranging from AA to F, Holy Cross professors ranked at Grade E, associates at Grade D, assistants at Grade C, and instructors at Grade B. "The Proposed Development Program at the College of the Holy Cross," [1962], Ropes and Gray Papers, CHCB 2, in ACHC, 16.1.

141. Faculty Notice, February 4, 1958, Faculty Meeting files, ACHC, 14.8.1A.

ited the campus in October of 1957 and reported that the College's unique character was connected with a strong tradition of Catholicism and discipline that made it "probably as deeply religiously oriented as any other Catholic institution in the country." Student life offered closer supervision than at most other schools and presented the "unique flavor of homelike and even parental atmosphere." Evaluators praised the classic liberal arts program; but they noted the unusually long probationary period (nine years) prior to tenure, the abnormally low salary scale, and the limited policy on academic freedom that differed materially from that of most other schools because it mandated immediate termination in case of "offense against Catholic doctrine or morality." The report offered nine recommendations, including better faculty salaries, a reexamination of promotion and tenure policies, a standing curriculum committee with faculty participation, a lay advisory council or lay trustees, and more delegation of responsibility by chief administrators.[142]

In January of 1958, as a follow-up to the report, Father Donaghy asked the Re-Evaluation Committee to assume responsibility for the "continuous reevaluation of academic policy and programs" in matters such as tenure, salaries, conditions of work, and curriculum. The members understood that the committee would be "a channel [of communication] between the faculty and administration." It would not serve as a grievance board, and it lacked the power to constitute and appoint members to faculty committees. Donaghy assented to this concept, granting the committee freedom to meet without his interference. He urged members to work out the scope of their interests and duties. Although Jesuit rules necessitated that policies and changes be passed through regular channels, he pledged his cooperation: recommendations would be rejected only reluctantly and with full explanation.[143] Because all members were appointed through the president's office, the Re-evaluation Committee represented only a limited sharing of responsibility, but it was a start. Between 1958 and 1960, the committee became a source of initiatives addressing important issues of academic life. In the addition to the 1960 proposal for higher salaries, it devised successful proposals for the adoption of a quality point system in grading, proposed a faculty Committee on Graduate Study

142. 1957 Reaccreditation Report, ACHC, 14.12.

143. Re-Evaluation Committee minutes, January 16 and February 24, 1958, ACHC, 12.24; Donaghy to Andrew McFadden [committee chair], January 20, 1958. ACHC, 14.12. As of February 3, 1958, the members of the committee included five Jesuits: Eugene Harrington (Philosophy), Paul Facey (Sociology), Joseph McGrady (Greek and Religion), Robert MacDonnell (Physics), and Andrew McFadden (Executive Assistant to the President). Lay members were Vincent McBrien (Mathematics), Thomas McDermott (Economics), Andrew Van Hook (Chemistry), and William Grattan (History).

and Scholarships, initiated catalog revisions and discussed the Honors program, proposed regular meetings of departmental chairs, discussed and suggested procedures for dismissal of the faculty, and initiated preparation of a faculty handbook.[144]

Faculty status at Holy Cross was the subject of a thoughtful report prepared in the spring of 1960 by Jesuit Thomas F. McQueeny, a faculty member at Fordham University, as part of a national study entitled "Faculty Recruitment, Professional Development and Stimulation in Jesuit Colleges and Universities in the United States." Apparently, the project was undertaken in response to a request from Father Janssens for a study of how well the Society's schools were achieving the goals of Jesuit education. The status of the lay faculty and the role of philosophy requirements were among the items singled out for examination. McQueeny visited Holy Cross in March to undertake his research; in late April he sent a copy of his "confidential" and "preliminary" report on Holy Cross to Father Donaghy.[145]

The document contained a blueprint designed to address the cluster of problems that had developed during the 1950s. There was "a great and urgent need to build up a young and strong faculty," including a hiring requirement of the Ph.D. or "A.B.D." (All But Dissertation completed toward Ph.D.), and an expectation that faculty members would participate in professional scholarly meetings. Administrators were urged to orient new faculty members to institutional traditions and aims, and to diminish the distinction between Jesuit and lay professors as faculty members, "but in no other way." Academic officers were advised to "insist on promotion through effort and scholarship, not solely through years of service." McQueeny advocated a prudent use of student evaluations, interdepartmental cooperation, and some classroom visitation by supervisors. Faculty research required more support through improved secretarial service, enhanced library collections, faculty seminars, reduced teaching loads "for those who can produce," and sabbaticals and funds to support research. New norms for promotion needed to be established and publicized as soon as possible. The faculty salary scale needed to be competitive, with insurance, loan benefits, and plans for pensions and tuition for faculty

144. Memo of A. H. McFadden [chair of Committee on Re-Evaluation] to Donaghy, June 9, 1959, ACHC, 12.24; Paul Facey to Raymond Swords, Worcester, September 10, 1960, ACHC, 14.12.

145. A note in the House Diary, March 13, 1960, says "Fr McQueeney [sic] guest here for a few days." Fr. Donaghy was away from campus during McQueeny's visit and was not interviewed by him. Donaghy to McQueeny, Worcester, April 28, 1960, ACHC, 12.23-1. The McQueeny report was sent on April 25, 1960, and may be found among Fr. Donaghy's papers, ACHC, 12.23-1. See also McQueeny to Donaghy, New York City, April 25, 1960, ACHC, 12.23-1, and FitzGerald, *Governance*, 149–52.

children. And, the system of faculty committees needed to be encouraged as a follow-through to the committee experience of the previous two years.

McQueeny's final point incorporated a set of suggestions, apparently gleaned from members of the faculty and administration during his visit, which echoed and amplified other parts of the statement: a change in traditional attitudes so that there would be "a clear and definite distinction between tradition and progress"; better communication with other schools; published statements of policy regarding the faculty; "removal of the distinction between Jesuit and lay faculty; more trust and confidence in lay members of faculty"; a re-examination of the curriculum, gradual faculty improvement; raising admissions standards; improvement in the library; "immediate improvement of the philosophy dept."; "less emphasis on disciplinary matters, and much more emphasis on the academic"; a re-examination of the role of extra-curricular activities; and "intellectual honesty in the approach to academic problems."

The McQueeny Report was a reasonably accurate reflection of the state of the College and a bold plan for re-shaping Holy Cross after a decade during which the problems had gradually intensified. The rapidity with which he delivered the assessment suggests that many of the problems—and anticipated solutions—were common to the institutions he had examined. Yet, the issues he identified and the recommended changes had their specific meaning for Holy Cross as they lay, confidentially, on Father Donaghy's desk. Clearly, his own thinking about the problems ran in another direction. The statement of educational philosophy, revised for the catalog during his last year in office, was an articulate justification of the *status quo*: "This traditional approach needs constant review to keep abreast of progress but *no basic revision* to subscribe to those educational expediencies which from day to day announce themselves as final educative solutions."[146]

By then Father Donaghy was worn out, drinking heavily, and ill. He had trouble comprehending the new spirit of Catholic openness to the broader world;[147] the double burden of confronting a set of institutional challenges he had only partially met and of leading an aging community of 103 Jesuit priests, brothers, and scholastics, had wearied him. By the summer of 1959, he was suffering recurring chest pains; his doctor attributed them to exhaustion and pre-

146. College catalog, 1960. Italics added.

147. In 1960, Donaghy expressed misgivings about speaking to the Rotary Club, as he confided to an acquaintance: "You can have this whole thing of intercreedalism. . . . I never 'bought' the idea that the Eternal Word of God would take . . . the trouble to establish a rummage sale of Religions." Letter to John F. Gannon, Worcester, February 4, 1960, WDA, Holy Cross, 1956–1960.

scribed a long rest.[148] By then, Father Coleran seems to have lost confidence in his leadership and was looking toward Raymond Swords, Chair of the Department of Mathematics, as the successor. Given the state of Donaghy's health, the provincial accelerated the transition. On June 13, 1960, Father Donaghy was informed that Father Swords would succeed him in three days.[149]

These circumstances help explain Fr. Donaghy's defensive response to the McQueeny Report. Although he prefaced his remarks with the disclaimer, "I agree with almost everything you say," the substance of his response made it clear that he found the implicit criticism of his leadership unfair and the suggestions unrealistic. He told McQueeny: "The cleavage, if there be one, between the Jesuit and Lay faculties is, to a degree in the very nature of things." Lay professors, he believed, had exaggerated the importance of this problem, since he had always been available to them as president to discuss institutional issues and as a priest to discuss their problems, "and the only time I see them is when they want an increase in salary." Yet, his concept of the relationship between administration and faculty was paternalistic: he claimed that he had made a great effort to provide faculty offices and "to improve their status." The rest of the proposals, he averred, were either impractical, or falsely based, or idealistic and impossible:

When you mention "a thorough examination of curricula," this must be taken in our context which is, I believe, unique. . . . Re-examination for its own sake is not necessarily symptomatic of sagacity. It would have to go forth in the light of our purposes and our traditions: I can see no necessary divorce between tradition and progress. Again, to build a better faculty is the desire of any academic administrator, as is the establishment of high entrance standards. These gleaming ideals, however, are overshadowed by grave realities — like money, the fact that Jesuits grow old, and the like. Similarly, a suggestion like the "immediate improvement of the Philosophy Department" is one that a man must necessarily salute but, if he sits in this uneasy swivel, he comes up bloody-nosed against the impenetrable "how precisely?" The implied dichotomy between emphasis on disciplinary as against academic matters is one that, frankly, I do not understand. Discipline is supposed to establish the climate and preserve the atmosphere in which the academic can flourish. Finally, "intellectual honesty in the approach to academic problems" — the lack of predication about this obviously desirable goal leads me to ask you whether you found that honesty lacking here: I am not aware that it is.[150]

148. Donaghy to Coleran, Poughkeepsie, June 17 and July 6, 1959, NEPA, HC-Rector; Donaghy to Coleran, Worcester, December 11, 1959, ACHC, 19.2-3.

149. Swords to Coleran, Worcester, June 17, 1959, ACHC, 19.2-3; Coleran to Donaghy, Boston, June 8 and 13, 1960, NEPA, HC-Rector.

150. Donaghy to McQueeny, Worcester, April 28, 1960, ACHC, 12.23-1.

"Grave realities"; "I do not understand"; "I am not aware"; "how precisely?"—certain phrases in Father Donaghy's response reveal more about the limits of traditional approaches than about shortcomings in the McQueeny Report. The record suggests that, after World War II, the second Holy Cross—the model Jesuit college where the *Ratio Studiorum* had been successfully refashioned according to twentieth-century norms for American higher education—could no longer be sustained. The Society of Jesus had too few members with the requisite qualifications to serve the needs of the expanded school; the quality and content of the academic program had become questionable; promising applicants were being lost; and many of the lay faculty, on whose efforts the College increasingly depended, were nettled by their inferior status. The network of control too often slowed progress and stifled initiative: everything from building projects to the curriculum was supposed to be reviewed—and approved—by outside authorities. John O'Brien and William Donaghy tried to defend the *status quo* by making adjustments and concessions. But good will and energetic application in the president's office fell short of putting the school back on a positive track; so did regular exhortations to the Jesuit faculty to be more academically productive. The "faculty" couldn't give what they didn't have; and, having been trained to live and teach at schools like the second Holy Cross, they couldn't easily adjust to the altered context. By 1960, the second Holy Cross had run out of momentum, a victim of its own success and of the assumption that what had worked well in the past was good enough for the present. But there were promising developments, particularly the insights of the McQueeny Report, the experience of the Committee on Re-Evaluation, and the untapped potential of the associate trustees. They were signposts to which Raymond Swords paid careful attention as he organized a new administration.

PART THREE

"This Remarkable Burst toward the Future"

CHAPTER NINE

Facing the Issues, 1960–1968

A FTER RAYMOND J. SWORDS assumed responsibility for Holy Cross in the summer of 1960, the context of institutional life changed dramatically. The sixties altered patterns of public life, brought the self-understanding of the Roman Catholic Church into the modern age, and redefined methods and goals of excellence in higher education. In the Society of Jesus, a new spirit of active engagement with contemporary culture "re-formed" the order in what one historian has called "a significant internal transformation, probably greater than any it had experienced in its previous four hundred years."[1] Some found these changes difficult to accept and sought to prevent their implementation; others pressed forward, determined to introduce the new spirit as quickly as possible. In the end, Father Swords had to choose sides, and he carried the College with him.

In the public arena, the confident patriotism of 1960 sustained Theodore White's judgment that, every four years, the political system offers voters "two men of exceptional ability" for the presidency.[2] Few would have taken exception to his optimism, or to the gender-exclusive twist. In the early sixties, a can-do spirit replaced the complacency of the "silent generation" with social activism, and postwar "Baby Boomers" generated their own distinct youth culture under the influence of a new permissiveness and economic affluence. At the same time, federal assistance to higher education facilitated the enlargement of physical plants and rising enrollments.[3] Yet, by 1968, anger and disillusionment were common responses to seemingly intractable problems like the protracted southeast Asian war, enduring racism, domestic violence, and self-serving ap-

---

1. Joseph M. Becker, *The Re-Formed Jesuits* (San Francisco, Ignatius Press, 1992), 11.

2. Theodore H. White, *The Making of the President, 1960* (New York: Pocket Books, Inc., 1961), 253.

3. Richard M. Feeland argues that federal aid promoted a "golden age" of American

Raymond J. Swords, College President from 1960 to 1970, under whose direction separate incorporation and other features of the third Holy Cross were put in place.

peals to law and order. Father Swords's challenge was to manage the conflicts, to seize the opportunities, and to assert a common spirit in this uncertain decade. His sense of the possibilities, and his willingness to act, moved the school decisively along the road from the second to the third Holy Cross—a process that reflected his personal growth in office. In a study of higher educa-

universities from 1945 to 1970. *Academia's Golden Age: Universities in Massachusetts, 1945–1970* (New York: Oxford University Press, 1992), 91–93. See also Rudolph, *American College*, 490–92.

tion published in 1967, Andrew Greeley asserted that effective administrative leadership was the most important factor in the academic improvement of Catholic institutions. The president had to symbolize institutional goals and generate confidence in their viability; he needed political skills and understanding of the educational field and his school's place in it; he had to choose competent assistants and be an effective fund-raiser.[4] Events were to prove Raymond Swords a successful leader according to most of those norms.

A native of Springfield, Swords graduated from Holy Cross *magna cum laude* as a classics major in 1938. He entered the Society of Jesus in 1940, taught mathematics and English at his alma mater during the war, and received an M.A. in mathematics from Harvard in 1947. He was ordained in 1950 and was assigned again to Holy Cross in 1952 to teach mathematics. Between 1953 and 1955, he served as director of admissions; he was chair of the Mathematics Department from 1955 to 1960.[5] When he assumed the presidency of Holy Cross, he was only 42 and had known privately for a year that he was under consideration to succeed to William Donaghy. New England Provincial James Coleran asked him in the spring of 1959 to think the matter over. Swords's first response was to decline—in his own judgment, he lacked the requisite experience and maturity. In a long, revealing letter, Swords told the provincial that he was willing to take any assignment, but offered several considerations against the projected appointment, including his tendency to internalize problems and to take criticism too seriously. He believed that his greatest abilities were in teaching and counseling. He found himself impatient at times, and marked by "an impetuous desire to . . . clear out the deadwood."[6] Contrary to Swords's expectations, these qualities probably helped persuade Father Coleran that he was the man for the job.

The short span of time between the announcement of Swords's succession on June 13 and his formal assumption of duty on June 16 left little time for preparing statements of goals. To the press, Swords stated blandly that he would be happy to be "one-tenth as good a rector as [Father Donaghy] has been."[7] In fact, his thoughts had been running in a different direction for some time. In a 1958 speech on the liberal arts, he endorsed the idea that the principle of adaptability stood at the core of Ignatius's thinking about schools. Adaptation was also the theme of his first address to the faculty in October of

---

4. Andrew Greeley, *The Changing Catholic College* (Chicago: Aldine Publishing Co., 1967), 71–72, 99, 147, 208–9.

5. Biographical data, Swords papers, ACHC, 12.24; HD, July 15, 1953.

6. Swords to Coleran, June 17, 1959, ACHC, 19.2-3.

7. Worcester *Telegram*, June 17, 1960.

1960: he announced a plan to construct two new residence halls, to attract competent faculty, to raise scholarship funds, and to keep the Re-evaluation Committee together as an academic advisory group. And he offered the reflection that the academic requirements were "too rigid . . . [and] too heavy for a student to carry if we are to expect him to be able to stop and think once in a while."[8]

Like his predecessors, Father Swords found the combination of responsibilities as Holy Cross president and rector of a community of 100 Jesuits impossible to manage. Between June and September of 1960, he wrote 37 letters to the provincial, many several pages long, on a variety of matters that included reports on sick Jesuits, personnel recommendations, reports on the College and its needs, and approval requests for the new student residences. He applied himself to his tasks with great energy, including regular exhortations to the Jesuits and preaching at student Masses. By November, he realized that the requirements of his two full-time jobs deprived him of time to think, and reduced him to being merely reactive to situations.[9] A few weeks later, he told Father Coleran that the situation was unfair: "The job of President is getting so big that, in my opinion, a man cannot handle it and be Superior to 100 Jesuits."[10] Nevertheless, he made the effort for two years, during which the Jesuit community reached its peak membership of 105. The House Diary during those years records Swords's *daily* visits to the sick at St. Vincent's Hospital, including one occasion when, after returning from a meeting at 11:30 P.M., he kept vigil with a dying Jesuit until 3:00 A.M. By June of 1962, when Swords departed for a vacation, the community minister noted: "By all physical and medical laws[,] he should have collapsed long ago from sheer fatigue."[11]

By then, Jesuit authorities had found a way to relieve Father Swords of some responsibility by appointing a separate religious superior to attend to the Jesuits as the rector's deputy. The concept of separating the presidency of colleges and universities from the rectorship of the Jesuit community had been under discussion since 1931, when Roman authorities became convinced that the relatively short tenure of presidents was a weakness in the Jesuit sys-

8. Manuscript notes for a speech on mathematics in the liberal arts curriculum [1958], and address to faculty, October 4, 1960, ACHC, 12.24. See also George Ganss, *Saint Ignatius' Idea of a Jesuit University*, cited in the preface.

9. Swords to Coleran, Worcester, November 4, 1960, NEPA, HC-Rector, and ACHC, 19.2-3.

10. Swords to Coleran, Lenox, November 27, 1961, ACHC, 19.2-3.

11. HD, October 23 and December 11, 1961, June 17, 1962. On May 4, 1963, the entry notes: "Tonight was the first night in well over seven years when there was no member of this community a patient in St. Vincent's [Hospital]."

tem. In 1934, the general authorized the separation of those offices; starting in 1940, Fordham University, Loyola University of Chicago, and the University of San Francisco experimentally adopted the system of separate leaders for school and community. By 1946, it seemed that a better solution was to appoint a rector/president (with both titles) whose primary responsibility was to be chief administrator of the school, while he delegated responsibility over the religious community to a superior who acted in his name. This plan was adopted at Georgetown University in 1952 and at Boston College in 1954. The same plan was introduced at Holy Cross in 1962, when William J. Casey, a member of the faculty since 1945, was appointed Jesuit superior.[12]

Father Swords sought additional assistance by re-activating the associate trustees early in 1962, with attorney Edward B. Hanify '33 as chair. The board comprised eight businessmen, six professionals from banking and finance, five from the legal profession, three medical doctors, and four representatives of the Church, including Worcester's second Catholic bishop, Bernard J. Flanagan '28. At the organizational meeting, Swords presented the challenges: keeping Holy Cross a small, liberal arts college; improving the faculty at a time when a large but aging Jesuit faculty would have to be replaced principally by lay professors; finding ways to attract gifted students despite the lack of endowment funds for scholarships; enlarging the physical plant. The associate trustees also discussed a proposed capital fund campaign and established four standing committees: Finance, Development, Planning, and Public Relations, plus an Executive Committee.[13] By the end of 1962, the associate trustees had become an important part of the administration. In December, the agenda included the application for a federal loan for the infirmary and faculty residence, tuition increases to cover a projected deficit, and several building projects. Despite their competence and the responsibility they were assuming, the associate trustees had only an advisory function. As at other Jesuit colleges and universities, the trustees of the College, all Jesuits, remained the legal governing board, with the power to accept or reject recommendations from the associates. The situation was archaic and begged for correction. By 1965, Father Swords was ready to move. "We would like to pioneer in the appointment of laymen to the College Board of Trustees," he told the associates.[14]

12. HD, June 10, 1962; FitzGerald, *Governance*, 110–19.

13. Associate Trustees' Minutes, January 21, 1962, ACHC, 11.1. Swords enhanced the Jesuits' sense of inclusion in the operation of the school by holding a meeting to discuss the financial condition of the College and describe the work of the Associate Trustees. HD, January 23, 1962.

14. Associate Trustees' Minutes, December 15, 1962, and December 11, 1965, ACHC, 11.1.

15. FitzGerald, *Governance*, 188–90, discusses the conciliar Declaration on Christian Edu-

Lay trusteeship was a novel idea in 1965; but the 28 Jesuit college and university presidents in the United States were already wrestling with the issue. Within the Jesuit Educational Association, they had gradually been increasing their freedom to direct their institutions by reducing interference from Jesuit authorities in America and Rome and gaining more assistance from lay advisors. In launching this initiative, the presidents drew support from Vatican II, with its understanding that apostolic work was appropriate to lay people who "have their own proper roles in building up the Church,"[15] and from the 31st General Congregation of the Jesuits held in 1965–66, which recommended "close collaboration" with lay associates:

Let Jesuits consider the importance for the Society itself of . . . collaboration with lay people, who will always be the natural interpreters for us of the modern world, and so will always give us effective help in this apostolate. Therefore, we should consider handing over to them the roles they are prepared to assume in the work of education, whether these be in teaching, in academic or business administration, or even on the board of directors. It will also be advantageous to consider whether it would not be helpful to establish in some of our institutions of higher education a board of trustees which is composed partly of Jesuits and partly of lay people; the responsibility both of ownership and of direction would pertain to this board.[16]

The same congregation elected a new general, Father Pedro Arrupe, who affirmed the quest to make Jesuit colleges academically excellent enterprises that stood in active relationship to the larger academic world, and endorsed the long-standing goal of Jesuit college administrators to have their faculties measure up to contemporary norms in scholarship and teaching.[17]

This fresh spirit stimulated the Jesuit college and university presidents to broaden administration at their institutions. As historian Paul FitzGerald put it, the presidents "had to keep pace with other American universities in the race for excellence and influence"; it was no longer possible to achieve that goal from the single platform of Jesuit structure and authority.[18] With the support of the regional Jesuit provincials, the presidents introduced a new policy that began to change the nature of the Jesuit Educational Association

cation. The quoted passage is from the Decree on the Apostolate of the Laity, cited in John Tracy Ellis, *American Catholicism* (2d ed., revised.; Chicago: The University of Chicago Press, 1969), 199.

16. Documents of the 31st General Congregation, Decree 28, nr. 27, (St. Louis: The Institute of Jesuit Sources, 1977), 237–38.

17. FitzGerald, *Governance*, 190–92.

18. Ibid., 187.

19. *Proceedings*, Commission on Colleges and Universities, Gonzaga University, June 1966, appendix L, p. 112, cited in FitzGerald, *Governance*, 198. See also 180–87 in FitzGerald's book.

from a supervisory agency to a service organization. In 1966, the presidents endorsed a statement noting that, because "the academic aims, structure and quality of our institutions rest in large part on criteria established by the accrediting agencies," the Society of Jesus would have to adapt to this reality. According to FitzGerald, they envisioned schools where "the authority of the appropriate academic officer would be paramount in all decisions and intrusion by the [Jesuit] provincial would be minimal." The provincials, several of whom had been higher education administrators, did not oppose this development.[19] In this context, lay trustees came to be understood as a vital part of the process of strengthening the institutions for the advantages their expertise and resources brought to schools, and for their usefulness as a balancing element in the effort to assert institutional autonomy within the structures of the Catholic Church.[20]

Father Swords's intention of introducing lay trustees gained momentum as the associate trustees made more and more recommendations on vital College matters.[21] At that time, the six Jesuit trustees included Swords as president of the board, the Jesuit minister as vice-president, the academic dean as secretary, and the College treasurer. Although Father Swords had succeeded in delegating much of the responsibility for managing the Jesuit community to a religious superior, the governance of community and College were still intermingled in the board of trustees. Appointing lay trustees would necessitate separate structures of governance, since lay trustees could not appropriately make decisions affecting the Jesuit community. What was at stake was the "separate incorporation" of the Jesuit community as an associated but distinct legal entity.

Early in 1967, Father Swords disclosed that the matter had been under active consideration for a year, and he expected the first lay trustee to be named by June. The president justified the plan by pointing out that other Catholic schools, including Notre Dame and Assumption College, were moving in the same direction. He envisioned a "gradual and careful expansion" of the board, with Jesuits in the majority. Lay trustees, he argued, would bring more openness and skill to the board and would enable Holy Cross to receive federal funds that were unavailable to religiously affiliated colleges.[22] At first, the process seemed to be on a fast track. In May, the Massachusetts General Court

20. FitzGerald, *Governance*, 188, 198–99. David O'Brien asserts: "Influential and generous lay advisors [were] a good counterweight for the strong presidents as they sought autonomy from ecclesiastical and order superiors for the sake of the institutions and their mission." Correspondence to the author, Pittsfield, July 27, 1995.

21. Associate Trustees' Minutes, May 21 and December 3, 1966, ACHC, 11.1.

22. Worcester *Telegram*, January 30, 1967; *Crusader*, January 30, 1967.

approved amendments to the charter, altering the number of trustees and their term of office. Then the trustees were forced to wait until approval arrived from Rome.[23]

The delay was associated with a widely expressed concern that lay trustees would foster secularization at Catholic colleges and a lessening of the Church's control.[24] Only one Jesuit institution, St. Louis University, achieved separate incorporation in 1967. Holy Cross was next in line, but Roman authorities wanted time to consider the make-up and operation of the two proposed corporations before ceding control of the College. During the summer of 1967, Father Swords consulted with Ed Hanify and worked with the trustees to draw up new by-laws. On August 31, the trustees accepted Chapter 289 of the Acts of Massachusetts of 1967, activating the new by-laws as of that date. The trustees asserted the College's religious affiliation by voting unanimously that College publications carry an official statement of "the purposes and character of the College as a Catholic institution of higher learning conducted by the Society of Jesus."[25] But because the process of separate incorporation was still awaiting Jesuit approval at the beginning of 1968, no lay persons were named to the board. Meanwhile, the associate trustees were providing many of the advantages that Father Swords hoped to gain by the change. In particular, he sought their advice in expanding the physical plant and in raising enrollment.

Student residences came first. Immediately after taking office, Father Swords told the provincial that he had not favored Father Donaghy's aborted plans for a campus center because of the need for housing for the students and Jesuit faculty; the College, he thought, could save money on new residence halls by utilizing architectural plans already in hand, duplicating Lehy and Hanselman.[26] Two buildings would provide rooms for 364 students and sixteen Jesuit "supervisors," allowing termination of residence for about 250 students in Campion House, Fenwick Hall, and O'Kane Hall. Late in 1960, a

23. Trustees' Minutes, February 27, April 22, May 29, 1967, ACHC, 11.0. On the delayed approval, see correspondence between Swords and Provincial J. V. O'Connor, August–October 1967, ACHC, 19.2-3.

24. A wide variety of clippings on the topic from Boston and Worcester newspapers may be found in the clipping files in ACHC, Book 80, pp. 1–5. See also FitzGerald, *Governance*, 204–5.

25. Trustees minutes, July 25, 26, and August 31, 1967, Hanify to Swords, Boston, August 11, 1967, ACHC, 11.0.

26. Swords to Coleran, Worcester, July 25, 1960, ACHC, 19.2-3.

27. "Evidence of Need Statement," ACHC, 16.1B; Michael Pierce to Ralph B. Cornell

Chart 9.1 Operating Budget, 1960–1972

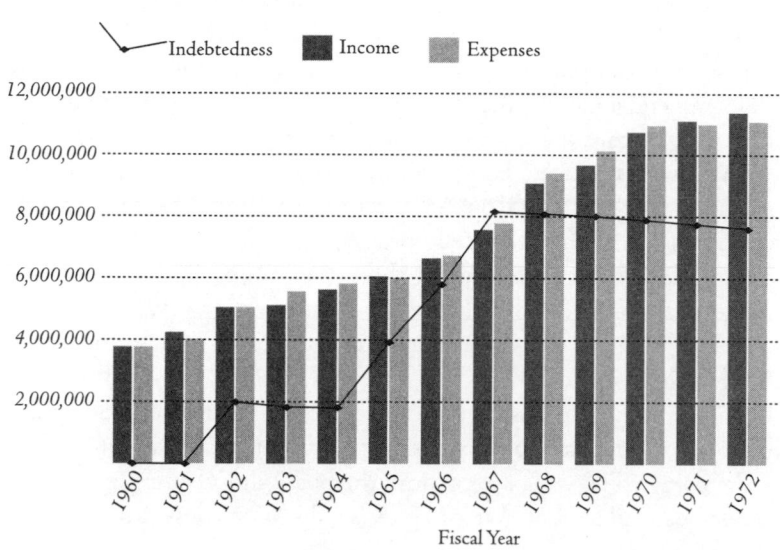

federal loan and approval from Jesuit authorities had come through. Ground was broken in the spring of 1961, and the buildings, named after James A. Healy and James Clark, were ready for occupancy in the fall of 1962.[27]

The additional space for resident students and the need for revenue prompted Father Swords to reconsider his position that Holy Cross should maintain enrollment at 1800. In 1963, new accounting procedures confirmed that the College was running a deficit. Between 1964 and 1968, in fact, the operating deficit exceeded $800,000 and had to be balanced from reserve funds (Chart 9.1). Tuition and room and board fees were raised six times during the decade 1960–70, from a combined total of $1750 to $3480 (Chart 9.2). That policy carried the burden of rising scholarship support. Other alternatives included raising unrestricted giving and enhancing the endowment—efforts that were only beginning to generate momentum during the 1960s. For a time, Father Swords considered adopting a trimester schedule "as a means of adding more students without adding to the present dormitory—and classroom —facilities."[28] But a larger enrollment on the semester system became his preference.

[Regional Administrator, HHFA], Worcester, August 25, 1960, ACHC, 16.1BTT-1; HD, July 26, 1960 and October 5, 1962.

28. *Crusader*, November 17, 1960; Report of George W. Nolan to the Associate Trustees,

Early in 1962, he told the trustees that he expected to raise the enrollment slightly. To facilitate the process, he hired a consulting firm to study the impact of the projected increase on campus facilities. The report, delivered in November, used a panoply of charts, graphs, and tables, plus a text of 353 pages to recommend a modest increase to 2000. A second report, released in September of 1963, considered the potential impact of 3000 and 4000 students.[29] Armed with this data, Father Swords approached the New England Jesuit provincial, Father J. V. O'Connor, and the associate trustees in November. Swords argued that the projected budgetary deficit could be covered by expanding enrollment to 2100 and using three-man rooms until another dormitory could be built. The dining hall, chapel, and heating plant could support expansion; such an enrollment increase could add $500,000 in room charges to the school's income.[30]

College Treasurer Father George Nolan offered three reasons for expansion: "the social and public relations' necessity" of addressing the educational needs of the rising college-age population; the possibility that changes in the National Defense Education Act of 1958 would attach less advantageous

Chart 9.2 Tuition, Room & Board Expenses, 1947–1972

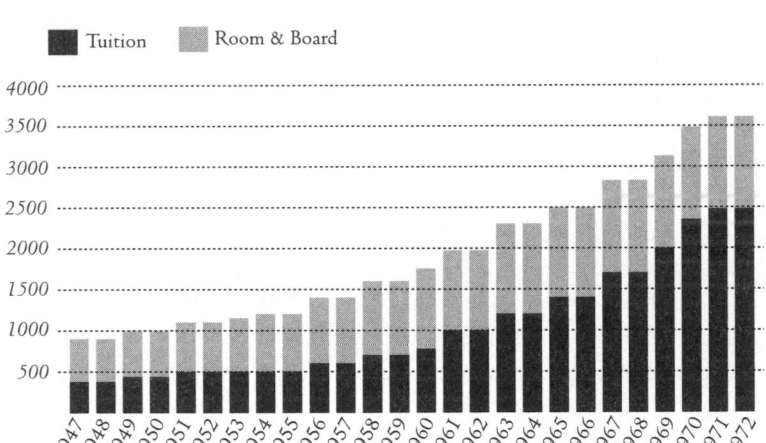

May 16, 1964, ACHC, 11.1; John E. Brooks to Robert R. Ramsey, Jr, Worcester, April 7, 1969, ACHC, 14.14; HD, May 17, 1963.

29. Trustees' Minutes, January 2, 1962; Swords to "Colleague," January 30, 1962. The consulting firm was Taylor, Lieberfeld and Heldman, Inc. ACHC, 11.0.

30. Swords to O'Connor, Worcester, November 20, 1963, ACHC, 19.2–3; Associate Trustees' Minutes, November 23, 1963, ACHC, 11.1.

terms to federal loans; and the fact that a rising standard of living was making a college education possible for a rising proportion of Catholic youth. His arguments captured the spirit of the dramatic rise in American college and university enrollments during the 1960s, when enrollments grew from 3.6 to 7.9 million, from 22 percent to 32 percent of college-aged youths; and the average institution of higher learning tripled in size.[31] Nolan also cited the prospect of budget deficits: he argued that tuition increases alone, without additional revenue-producing students, would price Holy Cross out of the market. The choice, he argued, was expansion in numbers or decline in quality:

This project is not a question of simple desire, but a very real question of ability to survive as a Liberal Arts College. If we do not increase our income to the point where we have a balanced budget, then I do not think it unlikely that the College will either be on the point of Receivership within ten years, or it will have changed its character . . . to that of a General Institution of the type of Boston College or Boston University with its proliferation of Undergraduates['] disciplines.[32]

Jesuit authorities withheld approval at first, requesting concrete plans for eliminating the deficit, lest the size of the College be determined primarily by a fiscal crisis. Father Swords replied by distinguishing between the ideal order and the economic realities that promoted expansion. He was convinced that time had caught up with the Holy Cross:

In the past fourteen years we have erected a Biology Building, another large Science and Classroom Building, four new dormitories, the College Infirmary, a Faculty Residence, a Maintenance Building. In addition to this, we have, of necessity, increased the number of lay faculty, have bettered their salaries and fringe benefits, have installed a meager pension plan for our other employees, have increased our maintenance staff greatly to take care of all these new buildings. And all the time we have not increased our principal economic base—the student body. When you look at the situation from this point of view, it really is remarkable that we have not been in difficulty before this.[33]

To phase in the projected increase, College officials planned to admit an additional 100 freshman boarders in the fall of 1964. Four new faculty would be hired immediately to sustain the increase.[34] In the same year, Father Swords

31. Freeland, *Golden Age*, 87–88.

32. Nolan to J. V. O'Connor, Worcester, December 6, 1963, ACHC, 16.1BM-1.

33. O'Connor to Swords, Boston, December 13, 1963, and Swords to O'Connor, Worcester, January 22, 1964, ACHC, 19.2-3.

34. [John O'Keefe] memo to George Nolan, December 6, 1963, ACHC, 16.1B. See also Dean of Students' file, 1964, ACHC, 12.24. Enrollment rose from 1826 in 1963 to 2002 in the fall of 1964. Registrar Records, series 3, ACHC, 14.3.

began planning a new residence hall with a capacity of about 350. By mid-May preliminary plans had been drawn up for a building with four wings whose shape resembled an elongated W.[35] By July, the Housing and Home Finance Agency (HHFA) had approved a loan of $2.3 million. Construction was begun in 1965, and the dormitory was ready for occupancy in the fall of 1966, at a total cost of $3.5 million, including furnishings. Following the suggestion of several members of the faculty, the building was named in memory of Thomas Mulledy.[36]

Afterwards, Father Swords had misgivings about the wisdom of raising the student population above 1800. The decision raised operating costs for faculty and other personnel without, in the short run, resolving the deficit. One effect was the increasing burden of scholarship aid—from 172 cases in his first year of office and a total of $102,000, to 700 cases in 1967/68 at a cost of $484,000. At a faculty meeting in 1968, Swords acknowledged that the enrollment increase had been "probably unwise" because of the unanticipated expenses. Early in his presidency, he admitted, he had been influenced by a representative of the Ford Foundation, who predicted the demise of many liberal arts colleges and recommended that "units of 1200 students were the soundest financially." On that basis, he had chosen to expand enrollment toward 2400.[37]

Improved housing for the Jesuit faculty, a goal that Father Dinand had hoped to achieve decades earlier, became instead the accomplishment of Father Swords. He turned his attention to the matter in the summer of 1961, when he realized that he should not expand the Jesuit quarters in Fenwick and O'Kane Halls after the students moved into the new dorms because fire hazard made renovation costly and impractical. Far better, Swords judged, to construct a new faculty residence.[38] Maginnis, Walsh, and Kennedy were too backed up to design plans speedily, so Father Swords engaged the New York firm Eggers and Higgins, whose services had been utilized in early discussions about the proposed gymnasium.[39] By February of 1962, preliminary plans were

35. Swords to Eugene Kennedy, Worcester, February 10, 1964, Swords's memo to Arthur Kennedy, February 23, 1964, and memo of Arthur Kennedy, April 1, 1964, ACHC, 16.1BM-1; Arthur Kennedy to Leo O'Connor, May 14, 1964, ACHC, 16.1B. Eugene Kennedy, of Maginnis, Walsh, and Kennedy was the architect.

36. Frank C. Trentacosti to Swords, New York, July 1, 1964. The name was suggested to Swords by Fr. William Lucey and Prof. William Grattan in letters of December 13 and 15, 1965. The name and cost were announced in a press release of February 16, 1966. ACHC, 16.1B. See also *Crusader*, September 13 and October 20, 1966.

37. Minutes of the special faculty meeting of February 5, 1968. ACHC, 14.12. The scholarship figures are in the Swords Papers, ACHC, 12.24.

38. Swords to Coleran, Worcester, August 14, 1961, ACHC, 19.2-3.

39. On Eggers and Higgins, see O'Connor's memo to Swords, December 28, 1961, and

available. The building was to be located behind the chapel, at the site of the old barn. Over Swords's objections, Jesuit authorities in Rome stipulated a larger number of rooms and a separate floor in the infirmary wing to serve members of the Society. The final plan contained 72 bedrooms in a five-story structure that included a chapel, library, dining room, visitors' parlors, offices, recreation rooms, and a tailor shop. The infirmary, three stories high, replaced the old unit of fourteen beds in a single ward; it contained seven four-bed units and four isolation rooms for students, plus seven rooms for Jesuits and a small chapel.[40] About $1.1 million was on hand for the project; Father Swords had authorization to negotiate a federal loan of $2.5 million to cover the balance,[41] but difficulties arose concerning the principle of separation of church and state.

A New York officer of the HHFA suggested that Holy Cross withdraw the loan petition because unit costs were too high and because of the "definite religious nature of parts of the proposed building."[42] On the latter point, the objection was the inclusion in the building of a chapel and of common rooms for Jesuits that constituted a *de facto* faculty union for religious personnel only. Attorney Charles Horgan '33 proposed a way around these difficulties by placing the chapel and common rooms in a separate building, financed through private sources. But eventually federal officials dropped their objection to the common rooms because, as one negotiator explained, the residence would be "the sole place where [the Jesuits] must live all day and every day. It must consequently contain facilities adequate to sustain . . . their individual lives and their community life and enable them to do the work that they have to do."[43] Preliminary approval for a loan for faculty rooms, an infirmary, and a "faculty union" arrived in January of 1963. The amount was later increased to reflect a revised determination of costs; and the chapel, which was built adjacent to the residence at a cost of about $680,000, was financed independently of the loan. The ultimate cost of the building and furnishings was $3.3 million. Loyola Hall was dedicated in September of 1965.[44]

Sullivan to Swords, February 7, 1962. ACHC, 16.1-B; and Swords to Coleran, Worcester, February 12, 1962, ACHC, 19.2-3.

40. Swords to Coleran, Worcester, February 12, April 2, and July 17, 1962, ACHC, 19.2-3; Swords to Consultors, Worcester, May 8, 1962, ACHC, 16.1-B; HD, February 1962–April 1963; Worcester *Gazette*, August 31, 1965.

41. J. V. O'Connor to Swords, September 8, 1962; Associate Trustees' Minutes, December 15, 1962, ACHC, 11.1.

42. Richardson J. Thompson to Swords, New York, November 30, 1962, ACHC, 16.1-B.

43. "Luke" O'Connor to Theodore Young, Worcester, March 22, 1963, ACHC, 16.1B.

44. Associate Trustees' Minutes, December 15, 1962, ACHC, 11.1; Richardson Thompson

Midway through his campaign to construct residence halls for students and Jesuits, Father Swords revived the campus center project. The report from the space utilization consultants offered compelling reasons for a new student center to incorporate the post office, bookstore, and dean of men's office from Kimball Hall. Funding was available from several sources. The account for the long-deferred gymnasium had risen to about $500,000; because of his desire to include bowling alleys, a billiards room, and squash and handball courts, Father Swords understood the project to be a legitimate application of the donors' desire for a recreation center. In addition, the College had $100,000 in unexpended plant funds, a major development drive underway, and hopes for a matching fund loan from the federal government.⁴⁵ Campus planners chose to take advantage again of the experience of Eggers and Higgins with public structures. The general plan combined two buildings: a five-story unit containing offices for campus organizations and a four-story building with large windows and spacious areas for public functions. The building was set on the slope above the library, with recreational facilities on the lowest floor, below ground level.⁴⁶ The estimated cost of the original plan necessitated scaling the project back and delayed it for about fourteen months, until early 1966, when a bid was accepted at just under the available funding.⁴⁷ Ground was broken immediately; at the dedication in October 1967 it was named for Henry M. Hogan '18, Vice-President and General Counsel of General Motors, who had served as national chairman of the College's fund drive. Father Swords called the Campus Center "the community center of the campus for all the College's constituencies— the faculty, the alumni, yes—and the area community—on occasion, and the student body . . . , the *living room* of the campus." He was careful to differentiate its function from ordinary student unions, since the Hogan Center was not the student dining room. Instead it was to house "a broad social, cultural and

to Swords, New York City, January 23, 1963, Thompson to Nolan, New York, October 7, 1973, and Swords to Paul L. O'Connor, Worcester, January 19, 1966, ACHC, 16.1B; *Crusader*, September 23, 1965. Objections about the cost of the building became moot in 1963 when studies showed that the cost per square foot was within the range then being allotted for dormitories and unions. Memo of Richard Burke to Swords, March 5, 1963, ACHC, 16.1B.

45. Swords to faculty meeting, Fall, 1962, ACHC, 12.24; Swords to J. V. O'Connor, September 16, 1963, ACHC, 19.2-3.

46. Swords to J. V. O'Connor, Worcester, September 12, 1963, ACHC, 19.2-3; Memo of Richard Burke to Swords, March 5, 1963, Swords to Eugene F. Kennedy, Jr., September 19, 1963, and Statement of Eggers and Higgins, ACHC, 16.1BP-1. Architect Appolinaire Osadca designed Loyola Hall and the campus center.

47. Letters between Eggers and Higgins and College officials on the modification of the plans may be found in ACHC, 16.1BP-1. Father Swords accepted the bid from Granger Construction Co. on February 9, 1966. Granger's bid of $3.563 million was $73,000 under the limit.

intellectual program, planned and organized by the students."[48] A full-time director administered the center in cooperation with a student chair and a board of directors to represent the College community in planning functions, and an advisory council to recommend major policies to the president.[49]

The Hogan Campus Center ended Father Swords's expansion of the physical plant. He had used low-cost federal loans to construct five major buildings in seven years. In addition, he sponsored construction of the maintenance building in 1964 and the renovation of Fenwick Theater, formally opened in 1965. He had a concept of future priorities in campus buildings—an addition to Dinand Library, a mathematics building, and a fine arts center.[50] These achievements, however, lay beyond his presidency. His immediate challenge, having committed Holy Cross to so massive an expansion, was to raise funds to balance the budget.

During its reaccreditation review in 1969, Holy Cross reported an endowment gain of $680,000 between 1958 and 1968, a successful fund drive of $7.5 million, and an increase in annual giving between 1967 and 1968 from $172,000 to $537,000. But the figures were misleading, and the carefully fostered impression of success concealed the difficulty of generating momentum for consistent fundraising. During his first year in office, Father Swords contemplated a major fund drive and hired a consulting firm to advise him on establishing a development office. By September of 1961, preliminary findings indicated "a very high percentage of the Alumni enthusiastic about establishing a development office and beginning a capital funds' drive," with a goal of raising $20 million. Within a month, Swords set up the Development Office, with Lewis Songer '55 as Public Relations Officer and James Q. Cobb '39 as Development Officer. By the end of 1961, preliminary plans were in place for a major fund drive, with a long range goal of $20.4 million, of which $7.5 million was targeted by June of 1964.[51]

48. Swords's address at Hogan Center Dedication, October 13, 1967, ACHC, 12.24; early Hogan Center leaflet, ACHC, 16.1BP-1; Worcester *Telegram*, October 14, 1967.

49. The first student chair was Frederick E. Bacon '68; John Duffek was the first full-time director. Early descriptive leaflet, Hogan Center Files, ACHC, 16.1PB-1.

50. George Nolan to J. V. O'Connor, Worcester, June 19, 1964, ACHC 16.1BG-1; HD, November 4 and 16, 1965; Swords to Francis J. McGrath, Worcester, May 17, 1966, ACHC, 12.24; Trustees' Minutes, June 5, 1968, ACHC, 11.0; *Alumnus*, August, 1964.

51. Reaccreditation Report, February 1, 1969, ACHC, 14.14; HD, August 2, 1960; Swords to Coleran, April 13, September 11, October 4, and November 21, 1961, Swords to J. V. O'Connor, November 22, 1963, ACHC, 19.2-1; Swords address to faculty, September 17, 1961, ACHC, 12.24.

Before entering the public phase of the campaign, Father Swords promoted the needs of the College among donors and organizers. His goal was to keep Holy Cross an undergraduate college whose reputation was "relatively high." The only path to that future was to carry out the building plan and increase the endowment beyond its current level of $3.25 million. Other needs included competitive salaries for the faculty and funds for scholarships. "We've run up our flag of distress," Swords stated. "I beg you to work with us to the point of sacrifice."[52] A dinner in Kimball Hall formally launched the drive on April 28, 1962. Speakers included Bishop Flanagan and Father Swords; Edward B. Hanify was the keynoter. Henry Hogan announced that over $1 million had already been pledged, including $56,465 from faculty and employees of the College.[53] Later, to regional alumni meetings, Father Swords confessed that, when he became president, he learned that the solvency of the College was "a terrible illusion." He repeated the list of needs, promising to use revenues to enhance their alma mater's prestige. Despite such earnest appeals, pledges came in slowly. By June of 1964, only $5.25 million had been pledged. In December of 1965, the associate trustees decided to wind down the capital campaign with a full-scale effort to meet the $7.5 million short-term goal, eighteen months late. In January of 1966, Father Swords reported that $7.8 million had been pledged and about $4 million paid in; the final yield was a disappointing $4.98 million.[54]

Afterwards, the associate trustees advised a reorganization of the development effort, greater emphasis being placed on class agents and personal solicitation. Father William Kelleher, Coordinator of Development in 1964 and 1965, was replaced in 1966 by George F. Dineen '37 as Vice-President for Development and College Relations. To provide a new focus, Dineen introduced

52. Swords to Regional Chairmen and Captains, [1962], ACHC, 12.24.

53. HD, April 28, 1962; Swords to Michael Walsh, April 11, 1962, and Paul E. Sadler '54 to Swords, Worcester, May 10, 1962, ACHC, 12.24. In the fall of 1962, Father Swords told the faculty that General Motors had given $25,000. General Tire and Rubber pledged $2 million over 10 years. ACHC, 12.24.

54. Associate Trustees' minutes, December 11, 1965, ACHC, 11.1; Swords's notes for talks at regional meetings [undated], Swords to Bishop Flanagan, Worcester, June 19, 1964, and Swords to Francis J. Vaas, January 5, 1966, ACHC, 12.24; Report of Accountants to Trustees, 1968, Development Office files. The grand total included a pledge of $1 million from Boston's Cardinal Richard Cushing. Late in 1966, Cushing reported that, because of illness and his impending retirement, he saw "no possibility of fulfilling this pledge in the foreseeable future. . . ." Father Swords replied: "You have been so extremely generous to the Society of Jesus and to so many good causes that I regret any embarrassment to you." Cushing to Swords, Brighton, November 28, 1966, and Swords to Cushing, Worcester, December 8, 1966, ACHC, 12.24. The Worcester Diocese contributed $100,000 to the drive. Swords to Bp. Flanagan, May 3, 1963, ACHC, 12.24.

Crossroads in 1967 as the publication for alumni news. The old *Alumnus* maga-zine, which became the *Holy Cross Quarterly*, featured book reviews, profiles, and literary articles.[55] Meeting with the associate trustees, Dineen spoke of in-creasing unrestricted revenue, collecting unpaid pledges, reactivating the Alumni Fund, and seeking funds from estate planning and from corporations and foundations. In 1967, the number of alumni donors passed 3000, for a total fund of $172,000, but contributed income was not alleviating the funda-mental problem that expenses were rising more quickly than income. Tuition increases were still regarded as a dangerous expedient because of a fear of dri-ving prospective students away.[56] When all was said and done, Father Nolan told the associates in 1967, "the financial survival of Holy Cross will depend on Government aid"[57]—an honest admission that an internally driven solu-tion no longer seemed possible.

In addition to relying increasingly on the associate trustees and alumni, Father Swords was promoting the concept of shared responsibility with the lay faculty for the academic program. At Holy Cross and elsewhere, it was a slow process, occasionally punctuated with frustration. The situation was complicated by the fact that there were two types of lay faculty members at most Catholic colleges, including Holy Cross, during the 1960s. The first was what Andrew Greeley characterized as the "old professor," a teacher with a master's degree or perhaps a doctorate from a Catholic university, who was in-tensely loyal to the institution and grateful to the religious order whose pa-tronage had promoted his or her career. The "new professors" were more ori-ented toward their professional colleagues than to the school, impatient with administrative mistakes, and resentful of criticism from the older group.[58] Je-suit faculty members also fell within both groups. These divisions were part of the human context within which Father Swords struggled to extend the re-sponsibilities of the lay faculty and to break down the institutional separation between "faculty" and "lay faculty," for the sake of academic improvement.

55. Jesuit House History, 1965–67, in ACHC, 19.7A-2. Edited by Matthew J. Quinn (1967–69) and Fr. William van Etten Casey (1969–75), the *Holy Cross Quarterly* included is-sues dedicated to the Berrigan brothers (1971), Worcester (1973), the Irish (1974), and a China issue (1975).

56. Swords to J. V. O'Connor, Worcester, September 18, 1965, ACHC, 19.2-3; Associate Trustees' Minutes, December 11, 1965, December 3, 1966, ACHC, 11.1; Swords memo to Fac-ulty, August 22, 1966, ACHC, 12.24; Thomas Ryan, "The Holy Cross Fund, 1948–1994," De-velopment Office files.

57. Associate Trustees' Minutes, December 3, 1967, ACHC, 11.1.

58. Greeley, *Changing*, 106–9.

The change was a matter of necessity; the Jesuits simply lacked the personnel to carry the enterprise forward. Father Swords told the trustees in 1962: "We have every reason to believe that we have reached the peak of the size of the [Jesuit] community—that it *will decline*—that we will not receive *replacements* for Jesuits *who* die or are assigned elsewhere."[59] Among the existing opportunities for "indoctrinating" the lay faculty with Jesuit ideas, he prized the free lunch that was still provided to the faculty in the lower Fenwick dining room. He emphasized to the Jesuit community that these lunches were an opportunity to acquaint their colleagues with "the nature and traditions of Holy Cross," and to profit from the presence of their colleagues and "not to let these men surpass us in dedication and devotion to our students and the academic life."[60] As a beginning of a structural approach to the problem, Swords made extensive use of the old Re-Evaluation Committee. By 1962, the Academic Advisory Committee, as it had been renamed, had five lay and five Jesuit members, all appointed by the president; they were advising him on salary and fringe benefits, rank and tenure procedures, the appointment of departmental chairs, and other academic matters. In 1960, Swords set up three additional faculty committees: Admission and Scholarships, Rank and Tenure, and Academic Standing.[61]

The effort to promote collaboration encountered a setback in 1965, when Father Swords attempted to appoint a layman, Stanley Idzerda, as academic dean. An alumnus of Notre Dame, Idzerda was director of the Honors Program at Michigan State University. Writing in support of the appointment, Father Joseph Donahue, the assistant dean, described the effort as "a unique opportunity to appropriate into our Jesuit tradition new vigor without risk of diluting our own traditions." The appointment would free the College from "a multiplicity of historical forces [that] so straitens the thinking of both professors and students that they view the educational process in its most limiting form: the students as a purely passive experience; the professor, as a mere exercise of magisterial precept."[62] Despite such passionate rhetoric, the proposal was not approved by the Jesuit provincial. Eight months later, when Swords nominated Father William Guindon (a former member of the Physics

59. Swords to Consultors and Trustees, May 8, 1962, ACHC, 11.0.

60. Swords to Jesuit Community, August 6, 1962, ACHC, 16.24.

61. Paul Facey to Swords, September 10, 1960, and Swords to V. O. McBrien, September 11, 1962, ACHC, 14.12; Swords addresses to faculty, October 4, 1960, September 17, 1961, Swords to John Long, December 15, 1960, and Swords to Robert McDonnell, June 7, 1961, ACHC, 12.24.

62. Swords to J. V. O'Connor, Worcester, February 27, 1965, ACHC, 19.2-3. The undated memo from Father Donahue was enclosed with the letter.

Department and the first director of the Data Processing Center) for the deanship, he defended lay collaboration again: "I do feel that we should bring laymen into the big administrative posts, and that we definitely should take steps to make laymen full trustees of this College. Until the day this happens we will not, in my opinion, be making the contributions to the Church and America which we should be making."[63] As a mark of his sensitivity, Father Swords announced Guindon's appointment at the annual faculty-staff banquet in June, before issuing the press release. The first word, he thought, should be given to the faculty.[64]

Frustrated along one line of development, Swords turned to another possibility: an enhanced role for the faculty in governance. He signaled his intention in 1964 by announcing that, henceforth, five of the ten members of the Academic Advisory Committee would be elected. He was assigning that committee the task of studying "the part which the faculty should play in the policy-making of the College." Centralization of power and decision making in the president's office, he asserted, was becoming obsolete; for the future, the quality of the faculty and of the school depended upon conferring "real academic responsibility" upon the faculty, subject to the Jesuit identity of Holy Cross:

We cannot lose sight of some broad restrictions which are placed upon us by the corporation which has a financial interest in the College and whose members founded the College and brought it to its present state of development. Nor can we overlook the regulations which make the President ultimately responsible for the spiritual, academic and financial well-being of the College. But within this framework we should be able to work out . . . a much more active voice and role for the faculty.[65]

In February of 1966, the Academic Affairs Committee proposed an interim committee "to develop proposals for Faculty Statutes governing the structure and operation of the College." The trustees accepted the proposal, which stipulated that they would retain the final authority to protect the College's objectives in identity, tenure, salaries, and budget.[66] Father Swords constituted the group at the faculty meeting in March; he would chair the committee and vote. By May, the faculty were summoned to a special meeting to

63. Swords to J. V. O'Connor, Worcester, October 19, 1965, ACHC, 19.2-3; Press Release on Guindon, June 10, 1966, ACHC, 12.24.

64. Swords to O'Connor, June 7, 1966, ACHC, 19.2-3.

65. Address to faculty, fall 1964, ACHC, 12.24.

66. Trustees' minutes, February 17, 1966, ACHC, 11.0. Besides Swords, the other members of the interim committee were Fathers Guindon (secretary), Reidy, William V. E. Casey, and Professors John Lynch, Robert McNerny, and Paul Rosenkrantz.

consider the first major proposal, namely, "the establishment of an educational policy committee, and the integration of faculty and administration on committees and in meetings." The new committee was to consist of the president and academic dean as *ex officio* members, and five elected members of the faculty. Its function was not to advise the administration, as the old Academic Affairs Committee had done, but to be the "central committee of the Faculty" and to report to the faculty. The faculty was defined to include those holding permanent faculty appointment, plus the president, academic dean, dean of students, assistant deans, the admissions director, registrar, librarian, and chairs of the Military Science departments. The new committee was overwhelmingly approved. When a lay professor asked: "Is the educational policy then made by the faculty," Father Swords answered, "Yes."[67]

The Educational Policy Committee began meeting in the fall of 1966 and submitted new statutes to the faculty in rapid order. In October, chaplains were added to the voting faculty, a recorder was chosen, and a schedule of four regular meetings per academic year was set. At the March meeting in 1967, the faculty accepted a proposal that sabbatical leaves and Faculty Fellowships be funded at 80 percent (not 50 percent) for a whole year, provided the courses could be covered without hiring replacements.[68] In October and November of 1967, the faculty accepted EPC recommendations for a new committee structure that established two more general committees, five standing committees, four College committees, four committees appointed by the president, four committees appointed by the academic dean, and three committees appointed by the dean of students. The trustees approved the new structure in November, thus setting in place the basic governance structure of the College in effect until 1994.[69] In 1967, controversy erupted over a line in the proposal for a policy on dismissal and academic freedom: "A member of the Faculty may be

67. Swords's memo to faculty, April 25, 1966, and minutes of Faculty Meeting, May 10, 1966, ACHC, 14.12.

68. Minutes of faculty meeting of October 18, 1966, and transcript of faculty meeting of March 13, 1967, ACHC, 14.12.

69. Minutes of faculty meetings of October 2 and November 6, 1967, ACHC, 14.18.1A; Trustees' Minutes, November 15, 1967, ACHC, 11.0. General committees of the faculty were the EPC, Nominations and Elections, and Professional Standards; standing committees were Academic Standing, Admissions, Curriculum, Library, and Research and Publication; College committees reporting to the trustees were the Alumni Board, the Athletic Council, the Budget Committee, and the Faculty Judicial Board; committees appointed by the president were Academic Advising, Campus Center Advisory Council, Financial Aid, and Student Activities; committees appointed by the academic dean were Graduate Studies, Junior Year Abroad, Premed/Predental, and Special Studies; and committees appointed by the Dean of Students were Film Series, Lectures and Concerts, and Student Personnel Policy Committee.

dismissed for serious neglect of his academic duties or for such public misconduct as to disqualify him from continued association with a Catholic College." The faculty voted to drop the words "a Catholic" on arguments that the
religious affiliation was sufficiently evident in the College's characterization of
itself and that the words were needlessly offensive to non-Catholic colleagues.
Faculty members also voted to retain wording requiring faculty members "to
respect the religious aims of the College."[70] In accepting the policy, the trustees
voted their understanding that "the religious orientation of Holy Cross does
not involve a limitation upon academic freedom." Afterwards, Father Swords
noted: "In the areas of the primary objectives of the College as a Catholic institution, rank and tenure, salaries and budget, the Board of Trustees reserves
the right to ratify, reject, or ratify with modifications, policies approved by the
Faculty." In event of modification, the trustees would defer a final vote, pending further discussion with the faculty.[71]

Related to the question of faculty governance were policies covering hiring
and promotion. To upgrade the faculty, Father Swords introduced in 1961 the
first major changes in tenure and promotion policy since 1949. Henceforth instructors needed a master's degree *and* plans for "proximate completion of the
doctorate," for a maximum of five, one-year appointments. Assistant professors now needed a Ph.D. and could retain their rank for a maximum of six
years, after which they were to be evaluated for "professionally recognized academic achievement." Full professors were required to show a record of "distinguished" academic achievement. Faculty fellowships for research, including
clerical help and subvention funding, were part of the new policy. With these
standards in place, the number of faculty holding doctorates rose from 22
percent in 1958 to 50 percent in 1969.[72] In response to a policy statement from
the American Association of University Professors (AAUP), the criteria were
adjusted again in 1964 to ensure that academic achievement for tenure and
promotion was carefully defined in terms of teaching, scholarship, and publication. Service to the College was considered a "supporting criterion." Pro-

70. Minutes of faculty meeting, November 6, 1967, ACHC, 14.12.

71. Trustees' minutes, November 15, 1967, and Swords's memo to faculty, November 22,
1967, ACHC, 11.0.

72. Norms for faculty appointment, promotion, rank, and tenure, 1961, ACHC, 12.24;
Report of Ad Hoc Committee on Faculty Resources and Educational Quality, 1989, ACHC,
14.12; Freeland, *Golden Age*, 96. As late as 1962, Father Swords judged that he had sufficient
grounds and authority to act unilaterally in promoting Fr. John Flavin of the Biology Department to associate professor. "I do not wish any publicity to be given to this promotion,"
he told the dean. "The simple changing of his rank in next year's Catalogue should take care
of the matter." Swords to Reidy, July 17, 1962, ACHC, 12.24.

motion to associate professor was considered separately from the conferral of tenure until 1966, when the two steps were linked.[73] In 1967, the faculty approved an elaborated set of policies for tenure and promotion. Each tenure case required proof of "scholarly teaching" and was to be considered by an *ad hoc* committee of three senior faculty members (a member of the candidate's department and representatives of a cognate field and of an unrelated field) approved jointly by the EPC, the president, and the academic dean. Father Guindon defined scholarly teaching as "direction of students, communication of intellectual attitudes, creative efforts, dissemination of . . . creative findings." Faculty members hired between 1961 and 1964 were granted the concession of gaining tenure as assistant professors.[74]

By the end of 1967, the faculty and administration had activated a plan of shared responsibility that seemed to promise greater institutional strength. The presence of twenty-three faculty committees, especially the influential Educational Policy Committee, indicated how fundamental the structural change really was. Summarizing the transformation, Father Guindon captured the mood of expectation:

It is to be noted that . . . [the Faculty] vote is deliberative and not consultative, and needs only the approval . . . of the Board of Trustees and *not* of the administrative officers (as was formerly the case.) In our opinion we seem to have the best faculty structure of any Catholic institution (certainly of any Jesuit institution) in the country.[75]

The dean's pride of accomplishment was understandable: he and his associates had achieved a reorganization that could scarcely have been imagined in 1960. To the alumni, Father Swords explained that presidents at church-related colleges had to share responsibility with the faculty because they supply more continuity and stability to the school than any other component. For that reason, he asserted: "It is the faculty and not the president that determines the academic quality and religious worth of the church college." The president's responsibility was to recruit, nurture, and retain a strong faculty.[76]

In retrospect, it is clear that necessity and opportunity worked hand in hand in the transference of more responsibility to the faculty. The professional credentials of the non-Jesuit faculty and staff represented an increasingly valu-

73. College Faculty Policies, January 15, 1964, and February 1, 1966, ACHC, 12.24; Freeland, *Golden Age*, 96.

74. Minutes of faculty meeting, May 1, 1967, ACHC, 14.12.

75. Associate Trustees' minutes, December 3, 1967, ACHC, 11.1.

76. From Swords's address to alumni in Garden City, N.Y., February 26, 1966, in *Alumnus*, Spring 1966.

able asset for the College and rendered the old designation of "lay faculty" offensive and obsolete. In the fall of 1963, the number of lay professors surpassed the number of Jesuit faculty members for the first time.[77] In 1966, Father Swords further delegated responsibility when he secured approval for the appointment of four vice-presidents—Father Guindon as Vice-President and Dean of the College; George Dineen as Vice-President for Development and College Relations; Father Charles Dunn (dean of men) as Vice-President for Student Affairs; and John F. O'Keefe '51 (treasurer) as Vice-President for Business Affairs.[78]

In addition to committing more responsibility to the faculty, Father Swords was also attentive to salary levels. In 1960, he announced that there would be no maximum salary for associate and full professors; in 1962, fringe benefits—health care, disability insurance, and new retirement benefits—were added to the wage package. In the fall of 1963, the president announced the beginning of a sabbatical policy "on a small basis." By 1964, using guidelines drawn up by the AAUP, Holy Cross ranked at the A level for non-tenured faculty, and at the B level for tenured ranks. In that year, additional funding was made available to support faculty research. Meanwhile, a Personnel Office was set up in 1961 to monitor and administer hiring, vacation, sick leave, and other policies applying to administrative and maintenance personnel.[79]

The spirit of change also affected the curriculum. Like the other innovations, these sprang from a variety of sources. In this case, Jesuit administrators initiated the plan, but the general movement for the reduction of requirements in American colleges and the overwhelming preference for the B.S. degree at Holy Cross hastened the process (Chart 8.2). The possibility for curricular reform opened up in the fall of 1958, when the Jesuit general authorized the granting of an A.B. without Latin by Jesuit schools, subject to certain conditions designed to protect the study of humanities. It was not a case of dropping Latin, Father Janssens asserted, but of "extending to other liberal programs the advantages and the prestige commonly attached to the A.B. degree."[80]

77. HD, September 19, 1963. See also Chart 8.5.

78. Trustees' Minutes, August 12, 1966, and Swords to Thomas Smith, August 19, 1966, ACHC, 11.0.

79. Swords to faculty, December 6, 1960, February 7, 1962, February 28, 1964, and his address to the faculty, fall 1963, Swords to Maurice Reidy, September 28, 1964, ACHC, 12.24; Swords to Coleran, Worcester, April 7, 1961, Coleran to Swords, Boston, April 10, 1961, ACHC, 19.2-3. The highest ranking on the AAUP's standard scales of compensation was AA, then A, B, and so on, down to F.

80. Edward B. Rooney to American Provincials, New York, November 12, 1958 (copy),

At Holy Cross, the question of the classics requirement was incorporated into a general consideration of curriculum reform that included the core requirements in philosophy and theology.[81] In his first address to the faculty, Father Swords set the tone, linking the need for good faculty with the question, "Why are we failing to stimulate so many of our students?" Two years later, he asked the Academic Affairs Committee to take up curriculum reform. Chaired by Mathematics Professor Vincent O. McBrien, the committee of six Jesuits and five laymen met 23 times during the 1962–63 academic year.[82]

Their report, delivered in May of 1963, characterized the curriculum as "the result of a series of substitutions and compromises resulting in a difficult-to-justify patchwork." Siding with Jesuit educators around the country, they asserted that neither philosophy nor theology should be considered sacred cows; both had to be justified academically. They proposed a reduction of the core to allow more ample preparation for graduate and professional school. They also advocated reduction of the ordinary course load from six to five per semester, a common curriculum in the first year, adding three-credit theology courses to the regular curriculum, and setting a B.A. requirement of six credit hours in history, English, and a classical *or* modern language, twelve hours in theology, and eighteen hours in philosophy. By then, the report indicated, a reduction in philosophy requirements had been effected in every Jesuit university and college except Holy Cross. Approval was granted in November for a three-year trial of the plan.[83] For the first time in its history, Holy Cross was prepared to award an A.B. without Latin; beginning in 1968, the degree of B.S. was eliminated. In March of 1966, the option of receiving an A.B. degree without Latin was extended to most graduates of 1966 and 1967.[84]

In addition to eliminating the Latin requirement, the new curriculum low-

---

ACHC, 19.8-1. In 1960, A.B. candidates at Holy Cross studied Latin during the first two years; B.S. candidates studied a modern language for two years. John Long to Coleran, Worcester, March 23, 1960, NEPA, Holy Cross-Varia. On the general reduction on non-major requirements, see Freeland, *Golden Age*, 109–11.

81. The Holy Cross committee met concurrently with a New England Province committee that considered core requirements. Minutes of New England Province Committee, May 30, 1963; James L. Burke to Maurice Reidy, Boston, June 5, 1963; Summary Report of Consultants' Meeting on Curriculum Revision in Philosophy and Theology in New England, June 21, 1963, J. V. O'Connor to College Rectors, Boston, February 4, 1964, ACHC, 19.8-1.

82. Swords's address to faculty, October 4, 1960, and fall 1962, ACHC, 12.24.

83. FitzGerald, *Governance*, 156–58; Report and Recommendations on the Core Curriculum, May 24, 1963, ACHC, 19.8-1; J. V. O'Connor to Swords, Boston, November 17, 1964, ACHC, 19.2-3; Swords to J. V. O'Connor, Worcester, July 27, 1964, ACHC, 12.24

84. Swords to Guindon, March 1, 1966, ACHC, 14.12; *Crusader*, March 10, 1966. Accounting majors, and a few students whose course selection was narrow, were excluded from the op-

ered the credits required for graduation from 136 to 120 and reduced required courses in philosophy and theology from 33 percent of the curriculum to 25 percent. At about the same time, the establishment of the Psychology Department enriched academic offerings in the social sciences.[85] The core curriculum now consisted of six semesters of philosophy, four of theology, and two each of English, history, and natural science, a language requirement of two to four semesters, and a non-credit requirement in composition. Majors required a maximum of twelve semester-long courses; free electives were to be chosen "under the direction of the chairman of the department in which the student is to major." The 1965–66 catalog was the last to mention the *Ratio Studiorum* as a foundation for degree requirements; in December of 1966, the faculty overwhelmingly endorsed a further reduction of the philosophy requirement from six to three courses.[86] To provide better academic advising, Father Swords directed in 1967 that each of the class deans was to stay with a designated class for four years to afford better counseling and "a closer relationship" between deans and students.[87]

Undoubtedly, the residual emphasis on philosophy and theology made this latest adaptation of the curriculum slightly more palatable to old guard elements who revered the traditional content of the *Ratio Studiorum*. Yet, in his drive toward academic excellence, Father Swords wanted to improve both the content of the curriculum and the academic competence of the faculty. Like his predecessors, he faced an uncomfortable dilemma in the case of Jesuit faculty who lacked professional training and pedagogical skills. As president, his aspirations for the College and his sense of obligation to the students left no choice but to terminate the teaching service of these men; but as rector, he was the leader of the Jesuit faculty, and removing some Jesuits from the class-

---

tion. The division reflected the New England Colleges Fund guidelines that a B.A. degree presumes at least 75 percent of courses in the liberal arts.

85. Worcester *Telegram*, September 20, 1964. William O'Halloran, S.J., led the movement for a separate Psychology Department. J. V. O'Connor to Swords, Boston, June 15, 1964, ACHC, 19.2-3.

86. The Philosophy Department generally supported the plan because, according to one of its members, professors were forced to teach the same thing over and over with little room for development. The fact that department members now offered different approaches also made it difficult for them to teach one system. Minutes of Faculty Meeting, December 5, 1966, ACHC, 14.8.1A. The new requirement, implemented in the fall of 1966, required Philosophy of Man, Metaphysics, and Ethics.

87. Swords to J. V. O'Connor, July 25, 1967, ACHC, 19.2-3. The first class deans were Fr. Owen Finnegan (seniors and juniors), Professor Charles Baker (sophomores), and Fr. Ambrose Mahoney (freshmen).

room was likely to raise problems of morale and polarization. Obvious solutions included reemphasizing the intellectual apostolate among younger Jesuits and relying on the help of the province prefect of studies in monitoring the quality of instruction.[88] But the present reality, he recognized, required decisive action.

In early 1963, he confided to the provincial that he was very disturbed by student complaints against the offerings in philosophy and theology: "A frightening number of [students] have told us that the Courses, for which they came to Holy Cross, turned out to be the poorest." The situation, he argued, had two worrisome dimensions—the obligation to provide students with the quality of instruction they paid for, and the prejudice against these disciplines being generated as a result of poor instruction. Swords was particularly upset because gifted students were objecting to the quality of the courses, a situation that harmed the reputation of the College. Terminating the teaching appointments of Jesuit teachers heretofore kept in place by a charitable regard for their feelings, Swords realized, was a drastic but necessary move:

It seems to me we must face up to the issue. . . . I am more aware than others of the problems that will be created by the solution we propose. I dread having to face the people who are involved. The emotional disturbance will not subside in any one or two months—and I have to live with it. Even more than the men involved are the others, who are close to them in age or friendship, who will be disturbed. Still, I think we have no alternative but to act as we think best before God.

After consultation with Roman authorities, Father Swords removed five Jesuits from the Philosophy Department in 1964. He also took steps to correct the jury-rigged system in the Theology Department that allowed instructors to cross fields to cover courses. Theology, he asserted, would require "quite a bit of changing" to reach the desired level: "We feel that it would be much better for us to drop the required Course in Senior Theology than to send our seniors out of here with the strong distaste for it they now have."[89] The provincial did his part to assist, assigning Father John E. Brooks, among oth-

88. Speech to Jesuit Presidents, 1961, ACHC, 12.24. As late as 1965, the prefect of studies, James E. Fitzgerald, was making the "official visitation" in the fall. HD, November 14, 1965.

89. Swords to O'Connor, Worcester, March 6, 1963, ACHC, 19.2-3. Swords was hardly exaggerating. The 1966 *Purple Patcher* (p. 28) referred to "the reports one hears [from the late 1950s] of widespread mediocrity and narrow-mindedness among the faculty, of occasional expressions of religious and ethnic bigotry in the classroom, of a general dissatisfaction and even bitterness among the students that continued well into the 1960s. We must try to un-

ers, to teach theology at Holy Cross in the fall of 1964. By November, Swords was requesting that Brooks be appointed chair, to assist in effecting the "strong measures" that Roman authorities had insisted upon as a remedy. The appointment was made in 1965.[90]

Soon, the Theology Department became the fulcrum of contention between advocates of tradition and proponents of a new Holy Cross. That Theology became the flashpoint of disagreement is not surprising. Theology departments were a justification for Catholic colleges; yet, as Andrew Greeley pointed out, theology was traditionally viewed as a non-developing area that could be taught by anyone who had gone through a seminary successfully. Required courses were often assigned to poor teachers who had failed at other work.[91] Removing ineffective teachers from Theology (and Philosophy, which was subject to similar conditions and assumptions) was only the first part of the battle to introduce academic respectability. The second task was to raise Theology from the status a service department for inculcating Roman Catholicism to the academic level of other departments. Both objectives required the collaboration of competent lay professors. Yet, until 1960, few Catholic educators considered the option that lay professors, particularly non-Catholics, could be employed at their schools to teach "religion." In the following decade, many Catholic colleges and universities successfully made the change.[92] At Holy Cross, the transition became, for a while, an international *cause célèbre*.

Controversy began in February 1967, when Father Brooks, as Theology chair, supported the hiring of two non-Catholic lay professors to teach Scripture studies. Carter Lindberg was a Lutheran with a Ph.D. from the University of Iowa; Alexander Stecker was a Mormon who was completing a doctorate in Old Testament studies at Brandeis University and was initially hired as a one-year replacement. Brooks defended the action on the grounds that modern

---

derstand how it was here then, in order adequately to appreciate all that has happened since." See also the statements cited in Robert M. Nicholson, "A Legacy in Transition: A Social Portrait of the Professoriate in a Liberal Arts College of the Catholic, Jesuit Tradition," Ed.D. Dissertation (Harvard University, 1991), 325.

90. Province Status, June 11, 1963, Swords to O'Connor, November 22, 1963, ACHC, 19.2-3. Seven Jesuits were retired or released from the Theology Department in 1965.

91. Greeley, *Changing*, 134–35.

92. Edward F. Maloney, "A Study of the Religious Orientation of Catholic Colleges and Universities in New York State from 1962 to 1972," Ph.D. dissertation (New York University, 1974), 64–70, 77–84. As late as 1965, an advisory group in the New England Province expressed reservations about the hiring of non-Catholics to teach required courses in philosophy and theology. Minutes of the Consultors of the New England Province Directors of Education, November 2, 1965, ACHC, 19.8-1.

biblical scholarship utilizes a methodology that transcends religious differences—a position also endorsed by Bishop Flanagan.[93] Immediately, protests
were filed by Jesuit members of the faculty, most notably Father Richard V.
Lawlor of the Theology Department.[94] To bolster his position, Brooks sought
support from eminent Jesuit scholars including George W. McRae (a professor of Scripture at the Jesuits' Weston College Theologate), William L. Moran
(Professor of Assyriology at Harvard University), and Frederick L. Moriarty
(a professor of Old Testament at Weston and at the Gregorian University in
Rome). Father Swords sent these statements to the trustees, to Bishop Flanagan, and to the provincial, along with his own statement of support for the
hirings. From the provincial offices, Father O'Connor commended Swords for
approaching the matter "with great care."[95]

At the beginning of April, the opponents launched their counterattack,
focusing particularly on Stecker. Father Lawlor urged the president to pay
Stecker off to spare Holy Cross unpleasant publicity "when this practice is
forbidden, as I am sure it has to be." The hiring, he warned, would contribute
to "the insanity and unorthodoxy of life in today's Church."[96] Lawlor sought
the assistance of a Weston College moral theologian, John C. Ford, in calling
the matter to the attention of authorities in Rome. Ford was a conservative
who opposed the recommendation of the papal commission on birth control
to modify the stand against artificial contraception.[97] Ford contacted Cardinal
Augustine Bea, a Jesuit who headed the Secretariat for the Promotion of
Christian Unity in Rome. And Bea, apparently, endorsed the spirit of opposition to the hirings at Holy Cross:

Non-Catholic professors, because of their general education and specific preparation,
neither give nor can give sufficient guarantees for the fulfillment of those requirements
of the Church which have been authoritatively set forth through its ordinary magisterium [teaching authority] and through the solemn magisterium of the Council. The
conclusion which should be drawn from this is obvious and obligatory.

93. Press release, April 21, 1967, and Swords to Bp. Flanagan, February 13, 1967, ACHC,
12.24; Flanagan to Swords, February 20, 1967, WDA, Holy Cross, 1966–1969.

94. The Brooks statement was issued on February 8, 1967; see also protests from Lawlor,
William Lucey, and John P. Haran, ACHC, 12.24.

95. Brooks to Swords, March 4, 1967; Swords to Trustees, March 9 and 10, 1967, ACHC,
12.24; O'Connor to Swords, Boston, March 13, 1967, ACHC, 19.2-3.

96. Lawlor to Swords, April 1, 1967, ACHC, 12.24.

97. Peter Hebbelthwaite, *Paul VI: The First Modern Pope* (New York: Paulist Press, 1993), 444,
469–72. Ford's efforts helped persuade the pope to oppose artificial birth control in *Humanae
Vitae* in 1968.

Father Arrupe communicated Bea's thoughts in a carefully worded memo to all Jesuit provincials in North America, urging them to communicate the statement to college administrators because of the issue's importance "in the mind of the cardinal."[98] Ten days later, Father Moriarty informed Father Brooks from Rome on reliable authority that Cardinal Bea's ideas had been misunderstood. His statement was a private, unofficial comment responding to an incomplete rationale; and therefore, Roman authorities were not forbidding the hirings. In fact, it later transpired that Bea had issued the statement without consulting his staff, who were then preparing a very different response to a similar question. When they pointed this out to him at a staff meeting, Bea gave an answer "very different from the private answer . . . sent to Fr. Ford."[99]

The controversy continued through the spring and summer of 1967. Fathers Lawlor and Ford continued to assert that the hirings were an affront to the proper exercise of teaching authority within the Catholic Church, while Fathers Brooks and Swords defended the action on a variety of grounds. For Father Brooks, the fundamental goal was to separate the teaching of theology as an academic discipline from the promotion of Roman Catholicism among students who sought religious instruction:

The task of religious instruction in the Catholic faith is incumbent upon *all* Jesuits assigned to Holy Cross, be they professors of theology or not. However the task is primarily that of . . . chaplains . . . as well as those who are working in the Chapel, on corridors, giving retreats, conducting prayer meetings, etc. on campus. The function of the Department of Theology is to serve as an *essential* part of the liberal arts program here at Holy Cross. This implies that the Department is interested *not* in expounding one particular confessional commitment, but rather in examining religious concepts and phenomena in order that the student might be assisted in his understanding of man, and in his own grappling with questions of ultimate concern and significance. The student studies Old and New Testaments not that he might be instructed in the Catholic faith, but that he might become acquainted with the entire Judaeo-Christian tradition, without which he could never come to an understanding of Western civilization.[100]

As directed by Father Arrupe, the American provincials discussed the matter at their meeting in the spring, but decided to take no action until the college

98. Ford to Swords, Weston, April 8, 1967, Bea's statement of March 20, 1967, and Arrupe's letter to the American Provincials of April 10, 1967, ACHC, 12.24.

99. Moriarty to Brooks, Rome, April 20, 1967, and Report of the Chairman of the J.E.A. Commission on Colleges and Universities (Washington, D.C., October 13, 1967), ACHC, 12.24. The report quoted a statement given in August at Holy Cross by a member of Bea's staff, Fr. Walter Abbott, S.J., who suggested that the cardinal would be "distressed" if he knew the use being made of his private statement.

100. Brooks to Swords, April 13, 1967, ACHC, 12.24.

and university presidents could consider the matter. Their hand was forced by John Ford, who continued circulating Bea's statement on the grounds that the cardinal had authorized him to make use of it. By August, the provincials had decided that, since they couldn't stop Ford from using a statement he was authorized to circulate, they needed a statement of their own. Two months later, the general endorsed this plan.[101] At the opening of school in September, Lawlor confronted Swords with his view that the hiring of a non-Catholic to teach theology at the College was "an objectively grave sin." He planned to advise students against taking such teachers.[102]

Such circumstances gave urgency to the preparation of a policy statement on the hiring of non-Catholics to teach theology. Representatives of the JEA Commission on Colleges and Universities prepared a rather timid proposal designed to foster professional expertise on theology faculties, provided that "the theology that forms the core of the department will remain Catholic."[103] The Jesuit presidents opposed these norms as "very embarrassing to them and possibly harmful to our institutions" because they were being imposed from outside. Theology hirings, the presidents insisted, should be exactly the same as hirings in other academic departments. The Jesuit provincials accepted the latter approach at their November meeting, and forwarded to the general a brief endorsement of the equal academic hirings. In practice, the general accepted their view: Theology was established at par with other academic departments.[104] Stecker remained on the Holy Cross faculty until 1971; Lindberg, until 1972.

The intensity of opposition to the theology hirings was partly a manifestation of the perceived diminution of Jesuit influence and traditional Catholic practice at the College. The new spirit that encouraged the participation of the faculty and brought the trustees to the brink of separate incorporation also introduced changes in student life. Nowhere was the change more dramatic than in the alteration of the rules for compulsory attendance at Mass and retreats. Father Donaghy's restoration of the weekday Mass obligation

101. Swords to William L. Moran, Worcester, June 14, 1967, John Ford to "Bill" [Guindon ?], Weston, July 18, 1967, and Edward Sponga to Swords, Baltimore, August 21 and October 10, 1967, ACHC, 12.24.

102. Lawlor to Swords, and Lawlor to Brooks, September 2, 1967, ACHC, 12.24.

103. Report of the Chairman of the JEA Commission on Colleges and Universities, Washington, D.C., October 13, 1967, ACHC, 12.24.

104. Edward Sponga to Arrupe, Baltimore, November 4, 1967, and the text, "Non Catholics as Teachers of Sacred Scripture in Jesuit Colleges: A Policy Statement," ACHC, 12.24; FitzGerald, *Governance*, 204–5.

(Sunday attendance was assumed because it was strictly sanctioned by Church law) failed to enhance religious fervor. Early in 1960, an observer complained that students streamed back to their rooms from the chapel after attendance was taken; on Sundays, many arrived for Mass very late. The situation created a morale problem for the conscientious students, because the slackers' behavior was ignored.[105] By then, the very assumption that students could be required to pray had been challenged by Father Janssens in Rome. In letters of 1958 and 1960, the general cited Ignatius's policy, set forth in the Jesuit Constitutions, that students should be encouraged to attend daily Mass, but not forced. Janssens counseled administrators to offer encouragement in the practice, but to leave undisturbed those who refused to comply, "until the Grace of God moves their hearts to better things."[106]

In early 1962, Father Swords met with his consultors and trustees to shape a new College policy. They were generally supportive of the change; with the present rules, one argued, "a love for daily Mass is not fostered, but rather a dislike for it."[107] By June, the president was convinced that all disciplinary sanctions involving Mass should be dropped, beginning that fall. To mitigate an overly abrupt change in policy, College authorities decided to maintain the requirement for freshmen "for a few years," after which the obligation was quietly dropped.[108] In 1967, the section devoted to campus Masses was moved from the first page of the Student Handbook to the middle, under the heading "Religious Opportunities." The same handbook replaced the statement that the goal of the College was to produce the "Christian man," with the assertion that the College was committed to the Liberal Arts for forming "the well-educated human person." Meanwhile, Father Swords asked the Jesuit community to foster appreciation of the Mass. By the fall of 1966, the time had also come to drop compulsory religious retreats for upperclassmen, replacing them with optional College-sponsored retreats.[109]

In the same years, the beginning of Mass in English as a result of the Vatican II reforms focused new attention on the liturgy, a development Father

105. The letter bears a notation dating it in April 1960. Commenting on the complaint several months later, New England Provincial James Coleran called the writer's tone "spiteful." Coleran to Michael Pierce, Boston, July 11, 1960, NEPA, HC Varia. Yet, oral tradition supports the accuracy of the statement.

106. Janssens's letters were quoted in Swords's letter to the Jesuit community, August 6, 1962, ACHC, 12.24. The general was referring to Part IV, Chapter 16 of the Jesuit Constitutions.

107. John Long to Swords, Worcester, March 12, 1962, ACHC, 12.24.

108. Swords to Coleran, Worcester, June 4 and July [1?], 1962, ACHC, 19.2-3.

109. Swords to the Jesuit Community, Worcester, August 6, 1962, ACHC, 12.24; Swords to J. V. O'Connor, Worcester, September 23, 1965, ACHC, 19.2-3; Student Handbook, 1966.

Swords promoted enthusiastically. Observing that students and faculty were "thrilled" with the innovation, Father Swords attended to the need for liturgical planning by requesting that Father Robert Lindsay be placed "in charge of the religious life on campus—a sort of overall chaplain."[110] The appointment of Lindsay as College chaplain, approved for the fall semester of 1965, revised somewhat the older concept of having a spiritual prefect. At the same time, Father Swords expressed his desire that the lay faculty be involved in the religious life and development of their students. In 1967, when Father John Walsh succeeded to the office of College chaplain, Father Swords pointed out the pressing need "to come up with a program replacing what was formerly taught in Theology courses, and giving our students an example of what an alive parish church should be."[111]

Another part of the established order at the College that fell under scrutiny in the 1960s was the tradition of Jesuit corridor prefects. In the spring of 1961, the trustees authorized the appointment of seniors to assist on corridors. The primary reason was the lack of a sufficient number of Jesuits to carry the responsibility, particularly with additional dormitories in the works. Two students were to be assigned to a prefect's room to oversee discipline and order and be accountable to the dean of men, with a Jesuit also on corridor as a spiritual counselor.[112] Father Swords announced the plan in early January 1962. It was to be tried on a limited basis, on freshman and sophomore corridors, but he anticipated that all dorms would eventually adopt the plan. In 1964, the plan was extended to junior corridors, and the designation was changed from student prefect to resident assistant. Two years later, hard realities prompted a move to cut back to one Jesuit per residence hall. Qualified candidates were scarce, and there were tensions between resident assistants, who were responsible for discipline, and Jesuits who found it difficult to stay clear of con-

---

110. Swords to Bishop Flanagan, Worcester, September 30, 1964, ACHC, 12.24; Swords to J. V. O'Connor, Worcester, July 30, 1964, ACHC, 19.2-3. The first campus Mass to use English was the May Day Mass in 1962, a Melkite Rite liturgy celebrated by Fr. Edmund Haddad, with a sermon by Bishop Flanagan—"a moving and pleasant experience for all." HD, May 1, 1962. English liturgies in the Roman Rite in the United States were slated to begin on the first Sunday of Advent in 1964, but Bishop Flanagan approved an English Mass at Holy Cross in September. Celebrated by Father Swords in the Field House, it was the first such Mass in the diocese. Worcester *Telegram*, September 24, 1964.

111. HD, September 11, 1965; Swords's address to faculty meeting, October 8, 1965, Swords to Walsh, August 29, 1967.

112. Trustees' Minutes, May 29, 1961, January 2 and May 8, 1962, ACHC, 11.0; Swords to Coleran, Worcester, December 26, 1961, ACHC, 19.2-3; Swords to Charles Dunn, Worcester, December 27, 1961, ACHC, 12.24.

frontational situations.[113] In 1968, Dr. John E. Shay, who became dean of men in 1967, recommended the appointment of dormitory chaplains instead of "housing reluctant Jesuits on student corridors." By then, the tradition of Jesuit corridor prefects was impossible to maintain. In some instances, their position within the residence hall had become marginal; for many of the teaching Jesuits, professional demands required that their time be devoted to other priorities. The tradition of reserving specific corridors for each class was overturned at about the same time; the policy of allowing students to choose rooms on the basis of seniority was introduced.[114]

Changes in residence hall life reflected the greater emphasis on personal responsibility that came to characterize the student code of conduct during the 1960s. In 1960, gambling and alcohol were still forbidden in the dormitories; lights out was enforced during the first three years; permission was required to leave campus at night; jackets and ties were required for classes and meals; classes (obligatory attendance) began with prayers, and meals started with grace; "odd and flamboyant dress" was not allowed. By 1962, juniors and seniors were allowed to receive guests in the lounges of the hill dorms; in 1965, responsibility for class-attendance policy was remanded to individual instructors. Greater changes arrived in 1966, when lights-out was dropped, students were allowed to entertain women in their rooms at designated times, and the dress code for Kimball Hall was relaxed. Lounges were now open to all students; women were allowed in the lounges without limit of time; students could leave campus by simply signing out in the dean of students' office. Finally, in 1967, College authorities dropped the rule forbidding students to have alcohol in their rooms, justifying the new policy as an approach that was designed to remove the glamor and danger associated with drinking, while allowing students to assume personal responsibility.[115]

"Holy Cross is catching up with the times," Father Swords told the literary editor of the 1968 *Purple Patcher*. College authorities no longer believed they had all the answers; therefore, they were determined to be open-minded toward change. But progress had its price. Swords was concerned about the lack of concern among students for the rights of others.[116] A report on campus discipline,

113. Trustees' Minutes, January 2, 1962, ACHC, 11.0; Dean of Students' Correspondence, 1961–1964, ACHC 15.2-14; *Crusader*, May 8, 1964; Swords to J.V. O'Connor, March 7, 1966, ACHC, 19.2-3.

114. John Shay to Swords, Annual Report, July 1, 1968, ACHC, 12.24; *Crusader*, May 12 and September 19, 1966, September 15, 1967.

115. Worcester *Gazette*, September 14, 1967; Student Handbooks, 1960–67.

116. Swords's hand-written notes in response to questions from Richard E. DiLallo '68, October 31, 1967, ACHC, 12.24.

issued in the summer of 1967, pointed to the issues. Resident assistants experienced problems with parietal violations, "obnoxious drinking," and physical damage to the dormitories. Noise was an increasing problem, particularly with the arrival of sound equipment in individual rooms. Support for parietal rules was dropping.[117] On the latter point, John Shay proposed shaping "a framework of reasonable regulations enforced primarily by responsible students in place of the rigid code of the past enforced by the dean of men." Peer pressure, he asserted, would require further relaxation of parietal rules, because students found the restrictions to rest on an "unreasonably conservative" idea that dorm rooms were merely bedrooms, while, in fact, they served a variety of functions. The same spirit of peer pressure, Shay argued, would regulate behavior in Kimball Hall far more effectively than sending authority figures out to patrol.[118]

Students had already tested standards of reasonable behavior in a confrontation with the administration in 1965. The episode started when John Hoban '65 appealed the D plus grade assigned to him in philosophy by Father Joseph Shea. Offended by the implied criticism, Shea directed the registrar to change the grade to an F. Hoban and others met several times with the academic dean, Father Maurice Reidy, in an unsuccessful effort to resolve the matter; eventually, Reidy upheld the failing grade.[119] Twelve days later, two of Hoban's classmates directed a letter of protest to Father Reidy, objecting that Hoban had passed a course "and was subsequently flunked for what could be termed criticism or, at most, insolence." They announced their intention to hold a public demonstration and leafleted the dormitories with their version of events surrounding the "*ex post facto* flunk." "Talk has failed," they argued, "so has Hoban. Now is the time to act." Organizers adopted the name, Ban Against Retroactive Flunking (BARF).[120] At least 1000 students (some in academic robes), plus media representatives, gathered at the library stairs on March 30 to hear the administration denounced for exercising "the heavy hand of paternalism, of *in loco parentis* discipline, of authoritarianism which at times evinces the attitude that a decision is just . . . due to the status of the person who made it." BARF sought restoration of the D plus for Hoban and the right of appealing grades without fear of intimidation.[121] Father Swords

117. Campus Discipline Report, July 1967, [issued by Fr. Maurice Reidy, Joseph Maguire '58, and Dennis Golden '63], ACHC, 11.0.

118. Shay's report to Swords, July 1, 1968, ACHC, 12.24.

119. Reidy to Hoban, Worcester, February 19, 1965, and circular to students from James Murphy, Jr. '66 and Edmund Carey, Jr. '65, [March 25, 1965], ACHC, 12.24.

120. Murphy and Carey to Reidy, March 24, 1965, and circular of [March 25, 1965], ACHC, 12.24.

121. Statements from the BARF demonstration are in the Swords Papers, ACHC, 12.24; *Crusader*, March 26 and April 1, 1965

handled the matter in his own fashion. He made no comment at the time of the protest; later, in his talk to students at the Easter Banquet, he promised that the administration and faculty would cooperate in "the current quest for a new understanding of the role and position of the students at Holy Cross." Hoban was allowed to graduate, despite the failing grade.[122]

On other fronts, College authorities were attempting to keep pace with the shifting cultural pattern. In 1960, when permission to leave campus for entertainment was still strictly regulated, the trustees approved construction of a ski tow on the back of the hill. In 1963, Campion House was converted to a pizza parlor; in 1966, pizza gave way to coffee, folk music, and jazz, when a student-run coffee house, Limbo, opened there.[123] Public affairs received a new emphasis in 1965 when Weston Howland, a Bay State textile manufacturer and benefactor of the College, anonymously established the Edward F. Hanify Memorial Lecture series, named after the distinguished alumnus of 1904 who served as a justice for the Superior Court of Massachusetts. Administered by students, the series aimed at attracting speakers whose careers modeled service in public affairs. After Howland's death, the lecture was renamed the Hanify-Howland Memorial Lecture.[124] Academic excellence received a new expression in 1966, when the Fenwick Scholar program was organized. Highly competitive, the program permits one outstanding senior (sometimes more) to work on a project during the academic year without reference to course requirements. The program was set up for Richard J. Pedersen '67, whose grade point average of 4.0, Father Guindon stated, "prompted the College to seek a fitting honorary award for conveying the college's pride in his achievement, and its confidence in his scholarly maturity."[125]

Signs of the times were evident, too, in the impact of great leaders on campus. In November of 1962, Martin Luther King, Jr., was a dinner guest of the Jesuit community and afterwards spoke to a large crowd in the field house. On the day of John Kennedy's funeral in 1963, Requiem Masses were offered simultaneously in the upper and lower chapels.[126] The following year, Lyndon Johnson was the commencement speaker. Local schools were closed on the day of his visit; 175,000 people lined the parade route from Worcester Airport

122. *Purple Patcher*, 1966.

123. Trustees' Minutes, September 22, 1960, ACHC, 11.0; *Crusader*, September 26, 1963; Worcester *Telegram*, April 9, 1967.

124. Report of Father George Higgins to Swords, August 1, 1967, ACHC, 14.75; Boston *Globe*, February 3, 1976. Edward F. Hanify '04 was the father of attorney Edward B. Hanify '33.

125. Worcester *Gazette*, September 13, 1966. Pederson also received a Rhodes Scholarship, the College's second. The first Rhodes Scholar was Francis Michael Buckley '66. *Crusader*, January 13, 1966; *Catholic Free Press*, December 23, 1966.

126. HD, November 19, 1962; Worcester *Telegram*, November 23 and 24, 1963. On King's speech, see the Worcester *Telegram* and *Gazette*, November 20, 1962.

A harbinger of change: Martin Luther King, Jr. addresses a large audience in the fieldhouse in 1962. The yearbook caption read: "Steve Bashwiner, representing every listener, expresses strong approval of the courage, conviction, and eloquence of Dr. Martin Luther King."

to the campus; 14,000 gathered at Fitton Field to hear the president appeal to the graduates to dedicate themselves to serve the welfare of all humanity and "to find new methods of improving the life of man."[127]

Like all other facets of campus life, the intercollegiate sports program encountered new realities during the 1960s. Two giants in the College's athletic

127. On LBJ's willingness to accept the honorary degree, see an undated telegram (copy) from Father Richard P. Burke expressing Sword's delight to have the president speak. Ken O'Donnell accepted for the president on April 14. A memo from Father Reidy to Swords, April 17, credits Congressman Harold Donohue with assisting the process. ACHC, 12.24. On the presidential visit to Worcester, see especially the Worcester *Gazette*, June 10, 1964. The commencement program may be found in WDA, Holy Cross, 1961–1965. The visit made political sense for Johnson in an election year; this was an opportunity to establish his credentials

tradition passed from the scene. Jack Barry died in 1961, having spent forty years as baseball coach.[128] Eddie Anderson retired at the end of the 1964 season, his twenty-first as head football coach. His successors, Mel Massucco (1965–66, 8–10–2) and Tom Boisture (1967–68, 8–11–1), were less successful; yet each season brought its thrills—especially the Boston College game in 1966, when Mike Kaminski '68 kicked two 44-yard field goals and the Purple won in the final minute with a touchdown pass from Jack Lentz '67 to Pete Kimener '67. In basketball, Frank Offtring '50, a standout student-athlete who had played on the 1948 NCAA championship team, succeeded Roy Leenig in 1961 and enjoyed four winning seasons (64–33), including Jack "The Shot" Foley's last season, when he averaged 33.3 points per game and was named an All-American. Offtring was succeeded in 1965 by Jack Donohue, whose teams maintained the winning tradition over seven seasons (106–66). In track, Art Dulong '70 won the National Invitational freshman mile run in 1967 in a new school record time of 4:04.8.[129]

Nevertheless, a shadow was slowly falling over the athletic program, because intercollegiate sports represented a questionable asset on the balance sheet, and because the drive to upgrade the academic quality of the school focused attention on the idea that athletes had to be scholastically competitive. In fiscal terms, intercollegiate athletics declined from 6.4 percent of the annual budget in 1960 to 3.3 percent in 1968. Basketball, using the Worcester Auditorium with a relatively small capacity, lost money every year. Football, which accounted for 86 percent of income from revenue sports, generated the lowest income in a decade during the 1961 season, prompting some hand-wringing from Father Swords about "how we can continue to sustain such a terrifying loss."[130] Given the generally precarious state of the school's finances, Swords monitored athletic scholarships carefully. In 1963, he directed the moderator of athletics to limit grants for the incoming class to 25 in football, 6 in basketball, and 2 in baseball. In 1964, he asked that the budgets for hockey and

---

with a heavily Catholic audience in a region where he was still somewhat unknown. John Kennedy had spoken at the Boston College centennial in 1963; Worcester was close enough to Boston to serve the same purpose, and more centrally located.

128. *Crusader*, April 27, 1961. Barry was succeeded by Albert D. "Hop" Riopel '24 (1961–66), Robert T. Curran '48 (1967–70) and Jack Whalen '48 (1971–). Holy Cross Baseball media guide, 1993.

129. Football and Basketball Media Guides, 1993; *Crusader*, March 16, 1967.

130. Swords to Joseph Glavin, December 12, 1961, and Arthur D. Little Memorandum I, December 16, 1968, ACHC, 12.24. Television revenues were slight: between 1959 and 1965, only the Syracuse game of 1964 was broadcast, with revenue of $85,000. Dougherty to Swords, April 19, 1968, ACHC, 12.24.

golf be reduced; the following year, he put monetary restrictions on scholar-ships for incoming athletes. At the same time, he directed Coach Massucco to cut back football grants, from 25 in 1965 to 20 in 1968 and thereafter. Under these conditions, football posted a net profit of $192,000 between 1963 and 1968.[131]

The academic implications of the College's athletic program emerged more slowly as a source of concern. At first, Father Swords lauded the school's reputation for athletic integrity and sportsmanship. In 1965, he characterized the athletic program as being modeled on the Ivy League, but "on a much more modest scale." Privately, he was worried about the academic qualifica-tions of some athletes, and he directed in 1965 that no scholarships be awarded unless students were athletically *and* academically qualified.[132] Late in 1966, he received SAT scores for varsity athletes from the Classes of 1964 through 1970 and learned that they averaged about 10 percent lower than other students. He was "quite surprised" by the figures, he told Athletic Director Vince Dougherty, and directed him to undertake "definite efforts to improve the academic qualifications of the athletes whom we are bringing into the col-lege." He feared a negative reaction from the faculty when these data became public.[133]

The two sets of considerations—financial and academic—brought to a head a movement for a grand review of the College's athletic policy. As early as 1958, Father Maurice Reidy of the History Department proposed making such a study part of the re-accreditation process. In 1961, when College au-thorities were still pessimistic about the land-taking, Father J. Leo Sullivan the College's business manager, proposed dropping football and reallocating the resources to intramural and other varsity sports. He feared sinking money into a new stadium, since old rivalries (and sources of income) could vanish if other schools dropped the sport. In 1965, Father Swords confided to Vince Dougherty that he hoped to sponsor a general study of the athletic pro-gram.[134] And in 1967, Mel Massucco's decision to take the head coaching job at Worcester Polytechnic Institute was taken as a signal by the local press that

131. Swords to Glavin, February 1, 1963, ACHC, 18.0-1; Swords to George Nolan, June 19, 1964, ACHC, 18.1-1; Swords to Richard P. Burke, February 15, 1965, and Swords to Massucco, September 7, 1965, A. D. Little Memorandum I, December 16, 1968, ACHC, 12.24.

132. Swords to Richard P. Burke, February 15, 1965, and Swords to Frederic O. Floberg '39, Worcester, December 14, 1965, ACHC, 12.24.

133. Swords to Dougherty, October 10, 1966, ACHC, 12.24.

134. Maurice Reidy to Andrew McFadden [Executive Assistant to Donaghy], March 8, 1958, ACHC, 14.12; J. L. Sullivan to Swords, December 12, 1961, and Swords to Dougherty, November 22, 1965, ACHC, 12.24.

Holy Cross might be on the verge of dropping football, as eight Jesuit colleges and universities did between 1950 and 1970.[135]

Responding to these concerns, the Educational Policy Committee voted in March of 1967 to establish a Joint Ad Hoc Committee on Athletics. Under the chairmanship of Professor V. O. McBrien, the committee included two Jesuits (the academic dean, and the executive assistant to Father Swords), four lay professors, and the athletic director. Their mandate was "to study the modes of faculty voice in the formulation of athletic policies having a bearing on the academic, with a view to recommending that mechanism most valuable to the welfare of the College."[136] The committee encountered difficulty almost immediately, when the trustees refused to collaborate, voting instead to *receive* a report. Faced with this reaction, the EPC in August set up a smaller Ad Hoc Committee on Athletics with a mandate to inquire into the nature and purpose of the Athletic Association, and the relationship of varsity sports to the general program of the College.[137] The bottom line of the investigation was the question of whether the school's athletic program was consistent with its academic ambition.

Shortly before the ad hoc committee began to meet, another faculty committee—the Special Committee on Admissions and Scholarships, which had been established in 1961—delivered a report that bristled with realism. The student body was characterized as selective but varying in quality "from excellent to extremely poor." The College badly needed to enhance its reputation: "It may be fairly stated that Holy Cross is not a 'prestige college' and does not have an outstanding national reputation. Its faculty has not achieved any noticeable preeminence." General recommendations included greater faculty involvement in the community, a campaign to correct the image of Holy Cross as a "training school for priests," and greater racial and geographic diversity among the students. The committee expressed satisfaction with the academic achievement of College athletes, but warned against "the danger of the excitement of big-time varsity athletics submerging the serious intellectual atmosphere of a small liberal

135. Worcester *Telegram*, March 7, 1967; Worcester *Gazette*, March 10, 1967. According to NCAA data, 86 schools dropped football during the 1950s, and 41 during the 1960s. Among these, fourteen were characterized as major college programs. NCAA data supplied to author, July 1995.

136. Guindon to faculty, March 15, 1967, ACHC, 14.8-1A.

137. V. O. McBrien to Guindon, April 25, 1967, Frank Petrella to Guindon, April 26, 1967, Ad Hoc Committee on Athletics file, ACHC 14.12; George Nolan to Swords, July 19, 1967, and Trustees' minutes, July 26, 1967, ACHC, 11.0. Members of the Ad Hoc Committee were William Green (History), Robert Ricci (Mathematics), Father Maurice Reidy (History), and Father Brooks as secretary.

arts college." To guarantee this atmosphere, they recommended that athletic scholarships be eliminated in favor of "College scholarships," which would be granted on a number of grounds, including athletic talent.[138]

With these recommendations in the air, Ad Hoc Committee on Athletics met weekly during the 1967–68 academic year. As they were gathering information, Mathematics Professor Vincent McBrien caused a stir by proposing abandonment of the major intercollegiate sports program in a letter featured prominently in the January 25, 1968, issue of the *Crusader*. McBrien advocated a scenario, common enough in those days, that Holy Cross should model itself academically on Williams or Amherst, abandoning "semi big-time athletics." Although he conceded that a small minority of students and alumni enjoyed the athletic program, he argued that it lost money, attracted comparatively little support within the Worcester community, removed Holy Cross from athletic competition with most Ivy League schools, and had a counterproductive influence on the academic reputation of the school. After publication of the McBrien letter, members of the ad hoc committee began considering a professional study as a means of grasping the ramifications of the current athletic policy and the options open to the College. By May, there was general consensus on hiring the Arthur D. Little firm to carry out the plan. As questions about the athletic program were being shaped, members of the administration suggested that other issues be included in the study, including coeducation and the size of the school. In September of 1968 the trustees endorsed the proposal. The study was announced to the press in November.[139] Thus, the athletic program, too, came under scrutiny, with the possibility of alteration in the old, familiar pattern.

There had been countless changes since 1960, changes that were transforming the school as its representatives struggled to understand and respond to contemporary challenges. Adaptation to persons, places, and times was a characteristically Jesuit trait—as defining for Father Swords and his associates in the 1960s as it had been for Ignatius and his companions over four hundred years earlier. Yet change is often difficult: it is easy to know what is being given up and difficult to trust that the new will serve its intended purpose. Justifying change, and evoking trust in the processes that supported it, were chal-

138. Report of Special Committee on College Admission Policy, June, 1967, ACHC, 11.0.

139. Minutes of the Ad Hoc Committee on Athletic Policy, 1967–1968, ACHC, 14.12. See also EPC Minutes, May 28, 1968, ACHC, 12.24. The trustees accepted the EPC recommendation in favor of the A. D. Little study on September 4, 1968. Brooks to Faculty and Administration, November 12, 1968. The press release was dated November 15. All documents in ACHC, 12.24.

lenges Father Swords faced continuously as he sought to create and express a new vision. To the incoming class in 1963, he said that the changes were for the sake of the students: "You and your contemporaries are so beyond the ken of our experience that you are causing us to do some basic rethinking."[140] To the provincial, he made a similar point, characterizing change as necessary liberation from self-serving inertia: "I would hope that we come gradually to a clearer conviction, which would carry over into actuality, that our institutions of learning . . . are not run for the sake of the Religious who own them but for the sake of the objects of our ministry."[141] He made vision the centerpiece of a talk to parents in 1968, arguing that the spirit of the documents of Vatican II required the College to be fully engaged in the world, a reversal of the nineteenth-century notion that withdrawal from the world was a higher ideal. Holy Cross, he asserted, "will last as long as it follows the lead of the Church and addresses itself to the problem of renewal, updating, making itself relevant to each succeeding age."[142]

Swords's fullest articulation of his vision of a modern Jesuit college was a speech given in September 1966 to new faculty at Georgetown University. In it, he discussed the supposed dilemma that secularization represented for a church-related institution because of an alleged contradiction between fidelity to the Church and adherence to the canons of the academy.[143] The Catholic identity, he stated, arises from adding the study of divinely revealed "mysteries of faith" to topics that can be known through the natural powers of intelligence. The Catholic university "affirms" that issues arising from faith and revelation deserve to be known because they encompass "truths that are vital to man's existence and destiny as a personal being . . . [and] should be freely and openly shared with all who earnestly seek the truth." A university that did not cultivate the study of theology as an intellectual discipline would not be Catholic. The Jesuit nature of the school had to do with "the harmonious integration within the human person and his world, of the sacred and the secular, of divine revelation and human reason, of theology and human science . . . , of knowledge and love."[144]

Inevitably, the strain of serving as the chief sponsor of change at Holy Cross took its toll on Raymond Swords. Expressions of support notwithstanding, he yearned for a release from responsibility. Midway through his an-

140. Swords' message to freshmen, 1963, ACHC, 12.24.

141. Swords to J. V. O'Connor, Worcester, October 19, 1965, ACHC, 19.2-3.

142. Swords's address at Parents Weekend, 1968, ACHC, 12.24.

143. Richard Freeland characterizes the dilemma succinctly: "how to be faithful to the Church and acceptable to the profession." *Golden Age*, 258.

144. Swords to new Georgetown faculty, September, 1966, ACHC, 12.24.

ticipated term of six years, William Grattan '38, Swords' classmate and a member of the History Department, praised his farsightedness and vision, and expressed the hope that "you will grace the office for twelve years rather than the customary six."[145] By 1965, however, Swords's thoughts were running in the opposite direction. Already in 1964, the term of Boston College's successful president Father Michael Walsh had been extended beyond the traditional six years; Swords must have intuited that a similar request would be put to him. And so he wrote to the provincial, asking to step down after six years. He was less able to respond to crises because the heavy burdens of office had diminished his resiliency, he argued; he was worried also that his decisions had alienated some members of the Jesuit community. From the perspective of the College, he suggested with remarkable humility that Holy Cross needed a more imaginative head: "It would have taken a man of pretty poor ability not to see what had to be accomplished, it was so apparent. . . . I admit that a fairly good road was selected at that time, but Holy Cross is truthfully at another crossroads, and it needs another type of person than I to do the leading now." In November of 1965, the Jesuit province consultors discussed the presidency of Holy Cross. Having reflected and prayed further about his status, he now softened his opposition to re-appointment: "I'll go whichever way [you] want me—even though my strong preferences lie in handing things over so someone else."[146] The province consultors voted unanimously to retain him because, as the provincial stated, "you are doing an excellent piece of work as President and Rector of Holy Cross." In response, Father Swords said simply: "I cannot say that I am happy about it, but I hope and pray that things will go well."[147]

Father Swords made a second attempt to leave office in 1967. He spoke with the provincial in July, following up the conversation with another personal letter, pleading weariness and personal distaste for responsibility as reasons for terminating his administration in 1968. He had achieved organizational reform, he stated; now the College needed strong educational leadership "and I am not an educational statesman." Finally—and most tellingly, given the context of institutional struggle—he indicated a willingness to stay on if that were the only means of ensuring that his reforms would not be overturned: "If my successor were to be one who would not support the trends and attitudes of the younger men in the Community I would wish—and

145. Grattan to Swords, June 5, 1963, Grattan Papers, ACHC, 14.8-3.

146. Swords to J.V. O'Connor, February 12 and November 6, 1965, ACHC, 19.2-3. On Walsh's extended term, see Freeland, *Golden Age*, 257.

147. J. V. O'Connor to Swords, Boston, November 12, 1965, and Swords to O'Connor, November 15, 1965, NEPA, HC-Rector.

strongly so—to stay on for a while."[148] Once again, Jesuit authorities overrode his desire to step down because his experience and expertise were deemed essential to pilot Holy Cross through the transition to separate incorporation.[149] For Raymond Swords, the cost of leadership was intense and private; the benefits were manifold, and public.

In October of 1964, Biology Department member Thomas Malumphy '21, reflecting on four decades of change at the College, observed: "As Harvard had its Eliot at the critical point of its development, we have been most fortunate in having our Father Swords."[150] That was hardly an understatement. Father Swords moved Holy Cross past its crossroads; his decisions positioned the school toward a dramatically brighter future. Every facet of the operation was affected: the quality and input of the faculty, the mode of Jesuit presence and influence on campus, the make-up of the curriculum, the role of the Theology Department, the emphasis on personal responsibility in student life, additions to the physical plant, a larger enrollment, the study of the varsity athletic program, and the anticipated transfer of responsibility for the College through separate incorporation. Already, he had achieved enormous gains by enlisting the responsible collaboration of professional lay persons, tapping their energy, expertise, and dedication for the good of Holy Cross. But the provincial was correct: the process wasn't finished. Raymond Swords accepted that judgment and braced himself to complete what he had begun.

148. Swords to O'Connor, Worcester, July 30, 1967, ACHC, 12.24.

149. "The hope that we could give separate incorporation a year of trial, and the wish to give the new Superior a year of experience as Superior before I left office, are the two principal reasons I agreed to remain in office for the present year." Swords to William Guindon, November 18, 1968, ACHC, 12.24. See also G. W. Nolan to J. V. O'Connor, Worcester, August 2, 1967, NEPA, HC-Varia.

150. Malumphy to Swords, Worcester, October 7, 1964, ACHC, 12.24.

CHAPTER TEN

The Shape of the Third Holy Cross, 1968–1972

B Y 1968, THE YEAR of its 125th jubilee, Holy Cross was positioned for a breakthrough into a new era, thanks to the leadership of Raymond Swords. Two years later, John Brooks, a major participant in the restructuring, assumed the presidency without interrupting momentum. In the four years that constituted the transition between two administrations, the third Holy Cross emerged. Separate incorporation, coeducation, the recruitment of minority students, a reformed curriculum, an improved faculty, a revitalized development office, commitment to liberal arts, and a Jesuit, Catholic identity disclosed its basic pattern. Radical politics, the unavoidable concomitant of higher education at that time, influenced the process without stopping it. As always, change brought conflict: both presidents had to mediate between those who wanted to accelerate the transition and those who were alarmed that so much was being left behind. Most of all, for those who participated in refashioning the school, the experience was exhilarating.

The jubilee in 1968 provided an opportunity to measure progress and look forward. A three-day celebration in October included a convocation at which Father Swords contrasted the austerity, discipline, and classicism of the old approach with the new emphasis on personal responsibility and faculty governance. Despite the changes, he argued, commitment to the values of Christian humanism remained strong.[1] The principal speaker, Harvard President Nathan M. Pusey, supported Swords's vision. He compared Holy Cross with Harvard: both schools were founded because of religious ideals, designed to provide clergy for their churches, and now educated students for a wide variety of ca-

1. This speech, and other materials from the jubilee, are in the 125th Anniversary File, ACHC, 17.1.

reers. He asserted that the goal of liberal education is not merely to transmit ancient learning, but "to awaken young minds to an imaginative understanding of the individual and personal nature of knowledge and to excite them to set out on voyages of discovery of their own." In that context, the special task of Holy Cross as a Catholic institution was to foster the spiritual development of its students, and through them to influence society. Pusey's endorsement of the College's approach and mission was a striking illustration that the battle that once pitted the *Ratio* against electivism had yielded to the common ground of humanism and the liberal arts, and respect for the religious mission of Holy Cross.

During 1968, the question of institutional affiliation was in the air as the drive toward separate incorporation neared its conclusion. Long a priority of Raymond Swords, the process had been initiated in 1966 and was now under review in Rome. One of the gains Father Swords anticipated was that separate incorporation would relieve Jesuits (and others) of the misapprehension that the Society of Jesus "owned" the institutions it sponsored. He and others accepted what came to be known as the McGrath Thesis,[2] a position that religious communities really only managed their schools in trust for the state. As College treasurer Father George Nolan put it, "neither the [Jesuit] Provincial nor the General has had any *legal* authority over Holy Cross College" since the charter was conferred in 1865.[3] Swords was convinced that the old system of governance, with Jesuit trustees serving mostly as rubber stamps for their religious superiors, confirmed the general impression "that the College was a type of private business rather than a public trust; . . . the ecclesiastical authority and the authority of the president could scarcely be distinguished."[4] Swords noted that Father Arrupe favored separate incorporation as "better for our spirit of poverty in the Community because it would bring home to [Jesuits] that our holdings are very limited."[5] He argued further that, after sep-

2. John J. McGrath, *Catholic Institutions in the United States: Canonical and Civil Law Status* (Washington: The Catholic University of America Press, 1968), 32–38; Joseph R. Preville, "Catholic Colleges, the Courts, and the Constitution: A Tale of Two Cases," in *Church History* 58 (June 1989), 201–4. The McGrath Thesis was attacked by some as inconsistent with Canon Law. James Coriden and Frederick McManus, "The Present State of Roman Catholic Canon Law regarding Colleges and Sponsoring Religious Bodies," in Philip R. Moots and Edward M. Gaffney, Jr., *Church and Campus* (Notre Dame: University of Notre Dame Press, 1979), 141–53.

3. Nolan to Swords, October 31, 1965, ACHC, 19.4-2.

4. Swords to Wernersville Conference, March 10–12, 1967, ACHC, 19.4-2. The impression among most Jesuits was that the College and the local Jesuit community had been incorporated by the same act, and that the Society "owned" the college and its assets.

5. Edward Sponga to Swords, Rome, October 16, 1966, and Swords's remarks at Round Hills meeting, May 1967, ACHC, 19.4-2.

aration, the contributed service of Jesuits would provide leverage for influence, and surplus income from the community could be earmarked for specific projects or goals. Swords also expected the change to afford retirement benefits to members of the Society.[6]

During the first half of 1967, Father Swords addressed the Jesuit community on the topic; associate trustee Charles Horgan and a nationally recognized Jesuit canon lawyer, James O'Connor, were present as experts. To supplement their input, Swords offered a set of points in support of change. Among the benefits, he cited guarantees that Jesuits could continue to reside on campus and clarification of the legal situation of the Jesuit community. Separate incorporation, he argued, would not weaken Jesuit influence; influence depended on the determination of the trustees to assert it and on the personal impact of Jesuits assigned to Holy Cross. Afterwards, written comments from the community ran about 3–1 in favor of the change.[7] As he prepared the Jesuits, Swords worked with the trustees and associate trustees about practical details. As members of the local Jesuit community, the trustees played a double role in preparing the legal groundwork and serving as facilitators of change during the many in-house discussions among Jesuits. They also discussed the many ramifications of separate incorporation—separate accounting procedures for College and Jesuit community, a formal agreement about Jesuit housing in Loyola Hall, the necessity for Jesuits to sign employment contracts, the need for the College to redefine its tax exemption as a "non-profit educational institution," and formation of a separate non-profit corporation for the Jesuit community.[8] Meanwhile, Swords kept pressing for approval from Father Arrupe, stressing that a majority of the community favored the change "(although they are somewhat timid about it)" and that the trustees were unanimously in favor. In April of 1967, he directed that practical steps be initiated: "a document of incorporation for the Community, By-Laws for the Community Corporation, and contractual arrangements between the College and the Community—so that we will be ready if and when an affirmative final decision is made."[9]

In July of 1967, New England Provincial J. V. O'Connor formally endorsed the petition and authorized Swords to draw up the necessary docu-

6. [Swords] to Reidy [March ?], 1967, ACHC, 19.4-2.

7. Swords to Jesuit community, May 10, 1967, ACHC, 12.24; Swords to Jesuit community, June 23, 1967, ACHC, 19.4-2. Written responses may be found in the Jesuits' separate incorporation file, ACHC, 19.4-2.

8. Nolan to Swords and College Trustees, December 21, 1966, ACHC, 19.4-2.

9. Swords' memo to Trustees and Jesuit consultors, April 25, 1967, ACHC, 12.24.

ments.[10] At the end of September, Father Arrupe sent his preliminary approval for lay trustees; but he asked for a number of clarifications "to chart changes at Holy Cross . . . and other colleges and universities, with full knowledge of the course which is being determined." Specifically, he wanted confirmation of his understanding that Jesuit authorities "would have no legal authority in or responsibility for Holy Cross College, except in exercising the rights granted by written contract to the Jesuit community and in fulfilling the correlative responsibility to these rights." He also requested copies of the proposed agreements between the Society and the College and clarification of the connection between pertinent sections of canon law and American civil law.[11]

Father Nolan was assigned to answer the general's questions. He confirmed that Catholic canon law held no status within the civil statutes of the United States, that all property belonged to the College corporation in virtue of the Massachusetts Charter, and that the separate incorporation of the Jesuit community would serve "as the basis of legality" and give "binding force" to any agreement between the Jesuit community corporation and the College.[12] Attorney Robert Donoghue '49 was commissioned to draw up by-laws for the Jesuit corporation and a proposed agreement between the trustees and the Jesuits.[13] In late 1967 and during the first half of 1968, a joint committee of trustees and community members, chaired by Father William J. Casey, worked out the agreement to define the relationship between the two corporations. On the Jesuit side, participants were carefully chosen to include several older members of the community who could interpret and explain to their contemporaries a set of changes that, at first, seemed threatening and destructive of a desirable arrangement.

The Separate Incorporation Committee met regularly, issued written progress reports after every meeting, and discussed their activities at community meetings. Gradually, they clarified the College's commitment to have Jesuits on the faculty to promote "Christian education and Jesuit ideals," to endorse the concept of theology as an academic discipline, to provide adequate living facilities for the Jesuit community, and to support the central role of worship in College life. The Jesuits pledged their presence, intellectual and financial support, and willingness to abide by the academic norms that applied to lay faculty. Practical details included decisions for the community to lease

10. O'Connor to Swords, Boston, July 14, 1967, ACHC, 19.2-3.
11. J. V. O'Connor to Swords, Boston, October 5, 1967, ACHC, 19.4-2. On the context of Arrupe's inquiries, see FitzGerald, *Governance*, 201–6.
12. Memo of George Nolan to Swords, October 31, 1967, ACHC, 19.4-2.
13. Swords memo to trustees, November 9, 1967, ACHC, 11.0.

rather than own Loyola Hall, for the College to maintain the campus cemetery, for the College administration (rather than Jesuit authorities) to supervise the work of the Chaplain's Office, and for the College to provide pension benefits for retired Jesuits. In a carefully written preamble, the trustees emphasized the historic relationship between the Society and the College and the mutual commitment that would keep Holy Cross a "Catholic College":

The College of the Holy Cross, through its trustees, recognizes the debt owed to the Society of Jesus for the origin, purpose, and development of the College; declares its intent and desire to retain the link between the College and the Society of Jesus, as represented by the incorporated Jesuit community at Holy Cross, so that the College . . . will remain a Catholic College conducted by Jesuits; and gladly repays some of the debt owed the Society of Jesus by the ways and means stipulated in this agreement.

From its side, the Jesuit community adopted articles of incorporation describing the new Jesuit corporation as "a non-profit, charitable, and educational corporation . . . for the promotion of higher education, and charitable and religious works." The document pledged to sustain the long relationship that bound the Society to the College, to supply financial aid, to pay a fair share of living expenses, and to supply personnel for academic, administrative, and pastoral needs.[14]

In the summer of 1968, Charles Horgan reviewed the foundation statement, by-laws, and articles of incorporation of the Jesuit corporation, and the agreement between the College and the Jesuits. In September, several changes were made at the request of William Guindon, who had left Holy Cross to take the office of New England provincial. In October, Guindon recommended to Father Arrupe that he accept separate incorporation at Holy Cross. The College corporation, Guindon argued, would now become "more clearly an educational establishment, rather than a religious one [but] the rights and responsibilities of the Society are spelled out through the contract." The agreement would guarantee "the maintenance of Society requirements for school and community, in a way recognized by civil and canon law."[15]

Privately, Father Swords used the fact that the separate incorporation process was nearing completion to renew his request for resignation. In September of 1968, he confided to the trustees that he intended to announce the

14. Minutes of the Joint Committee on Separate Incorporation, 1967–68, ACHC, 19.40-2. On the committee's work, see Swords to Guindon, August 16, 1968, ACHC, 19.4-2. The agreement between the College and the Jesuits, with Articles of Incorporation of the Jesuit corporation, by-laws, and foundation statements, is in ACHC, 19.4-2.

15. Swords to Robert J. Donoghue, August 19, 1968; Swords to Guindon, September 11, 1968; Guindon to Arrupe, Boston, October 2, 1968, ACHC, 19.4-2.

move after the 125th Convocation. On November 17, six weeks after the documents had been sent to Rome for approval, he asked Arrupe to expedite his decision on separate incorporation or, at least, on the separation of the College presidency from the rectorship of the Jesuit community, so that "we could forestall expected pressure and tension by announcing that the faculty will be involved in an advisory capacity in the selection of a new President."[16] Unexpectedly, then, the questions of separate incorporation and a change in the College presidency became linked. Raymond Swords believed he had done all he could for Holy Cross. He told the provincial that he was very tired and had nothing left to give.[17] But Fathers Arrupe and Guindon had other ideas. On November 25, the general sent his approval for separate incorporation, praising the "evidence of diligent and detailed planning." To the College, he communicated his blessing: "May this decision prosper the goals of this Jesuit College in Worcester and advance the apostolate of Catholic education as the College of the Holy Cross moves forward toward a second century."[18] But on the pending resignation, the general was temporarily silent. That gave Father Guindon time to dissuade Swords from his plan.

Immediately after learning of Swords's intention, Guindon wrote Arrupe in opposition to the plan and sent Swords a long, personal letter, written "in all sincerity and truth." Reviewing the record, he claimed that Swords had done "extraordinarily well" in development, physical growth, faculty improvement, and governance. Now, the introduction of separate incorporation—"this remarkable burst toward the future"—required Swords's continued leadership for a few more years, "if Holy Cross is to survive, as you, through these painful years, have striven to re-form it." Swords's leadership, he asserted, would preserve the reputation of the New England Province and avoid the impression that "the Society is opting out of Holy Cross." On campus, the trustees also requested Swords to stay on.[19] At the end of November, five days after approving separate incorporation, Father Arrupe also urged Swords to reconsider. Although he understood Swords's desire to be freed from an

16. Swords to Maurice Reidy, September 9, 1968, ACHC, 12.24; Swords to Arrupe, November 17, 1968, NEPA, Holy Cross.

17. Swords to Guindon, November 18, 1968, ACHC, 12.24; Guindon's notes on a conversation with Swords, November 27, 1968, NEPA, Holy Cross College.

18. Arrupe to Guindon, Rome, November 25, 1968, ACHC, 19.4-2.

19. Guindon to Swords, November 18, 1968, ACHC, 12.24; Executive Session of College trustees, November 19, 1968, ACHC, 11.0. Maurice Reidy, secretary of the trustees, had alerted Father Guindon of Swords's intentions, hoping to forestall the resignation by relieving the strain on Swords and keeping him in office for one or two more years. Guindon notes on conversation with Reidy, November 9, 1968, NEPA, Holy Cross College.

"onerous burden," he found Guindon's reasons against resignation to be of "singular cogency"; and he offered praise for "the fine work that you have done in the face of much misunderstanding." The general wrote to Guindon in the same tone, with appreciation that the criticism Swords had endured over changes in the Philosophy and Theology Departments "wears a man down to the breaking point."[20] By December, the trustees and provincial officials had worked out a plan to have Raymond Swords take a vacation, and he agreed to stay on for an extra year, until June of 1970.[21]

Father Swords's agreement to remain in office paved the way for effecting the structural changes at last. Early in 1969, William J. O'Halloran was named the first Jesuit rector at Holy Cross under the new plan, but the announcement was delayed until the rest of the pieces were in place. On the last day of January, articles of organization were filed for the new corporation, The Jesuits of Holy Cross, Incorporated. The new organization became effective on March 10. The final separation of the two corporations, and the inauguration of the agreement between them, took effect on March 25, 1969.[22] On that day, for the first time in the history of the College, the offices of president and rector, and the corporations they headed, were separate and distinct.

The conclusion of the legal process opened the way for the election of lay trustees. In May 1969, Father Swords solicited nominations from the Jesuit board members. One trustee welcomed the request because he thought institutional control was slipping rapidly from an ineffective board of Jesuit trustees, to lay faculty who lacked appreciation of the College's traditions. Stronger trustees, he believed, would rescue the College from precipitous change.[23] Father Nolan nominated trustees with diversified competence—Charles Horgan for his knowledge of law, and Donald P. Moriarty '52 for his knowledge of investments. On June 10, the trustees formally elected Horgan to be the

20. Arrupe to Guindon, November 18, 1968 (copy), Arrupe to Swords, Rome, November 30, 1968, ACHC, 12.24.

21. Guindon to Swords, Boston, December 6, 1968, Reidy to Swords, December 9, 1968, ACHC, 12.24.

22. Swords to Guindon, January 29, 1969, and Robert Donoghue to Swords, March 25, 1969, ACHC, 19.4-2. Four elected members served on the Jesuit board; the others were *ex officio* members as rector, minister, treasurer, and consultors of the community. Swords to Guindon, March 26, 1969, ACHC, 19.4-2. Guindon signed the papers of incorporation at Holy Cross on April 5, 1969. Swords had signed them earlier. Guindon to Arrupe, Boston, April 7, 1969, (copy), ACHC, 19.4-2.

23. Memo to Swords, May 21, 1996, unsigned but in the hand of Trustees' Secretary Maurice Reidy, who cited as a danger signal the faculty's skeptical attitude toward estimates for converting the physical plant for coeducation. In this instance, the faculty's skepticism was vindicated by later developments. ACHC, 11.0.

first lay trustee, a choice that was appropriate because of the service Horgan had rendered in facilitating separate incorporation.[24] Horgan attended his first meeting as a trustee in July. At that time the trustees organized themselves for the new system, setting regular meetings, drawing up an agenda for the annual meeting in September, defining the officers appointed by the trustees (president, vice-presidents, treasurer, academic dean, and dean of students), and distinguishing between faculty and College committees. In September, three laymen were added to the board: Edward B. Hanify, Donald P. Moriarty, and Jacob Hiatt, a Worcester businessman and philanthropist. In December of 1969, Charles Horgan was elected chair. "It's almost like having another Jesuit as Chairman," Swords told Bishop Flanagan.[25]

Father Swords' analysis of separate incorporation was optimistic, perhaps overly so:

[Separate Incorporation] strengthened the relationship of the Jesuits to the College and makes our position stronger in the event that the number of Jesuits on the campus grows smaller. Also, the Jesuit Community now stands on its own feet as a non-taxable charitable corporation with consequent rights and privileges. . . . Separate incorporation was so successful that no one appears to have any doubt as to the wisdom of the step.[26]

In fostering this achievement, he had an advantage he lacked in other situations during the latter years of his presidency: separate incorporation was largely an internal Jesuit matter, resolved through negotiation and discussion among representatives of several groups within the Society. Other challenges involved broader constituencies and issues that were beyond his control, like the struggle for racial justice, the movement for women's equality, the war in Vietnam, and student activism. In these instances, he was able to exercise authority with sensitivity to the human dimension, disclosing wisdom and magnanimity that might otherwise have remained hidden.

The first unavoidable issue was racism. Statistics about the racial composition of the student body before the late 1960s are hard to come by, but ev-

---

24. Swords to Horgan, February 11, 1969, ACHC, 19.4-2; Nolan to Reidy, May 13, 1969, trustees' minutes, June 10, and July 30–31, 1969, ACHC, 11.0.

25. Trustees' minutes, July 30–31, September 8–9, 1969, ACHC, 11.0; Worcester *Gazette*, September 10, 1969, Swords to Flanagan, December 31, 1969, WDA, Holy Cross College. Swords stepped down to remove the possibility of being in a position superior to his successor, then in the process of being chosen (Trustees' minutes, December 12, 1969, ACHC, 11.0).

26. Swords to Patrick O'Leary, September 29, 1969, ACHC, 12.24.

idence suggests that few minority students attended Holy Cross between 1860 and 1965. To be sure, there were efforts to position the College on the side of enlightenment. In 1947, William Healy was the only clergyman to attend a State House hearing on a Fair Educational Practice Bill. He endorsed Branch Rickey's experiment of integrating professional baseball and sought the integration of Holy Cross, writing, "No boy will ever be denied admission to Holy Cross because of his color." Ten years later, William Donaghy used the athletic program to promote equality by prohibiting competition against segregated teams.[27] But favorable policies could not, by themselves, attract qualified African-American applicants. In 1965, Father Swords reported that minority enrollment stood at about twelve. Although he wanted to do more, he conceded that "some very sad [academic] experiences . . . cause us to be cautious—maybe too cautious."[28] Then, slowly, the civil rights movement altered circumstances. In 1968, about 700 students marched to a local demonstration following the death of Martin Luther King, Jr.; the following year, Holy Cross became the first large school in the country to join Project Equality, an organization that urged the boycott of business that discriminated against minorities. By then, most traditionally non-black colleges and universities in the North had been won over to the idea that minority students are an asset to the learning environment and that they are deserving of assistance; many schools adopted appropriate admissions and financial aid policies.[29]

This movement received a tremendous boost on Jesuit campuses in November of 1967, when Pedro Arrupe issued a letter on the racial crisis in the United States. Linking blacks and Hispanics together as victims of "racial injustice and grinding poverty," he pointed out that American Jesuits had a mixed record in opposing racism: "It is embarrassing to note that, up to the present, some of our institutions have effected what seems to be little more than token integration of the Negro." This weakness, Arrupe argued, was connected with an erroneous view of human nature, a tendency to accept stereotypes, to be isolated from the poor, and to accept prevailing attitudes uncritically. The result was "our past failure adequately to realize, to preach, to teach, and to practice the Christian truths of interracial justice and charity, according to our Jesuit vocations." To remedy the situation, Arrupe set forth ten new policies, including renewed efforts to increase minority enrollment, re-

27. Healy to John McEleney, August 13, 1947, NEPA, HC-Rector; Donaghy to Andrew McFadden, Rome, September 9, 1957, ACHC, 12.23.

28. Swords to Walter C. Tisdell '40, March 26, 1965, ACHC, 12.24.

29. *Crusader*, April 9, 1968; Boston *Globe*, November 16, 1969; Horowitz, *Campus Life*, 241

cruitment of minority faculty and administrators, and the obligation to teach that racial justice is integral to the Christian commitment.[30]

At Holy Cross, the response to the general's challenge was energetic. In the spring of 1968, Father Swords appointed an Ad Hoc Committee on the College's Responsibility to the Negro to promote awareness about racism. After the King assassination, Swords announced the establishment of a memorial scholarship fund for minority students, to be sustained by offerings from students, faculty, and administrators.[31] With the recruiting year nearing its end, Father Brooks traveled to East Coast cities in an effort to attract African-American students. Eventually, nineteen black students enrolled at the College in the fall of 1968. Approximately $35,000 in financial aid supported these students—the equivalent of about thirteen full scholarships, or 6.4 percent of all aid given, exclusive of athletic scholarships.[32]

The nineteen new minority students, plus the nine veterans, constituted a nucleus for discussion and planning about the needs and concerns of African-American students on the overwhelmingly white campus. Throughout the 1968–69 academic year, Fathers Swords and Ad Hoc Committee members John Shay (dean of students), Father Brooks (appointed academic dean in 1968),[33] and Paul Rosenkrantz (Psychology) dined weekly with black students, working at their task with a sense of making up for lost time.[34] Out of their discussions grew a commitment to add courses in African-American literature, art, history, theology, and economics, to cooperate in the recruitment of more minority students, and to find ways to include these students specifically in the work of faculty-student committees. In March, the students won formal recognition for the Black Student Union (BSU); by the end of the academic year, Father Swords pledged $55,000 in financial aid (about 10 percent of the total available) for black students for the coming year. He also honored petitions to eliminate the reference to Old Black Joe from the school song, "Mamie Reilly," and to set up a separate corridor in

30. Arrupe to Jesuits in the American Assistancy, November 1, 1967, ACHC, 19.2-3.

31. Undated memo [1968] from John Shay to Swords, and Swords to Holy Cross community, February 26, 1969, ACHC, 12.24; Worcester *Telegram*, December 21, 1969.

32. Statement on financial assistance, 1968–69, ACHC, 12.24.

33. In the spring of 1968, after William Guindon resigned as academic dean to head the Jesuit Province of New England, Father Swords asked the elected members of the EPC for suggestions. They proposed six names, from which Swords chose Brooks. Swords memo, May 22, 1968, ACHC, 12.24.

34. Shay memo to Swords, February 18, 1969; Brooks's notes on meetings with black student representatives, February–May 1969, ACHC, 12.24; Worcester *Telegram*, December 21, 1969.

Healy Hall.[35] To pave the way for the black corridor, he made racism the topic of his address at the Easter Banquet. Characterizing it as "a sanctimonious second-guessing of God's certified estimate of all his children—and therefore a blasphemy," he urged the students to promote the good cause: "Holy Cross expects, yes demands, of her sons . . . the concrete pursuit of racial justice."[36] Happily, the response to the black corridor was generally positive; among white students, there were far more applicants than could be accommodated in the spaces remaining after black students were housed. After active recruitment, the new African-Americans who enrolled at the College in the fall of 1969 raised the total to 68.[37]

That year, the director of the Civil Rights Office in Boston visited the campus to investigate compliance with the Civil Rights Act of 1964. The report included eleven recommendations, including the institution of a written policy on non-discrimination, the hiring of more minority faculty, greater recruitment of local minority students, and campus sensitivity training on racism. During the summer, an African-American had been hired through the Worcester college consortium to teach black literature at Assumption, Clark, and Holy Cross, and incoming students were assigned to read accounts of the African-American experience. During the fall orientation, black students led seminars, and Dick Gregory spoke on campus. Officials deemed these efforts sufficient to constitute compliance with federal laws.[38] But the situation was not as rosy as it seemed. December 1969 brought the largest and most serious student protest in the history of the College, when about 60 black and 50 white students walked out of Holy Cross. The confrontation concerned racism and the limits of political activism.

Among the analysts of campus activism during the late 1960s, David Riesman has summarized the movement's particular impact on Catholic institutions:

35. Brooks's minutes of a meeting between administration and black students, March 10, 1969, ACHC, 12.24; associate trustees' minutes, May 13, 1969, ACHC, 11.1. Until that time, the conclusion of "Mamie Reilly" read: "Down in Old Kentucky / Old Black Joe / O Mamie, Mamie, Mamie Reilly." Although some favored "Way Down South" as a substitute for the offending phrase, a happier solution was found with the words "Go Cross Go," suggested by Donald Karal '49. Memo to author from John Brooks, November 1995.

36. Swords's address to student banquet, March 25, 1969, ACHC, 12.24.

37. Brooks minutes of a meeting with black students, April 30, 1969, Swords's notes on recruiting for black students for fall 1969 [undated], and James Halpin memo to Swords, May 27, 1969, ACHC, 12.24.

38. John G. Bynoe to Swords, Boston, April 24, 1969, Swords to Bynoe, April 28, 1969, Marcus Brewster to Swords, Boston, September 11, 1969, Swords to Brewster, December 2, 1969, and Bynoe to Swords, December 9, 1960, ACHC, 12.24; Worcester *Telegram*, August 2, 1969. Students read *The Autobiography of Malcolm X* and Eldridge Cleaver's *Soul on Ice*.

At the outset, the counterculture, as it came to be called, and political activism came to be allied: both movements sought freedom from the constraints of university life, whether in the curriculum or in the extracurriculum (*in loco parentis* vanished with astonishing speed, with the Catholic colleges not far behind the secular ones—a tacit alignment between faculty and students, convenient in freeing the former from disagreeable supervisory tasks in dormitories or extracurricular life generally).[39]

At Holy Cross, student activism at first prompted the creation of structures to give more voice and responsibility to students for aspects of their own lives—essentially, an evolution from the traditional emphasis on discipline that transformed the College from a "Catholic West Point" to a more typical undergraduate institution.

Student government was a case in point. From 1947 to 1968, the Student Congress comprised House Councils and a Student Senate. Corridor representatives sat on house councils, which helped coordinate residence hall activities and acted "in a legislative and judicial manner in all matters that affect the peace of the House"—e.g., parietal violations, drinking, and vandalism. Each residence hall also elected two senators (because of its larger size, Mulledy elected three) to constitute a general student government. The president and dean of discipline held power to nullify any act of the Congress.[40] In the fall of 1968, the old system was supplanted by the Inter-House Council, through which more responsibility was put into the hands of students. The shift was part of a general movement to include students in College governance and in the work of academic departments.[41] The Inter-House Council held the responsibility for granting (and revoking) charters to student organizations and took on a prominent role in the discussion about parietal rules, coeducation, and anti-war activities.

In the late 1960s, student opposition to parietal rules grew rapidly. The issue became a test case of student rights, a challenge against claims that the College stood *in loco parentis*, and a measure of the influence of the new student culture. In 1967, the Student Senate called for extended parietal hours on weekends, resting the case on the argument that dorm rooms are social gathering places as well as bedrooms, on the conviction that the College should not "dictate morality," and on the theory that softer parietal rules would not

39. David Riesman, *On Higher Education: The Academic Enterprise in an Era of Rising Student Consumerism* (San Francisco: Jossey-Bass Publishers, 1980), 82–83.

40. Letter from Timothy L Porter '68 to Resident Assistants, September 18, 1967, SGA Handbook, 1976–77, ACHC, 15.1.

41. Faculty meeting minutes, May 6, 1968, ACHC, 14.12. A full description of the structure of the Inter-House Council is located in a subject file. ACHC, 15.1, box 7.

harm the reputation of the school—already there were "motel incidents" and "pigging" (described as "a relatively common practice of waiting at the bottom of College Hill for a young woman, whom you've never met before, to drive by and pick you up"). John Shay endorsed the proposal and submitted it to Father Swords.[42] But the administration held firm for two more years; only in the fall of 1969 were parietal hours extended on weekends.

By then, even these rules were widely regarded as "unrealistic and unenforceable" because of peer pressure.[43] In the spring of 1970, calling the present rules "unnatural, hindering, even stifling to the maturing process," the Inter-House Council asked the trustees to authorize each residence hall to determine its own parietal hours. The petitioners attempted an elevated tone in an effort to persuade:

The gentlemen of Holy Cross, searching and questioning, have finally begun the evolution in which a girl is being transformed from an object to a person. . . . The atmosphere of the houses can become less social [sic] only when women become a more frequent and more natural sight on the corridor. A woman's humanity will shine through[,] given enough time.

Unmoved by such rhetoric and by Father Brooks's assessment that "you have to face the fact that you cannot enforce the present parietal rules," the trustees held the line, opting for a policy "consistent with the religious, moral and social heritage of the College."[44] The decision put administrators in a difficult position. John Shay attempted to make the best of it by asking students to view the rules "as a question of educational desirability rather than one of legislative authority."[45] In 1970, visitation hours were relaxed again, but only in 1972, with the introduction of coeducation, were parietal rules dropped in favor of a policy forbidding cohabitation as contrary to civil law and the standards of the College.

Confrontations over parietals notwithstanding, students were pleased with other changes, including the high level of campus entertainment. Judy Collins

42. "An Experimental Proposal for Parietal Hours," signed by Timothy L. Porter '68 (Student President) and approved by Student Senate, October 25, 1967, and Shay to Swords, December 27, 1967, ACHC, 11.0.

43. Minutes of Head Resident Assistants' Meeting, October 22, 1969, ACHC, 11.0; *Today*, October 21, 1969. In his annual report to Father Swords for 1968–69, John Shay reported that marijuana use was "clustered on certain corridors" and was tolerated by student opinion, as were drinking and the presence of women in rooms. Shay to Swords, July 1, 1969, ACHC, 12.24.

44. Trustees' "Parietals" file, trustees' minutes, August 6, and September 9, 1970, ACHC, 11.0.

45. Shay to students, February 23, 1970, ACHC, 11.0.

led a parade of nationally known performers to the fieldhouse in 1968. The following year, The Who performed for Homecoming; and The Fifth Dimension entertained the Winter Weekend crowd in February of 1970. Later that year, a concert by the rock group Chicago led to violence that was stilled only after the local police were called.[46] New tolerance of student drinking was reflected in the 1968 Student Handbook, which merely warned against using alcohol irresponsibly. A drug policy, first published in 1968, reminded students that they were subject to civil laws and offered information on drug abuse. By 1972, school policy seemed almost apologetic: "Despite the uncertainty of the effects of drug use on members of the community, a response by the College is required." That response was non-interference with legal authorities, and an offer of counsel to students affected by drug use.[47] Handbooks endeavored, for a while, to hold the line on dress. Until 1970, students were "urged to follow the normal canons of good grooming at all times while on campus," and jackets and ties were still "recommended" for classes, chapel, and meals. Thereafter, jackets and ties disappeared from the handbook. By then, the idea of dressing for meals had a further reason for discontinuation: increased enrollment had strained the capacity of Kimball Hall. By 1969, twelve students were crowded at tables meant for ten at family-style meals. Students stayed at table for an average of seventeen minutes, according to one survey. In the fall of that year, in an effort to maintain the tradition of sit-down meals, the dean of students directed that food be served "family style on a continuous basis," instead of serving the entire room at designated times. But even that system failed to maintain the atmosphere of good order and table fellowship associated with the old system. Finally, in 1971, a cafeteria system was introduced as a more satisfactory solution.[48]

Students gained formal influence in governance structures when a faculty resolution of May 1968 approved their inclusion in the faculty meeting and on appropriate committees. The resolution endorsed student involvement in decisions affecting their academic and social lives, with membership on relevant committees, and voice—but not vote—at regular faculty meetings.[49]

46. *Crusader*, September 27, 1968, October 3, 1969, February 6, and October 16, 1970.

47. On drugs and the counterculture see David Farber, *The Age of Great Dreams: America in the 1960s* (New York: Hill and Wang, 1994), 173–83. David Steigerwald, in *The Sixties and the End of Modern America* (New York: St. Martin's Press, 1995), 154–86, summarizes the spirit of sex, drugs, rock 'n' roll.

48. Report of Ad Hoc Committee to Study Student Dining at Holy Cross, May 1, 1969, John Shay to Students, September 5, 1969, ACHC, 16.1BN-1; Kimball Manager File, ACHC, 16.5-1.

49. Faculty meeting minutes, May 6, 1968, ACHC, 14.12. Committees open to students were Admissions, Curriculum, Library, Student Activities, Budget, Film Series, Concert and

The following year, the faculty extended a full vote on the EPC to student members and gave all student members of faculty committees the right to vote at the faculty meeting. Under this plan, which was adopted for a two-year trial period, students constituted about 14 percent of the Faculty-Student Assembly. The faculty also set up student advisory committees in each academic department to assist with hiring and teaching evaluation. In 1969, the faculty added two students to the Student Judicial Board, the body that had responsibility for determining sanctions when disciplinary rules were violated. By then, a Boston broadcaster had characterized Holy Cross as "one of the most liberal colleges in the East" in terms of student participation in governance.[50] In 1971, the successful experiment with student participation prompted the assembly to raise the number of voting students to 48 (or about 20 percent of the total membership).[51]

Clashes between student activists and agents of authority were a condition of life by the late 1960s. A major source of the confrontational spirit was the Port Huron Statement adopted in 1962 by the Students for a Democratic Society (SDS). Essentially an adaptation of the ideas of C. Wright Mills,[52] the platform endorsed "participatory democracy" as a method of cooperation to shape and influence policy. The student movement represented a cultural ethos as well as a pattern of radical thought. As one interpreter put it, "Protesters of the 1960s were acting not merely out of individual conscience, but from within a collegiate culture with its own ethos and codes of behavior."[53] Although these ideas surfaced in the early 1960s, the presence of the draft and the escalation of the War in Vietnam popularized their appeal by associating

Lecture, the Campus Center Advisory Committee, and the Student Judicial Board. Students would have an advisory presence on the Educational Policy Committee.

50. Unidentified clipping [May 1969], Swords Papers, and Swords remarks to faculty meeting, [May 1969], ACHC, 12.24; *Crusader*, May 9, 1969; Faculty-Student Assembly minutes, October 6, 1969 and April 19, 1971, ACHC, 14.12.

51. Faculty-Student Assembly minutes, April 19 and May 3, 1971, ACHC, 14.12. In addition to student committee members, representatives were chosen from constituencies including the Inter-House Council, the BSU, the various residence halls, and eight at-large students.

52. In books like *The New Men of Power* (1948), *White Collar* (1952), and *The Power Elite* (1956), Mills argued that the concentration of power in American society had overturned the promise of true democracy and promoted the powerlessness of intellectuals. Mills's ideas were a powerful stimulus for Tom Hayden and other radical student leaders of the 1960s. James Miller, *"Democracy Is in the Streets": From Port Huron to the Siege of Chicago* (Cambridge: Harvard University Press, 1994), 78–85.

53. Horowitz, *Campus Life*, 228–29, 236.

authority with the abuse of power.[54] By the middle of the decade, challenging authority was a hallmark of student radicalism; frequently that authority was personified by college administrators (and their allies on the faculty), who were vilified for pandering to self-serving interests, including the federal government, whose policies were seen to compromise educational ideals. Campus confrontations reached their peak in the 1969–70 academic year, when 9408 confrontational outbreaks occurred on American campuses; 731 involved police intervention, including, tragically, the deaths at Kent State University. Afterwards, with the de-escalation of the war, student unrest dissipated slowly.[55] Holy Cross was immune from none of these influences; yet the playing out of conflict on Pakachoag had a distinctive dimension because the spirit of "us" versus "them," with its telltale invocation of administrative authority in the name of good order, did not prevail. That, in itself, was a tribute to the inclusive pattern of governance and to Raymond Swords's ability as a diplomat.

At Holy Cross, concern about Vietnam surfaced early in 1965, when six faculty members joined colleagues throughout the Northeast in petitioning Lyndon Johnson to negotiate a peace "while there is still time."[56] In January of 1968, an orderly demonstration took place outside the Placement Services office in O'Kane Hall against recruiters from the Dow Chemical Company (a manufacturer of napalm).[57] The demonstration followed a new three-point policy adopted by the trustees to preserve free expression and good order: individuals or groups invited to campus by the College or recognized student organizations had guaranteed access to campus facilities; individual students were free to promote causes and distribute literature as long as their activities did not offend against propriety; and members of the campus community were free to demonstrate peacefully as long as normal activities were not hampered. The trustees were determined to preserve freedom of expression, mutual respect, and good order, and especially to forbid "advocates of any cause to deny freedom to anyone with whom they may disagree."[58]

54. According to David O'Brien, the draft, "along with assassinations and urban riots[,] had accentuated [a] sense of crisis and delegitimated authority. . . . And now the Church and the professors agreed [that] each one had to decide. All this set a distance with parents, and made peer bonds all the more important." Correspondence to the author, November 1995.

55. Ibid., 234, 244; Riesman, *Higher Education*, 67–70. Among the larger schools in eastern Massachusetts, strikes and other manifestations of student unrest occurred as follows: Boston College (1970), Brandeis (1967 and 1969), Harvard (1969), MIT (1969), Northeastern (1968 and 1970). Freeland, *Golden Age*, 98.

56. Swords to William F. Dowling, Jr., Worcester, March 8, 1965, ACHC, 12.24.

57. *Crusader*, January 19, 1968.

58. "College Policy on Demonstrations," November 20, 1967, Trustees' Subject File, ACHC, 11.0.

Presumably, the policy was devised at least partly in response to the organization of a campus chapter of SDS at about the same time. SDS was affiliated with the more moderate Student Action Committee, as its left wing to advocate more extreme positions and sponsor actions. Its immediate goals were to eliminate academic credit for ROTC courses and to stop campus recruitment for officer candidate schools by representatives of the Armed Forces. In December, a campus demonstration, plus the threat of a disruptive SDS rally, prompted recruiters from the Central Intelligence Agency to cancel a recruiting visit.[59] SDS benefited from protection afforded by the College. Early in 1969, John Shay refused a police request for a membership list because "the undergraduate years are a time when students should be free to test out their ideas without fear that what they say now will be held against them . . . later."[60] In March of that year, about 30 SDS members and sympathizers conducted a peaceful demonstration in the lobby of the Hogan Center against Marine recruiters. Afterwards, Father Swords expressed his satisfaction that the event had been an "extremely mild" exercise in freedom. In May, he told the associate trustees, with evident satisfaction, that there had been no outbreaks of campus unrest at Holy Cross: "In the main, we find our students quite reasonable."[61]

Despite this record of good order, John Shay warned of stronger confrontations from groups whose tactics might dictate that "the clash itself is central." He consulted the College attorney about legal options, including the use of court injunctions to evict students who might occupy a building.[62] Swords was inclined to agree about the need to be prepared; after school opened in the fall of 1969, he monitored the work of an ad hoc committee appointed by the EPC to draw up a set of principles for use in case of disorder. In October, the committee offered a nine-page report that was assailed by crit-

59. *Crusader*, October 18 and December 6, 1968. The tone of the debate (and a sign of the times) may be found in an open letter from SDS to the student body in 1968 that characterized ROTC recruiting literature as "the same abstract bullshit about the military that they've been shoving down your throats since kindergarten. The only honest piece of information in these booklets concerns the size of the bribe they're offering in return for your ass. . . . The military doesn't just take your ass . . . , it robs you of your humanity. . . . By joining the ROTC you will be giving up a good part of your life to the cause of crushing popular revolution and bolstering fascistic governments in every corner of the globe." The records of Holy Cross SDS are in the student organization file, ACHC, 15.1T.

60. Shay to Swords, January 21, 1969, ACHC, 12.24.

61. *Crusader*, March 21, 1969; Swords to Robert Pollock, March 26, 1969, ACHC, 12.24; associate trustees' minutes, May 3, 1969, ACHC, 11.1.

62. Shay to Swords, July 1, 1968, and April 29, 1969, and Robert J. Donoghue to Shay, August 22, 1969, ACHC, 12.24.

ics for being too exclusively concerned with students' rights. After inconclusive discussion, the Faculty-Student Assembly instructed the committee to draw up a "concise, philosophical statement of student, faculty, and administrative rights and freedom."[63]

As the academic year progressed, the peaceful pattern seemed to be holding. In September, a peace sign was painted on the roof of what the perpetrators erroneously believed to be the Air Force ROTC building.[64] By then, Father Swords had adopted a public anti-war position, joining 75 college presidents in calling for military withdrawal from Vietnam. That fall, 65 faculty members pledged support for a nation-wide Vietnam Moratorium Day on October 15. Father Swords invited members of the campus community to respond to the event according to their consciences. Among the special moratorium events, about 1500 people attended a Mass for Peace on the steps of Dinand Library. Afterwards, Father Swords told a crowd of about 15,000 at Worcester Common that the war was unjust and that "the moral course of action [speedy withdrawal from Vietnam] is also the honorable course of action."[65]

As John Shay had predicted, a new group, the Revolutionary Students Union (RSU), was organized in September of 1969 to take confrontational stances on campus and national issues.[66] With an active membership estimated between twenty and forty, the RSU announced its intention to disrupt Marine recruitment in November. Under these circumstances, the Student Personnel Policies Committee recommended unanimously that the Marine visit

63. John Shay to Swords, September 26, 1969, ACHC, 12.24; Faculty-Student Assembly minutes, October 6, 1969, ACHC, 14.12.

64. Copy of a letter from Gary Lednar '72 to his family, September 20, 1969, in the Swords Papers, ACHC, 12.24. The symbol was actually painted on the roof of a storage building behind the Air Force building. Sometime later, other students—perhaps believing the peace sign to be a sacrilegious inverted cross, or perhaps to associate peace specifically with the College—painted a cross in the upper left part of the symbol. The emblem remains in place to this day, though the building has been incorporated into the Millard Art Center. The peace sign apparently originated from the semaphore positions for the letters N and D, and was used by Bertrand Russell in the 1950s in his movement for nuclear disarmament.

65. Holy Cross press release of October 10, 1969, Swords's Moratorium Day speech at Worcester Common, October 14, 1969, ACHC, 12.24; Worcester *Free Press*, October 17, 1969; *Crusader*, October 10, 1969.

66. An undated copy of the RSU Charter, marked "pending approval" and deposited with the Trustees' records, defines the group as "an organization of young Socialists and Communists" dedicated to supplanting capitalism with socialist democracy, and combating "racism, male supremacy, and private property. . . . We openly declare that our ends can only be achieved by the forcible overthrow of all existing social conditions." ACHC, 11.0.

be postponed "until the policies on campus recruiting and demonstrations could be considered by the faculty."[67] On December 1, a large majority of the Faculty-Student Assembly endorsed the principle of an "open campus":

Any device which allows a majority of the community to prevent a minority of students from securing access to career counselors, representing legitimate (those legally operating in Massachusetts) business firms or government agencies, constitutes an infringement upon the rights and privileges of that minority.

Father Swords interpreted the vote as an assertion of "responsible free speech [and] free access." Afterwards, the RSU announced its intention to obstruct recruiting by representatives of General Electric, scheduled for Wednesday, December 10.[68]

On that day, after the recruiters were escorted to their room in the Hogan Center, a crowd gathered in the corridor outside, and demonstrators gathered at the doorway to block access. By locking arms and turning their backs, they prevented several students from seeing the recruiters and also refused access to Donald McClain, the dean of men, amid chanting and counter-chanting of slogans. McClain then announced that the matter would be referred to the College Judicial Board and that the recruiters would be asked to leave campus, since recruiting had become impossible. During the encounter, staff members of the Dean of Men's Office made "visual identification" of sixteen demonstrators.[69]

The Judicial Board met the next day with a sense of urgency, because Marine recruiters were slated to return to campus the following week. Deliberations lasted fourteen hours and became an agonizing exercise when two distinct issues became entangled: violations of the open campus policy, and a sense of betrayal by members of the BSU who alleged that the process was tainted by racism. Fifty-four students had been involved in the demonstration; 49 were white and 5 were black—yet, only twelve of the white students (24 percent) were being charged, while four of the blacks (80 percent) faced penalties. Even so, the Judicial Board determined that the black students were responsible for "high spatial visibility" because of the nature of their participation: all sixteen students were recommended for suspension. When the outcome was announced at 3:00 A.M., many students voiced displeasure; BSU

---

67. "A Special Report from the President," issued in December of 1969 by Raymond Swords after the G. E. Recruiting Crisis, summarizes the events. Unless otherwise noted, the following account of the crisis draws upon that source. ACHC, 12.24.

68. Faculty-Student Assembly minutes, December 1, 1969, ACHC, 14.12.

69. Details on the flawed process of identifying the sixteen demonstrators were described in a class letter by James R. Matthews '70 in 1994. Copy in possession of the author.

representative Theodore V. (Ted) Wells '72 "denounced the decision as racist and the product of warped minds [and] stated that the members of the BSU would withdraw from the college since it was a racist institution." That set the stage for the second phase of the crisis.

On Friday morning, the BSU held a widely publicized press conference in the Hogan ballroom. Ted Wells read "a brief declaration of intention for the group[,] after which all the BSU members tossed their student identification cards on the table and promptly walked out to a caravan of waiting cars which transported them off campus." At least sixty black students, joined by fifty white sympathizers, participated in the action. Only about 200 students attended class that day as a crisis atmosphere enveloped the campus. Hundreds of students and faculty met continuously in the Hogan Ballroom; and many members of the Judicial Board petitioned Father Swords to lessen the sanctions for the good of the College. On the same day, by coincidence, the trustees were holding a regular meeting on campus. Swords told them that the BSU had actually voted *against* backing the GE protest. He defended Wells and his BSU associate Arthur Martin '70 as "two great leaders," accepted Father Brooks's suggestion that a quick review be undertaken to avoid an intensification of the problem, and asserted that the situation was "dangerous in the sense of widespread splitting of the campus—the one thing we are trying to avoid."[70]

To repair the situation, Father Swords canceled classes on Monday and called for a day of discussion. He expressed sympathy for the BSU: "I agree with the Black Students Union that the procedures were not ideal. . . . [The College] will consider more adequate methods of identifying all students involved in future obstructive demonstrations." He postponed all outside recruiting, pending a further examination of the issue by a committee established by the Educational Policy Committee a week earlier. Finally, he utilized the services of John F. Scott,[71] director of the Worcester Youth Guidance Center, as an intermediary between the alienated students (many of whom had

70. Transcript of trustees' meeting, December 12, 1969, ACHC, 11.0; personal correspondence from David O'Brien, November 1995. The petition for clemency asked Swords to "move immediately to lessen the sanctions." "Special Report," ACHC, 12.24.

71. John Scott, Ph.D., had refused an invitation to join the Holy Cross Trustees earlier in 1969 because of the pressure of work. But he told Father Swords: "If there are things that from time to time you feel I might be of some help with, please feel free to call on me." Swords replied: "I appreciate your offer of assistance. I am certain that we will be taking advantage of it. I feel unqualified to handle the problems which I am sure will arise as we increase the number of Black Students at Holy Cross." Scott to Swords, September 12, 1969, and Swords to Scott, September 15, 1969, ACHC, 11.0.

found temporary lodging at Clark University) and the College administration. Meanwhile, Swords continued to consult with the trustees and with an advisory group that included Charles Horgan, John Scott, faculty members, administrators, and an ad hoc committee of students.

Soon, a general solution emerged. The BSU was demanding amnesty for the four black students as the price of returning to campus. John Scott pleaded successfully with the black students to stay in Worcester so that negotiations could take place. They convinced him that they were in earnest about leaving the College because of "a public humiliation they could not accept." His advice to Swords was blunt: "Holy Cross had the option, if it wanted, to see itself as an all-white school, with that public image, or of conceding to this request for amnesty." As discussions continued, the concept of amnesty won support as a reasonable response to the racial disparity involved in the disciplinary proceedings. Charles Horgan assured Swords of the personal support of the Trustees, despite the fact that not all favored clemency.[72] On Sunday evening, Father Swords announced his decision in the crowded Hogan ballroom: amnesty for all students involved in the previous week's confrontation, and a new study of recruitment by the blue-ribbon committee already established by the Educational Policy Committee.

As students, faculty, and administrators departed into the snowy night after three days of meetings, the crisis was palpably relieved. A news release issued by student leaders distinguished amnesty from exoneration; the Judicial Board, they claimed, had upheld the letter of the law, and Swords had upheld its spirit as the only individual in a position "to correct the violations against human rights" that stood at the center of the conflict. "We applaud his decision as a living example of the values upon which this college is founded."[73] The faculty was informed of the decision on Monday at a special meeting that included an appearance by John Scott. Some opposed Swords's decision; others praised his moral integrity. Afterwards, a faculty member described "the deep sense of loyalty and belief in Holy Cross that many faculty feel as a result of his decision."[74] Reaction in the press was mixed. On December 16, the Worcester *Telegram* called it "an extremely dangerous and troublesome precedent . . . [which] severely damaged the credibility of the college administration" by compromising the open campus policy. But in the Diocese of

72. Trustees and associate trustees minutes, December 13, 1969, ACHC, 11.1; 73. Student Resolution of December 13, 1969, trustees' files, ACHC, 11.0; Horgan to Trustees, New York, December 19, 1969, ACHC, 12.24.

73. "Student News Release," [December 14 or 15, 1969], ACHC, 12.24.

74. From anonymous comments submitted to the Presidential Search Committee, 1970, Trustees' Files, ACHC, 11.0.

Worcester, the *Catholic Free Press* praised Swords for holding out against "anti-Black, anti-union, anti-intellectual, anti-youth sentiments."[75]

Father Swords sent a special report to alumni, parents, and friends of the College, offering a chronology of events and a rationale for his decisions. He conceded that he would not have granted amnesty had only white students been involved, but the "de facto mathematical disproportion of the Blacks who were identified" left no choice but to grant amnesty to those four "and consequent on that—grudgingly but ineluctably—to the 12 whites." To have punished them while granting amnesty to the others would have opened the administration to charges of reverse racism. Swords admitted his concern that some alumni would be alienated by his decision—those "who are already deeply wounded by changes that have taken place at Holy Cross over the past decade. I realized that our graduates, brought up at Holy Cross on discipline based on respect for authority, would be inclined to consider . . . amnesty as a surrender of principle." Nevertheless, he had come to the conclusion that the black students had been "deeply hurt" by the course of events. "I finally accepted the fact of their hurt," he said; the need to remedy it was imperative for the good of the school. Finally, he reported that he had never experienced such unity at Holy Cross as during the crisis. The outcome upheld his confidence in the quality of the students, "and if ever I had any question as to the value of a Catholic College, these were dispelled by the happenings of our recent crisis."

Father Swords received many letters of support from alumni and friends, including Bishop Bernard Flanagan of Worcester ("a wise as well as merciful decision"); U.S. District Judge W. Arthur Garrity, Jr. '41 (the issues were "not worth rending the fabric of the Holy Cross community"); and Worcester City Manager Francis McGrath '30. Yet there was criticism, too. In all, 312 alumni responded to the report. Of these, 207 expressed support, and 99 (including two anonymous writers) were critical, even harsh. Among the students, all but two of 53 who wrote to Swords voiced support.[76] Near the end of December, for the record, Swords recorded his own analysis:

The HC student body is a law-abiding stud[ent] body. A large majority backed the administrat[ion] in the original punishments decreed for the violators. It was only when the students felt an injustice had been inflicted on the blacks that they protested—and then in such an orderly fashion that they attended discussion sessions for four days[,] even though they could have left early for their Christmas hol-

75. The *Catholic Free Press* editorial is in the Swords Papers, Box 14, folder 1, ACHC, 12.24.

76. Letters from Bishop Flanagan (December 24, 1969), W. Arthur Garrity, Jr. (January 7, 1970), and Francis McGrath (December 30, 1969) are in the Swords Papers, Box 14, folder 1, ACHC, 12.24.

College Dean John E. Brooks facing demonstrators at the Air Force ROTC building in the spring of 1970.

idays. Instead of disunity on campus there was evident solidarity as a result of the disturbance. There was no "we'll bring them to their knees mentality," nor post factum boasting about victory over the administration, but rather a sense of unity.[77]

For Raymond Swords, unity and community spirit were the bottom line. His ability to hold to that mark guided the College through its worst crisis. The committee reviewing recruitment policy met through the winter and spring of 1970. At a four-hour meeting in May, the Student-Faculty Assembly endorsed the majority recommendation that "unrestricted, on-campus recruiting" be maintained as "an integral part of the educational process." The plan also set up a standing committee of faculty and students to advise the president if a recruiter's visit should be postponed, using "the well-being of the College community" as the sole criterion.[78]

The hard-gained spirit of unity was tested in May of 1970 after the Cambodia invasion and the student deaths at Kent State University and Jackson State College. College campuses throughout the country erupted with protests and student strikes; and 24 ROTC buildings on various campuses were bombed or burned.[79] At Holy Cross, the protests began on Monday, May 4, when the Faculty-Student Assembly voted to join other schools in suspending classes for a week, after which the group would determine "whether it will be more fruitful to continue cessation of classes during the last week of school [May 11–15]." For the rest of the week, 53 members of the faculty and over 1100 students participated in workshops, panels, and symposia.[80] Because of the threat of violence, Father Swords hired four off-duty policemen as extra security guards to protect the ROTC facilities, particularly the Air Force ROTC building, a vulnerable, wooden structure near Loyola Hall. On the evening of May 5, after a symposium on excluding ROTC programs from campus, about 200 students massed outside the AFROTC building with torches, protesting the presence of policemen. With Father Brooks standing at the door of the building to block the way, Father Swords explained that

77. Swords's handwritten note on a copy of a letter from Jacob Hiatt to Robert W. Stoddard, Leominster, December 26, 1969, ACHC, 12.24.

78. Minutes of trustees and associate trustees, May 8, 1970, ACHC, 11.1; Faculty-Student Assembly minutes, May 20, 1970, ACHC, 14.12; undated press release [1970], ACHC, 12.24; *Crusader*, September 25, 1970. The standing committee was dissolved in 1972.

79. George Donelson Moss, *Vietnam: An American Ordeal* (Englewood Cliffs, N.J.: Prentice-Hall, Inc., 1990), 320.

80. Faculty-Student Assembly minutes, May 4, 1970, ACHC, 14.12; "Schedule for Wednesday" [May 6, 1970], and memo from Brooks to Swords, May 6, 1970, ACHC, 12.24; John Day '70 and Tom Dougherty '70, "A Short History of the Week's Activities" (mimeograph), ACHC, 14.8.1A.

he had hired guards only to give warning of vandalism or destruction, and not to harass students. In the end, the building was spared; Swords agreed to hire no more off-duty policemen. After a second demonstration the following evening, Swords promised to expedite the study of ROTC that was then in progress.[81]

During the week, the practical problem of justifying the cessation of classes arose. From the Dean's Office, Father Brooks and the assistant deans sent a letter to parents to explain the educational value of the moratorium for responsible citizenship and the Christian imperative "to take at these most critical times a radical stance." Parents received a copy of that week's *Crusader* to help explain "the effect of this move on the education of your son."[82] The trustees and associate trustees discussed the moratorium at the end of the week. After defeating a proposal to threaten the faculty with breach of contract for canceling classes, they adopted a policy distancing the institution from a specific position on the war. They also expressed concern about lawsuits for breach of contract, expressed confidence that "the Faculty will exercise its judgment in a fashion which will guarantee that students are not denied their legitimate expectations of a profitable educational experience," and mandated the faculty to "institute procedures which will assure students a satisfactory completion of their semester."[83] On May 11, the Faculty-Student Assembly discussed the best means for concluding the academic year. Despite a student poll favoring a continued strike, faculty shared the concern about possible lawsuits and a demand for rebates if classes were not resumed. In the end, the body adopted a plan requiring class meetings during the rest of the week, and offering students several options for completing their course work. Most teachers met their classes for the rest of the week. But the mail ran heavily against the administration's handling of events.[84]

81. "Clarification of Last Evening's Incident," May 6, 1970, ACHC, 12.24; Minutes of trustees and associate trustees, May 8, 1970, ACHC, 11.1; Day and Dougherty, "Short History," ACHC, 14.8.1A.

82. Letter to Parents from Brooks and Assistant Deans, May 7, 1970, ACHC, 11.0. About 27,000 copies of the May 8, 1970, edition of *The Crusader* were printed, instead of the usual run of 3000. Besides the copies distributed to students and parents, over 18,000 were sent to alumni and 4000 were distributed in Worcester. That issue also reported the findings of the A. D. Little study on the athletic program.

83. Trustees' minutes, May 9, 1970, ACHC, 11.0.

84. Faculty-Student Assembly minutes, May 5, 1970, ACHC, 14.12; Brooks to Student Body, May 11, 1970, published in the bulletin *Today*, ACHC, 12.24; Swords to Trustees, May 12, 1970, ACHC, 11.0. The mail ran 79–9 against the administration. Negative writers echoed the view that demonstrations gave support to communism. Some requested tuition refunds. Swords Papers, Box 12, folder 10, ACHC, 12.24.

The drama and criticism connected with the late 1960s prompted Raymond Swords to activate his plan for resignation. During 1968, he was weary of "constant confrontations with students and faculty" over athletic policy, political activism, parietals, and religious discipline.[85] Swords was particularly discouraged by alumni criticism: "The opposition has become more and more vocal, to the point where one sometimes wonders whether it is worth undergoing the strain."[86] By February of 1969, his mind was made up. He told the trustees: "I am asking to be relieved of my office as President of Holy Cross as soon as possible, and not later than July 1, 1970." He asked that the search for his successor begin immediately after separate incorporation was finalized.[87] Late in August, after the organization of the new board of trustees, Swords announced his resignation publicly and asked the faculty "to begin immediately consideration of the qualities and qualifications you judge proper for my successor and to prepare, for reference to the Trustees, a list of possible candidates."[88]

In September, the trustees set up a search committee comprised of three elected faculty members, two alumni, one associate trustee and one student. They endorsed the suggestion of Charles Horgan that administrative responsibilities be divided, with the new president attending to internal responsibilities regarding students, faculty, and the academic program, while a chancellor (presumably Raymond Swords) attended to external duties with alumni, fund-raising, and community relations.[89] During the autumn months, faculty members expressed preference for a president who fostered excellence in teaching, involvement in student life, and collaborative governance. About 55 percent of the students favored John Brooks, but there were a smattering of votes for other Jesuit and lay professors and for public personalities. A significant number of students and faculty suggested that the office need not be restricted to a Jesuit; 89 of the faculty signed a petition calling the Jesuit requirement "unrealistic" and asking for the appointment of the best candidate without reference to clerical status. But the trustees insisted that an excellent

85. Swords to John G. Deedy '48, March 11, 1968, ACHC, 12.24.

86. Swords to Frank O'Hare '47, July 15, 1968, ACHC, 12.24.

87. Swords to Reidy, February 1, 1969, ACHC, 12.24.

88. Swords to Trustees, William Guindon, Faculty, and "Close Friends and Special Benefactors," August 26, 1969, ACHC, 12.24.

89. Horgan to Trustees, New York City, August 29, 1969, and Trustees' minutes, September 8–9, 1969, ACHC, 11.0. Three Jesuits, William Healy, F. P. Greaney, and William van Etten Casey, were elected by the faculty to join alumni Austin Keane '47 and William Cousins, Jr. '45, Associate Trustee Howard Jefferson, and student Paul DelColle '72. Minutes of trustees and associate trustees, December 13, 1969, ACHC, 11.1.

candidate would be chosen "within a context of the College's distinctive characteristics."[90]

The trustees completed the search at a special meeting on May 25. By then, the 54 recommended Jesuits had been narrowed to two—John Brooks and Raymond Baumhart (executive vice-president at Loyola University of Chicago.) The report on Brooks praised his "concern for faculty excellence," his recruitment of minority students, his willingness "to think and read about the fundamental problems of higher education . . . ," and his familiarity with Holy Cross.[91] The trustees were also influenced by Father Swords's sense that a strong president was needed: "I should have been more firm with the faculty; leadership is needed; a strong Dean is needed." After interviews and a secret ballot, Charles Horgan counted the ballots and announced Father Brooks as victor.[92]

Although antiwar activism absorbed a great deal of Father Swords's energy during his final years in office, protecting the campus from violence was not his principal concern. The years 1969 and 1970 stand out as a critical time during which institutional nerve endings became sensitized around a set of issues—curriculum, coeducation, the athletic program, and fiscal management—that were at the heart of the College's identity and well-being. Lay trustees, for the first time, were directing the affairs of the College. The Faculty-Student Assembly met thirteen times during the 1969–70 academic year, experiencing unprecedented preeminence as a forum of discussion and policy making. Alumni, too, their support crucial to the economic stability and morale of Holy Cross, kept registering strong responses. In the midst of dialogue and disagreement, a new process of accountability gradually took shape. It reflected the technical requirements of separate incorporation and foreshadowed unprecedented strength through cooperation.

Curriculum reform was a response to the reaccreditation report received in March 1969. The evaluators noted with satisfaction the many positive changes that had occurred within a decade: the faculty had expanded from 128 to 188 (the number of Jesuits was down from 91 to 54); enrollment had increased; the faculty teaching load had been reduced; every faculty member now had a pri-

90. Faculty and student polls, and faculty petition, fall 1969, trustees' files, trustees' minutes, December 12, 1969, ACHC, 11.0. Joseph Fallon was the only Jesuit to sign the petition. Three individuals signed twice.

91. Candidates' list (November 10, 1969), confidential memo from Presidential Evaluation Committee to trustees (March 2, 1970), and committee profile on John Brooks (April 17, 1970), ACHC, 11.0.

92. Trustees' minutes, May 25, 1970, ACHC, 11.0.

vate office; a democratic model of governance was in place; separate incorporation, "an enormous improvement," had brought Holy Cross into line with other excellent institutions. The report stressed the beneficial effect of higher academic standards on campus morale: faculty members "seemed to believe in themselves, their students, and their president in the most positive way"; students "appeared proud of Holy Cross, involved in their work, and at odds neither with themselves nor their institution." Areas targeted for examination included the proliferation of courses, a reduction of the standard student course load from five to four in imitation of "leading institutions," coeducation, the diversity of the student body, library space, and the endowment.[93]

The report prompted the Curriculum Committee to undertake a general study of the curriculum. By early 1970, they had readied two proposals. The first called for adoption of the four-course plan of studies in imitation of "all the better colleges and universities" to enhance flexibility and experimentation. The second proposal called for a reduction of the core requirement to six courses (two in literature or fine arts, two in history or social science, and two in theology). The goal was to eliminate unsatisfactory introductory courses, foster competition among professors and academic departments, and free professors from the repetitive obligation of required courses. The course reduction plan was adopted overwhelmingly in March. The debate on the core curriculum was deferred as assembly members studied five alternative plans, ranging from the status quo to a complete abandonment of core and distribution requirements. Although defenders of the status quo stressed its value in maintaining the tradition of liberal arts, many faculty believed that a strong advisory system would guarantee the same goals more effectively; a proposal to drop all required courses and institute a strong advisory system was adopted by a large margin.[94] Adoption of the open curriculum was a stunning victory for the concept of guided electivism, but the triumph wasn't permanent. In the 1980s, the faculty would return to the concept of distribution and language requirements.

The curriculum reorganization of 1970 completed a set of revisions that had started after the reaccreditation report of 1958, when the Business Administration major was dropped and the Departments of Philosophy, Psychology, Fine Arts and Music, and Theology were added.[95] An important

93. 1969 New England States Accreditation Report, March 26, 1969, ACHC, 14.12.

94. Curriculum Committee proposal on curriculum reform [February, 1970], Faculty-Student Assembly minutes, March 2 and 23, and April 6, 1970, ACHC, 14.12; Swords to George M. Moran, April 13, 1970, ACHC, 12.24.

95. Holy Cross Reaccreditation Study, February 1, 1969, ACHC, 14.12; Minutes of Student-Faculty Assembly, January 20, 1969, ACHC, 14.12; trustees' minutes, January 21, 1969, ACHC, 11.0.

source of support for the academic program came from the Charles and Rosanna Batchelor Foundation, which provided a nucleus of $950,000 in 1968 and 1969 to create a fund for faculty research.[96] And a final curricular asset was the initiation, in 1967, of coordinated planning and cooperation among six Worcester area colleges. In 1969, the Worcester Consortium for Higher Education, Inc., was formally organized, with Raymond Swords as its first chair. The consortium was modeled on similar groups in the Connecticut Valley and Washington, D.C.[97]

Compared with the relatively smooth progress of curriculum reform, the decision for coeducation was complicated. For some, coeducation threatened a key element of the school's identity and traditions; for others, it represented a hurdle in the drive to enhance academic quality and bring the school into the mainstream of American higher education. The possibility of change had been in the air for decades, but momentum gathered only in the 1960s, when the issue began to be discussed in connection with the campaign to ease parietal rules.[98] A faculty-student conference in January of 1967 disclosed considerable support for coeducation. That fall, the first women were hired as full-time faculty members, and an experimental Co-Education Day, sponsored by student government, drew 400 female students to campus for classes and meals.[99] At the same time, the Faculty-Student Assembly mandated a special committee to study the topic.[100]

In May of 1968, the special committee presented its final report. Members

96. Swords's notes on copy of application to the Batchelor Foundation, undated. Swords recorded that the foundation had given $90,000 between 1959 and 1968 and that "all these gifts were obtained through intercession of Bill Beasley ['37]." Swords announced the grant to the faculty in a notice on January 8, 1969. ACHC, 12.24.

97. Swords's memo to faculty, September 27, 1967, and Articles of Organization, July 29, 1969, ACHC, 12.24.

98. In November 1931, a *Purple* editorial characterized the campus environment as "terrifyingly male," but the situation was irreversible: "Holy Cross will have co-eds when debutantes can join the Marines." A formal campus debate on the issue in 1938 had yielded an affirmative vote. *Tomahawk*, December 13, 1938.

99. Report of Faculty and Student Conference, January 29, 1967, ACHC, 12.24; Worcester *Telegram*, September 13, 1967; *Crusader*, October 13, 1967. The first full-time women faculty members were Drusilla Boelcskevy (Modern Languages) and Sharon Tumulty (English). Four years earlier, Maureen Begley Zlody was the first woman to serve formally on the faculty. She was hired on a substitute basis in the Psychology Department in 1963 after the death of Father George McKeon. *Crusader*, January 31, 1963.

100. Faculty meeting minutes, October 2, 1967, ACHC, 14.12. For a detailed account of the debate over coeducation, see Ann J. Cahill, *Women on the Hill: Alumnae Reflect on Twenty Years at Holy Cross* (Worcester: Holy Cross Center for Interdisciplinary and Special Studies, 1993), 3–20.

unanimously endorsed coeducation, though two argued that the time was not yet opportune. The report incorporated stereotypes that patronized women even as it saluted progress in gender equality: "We feel that there are talented women just as there are talented men and that women will more and more hold positions of responsibility in society." The committee advocated a ratio of 20 to 40 percent women "to avoid tokenism." The unwillingness to endorse full equality in admissions arose from the impression that fewer women than men used college as a springboard to advanced studies in the professions: "Should Holy Cross exclude . . . 700 men, and thus 700 potential leaders, and have their places taken by 700 women whose aims may be home making? . . . Is the goal of education solely leadership, or is it also the means to obtain a more interesting and richer life, regardless of occupation?" Finally, the committee argued, women would enhance the academic level of the school by increasing the pool of applicants. On a show of hands, the faculty indicated wide support for coeducation. Afterwards, Father Swords noted that the report had failed to consider specific costs and changes; but the process moved forward.[101]

The next development was Co-Ed Week, held February 23–28, 1969. Housed in three residence halls, about 250 women (the listing of events called them "girls") shared a week of classes, discussions, and athletic events.[102] The experience confirmed opinions, pro and con; hard facts of costs and impact were harder to come by. During 1967–68, John Shay and Father Brooks conducted a study of women's colleges to determine what alterations to the curriculum and physical plant would be necessary. The lack of familiarity with women's preferences and the cultural assumptions under which some administrators labored produced an exaggerated list of requirements.[103] The Faculty-Student Assembly received a progress report at its March meeting in 1969. Father Swords presented the state of the question, stressing the point that women were perceived to be more open to the liberal arts and academically equal to, or better than, men. He noted that 50 percent of successful applicants who later rejected Holy Cross specified the lack of coeducation as a rea-

101. Preliminary and Final Reports of Ad Hoc Committee on Co-Education (October, 1967 and May, 1968), minutes of faculty meetings November 6 and December 4, 1967, and May 6, 1968, ACHC, 14.12; Swords's notes for faculty meeting, [March 10], 1968, and Swords to Trustee Committee on Coeducation, July 14, 1970, ACHC, 11.0.

102. Memo of the Co-Ed Committee to the Holy Cross community on Co-Ed Week, February 21, 1969, ACHC, 12.24; *Crusader*, February 28, 1969.

103. John Shay to J. Leo Sullivan, November 19, 1968, ACHC, 11.0; Brooks's jottings on conversation with Ursuline Sisters at New Rochelle, November 27, 1968, ACHC, 11.0, series 2.

son. He expected the presence of women to have a beneficial effect on "the rough conduct of an all-male campus," and to answer students' complaints that the gender-exclusive atmosphere was "a fairly serious defect in their educational experience." Swords was attracted by the prospect of a better educational atmosphere; but he was concerned about the possibility of negative alumni reaction and the desirability of keeping Holy Cross distinctive, and he worried that conversion costs would divert money from other priorities. Father Brooks added that the College had to choose coeducation or the status quo, since no women's college was interested in relocating to Pakachoag. John Shay discussed changes in facilities and lamented the dehumanizing "cattle calls" as female guests emerged from the busses that transported them to campus for social events.[104]

The faculty and the student representatives heard cost estimates at a second meeting on coeducation in April—a session that became the platform for a counterattack by the forces opposed to change. Father Swords presented a pessimistic memo from Father Nolan, the college treasurer, suggesting that, because women graduates tend to contribute less to their colleges, there was potential for a loss of 30 percent in annual giving, a financial risk the College couldn't afford.[105] An elaborate conversion study, prepared by Father "Luke" O'Connor, director of plant planning, indicated costs of about $2 million for mirrors, bathtubs, lingerie and shampoo sinks, and accommodations for house mothers—a strain the College budget could not endure. The same meeting received a 26-page dissenting view from Patrick Shanahan of the Mathematics Department, appealing to tradition and the need for variety in higher education. Once the novelty of attending a formerly men's college had worn out, he warned, women would realize that they had been brought in "to solve the problem of a dreary campus life, and their reaction would be predictable and justifiable."[106]

On May 5, the faculty met a third time on the issue and adopted the following resolution:

We reaffirm our previous endorsement of coeducation and recommend that the class entering Holy Cross in September 1971 be composed of no less than 30% and no more than 40% women students.

We also ask that the Board of Trustees before acting on our recommendation review the *Preliminary Report of Cost Estimates for Conversion to Coeducation* with an eye to reassessing the costs essential to such a conversion.

104. Faculty-Student Assembly minutes, March 10, 1969, ACHC, 14.12.

105. Nolan to Swords, April 14, 1969, ACHC, 11.0.

106. Transcript of Faculty-Student Assembly meeting, April 14, 1969, and documents from O'Connor and Shanahan, ACHC, 14.12.

Further, we ask that the Board of Trustees ... direct the officers of development to initiate in addition to their regular operation a concerted effort to obtain the financial support necessary for the funding of coeducation.

The roll call vote taken that day was an anomaly: the governance system was still so new that nobody realized the vote should have been a secret ballot. Coeducation won by a margin of 95–53, with six abstentions. Nine Jesuits, including Father Brooks, voted yes. Fathers Swords and Reidy, both trustees, voted no.[107] To his credit, Swords had defended the freedom of the faculty a few days earlier when an associate trustee suggested avoiding a faculty vote. Swords answered: "The faculty have the prime say in determining our educational policy since they know better than the rest of us what is best for the classroom. ... We have a good thing going. We could really ruin it by changing it."[108]

Coeducation became one of the first items on the agenda of the newly configured board of trustees. In December 1969, the trustees and associate trustees appointed a joint committee to study the matter. Father Swords conceded that the original cost estimates were inflated, and took note of faculty and student support for change. Already, data coming in from the Arthur D. Little study indicated that 64 percent of the lay faculty and 27 percent of the clerical faculty favored the change. Among alumni respondents, 27 percent favored coeducation, but support was far higher among recent graduates.[109] The trustees deferred a final decision during the 1969–70 academic year because of the press of other matters, including the selection of a new president.

Finding the right niche for the College's intercollegiate athletic program provided another difficult challenge. The Ad Hoc Committee on Athletics met weekly during three academic years, starting in 1967. During the first year, they made the case for commissioning a study by Arthur D. Little, Inc., of Cambridge. During the middle year, they worked with the Little team on six

107. Faculty-Student Assembly minutes, May 5, 1969, ACHC, 14.12; *Crusader*, May 9, 1969. Swords's vote was a function of his fear that alumni would be alienated by forcing the decision too rapidly and by his standing position that coeducation would become necessary if the lack of women made the College unattractive to qualified male applicants. That year, the incoming class totaled 777, about 25 percent higher than the admissions office target; students again had to be housed in Campion and Fenwick IV. At the moment, then, there seemed to be no economic or academic need for the change. Associate trustees' minutes, May 3 and December 12, 1969, ACHC, 11.1; Worcester *Telegram*, September 7, 1969; Swords to Lloyd Smith, September 3, 1969, ACHC, 12.24.

108. Associate trustees' minutes, May 3, 1969, ACHC, 11.1.

109. Minutes of joint meeting of trustees and associate trustees, December 13, 1969, ACHC, 11.1; Arthur D. Little Memos 5 and 6, ACHC, 12.24.

memoranda that conveyed the findings. During the final year, the committee analyzed the data and framed recommendations in a report discussed by the faculty during the spring of 1970. Early in their deliberations, they learned from Father Nolan that the potential savings from dropping football scholarships would be negligible.[110] From the Development Office, George Dinneen reported strong objections from alumni who were upset about the Little study. For some, this latest development only exacerbated a sense of disappointment about the College:

> In all my years of alumni involvement, I have never heard so much criticism. There is still much conversation about the changes in the curriculum, especially in the areas of theology and philosophy, the rules concerning attendance at daily Mass, drinking in the dormitories, and girls in the rooms. The ADL study has now taken preference.
>
> . . . . .
>
> [There is] substantial criticism of faculty members for trying to make Holy Cross into something, "It is not and could not be in the next 100 years. Getting tired of hearing from our new lay faculty that we did not receive a good education at Holy Cross." [sic][111]

In December of 1968, the first memorandum from the Little study confirmed the existence of two cultures at Holy Cross. The academic side was concerned that the athletic program, particularly football, worked to the detriment of excellence in the academic program and tended to create "a 'circus-like' atmosphere." The athletic side favored football and other sports for sustaining campus spirit and symbolizing tradition. The memorandum held the administration at fault for not promoting better contact between the two sides, which "have not been in communication for a long time."[112] In fact, the contest had become a tug-of-war between proponents of the new Holy Cross, many of whom lacked experience and understanding of the older institution then in the process of being redefined, and defenders of the old order, who believed that precipitous change was overturning every aspect of the College that claimed their loyalty. In jeopardy was the middle ground where innovation and tradition could be harmonized by sustaining athletic (and other) traditions without impeding the drive toward academic excellence. Meanwhile, about two-thirds of the students were participating in organized athletics, including intramural sports, and all had legitimate claims on institutional resources. Other findings disclosed that the school's athletic reputation was less significant to outsiders than to people

110. In a letter to Swords dated February 19, 1968, George Nolan estimated a net savings of $375 by 1971–72 if athletic scholarships were eliminated. ACHC, 12.24.

111. Memo from George Dinneen to Maurice Reidy, December 4, 1968, ACHC, 11.0.

112. Arthur D. Little Memorandum I, December 16, 1968, ACHC, 12.24.

associated with the College, and that Holy Cross had the highest athletic program cost per capita among schools in a comparison group.[113]

Everybody recognized that the football program, with its high visibility and costly scholarships, was the flashpoint of the controversy. With its standing and reputation under intense scrutiny, the program suffered two unexpected blows. The first was a private censure by the NCAA, the result of alleged recruiting infractions by the Holy Cross Club of Plymouth County, and illegal pre-season practices held in Canada in August 1968. When College authorities learned of the violations, they requested, and received, the resignation of Head Coach Tom Boisture and "forcefully instructed" the Plymouth County club to halt its recruiting efforts. In June 1969, Athletic Director Vincent Dougherty and Father Raymond Cahill of the Economics Department represented the College at a meeting with NCAA authorities, pleading that, under the circumstances, "adverse publicity would be tantamount to throwing gasoline on the fire." NCAA authorities agreed to issue "private reprimands and censures" because of the College's initiative in investigating the infractions and acting on them.[114] The matter had no visible effect on the debate about athletics, but the willingness to deal with it privately spared football's reputation.

The second blow was a hepatitis outbreak. The first player became ill on September 25, 1969. By October 6, the entire varsity team, plus several coaches and managers had contracted the illness. Medical investigators traced the problem to a practice field drinking faucet that had been contaminated during the summer by neighborhood children.[115] After losses in the first two games, the rest of the season was canceled, with an estimated revenue loss of $102,500. The College received contributions from Dartmouth, Boston College, and other schools; and over 1000 alumni contributed $35,000 toward the shortfall. Father Swords assured alumni that the experience outbreak would not influence the trustees' decision on football.[116] Nevertheless, the plight of the vic-

113. Arthur D. Little Memorandums II and III, March 10 and March 11, 1969, ACHC, 12.24.

114. Arthur J. Bergstrom [Sec'y NCAA Committee on Infractions] to Swords, Kansas City, May 14 and September 15, 1969, Swords to Bergstrom, June 3, 1969, Vincent Dougherty minutes on Chicago meeting, June 7, 1969, and Raymond Cahill to Swords, August 22, 1969, ACHC, 12.24. According to Dougherty, the illegal practices involved eight or nine players doing conditioning, and running and passing drills for about two days.

115. John Shay to Swords, October 16, 1969, ACHC, 12.24. A chronology of hepatitis outbreak was included in a statement prepared for the NCAA/ECAC in an effort to extend eligibility for affected players. Ibid.

116. Dougherty to Swords, October 16, 1969, Swords to James J. O'Connor '58, October 20, 1969, and memo of Swords to Joseph Shea, January 22, 1970, ACHC, 12.24; *Worcester Telegram*, November 21, 1969; Trustees' minutes, December 12, 1969, ACHC, 11.0.

tims and the experience of a fall season (almost) without football drew attention to the program and its importance.

Throughout the winter of 1969–70, the sense deepened that the athletic program would have to be altered. In December, a new A. D. Little memorandum indicated that 77 percent of the faculty and 66 percent of students felt that football was too prominent. Among the alumni, however, 40 percent wanted the program strengthened and another 31 percent thought the emphasis on football was about right.[117] Father Maurice Reidy, a member of the committee, predicted: "The more I look into this, I feel we are going to have to go out of athletic scholarships entirely."[118] A month later, Father Nolan revised his earlier estimates about the cost of the football program and suggested that Father Swords "seriously consider withdrawing from all formal participation in Intercollegiate Football" to maintain the commitment to academic financial aid.[119]

These reports and expectations created the context for the final report of the Ad Hoc Committee on Athletics in April of 1970. The 83 pages of analysis and recommendations were grounded in a recognition that programs feasible for large universities were not appropriate for smaller schools like Holy Cross. There were three specific proposals: first, establishment of an Athletic Council (including representatives from the trustees, alumni, administration, faculty, athletic association and treasurer's office) "with authority to advise, consult, recommend and act in matters of athletic policy"; second, elimination, by the fall of 1971, of full athletic grants-in-aid in favor of need-based financial aid for all students; third, a re-prioritization of funds to give better support to recreational, intramural, and non-revenue-producing varsity sports, with a continuation of the current emphasis on basketball, track, and baseball. The committee lamented the College's poor intramural facilities: in comparison with other schools, Holy Cross had "the highest athletic program costs per undergraduate . . . , yet it had the least commodious and least valuable athletic plant." They suggested grading the hilltop to provide more playing fields and building a new athletic complex with an arena, pool, and squash courts. Athletic scholarships had to be eliminated, they argued, because of the "serious imbalance in the distribution of financial aid to students: it contradicts the principle of financial aid . . . awarded . . . equally on the basis of need; it results in unduly heavy financial support for the single extra-curricular activity of athletics; and given the current financial condition of the College, it is

117. Arthur D. Little Memorandum V, December, 1969, ACHC, 12.24.
118. Trustees' minutes, December 12, 1969, ACHC, 11.0.
119. Nolan to Swords, January 21, 1970, ACHC, 11.0.

a program which is inadvisable, perhaps impossible to maintain." Their statistics indicated that 28 percent of financial aid went to varsity athletes who were five percent of the student body. Under the circumstances, the committee foresaw the possibility of de-emphasizing the football program, perhaps even to the level of club football—a step that was preferable to having "the educational program diminished for lack of funds."[120] To members of the Varsity Club on May 1, Father Swords stated that the future of athletics at Holy Cross did not look good.[121]

The Faculty-Student Assembly discussed the report on May 26. Father Swords acceded to a request from the Athletic Association for representation at the meeting and invited Head Basketball Coach Jack Donohue, Bill Whitton (who had succeeded Boisture as head football coach), and Vincent Dougherty to represent their views and answer questions. A sixteen-page rebuttal of the report, offered by the Holy Cross Club of Boston, argued that the faculty lacked understanding of the College and of the tangible and intangible benefits of the football program.[122] Discussion centered on the desire for equitable, need-based assistance, on the sense that Holy Cross should assume leadership in a difficult area, and on survey results from A. D. Little indicating that large donors would be more generous if varsity sports were de-emphasized. Coach Whitton and others asserted that the program had already been pared down as far as possible, while Father Brooks pointed out that canceling athletic scholarships would not automatically produce money for needy students. In the end, the assembly endorsed by a substantial margin the recommendation to abolish athletic grants-in-aid. A motion to create an Athletic Council also passed easily. At the end of the meeting, Father Swords announced that the trustees had chosen John Brooks as president.[123]

During Father Swords's final month in office, alumni opposition to the faculty recommendation continued to grow. Already the General Alumni Association had endorsed the status quo. Varsity Club President Peter P. Karpawich '36 described for the press a general feeling that "the lay faculty is taking over the conduct of the College and its extra curricula[r] activities to

120. Report of Ad Hoc Committee on Athletics, April 1970, and Press Release, May 7, 1970, Swords to trustees and associate trustees, May 1, 1970, ACHC, 12.24.

121. *Crusader*, May 1, 1970.

122. Swords to Vincent Dougherty, May 18, 1970; Holy Cross Club of Boston, Student Aid Committee, undated rebuttal, ACHC, 12.24. William Ziobro '66 of the Classics Department also submitted a memo, May 22, 1970, arguing for a more practical and cautious approach. Ibid.

123. Faculty-Student Assembly minutes, May 26, 1970, ACHC, 14.12.

such an extent that the alumni no longer has [sic] a voice."[124] The Varsity Club issued a letter contending that the ad hoc committee report was "misleading," and "potentially catastrophic"—academic standards had already been raised without sacrificing a "healthy, modest and interesting" varsity sports program that included football. And they voiced the fear that alumni contributions would fall if the trustees adopted the faculty plan.[125] Even the Worcester City Council urged the College "to think of what a great force for community good the football teams of Holy Cross have been and to make every effort to maintain a team at the same level as in the past."[126] On the first of July, the issue became Father Brooks's responsibility, a difficult choice aptly described by a local sports writer: "He takes office caught between two fires—a faculty which has instigated and seems in the driver's seat for the de-emphasis of HC football, and an aroused alumni, which wants the continuance of sports and may be forgotten in the revolution which is sweeping college campuses."[127]

As John Brooks pondered his options, Raymond Swords looked back with the hope of justifying his leadership. He presented his case during a round of alumni talks, attempting to explain the principles that sustained the new Holy Cross. He was particularly impatient with unreasonable attacks on issues like parietal changes: the students were, after all, the products of a permissive atmosphere and often "the parents want us to do what they wish they could do with their children." Students, he asserted, were "not cut in the same pattern as the older generation" and could not be directed in their personal conduct by appealing to authority; already, they had seen civil rights demonstrations, strikes and protests for concessions, and confusion about authority in the Church. Most of all, Swords insisted, the modern student had to be understood:

Whatever bad there is in him, what we do not like in him, we have mostly ourselves to blame for. He did not create the present conditions of this world. The wonder is that he is as good as he is. And he is good. He has very high ideals. He is extremely generous. He hates dishonesty. He is very sensitive to hypocrisy.

Perhaps to anticipate the objections of those who found his characterization idealistic or mawkish, he argued that the best way to develop responsibility was to allow students to exercise it. He quoted Cardinal Newman's aphorism that people are not prepared for troubled waters by being protected from

124. Worcester *Gazette*, May 28, 1970.

125. Letter of Peter P. Karpawich and Joseph Fay, June 10, 1970. The letter was written on Varsity Club stationery and distributed within the Holy Cross community and to the local media. ACHC, 11.0.

126. Resolution of Worcester City Council, July 21, 1970, ACHC, 11.0.

127. Roy Mumpton in the Worcester *Gazette*, May 28, 1970.

them, and echoed Pedro Arrupe's plea not to fear the new world, because God is there.[128] The presentations were vintage Swords, a strong assertion of the connection between the inevitability of change, the spirit of the young, and the Jesuit principle of adaptation for the sake of the *magis*. Raymond Swords wore his heart on his sleeve facing his critics. They were no less forthright in responding.

Father Swords told members of the student government that he had been "severely criticized" by some of the alumni, and "sometimes treated in a very rude fashion." He had been verbally attacked because of all the changes; special meetings had been called against him; he had lost friends because his policies were deemed too permissive:

Let me tell you, I returned from this last trip, bloody and beaten after a couple of those evenings. The principal point of my talk to parents and alumni has been that you *are* different from the students of ten years ago, and you should be treated differently.[129]

To Bishop Flanagan, he confided his sense of anguish:

No one in this area knows better than you how trying these days are, and how difficult it is to decide what is the correct position to take and then to take it when you know the guns are pointing right at you. I find all this an unexpected answer to the self-immolation I vowed and a martyrdom of a far more difficult type than I bargained for.[130]

In his final address to the Worcester County Alumni, he admitted: "If anyone has changed in the course of this decade it was I. . . . I'm not only involved in educating young people; these young people have been educating me." Did his outreach to the alumni succeed? Despite his sensitivity to criticism, the Arthur D. Little survey disclosed that 70 percent of the alumni were highly or moderately satisfied with changes at the College—a vote of confidence that must have pleased him.[131]

The outgoing president was also pleased when the Class of 1970 invited

128. Swords's address to alumni groups, spring 1968, ACHC, 12.24.

129. Swords's notes for talk with Student Government, February 2, 1968, ACHC, 12.24.

130. Swords to Flanagan, March 7, 1968, WDA, Holy Cross, 1966–1969. Two years later, in his final address to the Worcester County club, Swords offered lavish praise to Flanagan for his exceptional understanding and support of the College. At the bottom of the file copy of the speech, Swords penned a note for historians: "(I meant every word and much more.) He has been simply wonderful in his understanding, in trusting us, and in not interfering with the College.)" [punct. sic] Address to Worcester County Alumni, February 15, 1970, ACHC, 12.24.

131. Arthur D. Little Memorandum VI, March, 1970, ACHC, 12.24.

him to break the tradition of having the governor deliver the commencement address, by speaking to the graduates himself. At first, he sought assurance that there was consensus among the seniors. A few days after the amnesty announcement of December 1969, he received this response: "It is our desire now, more than ever[,] in light of your courageous decision of December 14, that you address us at graduation."[132] Father Swords did not disappoint. He offered the graduates a ringing challenge to be committed to change, to promote justice. The campus response to the Vietnam tragedy and other contemporary events, he told them, "revealed the depth of your feeling and the authenticity of your concerns. From this point on, there is no turning back, no copping-out." He urged them to stand "for life, for peace, for justice" and to fight against poverty and racism. He would not have spoken thus a decade earlier. The challenges had matured him, and deepened his convictions. When he finished speaking, he received a prolonged, "thunderous" standing ovation.[133]

Less than a month later, John Brooks assumed the presidency of Holy Cross. He was 46 years old and experienced in administration because of his duties in the Theology Department and as vice-president and academic dean since 1968. After his election, he expressed his hope to deal with student unrest in a reasonable way and acknowledged that fiscal issues, common on college campuses at that time, were a difficult challenge at Holy Cross. He also indicated his intention to stress accountability as a necessary condition within the governance structure.[134] He moved decisively to fashion an administration reflective of his priorities and style. He declined the option of having a chancellor, preferring instead to maintain hands-on responsibility for internal and external matters. He appointed Father Joseph Donahue as executive vice-president "as a means of distributing the burdens of the President's Office," and to function as president in his absence.[135] During the first summer, Father Joseph Fahey, a member of the Economics Department since 1968 and acting dean after Father Brooks vacated the office, was appointed

132. Marc Young '70 to Swords, November 25 and December 18, 1969, ACHC, 12.24; Worcester *Telegram*, May 18, 1970.

133. Commencement address, June 10, 1970, ACHC, 12.24; Worcester *Telegram*, June 11, 1970; Nicholson, "Legacy," 197.

134. Boston *Evening Globe*, June 3, 1970.

135. Trustees' minutes, August 6, 1970, ACHC, 11.0. At the time of Brooks's selection, Father Swords himself expressed doubts about becoming chancellor "since the new President might have the impression that an ex-president is 'looking over his shoulder.'" Trustees' minutes, May 25, 1970, ACHC, 11.0. The principal issue, however, seems to have been Brooks's leadership style, which limited the appeal of a chancellor, as the trustees envisioned it.

dean; John F. O'Keefe, vice-president for business affairs was also appointed treasurer. In 1971, Donald T. McClain replaced John Shay as dean of students; Father Paul Harman was appointed associate dean of the College; and faculty members Joseph Maguire '58 and William Ziobro '66 became assistant deans.[136]

As he assembled his staff, Father Brooks had to come to terms with a variety of unresolved issues. Among them was the need to work with the trustees in responding to faculty votes on athletic scholarships and coeducation, to guide the College through the final years of activism associated with the civil rights movement and the Vietnam War, and to resolve a fiscal crisis that had led to five straight deficit budgets. Brooks worked first of all to expand the number of trustees—from fourteen (nine Jesuit, five lay) in his first year of office, to the mandated limit of 25 by 1973, by which time lay trustees constituted a majority. In 1970, the trustees voted to add a June graduate to the board each year, for a two-year term, as a means of adding an immediate, fresh perspective to the group.[137]

At a special meeting in October of 1970, the trustees considered the faculty vote on athletics, accepting the proposal for an Athletic Council and rejecting the proposal to end athletic grants-in-aid. The major reason for the second vote was fiscal. Dropping the current level of football, they believed, would sacrifice revenue at a time when the College was facing a large deficit. The following day, Father Brooks told the President's Council that football had made $208,000 during the six seasons preceding the hepatitis outbreak. For the sake of this income, the current program had to be maintained. The trustees advanced the same argument to the faculty:

If our financial situation at a later date suggests a reconsideration, the question can be opened again. We are convinced that our athletic program is a healthy and wholesome aspect of Holy Cross life. Improvement of the recreational, intramural and minor sports programs, which our students legitimately regard as part of their total college experience, will be a major objective of the proposed Athletic Council.[138]

The Faculty-Student Assembly objected to this response, requesting the report of the trustee's Committee on Athletics and other information; but this request was refused. Instead, the trustees issued a statement that the question

136. Trustees' minutes, January 4, 1971, ACHC, 11.0; *Crusader*, September 25, 1970, and September 24, 1971.

137. Trustees' minutes, September 9, 1970, ACHC, 11.0; *Crusader*, September 25, 1970. Brian O'Connell '71 was the first new graduate to assume responsibility as a trustee.

138. Trustees' minutes, August 6 and October 2, 1970, and Brooks's memo to faculty, October 3, 1970, ACHC, 11.0; Worcester *Gazette*, October 3, 1970.

of athletic scholarships was closed. In February of 1971, the Educational Policy Committee made another effort to move the trustees by objecting that the proffered explanation of policy was not "sufficient and acceptable."[139] But the trustees' decision was truly closed. That might not have been the case under Father Swords; but Father Brooks and the trustees used the case as an opportunity to assert their ultimate responsibility for the direction of the school.

Even so, Father Brooks and the trustees were not unappreciative of the idea of need-based athletic scholarships. In 1971, they debated the possibility of moving to need-based grants, because, as Brooks put it, a principle was involved: "There is a *moral* question of giving money to people who don't need it." In August, the College joined the Yankee Conference after securing a commitment to explore the possibility of basing athletic grants upon need. The move was promoted as an effort to cut athletic expenses, expand competition in minor sports, and eliminate the problems of remaining an independent school.[140] Meanwhile, there were shake-ups in the athletic program. In December 1971, the contracts of Basketball Coach Jack Donohue and Athletic Director Vincent Dougherty were not renewed. The following spring, Ronald Perry '54 was named athletic director. He told the trustees that morale was low in the Athletic Association and requested an "all-purpose athletic facility" as a high priority.[141] At the same time, George Blaney '61 became head basketball coach. In football, Bill Whitton's squad was unable to win a victory during the 1970 season as they struggled to come back from the canceled season. Whitton resigned in February 1971, citing health and family reasons, and was replaced by Ed Doherty, who was named New England Coach of the Year for leading Holy Cross to four victories in his first season. In baseball, Jack Whalen '48, another product of the Jack Barry era, succeeded Bob Curran as coach.[142]

The extraordinary succession of events that required the trustees' attention during 1969–70 delayed discussion of coeducation; but, after meeting with members of the faculty, admissions officers, and the dean of students, a trustees' committee readied a report for a special meeting in January of 1971. The committee found that the cost of conversion would be about $500,000 for "minimal, not spartan" arrangements. On the crucial question, "that the College of the Holy Cross admit full-time resident women students in the fall of

139. Trustees' minutes, December 5, 1970, EPC to Horgan, February 19, 1971, ACHC, 11.0.
140. Trustees' minutes, May 7 and August 7, 1971, ACHC, 11.0; *Crusader*, September 24, 1971.
141. *Crusader*, January 28 and April 14, 1972; Trustees' minutes, May 5, 1972, ACHC, 11.0.
142. *Crusader*, February 12, March 19, and December 3, 1971, April 14, 1972.

Co-education at last: newly admitted Holy Cross students look forward to the start of a new era in the fall of 1972.

1972 without increasing the size of the student body," the vote carried easily.[143] Father Brooks announced the decision on January 11, citing four reasons for the change: women's attraction to the College's strong liberal arts program, the prospect of "mutual enrichment" in a coeducational learning environment, "healthier mutuality of respect and Christian regard between the sexes," and the expectation that the College would help prepare women for prominence in professional and public life. Alumni response was relatively muted. Fewer than sixty wrote to him; among these, about sixty percent were favorable.[144]

Coeducation required some modifications to the physical plant, and pro-

143. Paul Schweitzer to Maurice Reidy, Princeton, October 13, 1970, and minutes of trustees' meeting, January 4, 1971, ACHC, 11.0.

144. Brooks's statement on coeducation, January 11, 1971, ACHC, 11.0; Coeducation File, Brooks Papers, ACHC, 12.25.

vided the opportunity to hire women in administrative offices. In the summer of 1972, Marilyn Boucher was named associate dean of students, Eileen Dooley became associate director of student activities, and Jeanmarie Early became an admissions counselor. The admission of women doubled the applicant pool, with the result that the academic qualifications of the student body increased: about 50 percent of the Class of 1974 ranked in the top fifth of their high school class; for the Class of 1976, the figure was 71.5 percent. The first women arrived on campus in September 1972 as third-year and second-year transfer students, and as incoming members of the Class of 1976. A brief article in *The Crusader* noted simply that the transition had occurred "rather smoothly."[145]

Radical campus activism maintained its presence until the end of the Vietnam War in January 1973. In 1970, the fall calendar was altered to set up a four-day holiday just before the national election so that interested parties could participate.[146] In May 1971, the Faculty-Student Assembly supported a national Anti-War Moratorium. The endorsement was less ringing than in the previous year: there were various interpretations about student absence, but Father Brooks made it clear he expected the faculty to be in class. A year later, the assembly passed its final resolution in opposition to the war.[147] The Faculty-Student Assembly eventually took up the issue of dropping ROTC from the curriculum. Dozens of campuses, including Harvard, did drop their programs. At Holy Cross, military units were conducting drill off campus to keep a low profile. The movement to drop ROTC gained attention during the 1969–70 academic year, when an ad hoc committee composed of two faculty members, two students, and one trustee considered the issue. In September 1970, they recommended 3–2 (the majority included both students) to recommend phasing the program out. But the assembly disagreed by a margin of three to two. Most telling for the majority were arguments that the program aided poor students and that it helped add a well-educated element into the corps of officers. The faculty did take steps, however, to ensure that ROTC courses would be held up to the same academic criteria as all other courses.[148]

145. Brooks memo to faculty, August 7, 1972, ACHC, 14.12; Alice D. Sloan, "The Admission of Women to the College of the Holy Cross Has Upgraded the Academic Atmosphere" (Providence College, Department of Education Research Study, July 1974), in Coeducation File, Brooks Papers, ACHC, 12.25; *Crusader*, September 22, 1972. See also Cahill, *Women on the Hill*, 25–39.

146. Brooks memo to Faculty, Students, Administrative Officers, [September 1970], ACHC, 14.12.

147. Faculty-Student Assembly minutes, May 5, 1971, and May 12, 1972, ACHC, 14.12.

148. Minutes of trustees and associate trustees, May 8, 1970, ACHC, 11.1; *Crusader*, September 25, 1970; Minutes of Faculty-Student Assembly, October 12, 1970 and March 29, 1971,

During and after the debate, campus radicals, led by the RSU, made a final effort to oust the Air Force ROTC unit. A potentially serious episode occurred in November 1971, when Marine recruiters came to campus for two days. At the end of the first day, about 200 protesters gathered between Loyola Hall and the Air Force building, threatening to destroy the ROTC structure unless the second day of recruiting was postponed. A number of other students also gathered, prepared to defend the building. Campus authorities were convinced that summoning the police would provoke violence. In the absence of Father Brooks, Father Donahue consulted the Advisory Committee on Campus Recruiting and accepted their decision to postpone the second day of the visit. Four students were brought before the College Judicial Board for threatening violence, and acquitted. Father Brooks told the trustees that he would abide by the verdict, that the "open campus" policy remained in force, and that violence and the threat of violence would not be tolerated.[149]

The last of the protests started on the morning of May 3, 1972, when members of the Black Student Union occupied Fenwick and O'Kane Halls to dramatize grievances against the College. The BSU issued a news release, listing demands that included increasing the number of black students, a stronger commitment to hiring black faculty and administrators, better financial aid, elimination of alleged hiring discrimination in Kimball Hall, and a challenge to certain holdings in the College's stock portfolio. In meetings with the protesters, Father Brooks explained the constraints of limited funds and the impossibility of forcing academic departments to make specific hires, but he pledged to resolve issues that lay within his control, especially Kimball policies. He also insisted that the building be released. At 5 P.M. the BSU agreed, and the crisis ended. At a special meeting on May 12, the Faculty-Student Assembly adopted a set of policies to promote the hiring of black faculty.[150]

ACHC, 14.8.1A; Moss, *Vietnam*, 312; Freeland, *Golden Age*, 174. In fact, the Arthur D. Little survey showed campus opinion divided on dropping ROTC, with a slight majority of students and faculty in favor of keeping ROTC. Alumni and administrators were far more inclined to support the program. Data given with materials for faculty discussion, [1970], ACHC, 14.12.

149. Memo to trustees and associate trustees, November 3, 1971, and trustees' minutes, December 4, 1971, ACHC, 11.0; *Crusader*, December 4, 1970, November 5, 1971, April 21, 1972. In the fall of 1970, the RSU attempted to stir up opposition to ROTC programs in a booklet of deliberately offensive articles, "Holy Cross, Holy Shit." ACHC, 15.1T. The RSU had died out by 1977.

150. Trustees' minutes, May 5, 1972, ACHC, 11.0; *Crusader*, May 5, 1972; Faculty-Student Assembly minutes, May 12, 1972, ACHC, 14.12.

Conflict over coeducation and the athletic program, and finding ways to accommodate African-American students, were growing pains of a new era; but the fiscal crisis that developed during the late 1960s betrayed a fundamental weakness that threatened all the gains (Chart 9.1). In the spring of 1968, the trustees and associate trustees received confidential letter from Father Nolan, warning: "It appears highly unlikely to me that the Development Program and the Alumni Fund will be able to produce enough income over the near term, to forestall disastrous financial deficits and to permit the College to continue the growth process in which it is engaged."[151] Income for the year was up by 2 percent, while expenses, reflecting an annual inflation rate that ran close to 6 percent between 1969 and 1973, had risen by 8.8 percent. The deficit was projected at $450,000 after drastic cuts in budget requests. The problem was blamed on lower-than-expected enrollments (2300) and the rising cost of financial aid. To meet the shortfall, the trustees authorized taking the money from reserve funds; meanwhile, they mandated "substantial economies."[152]

The fiscal crisis worsened toward the end of 1969, when projections showed that continuing the deficit operation at the current level would deplete the endowment in five years. The total deficit from 1968 to 1970 was $1.8 million, of which $1.5 million was raised by liquidating financial holdings; the trustees projected an operating deficit of $200,000 for fiscal year 1971.[153] The particular seriousness of the crisis became clear with the publication of a study of private colleges in Massachusetts, undertaken in 1970 by McKinsey and Company for a committee appointed by the governor. John T. Garrity '45, a managing partner in the firm, prepared a separate analysis for the Holy Cross trustees, presenting the problem in sobering detail. Holy Cross had the highest deficit of any comparable institution in absolute dollars and as a percentage of current expenditures. The College's overhead expenditures and general administrative costs were "inordinately high." The $1.06 million student aid program, accounting for more than 10 percent of expenses, ran ahead of similar schools by as much as 40 percent. Auxiliary enterprise costs ($520 per student, as against $200 at comparable schools) would begin to run deficits if not altered.[154]

151. Nolan to Swords, April 11, 1968, ACHC, 11.0. Again in late summer Nolan advocated dropping intercollegiate football, arguing that 25 percent of all financial aid assigned to the incoming class was reserved for athletic grants-in-aid. Trustees' minutes, September 11, 1968, ACHC, 11.0.

152. Associate trustees' minutes, May 26, 1968, ACHC, 11.1; Swords to Blaise Drayton, July 16, 1968, ACHC, 12.24; Trustees' minutes, August 1–2, 1968, ACHC, 11.0.

153. Trustees' and associate trustees' minutes, December 13, 1969, and May 8, 1970, ACHC 11.1; trustees' minutes, March 13–14, 1970, ACHC, 11.0; *Crusader*, October 2, 1970.

154. John Garrity's "observations" on the financial situation at Holy Cross, January 14, 1970, ACHC, 11.0. See also George Nolan to Swords, January 21, 1970, ACHC, 11.0.

Chart 10.1 The Holy Cross Fund, 1960–1972

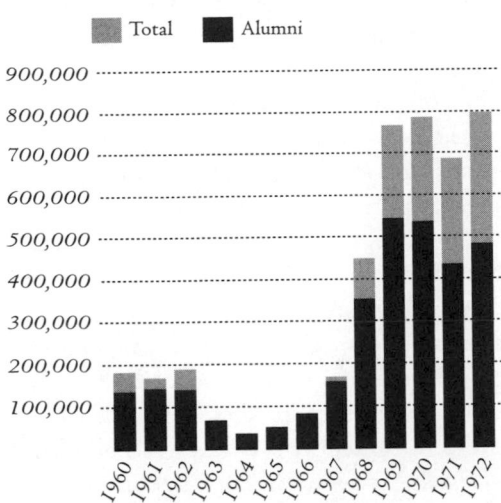

The study clarified the most glaring weakness of the Swords administration—an inability to fund ambitious plans. When he left office in the summer of 1970, the crisis was at its peak. Yet, in retrospect, it is clear that he had already found several solutions to help pull the College back toward solvency. One insight involved annual tuition increases, a policy he adopted in 1969 (Chart 9.2). Almost half of the students were receiving financial aid, and the tuition increase added only 10 percent to the funding available for scholarships.[155] The consequences of such increases were mitigated by the availability of low-cost educational loans from the federal government and other sources. The National Defense Education Act of 1958, the Higher Education Act of 1965, and the Higher Education Amendments of 1972 funded student loans and work/study programs that made higher education costs more manageable.[156]

Tuition increases helped with the shortfall, but circumstances also required re-invigoration of the fund-raising effort. After the unsuccessful fund drive that ended in 1965, the Holy Cross Fund was re-emphasized and grew to $790,000 in 1970 (Chart 10.1). Then, unexpectedly, the fund fell—to

155. Trustees' minutes, March 14, 1970, ACHC, 11.0; Swords to Parents and Undergraduates, March 16, 1970, ACHC, 12.24; Swords to Bishop Flanagan, March 20, 1970.

156. Until 1958, federal aid to higher education was largely restricted to land-grant colleges. Russian success with Sputnik prompted the legislation of 1958; subsequent acts were part of the Great Society and its aftermath. Lewis R. Mayhew, *Legacy of the Seventies: Experiment, Economy, Equality, and Expediency in American Higher Education* (San Francisco: Jossey-Bass Publish-

$690,000 in 1971, as alumni giving declined by about 20 percent in two years. The fall-off, attributed to a weak national economy and to alumni dissatisfaction with changes at the College, exacerbated the sense of crisis during the presidential transition.[157] To reverse the process, Father Swords adopted several expedients. First, he introduced better management of the College's portfolio of liquid assets, once dominated by General Motors and General Tire and Rubber stock. Next, he organized the President's Council in 1968 "to bring under one banner all who are committed to an exemplary level of support." Council members, who contributed $1000 annually, numbered 192 in the first year and 250 in the second. Finally, he opened the office of Alumni Relations in 1969, with Patrick McCarthy '63 as director.[158]

When Father Brooks assumed the presidency, the trustees directed him to limit the deficit to $382,000 during fiscal year 1971. To the Student-Faculty Assembly, he disclosed the seriousness of the crisis. He predicted that the school had the resources to remain solvent for one more year unless fiscal problems were brought under control. He pledged that he would not deny promotions as a means of saving money, but he was investigating cuts in administrative staff and in sabbatical leaves and increasing teacher workloads.[159] When, in December, the trustees mandated a balanced budget beginning in fiscal year 1972, Father Brooks told the faculty that he would have to reduce expenses, increase giving, raise tuition again, and hold faculty raises to a maximum of 4 percent—a level below the rate of inflation.[160]

---

ers, 1977), 272–75. In 1969, the Presidential Task Force on Higher Education found a "growing need for methods of federal institutional assistance to sustain high-quality four-year colleges" and asked for federal financial assistance "in the immediate future." The federal student aid program in FY 1969 included $145 million in Educational Opportunity Grants; $143 million in work/study support; $186 million in NDEA loans; and $45 million in student loan guarantees. President's Task Force on Higher Education, *Priorities in Higher Education* (Washington, D.C.: GPO, August 1970), 11, 31. By 1970, private schools were receiving, on average, 23 percent of their operating budgets through federal programs that included student aid and research support. Freeland, *Golden Age*, 92.

157. Thomas Ryan '76, Holy Cross Fund figures, 1948–94; *Crusader*, October 1, 1971.

158. Minutes of faculty meeting, February 5, 1968, ACHC, 14.12; Swords's notes for talk at first President's Council dinner, September 27, 1968, ACHC, 12.24; George Dinneen to Council members, September 16, 1969, WDA, Holy Cross, 1966–1969; College press release, May 29, 1969, ACHC, 12.24; President's Council brochure, September 27, 1968, ACHC, 17.3D-1.

159. Faculty-Student Assembly minutes, October 4, 1971, ACHC, 14.12; *The Catholic Observer*, November 20, 1970; New Orleans *Clarion-Herald*, November 26, 1970.

160. Trustees' minutes, December 5, 1970, and College press release, December 9, 1970, ACHC, 11.0.

The decision to limit salary increments as part of the strategy for solving the deficit prompted the local chapter of the AAUP to register displeasure as early as 1970, when members petitioned the trustees to "immediately allocate a greater percentage of the College budget to faculty salaries to improve the faculty salary situation and the College's comparative external profile."[161] After assuming office, Father Brooks kept the faculty informed of the trustees' actions. By 1971, they were able to increase salary allotments 6 percent for fiscal year 1973. They agreed to assign a high priority to improving salaries, but as long as the fiscal crisis lasted, the options were limited. Meanwhile, the "Ph.D. glut" of the early 1970s somewhat reduced the bargaining power of the faculty.[162] Nevertheless, with a membership of 68 in 1971, the AAUP represented a significant bloc of the faculty; their morale and confidence could not be alienated but at cost to the well-being of the College.

The draconian measures adopted during 1970 produced the intended effect and brought a balanced budget during Brooks's first year in office. This outcome had several causes, including increased giving from non-alumni sources, increased rentals, and $215,000 from the Jesuit community (a gift of $125,000, plus a renegotiation of the agreement covering overhead expenses).[163] A year later, Father Brooks reported another balanced budget, financed by a tuition increase and a rise in annual giving. The budget included $300,000 set aside for renovations to Carlin, Alumni, and Beaven Halls. He thanked the faculty for helping to hold down expenses, but he also sounded a warning: "We have struggled and gained some breathing space, but we are not affluent."[164] In time, the faculty received a share of the emerging institutional prosperity. In 1972, the trustees increased salary allotments by 7.5 percent for fiscal year 1974. They also adopted procedures to give greater responsibility to the dean and departmental chairs in determining individual increments.[165]

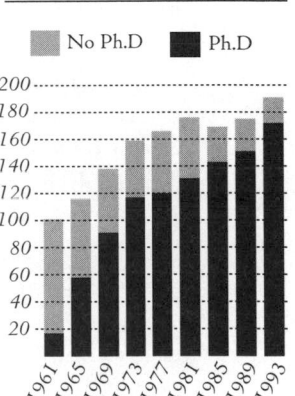

Chart 10.2 Faculty at Assistant Professor or Above, 1961–1993

161. AAUP minutes, February 13, March 4, November 13, and November 29, 1971, ACHC, 14.12-1.

162. Faculty-Student Assembly minutes, October 4 and December 13, 1971, ACHC, 14.12. See Freeland, *Golden Age*, 381–82, on the effects of the oversupply of Ph.D.s in the United States.

163. Brooks to Faculty-Student Assembly, October 4, 1971, ACHC, 14.8.1A.

164. Brooks to Faculty-Student Assembly, October 2, 1972, ACHC, 14.12.

165. Brooks to Faculty, September 18 and September 26, 1972, ACHC, 14.12.

The number of faculty members had increased by about 50 since 1961 (Chart 10.2). After 1965, faculty members with the Ph.D. constituted a majority of the permanent faculty. One implication of this development was that more of the faculty were highly specialized in their fields of expertise, and the number of semester courses proliferated to about 675 by 1972—a "luxury" Father Brooks opposed by advocating the cycling of more courses and the discontinuation of others that drew small enrollments.[166] Moving along another avenue, the faculty endorsed a new Center for Interdisciplinary and Special Studies in 1971 "to revitalize the educational process" by allowing students more responsibility and independence. The program sponsored interdisciplinary courses and seminars, fieldwork opportunities including internships, student-designed plans of study, and exchange programs. The Special Studies Committee had oversight of the center which, in time, assumed sponsorship of the Honors Program, multidisciplinary majors, the Washington Semester program, academic internships, the Fenwick Scholar program, and a series of academic concentrations. Other effects of the size and specialization of the faculty occurred in 1971, when the History and Political Science Departments became distinct entities and majors, and the major in European Literature was introduced.[167]

Between 1968 and 1972, the third Holy Cross came into existence, the product of fruitful collaboration between trustees, faculty, administrators, alumni, students, and two determined presidents. In the spring of 1970, Father Swords admitted that he was counting the days until he could surrender a set of responsibilities that had become increasingly heavy.[168] He was worn out, but his importance for the development of the College was widely appreciated. In his place, John Brooks brought new energy, a more sophisticated approach to the fiscal operation, and a commitment to follow through on what had been set in place. Brooks's selection meant that the changes of the 1960s would be permanent: he pledged to stay the course, guided—as he frequently said—by the desire for academic excellence and the full ideals of the College's Catholic and Jesuit traditions. In his time, the challenge was not to invent a new Holy Cross but to assert its potential.

166. Trustees' minutes, December 4, 1971, ACHC, 11.0.

167. Faculty-Student Assembly minutes, March 29, 1971, ACHC, 14.12; *Crusader*, October 16, 1970 and October 8, 1971.

168. Swords to Hanify, April 28, 1970, ACHC, 11.0.

CHAPTER ELEVEN

Toward a History of the
Brooks Administration, 1970–1994

H ERE THIS HISTORY OF HOLY CROSS ends. The administration of John Brooks is too recent to be an appropriate subject of historical analysis. Yet, the book would be incomplete without a record of his presidency. By common agreement, Father Brooks followed through on the initiatives of the Swords years, leading the College in pursuit of the potential of its third age. His work in building the endowment, enhancing the physical plant, attending to faculty development and the selectivity of the student body, confronting the challenge of athleticism, combating discrimination, and securing a broadly accepted mission statement made Holy Cross substantially stronger. That record can be described, even though its closeness in time distorts the perspective. This account moves toward a history of an administration that is too recent to be historical and too important to be left out.

By the fall of 1972, Father Brooks had attended to the unfinished agenda of the Swords years, bringing the operating budget into balance, facilitating the transition to coeducation, and setting a policy for the athletic program. Beyond specific policies, his goal, as he stated frequently, was to make Holy Cross "the best undergraduate, Jesuit liberal arts college it can possibly be." Brooks had the breadth, experience, and temperament to act on his challenge. A graduate of the Boston Latin School, he entered Holy Cross in 1942, but left the same year to serve in the U.S. Army. He returned to the College after the war and graduated in 1949. After a year of graduate studies in geophysics at Penn State University, he entered the Society of Jesus. As a Jesuit scholastic, he taught mathematics and physics at his alma mater from 1954 to 1956. He was ordained to the priesthood in 1959, and afterwards studied theology at the

Gregorian University in Rome, where he earned an S.T.D.[1] The fourth successive alumnus in the College presidency, John Brooks brought to the job an intimate knowledge of the changes he had helped Raymond Swords to put in place.

Father Brooks had the advantage of beginning his work with a board of lay trustees who were dedicated to the school and accustomed to the fact that the Jesuits no longer held exclusive control. Until 1974, the board enjoyed the leadership of Charles Horgan, a popular alumnus whose wise counsel had eased the transition to separate incorporation. Horgan was succeeded by Donald P. Moriarty '52; Moriarty was followed by Charles E. F. Millard '54, in 1977.[2] In 1973, the board dropped the requirement of a Jesuit majority, a precaution undertaken to safeguard eligibility for federal and state funding. In 1975, the associate trustees, who had been meeting in conjunction with the board of trustees since 1969, were disbanded on their own initiative because their original purpose of serving as lay advisors to Jesuit trustees no longer existed.[3]

Among the new trustees elected during the 1970s, none was better known than the Washington trial lawyer Edward Bennett Williams '41. When Williams joined the board in 1976, he told Father Brooks, "I'll give you my very best on the condition that Holy Cross commit itself to excellence, to being the very best."[4] His comment described the tenor of his service to Holy Cross for the rest of his life. In 1977, he was elected vice-chairman; and, in 1982, he succeeded Charles Millard as chair. He wanted always to keep building, expanding, moving ahead. During his twelve years on the board, the College undertook its most ambitious building program since the 1920s. Williams's network of contacts brought a group of distinguished visitors to the campus: Ben Bradlee, Art Buchwald, Mario Cuomo, Helen Hayes, George Will, Eunice Kennedy Shriver, Sargent Shriver, Lane Kirkland, Joe DiMaggio, and Alexander Solzhenitsyn, among others. Beyond his leadership, he was a generous donor, and on his death from cancer in 1988 he left $2 million to the College. His generosity inspired trustees and other friends to establish the

1. *Crusader*, September 25, 1970.
2. *Crusader*, September 13, 1974, and September 16, 1977. Donald Moriarty was a partner in the New York investment firm William A. M. Burden & Co. Charles E. F. Millard was chief executive officer of Coca-Cola Bottling of New York, Inc.
3. The policy specified that "a reasonable number" of Jesuits would serve on the Board. Executive Committee minutes, February 5, 1973, and Trustees' minutes, May 5, 1973, ACHC, 12.25; trustees' minutes, May 5, 1972, and September 9, 1975, ACHC, 11.0.
4. Brooks address to faculty, October 4, 1988, ACHC, 14.12.

John E. Brooks, College President from 1970 to 1994, who worked successfully for fiscal solvency, greater social diversity, and an enhanced academic reputation. "I want Holy Cross to be the best Jesuit under- graduate liberal arts college it can possibly be," he frequently said.

Edward Bennett Williams Professorship in his memory.[5] Williams was succeeded by John P. Brogan '66, the last trustees' chair during the Brooks presidency.[6]

During the 1970s, Holy Cross survived economically, but the lack of a substantial endowment impeded progress somewhat. Between 1972 and 1975, in fact, the endowment dropped from $7.1 to $6.2 million (Chart 11.1). In 1973, Father Brooks secured the help of Father Francis X. Miller '46 as vice-president for development and college relations. Father Miller, who had been the College treasurer from 1961 to 1963, built up the program in annual giving. During his first year, alumni participation in the annual giving program rose to 33 per cent; alumni contributed $581,000 toward an annual Holy Cross Fund total of $1.3 million—the first time the fund topped one million dollars. In 1981, alumni giving passed 50 percent for the first time; between 1983 and 1994, the participation rate remained above 55 percent. In 1991, the total annual fund reached $6 million.[7] Under these circumstances, confidence grew. In 1979, when the total Holy Cross Fund topped $2 million for the first time, the trustees decided on a new capital fund campaign—the first since the failed

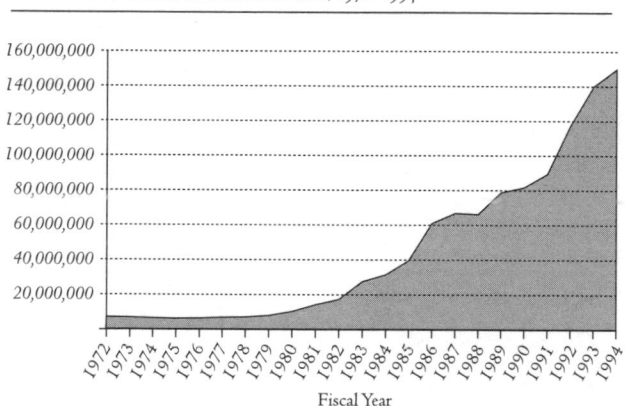

Chart 11.1 Endowment and Similar Funds, 1972–1994

Fiscal Year

5. Thomas, *The Man to See,* 388–89; Worcester *Telegram,* October 4, 1982; *Crossroads,* July/August 1989.

6. *Crossroads,* September/October 1988. John P. Brogan was president of The Brogan Company, a venture capital firm.

7. The Holy Cross Fund, 1948–1994, Development Office files; *Crusader,* February 2, 1973. In 1989, alumni giving reached a peak of 58 percent, a figure that placed Holy Cross among the top eleven institutions in the country in that category. 1990 reaccreditation self-study, ACHC, 14.12.

drive of the mid-1960s. Edward Bennett Williams was the national chairman; the goal was $20 million in new funds by 1983, including $14.5 million for the endowment. With good organization and excellent management, the drive surpassed its goal, raising almost $23 million. And the endowment, which stood at $7.9 million in 1979, rose to $27.7 million in 1983.[8]

The quest for capital endowment continued throughout the Brooks years. In addition to governmental grants of $2.4 million, the College received grants of $4.6 million from private sources. One of the most important, in terms of academic impact, was a challenge grant of $500,000 in 1982 from the Charles A. Dana Foundation to provide a restricted endowment for the support of a group of Dana Scholars, students required to give evidence of outstanding academic achievement, good character, and leadership.[9] The following year, challenge grants totaling $200,000 from the William and Flora Hewlett and the Andrew W. Mellon Foundations supported the creation of a presidential discretionary fund of $800,000, whose income is reserved for faculty and curriculum development. And in 1987, the Henry R. Luce Foundation provided $450,000 to establish the Luce Professorship in Religion, Economic Development, and Social Justice—a position filled in 1989 by Professor Diane Bell, an Australian scholar widely known for her work in Aboriginal studies. A further anonymous gift of over $1 million in 1989 funded the William H. P. Jenks Chair in English Literature.[10] By 1989, the endowment had risen to $79.9 million, a tenfold increase during a remarkably successful decade. As the final fund-raising effort of the Brooks years, the trustees initiated a new campaign in connection with the Holy Cross Sesquicentennial in 1993–94. Under the leadership of Charles E. F. Millard, the drive's goal was $60 million by June 30, 1994. The drive closed with a final figure of $76.6 million—27 per cent over the goal. By then, the endowment surpassed $150 million. Rising income allowed the College to balance the budget and even generate a surplus for the endowment in some years.[11]

8. Brooks reports to faculty, September 24, 1979, February 23, 1981, and September 26, 1983, reaccreditation self-study, 1980, ACHC, 14.12; Trustees' minutes, May 10, 1980, ACHC, 12.25.

9. In 1977, only fifteen colleges hosted Dana programs. Brooks report to Faculty-Student Assembly, September 27, 1982, and September 26, 1983, 1990 reaccreditation self-study, ACHC, 14.12.

10. Trustees' minutes, December 10, 1983, ACHC, 12.25; Brooks reports to faculty, September 23, 1985, September 23, 1986, and October 6, 1987; 1990 reaccreditation self-study, ACHC, 14.12; *Crusader*, January 27, 1989.

11. The 1990 self-study noted an annual operating surplus of 10 percent at the end of the 1980s as a source of revenue for the endowment. ACHC, 14.12.

Chart 11.2 Operating Budget, 1972–1994

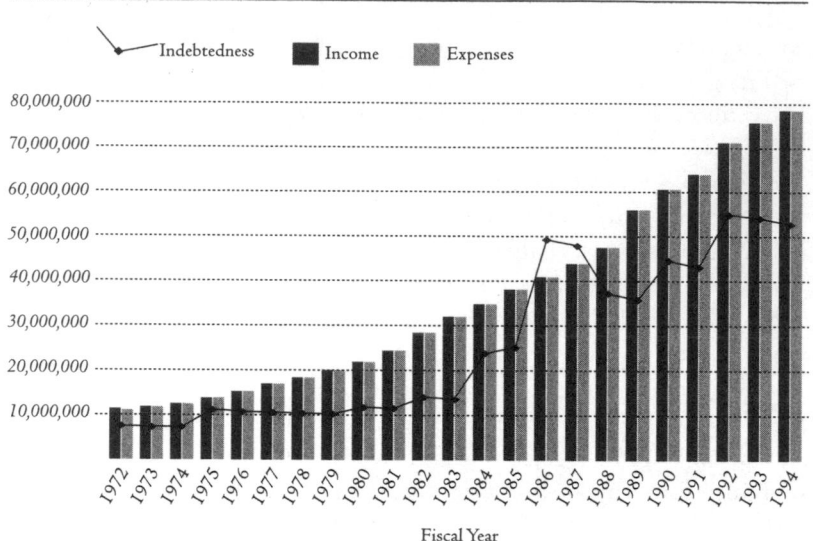

Fiscal Year

Despite the dramatic improvement, fiscal assets still lagged behind those of other highly rated Eastern colleges. College Treasurer William P. Durgin noted in 1991 that the endowment came to about $30,000 per student, whereas schools like Amherst and Harvard had up to $160,000 per student. In that year, the actual cost of educating a Holy Cross student was over $26,700, while tuition and room and board supplied $20,900. The difference was supplied from endowment income and gifts to the College. Debt service to finance the ambitious building program was also comparatively high (Chart 11.2).[12] These circumstances persuaded administrators and trustees that a larger endowment was essential. Meanwhile, tuition continued to be the major source of revenue, a source College authorities needed to exploit. Tuition and room and board charges rose quickly: to $10,000 in 1983, and $20,000 in 1991. By 1993, the figure stood at $23,500 (Chart 11.3).

Additional tuition revenue was offset, however, by the need to provide more funding for student aid, especially after the adoption of a need-blind admissions policy in 1986 committed the College to supply the full financial need of every admitted student through a package of grants, work/study funding, and student loans (Chart 9.3). Even so, hard-pressed parents and students pointed to the fact that college expenses tended to run ahead of the in-

12. *Crusader*, February 17, 1989, and November 8, 1991.

flation rate (Chart 11.4). College representatives responded that they had no alternative if they wanted to offer competitive salaries, support necessary maintenance and building programs, and come to terms with reduced federal funding.[13] By the 1990s, the cost of private education was forcing administrators to limit further tuition increases as they searched for ways to sustain the school without pricing it beyond the means of consumers.

The fund-raising efforts sustained an extensive building program. The first priority fell to the long-delayed athletic facility. With the recommendations of the Arthur D. Little study on the table, the trustees gave preliminary approval in 1973 for a recreational building adjacent to the fieldhouse, running downhill along College Street, with an arena and swimming pool.[14] Then, as had happened so often in the past, plans for an athletic facility encountered difficulty. When cutbacks in support for the Department of Housing and Urban Development precluded federal funding, College representatives attempted to raise private funds for the project; but results were disappointing. Although these circumstances forced a delay, the situation was a blessing in disguise.[15] The year that was lost in acquiring a recreation center was well spent in re-thinking the facility's features and location.

An important initiative came from students who suggested substituting a

Chart 11.3 Tuition, Room and Board Costs, 1971–1993

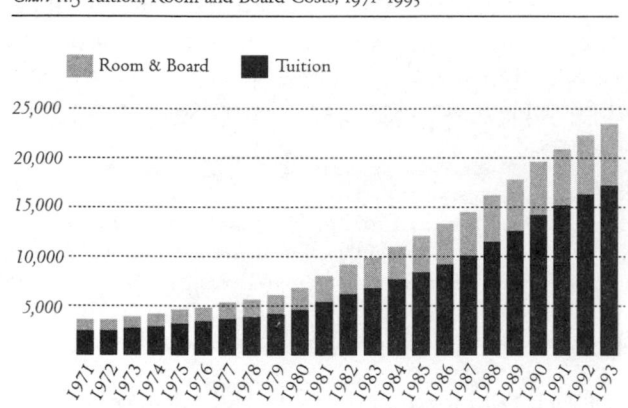

13. These justifications were cited by Father Brooks in 1987. *Crusader*, February 27, 1987.

14. Memo of John Brooks, January 22, 1973, ACHC, 16.1B; Worcester *Gazette*, January 23, 1973.

15. Executive Committee minutes, February 5, 1973, ACHC, 12.25; Trustees' minutes, May 5, 1973 ACHC, 16.1B; Worcester *Telegram*, May 6, 1973.

Chart 11.4 Tuition, Room and Board Increases vs. Inflation Rate, 1961–1991

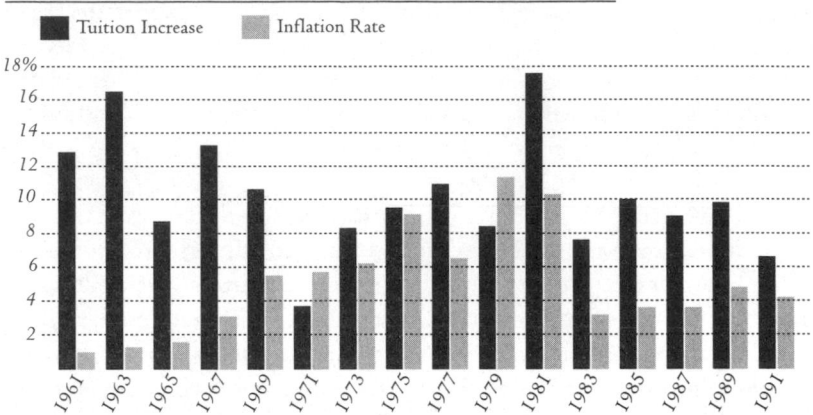

hockey rink for the swimming pool. A student poll endorsed the concept; Patrick Butler '76 and James Longley '74 made a formal presentation to the trustees' Executive Committee. The popularity of the idea, and the practical consideration that ice rental would help meet the operating costs of the building, eventually prevailed. Meanwhile, a planning committee recommended placing the facility at the top of the hill, near the athletic fields.[16] Finally, in 1974, the Trustees adopted plans for a recreational facility incorporating a basketball arena with seating for 3500, and a hockey rink seating about 950. Revenue bonds financed through the Massachusetts Health and Educational Facilities Authority (HEFA), supported the project.[17] As construction was underway, the Trustees voted to name the building for Father Francis Hart, long-time director of intramural athletics.[18] The Hart Recreation Center opened on December 1, 1975.

16. David F. Farrell, Jr., to Brooks, March 12, 1973, Brooks notes in Executive Committee Meeting, July 17, 1973, and Brooks to John J. Cummings, Jr., August 28, 1973, ACHC, 11.0; James B. Longley, Jr. and Patrick Butler to Brooks, May 18, 1973, Executive Committee Minutes, June 12, 1973, ACHC, 12.25; J. Leo Sullivan to John Cummings, October 19, 1973, and Minutes of Ad Hoc Committee on Recreational Facilities, October 30 and November 10, 1973, ACHC, 11.0.

17. Barbara Green to William L. Kelleher, September 11, 1974, HEFA Revenue Bond statement, October 23, 1974, Trustees' minutes, December 8, 1973, and May 4, 1974, Trustees' Executive Committee minutes, September 10, 1974, ACHC, 12.25; Worcester *Telegram*, May 6, 1974.

18. Brooks notes on meeting with Paul McMaster, Athletic Council Chair, December 28, 1971, Executive Committee minutes, October 17, 1974, ACHC, 12.25; Worcester *Telegram*, December 8, 1974. Father Hart's motives for accepting the recognition are a matter of conjec-

While the Hart Center was under construction, the trustees authorized a study on the feasibility of expanding the Dinand Library. The report confirmed that the building was operating at capacity with 330,000 volumes and no space for expansion. To address the need, library architect Paul Peng-Chen Sun was commissioned to prepare plans "to provide functional and efficiently used space and increase the library capacities to modern college library standards." Working with the Library Committee, he drew up an imaginative design with "two basically underground skylit rooms closely attached to each side of the present reading room ell."[19] The final plan, costing about $2.85 million, also altered existing space for administrative services, the reserve room, the archives, and a new circulation desk.[20] Among the trustees, the addition had no more enthusiastic supporter than Jacob Hiatt, who promoted the project and contributed generously to it.[21] Nevertheless, Hiatt was surprised when Father Brooks announced that the building would be dedicated to the memory of his parents and the other victims of the Holocaust, as an affirmation of the College's commitment to teach the young about justice and the importance of moral choices. Brooks also announced that the library would henceforth house "a special collection of books and reference materials on the Holocaust."[22] The Joshua and Leah Hiatt Wings in Memory of the Vic-

ture. In 1967, the trustees voted to name the fieldhouse in his honor, but Hart refused. [Trustees' minutes, August 31 and November 15, 1967, ACHC, 11.0.] In 1974, he seemed more compliant. The trustees may have acted without giving him an opportunity to veto the idea, or (as some pundits have impishly suggested) he may have been holding out for a better building.

19. Trustees' Executive Committee minutes, November 14, 1974, and Trustees' minutes, September 9, 1975, ACHC, 12.25; Library Feasibility Survey, June 1975, preliminary library design, April 7, 1976, and a brochure, "The Dinand Library Tomorrow" [1977], ACHC, 16.1B-1; Boston *Globe*, December 10, 1986. Sun was associated with Shepley, Bulfinch, Richardson and Abbott in Boston.

20. Brooks notes for trustees' meeting, May 7, 1977, ACHC, 12.25; *Crossroads*, May/June 1977. As construction was underway, the College received additional funding in the form of a challenge grant of $150,000 from the Kresge Foundation and a grant of $225,000 from the National Endowment for the Humanities. Unidentified press clipping, September 8, 1978, and Worcester *Gazette*, October 21, 1978, ACHC, 16.1B.

21. Trustees' minutes, September 14, 1976, cited in a letter to Hiatt from Barbara Green, March 7, 1979, ACHC, 16.1B; personal interview, Francis X. Miller, December 18, 1995.

22. Press release, February 7, 1979, and Brooks memo of a phone conversation with Donald Campion, March 12, 1979, ACHC, 16.1B; Worcester *Gazette*, February 7, 1979; *Crossroads*, May/June 1979. Both of Hiatt's parents and thirty other family members perished in the Holocaust. Brooks to Bishop Flanagan [1979]. ACHC, 16.1B. During the Brooks years, the Coordinator of the Holocaust Collection was Vincent A. Lapomarda, S.J.

tims of the Holocaust were dedicated in May 1979. Among the speakers, Holocaust author Elie Wiesel described the importance of libraries to foster remembrance: "Nothing can be more urgent for our generation than to remember those days. Not to remember would turn us into accomplices of the killers."[23]

To maintain momentum, the trustees drafted a strategy for further expansion of the physical plant: a new science building connecting O'Neil and Haberlin Halls, and an addition to the Hart Center. Both plans were made public in 1981. Cost estimates came to $3.5 million for the Hart Center addition, $7.5 million for the new science building.[24] Quickly, plans were drawn up to expand the Hart Center by adding an Olympic-sized swimming pool, a rowing tank, locker and physical therapy rooms, and squash and handball courts. Efficient management by the Perini Corporation reduced the building's cost to $3.1 million. The addition opened in January 1983. Four years later, the facility was enhanced by grading the top of the hill to create a series of athletic fields, one of which was surfaced with artificial turf and a rubberized running track.[25]

Site preparation for the science building started in 1983. The need to provide structural reinforcement to Haberlin Hall added to the expense of the project, whose final cost, with furnishings, was $10.5 million. The new building housed the Department of Mathematics and allowed for the expansion of facilities for the Biology Department. The building also housed classrooms, a computer library, laboratories, a greenhouse, and a new science library, and featured a courtyard entrance and atriums on both sides, where it was joined to O'Neil and Haberlin.[26] At the request of faculty, alumni, and friends, the building was named for Raymond Swords and dedicated in 1985.[27]

23. Dedication materials, May 11, 1979, ACHC, 16.1B.

24. Executive Committee minutes, October 31, 1980, trustees' minutes, December 12, 1980, and December 12, 1981, ACHC, 12.25.

25. Funds for the Hart Center expansion were raised mostly through a HEFA bond issue of $3 million. Brooks to David Perini, March 6, 1981, John Perry to Perini, March 31, 1981, Frank Cariglia to Brooks, Framingham, May 4, 1983, ACHC, 12.25; Worcester *Gazette*, January 5, 1983; *Crossroads*, January/February 1983 and March/April 1987. The addition was designed by John Orcutt of Sasaki Associates of Watertown.

26. Swords Hall was designed by Shepley, Bulfinch, Richardson and Abbot. Brooks's notes on science building, September 7, 1983, Frank Cariglia to Brooks, Framingham, April 26, 1985; ACHC, 12.25; James Ford Clapp Jr., "A Science Center for the College of the Holy Cross," [1983], press release, April 25, 1985, ACHC, 16.1B; Brooks report to faculty, September 26, 1983, 1980 reaccreditation self-study, ACHC, 14.12.

27. Brooks report to faculty, September 24, 1984, ACHC, 14.12; *Crossroads*, May/June 1985.

Shortly after the dedication of Swords Hall, Father Brooks announced that the College would build a new office and classroom building, convert the classroom and office space on the lower floors of Carlin and Alumni Halls into student residential suites, and renovate the wooden stands in Fitton Field. The new building was located on the parking lot west of Carlin Hall and had a T-shaped design that harmonized with the surrounding buildings. Constructed at a cost of $8 million, it incorporated 35 classrooms and offices for the Departments of Economics, Modern Languages and Literature, and Religious Studies.[28] The structure was named Edith Stein Hall in memory of a German, Jewish-born woman who converted to Catholicism and became a Carmelite nun, established a strong reputation as a philosopher, and perished at Auschwitz in 1942. Edith Stein Hall opened in January of 1988.[29] Once the three academic departments had been relocated, the two lower floors of Carlin and Alumni Halls were converted to multiple-bedroom suites.[30] The Fitton Field renovation, the third part of the 1985 initiative, was completed in 1985 and 1986 at a cost of about $3.6 million. The old wooden seats were replaced with aluminum plank seats and stands were added at the northeast corner to complete the horseshoe pattern and allow for the removal of bleacher seats behind the west goal post. The renovated stadium had seating for 22,242 spectators.[31]

Among the renovations to the physical plant, several were geared toward the enhancement of the fine arts. The old O'Kane parlor and switchboard area was converted in 1983 into an art gallery through the benefaction of Iris and B. Gerald Cantor, philanthropists and collectors of sculpture and paintings, especially the works of Auguste Rodin. In 1979, sculptor Enzo Plazzotta and his patron B. Gerald Cantor, formally presented *The Hand Of Christ*, which graces the stairs of Dinand Library. The following year, the College received castings of Rodin's bust *Benedict XV* and *The Head of John the Baptist* for the library foyer. The Iris and B. Gerald Cantor Art Gallery was opened in October of 1983 with an exhibit featuring 31 bronze sculptures by Rodin, including the monumental figure of Eustache de S. Pierre from *The Burghers of Calais*. In 1985, the latter fig-

28. Brooks address to faculty, September 23, 1985, ACHC, 14.12; press release, June 2, 1986, ACHC, 16.1B.

29. Brooks address to faculty, September 23, 1986, ACHC, 14,12; *Crossroads*, May/June 1986 and January/February, 1988. On Edith Stein, see Waltrud Herbstrith, *Edith Stein, A Biography*, trans. Bernard Bonowitz (San Francisco: Harper and Row, 1985).

30. *Crusader*, January 29, 1988, and February 3, 1989; *Purple Patcher*, 1988.

31. Perini Company status report, March, 1986, ACHC, 12.25; *Perini News*, July/August 1986, ACHC, 16.1B. Evan Thomas reported that oilman Marvin Davis contributed $300,000 toward the Fitton Field renovation. Williams was Davis's attorney for the purchase of Twentieth Century Fox in 1981. *The Man to See*, 378–80.

The central part of the campus about 1990. Compare with photo on page 249 for a sense of the physical expansion since 1925.

ure was given permanently to Holy Cross.[32] Fine arts received an additional boost with the replacement of the chapel's original Cassavant organ. In 1980, following the recommendation of organist James David Christie, the College contracted for a new tracker organ with the Taylor and Boody Company of Virginia. Containing 3814 pipes, the new instrument followed the style of Dutch and North German organs of the seventeenth century and exceeded $400,000 in cost. The organ was dedicated in March of 1986; by then, extensive renovations had restored the chapel's original lighting and painting.[33]

32. Trustees' minutes, December 8, 1979, and September 9, 1980, and Brooks to Ellen Lawrence, April 18, 1985, ACHC, 12.25; *Crossroads*, September/October 1979; *Crusader*, October 22, 1982.

33. Executive Committee minutes, September 4, 1980, ACHC, 12.25; Brooks report to faculty/student assembly, September 26, 1983, ACHC, 14.12; Worcester *Telegram*, March 10, 1993. See also the feature article in *The American Organist* 19 (March 1985).

The last major building effort during the Brooks years was finalized in 1989, when the College arranged a $10 million bond issue to cover several large projects. A new residence with 34 bedrooms, named Ciampi Hall, was built for the Jesuit community on College-owned property adjacent to the campus on City View Street. After the Jesuits vacated Loyola Hall, it was converted to student housing. Beaven Hall, meanwhile, was converted to offices, classrooms, and laboratories for the Departments of Psychology and Sociology. Other projects included a renovation of the upper floors of Carlin and Alumni halls into three-room suites, and a major renovation of Kimball Hall.[34] At the same time, the wooden Air Force ROTC building and the maintenance shed behind it were converted into a facility for studio art. The completed project was dedicated in May of 1993 as the Millard Art Center, in memory of Rev. Daniel Millard '47, the brother of Charles E. F. Millard.[35] A further renovation converted the old Fenwick chapel into a concert and convocation hall. The project was completed in 1994 and named in recognition of Father Brooks.[36]

Physically enhanced during the Brooks years, the campus still fostered a quality of student life that tended to justify the claims of individual attention that were emphasized in the promotional literature. Beyond the contact with members of the faculty, administration, and staff, students bonded with each other and their alma mater through campus activities. Varsity and intramural athletics continued to engage a large proportion of students. Publications, student government, religious activities, and SPUD (Student Programs for Urban Development, a community outreach program) also attracted large numbers.[37] Self-studies in 1980 and 1990 disclosed that about 20 percent of students were involved in SPUD activities, and a significant number participated in the Committee for Campus Ministry. Student government was re-organized in 1975, when the Inter-House Council was succeeded by the Student Government Association (SGA), a group that incorporated a larger number of student representatives and held the power of voting appropriations to various student organizations from the student activities fee.[38] *The Crusader* gained

34. Worcester *Telegram and Gazette*, July 13, 1989; Brooks report to faculty, September 26, 1989, ACHC, 14.12.; *Crusader*, September 11, 1992. The bond issue was floated through the Massachusetts Industrial Finance Agency

35. Brooks report to faculty, September 25, 1990, ACHC, 14.12. A copy of Father Millard's obituary, carried by the Patterson *Morning News*, May 30, 1973, may be found in ACHC, 16.1B.

36. Funding came through a $500,000 challenge grant from the Davis Educational Foundation. Brooks report to faculty, September 24, 1991, ACHC, 14.12; *Crusader*, September 27, 1991.

37. Nicholson, "A Legacy in Transition," 107; unrevised MS, Chart 11.5.

38. Funding decisions sometimes generated controversy. In 1991, for instance, the SGA voted (26-19) to recognize the Pro-Choice campus group; but the administration exercised its

a campus rival in December 1989 with the appearance of a privately funded journal of conservative opinion, *The Fenwick Review*. Founding co-editors-in-chief Kevin S. O'Scannlain '92 and Paul D. Scalia '92 expressed their determination "to publish a journal of opinion, in which we hope to provoke intellectual discussion and stimulate ideas."

Within the office of the dean of students, drinking and alcohol abuse, a reflection of the national student culture, remained a constant concern. After the legal drinking age was lowered to 18 in 1973, bars sprouted in the residence hall social rooms as a source of revenue for social activities sponsored by dormitory councils. A campus pub opened in space formerly occupied by bowling alleys in the Hogan Center and became another focus of social life. In 1977, the state government began to enforce license laws more strictly, forcing closure of the social room bars. Gradually, the drinking age was raised—to 20 in 1979, and 21 in 1985. The reduced number of students legally able to patronize the campus pub prompted school authorities to relocate it to a smaller space and install a pizza parlor in the vacated area. It fell to Father Earle Markey, who was appointed associate dean of students in 1976 and dean of students in 1979, to come to terms with students' use of alcohol. Among the solutions was the introduction in 1981 of student alcohol advisors as peer counselors in the residence halls.[39]

By then, the practice of having Jesuits live on residence hall corridors as chaplains and prefects had largely been abandoned. A new model of Jesuit presence was developed at Campion House, which became the chaplain's residence in 1971, when Father Robert E. Manning was appointed College chaplain. Manning lived with two other Jesuits on the second floor; downstairs rooms were open for meetings and quiet study. When Manning became community rector in 1983, Father Michael Boughton succeeded him as head chaplain. Ten years later, Kathryn McElaney '76, who had worked in the Chaplains' office since 1985, was appointed director of the office of college chaplains. During these years, the

---

prerogative to deny recognition. Father Brooks asserted that Holy Cross "wishes publicly to affirm and bear witness to Catholic Christianity's longstanding insight that all of human life is sacred in the mystery of its origins and that abortion thus cannot be condoned." The group was allowed to meet on campus, but was ruled ineligible for College funding. *Crusader*, April 18, 1975, and December 5, 1986; Worcester *Telegram and Gazette*, May 4, 1991; Boston *Globe*, December 5, 1991.

39. Cahill, *Women on the Hill*, 102–3; *Crusader*, February 16, 1973, and September 26, 1986; *Crossroads*, May/June 1976 and May/June 1979; 1980 reaccreditation self-study, ACHC, 14.12; Dean of Students Office, "The Student Alcohol Advisor Program: History, Philosophy Evaluation" [1996].

Chart 11.5 Student Origins, 1947–1990

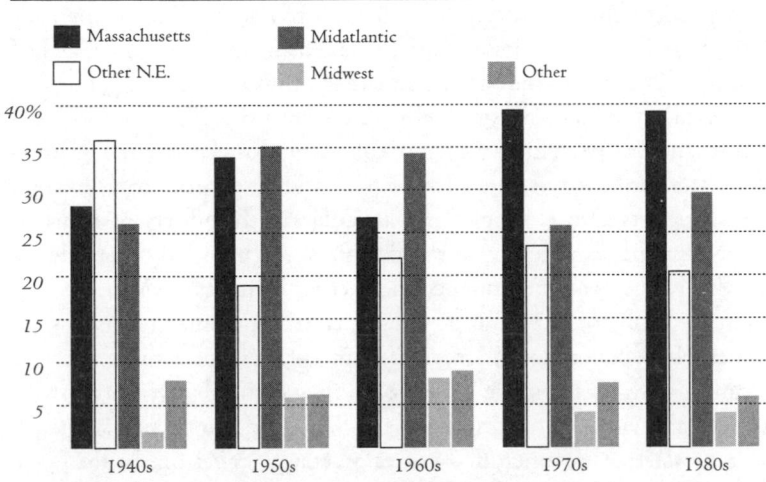

chaplains sponsored service projects to Appalachia during the spring recess and an annual consciousness-raising program in Latin America in June. The retreat program retained its strength through the efforts of Father Joseph LaBran, who took students to Gloucester and later to Narragansett, Rhode Island, for a silent five-day adaptation of the Spiritual Exercises of Ignatius of Loyola. By the 1990s, as many as 250 students were making the Narragansett retreats each year, in addition to those availing themselves of shorter retreats and spiritual direction. Meanwhile, Campion House was modified in 1989 by incorporating the first-floor rooms into the residence; afterwards, as many as seven Jesuits (including chaplains) could live there and share in pastoral work.[40]

During the Brooks years, College authorities endeavored to enhance diversity within the student body. Inevitably, the Admissions Office was more successful in some categories than in others. Data sampling shows a remarkable continuity in the geographic origins of the students throughout the postwar era (Chart 11.5). Well over half of the students came from the New England states; nearly 40 percent traced origins to Massachusetts in the samples from the 1970s and 1980s. Holy Cross also remained an attractive option for students from the Mid-Atlantic states.[41]

40. Personal interviews, Kathryn McElaney, February 29, 1996, and Robert Manning, March 1, 1996.

41. In 1989, 37 percent of students were from Massachusetts; 19 percent from New York State; and 10.5 percent from Connecticut. 1990 reaccreditation self-study, ACHC, 14.12.

Gender diversity was guaranteed by the decision for coeducation, but questions of gender equality proved more difficult to address. The women admitted in the fall of 1972 as transfer students and as members of the Class of 1976 constituted about 10 percent of the student body. Over the years, the percentage of female students rose gradually, until, with the Class of 1984, the proportion reached 50 percent—a ratio deliberately fostered by the Admissions Office afterwards. Adjustment issues were addressed primarily through the Dean of Students Office, thanks, in particular, to the efforts of Marilyn Boucher. But gender bias inherent in the culture sometimes led to problems. To address this reality, women students and faculty formed the Women's Organization in the spring of 1973, "to provide an arena for women to discuss . . . campus issues which concerned them," and to integrate women more successfully into campus life. To promote those goals, they focused attention on sexual harassment and violence, promoted the use of gender-inclusive language, and issued a newsletter that included essays, poetry, and fiction. In 1984, the name was changed to the Women's Forum.[42]

Gradually, women achieved recognition and leadership. In 1974, Joan Sinopoli '76 was elected *Crusader* editor. The following year, Mabel L. Lang, a renowned classicist at Bryn Mawr College, became the first female commencement speaker. In 1976, Jane M. Hawkins became the first woman valedictorian; in 1980, Ann Gallagher '81 became the first woman to head the Student Government Association.[43] The number of women on the faculty and administration also grew. In 1974, Sister Anna Marie Kane, S.S.J., became the first woman chaplain, and Professor Caren Dubnoff of the Political Science Department became the first woman to chair an academic department. Slow turnover made gender equality on the faculty a long process. In 1972 women comprised five percent of the total; by the early 1990s, they accounted for about one-third. In 1990, Professor Victoria L. Swigert (Sociology) became the first woman appointed an assistant dean.[44]

Women's athletics posed another set of issues. Given the College's strong tradition in men's sports, the lopsided gender ratio before 1983, and the limited space for practice and team sports before the opening of the Hart Center, women's sports advanced slowly. During the first year of coeducation, the College sponsored nine activities for women, ranging from modern dance to

42. Cahill, *Women on the Hill*, 29–30, 150–53. Graphs depicting student gender ratios are on p. 28.

43. Worcester *Telegram*, November 23, 1974; *Crossroads*, March/April 1975 and May/June 1976; *Crusader*, April 25, 1980.

44. Cahill, *Women on the Hill*, 56–58; *Crossroads*, September/October 1974 and March/April 1987.

track and crew. In 1973, a part-time coordinator of women's athletics was hired. By 1976, intercollegiate teams were being fielded in basketball, crew, fencing, field hockey, tennis, track, volleyball and swimming. Although the number of teams and coaches gradually expanded, women pressed for new sports, access to practice facilities, and even uniforms.[45] The picture brightened after 1975, when Title IX of the 1972 federal civil rights law was interpreted as a mandate for equal athletic opportunities at schools receiving federal funding. At Holy Cross, the legislation prompted the introduction of athletic scholarships for female basketball players, whose program was upgraded from Division III to Division II in the fall of 1980, and to Division I in 1982.[46]

In 1980, Father Brooks implemented a request of the Faculty-Student Assembly to appoint an Ad Hoc Committee on the Status of Women at Holy Cross.[47] The committee of eight women included students, faculty and administrators. Meeting from 1980 to 1984, members designed or strengthened policies covering gender-inclusive language, maternity leave, and sexual harassment. In 1984, the group was replaced by a new standing Committee on Social Concerns. Despite such manifest progress, occasional episodes of violence necessitated decisive responses that included the installation of a new and effective campus security system in 1988.[48] Coeducation transformed the campus in positive ways. To recognize that fact, a ten-year celebration in 1982 featured a talk by Gloria Steinem. Ten years later, alumnae returned to campus for a weekend celebration co-ordinated by Luce Professor Diane Bell.[49]

Equality issues extended to race as well as gender. At Holy Cross, women students had reached numerical equality by 1983. For African-Americans and other minorities, the issue of campus diversity proved more difficult. Fall enrollment statistics show the pattern, and the problem (Chart 11.6). The proportion of African-American students peaked in 1972 at less than five percent;

45. Ronald Perry to Brooks, October 4, 1972, Brooks notes on conference with Perry, February 19, 1975, ACHC, 12.25; Cahill, *Women on the Hill*, 114–15.

46. Cahill, *Women on the Hill*, 120–24; Women's Basketball Media Guide, 1994–95. On Title IX, see John R. Thelin, *Games Colleges Play: Scandal and Reform in Intercollegiate Athletics* (Baltimore: The Johns Hopkins University Press, 1994), 171, 193–94.

47. Presenting the motion, Professor Theresa McBride (History) stated: "We're very concerned that we begin to open up discussion now, eight years after co-education, to talk about whether or not women really are considered a vital part of the College and its life." Minutes of Faculty-Student Assembly, April 28, 1980, ACHC, 14.12.

48. Brooks memo on Ad Hoc Committee on the Status of Women [spring 1980], ACHC, 12.25; Cahill, *Women on the Hill*, 140–41, 153–59; minutes of Faculty-Student Assembly, February 23, 1981, and February 22, 1982, ACHC, 14.12.

49. *Crossroads*, January/February 1982 and January/February 1993.

thereafter, successive waves that crested in 1980 and 1991 fell short of that number. In the spring of 1976, Black Students' Advisor and Sociology Professor Ogretta McNeil called the attention of the Faculty-Student Assembly to the fact that, despite the 1972 resolution mandating an increase in the number of minority students and faculty, the number of African-American students was decreasing.[50] In fact, Holy Cross had to compete with wealthier schools that could offer more attractive financial aid packages to successful applicants; and the very size of the African-American group on campus became itself an issue in attracting new students. Between 1976 and 1978, members of the Black Student Union adopted a more assertive stance concerning student recruitment, hirings in the faculty and administration, and representation on student committees. This activism engendered a backlash among some students and the situation became volatile. In response, the trustees added Ted Wells to the board in 1976; and in 1977, Father Brooks addressed a letter to the campus community, insisting that recent campus tensions had been "deeply rooted in racism," a phenomenon he characterized as "the most destructive sin." As a remedy, he challenged the community to open-hearted acceptance of all members of the human family. Brooks also took steps to foster recruitment of black faculty, to hire a black admissions counselor, and to add funding for the BSU.[51]

Chart 11.6 Fall Minority Enrollments, 1967–1993

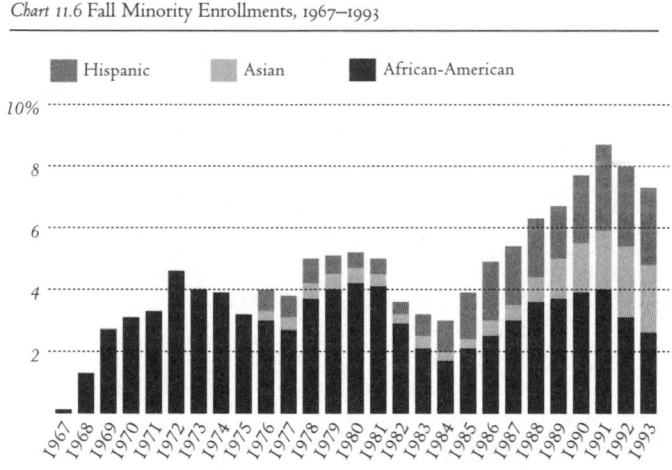

50. Minutes of Faculty-Student Assembly, April 29, 1972, ACHC, 14.12.

51. Trustees' minutes, December 4, 1976, May 7, 1977, Brooks to Trustees, September 13, 1977, Executive Committee minutes, March 16, 1977, and June 1, 1977, Brooks to Holy Cross Community, September 1977, ACHC, 12.25; *Crusader*, 1976–78.

The advantages of diversity: minority students and women have immeasurably expanded the potential of the College in its third age.

In the ensuing years, two episodes challenged the campus community to growth in racial solidarity. The first involved members of the men's basketball team and started with a fight at a practice near the end of December 1985. Ron Perry mediated the situation, but the case generated publicity and gave rise to a demonstration after students returned to campus.[52] The second incident oc-

52. Alleging discriminatory treatment from Coach George Blaney and racist behavior on the part of some players, four black players left the team. The charges were denied by other players and by the black student manager. Two of the protesting players were dismissed from the team but retained their scholarships to the end of the academic year. The other two were invited back. Perry to Brooks, January 10, 1985, Brooks notes, January 16, 1985, and Blaney to Brooks, January 24, 1985, ACHC, 12.25; Worcester *Gazette*, January 3, 1985; New York *Times*,

curred in May of 1992, when two black students found on their answering machine an obscene message threatening violence. Responding in a strong letter, Father Markey invited the campus community to an open discussion with members of the administration.[53] In addition to a formal session in the Hogan Center ballroom, informal discussions gave students an unanticipated opportunity to promote understanding across racial lines. The issue was addressed again the following September in a convocation featuring addresses from Trustees Theodore Wells and Katherine McCarthy on racial and gender discrimination. At the same time, Father Brooks set up a new Task Force on Race and Gender to advise him on diversity and violence on campus, and on effective responses to racist and sexist acts.[54]

The presence of Latin American and Asian minority groups presented additional opportunities and challenges. Campus authorities began charting those groups in the fall of 1976, when both represented small but stable minorities (Chart 11.6). During the mid 1980s, the number of Hispanic students started to rise; five years later, the number of Asian students began to show a similar increase. During the 1991–92 academic year, both groups gained formal recognition and eligibility for funding—the Latin American Students' Organization (LASO), and All Students Interested in Asia (ASIA). To support these and other groups, Thomas Stokes moved from the Admissions Office to become assistant dean and director of multicultural affairs, with the responsibility to promote cultural diversity and to help recruit, retain, and assimilate minority students.[55] If nothing else, a quarter century of experience made clear that the College was vulnerable to larger social problems concerning race and gender; the response had to be strong, consistent, and periodically renewed.

Integrity and balance of another sort were at stake as College officials continued the effort to harmonize the school's athletic tradition with the realities of college sports in the television age. Analyst John Thelin has called varsity athletics the "peculiar institution" of American higher education, an area that has constantly challenged presidents to sustain institutional integrity. Sum-

---

January 6, 1985; *Crusader*, January 25, 1985. See also Perry's chronology of the episode, ACHC, 12.25.

53. Markey to the Holy Cross Community, May 1992, DOS file, ACHC, 15.0.

54. Brooks to Holy Cross Faculty, September 29, 1992, ACHC, 14.12; *Crusader*, September 11, 1992.

55. *Crusader*, February 7 and November 20, 1992; Peter Simonds, personal interview, February 20, 1996.

marizing four major efforts to reform intercollegiate sports between 1929 and 1991, Thelin found constant elements: the importance of varsity athletics in the college experience, the ideal of the student-athlete, the mentoring role of coaches, presidential direction of the athletic program, a refusal of commercialization, and avoidance of excess in recruitment and special privileges for athletes.[56] During his presidency, John Brooks attempted to keep Holy Cross aligned with these priorities.

Because of its high profile and problems associated with scheduling, football drew the first attention. After Holy Cross joined the Yankee Conference in 1971, Father Brooks attempted to follow through on a point of attraction, a commitment to move toward need-based athletic scholarships. He raised the matter with Yankee Conference presidents in 1971; but opposition surfaced at several of the conference's state universities. The difficulty of reconciling the Yankee Conference schedule with Holy Cross's long-standing football and basketball series with Ivy League schools raised a further difficulty.[57] In September of 1972, the Athletic Council endorsed resignation from the conference; after confirming the extent of opposition to need-based athletic grants-in-aid, Father Brooks withdrew from the Yankee Conference in October, after an affiliation of eighteen months.[58] To an alumnus who inquired about his policies, Father Brooks responded: "I strongly support a modest football program which fully respects the academic priorities of Holy Cross."[59]

Departure from the Yankee Conference placed Holy Cross again in the ranks of independent schools, a position that required continuation of athletic scholarships for the sake of balanced competition. Nevertheless, in 1975, Father Brooks directed that the number of athletic scholarships be reduced from 110 to 102 over a three-year period. In 1978, as a response to Title IX regulations, athletic scholarships were dropped in the non-revenue sports of track and baseball.[60] These cuts left the football program relatively untouched,

56. Thelin, *Games Colleges Play*, 1–2, 197.

57. Brooks notes on meeting with Yankee Conference representatives, February 27, 1971, minutes of Yankee Conference presidents, June 18, 1971, Brooks to Adolph Samborski, June 28, 1971, Brooks notes on conversations with Yankee Conference presidents, March 30, 1972, Perry to Brooks, May 30, 1972, ACHC, 12.25.

58. Perry to Brooks, July 24, 1972, Athletic Council minutes, September 13, 1972, Thomas Bonner to Brooks, Durham, NH, September 21, 1972, and Brooks to Bonner, November 13, 1972, ACHC, 12.25. Brooks's letter of resignation to Yankee Conference presidents was dated October 31.

59. Brooks to Frank A. Kelley '70, February 23, 1973, ACHC, 12.25.

60. Brooks to Perry, January 28, 1975, Christian Ciabotti '80 and Mary Noonan '80 to Perry, October 3, 1977, ACHC, 12.25; *Crusader*, February 17, 1988.

but struggling nevertheless to achieve a winning record. In November of 1975, Coach Ed Doherty resigned after a 1–10 season and a five-year record of 20–31–2. Doherty was succeeded by Neil Wheelwright, whose teams achieved back-to-back wins over Boston College in 1977 and 1978, the Crusaders' last victories in the series. He was relieved of his duties after a 3–8 season in 1980, having compiled a record of 20–35. Rick Carter, 1980 Coach of the Year for his work with the national championship team at the University of Dayton, succeeded Wheelwright and turned the program around during his first two years.[61] Meanwhile, the scene in intercollegiate football was changing rapidly. In 1981, 62 universities with large football programs formed the College Football Association to gain priority for their programs and, eventually, to negotiate an exclusive television package. The possibility of their withdrawal from the NCAA prompted the organization to divide football programs into two divisions, designated I-A and I-AA, depending on stadium size and average attendance. In 1983, the Crusaders qualified for the Division I-AA playoffs.[62]

In basketball, Father Brooks and Ron Perry discussed the possibility of affiliation with the nascent Big East Conference in 1979. Brooks was wary because of his conviction that other member schools would have a lower academic threshold for athletes. A year later, an invitation to join the Metro Atlantic Athletic Conference (MAAC) was also rejected when Brooks argued that the proliferation of leagues was partly a device to gain shares of revenue from the NCAA Tournament, whereas using sports for revenue was a goal he rejected for Holy Cross.[63] By 1982, however, the proliferation of leagues was creating scheduling difficulties; in 1983 Holy Cross joined the MAAC after all, because, as Ron Perry expressed it, there was an "absolute necessity of conference affiliation in collegiate basketball."[64]

League affiliation for football was also in the wind by then. In the fall of 1981, Dartmouth's athletic director inquired informally whether Holy Cross would be interested in Ivy League membership. Father Brooks and several trustees, including Edward Bennett Williams, Charles E. F. Millard, and Eunice Shriver, pursued the possibility through their networks of contacts.[65]

61. 1995 Football Media Guide; *Crusader,* November 7, 1975, and December 5, 1980.

62. Thelin, *Games Colleges Play,* 185; 1995 Football Media Guide.

63. Brooks notes on conversation with Perry, May 25, 1979, Executive Committee minutes, September 4, 1980, ACHC 12.25.

64. Executive Committee minutes, August 4, 1982, ACHC, 12.25; *Crusader,* February 4, 1983. Other MAAC schools were Army, Fairfield, Fordham, Iona, LaSalle, Manhattan, and St. Peter's.

65 Brooks's chronology of Ivy League contact, January 18, 1982, ACHC, 12.25; New York *Times,* January 10, 1982.

Rather quickly, however, Ivy League presidents made it clear that their goal was not to expand their league but to increase the list of schools available for regular competition within Division I-AA. Brown University President Howard Swearer told Father Brooks that the Ivy presidents wanted "to identify colleges with similar philosophies and interests with which to compete."[66] The Ivy League's search took in about twenty schools, and by March of 1983, consensus was growing about the formation of a new athletic conference (including Bucknell, Colgate, Holy Cross, Lafayette, Lehigh, and, initially, Tufts) whose academic standards and level of athletic competition were compatible with the Ivy League. For Holy Cross, the alternative was to join the new league or to give up games with Ivy schools. Brooks viewed the situation as a welcome opportunity to collaborate in developing an alliance that would "speak loudly and clearly to the academic community, and might lead others to correct the many abuses we're presently seeing."[67] In April, the Ivy presidents met with presidents of schools in the proposed league and drove the project forward. A preliminary announcement, issued in September, disclosed the plans and included a statement of support from the Ivy presidents.[68]

Holy Cross's affiliation with the new league drew a mixed reaction in the press and within the College community because of the likelihood that football scholarships would eventually be dropped. Privately, Rick Carter opposed the possible move to need-based aid and pointed out that travel in the new conference would be "somewhat lengthy."[69] But Father Brooks defended the arrangement at Fall Homecoming in 1983. Reviewing the status of college sports, he admitted that the issues were complex; but he defended the goal of having athletes who would be "truly representative" of the student body, participating in a "reasonably competitive" league in which the presidents would hold final authority. With characteristic vigor, he also assailed his opponents:

The press, with its narrow vision, has failed to see the academic thrust our deliberations have taken, has failed to understand that I have no intention whatsoever of jeopardizing the well-earned academic reputation Holy Cross now enjoys by adopting a "bread and circus" attitude towards our sports programs, has failed to

66. Swearer to Brooks, Providence, March 4, 1982, Brooks's jottings of conference call with Charles E. F. Millard and Donald P. Moriarty, January 26, 1982, ACHC, 12.25.

67. Brooks notes on conversations with A. J. Marucha, October 25, 1982, and March 15, 1983, ACHC, 12.25.

68. Brooks notes on meeting of Ivy and affiliate league presidents, April 17, 1983, notes on conversation with A. J. Marucha, July 12, 1983, notes on meeting of affiliate league presidents, August 11, 1983, preliminary notice of new league, September 23, 1983, ACHC, 12.25.

69. Carter to Brooks, September 19, 1983, ACHC, 12.25.

grasp that were we not to join the Colonial League . . . , we would no longer be scheduling the Browns, the Dartmouths, the Harvards, and the Columbias that are the guts and strengths of our football schedule each year. Instead, they have chosen to focus exclusively on the question of grants-in-aid—a matter which, though important, is going to take considerable time to resolve if the league is to be truly competitive.[70]

In fact, the Colonial League's Statement of Principles, adopted in 1984, acknowledged "significant differences" among the schools on the question of grants-in-aid. Because of a stipulation initially imposed by the Ivy presidents, the statement specified that programs would be need-based or comparable with need-based aid. Holy Cross agreed to review its current policy "with a view toward defining and adhering to a policy that is compatible with the academic and athletic policy of the Colonial League." On the other principles, there was agreement from the start: academic programs held paramount importance; players would be representative of the student body; member schools would share information about admissions and financial aid; the presidents would exercise full responsibility. In the summer of 1985, Holy Cross agreed that, beginning in 1989, incoming football players would have need-based aid. To assert the primacy of academics, the College withdrew from eligibility for the Division I-AA playoffs. By then, Davidson College had established itself as the sixth member school. On September 13, 1986, the first Colonial League game was played at Fitton Field. Holy Cross defeated Lehigh, 17–14.[71]

The period of launching the Colonial League brought other changes in the football program. In February of 1986, after the conclusion of his only losing season at Holy Cross, Coach Rick Carter committed suicide, having compiled a record of 35-19-2 in five seasons. He was succeeded by his associate head coach and defensive coordinator, Mark Duffner, who achieved a record of 60-5-1 over the next six seasons, including undefeated seasons in 1987 and 1991, and league championships in every year except 1988. The temporary continuation of athletic scholarships gave Holy Cross an advantage during those years, as did the participation of two-way player Gordie Lockbaum '87, who placed fifth in Heisman Trophy voting as a junior, and third

70. Statement at Fall Homecoming, [1983], ACHC, 12.25.

71. 1984 Colonial League Statement of Principles, Brooks to Colonial League Presidents, April 24, 1984, press release, August 12, 1985, ACHC, 12.25; Worcester *Gazette*, May 4, 1985. As late as 1988, Father Brooks assured Cornell President Frank Rhodes that Holy Cross would keep its commitment to drop football scholarships: "My own integrity and reputation ride on this commitment." Brooks to Rhodes, March 31, 1988, ibid.

as a senior.[72] The undefeated seasons occurred after Father Brooks's decision to discontinue the annual series with Division I-A rival Boston College. Despite its long tradition, the series had become an unequal contest between programs with divergent methods and goals.[73]

The early success of the Colonial League prompted the presidents to consider expansion into other sports. In 1988, they concluded an interim agreement to begin league competition in 1990–91 in ten men's and women's sports, including basketball. Schools with athletic scholarships in these sports pledged to conform to league policy "on a schedule to be determined by the . . . presidents." In the same year, Fordham University's long-standing application for membership was accepted, and Army was granted league membership, except for football and baseball.[74] When the new schedule went into effect, Holy Cross withdrew from the MAAC and agreed to drop grants-in-aid in basketball, starting in 1990. Other changes in 1988 included the decision by Davidson trustees to drop membership, and a change of name to the Patriot League, necessitated by confusion with the Colonial Athletic Association.[75] In 1990, Navy was accepted for league membership on the same basis as Army; in the same year, the league tournament champion in men's basketball was granted an automatic bid by the NCAA to the national tournament.[76] By 1991, the Patriot League was able to stand on its own, free from formal agreements with the Ivy League on specific policies. Taking note of this progress, University of Pennsylvania President Sheldon Hackney and Lehigh President Peter Likins issued a joint statement affirming "mutual respect" between the two leagues: "We believe that our two leagues will develop together most ef-

72. *Crossroads*, January/February 1986; 1995 Football Media Guide. A thoughtful look at Rick Carter and his legacy was offered by sports writer John Gearan '65, Worcester *Telegram and Gazette*, February 2, 1996.

73. Brooks to Monan, February 11, 1987, ACHC, 12.25. For perceptive analysis of the devolution of the series into a lopsided mismatch, see "Sports Corner" columns by Clark Booth '61 in the Boston *Pilot*, December 7, 1984, and November 28, 1986.

74. George Langdon, Jr., to Colonial League Presidents, May 27, 1987, Colonial League press release, July 22, 1988; Alan W. Childs to Brooks, Easton, PA, August 4, 1988, ACHC, 12.25.

75. John Kuykendall to David W. Ellis, Davidson, NC, December 19, 1988, Brooks notes on Colonial League meeting, December 15, 1989, Patriot League press release, December 21, 1989, ACHC, 12.25.

76. Revised Patriot League Agreement, June 5, 1990. ACHC, 12.25. In a memo to the NCAA Administrative Committee dated June 5, 1990, the Patriot League presidents admitted that they had taken a risk of being excluded from the tournament "in order to achieve important ideals. . . . The decision of the NCAA Men's Basketball committee justified our faith in the system, and vindicated our judgment." ACHC, 12.25.

fectively if we rely upon our natural affinities, and set aside any past agreements that permit either league to constrain the policies of the other."[77]

The move to need-based athletic scholarships affected the football and basketball teams in different ways. In football, Mark Duffner resigned at the end of the undefeated 1991 season, when the era of scholarship athletes in football ended. His successor was Peter Vaas '74, whose teams compiled records of 6–5 and 3–8 during his first two years. In men's basketball, George Blaney took teams to the NCAA Tournament in 1977, 1980, and 1993. The latter team represented the Patriot League and was one of seven Blaney-coached teams to win at least twenty games. During Blaney's tenure, Ronnie Perry '80 set a new Holy Cross scoring record with 2542 points. After the move to Division I in 1980, women's basketball became the College's most consistently successful athletic team. Togo Palazzi '54 coached the Lady Crusaders for five years, including four seasons with twenty or more victories, thanks to the play of Sherry Levin '84, who scored 2253 points in her career. Under Bill Gibbons, appointed head coach in 1985, the program remained successful. By the end of the 1993–94 season, Gibbons's teams had compiled a record of 180–85, including six twenty-victory seasons and Patriot League championships in 1991 and 1993.[78]

During the Brooks years, the academic program was also subject to adjustment, as commitment to the liberal arts stimulated reassessment and change. The addition of new academic departments was one avenue of development. In 1979, the Fine Arts Department became the Visual Arts Department and Music and Theatre Arts were constituted as separate departments. The Music major was introduced in 1982, and the Theatre major in 1987.[79] Interdisciplinary studies were enhanced in 1975, thanks to successive grants from the National Endowment for the Humanities. The Humanities Sequence program featured paired courses sponsored by two academic departments. The two instructors helped model "integrated interdisciplinary study of common themes, problems, or historic eras."[80] Other developments included renaming the Theology Department as Religious Studies (1972), the establishment of a local chapter of Phi Beta Kappa (1974), and the introduction of a five-year coop-

77. Hackney and Likins to "Colleagues," June 3, 1991, ACHC, 12.25.

78. 1995 Media Guides for Football, and Men's and Women's Basketball.

79. Trustees' minutes, September 11, 1979, and May 9, 1981, ACHC, 12.25; minutes of Faculty-Student Assembly, May 7, 1979, April 27, 1981, December 2, 1986, ACHC, 14.12; *Crossroads*, January/February 1987.

80. 1980 reaccreditation self-study, ACHC, 14.12; Brooks report to faculty, September 25, 1978, ACHC, 14.12.

erative program with Worcester Polytechnic Institute that allowed students to earn degrees in engineering and the liberal arts.[81] In 1982, the Writing-Across-the-Curriculum Program organized a cluster of writing-intensive courses, which featured support for teachers and students. By 1990, 122 such courses had been offered in twelve academic departments. Meanwhile, interdisciplinary concentrations opened in African-American Studies, International Studies, Peace and Conflict Studies, and Women's Studies. Audio-Visual Services, which started in 1974 with a part-time coordinator, received a full-time director in 1980. The office for Computer and Information Service, which had relied on a mainframe for faculty and student word processing until 1987, began to emphasize personal computers thereafter. By the end of the decade, Edith Stein Hall had a classroom computer facility; additional personal computers were available to students in O'Kane and Swords Halls, and the staff had grown to include fourteen professionals.[82]

Second thoughts about the open curriculum arose in connection with the decennial evaluation in 1980. The Curriculum Committee opened the discussion in 1976 with a series of recommendations that emphasized the need for better academic advising and policies to encourage more study in mathematics, sciences, and languages. Two years later, the assembly considered a recommendation for distribution requirements, but the debate was inconclusive.[83] Then the curriculum drew extensive comment in the reaccreditation report. Evaluators expressed surprise that students could graduate without a course in religious studies and without significant exposure to science or mathematics; the lack of a core or distribution system, they found, left many students with "serious gaps in their liberal education."[84] Such criticism reinforced the sense that the curriculum needed attention, but progress was slow. Finally, in 1982, the trustees formally requested the faculty to consider curriculum reform. To bring closure to the issue, the Curriculum Committee recommended a plan with ten distribution requirements in six curricular areas: The Arts, Language and Literature; Religious and Philosophical Studies; Historical Studies; Cross-Cultural Studies [courses in "contemporary societies and cultures other than one's own"]; Social Sciences; and Natural and Mathematical Sciences. Proponents stressed the plan's broad exposure to the liberal arts, flexibility of choice, and interdisciplinary nature, and the proposal passed easily and took effect

81. Trustees' Executive Committee minutes, June 7, 1972, ACHC, 12.25; *Crusader*, September 14, 1973; Worcester *Telegram*, November 14, 1973.

82. 1990 reaccreditation self-study, ACHC, 14.12.

83. 1980 reaccreditation self-study, ACHC, 14.12.

84. Ibid.

with the Class of 1988.[85] When the policy was reviewed in 1988, faculty and students offered overwhelming support.[86]

The success of the distribution requirement created the context for consideration of foreign languages in the curriculum. The matter came up in 1984, when a language requirement was rejected by the Faculty-Student Assembly.[87] Several years later, after the History Department adopted a language requirement within the major, the EPC appointed a new committee to study the issue. In 1989, its members recommended a competency requirement that would obligate students to intermediate knowledge of one foreign language. The rationale cited requirements at comparable schools, the "national myopia" regarding foreign languages, the rising emphasis on international studies, and the value of language studies in facilitating service "for others." The motion passed, and the requirement took effect with the Class of 1994.[88]

Questions surrounding governance and responsibility remained in the air during the Brooks years. The sharpest controversy occurred in 1976, when the trustees' Executive Committee overturned several recommendations submitted by a newly created Committee on Tenure and Promotion (CTP). The CTP, initiated with little opposition from the faculty and none from the trustees, was intended to supply uniformity of judgment that had been lacking in the old system of ad hoc committees. It had ten members—eight elected members of the senior faculty who served staggered two-year terms, the dean *ex officio*, and, as non-voting chair, the president, who had the responsibility of conveying the recommendations to the trustees for final determination. In the fall of 1976, the CTP considered eleven individuals—three appeals for promotion to full professor, and eight cases of promotion to associate professor with tenure. The latter cases became the flashpoint of controversy in early February, when the campus community learned that five of

85. Sponsors estimated that about 20 percent of students, who were not then conforming to the proposed requirements, would be affected. Brooks address to faculty, September 27, 1982, Minutes of Faculty-Student Assembly, April 28, 1980, April 26, 1982, December 6, 1982, and April 25, 1983, ACHC, 14.12.

86. In a 1988 survey, 66 percent of students reported that the distribution requirement had enhanced their education. Minutes of Faculty-Student Assembly, April 26, 1988, ACHC, 14.12.

87. Minutes of Faculty-Student Assembly, April 30 and December 3, 1984, ACHC, 14.12.

88. Minutes of Faculty-Student Assembly, March 7, 1989, 1990 reaccreditation self-study, ACHC, 14.12. In 1988, Modern Language studies had been enhanced by the addition of native-speaking language assistants from France, Germany, Spain, China, and the Soviet Union (Russia).

the eight CTP recommendations had been reversed.[89] The Student Government Association initiated the confrontation by voting "no confidence" in the administration and trustee's Executive Committee; then the elected members of the CTP resigned, asking Father Brooks to initiate an investigation of the overturned cases by the full board of trustees.

On the faculty side, the confrontation was an effort to have the trustees endorse the "professional judgment of the faculty," particularly in personnel decisions, and to discover whether extrastatutory criteria had been used in reversing the recommendations. As a first step, the trustees were requested to review the eight disputed decisions.[90] In April, the Faculty-Student Assembly set up a committee to discuss outstanding issues with the trustees. The assembly acknowledged the trustees' legal power to grant tenure and promotion, but asserted the faculty's primacy as the "ordinary vehicle" by which such decisions are made.[91] During the spring, many of the trustees visited the campus to discuss the crisis. In May, they adopted a resolution deploring the "misunderstandings" and pledging to work toward a solution that respected "the nature and mission of the College." The trustees recognized "the competence of the faculty . . . to make professional judgments about their peers," but stopped short of endorsing a ten-year-old AAUP statement on faculty primacy in tenure and promotion. Finally, they agreed to review all eleven promotion cases.[92]

This response did not allay the crisis. The former members of the CTP stated that the trustees' statement "does not restore our confidence in the Ex-

89. Trustees' minutes, September 9, 1975, Executive Committee to Trustees, April 15, 1976, ACHC, 12.25.

90. The chronology was supplied to the Trustees by the Executive Committee, April 15, 1976, ACHC, 12.25. See also the report given to the Faculty-Student Assembly, March 15, 1976, ACHC, 14.12 According to Robert Nicholson, speculation about a fourth criterion focused on two possibilities: "a commitment to the College community," or "a loyalty and allegiance to the Catholic, or perhaps religious, purposes of the College." "A Legacy in Transition," 74–75.

91. Mi nutes of Faculty-Student Assembly, April 9, 1976, ACHC, 14.12.

92. Trustees' minutes, May 5, 1976, ACHC, 12.25. Part of the reason for the trustees' response on the AAUP statement of 1966 may have been a reflection of Brooks's view that the trustees' authority in tenure cases had not been altered by the creation of the CTP. For him, the issue concerned the trustees' responsibility to give direction to the institution, defending it, if necessary, from "a very small group of people who wish to change the institution from a Jesuit Catholic college." Transcript of Executive Committee meeting, May 1, 1976, ACHC, 12.25. Father Brooks told the trustees that, in conversations with eleven presidents of schools, including Dartmouth, Colgate, Bowdoin, Amherst, and Georgetown, he learned that only Franklin and Marshall College had formally adopted the 1966 AAUP statement as institutional policy. Brooks notes for trustees' meeting, May 5, 1976, ACHC, 12.25.

ecutive Committee," and the assembly endorsed a resolution characterizing the trustees' response as "evasive" and "unacceptable" because it avoided a definitive response on the issue of primacy in personnel matters.[93] During the summer and fall, the crisis cooled. At a special meeting in July, the trustees examined the cases, concluded that statutory procedures had been followed, and invited the faculty to join in a committee to study the connection between faculty primacy in personnel matters and the ultimate responsibility of trustees for the management of the college.[94] But in September the Faculty-Student Assembly refused to participate. Afterwards, the trustees directed Father Brooks to work with the 1976–77 CTP on practical changes for clarifying communication and reducing tension.[95]

The smoother operation of the decision-making process that year opened the way for a joint committee of faculty and trustees to study the questions "Who governs?" and "According to what criteria?"[96] From March of 1978 until May of 1981, a committee of the entire teaching faculty (The Ad Hoc Committee of the Teaching Faculty), steered by the faculty members of the trustees' joint committee, discussed governance issues and succeeded in adopting new grievance procedures in 1979. Ultimately, the discussions also adjusted the procedures for tenure and promotion.[97] These modifications, and the lack of further wholesale overturns by the trustees, brought stability to the system of promotion and tenure. Under these circumstances, the question of primacy in the granting of tenure lost its urgency and both sides seemed willing to avoid further confrontation.[98]

The tenure crisis raised the larger issue of the meaning of the school's

93. Minutes of Faculty-Student Assembly, May 6, 1976, ACHC, 14.12.

94. Trustees' minutes, July 19, 1976, and Brooks memo to faculty, August 13, 1976, ACHC, 12.25. In the fall, an outside examiner invited by the local AAUP chapter found no grounds for a formal investigation, but recommended further study to clarify the impasse. Trustees' minutes, May 7, 1977, ACHC, 12.25

95. Minutes of Faculty-Student Assembly, September 13, 1976, ACHC, 14.12; trustees' minutes, September 14, 1976, ACHC, 12.25.

96. Minutes of Faculty-Student Assembly, April 18 and May 2, 1977, ACHC, 14.12; trustees' minutes, May 7, 1977, ACHC, 12.25.

97. Under the revised procedure, candidates received unsigned copies of majority and minority reports of the CTP by January 1 to afford them an opportunity to prepare a response for the Executive Committee; the president announced his own recommendation in each case to the CTP prior to the meeting of the Executive Committee. Minutes of Faculty-Student Assembly, March 13 and May 1, 1978, May 7, 1979, ACHC, 14.12.

98. David O'Brien asserts: "The administration and inexperienced trustees insisted on their ultimate authority, required to protect the college's Jesuit and Catholic character. Because the faculty had no stomach for decisive action, the dispute had no decisive resolution,

Catholic and Jesuit identity, and how it was to be appropriately identified and maintained—if at all—in the era of separate incorporation and extended faculty responsibility. The question attracted attention from contemporary analysts. Among them, Jesuit Edward F. Maloney described a weakening ability to articulate "religious objectives" at Catholic colleges and universities.[99] William Henry Dixon described a crisis involving "lack of clarity about educational objectives" and a weakening of the ideal of Christian humanism at Jesuit colleges and universities: "The question has been strongly raised as to the identity of such institutions, particularly as to how they may be distinguished from secular universities. Given the strength of the secular university today, it has even been asked whether the Jesuit institutions should be kept in existence any more."[100] Facing the issue of what it meant to be Jesuit and Catholic was unavoidable during the Brooks years. The lack of perspective made answers hard to find.

At Holy Cross, the question came into focus in 1976, when the assembly was discussing the overturned tenure decisions. Professor John Wilson made the point clearly:

We really have no consensus as to what kind of institution we want this to be; we don't know what the proper way is to maintain our Catholic, Christian, Jesuit identity, or even whether we wish to retain just that identity. There is obviously disagreement about all these questions among the administration and the Board of Trustees, as well as among students and faculty. And the latter have no way of being assured that the administration and trustees are necessarily being guided . . . by an understanding shared by all.[101]

An AAUP consultant who visited the campus in the spring of 1977 also recommended study of identity questions; in December, in their ongoing discussion of the tenure crisis, the trustees concluded that a mission statement would facilitate consensus on governance. The idea was formalized in 1978,

---

which meant victory for the trustees and administration." *From the Heart of the American Church: Catholic Higher Education and American Culture* (Maryknoll, NY: Orbis Books, 1994), 127–29. See also O'Brien's discussion, "The Holy Cross Case," in *Commonweal* (October 8, 1976), 647–53, and the responses in *Commonweal* (January 21, 1977), 45–48.

99. Edward F. Maloney, "A Study of the Religious Orientation of Catholic Colleges and Universities in New York State from 1962 to 1972" (unpublished Ph.D. dissertation: New York University, 1974), 1–3.

100. William Henry Dixon, "An Historical Survey of Jesuit Higher Education in the United States with Particular Reference to the Objectives of Education" (unpublished Ph.D. dissertation, Arizona State University, 1974), v, 93.

101. Minutes of the Faculty-Student Assembly, March 15, 1976, ACHC, 14.12.

when the Ad Hoc Committee of the Teaching Faculty set up a Subcommittee on the Jesuit and Catholic Mission of Holy Cross. Its mandate was left "deliberately vague," with the implication that a discussion would be valuable, even if no concrete proposal resulted.[102] The final report, delivered in August of 1980, discussed "the mission issue" without specifying solutions. The study disclosed that a lack of consensus involved Holy Cross in a "religious and secular humanistic dualism" and that the lack of agreement about mission had wide repercussions. All faculty, regardless of background, had somehow to come to terms with the school's Catholic identity—often with little guidance, and sometimes under the impression that "compatibility" was an issue with some administrators and colleagues. The report suggested possible solution in a value-oriented program "somewhere between the Jesuit education of the recent past and a fully secularized version of liberal arts."

There, for the time being, the matter rested, although efforts were made through the Jesuit community to sponsor dialogue about the school's Jesuit character. Father Joseph Ryan, who served as community rector from 1977 to 1983, initiated a series of "Jesuit Evenings" for lay faculty and administrators at Loyola Hall. They featured a lecture on an aspect of Jesuit identity, followed by a social hour and dinner. The series was continued during the rectorships of Fathers Robert E. Manning (1983–85) and William E. Reiser (1985–91). After a number of years, Father Reiser replaced the dinners with community-sponsored "Jesuit Weekends"—overnight dialogues between Jesuit and lay members of the faculty and administration. That series was continued by Reiser's successor, Father David Gill (1991–94). Through these efforts, the Jesuit community sought to promote understanding about institutional mission, though responsibility for a mission statement remained, ultimately, with the College administration.

The administration itself was subject to turnover as new associates joined Father Brooks. In 1975, the associate dean, Father Paul Harman, succeeded Father Joseph Donahue as vice-president of the College. Father Harman, in turn, was succeeded in 1984 by Father William O'Halloran, who had been the Jesuit rector at the time of separate incorporation and afterwards served several years as president of LeMoyne College.[103] Also in 1984, William R. Durgin succeeded John O'Keefe as College treasurer and vice-president for business affairs. In the Dean's Office, Father Joseph Fahey was succeeded in 1981 by Father Raymond A. Schroth, former academic dean at Rockhurst Col-

102. Files of 1980 Subcommittee on the Jesuit and Catholic Mission, personal files of David O'Brien.

103. *Crusader*, September 12, 1975; *Crossroads*, May/June 1984.

lege.[104] Father Schroth encountered difficulties in 1985 when he directed members of the Economics Department to hire someone "sympathetic with" (later altered to "conversant with") principles articulated in the recently issued American Bishops' Pastoral Letter on the Economy. There was a strong reaction on the part of many faculty who deemed the directive a violation of academic freedom, and Schroth resigned, citing insufficient support for his leadership.[105] Frank Vellaccio of the Chemistry Department replaced him and, in 1987, was named vice-president for academic affairs at the same time that Father Earle Markey was named vice-president for student affairs.[106]

Frank Vellaccio's status as the first lay dean of the College was another sign that the pool of Jesuits available for administrative and faculty positions had shrunk. Nationally, the number of Jesuits declined by 38 percent in the quarter century after Vatican II, a movement that had implications at Holy Cross. In 1970, there were 55 Jesuit faculty members; by 1992, there were ten Jesuits teaching full-time and four part-time, and ten more working as administrators or chaplains. These two dozen men, plus a number of retired Jesuit residents, constituted what Robert Nicholson called "Holy Cross's living legacy" in a study completed in 1991. Nicholson pointed out that Holy Cross depended in important ways on the Jesuit presence described in the separate incorporation agreement of 1969. Jesuits carried the responsibility for personifying a distinctive aspect of the school's identity; many did so in ways that made a difference for students and graduates through pastoral care, pedagogical dedication, and a willingness to engage with students in mentoring relationships. Many people, Nicholson concluded, "associate the unique excellence of Holy Cross with the presence of the Jesuits."[107]

During the Brooks years, the investment in faculty development was paying dividends as the quality of the faculty and the reputation of the College continued to rise. By 1989, when the number of faculty with doctorates had risen to 90 percent, the Holy Cross professoriate compared favorably in

---

104. *Crossroads*, January/February and July/August 1981.

105. Schroth to John R. Carter, December 11 and 21, 1984, ACHC, 14.0; *Crusader*, February 22 and April 3, 1985; *Crossroads*, March/April 1985. David O'Brien, who sympathized with Schroth's goal, argued that the dean was "driven from a school for his attempt to hire faculty committed to the dialogue of faith and culture." *Heart of the American Church*, 118.

106. *Crossroads*, May/June 1985 and January/February 1986; *Crusader*, February 13, 1987.

107. Nicholson, "Legacy in Transition," 62, 248–49; Philip Gleason, *Contending with Modernity: Catholic Higher Education in the Twentieth Century* (New York: Oxford University Press, 1995), 319.

scholarly publication with colleagues at comparable schools; they also carried an average teaching load of 68 students, offered three courses per semester, and enjoyed an open sabbatical policy.[108] Administrators and trustees worked to keep salaries and benefits competitive. The 1990 reaccreditation report praised the gains in faculty salaries and the full-need commitment to students. Evaluators found the faculty "highly qualified . . . , dedicated, hard working, and productive." Yet an internal study conducted by the Faculty Resources Committee in 1989 cited "unrealistic demands" on the faculty: although the school ranked high in support for faculty research, it stood low among comparable schools in faculty/student ratio (1:16), class size, and teaching load.[109] Concern about other matters was focused through a cluster of self-studies covering the curriculum, student life, and the institutional mission, undertaken in connection with the 1990 reaccreditation. Delivered between June and September of 1989, these reports, plus the reports of the Faculty Resources Committee, constituted a nexus of data, ideas, and recommendations for utilizing the strengths of the College and addressing its outstanding issues.[110]

The Ad Hoc Curriculum Committee advocated creative approaches to the liberal arts and better communication within the campus community. Academic departments were challenged to improve teaching methods and to prepare students more effectively for graduate school. To achieve these goals, the report endorsed more concentrations and minors, an improved advising system, and a more diverse student body. Committee members stressed the formative value of the liberal arts and called for "institutional efforts to refashion a tradition of integrated learning . . . which refuses to surrender to the entrenched separation between learning and campus life which exists here and on most American campuses." In words that echoed the spirit of Jesuit adaptation, the committee endorsed mentoring relationships that were re-

108. 1980 reaccreditation self-study, 1990 reaccreditation self-study, Faculty-Student Assembly minutes, October 17, 1989, ACHC, 14.12.

109. Report of Ad Hoc Committee on Faculty Resources and Educational Quality (September 1989), and 1990 reaccreditation report, ACHC, 14.12. Among the features of faculty research support was the introduction in 1988–89 of one-semester salaried research leaves for junior faculty, normally given in the third year after hiring. Minutes of the Faculty-Student Assembly, April 25, 1989, ACHC, 14.12.

110. Brooks address to faculty, October 4, 1988, ACHC, 14.12. The Faculty Resources Committee offered recommendations designed to ease pressure on an overextended faculty: increasing the faculty by thirty, adopting a 3–2 teaching load, reducing enrollment to 2400, coordinating academic leaves more effectively, and giving an annual teaching award. ACHC, 14.12.

sponsive to student culture: "It is the faculty's obligation not to contribute to [student anti-intellectualism] through a too narrowly defined concept of professionalism which gives sole priority to classroom and research activities and ignores educating the whole person."[111] A similar theme emerged in the report of the Ad Hoc Committee on Student Life, a document that examined the separation between student culture and the intellectual, extracurricular, and religious life of the campus. Too often, the committee argued, campus life had been shaped by eighteen-year-olds, "in isolation from the other dimensions of campus life"—a situation that jeopardized the goal of integrated campus life, "a culture where belongingness and community are facts, not anxieties." Recommendations included a permanent committee on student life, more contact among students and faculty, more small-group courses, and a first-year program.[112]

The Committee on the College Mission was constituted by Father Brooks "to formulate and carry out the process by which an institutional mission statement is developed—one that enjoys the strong support of the faculty, administration and trustees, and one that reflects the determination of this College to remove, to every extent it possibly can, the shameful and abhorrent cultural and economic inequalities . . . [that] are responsible for the wholesale destruction of a significant segment of God's people." Brooks assigned the committee the task of articulating the mission in a way that was respectful of the College's history and Jesuit character, reflective of the goals and purposes of Jesuit education, open to ecumenical approaches, and linked strongly to "the great educational ideals."[113] Under the direction of Professor David O'Brien, committee members sponsored a series of meetings to collect input from various components of the community. Commitment to the liberal arts and to education for social justice enjoyed broad support, but specific meanings for liberal arts and Catholic education proved elusive. Afterwards, O'Brien admitted that task was complicated by the fact that separate incorporation, the professionalization of the faculty, and diversity within the school "made it difficult to articulate a compelling Catholic position for the Catholic university as a whole." The solution was to conceive of Catholicism, not as a dis-

111. Report of the Ad Hoc Curriculum Committee, August 18, 1989, ACHC, 14.12.

112. Report of the *Ad Hoc* Committee on Student Life, July 31, 1989, minutes of Faculty-Student Assembly, December 4, 1989, ACHC, 14.12.

113. Committee members were Maurice Geracht and James Kee of the English Department, Theresa McBride and David O'Brien of the History Department, and Father John MacDonnell of the Mathematics Department. Brooks address to Faculty-Student Assembly, October 4, 1988, ACHC, 14.12.

tinguishing attribute, but as a source of insights and resources to help define and defend the common good.[114]

In June of 1989, the committee delivered a twelve-page report. The centerpiece was a draft mission statement of five paragraphs, summarized by Father Brooks as pledging "to make the best of our talents, to work together, to serve others, to seek justice, and in so doing, to 'create a setting where Catholics and others can learn to give an account of their beliefs, not apart from other communities of meaning and value, but among them.'"[115] In transmitting the draft statement, committee members noted the difficulty in discussing concepts for which adequate shared language was lacking: "'Liberal arts,' 'religion,' 'faith,' 'reason,' 'values,'—not to mention 'God'—mean different things to different people. We believe that our commitment to the liberal arts, to say nothing of our Catholic and Jesuit heritage, requires us to recognize and honor these differences but still push beyond a live-and-let-live pluralism." A mission statement, they concluded, had to be an open-ended invitation to dialogue.[116]

These reports, and ongoing discussion about a first-year program, enabled the Reaccreditation Steering Committee to offer the evaluators more data and analysis than had been available at any time since the founding of the College. The self-study noted that enrollment had increased to 2684, and SAT averages had risen about 50 points during the 1980s, to 1206 for the Class of 1993. The commitment to full-demonstrated need for admitted students was proving costly, though the school came close to meeting the criteria between 1987 and 1989, the final years included in the self-study. For fiscal year 1991, $7.88 million was budgeted for financial aid, a figure that included money formerly reserved for athletic scholarships.[117] Such statistics won favorable notice in the 1990 reaccreditation report. Evaluators praised the salutary effect of distribution requirements on the academic program, the language requirements, and interdisciplinary studies. They praised the faculty's dedication, the leadership of Father Brooks, the counseling center and library, the school's prudent fiscal management, and the level of maintenance of the physical plant. Concerns included the failure to adopt a mission statement, a governance structure and presiden-

114. O'Brien memo to Mission Committee, November 21, 1988, Statement of *Ad Hoc* Mission Committee, June 15, 1989, O'Brien papers; O'Brien, *Heart of the American Church*, 118, 121.

115. Brooks report to Faculty-Student Assembly, September 26, 1989, ACHC, 14.12.

116. Report of the Ad Hoc Committee on the College Mission, June 15, 1989, O'Brien papers. See also O'Brien, *Heart of the American Church*, 122–24.

117. 1990 reaccreditation self-study, ACHC, 14.12. $2.6 million had been reserved for athletic scholarships in 1989, the last budget before the phase-out.

tial style that hindered communication,[118] a faculty-student ratio that compared unfavorably with similar schools, overcrowded residence halls, and the absence of women in high administrative posts.

As immediate objectives, the evaluators emphasized governance reform and enhancement of student life "so as to achieve what the College itself calls the goals of a just community."[119] But the report was particularly emphatic in asserting that the lack of a mission statement was complicating the ability to come to terms with important policy issues. Ad hoc responses to such issues, the evaluators warned, could "unwittingly create centrifugal forces that promote conflicting goals." The declining number of Jesuits made such a statement even more necessary "to institutionalize new means of insuring the traditions and distinctiveness of the College."

The first response to the self-study associated with the 1990 re-evaluation was the adoption of a priorities statement, "Planning for Excellence," designed by the Educational Policy Committee and passed by the faculty in May of 1990 by an almost unanimous vote. The document incorporated elements drawn from the ad hoc committee reports and the discussions that ensued. The preamble affirmed the centrality of the liberal arts and the College's identity "as a Jesuit college which regards its relationships with the Society of Jesus and with the Roman Catholic community as enriching elements of its life and work." The document set integrated priorities for the 1990s that included a better governance structure, an increase of thirty faculty positions and the possible introduction of a 3/2 teaching load, better integration of the curriculum and the co-curricular life of the students, and a commitment to explore mission-related opportunities and issues.[120] In September, Father Brooks told the faculty that the trustees had given serious consideration to the document, which they understood as "an expression of faculty commitment to using new resources for the purposes of (1) strengthening the Jesuit Mission of Holy Cross—a goal which should include the completion and adoption of a Mission statement; (2) the continued professional development of the faculty; and (3) curricular reform, including the adoption of a First-Year Program." Father Brooks added his own expression of satisfaction that the program arose from initiative within the College community, rather than being imitative of other schools.[121]

118. Reaccreditation reports in 1980 and 1990 drew attention to issues in communication and collaborative planning.

119. The report was transmitted to Holy Cross on November 27, 1990. The chair of the evaluation committee was Mary Maples Dunn, president of Smith College. ACHC, 14.12.

120. The Planning for Excellence report was passed by the Faculty-Student Assembly on May 4, 1990, by a vote of 140–3–3. ACHC, 14.12.

121. Brooks address to faculty, September 25, 1990, ACHC, 14.12.

To formulate a response to Planning for Excellence, the trustees authorized a Task Force on Resources, Needs and Priorities whose members included three trustees, three members of the faculty, the five vice-presidents, and Father Brooks. Their report, issued in 1992, was grounded in fiscal realism. In response to calls for a larger faculty, the report cited "the effects of a worsening recession and growing criticism of higher education's inability to curb rising costs." With a budget constrained by an inability to raise tuition much more quickly than inflation and the expectation that annual giving would remain flat, growth in endowment income was made a paramount objective. Other resources would be earmarked for faculty salaries and fringe benefits, full-need commitment to admitted students, and enhancement of library resources. Other needs would be addressed through growth by substitution and "only modest budget increases." The statement closed with a defense of limited but feasible priorities.[122]

In the spring of 1991, a multidisciplinary first-year program, the final major curricular innovation of the Brooks years, was adopted after five years of discussion and refinement. The program's goals — to establish a student intellectual community, to promote discussion among participants, and to encourage active student participation — would be fostered by having students live in the same residence hall and take one course in the program each semester, in groups limited to fifteen. Faculty participants received a one-course reduction in teaching load to facilitate student writing and speaking and to be able to collaborate in developing a common theme inspired by Leo Tolstoy's question, "How then shall we live?" The proposal was designed as a pilot project, involving part of the first-year class. During the inaugural year, 1992–93, 165 student participants and seven faculty (four of whom taught two sections) considered the question: "How then shall we live meaningfully in a world with so many different claims of what is good and true?"[123]

In response to the 1990 reaccreditation report, Father Brooks re-constituted the Mission Committee in the fall of 1991 and requested the faculty to approve a statement for submission to the trustees the following May. Once again, the committee sponsored a series of meetings that produced a modified statement that rearranged some of the material of the 1989 draft (Appendix I).[124] The

122. Report of the Task Force on Resources, Needs and Priorities, copy in possession of the author. An indication of faculty reaction to the report may be found in O'Brien, *Heart of the American Church*, 135–36.

123. Minutes of Faculty-Student Assembly, May 13, 1991, and December 8, 1992, ACHC, 14.12.

124. Brooks address to faculty, September 24, 1991, and minutes of Faculty-Student Assembly, December 3, 1991, ACHC, 14.12.

final draft avoided the expression "Catholic college" as ambiguous and divisive. Instead, the statement reflected a general consensus about the College's Jesuit identity and what David O'Brien called "a practical commitment to provide concrete service to Catholic students and to the church, which could easily provide the foundation for programs and for hiring faculty interested in Catholicism."[125] When the final draft was presented to the Faculty-Student Assembly in February of 1992, Father Brooks stepped down from the chair to advocate adoption. He asserted that the goals of his presidency were "precisely those embodied in the Mission Statement that is on the table now . . . , a specific articulation of the principles upon which the College has successfully built its current strengths and upon which it has earned its current reputation."[126] The Mission Statement was endorsed overwhelmingly by the assembly and quickly approved by the trustees. Afterwards, David O'Brien analyzed the document and the process that produced it: the statement was approved by the faculty; it was honest about the lack of agreement in defining the liberal arts and therefore made conversation a pervasive theme; it asserted that the liberal arts move individuals toward integrated lives; it placed fundamental religious and philosophical questions at the heart of a liberal arts education; it endorsed the importance of shared responsibility for the College's mission; and it recognized a special responsibility "to enable all students who wish to do so to enter into the life and mission of the Catholic church."[127]

Governance was another area singled out for attention in the 1990 reaccreditation report. The 1980 self-study had already produced one minor reform, a reduction of the number of student representatives in the Faculty-Student Assembly from 48 to 12, as a means of "re-establishing the appropriate authority of the faculty" in its distinct areas of responsibility.[128] But other issues were accumulating: the system adopted during the Swords administration

125. O'Brien, *Heart of the American Church*, 136. In his magisterial study of Catholic higher education in the twentieth century, Philip Gleason underscored the difficulty in coming to terms with the definition of a Catholic college: "The identity problem that persists is . . . not institutional or organizational, but ideological. That is, it consists in a lack of consensus as to the substantive content of the ensemble of religious beliefs, moral commitments, and academic assumptions that supposedly constitute Catholic identity, and a consequent inability to specify what that identity entails for the practical functioning of Catholic colleges and universities. More briefly put, the crisis is not that Catholic educators do not want their institutions to remain Catholic, but that they are no longer sure what remaining Catholic means." *Contending with Modernity*, 320.

126. Minutes of Faculty-Student Assembly, February 25, 1992, ACHC, 14.12.

127. O'Brien, *Heart of the American Church*, 136–40.

128. 1980 reaccreditation self-study, Faculty-Student Assembly minutes, February 24 and April 14, 1986, ACHC, 14.12.

and modified over more than two decades needed re-examination and reform. These needs were spelled out in reports and recommendations of the various ad hoc committees in 1989. Accordingly, the Educational Policy Committee appointed an Ad Hoc Committee on Governance, charged with making proposals for the function of the faculty-student assembly, the role of the academic dean, the relationship between faculty governance and student government, and the role of faculty governance in institutional planning. A basic outline of the new governance structure was approved by the Faculty-Student Assembly in April of 1991: final adoption was voted two years later and the new system took effect in 1994.[129] The plan was designed to streamline governance, facilitate communication, and introduce a more collegial approach. It featured three major committees, designated as the Finance and Planning Council,[130] the Student Life Council,[131] and the Academic Affairs Council,[132] all of which reported to the Faculty Assembly that was chaired by a newly created Speaker of the Faculty. The Speaker also served *ex officio* as a member of the Academic Affairs Council and represented the assembly to the president and trustees.

The new governance structure, the final organizational accomplishment of the Brooks administration, further expressed the collaborative approach to academics and student life. Other parts of his legacy, especially the endowment, the physical plant, enhanced academic reputation, the stand for integrity in athletics, the Mission Statement, were also in place. The Brooks legacy also encompassed an important but intangible element: his impact on the spirit of the campus. Nowhere was that influence more evident than in his annual addresses to the Faculty-Student Assembly, talks that combined elements of sermon, apodictic discourse, academic lecture, and pep talk—appeals to be energized and uplifted by the challenge of teaching and learning

129. Minutes of Faculty-Student Assembly, February 27 and December 4, 1990, April 30, 1991, and April 27, 1993, ACHC, 14.12.

130. The Finance and Planning Council was set up "to advise the president on long-term financial planning needs and on general budget policy," and to "discuss priorities, make recommendations, and hear explanations of budget and planning decisions made by the president."

131. The Student Life Council advised the Dean of Students on College policy and made recommendations on student life issues to the Dean of Students and the Finance and Planning Council.

132. The Academic Affairs Council was a faculty senate, described as "the principal body of the faculty in all matters concerned with the faculty and the academic life of the College." This council was also designed to facilitate communication within the campus community, to represent academic needs to the Finance and Planning council, and to set the agenda for meetings of the Faculty Assembly.

at Holy Cross, to serve the old ideal of the *magis*, now expressed in the words of Pedro Arrupe: educating "men and women for others."

The 1983 address made the point by associating moral training with academic excellence. Citing Cardinal Newman's assertion that teachers are called to the exacting task of representing truth, Brooks insisted that the educational process should be imbued with clear values:

> As teachers and administrators in a liberal arts college bent on excellence, we must go beyond the pedagogy of skills and quantitative objectives, and profess our own values through our behavior and through our expectations for our students. We teach values when we refuse to tolerate procrastination, self-indulgence, laziness, or the lack of any sense of priorities.
>
> . . . . .
>
> There is no need for pessimism about the future of Holy Cross provided we— faculty and administrators—summon the courage and steadfastness to hold tenaciously to the basic purposes and goals of this college: the pursuit of truth, the relentless pursuit of academic excellence, and the development of strong moral principles. To think otherwise would be to betray the virtue of hope—and without hope, one is already dead.[133]

Two years later, Brooks returned to the theme, asking faculty to promote a "holy disobedience" that prized justice in a world of scientifically and economically driven values. That was the essence of education at Holy Cross, in the richness of its Jesuit and Catholic heritage:

> Education is expected to be sensitive to the courage, compassion, and the critical consciousness of Christ. What we desperately want and strive to achieve at Holy Cross is an education: that leads rather than follows; that contributes to a just future rather than simply to an economically satisfying present; that is willing to question whether or not what is scientifically, organizationally or economically possible is also humanly appropriate; that is built on curricula of conscience, not just curricula of content; that knows that peace is based on justice and bends itself to build it; that realizes that freedom is owed to all human beings and is intended to reflect the equality conferred by God.

Brooks concluded with an appeal to aspire beyond academic excellence to achieving "a community seriously committed to peace, to freedom, to equality, to social justice for all."[134]

In April of 1994, Father Brooks made his final appearance at the Faculty-Student Assembly as president. Because of the forthcoming change in governance, it was also the last faculty meeting presided over by the College presi-

---

133. Brooks address to Faculty-Student Assembly, September 26, 1983, ACHC, 14.12.
134. Brooks address to Faculty-Student Assembly, September 23, 1985, ACHC, 14.12.

Celebrating the sesquicentennial on November 1, 1993, worshipers from the College community enter the chapel under the banner of Ignatius of Loyola. The homily was offered by Cardinal Joseph Bernardin, who had delivered the commencement address and received an honorary degree ten years earlier.

dent. At that meeting, Frank Vellaccio presented his third annual report to the assembly as academic dean, a procedure introduced two years earlier at the request of the Educational Policy Committee. After reviewing the year's accomplishments and forthcoming challenges, Vellaccio turned his attention to Father Brooks. There were stories of his wisdom and humor, praise for his accomplishments, and a conclusion that expressed the sentiments of the audience with deliberate understatement: "In the end, the only thing left to say is thank you, Father."[135] The ovation was prolonged and enthusiastic.

By then, the celebration of the College sesquicentennial was well under

135. Minutes of Faculty-Student Assembly, May 14, 1992, and April 26, 1994, ACHC, 14.12.

way: a convocation had tested the oratorical abilities of representatives of church and academy, city and state; Cardinal Bernardin had journeyed from Chicago to preach the jubilee sermon; distinguished graduates had returned to campus for a special lecture series; an alumni reunion had recognized the milestone; a federal postcard with a picture of O'Kane Hall had been issued; anniversary cake and special wine had enhanced the spirit of merriment; the major fund drive had gone over the top; and a new president, Father Gerard Reedy, had been chosen. Among the many events, one occurred on June 21, 1993—the 150th anniversary of the cornerstone laying of Fenwick Hall. That afternoon, members of the Jesuit community, joined by the three Catholic bishops in Worcester, celebrated Mass in Ciampi Hall and intoned the *Te Deum* to offer thanks for a century and a half of accomplishment in the work of education. Father Brooks presided at the liturgical gathering. Few of those present were aware that the letter announcing his intent to resign the presidency, bearing the same date, was in the mail. Afterwards the celebration continued with a festive dinner at which the College—past, present, and future—was saluted and toasted. In an atmosphere of gratitude, fellowship, and expectation, Holy Cross entered its one hundred and fifty-first year.

Mission Statement

T HE COLLEGE OF the Holy Cross is, by tradition and choice, a Jesuit liberal arts college serving the Catholic community, American society and the wider world. To participate in the life of Holy Cross is to accept an invitation to join in dialogue about basic human questions: What is the moral character of learning and teaching? How do we find meaning in life and history? What are our obligations to one another? What is our special responsibility to the world's poor and powerless?

As a liberal arts college, Holy Cross pursues excellence in teaching, learning and research. All who share its life are challenged to be open to new ideas, to be patient with ambiguity and uncertainty, to combine a passion for truth with respect for the views of others. Informed by the presence of diverse interpretations of the human experience, Holy Cross seeks to build a community marked by freedom, mutual respect and civility. Because the search for meaning and value is at the heart of the intellectual life, critical examination of fundamental religious and philosophical questions is integral to liberal arts education. Dialogue about these questions among people from diverse academic disciplines and religious traditions requires everyone to acknowledge and respect differences. Dialogue also requires us to remain open to that sense of the whole which calls us to transcend ourselves and challenges us to seek that which might constitute our common humanity.

The faculty and staff of Holy Cross, now primarily lay and religiously and culturally diverse, also affirm the mission of Holy Cross as a Jesuit college. As such, Holy Cross seeks to exemplify the longstanding dedication of the Society of Jesus to intellectual life and its commitment to the service of faith and promotion of justice. The College is dedicated to forming a community which supports the intellectual growth of all its members while offering them opportunities for spiritual and moral development. In a special way, the College must enable all who choose to do so to encounter the intellectual heritage of Catholicism, to form an active worshipping community and to become engaged in the life and work of the contemporary church.

Since 1843, Holy Cross has sought to educate students who, as leaders in business, professional and civic life, would live by the highest intellectual and ethical standards.

In service of the ideal, Holy Cross endeavors to create an environment in which integrated learning is a shared responsibility, pursued in classroom and laboratory, studio and theater, residence and chapel. Shared responsibility for the life and governance of the College should lead all its members to make the best of their own talents, to work together, to be sensitive to one another, to serve others and to seek justice within and beyond the Holy Cross community.

(Adopted 1992)

Presidents of the College of the Holy Cross

Thomas F. Mulledy (1843–1845)
James Ryder (1845–1848)
John Early (1848–1851)
Anthony F. Ciampi (1851–1854)
Peter J. Blenkinsop (1854–1857)
Anthony F. Ciampi (1857–1861)
James Clark (1861–1867)
Robert W. Brady (1867–1869)
Anthony F. Ciampi (1867–1873)
Joseph B. O'Hagan (1873–1878)
Edward D. Boone (1878–1883)
Robert W. Brady (1883–1887)
Samuel Cahill (1887–1889)
Michael A. O'Kane (1889–1893)
Edward A. McGurk (1893–1895)
John F. Lehy (1895–1901)
Joseph F. Hanselman (1901–1906)
Thomas E. Murphy (1906–1911)
Joseph N. Dinand (1911–1918)
James J. Carlin (1918–1924)
Joseph N. Dinand (1924–1927)
John M. Fox (1927–1933)
Francis J. Dolan (1933–1939)
Joseph R. N. Maxwell (1939–1945)
William J. Healy (1945–1948)
John A. O'Brien (1948–1954)
William A. Donaghy (1954–1960)
Raymond J. Swords (1960–1970)
John E. Brooks (1970–1994)
Gerard Reedy (1994–)

Jesuit Leaders, 1843–1994

Generals of the Society of Jesus

Jan Roothaan (1829–1853)
Peter Beckx (1853–1887)
Anton Anderledy
   Vicar (1883–1887)
   General (1887–1892)

Luis Martin (1892–1906)
Franz Wernz (1906–1914)
Wlodimir Ledochowski (1915–1942)
John Baptist Janssens (1946–1964)
Pedro Arrupe (1965–1983)
Peter-Hans Kolvenbach (1983–)

Regional Provincials

Maryland Province

Francis Dzierozynski, Acting (1840–1843)
James Ryder (1843–1845)
Peter Verhaegen (1845–1848)
Ignatius Brocard (1848–1852)
Joseph Aschwanden, Acting (1852)
Charles H. Stonestreet (1852–1858)

Burchard Villiger (1858–1859)
Felix Sopranis, Visitor (1859–1861)
Angelo Paresce (1861–1869)
Joseph E. Keller (1869–1877)
Robert Brady (1877–1879)

Maryland-New York Province

Robert Brady (1879–1882)
Robert Fulton (1882–1889)
Thomas J. Campbell (1889–1893)
William Pardow (1893–1897)
Edward Purbrick (1897–1901)

Thomas J. Gannon (1901–1906)
Joseph Hanselman (1906–1912)
Anthony Maas (1912–1918)
Joseph Rockwell (1918–1922)
Lawrence Kelly (1922–1928)

New England Province

Patrick F. O'Gorman
   Vice-Provincial (1921–1924)
James M. Kilroy
   Vice-Provincial (1924–1926)
   Provincial (1926–1932)

James T. McCormick (1932–1937)
James H. Dolan (1937–1944)
John J. McEleney (1944–1950)
William E. FitzGerald (1950–1956)
James E. Coleran (1956–1962)

New England Province (continued)

John V. O'Connor (1962–1968)

William G. Guindon (1968–1974)

Richard T. Cleary (1974–1979)

Edward M. O'Flaherty (1979–1985)

Robert E. Manning (1985–1991)

William A. Barry (1991–1997)

Holy Cross Rectors after Separate Incorporation

William J. O'Halloran (1969–1974)

John T. Seery (1974–1977)

Joseph L. Ryan (1977–1983)

Robert E. Manning (1983–1985)

William E. Reiser (1985–1991)

David H. Gill (1991–1994)

INDEX